JUDENMORD

JUDENMORD

Art and the Holocaust in Post-war Germany

Kathrin Hoffmann-Curtius

with Sigrid Philipps

REAKTION BOOKS

In Memory of
my Grandmother Emma Hummel née Reis,
Mainz, 27 September 1880 – Krefeld, 3 April 1962
and my great-aunt Barbara Fischer née Reis,
Mainz, 9 January 1895 – Auschwitz, 20 October 1943

Published by
REAKTION BOOKS LTD
Unit 32, Waterside
44–48 Wharf Road
London N1 7UX, UK
www.reaktionbooks.co.uk

First published by Reaktion Books in 2018

English translation by Anthony Mathews

Originally published by Jonas Verlag, Marburg, 2014

The translation of this work was funded by Geisteswissenschaften International – Translation Funding for Humanities and Social Sciences from Germany, a joint initiative of the Fritz Thyssen Foundation, the German Federal Foreign Office, the collecting society VG WORT and the Börsenverein des Deutschen Buchhandels (German Publishers & Booksellers Association). The author acknowledges additional support by the Akademie der Künste, Berlin, Kunstsammlung.

Printed and bound in China by 1010 Printing International Ltd

A catalogue record for this book is available from the British Library

ISBN 978 1 78023 907 1

Contents

Foreword to the English Edition

Continuing to work on the subject of this book, along with the translation by Tony Mathews, made it easier to gain a certain distance from the German text and called for renewed reflection upon the period after the Second World War. For the English edition I have therefore more clearly elaborated the various phases of the reception of the Nazi regime in Germany, as these have also affected the production of the images. At the start of the immediate post-war period, the acts committed by the tyrannical regime were still obvious to the whole population and shown in films and photographs. With the Cold War and the founding of two distinct political systems, the Federal Republic of Germany (FRG) in the West and the German Democratic Republic (GDR) in the East, resources began to be directed towards the rebuilding and construction of society, at the same time as repressing the past. Exclusion of the Jews, hatred towards them and their murder did not start in 1933 or stop after 1945, but this fact was hardly discussed in public up until the Auschwitz trial. After the reunification of the two competing German states in 1989, it again became clear how relations between them were interwoven and how much they had been engaging in propaganda against one another in dealing with the past; acknowledgement of the murder of the Jews was blocked in both states. Whereas the GDR saw the Federal Republic as a continuation of the Nazi regime, West Germany was confirmed in its view of the GDR as continuing Stalinism.

The historical background to the general situation of cultural politics is more strongly defined in this edition, and the prehistory of hostility towards the Jews in Germany has been given a separate chapter on the representations of pogroms.

I have added to the enlarged English edition artistic commentaries obtained from further reading and visits to museums: two posters by Jewish artists appealing to all survivors in the displaced person camps in occupied Germany in 1947, Bazon Brock's art installation as well as two of his works made of paper from 1959–60, and the four abstract paintings *Birkenau* that Gerhard Richter published in 2015.

Kathrin Hoffmann-Curtius, Berlin, December 2016

Introduction

We murdered them in their hundreds of thousands – no denials in the world can get around that fact – since it was nothing but murder, this 'solution' to the question of the Jews who could not defend themselves![1]

Entry in the war diary of the German Army judge Werner Otto Müller-Hill, 6 February 1945

Remembering the murder of the Jews during the period of National Socialism, one thinks immediately of photographs. The visual art of the post-war period is closely associated with abstract painting, with pictures devoted to the building of socialism and with modernism, something previously dismissed as 'entartete Kunst' (degenerate art). Early on, however, there were attempts by artists to deal with the subject, even if art history has paid little attention to them. There were not a great many, however. Those who had been opposed to National Socialism from the start portrayed the crimes of violence while the war was still going on, and immediately after the end of the war they exhibited pictures showing the murder of the Jews in the perpetrators' own country. Their drawings, etchings and paintings were often based on traditional representations of violence, at the same time introducing new pictorial motifs that, coexisting and interacting with photography, have shaped how we remember the events. The pictures, along with the poetry of Nelly Sachs and Paul Celan, already contained those signifiers that have become symbols of mass murder. They contradict Theodor W. Adorno's sweeping assertion that there can be no poetry after Auschwitz and the recently reargued claim that it is not possible to represent the Shoah.[2]

Central to this current study is the question of how the crimes were represented during the first twenty years after the end of the war. How did artists deal with their own experiences and relate these to what they saw, heard and read, and in what ways did they develop their ideas? What images of the Jews, at first excluded and then murdered on an industrial scale, were presented to the Germans after the end of the brutal regime? These were Germans who, even if they had not taken part in the persecution themselves, had nevertheless witnessed it and had for the most part tolerated and approved of it. What scenes were represented in the drawings and paintings that were derived from the photographs and films taken at the liberation of the concentration camps and shown after the end of the war, and then again at the time of the Auschwitz trial? What do the images have in common and where do they differ? And not the least interesting thing to explore is how much the works of art and the ways they were received were related to the punishment of the perpetrators, the re-education of people and new ways of thinking in both East and West, as well as how much they contributed to the culture of memory and the way in which this gradually changed.

Now that the Cold War is over, it is possible and indeed necessary to examine how the then-recent German past was remembered and built into the founding narratives of the West German FRG and the East German GDR and how the different values of the two states and their ideas of citizenship were developed. In the ensuing period the ideological positions have admittedly gone through changes, but wars and conflicts are still being justified based on the ideological perception of enemies. It still remains highly relevant to examine how artists reacted to injustice in a social situation where the majority stayed silent.

The Production and Criticism of Art

The works discussed here illustrate the extent to which the production of art in the East and the West was conditioned by politics, particularly in the period when in the West it was thought that art at least could be isolated from politics as a separate sphere. In all the occupation zones in the period immediately after the war, when the industries were not yet churning out consumer goods and entertainment offered very little, there was a lively interest in art, and exhibitions were attended by a large number of different sections of the population. In 1946 the *Allgemeine Deutsche Kunstausstellung* (General German Art Exhibition) took place in Dresden, aimed at the whole German population and showing figurative as well as abstract painting. Following this, in the Soviet occupation zone the pressure in favour of Socialist Realism became more and more intense.[3] The Western zones, particularly after the two states were set up, developed abstract art into a key symbol of representative democracy and this was true above all of the discourse during the early years of the West German FRG.[4] Non-figurative painting, after all, held the promise of opening up new perspectives and turning away from old ones.

In all the zones there was at first a dominant cultural policy led by the Kulturbund zur Demokratischen Erneuerung Deutschlands (Cultural Union for the Democratic Renewal of Germany),[5] the trade unions and the departments of culture. This was an attempt to appeal to a broad cross-section of the population. It was not long, however, before the policy of the Soviet zone/GDR focused public awareness exclusively on the heroic struggle against fascism and the prospects for the future. Even before the setting up of the state in 1949, an authoritarian artistic policy following the Stalinist battle-cry of 'the struggle against Formalism' had sought to shape the victory over fascism and the construction of the new state in line with the conventional subject-matter of pictures.[6] The difficulty artists had in creating works that did not fit in with this ruling can be seen from the biography of Horst Strempel. In *Night over Germany* (see illus. 10) he linked together the recent past and the present-day state of the nation, in so doing creating what is probably the most important painting depicting the state of Germany in 1945. Despite initially being recognized for his work, he was caught up in the crossfire between the two political opponents.

The immediate post-war period saw the growth of a large number of art galleries, and publishers released albums of graphic art making artists' comments on the recent past accessible to broad sections of the population. The long-term focus of art history in the West on stylistic innovation, however, has diverted attention away from the variety of the post-war cultural landscape. Given what had become a preference for abstract painting in regard to taste and judgement of quality, policy towards collecting and exhibiting excluded anything dealing with war crimes as narrative and figurative subject-matter.[7] The basis for this was the tendency already present in art historical reviews of early art exhibitions, in which the authors concentrated on questions of style and either did not mention any direct relation of the pictures to the crimes of the immediate past or mentioned them only in passing. The forewords and accompanying texts to the works in albums, by contrast, were concerned not just with discussions on art, but with the subject-matter in the context of the Nazi past. The failure of the West German debate on art to link together the memory of National Socialism and mass murder was equally convenient for art historians, curators and artists, allowing them to suppress the past and the equally inevitable question of personal guilt.[8]

Research into the Culture of Memory

This present study was inspired by the research carried out by Ziva Amishai-Maisels in her 1993 book *Depiction and Interpretation: The Influence of the Holocaust on the Visual Arts*.[9] Her basic compendium of material encouraged me to look more closely at production and reception in Germany. The reason why the immense literature on National Socialism and the available visual documentary record have hardly taken art into account up until now can be explained in terms of the fact that the idea of research has been slow to evolve. For a long time art historians concentrated on questions of form, and the prevailing judgements of quality after 1945, which were often politically motivated, prevented them from relating aesthetics to the recent German past. In the West the exclusion of paintings and drawings from the canon affected figurative art in the tradition of left-wing realism, particularly in view of the fact that it had been adopted by artists most of whom had decided to live in the Soviet occupation zone.[10] In their condemnations of Nazism these artists were above all reminding the world of the persecution of the Jews. For that reason it was in the Soviet occupation zone that pictures showing the horrors of the Nazi period were exhibited, discussed and incorporated within the canon of art in the GDR. This took place despite the 'debate about formalism' and the expectation that they would follow the 'Bitterfeld way' of art working on the image of the 'Neuer Mensch' (the 'New Human').[11]

Only one exhibition at the Frankfurt Kunstverein in 1980, *Zwischen Krieg und Frieden – Gegenständliche und realistische Tendenzen in der Kunst ach 45* (Between War and Peace – Objective and Realistic Tendencies in Art after 1945), departed from the prevailing canon;[12] it came out of research by critical, leftist, West German art historians on artistic production in the two parts of Germany. In her analysis of the 'drawing of parallels between National Socialism and the story of the Passion as the basis of significance for aesthetic practice', the organizer, Gabriele Schultheiss, took it for granted that this also included the representation of the Jews in paintings by Grundig and Strempel from Leipzig and East Berlin respectively.[13] This appeal for recognition of texts and pictures by the West German art establishment of the time was, however, dismissed as GDR propaganda and largely fell on deaf ears as regards the influential art scene.[14]

It was not until the reunification of Germany, when taking an interest in the art of the other part of the country was no longer considered to be treasonable, that it became possible to make an overall comparison of the two sides rather than just praising the other side's dissidents. Eckhart Gillen in his 2009 book *Feindliche Brüder?* (Warring Brothers?) described this hostility and simultaneously set out to deconstruct it. Both that publication and, in the same year, the exhibition *Kunst und Kalter Krieg. Deutsche Positionen 1945–89* (Art of Two Germanys/Cold War Cultures) contained contributions from post-war art on the subject of the Nazi tyranny.[15]

In research devoted to the history of the reception of the Nazi period, the contribution made by artists in the first twenty years after the end of the war has been largely ignored.[16] This despite the fact that West German art historians were involved in organizing the 1995 exhibition *Representations of Auschwitz* in Krakow, a relatively early examination into the origin of the 'historical image' of Auschwitz and the fact 'that our understanding of history is mediated by how it is represented to us'.[17] The group of international scholars headed by Detlef Hoffmann and Jonathan Webber looked at examples from a whole range of media of the early period: literature, films, photography, comics and drawings. Of these, the ones falling within the period of analysis were produced by concentration camp inmates, mostly while they were imprisoned, and the pictures are still in Auschwitz. The collection that appeared in the 1997 book *Bilder des Holocaust* (Pictures of the Holocaust),[18] whose subtitle specifically mentions fine art, is nevertheless entirely devoted to art of the 1970s and '80s. In the 2007 *Lexikon der 'Vergangenheitsbewältigung' in Deutschland* (Lexicon of 'Coming to Terms with the Past' in Germany) discussion is limited to the rehabilitation of so-called 'degenerate art'.[19] The promising title of the volume *Die Shoah im Bild* (The Shoah in the Picture) of 2003[20] deals only with film, photography and literature, apart from Detlef Hoffmann's contribution on symbolic strategies.[21] The exhibition held in 2004 recalling the Auschwitz trial and its contemporary reception displayed commentaries by visual artists dealing with the topic in the twenty-first century, but the period of the trial was only documented through reactions in the press, literature and philosophy. And as late as 2016 Buchloh writes about 'the few big exceptions' in pictorial art where you find 'reflection on history after Auschwitz'. He mentions four 'important examples'[22] in comparison with the 'innumerable purely referential or anecdotally illustrative works'. In the field of literary studies *Die ersten Stimmen, deutschsprachige Texte zur Shoah* (The First Voices, German Writing on the Shoah)[23] has drawn some attention recently. *Die andere Erinnerung* (The Other Memory)[24] by exiles and survivors clearly stands out as regards content and the frequency with which non-Jewish authors in Germany mention the persecution of the Jews.[25] In so doing, texts do make reference to other texts, but they are hardly ever seen in relation to contributions by graphic artists and painters.

In summaries of the art of the first post-war years written after the reunification of Germany, the pictures discussed here are almost totally absent up until 2012. Admittedly, Wolf Goeltzer, the curator of the 1998 Stuttgart exhibition *Stunde Null* (Year Zero), mentions in his introduction 'three huge negative factors affecting everything: the Nazi tyranny, Auschwitz and Hiroshima'.[26] Nevertheless, these were not in evidence in the titles of the pictures in the collections displayed at the Staatsgalerie, nor is there any sign of any direct reference to the mass murder in the artworks on display. In the recent exhibition *Gegenwartskunst von 1945 bis heute* (Contemporary Art from 1945 until the Present), put on at the Staedel in Frankfurt am Main in 2012, out of 'nearly 300 works of art' there were only two from the period 1945–9 – *Spatial Refraction of a Rectangle* by Hermann Glöckner from 1945 and *Pleasant Landscape IV* by Willi Baumeister from 1949 – and in both cases the works fitted in with the dominant trends in the West,[27] constructivism and abstraction.

Much more nuanced was the arrangement in the first room of the exhibition *Der geteilte Himmel* (The Divided Heaven),[28] put on at the Neue Nationalgalerie in Berlin in 2012 and displaying the art history of the period immediately after the end of the war. Thanks to the totally different purchasing policy of the GDR, whose Staatliche Museen (State Museums) had been incorporated within the Stiftung Preussischer Kulturbesitz (Foundation for Prussian Cultural Property), it was possible in that case to exhibit abstract art, figurative art and even early informal painting all together alongside and in contrast to one another. The cultural policy of state control which, unlike that in the West, did not have to compete with the closed shop nature of the art world had resulted immediately after the war in the appearance in museums of the major works of post-war art, which later came to be severely criticized, such as Stempel's *Night over Germany* (see illus. 10), *Auschwitz* by Heinrich Ehmsen (see illus. 123) and *To the Victims of Fascism 2* by Hans Grundig (see illus. 114) and later works by Werner Tübke. Focusing on Heinrich Ehmsen's satirical image of clowns turning somersaults among the ruins,[29] the display called for a new way of looking at things. The exhibits included Wols's *Yellow Composition*,[30] the colouring of which reminds one of the quotation from Paul Klee 'abstract with memories',[31] Ehmsen's figurative picture of Auschwitz (see illus. 123), Harald Metzke's *The Shark*[32] and Wolfgang Frankenstein's abstract *Invasion of the Brown Animals*,[33] disturbing urban impressions by Werner Heldt,[34] a self-portrait by Hans Grundig,[35] the first design for the Buchenwald Memorial[36] by Fritz Cremer from 1952 and a sculpture by Alfred Lörcher.[37] These are Eastern as well as Western artworks, and only those from the East reveal any direct attempt to come to terms with recent history and, in the case of Ehmsen's absurd clowns and Grundig's self-portrait, the insecure position of the artists.

Selection of Contributions

Despite a large number of sources[38] having been drawn upon for the drawings, paintings and sculptures[39] analysed here, this present volume does not deal with a vast amount of material. This is because the majority of the artworks exhibited at that time depicted landscapes, still-lifes and bouquets of flowers, portraits and female nudes using a discreet form of naturalism. Among them were some isolated images of lamentation and grief, scenes of devastation and themes from ancient mythology.[40] As timeless art, often published without any indication of the original dates, they come across as scenes of harmless everyday life or nature evolving according to the rhythm of the seasons, soothing the population out of their fears and worries, either under the hail of bombs or after it was all over, and generally appealing to the consumer.[41] But even those who had survived the concentration camps, according to the 'analysis of the subject-matter of the works on display' in the description of an exhibition of art by displaced persons in Munich in 1947, painted figurative compositions, landscapes and still-lifes: 'in their immediate presentation they reveal nothing of the tragic reminiscences of their creators . . . What is noticeable is a certain motivation to forget everything and not reawaken anything of the earlier pain and suffering.'[42]

This present study looks at paintings, drawings and etchings that bring to light the persecution of the Jews, including images that follow the usual style trends and the collecting policies of museums and those that do not. The pictures of the persecution of the Sinti and Roma that have come to our knowledge during research will also be considered, people that it seems only Otto Pankok thought worthy of being represented up to now. Images of the suffering of the Jehovah's Witnesses only became known about in the 1970s,[43] and Gerhard Richter is probably the only one to make any reference in art to the murder of the disabled.

There is a problem in relation to the way images represent 'Jewishness', a Jewishness that can be indicated in pictures only by means of names or religious symbols. Visually signifying a Jew runs the risk of harking back to anti-Semitic stereotypes and the Nazi system of racial classification. This dilemma arose for those artists who were trying to distinguish the murder of the Jews from the many others carried out by the Nazis, as it did for those who wrote about these murders, the only solution to this problem being to put the characterization into context. One also admittedly has to take into account the fact that the early illustrated reports by the Allies, which made the scale of the crimes known to the public for the first time, refer to the various nations and 'foreign workers', whereas the term 'Jew' is not mentioned.[44] In the Nuremberg trials and for some time afterwards, the crimes against the Jews were lumped together with other German war crimes.[45] Even the film *Night and Fog* (see p. 171),[46] which considerably influenced the perception of the Nazi period and the way it has been portrayed in art since 1957, only mentions 'deportees'; those being persecuted as Jews are nevertheless clearly distinguished by the yellow star.

In West Germany, where anti-Semitism was slow to disappear, there remained long after the war a certain reluctance to use the word 'Jew' at all or refer to anyone as a Jew.[47] The habit of disparagement ran deep and there was considerable anxiety about not behaving in the correct manner. When anti-Semitism was condemned after the war, most people had no words to hand for speaking about the Jews.

In the GDR, officially, there was no recognition of religious affiliation, hence no denomination of Judaism either. This state saw itself as liberated from the legacy of fascism and from its anti-Semitic burden, claiming allegiance to the tradition of anti-fascist resistance. This led to the Communists, in their policy as regards imagery, identifying the victims mainly as 'politicals' and paying no special attention to those who had been persecuted for racial or religious reasons.

For the present study the question that had inevitably to be addressed was that of the definitions that have been applied to Nazi crimes since 1945. Whenever the genocide of the Jews was mentioned at all in speeches and in the press up until the end of the 1950s, the word *Ausrottung* (eradication) was used; the expression used most frequently by the Nazis, *Ausmerze* (eliminations), was considered to be tainted by association, which was not the case, however, with the verb *ausmerzen* and the noun derived from it,

Ausmerzung.[48] Of the many terms, such as 'extermination', 'annihilation', 'Hitler's barbarism' and 'Auschwitz', the one chosen was whichever sums up the events as precisely as possible, even though the word 'Holocaust'[49] has in the meantime become the usual term for the Judenmord. Despite becoming internationally known following the 1979 American television series of the same name, 'right from the start the meaning of the term' has had 'historically a slightly anti-Jewish tinge' and introduces a religious justification for the events.[50] In addition, the term borrowed from English makes it possible for everyone in the world to know immediately what they are talking about, but at the same time allows every German to talk about it with German history kept at one remove.

The images discussed are mainly those that have been exhibited in Germany or at least have been made available in publications. This is because only by looking at their reception can one discover the significance of these works to the public in the country of the perpetrators. Works that were created in the concentration camps or after 1945 by exiles are included for consideration only if they fit in with this criterion. There are, however, exceptions: Ludwig Meidner's works in London on the massacres in Poland, despite their having been exhibited only in fragments and then not before the 1970s, are discussed alongside the cycles by Lea Grundig, a communist artist from a Jewish family who fled to Palestine in 1939, returned to Eastern Germany in 1949 and for many years reminded the world about anti-Semitism and its consequences.

Because of the now popular association of 'Auschwitz' with the 'murder of the Jews', works with that word in the title have been included even though at first glance they might appear to have nothing to do with the genocide. Likewise included are pictures referring to photographs of the liberation of the camps and other scenes clearly associated with persecution and extermination.

The Auschwitz trial in Frankfurt am Main in 1963–5 marked a turning point in the politics of memory to which the artists discussed here had contributed and the study ends with the works of art commenting on it. It was accompanied by a programme of exhibitions, and the daily press and the radio reported in detail on the trial. The commentators in the GDR continually added extra names to the list of the accused in West Germany, and in the Western media the 'extreme acts dominated the public reception'.[51] What became clear was that the accused had continued to live a normal bourgeois existence as salesmen, chemists or other employees. This started a public debate about the torture and murders; nevertheless even by 2002, as a result of many families keeping quiet on the subject, many young people still believed that there had been no Nazis in their family.[52] It was only later that biographical studies appeared by children of the generation of perpetrators. In the fine arts Gerhard Richter revealed that families were involved early on, but he mentioned only names, and neither deeds nor sufferings.

The question about what the selected works show of the history of the persecution and murder of the Jews under the Nazis can be answered as follows:

discrimination, deportation, imprisonment in camps, torture, shooting, hanging, gas chambers, *Todesmärsche* ('death marches', that is, evacuations from the camps) and grief for the dead. In the images were torturers and the tortured, murderers and the murdered, violence, voyeurism and the eroticism of violence. This book could have been composed following one of these lists. Yet what is being addressed over and over again is how the artists in differing social situations portrayed fear, suffering and human worth and worthlessness and how those observing were made into, and were accused of being, witnesses to inhuman acts. In order to put into context the role of artists in the history of how the Nazi period is viewed, the works of art are therefore presented in chronological order. This principle is adhered to even if it leaves out the individual sequence of each artist's production. Each chapter begins by summarizing the changes in the culture of memory in the light above all of the publicly available visual documentation with which the producers and the recipients of the art would have been familiar. The particular social situation of each artist is discussed. In separate essays the works are seen in the context of their time. In each case the length of the section varies considerably according to the amount of available material and the state of research. Until we have access to the complete works of the many now-forgotten artists, this present study must be seen as a first step towards further analysis and discussion.

Commentaries on the Selection

All of the artists whose works are analysed and discussed here belong to the generation that lived through the Nazi period. They served in the Wehrmacht or they were able to survive on account of their age and despite their rejection of the system in Germany; many of them were still at school. Jews and Communists and the Jewish Communists among them were imprisoned in concentration camps or forced to emigrate. Many of the works exhibited in the period 1945–9 were completed while the war was still being fought. The pictures concealed from the Nazis comment on the exclusion and deportation witnessed by everybody in Germany but soon deliberately forgotten by the majority. Artists went against the official line of interpretation trotted out in reading material and radio reports about this exclusion and deportation and expressed grief about the loss of friends. In Nazi Germany it was a risky thing to show empathy with the persecuted Jews and Sinti in paintings; pictures were hidden or, as in the case of Fritz Ketz, carried around as treasured objects. Those artists who confronted the horror they were going through again and again in sketches while still imprisoned were risking their lives. In the first few years after the war they bore witness, often in albums of graphic art, particularly to the suffering in the concentration camps. All the pictures illustrate life and death, no matter whether those who painted them, such as Hermann Bruse, Leo Haas, Peter Edel, Karl Schwesig and Jerzy Zielezinski, were themselves imprisoned or were in exile, like Lea Grundig, Ludwig Meidner and Teo Otto, who had heard and read about the suffering. Together with artists such as Willi Geiger, Carl Lauterbach, Otto Pankok and Eduard Winkler, who had remained in the country and devoted only individual prints and drawings to the events in the camps and on the marches, they cried out the warning: 'Nie wieder!', 'Never again!'

Reports from the occupied territories, scenes in films and photographs published in booklets about the liberation of the camps are there in works of art; they correspond to what many had experienced; images seen and situations lived through are closely interwoven. In the early years the images – in speech, drawings, paintings and photographs – still reveal the search for an appropriate language that allows one to recognize a form of brutality and inhumanity that had never been seen before. The metaphorical language arising at the time, be that of the 'living corpses',[53] the 'death factory'[54] or the association, unknown up until then, of gas and smoke with mass murder, makes clear the close interrelation between speaking, writing, seeing and showing. What they had already got from the news about the German atrocities, images of violence from Christian iconography and paintings of battles influenced the way photographers used their cameras to record the conditions in the liberated camps. These early visualizations were developed and distributed and became established in news reports, literature, political analysis and art.

The prominent role that photography played in the way people remembered the atrocities came about as a result of the re-education measures instituted by the Allies using posters, booklets and films,[55] and this was accentuated by the trials. Documents using pen or brush were rarely[56] taken to be evidence. In the Nuremberg trials even more weight was attributed to photographs than to witness statements. In her analysis of the judgements in the media, Cornelia Vismann demonstrated the importance given to the innovation of showing films:

> At least for the American Allies the crucial thing right from the start was to show the war and the extermination in images . . . Referred to as the 'architect of the tribunal', the principal prosecutor Robert H. Jackson introduces the use of technology into the process, illustrating the trust on the part of the Americans in photographed evidence and the associated mistrust in the spoken word, to the extent that he shows films rather than listen to the witnesses.[57]

Allied information campaigns are almost exclusively based on photographs, very much in line with Roland Barthes' observation that 'every photograph is a certificate of presence' of the referent '("This has been")'.[58]

Reading against the grain, this tendency reveals how necessary it was and sometimes still is to confront the Germans with images that appear as incontrovertible as possible, the majority of people having again and again sought to hide behind the claim that they knew nothing about it all.[59] The surviving photographs, however, also document the fact that the way the crimes were to be remembered was determined by the Allies' view of things right from the start. They were reproduced in enormous quantities. In addition, there are the photographs taken by the perpetrators themselves, such as the photographs in the Stroop Report, often shown without any commentary.[60]

The paintings produced in this period raise to another level what had happened as seen from different perspectives and concentrate the events into one single representation. Strempel took the viewer beyond the barbed wire towards the devastated landscape and, in the images from the triptych *Night over Germany*, he combined all the sufferings of the Jews, those imprisoned and children so as to show the horrendous effects of the regime based on the system of camps. Edgar Jené, closely associated with Paul Celan at the time, demonstrated that exclusion and extermination could also be visualized surrealistically. In his painting, phantasmagorical figures move about among stylized railway lines and watchtowers. Whereas Mathias Barz, Henry Koerner, Hans Grundig, Dore Meyer-Vax, Max Lachnit and even to a certain extent Otto Pankok with his melancholy memories generalized their individual grief and pain at the loss of friends, Heinrich Ehmsen, like Strempel pictorially taking one beyond the barbed wire, attempted to characterize the concentration camp as a 'death factory'. Karl Hubbuch pointed the finger at those responsible for the extermination and drew a sarcastic caricature showing a cremation oven as the entrance gate to the Nazi stronghold. The pictures by Strempel, Ehmsen and Hubbuch emphasize the political concept; those by former camp inmates additionally reveal the vile function from the inside. They are the only ones who can demonstrate that hunger can reduce human beings to grubbing in the mire for food, and it is they above all who show brutal scenes of torture. One single example of a confession in a painting by a former member of the Nazi Party was revealed by research. Hanns Georgi painted his nightmare of being persecuted himself for once.

In the case of the representations in the pictures mentioned so far, the style was mostly realistic and figurative. Carl Buchheister was the only one in the 1950s to use abstract painting to draw attention to the theme of violence in the concentration camps, though this becomes clear to the viewer only from the title.[61] When Gerhard Richter (1998–2017) introduced his abstract representations of the inseparable German-Jewish history in a slowly accelerating process, he had anticipated the impossibility of conveying a narration non-verbally as well. It would be worthwhile to undertake further research into pictures falling under the heading of abstract, informal and surreal painting.[62] It might also be worth enquiring into how the perceived increase in the use of the colour black[63] and the mistreatment of the surface of paintings[64] of the late 1940s and the 1950s relate to despair after the experience of violence. Likewise, it might be worthwhile looking for an explanation of how the colours yellow and brown came to be overwritten with a new significance. In this study, the section headed 'Deconstructed Likeness' (see p. 60) will deal only briefly and in passing with the question of how the catastrophe was treated by artists who felt the traditional model of intact bodies was no longer appropriate. Also under the heading 'Remembering in the 1950s' Carlfriedrich Claus is the only representative of an artist working in a non-objective style, as Helmut Wolff's Cubist plan (see illus. 141) for a memorial for Auschwitz-Birkenau remained just as unfinished as the figurative ones by Joseph Henry Lonas and Lidy von Lüttwitz (see illus. 140) or the installation by Joseph Beuys (see illus. 143).

The few artists who in the 1950s worked on pictures of the persecution and murder of the Jews were no longer involved in the public debate about the events because in West Germany all those who died in the Second World War were remembered together and, in the GDR, there was an emphasis on the connection between the resistance victims and the new state. Individual memories by Gerd Baukhage of having taken part in the war have survived. A long time before it became a matter of public debate following the exhibition *Verbrechen der Wehrmact* (Crimes of the Wehrmacht),[65] two of his coloured drawings showed bodies of the hanged among the corpses of horses and other subjects in the style of standard paintings reporting on warfare, one of which was entitled *Hanged Jew with a Hat On* (see illus. 136). Over a period of several years, Willi Sitte studied and drew on Nazi photos of the crimes for a painting about the massacre at Lidice which mysteriously disappeared after completion. In hitherto unpublished drawings Gerhard Richter interpreted Anne Frank's *Diary*. None of these was purchased for any public collection. The aged Pankok composed a memorial to Jews, Sinti and those who had lost their homeland but this was displayed only in the museum; Arie Goral did a painting with an allegorical sacrifice appearing as a warning above Hamburg; and during the debate about the National Memorial at Buchenwald as a place of resistance, Lea Grundig recalled the Jews murdered in the concentration camp.

In the late 1950s and early '60s, at the time of the trial of Adolf Eichmann, the full extent of the murder of the Jews became such a topic that the media found it impossible to overlook. The close connection from then on between German history and the Second World War and the extermination of the Jews was made clear by Werner Tübke in a cycle dedicated to the historical background of the GDR and paying tribute to the labour movement. He not only recalled scenes of heroism but honoured the dead of Stalingrad and of the camps. Lea Grundig worked on a new cycle accusing the West of continuing to cover up for the perpetrators. Dore Meyer-Vax began to work on a monumental linocut on the violent history of the twentieth century.

Some of the pictures and objects that date from the period when the surviving perpetrators were put on trial in Frankfurt am Main and Düsseldorf hark back in their choice of subject-matter to the documentary model that was aimed at immediately after the war. The do often, however, mark a new turn by calling into question the way atrocities had been recalled up until that time. Bazon Brock drew many lines between past and present times using photographs of Nazi atrocities. Joseph Beuys continued to work with photographs familiar to him from the Auschwitz competition but linked them to everyday objects of esoteric healing therapy. In the case of Otto Schubert there is a focus on violence and sex in documenting the narrative of Auschwitz, something only hinted at by Haas, and Hubert Berke in his paintings used the images of maltreated female bodies made familiar by the reports at the Frankfurt trial. Wolf Vostell made use of current photographs, ones from the Nazi period and material that had been thrown away; in his assemblages named after the concentration camps he combined criticism of consumer society with reminders of the crimes, and linked newspaper reports of a sexual scandal to bodies from Dachau. Werner Tübke too confronted the issue of erotic seduction in relation to those being abused. His paintings are composed of action shots depicted from photographs and used like witness statements; thus he stages the ongoing discourse of the trials to question the way the legal system and individuals deal with history. Rolf Szymanski re-evaluated the inferiority of the Synagoga defeated by Ecclesia. His sculptured allegory stands free, alone and, in contrast to the Christian tradition, upright. The fact that towards the end of the twentieth century the murder of the Jews formed an integral part of German history is demonstrated by Gerhard Richter's design for the Reichstag when it became the seat of the German Federal Parliament. On the wall made available to him, the only images he planned to install were blown-up photographs of ss prisoners and concentration camp inmates. Admittedly he gave up the design, but he published it nonetheless. In 2017, at least part of his work *Birkenau* can be seen in the same hall.

The prominent role of photography in relation to remembrance of the past was increased by the publication in 1960 of *Der gelbe Stern – Judenverfolgung in Europa 1933–1945* (The Yellow Star: The Persecution of the Jews in Europe, 1933–1945), which has since become one of the *Klassiker der Zeitgeschichte* (Classics of Contemporary History).[66] This book by Gerhard Schoenberner republished photographs from documentary sources belonging to the Allies and the Nazis, the private possessions of German soldiers and 'illegal photos of members of the resistance movement', becoming the most well-known illustrated volume in Germany.[67] The images displayed in this book can be found either as clearly recognizable or as hidden references in many works of art.

By 1944, however, the place of photographs as evidence had already been challenged by drawings. Bedřich Fritta, an inmate of Theresienstadt/Terezin, in the ink drawing presumably later given the title *Film and Reality* (illus. 1), showed the staging of a scene for the medium of film,[68] revealing the manipulation of photography by means of the selective use of the camera. The

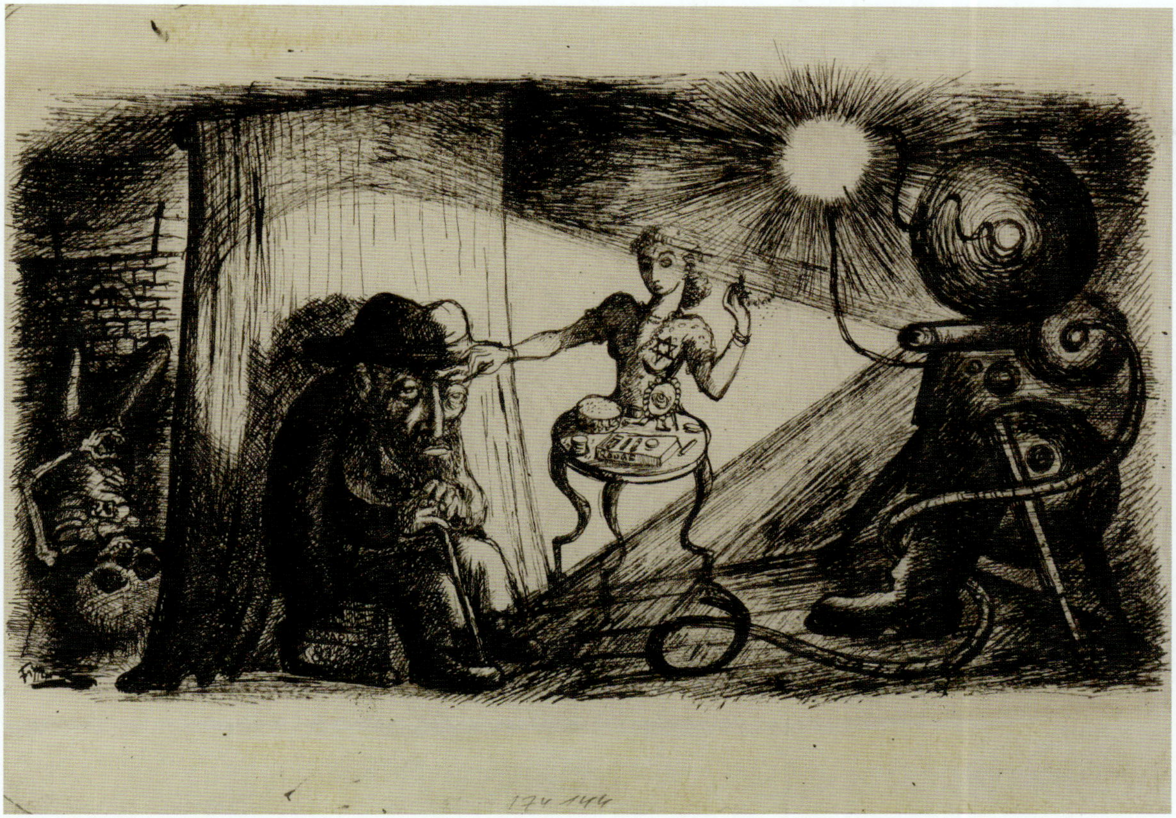

1 Bedřich Fritta, *Film and Reality*, Theresienstadt, 1944, pen and black ink.

robot-like Nazi cameraman in jackboots is filming a prettified aspect of the ghetto: the Jew, correctly made up, on one side, along with the make-up girl, identified as being Jewish by the Star of David and given a make-up table by Fritta in place of a lower body. The camera shot reaches only as far as the curtain; the skeleton lying there is not visible. Only in the traditional medium of drawing – done in secret – was it possible to reveal the selection of the image by the Nazis in the ghetto.[69]

1 Prequel Images

The Nazi period was not the first time that Jews were subjected to deadly attacks; quite early on pogroms were captured in images and widely known about. The question is whether this German history of anti-Judaism and anti-Semitism is also reflected in the drawings and paintings that were made after 1945.[1]

As early as 1493 the same woodcut of Jews being burned alive was shown as many as three times in the Nuremberg chronicle of the world by Hartmann Schedel (illus. 2). The illustration was inserted into the text whenever 'evil deeds' are mentioned that were attributed to the Jews and whenever there are reports of their alleged desecrations of the Sacred Host in various German towns.[2] This extremely realistic portrayal of the burning alive of Jews has remained in the popular mind right up until modern times, and is recalled in the graphic representations of gassing by both Lea Grundig and Ludwig Meidner (see illus. 41 and 42). Whereas, however, the image in the late medieval illustrated book of world history was understood in relation to the torments in Hell as an inevitable punishment, in their 1940s graphics the two exiled Jewish artists expressed sorrow at the terrible suffering of their people. In this sense they were countering the anti-Semitic imagery of the Nazi propaganda that did not so much portray acts of violence as emphasize the alleged danger that the Jews presented. In the 1950s Lidy von Lüttwitz (see illus. 140) used the ancient woodcut as a model for the memorial at Auschwitz.

In Germany the few other representations of pogroms before 1933 referred mainly to the cruel acts of persecution in Tsarist Russia in the 1880s and those carried out during the civil wars there.[3] As images of grief and forewarning, they have been represented principally by Jewish artists. In 1904 in *Exile* (illus. 3), Samuel Hirszenberg portrayed the mass exodus following the

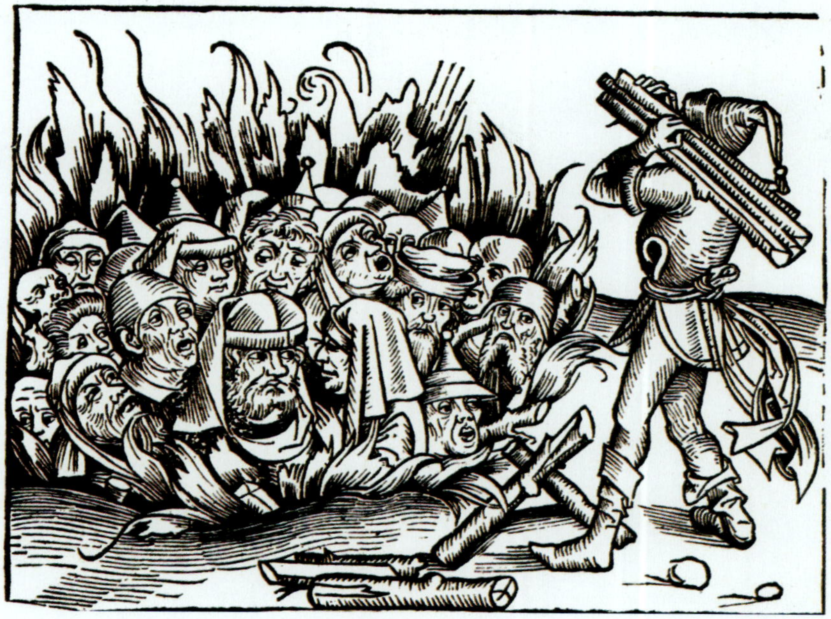

2 Hartmann Schedel, 'Burning Alive of Jews', from *Schedelsche Weltchronik* (Nuremberg, 1493), woodcut.

pogroms of 1903.[4] In a large painting a long procession of male and female figures is moving through a hostile-looking landscape. Their clothing and headgear are varied and indicate a range of social classes, all walking close together, sharing the same fate. The painting has disappeared; in the interim it was widely distributed as a postcard bearing the title *Golus* and referring to any exile since the destruction of the Second Temple.[5] It became a prototype for the representation of Jewish refugees and has clearly influenced the works of art discussed in this book more than Hirszenberg's *Wandering Jew* of 1899, portraying a massacre.[6]

For Jakob Steinhardt in 1913, it may have been both the contemporary accusations of ritual murder current in Russia at the time and those in Zerkow in Poland in his youth that were the motivation behind his two woodcuts[7] and the dry-point etching (illus. 4) depicting pogroms. The compositional arrangement of these works, Lea Weik concluded, harked back to the copper engraving by Johann Michael Voltz on the bloody acts of violence against Jews in Frankfurt am Main in 1819.[8] In this drawing, and in one of the two woodcuts of 1913, gangs approaching from the left are attacking Jews on the right who are already overpowered, while in the right-hand foreground, among those that have been clubbed, there is an old bearded Jew holding up his hands to the heavens, representing the lamenting Jew and prophet, a grieving figure that Steinhardt was particularly preoccupied with at the time.[9] With what seem wildly rapid strokes, the whole event is etched into a city street scene, as in the case of Voltz, but significantly Steinhardt added on the horizon a church tower topped by a cross.

In a 1914 lithograph Max Liebermann recalled the pogrom in Bessarabia ten years previously. Only in the background did he suggest the attacks by

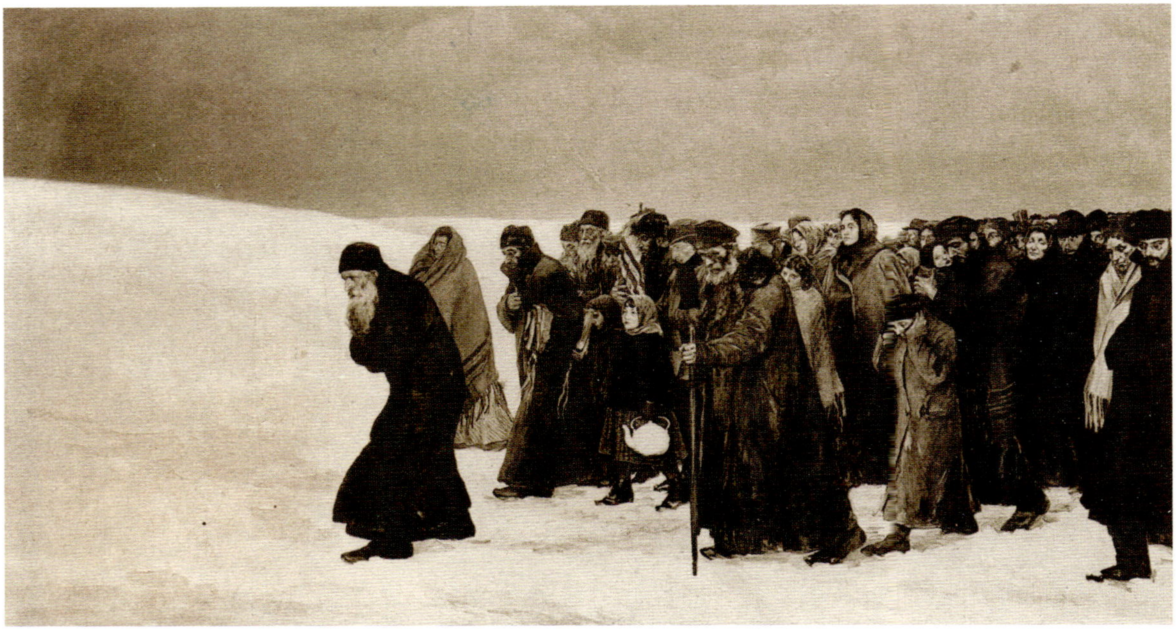

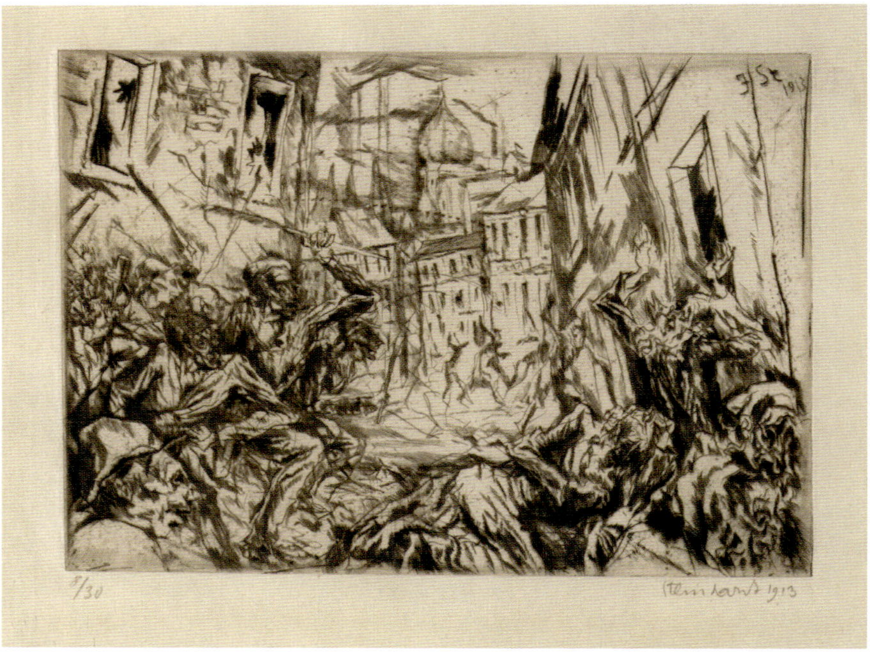

3 Samuel Hirszenberg, *Exile*, 1904, postcard.

4 Jakob Steinhardt, *Pogrom*, 1913, dry-point etching.

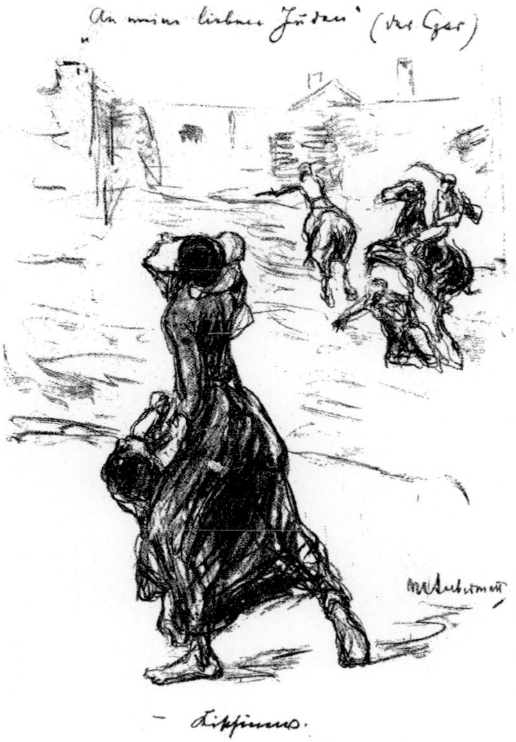

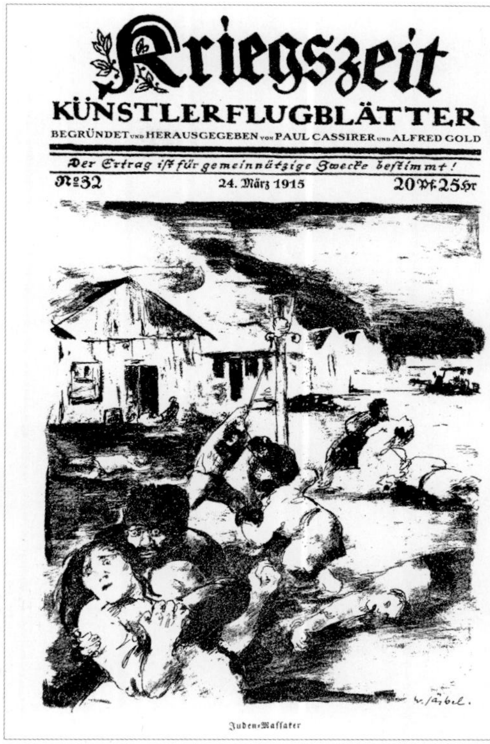

5 Max Liebermann, *Kischinew: To my Beloved Jews (The Czar)*, from *Kriegszeit Künstlerflugblätter*, III/16 (September 1916), lithograph.

6 Willy Jaeckel, *Massacre of the Jews*, from *Kriegszeit Künstlerflugblätter*, XXXII/24 (March 1915), lithograph.

the military on horseback, whereas he placed a monumental female figure in the centre of the picture following a pictorial arrangement that he often used (see illus. 218). Fleeing from her assailants out for plunder and carrying her child and all her belongings in her arms, she can be viewed as an allegory of the persecuted Jews. The print with the title *Kischinew* (illus. 5)[10] appeared in the magazine *Kriegszeit* in 1914 published by Paul Cassirer and justified the German attack on Tsarist Russia. In the same series of *Künstlerflugblätter* (artists' flyers) the non-Jewish Willy Jaeckel also published the drawing *Massacre of the Jews* of 1915 (illus. 6). He emphasized the rape of Jewish women by men with fur caps, here presumably indicating Russians; at the time Russia was at war with the German Reich. The artist was harking back to a popular image in war propaganda, using the defilement of women in war as a means of blackening the enemy.[11]

Lea Grundig, after her first arrest and under the influence of the Nuremberg Race Laws in Germany around 1935 or perhaps during her stay in Switzerland, etched *Pogrom* (illus. 7) as part of the series *The Jew is Guilty* about the persecution at the time in Poland.[12] The same gesture by a boy terrified to death is documented in the well-known photograph from the Stroop Report on the Warsaw Ghetto Uprising, with which the SS demonstrated their victory over the Jews in 1943 (see illus. 153). Grundig placed the viewer in the same position as the firing squad and so presented him with the threat of murder of the extended family before his very eyes.

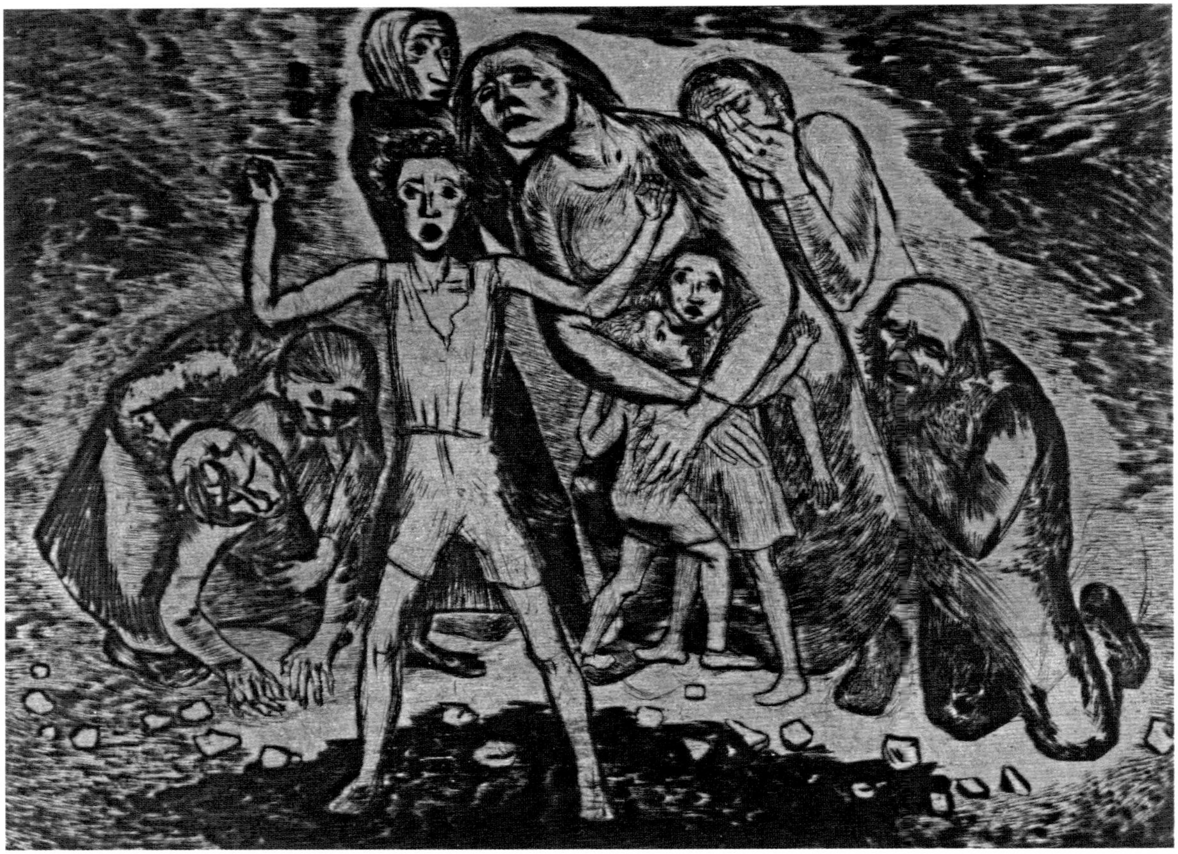

7 Lea Grundig, *Pogrom*, drawing 5 from the series *The Jew is Guilty*, 1935, etching.

Even though many artists witnessed the start of assaults by the Nazis after 1933, apart from Grundig there are not many other commentaries on them. The painter Ludwig Meidner, libelled and driven into exile by the Nazis, and who in Cologne had experienced the pogrom against Jews and their property on *Reichskristallnacht* in 1938, devoted an impressive drawing[13] (illus. 8) as a memorial to these aggressive acts by the Nazis. Two religious Jews, presumably rabbis, lamenting in the midst of destroyed and burning synagogues and the remains of their contents, are juxtaposed by Meidner with an angel-like vision in a bright robe and with curly hair. This figure is pointing its right forefinger at Hebrew letters[14] resembling the Writing on the Wall at Belshazzar's Feast, but indicating on a white scroll – not on the wall as in Daniel 5:5 – the date equivalent to 10 November 1938 in the Jewish calendar. By inscribing this on a scroll, Meidner was writing the date into the long history of persecution of the Jewish people. He was linking Jewish history to contemporary politics in Germany by making reference back to the text of the prophet Daniel and the subsequent tradition of Christian iconography. Its message is that the figure pointing to the scripture is intended to be the prophet Daniel, who is interpreting the writing as a prophecy of the coming end of Belshazzar's rule. Opposite him, in the way the scene is normally

8 Ludwig Meidner, *In Memory of our Destroyed Synagogues in Germany*, 1939, chalk and charcoal on paper.

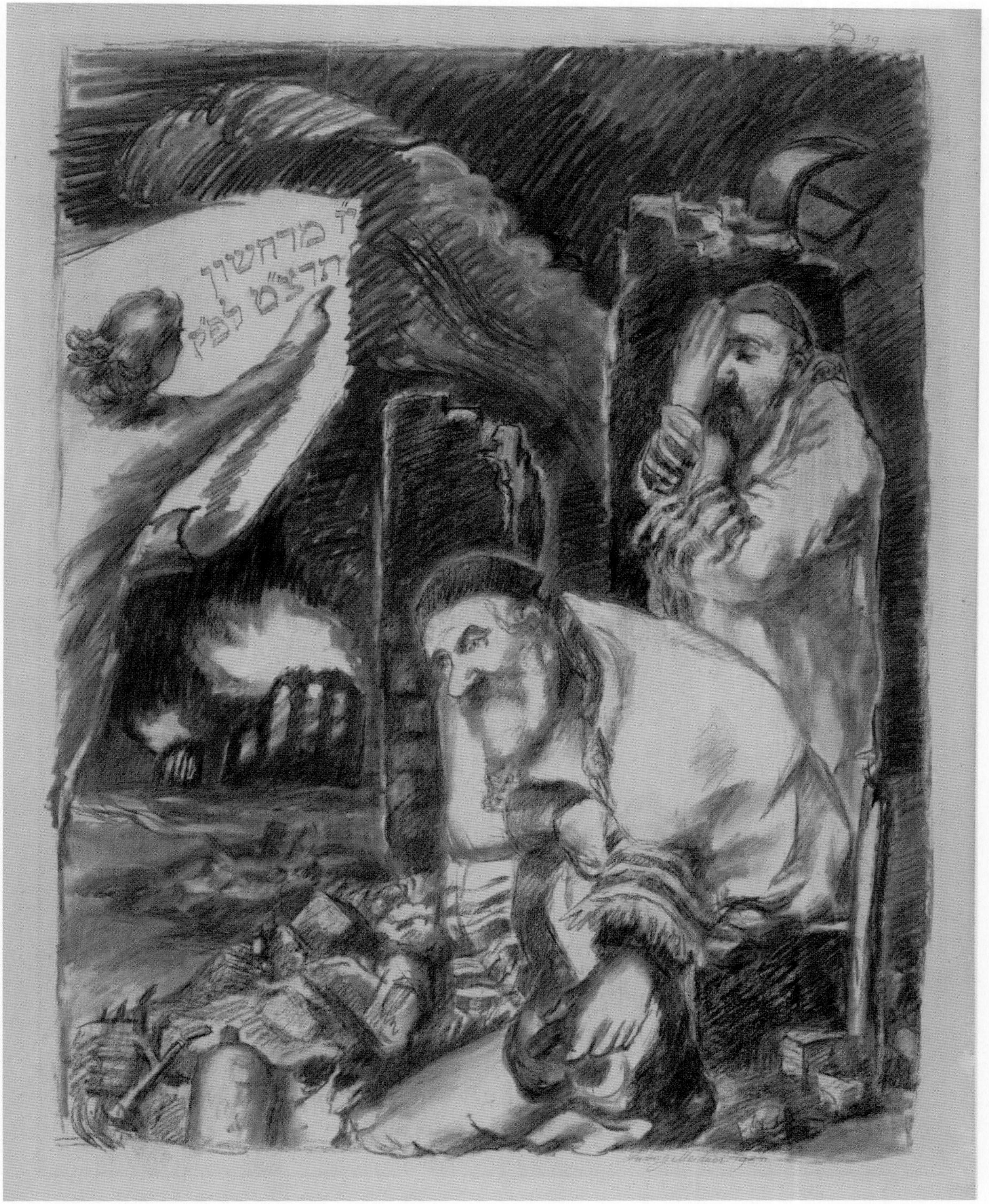
ז״ מרחשון
תרצ״ט לפ״ק

represented, is the terrified king, the only one to see the message. But in this position Meidner placed the despairing rabbis bewailing the burning of the synagogues, heedless of the written signs. The viewer is left to interpret the reference to Daniel's prophecy of the coming fall of the brutal tyranny as words of consolation for the Jews. The signs and the burning synagogues can, however, be read as a forewarning from 1939 of destruction still to come in the course of what was at the time the unpredictable end of the German policy of conquest.

In Germany Otto Pankok was the only non-Jewish artist to give the title *Pogrom* (see illus. 16 and 23) to works, though this was a picture portraying only the recently committed atrocities.[15] In the charcoal drawing of 1940, he indicated the place of the assaults and, by the way the picture was constructed, he put the viewer in the position of bystanders. Even though it bears the title *Massacre II*, Sitte's memorial image for Lidice (see illus. 134) must also be mentioned here.

Despite the incomparable extent of the murder of six million Jews by the Nazis, historical representations of pogroms were also referred to after the end of the Nazi tyranny. But it is not the history of German anti-Semitism and the recently experienced terror that is reflected in a poster appealing for the collecting of memories of Nazi tyranny. Instead it places these within the history of the people of Israel, thus taking up a position that was highly controversial among the surviving Jews.[16] P. Shuldenreyn, presumed to be a Jew living in a camp for displaced persons (DPs) in occupied Germany, designed a poster in 1947 that won the second prize[17] in the competition 'Collect and Record!' (illus. 9), organized by the Central Historical Commission of Liberated Jews in the American Zone of Occupation in Germany for all the DPs in the Western zones.[18] In this, Shuldenreyn referred to the history of his people and emphasized what was for them the 'religious imperative'[19]: 'Remember what Amalek did to you!' The lines from Deuteronomy 25:17 that can also be taken as a call for self-defence are shown as a two-row heading in large red Hebrew letters at the top of the poster. The course of the Jewish diaspora is represented by four scenes on the face of a clock. In each case, together with a written document, they indicate the appeal for *Zameln*, the collecting of images and accounts, the written word. In front of the pyramids at the top left-hand side, a group of building workers in line with the book of Haggadah recount the slavery in exile and the exodus out of Egypt. Opposite on the side there appears the destruction of the First Temple in Jerusalem and the people bewailing the event; here Shuldenreyn has the Menora tumbling onto the scroll of the Lamentations of Jeremiah. At the bottom left, there is a reminder of the pogrom of Jews in 1648 during the Khmelnytsky Uprising, recorded in the book *Yawen Mezulah* by Nathan Nata Hannover. At the same level as this on the right, there is an equally large book with the title *The Vale of Lamentation*, with the words above commenting on the representation of the procession of wandering Jews through the *Valley of Tears*.[20] This does not, however, refer

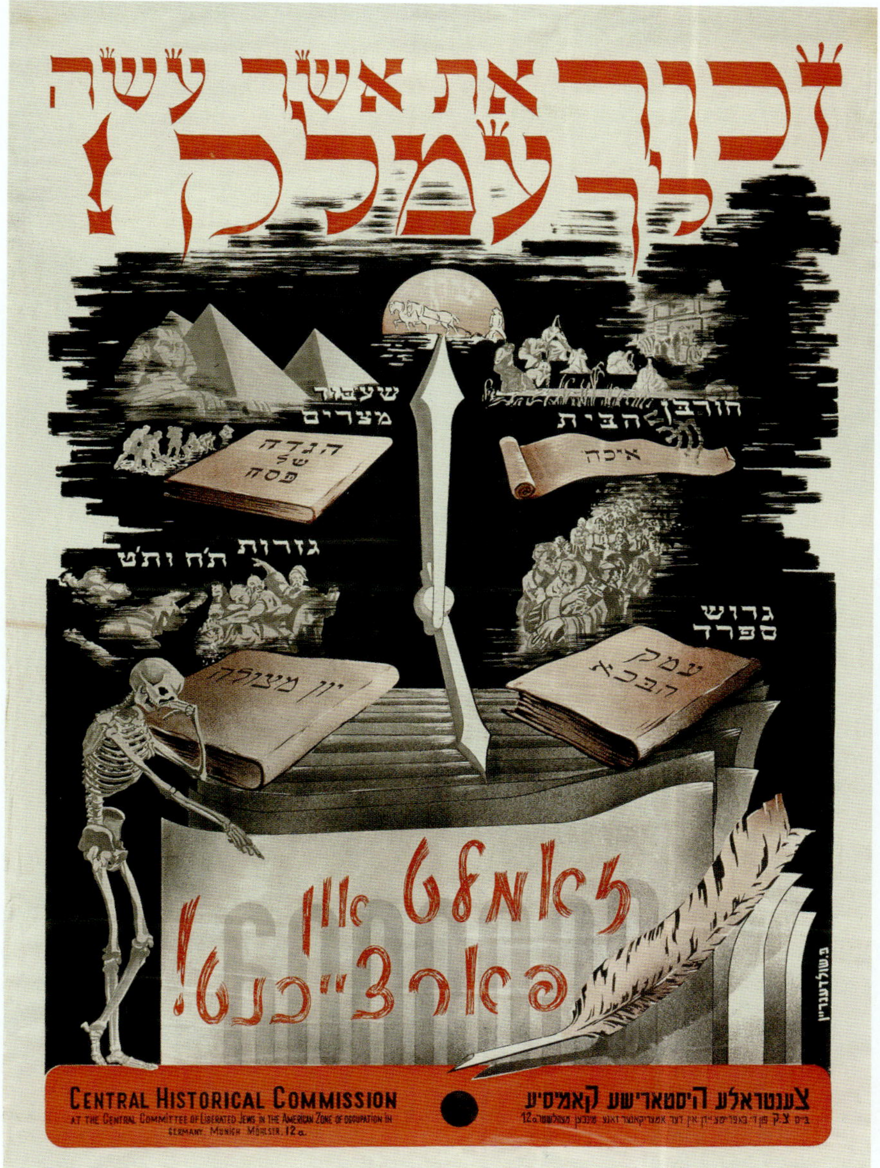

9 P. Shuldenreyn, *Remember What Amalek Did to You*, for the competition 'Collect and Record!', Munich, 1947, poster.

to the biblical exodus through the desert but to the results of the 'Alhambra Edict', the expulsion of the Jews from Spain in 1492. The bearded man leading with the tallith and Torah scroll on his arm reminds the viewer of one of the attempts to save the Holy Scriptures that Samuel Hirszenberg also refers to in the famous painting *Exile* of 1904 (see illus. 3).

The book on the pogroms in the Ukraine, Belarus and Moldova, from where many of those addressed by the poster had fled, and the writing on the journey of the Jews across the desert are to be found on a large stack of papers standing in an upright position. On the first one, written in printed Hebrew letters, are the Yiddish words 'Zamelt un farzjjchnet!' (Collect and Record!)

The red letters are written, as in blood, above the stark figure of 6,000,000. They and the quill-pen at bottom right appeal to the viewer of the poster to record, within the continuity of the scriptures, their suffering, their *Valley of Lamentation* and their 'journey through the desert' and thus to preserve for 'eternity' their recent history, just as stated in the appeal by the Central Historical Commission in Munich.[21] The skeleton on the left copied from Vesalius,[22] whose stance also reminds us of 'the living dead', one of the then widespread terms applied to concentration camp inmates, as an embodiment of the Six Million signifies both them and also the appeal for documentation. The small hand of the clock points towards the appeal, and the big hand points towards the sunrise, with the imprinted letters for 'Zion'. In front of the red semi-circle, a farmer can be made out, working the land with his horses and plough. This reference to the widely circulated memorial drawing *From the Ghetto to Zion* by Ephraim Moses Lilien[23] from the 1901 Zionist Congress in Basel with the prophecy 'and will gather them on every side, and bring them into their own land' (Ezekiel 37:21) was for the DPs in the occupied Germany of 1947 the promise of a shining future in Palestine. This promise is emphasized by the fifth hour, the moment of sunrise. By using a further reference, Shuldenreyn continued the association with the history of the pogroms and the tradition of representing them, since the darkened sun appears in a drawing by Ephraim Moses Lilien as a memorial for the martyrs of Kishinev,[24] like a halo above the Jew who is bound onto a stake with a tallith. The disc of the sun, already semi-visible in Shuldenreyn's poster on the other hand, could be taken as a confident answer to Lilien's drawing. After all, the memory of the catastrophe of the history of the Jews from their enslavement in Egypt up to the recent past was linked to the prophecy that the sun would rise for the Jews in Zion. There is no representation of a 'timeless cycles of atrocities'[25] but a religiously motivated remembrance of Jewish history from the beginnings in slavery up to the imminent prospect of being able and free to migrate to the Promised Land. 'Khurbn',[26] the catastrophe that all displaced persons had been through, and the murder of six million Jews were not shown, only the appeal to write everything down.

These representations of pogroms could also have served after 1945 as models for artists of Christian origin in order to contextualize the new and horrendous events they saw themselves confronted with and enable them to gain some distance from them. However, the earlier murders were not taken as subject-matter. Most of the artists referred to the contemporary media, photographs and films of the liberated camps. Apart from some scenes of violence that had already served as a basis for photography in the construction of the imagery, older representations were not referred to. The photographs from the liberated camps that promised an overwhelming degree of authenticity and uniqueness led to people forgetting images of the earlier pogroms.

This was not the case for Jewish survivors. After the Second World War and the murder of millions, they were left in no doubt that they were seen as Jews.

Having barely come out of it alive, deprived of their rights and homeless, they found that the memory of the history of the people of Israel held out to them the prospect of a common identity. This tendency to think in terms of the tradition of expulsion has also been identified by Mirjam Rajner in the images of flight and deportation ranging from Hirszenberg's *Exile* (see illus. 3) to the relief on the rear face of the 1948 monument to the Warsaw Ghetto by Nathan Rapoport.[27] The procession of fleeing people on Leo Haas's *Death March* (see illus. 85) and Lea Grundig's *The Way into the Gas* (see illus. 58) contain echoes of this. Arie Goral transferred Chagall's paintings of the pogrom at Vitebsk to Hamburg (see illus. 148 and 149).

Particularly artists of Jewish origin reminded people of the long history of hostility to the Jews. Otto Pankok was the only non-Jewish artist who, in the 1957 sculpture *Jew Walking* (see illus. 133), made a connection with earlier pogroms and persecutions.

2 The Human Figure, 1945–9

With the end of the Second World War on 8 May 1945, information was published about the murder of the Jews that had previously only been circulating secretly. As early as 1947 Victor Klemperer had recognized that, for the large majority of Germans, anti-Semitism and racial doctrine were synonymous and, as he analysed in his writing, anti-Semitism had formed 'the kernel and in every respect the prime motivation behind the whole of Nazism'.[1] Only gradually did this view come to be accepted amongst historians,[2] and it was totally absent from the programme of re-education immediately following the liberation. Echoes of this thesis, on the other hand, are already to be found in Horst Strempel's four-part picture *Night over Germany* (see illus. 10) and in the work of Karl Hubbuch. The actively promoted process of public education confronted the 'superior race' with their crimes, revealing what had been suppressed. 'With your own ears you heard about the horror. With your own eyes you saw in Berlin and other towns near the concentration camps the emaciated, numbered figures formed into bomb-disposal units and detonation squads,' wrote the former prisoner Ottomar Geschke, now a member of the Berlin City Council and head of the department of social affairs, in the *Berliner Zeitung* on 4 May 1945 about the attitude of the German people; 'you closed your eyes and covered your ears, because you knew what was going on and you nevertheless tried to claim that you didn't know.'

The writer Erich Kästner, who was himself persecuted during the Nazi period but had never been able to suppress what he knew, nevertheless had trouble finding words to express the scale of the murder. 'Es ist Nacht' (It is Night) is how each of his paragraphs began when he wrote about the film *Todesmühlen* (Death Mills) in the *Neue Zeitung* on 2 February 1946. And this was not simply referring to the ruined cities whose streets and apartments, where there still were any at all, were in darkness, 'often reminding one of film images. What took place in the camps is so dreadful that one cannot stay silent about it and one cannot find the words.' Horst Strempel gave a similar title to the painting with which he attempted to sum up the state of the country and the oppressive images and reports: *Night over Germany*.

The former Buchenwald inmate Jorge Semprun described the, for him, bewildering confrontation between the images he remembered and the Allied film clips: 'In the quiet of the movie theatre . . . these intimate images became foreign to me . . . They ceased being my property and my torment.' But the films, he wrote later, were silent 'because they said nothing precise about the reality they observed, because they delivered only confused scraps of meaning . . . What was really needed was commentary on the images, to decipher them, to situate them not only in a historical context, but within a continuity of feelings and agitations.'[3] In this context one's limited ability to express experiences of suffering begins to falter.

Meanwhile, there was no shortage of facts to be seen and read. Every day there was at least one article in the newspapers describing the conditions in one or more of the camps. In their poster bulletins and leaflets, the American military administration published photographs of piles of corpses, ovens opened up in the crematoria and 'living skeletons'. In addition, they ordered compulsory visits to the liberated camps.[4] The Soviet military authorities in the newspapers they controlled relied totally on the power of the word.[5] Without a doubt, every newspaper reader, cinema-goer and radio listener in Germany had been informed about the German crimes against the Jews in the first three months after the end of the war. However, along with the revelations of genocide, there was pressure for a line to be drawn under the events. Even shortly after the first revelations, on 4 June 1945, the *Berliner Zeitung* quoted a letter from a lady reader who, while deeply upset about the concentration camps, nevertheless requested them not to publish any more descriptions and was of the opinion that 'a final line should be drawn under everything that has happened. We must all begin things anew.' 'Expression of a Nazi guilty conscience' is how the *Frankfurter Rundschau* even then described the unwillingness to know about what had happened (22 September 1945).

But there was also the joy of the liberated opponents of the regime and mourning at the millions of deaths. One of the earliest memorial sites was the sports stadium bordering Tempelhof airport in the area of Berlin Neukölln in July 1945. At its reopening it was named after the communist resistance fighter and German boxing champion Werner Seelenbinder.[6] The inauguration of a commemorative site as early as autumn 1945 set the tone for the culture of memory in the GDR, and contrary to the usual practice it was reported entirely in pictures. The City Council established by the Red Army together with the Chief Committee of the Victims of Fascism (OdF), the organization responsible for the clarification of the former prisioners in regard to the allocation of housing, employment and, where possible, financial aid announced another commemoration in this stadium for the second Sunday in September. Those being honoured had been active in the political resistance. The architect Hans Scharoun, at the time still a member of the City Council, had designed a temporary memorial,[7] the central symbol of which was a single triangle that all concentration camp inmates had to wear as a badge in various colours.[8] The triangle of the memorial placed in front of a 60-m-long wall bearing the letters K and Z (that is, *Konzentrationslager*, or concentration camp) was red, like the stripe of the political prisoners,[9] and formed the model for the many simple stones in the GDR that from then on marked the route of the death marches after the evacuation of the concentration camps. This commemoration on its own symbolized the hierarchy of victims that was to be characteristic of the politics of remembrance and *Wiedergutmachung* (reparations, that is, making up for the past) in the two German states up to the reunification. While the GDR gave priority to *Kämpfer* (resistance fighters), in the FRG, on the other hand, the resistance was soon to be exclusively associated with the failed attempt on Hitler's life on 20 July 1944. In the East, figures of the *Kämpfer* or the inmates' badge, mainly coloured red, predominated, even on later memorials. For that very reason, in the West the triangle could not become a symbol of the Nazi crimes.

The Jewish religious community in Berlin remembered those among them who had been murdered by laying a foundation stone a week later for a memorial in the Jewish cemetery at Weissensee. The ceremony was a reminder not only of the dead, but of the feelings of envy harboured by the Germans towards successful Jews and the Germans' 'racial fanaticism. With six million murdered by Nazism, the Jewish community have been of all peoples the greatest victims, a fact that deserves to be respected and demands the recognition of the extent of Jewish victimhood' (*Berliner Zeitung*, 19 September 1945).

Horst Strempel: *Night over Germany*

Germany being a landscape of camps at the end of the war in 1945–6, Horst Strempel[10] painted the triptych *Night over Germany* (illus. 10), in oil on sackcloth, showing the destruction of the country and its people. Like a large-scale Christian winged altarpiece, the symbolic view of night consists of several panels. On the central one, one sees a large male figure in the middle and a smaller one on the left side hanging on barbed wire; on the right side are children with their arms raised and open hands, displaying red tattoos. The panel below is devoted to the prisoners attempting to communicate by knocking sounds. On the right-hand wing, Strempel painted a Jewish family, indicated by the yellow patch on the man's chest;[11] on the left-hand wing, a figure squatting in the dark, looking anxiously out of the picture. Strempel did not

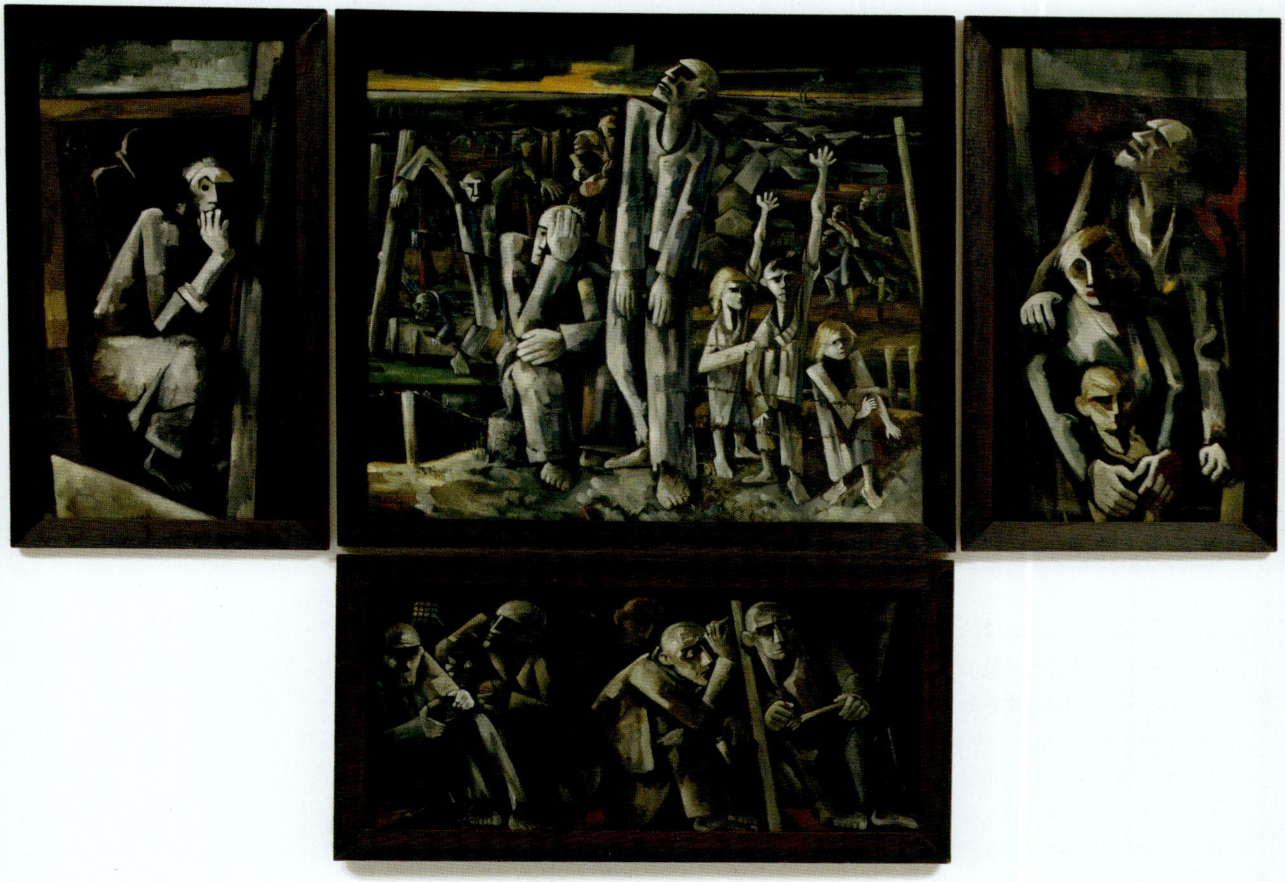

10 Horst Strempel,
Night over Germany,
1946, oil on sack-cloth.

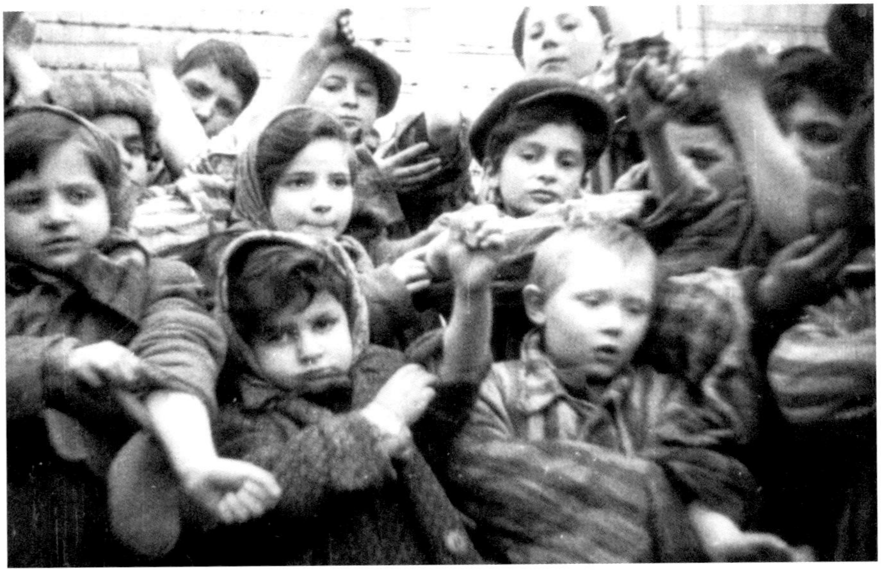

11 *Liberation of Auschwitz, Poland, 1945*, part of the film *Death Mills*. Dialogue of the German version: 'Children in Auschwitz: their parents and relatives were gassed long ago: they have forgotten their names, they are nothing but numbers, burned on their arms.'

limit his perspective to the misery and the ruins, as portrayed at the same period by his teacher Carl Hofer in the *Deutsche Kunstausstellung* (German Art Exhibition) in Berlin.[12] In the way he presented things, Germany is not just characterized as a nocturnal landscape according to the natural sequence of day and night but as a dismal crime scene where even children are not spared, whether their parents are Jewish, Sinti or Roma. Strempel portrayed the places which many Germans were now taken to visit as part of the re-education programme, places that were already familiar to those who lived nearby, having been after all workplaces and places to go to for Sunday outings.[13]

Strempel brought together different groups and individual people, such as the cowering man and the man committing suicide on the electrically charged barbed wire,[14] among them a body lying dead, a mother with a child and the three children right in the foreground of the central panel. They nevertheless stand on their own; they are not unified by any common activity. The viewer is called upon to respond to the gaze emanating from the dark eye sockets. One is conscious of the figures being set against the background of smoking chimneys on the horizon which are repeated even larger on the right-hand panel and could represent the chimneys of the crematoria at Auschwitz-Birkenau (see illus. 101).

The artist used as the basis for his portrayal what was available in the contemporary documentation in the form of photographs and on film. A child like the one in the central panel with his sleeve rolled up and displaying his tattoo can be seen in the film *Death Mills*,[15] which many Germans had to watch as part of the re-education programme (illus. 11). Marks reminiscent of the camp numbers tattooed on after deportation are to be seen on the raised arms of the other children portrayed and, along with their clothing, show them to be former inmates. Strempel was not the only artist to refer

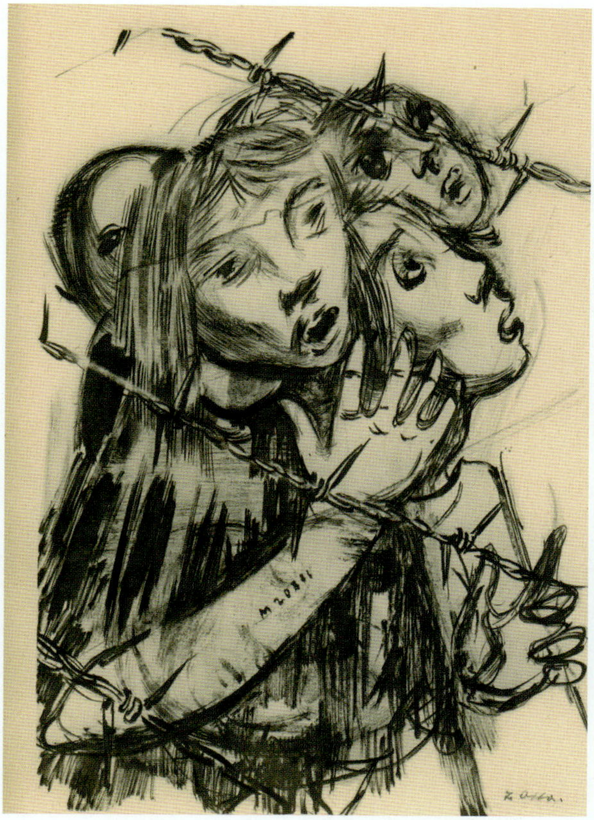

12 Teo Otto, *Children in the camp*, from *Nie Wieder. Tagebuch in Bildern* (Berlin, 1949), photo-lithograph.

to these tattoos on children's arms from the film. Teo Otto devoted a page, *Children in the camp* (illus. 12), to them in his *Tagebuch in Bildern* (Journal in Images), as did Peter Edel with his drawing in coloured chalk *Children in Auschwitz-Birkenau*[16] (illus. 13). Just how much not just the painters but the people of the time were affected by the scene in the film can be gleaned from one of the reports, entitled *Zum Tage* (Thought for the Day), by Axel Eggebrecht on Northwest German Radio about the first Belsen trial in the autumn of 1945. He described his 'vision' referring to the documentary film of the children and, at the same time, casting a shadow over it: 'I saw these at the time eight- and ten-year-olds as old people. Around the end of this century. Telling their grandchildren about the decade of humiliation – and revealing their left arms, as evidence of that which a more fortunate generation will not be able to comprehend. Will not be allowed to comprehend!'[17]

On the left side of Strempel's central panel, a cowering man, identified as a Jew by a yellow patch, is turning his upper body away from the scene with the child prisoners, a gesture further heightened by his covering his eye. Male figures sitting like this one, seemingly aware of nothing but their own despair, were characteristic of many of the artworks produced in West Germany in the 1950s, particularly sculptures that sought to interpret the war and its aftermath.[18] Strempel derived the key image, the large looming figure in the centre of the picture, from socialist iconography, but in his image it is not simply interpretable as a heroic ideal: this is no model of a leader of the workers' movement that we see here. It is left up to the viewer whether they see in the figure a prisoner who is rising up to greet the shaft of light on the horizon, or a German Nazi attempting to stumble forward in the dark.

The stance of the body of the male figure in the right-hand panel and the direction in which he is looking correspond to those of the central figure in the middle panel, and these too do not indicate any fundamental change. The uncertainty is made even clearer by the figure looking out of the left-hand panel with eyes wide open. No hint of an end to the terror is given either by the scene in the predella, in what the bars indicate to be a prison, showing the male figures in striped prison clothing as prisoners at various occupations and activities. The figure cowering in the left-hand corner is clutching an empty plate; his sunken face, like those of many of the emaciated camp inmates seen

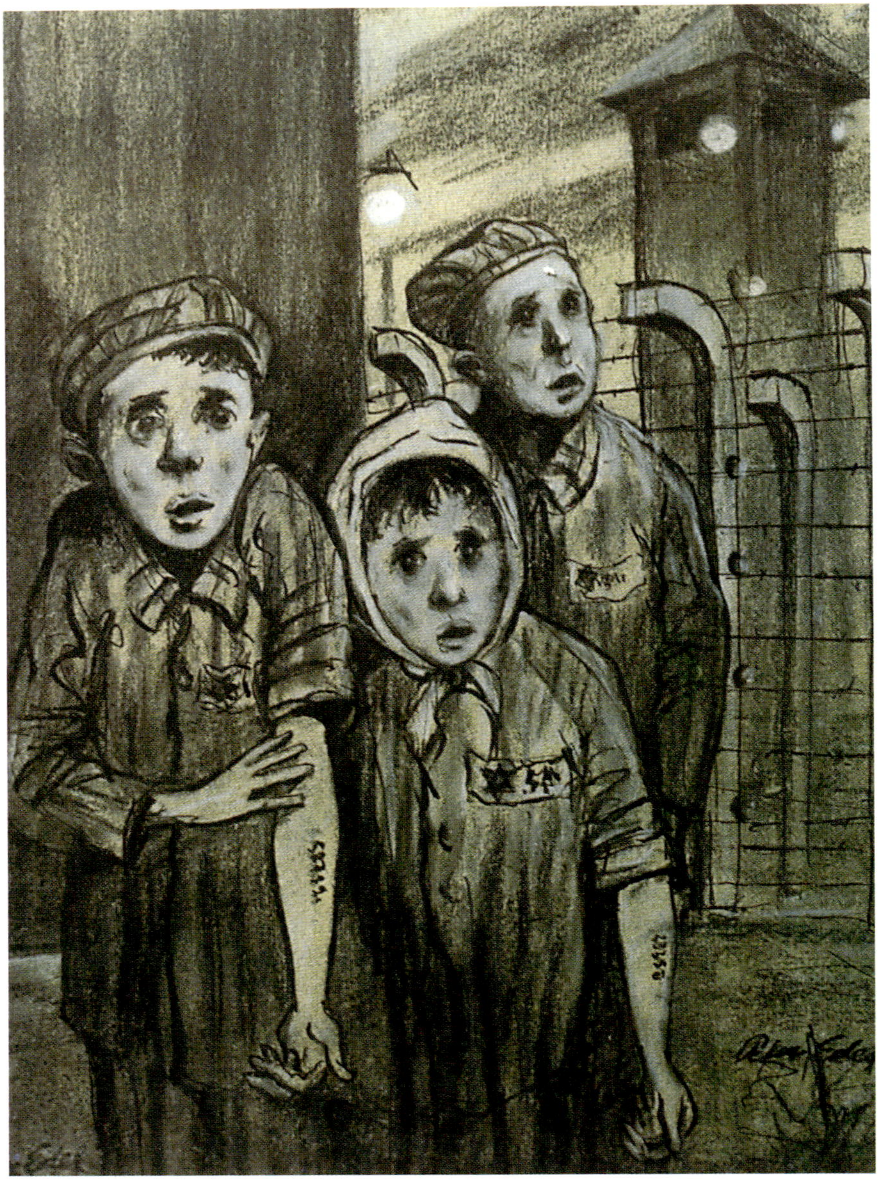

13 Peter Edel, *Children in Auschwitz-Birkenau*, 1944, fol. 14 from *Wenn es ans Leben geht* (Berlin, 1983), drawing.

in the photographs and films at the liberation, resembles a skull. It represents prisoners characterized as suffering from 'extreme physical and mental exhaustion' and referred to in the concentration and extermination camps by the term *Muselman*.[19] This is suggested by the fact that he does not react to the figure next to him. It is the only time that bread, as a sign of hunger, is seen in the panels and here it is not accepted. In an emphasized position at the intersection of the central panel and predella, but in the darkness, a fifth figure can be made out, distinguished from the others by blue clothing, with his right hand clenched into a fist. He could symbolize the impotent position of the Communists within fascism. Strempel refers to figures formulated in

Christian iconography and in the arts of the workers' movement and brings them up to date with current events. The dramatis personae of his triptych are figures that became familiar in later representations of the Nazi period.

Contemporary art critics at the first exhibition saw a work that 'sums up everything that is terrifying, miserable and grey . . . grey upon grey',[20] and called it 'Germany destroyed'.[21] The picture was purchased immediately on completion by Berlin city council, but then disappeared from public view until the 1970s. Initial recognition of the work was soon followed by rejection, and the artist fell foul of the opposition between the two sides in the Cold War and the debate over politics and art. After returning from being a prisoner of war, he was given an apartment in West Berlin in 1945. In 1947 he was appointed as a lecturer at the Academy of Applied Art in Berlin-Weissensee, then a part of the Eastern zone. His pictorial work *Night over Germany* was highlighted in 1947 at the exhibition of the *Meisterwerke deutscher Bildhauerei und Malerei* (Masterworks of German Sculpture and Painting) at the Zeughaus in Berlin, then belonging to the Soviet sector. He was commissioned to produce a mural, *Aufbau* (Construction), for Friedrichstrasse Station, also in the east of the city. With the change in cultural policy and the start of the debate around formalism, he came in for some heavy criticism, nevertheless still being appointed professor at the Weissensee Academy in 1949. During the exhibition of his works in West Berlin, the reports in the Western press went in for some schadenfreude at the criticism of him in the East. In 1951 in the debate around formalism in the GDR, Strempel was held up as a negative example for whom the human being was not an individual but only 'a mark in the composition',[22] and shortly afterwards his mural at Friedrichstrasse Station was painted over. In 1952 another mural by Strempel in Ballenstedt was removed. After accusations that he was involved in sabotage, Strempel escaped to the West without any possessions where, this time, an application to be allowed to stay given the extreme circumstances was refused.[23] Not until 1977 was *Night over Germany* shown in public again,[24] and in the 1980s it was even reinstated in the canon of the 'most impressive achievements' of the early development of art in the GDR[25] – an assessment that has held good even after the Fall of the Berlin Wall.

Compared with *The Camp* by Edgar Jené (see illus. 106) of the same year and his surrealistic figurines representing the camp inmates, one can see how Strempel managed to portray the oppressive reality of the camp, now applied to the whole of the country, using traditional stylistic means and familiar iconographic models as well as references to the present. Like Otto Dix in his 1932 painting of the destruction of the First World War recalling Matthias Grünewald's Isenheim Altar[26] and Hans Grundig in his 1936 picture of the destruction of *The Thousand Year Reich*,[27] the artist was referring back to a standard image of Christian devotion, a triptych with a predella. But he was not painting any religious message of salvation. Instead, he was echoing the political warnings by the artists named and transforming the particular pathos of Christian iconography into a representation of suffering without any hope of salvation. Rather, the long transition from war to peace characterizes *Night over Germany*; it is still uncertain whether the people are expecting an end to the deadly system or continuing to react, as if paralysed, to this event.

Night over Germany was not to be the only work by Strempel on the persecution of the Jews under the Nazis. Under the title *Pogrom*, he finished nine separate pictures in 1946–7, some of which are presumed to have been lost.[28] As far as Gabriele Saure could find out, he was here developing several scenes from this polyptych into paintings:[29] *Fear*, *The Yellow Star*, *The Camp*, *On the Wire*, *Forced Labour*, *Children*, *Transportees*, *Prisoners* and an oil sketch, *Pogrom*.

Peter Edel

Esther

The pencil drawing that Peter Edel made of his wife, murdered in Auschwitz-Birkenau, as the portrait of 'the young painter Esther' (illus. 15) was published in the GDR, at the latest at the time of the dedication of the memorial site at Sachsenhausen (on 23 April 1961), in the newspaper *Märkische Volksstimme* of 16 April 1961.[30] The writer and graphic artist, the son of a Catholic mother and a Jewish father, survived the camps at Grossbeeren, Auschwitz, Sachsenhausen, Mauthausen and Ebensee because he was still useful in being able to draw dollar bills,[31] and after the war he became a Communist, a highly respected citizen of the GDR and in 1978 an unofficial member of the Ministry of State Security (STASI).[32] His drawing catches the reader's eye, drawing attention to the page, and is placed above his double-column report on resistance activities in the forgery workshop in Sachsenhausen, entitled *Block 19 Death Squad*. On the left side of the newspaper, one can read a report covering two whole columns by two communist former prisoners in the same camp about solidarity among the comrades and their resistance. Esther, persecuted for being a resistance fighter and murdered for being a Jew, by contrast is presented in the drawing as resistance in the form of a beautiful person. The caption to the picture ends with the statement: 'No acts of cruelty on the part of the SS torturers were able to break this woman. She remained a human being, the really beautiful person of that time.'

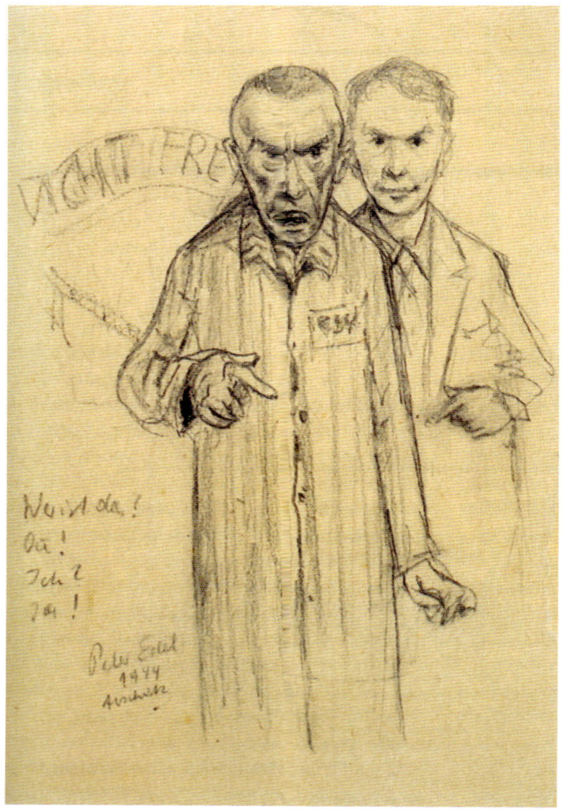

14 Peter Edel, *Self-portrait*, 1944, pencil on cardboard.

Peter Edel had written a book about her immediately after the war: *Schwester der Nacht* (Sister of

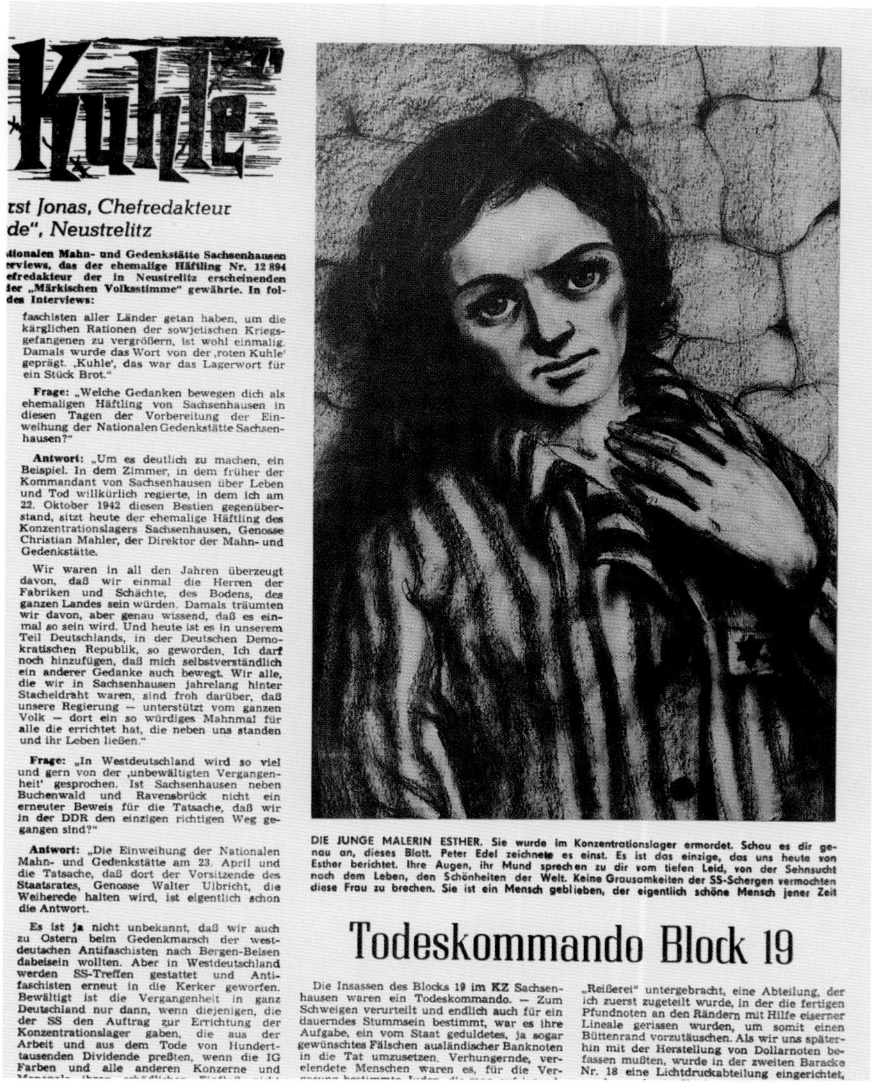

„Kuhle"

…rst Jonas, Chefredakteur
…de", Neustrelitz

…tionalen Mahn- und Gedenkstätte Sachsenhausen …rviews, das der ehemalige Häftling Nr. 12 894 …efredakteur der in Neustrelitz erscheinenden …der „Märkischen Volksstimme" gewährte. In fol… des Interviews:

faschisten aller Länder getan haben, um die kärglichen Rationen der sowjetischen Kriegsgefangenen zu vergrößern, ist wohl einmalig. Damals wurde das Wort von der ‚roten Kuhle' geprägt. ‚Kuhle', das war das Lagerwort für ein Stück Brot."

Frage: „Welche Gedanken bewegen dich als ehemaligen Häftling von Sachsenhausen in diesen Tagen der Vorbereitung der Einweihung der Nationalen Gedenkstätte Sachsenhausen?"

Antwort: „Um es deutlich zu machen, ein Beispiel. In dem Zimmer, in dem früher der Kommandant von Sachsenhausen über Leben und Tod willkürlich regierte, in dem ich am 22. Oktober 1942 diesen Bestien gegenüberstand, sitzt heute der ehemalige Häftling des Konzentrationslagers Sachsenhausen, Genosse Christian Mahler, der Direktor der Mahn- und Gedenkstätte.

Wir waren in all den Jahren überzeugt davon, daß wir einmal die Herren der Fabriken und Schächte, des Bodens, des ganzen Landes sein würden. Damals träumten wir davon, aber genau wissend, daß es einmal so sein wird. Und heute ist es in unserem Teil Deutschlands, in der Deutschen Demokratischen Republik, so geworden. Ich darf noch hinzufügen, daß mich selbstverständlich ein anderer Gedanke auch bewegt. Wir alle, die wir in Sachsenhausen jahrelang hinter Stacheldraht waren, sind froh darüber, daß unsere Regierung – unterstützt vom ganzen Volk – dort ein so würdiges Mahnmal für alle die errichtet hat, die neben uns standen und ihr Leben ließen."

Frage: „In Westdeutschland wird so viel und gern von der ‚unbewältigten Vergangenheit' gesprochen. Ist Sachsenhausen neben Buchenwald und Ravensbrück nicht ein erneuter Beweis für die Tatsache, daß wir in der DDR den einzigen richtigen Weg gegangen sind?"

Antwort: „Die Einweihung der Nationalen Mahn- und Gedenkstätte am 23. April und die Tatsache, daß dort der Vorsitzende des Staatsrates, Genosse Walter Ulbricht, die Weiherede halten wird, ist eigentlich schon die Antwort.

Es ist ja nicht unbekannt, daß wir auch zu Ostern beim Gedenkmarsch der westdeutschen Antifaschisten nach Bergen-Belsen dabeisein wollten. Aber in Westdeutschland werden SS-Treffen gestattet und Antifaschisten erneut in die Kerker geworfen. Bewältigt ist die Vergangenheit in ganz Deutschland nur dann, wenn diejenigen, die der SS den Auftrag zur Errichtung der Konzentrationslager gaben, die aus der Arbeit und aus dem Tode von Hunderttausenden Dividende preßten, wenn die IG Farben und alle anderen Konzerne und

DIE JUNGE MALERIN ESTHER. Sie wurde im Konzentrationslager ermordet. Schau es dir genau an, dieses Blatt. Peter Edel zeichnete es einst. Es ist das einzige, das uns heute von Esther berichtet. Ihre Augen, ihr Mund sprechen zu dir vom tiefen Leid, von der Sehnsucht nach dem Leben, den Schönheiten der Welt. Keine Grausamkeiten der SS-Schergen vermochten diese Frau zu brechen. Sie ist ein Mensch geblieben, der eigentlich schöne Mensch jener Zeit

Todeskommando Block 19

Die Insassen des Blocks 19 im KZ Sachsenhausen waren ein Todeskommando. – Zum Schweigen verurteilt und endlich auch für ein dauerndes Stummsein bestimmt, war es ihre Aufgabe, ein vom Staat geduldetes, ja sogar gewünschtes Fälschen ausländischer Banknoten in die Tat umzusetzen. Verhungernde, verelendete Menschen waren es, für die Ver-

„Reißerei" untergebracht, eine Abteilung, der ich zuerst zugeteilt wurde, in der die fertigen Pfundnoten an den Rändern mit Hilfe eiserner Lineale gerissen wurden, um somit einen Büttenrand vorzutäuschen. Als wir uns späterhin mit der Herstellung von Dollarnoten befassen mußten, wurde in der zweiten Baracke Nr. 18 eine Lichtdruckabteilung eingerichtet,

15 Peter Edel, *Esther*, 1944, from *Märkische Volksstimme* (16 April 1961).

the Night).[33] In the novel the figure of 'comrade' Esther, recalling his deported wife under the fictional name Marion (p. 52),[34] becomes 'a symbol for millions of young girls who followed the same way as her' (pp. 7, 199). He described her persecution in detail through the various stages, starting with escape from where she was living, via the Gestapo torture cells, deportation from there on to their meeting up again in Mauthausen concentration camp, the expression of her eyes, her face and her maltreated body which, however, he drew as being purely unscathed.

The date of the pencil drawing on paper that was frequently published and probably also shown in exhibitions is variously given in the publications and cannot be precisely established from Edel's fictional accounts.[35] The pencil drawing must date at the latest from shortly after his liberation in Austria, along with the writing of *Schwester der Nacht*. The 1947 novel has autobiographical elements, and in the foreword, Edel specifically emphasizes its claim to be realistic: 'The action of the novel is not made up. Everything related in this book unfortunately took place exactly as it is recorded.' Here for the first time, not later in his autobiography published in 1969, he described Esther's characteristic pose in which he drew her: 'Oh, how broad and heavy her hand was, placed so casually on the lapel of her jacket. Her fine, white artist's hand that I saw so often holding the palette' (p. 198). Edel's picture showed no cut wounds or red marks on Esther's body that had been described earlier, during and after torture, as completely disfigured: 'a naked human question mark on the damp concrete floor, battered and abused . . . she is an animal breathing its last' (pp. 117–18).

Just as, at the same moment in France, the painter Jean Fautrier was in hiding, portraying a Jewish woman as a barely recognizable amorphous mass representing a hostage presumed to have been shot,[36] on the contrary Edel, for the image, returned to the theme of the intact female body. Edel followed the ancient desire of human beings to keep a familiar likeness of the dead person concerned, as in this case he imagined Esther here with her slightly downcast head and her slender body. His drawing was intended to make one forget Esther's wounds. As a portrait recalling the murdered woman that was to symbolize millions of other Jewish women, with Esther's face, her dark hair, her prominent eyebrows, her big eyes and her fulsome mouth,[37] Edel was emphasizing the stereotype of the 'beautiful Jewess',[38] even in the emaciated form in prison garb.

Self-portrait

His own facial features and their transformation into an alien out-of-body state, on the other hand, he was to capture in Auschwitz in a pencil drawing on cardboard. On the left in the background a fragment of the motto from the entrance of Auschwitz and other Concentration Camps, 'ARBEIT MACHT FREI' (literally, 'work makes free'), is visible, but without the word 'ARBEIT', thus becoming the outcry 'liberate'. The drawing can be seen as a desperate attempt at self-recognition, at capturing one's identity in a concentration camp (illus. 14). 'Who is that?' he wrote next to the figure of himself as a hunched prisoner and, alongside his prematurely aged, haggard face, he drew his well-formed portrait as in the days gone by. Pointing at one another, both figures, in search of that which has become alien in the other's gaze, while looking, find themselves subject to the gaze: 'You! I! Yes! Peter Edel 1944 Auschwitz'.[39]

Otto Pankok

Immediately after the war, the artist Otto Pankok, who had been banned by the Nazis, was reinstated thanks to the occupying powers.[40] He was

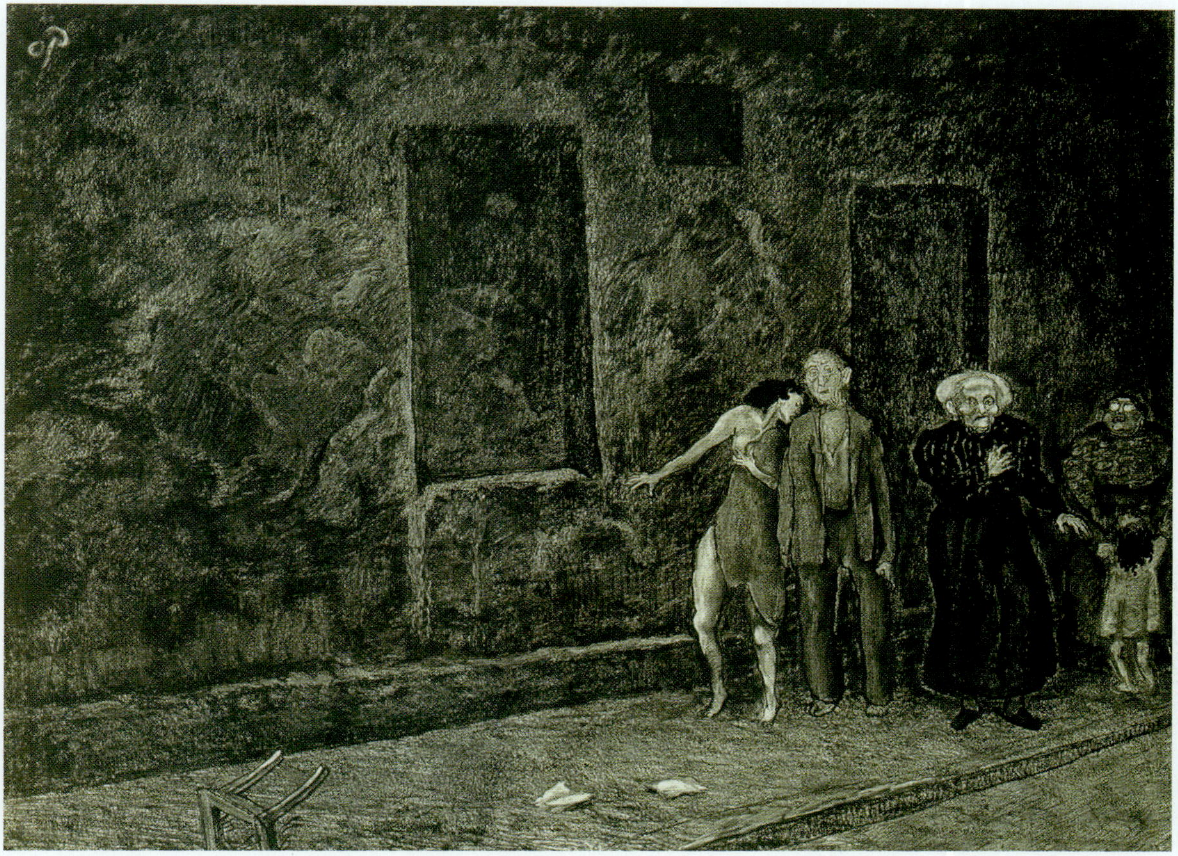

16 Otto Pankok, *Pogrom in Düsseldorf*, 1940, charcoal on paper.

immediately given a professorship at the national Art Academy in Düsseldorf, and his works were displayed in a number of exhibitions in the first few years after the war.[41] Now he was able to show the public the pictures concerning the fate of the Jews he had produced from the beginning of the Second World War, even under serious threat. The first exhibition of his works after the war, indeed the very first one, in Aachen, which had already been liberated as early as 1944, received the review: 'The pictures entitled "Mass Murder"[42] and "Pogrom in Düsseldorf" remind us of the horrific way the Nazis treated the Jews; Pankok is here the implacable accuser and defender of humanity. One feels that the last thing he is aiming at is producing cheap effects.'[43]

Pankok's choice of images for the early exhibitions, in Aachen in 1945, Düsseldorf in 1946–7 and Hamburg in 1947, consisted solely of those concerning the story of the Jews; *Pogrom in Düsseldorf* (illus. 16) was on display at all three. In the first exhibition of the re-established Rheinische Sezession in 1946 in Düsseldorf, nine out of the ten Pankok works chosen were devoted to the Jews and their persecution.[44] As the Hamburg catalogue records, in September and October 1947 'at the galleries of the art circle in the Hamburg Alsterhaus' the visitors to the museum were presented with a total of 61 paintings, 114 woodcuts, 22 etchings, 18 lithographs and 35 sculptures by Pankok,

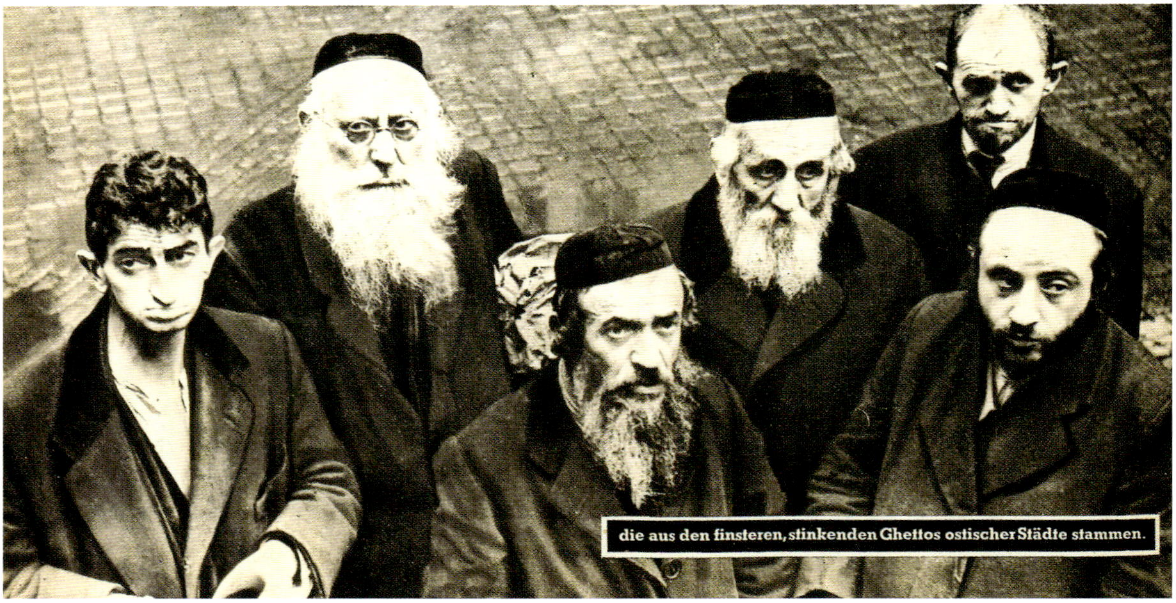

17 'Those coming from the dark, stinking ghettos of Eastern cities', in *Der Untermensch*, ed. Reichsführer SS Office (Berlin, 1942).

among which were seven paintings, seven woodcuts and two sculptures portraying Jews.[45] At the 1948 exhibition in Mannheim, only three of the 79 titles were portraits of Jews; *Pogrom in Düsseldorf* was not exhibited.[46] As Pankok drew men only in the dress of the inhabitants of East European shtetls, consisting of a long coat with a hat and a beard, it was clear to the museum public that they were looking at images of a group of people who had been stigmatized and systematically exterminated by the Germans as *Untermenschen*.[47] The Hamburg exhibition displayed four of the sketches consisting of charcoal drawings, appearing under the heading *Paintings*, that not only show individual Jews, but record the indignities the Jews had to submit to at the hands of the Nazis right at the start of their persecution, in full view of all the local inhabitants: *The Synagogue* (see illus. 19), *Street in the Ghetto*, *Pogrom in Düsseldorf* (see illus. 16), *The House for the Jews* (see illus. 24).

Jews

For his images of the suffering of the Jews Pankok drew on the most varied sources of imagery and had no hesitation in using references to extremely malicious literature against the grain of their authors' intentions. His interpretation of photos showing Jews from the Nazi propaganda publication *Der Untermensch* that appeared with blatantly dehumanizing captions such as 'coming out of the dark, stinking ghettos of Eastern cities' (illus. 17) or 'Animals in human form' turned them into memorable towering studies of elderly Jewish men, as for example in *Rabbi 2* (illus. 18) of 1942.[48]

The Synagogue (illus. 19) of 1940 is presumably the same charcoal drawing on paper which was later frequently reproduced with the addition of *zerstörte* (destroyed), and was classified under the collection of subjects dealing with *Jewish*

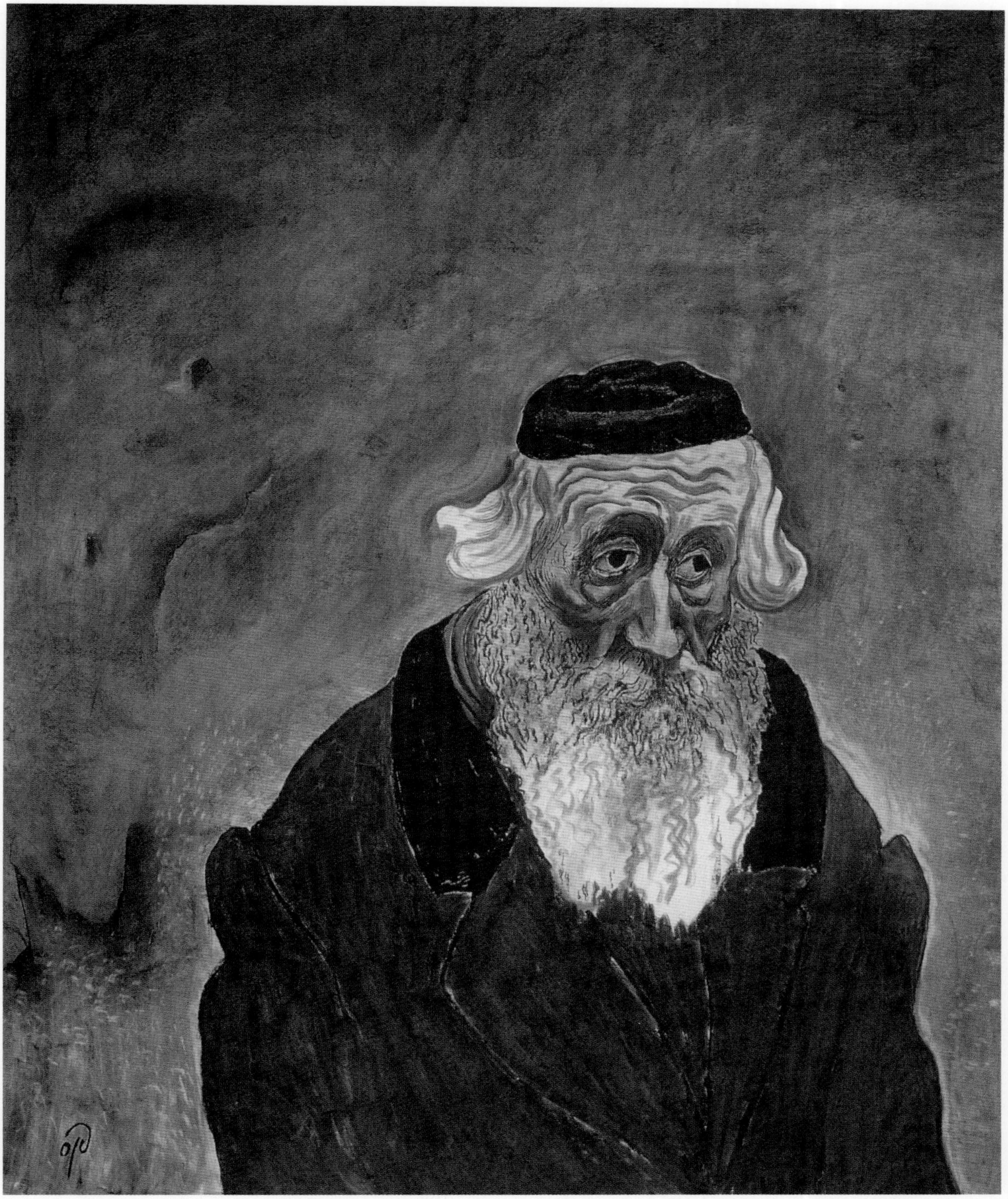

18 Otto Pankok, *Rabbi 2*,
1942, charcoal on paper.

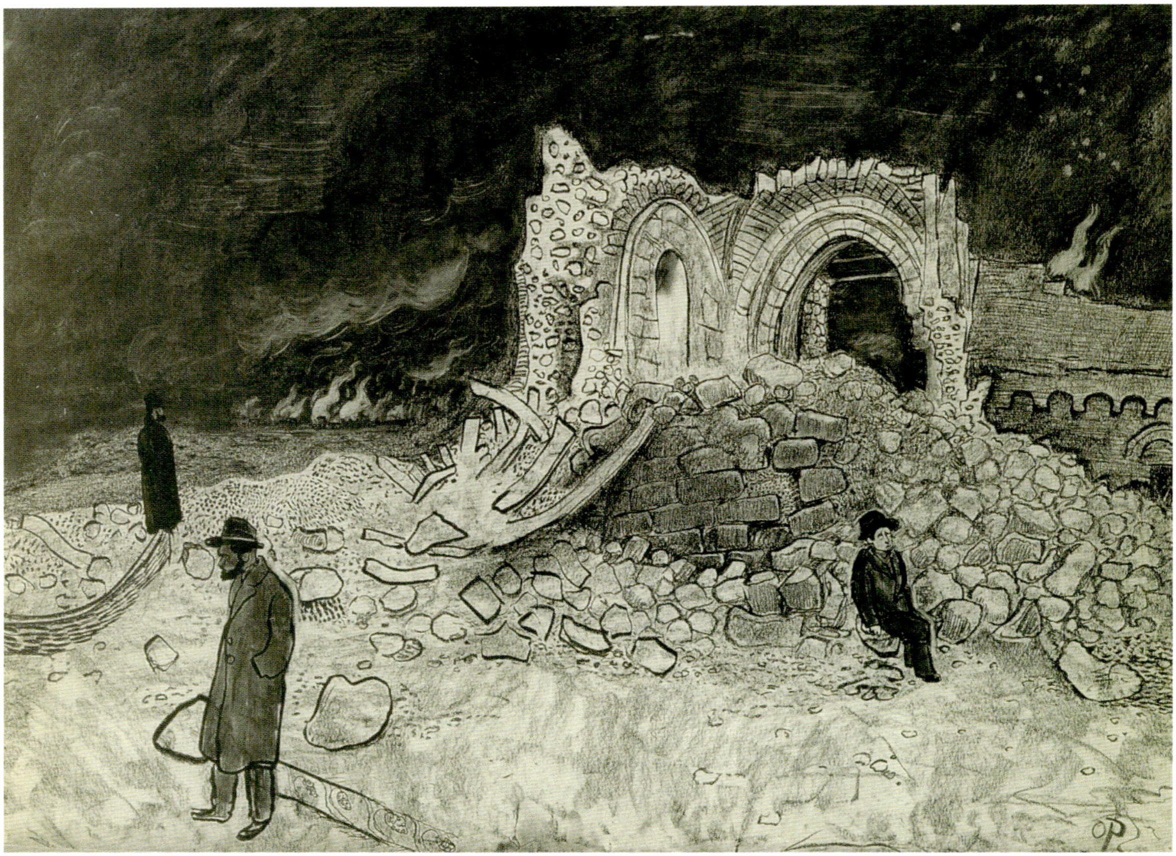

19 Otto Pankok,
The Synagogue, 1940,
charcoal on paper.

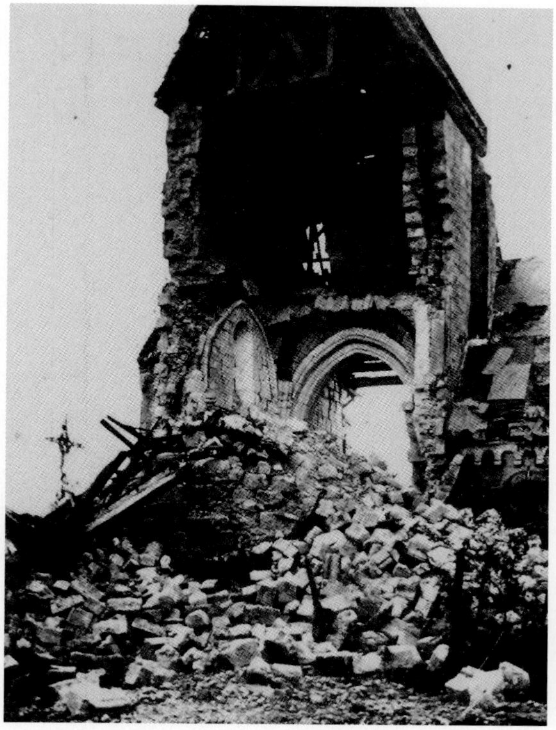

20 'Behold the Constructive Work of Capitalism', in Ernst Friedrich, *Krieg dem Kriege!* (Berlin, 1924).

Fates that does not represent a planned cycle but arose only in the course of the many exhibitions in East and West Germany.[49] Pankok the pacifist copied the three isolated figures from a photo by Walter Gircke, already in the 1920s a sought-after photographer, who had contributed in many magazines to the image of the criminal or at least questionable and backward Eastern Jew (illus. 21).[50] The pile of rubble against a dark background is inspired by a photograph of a destroyed church from a book by the left-wing author Ernst Friedrich, *Krieg dem Kriege!* (War on War!)[51] (illus. 20). Understandably, signs of the Christian church, as well as the central tower above the grooved Gothic arch, have been left out, and the outline of a cross against a light background has given way to a sea of flames on the horizon. The drawing, however, is in accord with Friedrich's pacifist intention, condemning deliberate destruction. Friedrich had used this photo from the First World War as a sarcastic illustration of capitalism and war: 'Behold the constructive work of capitalism.' Pankok in his turn was recycling this to show the brutal destruction of Jewish culture and religion at the start of the following war.

He now frequently turned to the fate of the Jews, again referring back to Walter Gircke's 1928 photo of the Berlin Scheunenviertel for the two drawings of waiting men: *Ghetto* with four men[52] and *Men Waiting (Ghetto)* (illus. 22). He did not put the two men with walking sticks talking in Gircke's photo into the second drawing. Using the medium of drawing, he transformed the everyday snapshot in the Grenadierstrasse in Berlin[53] into an image of the continuing desperate situation of the ghettos in the German-occupied territories and distanced it from the hate campaign of the period, couched in terms such as 'The Focus of Contagion for Europe: The Polish Ghetto'.[54] The individual bystanders in the Berlin street scene, the first with his hand in his coat pocket, the fifth and the fourth man from the right, become three isolated men waiting in long coats, and with beards and hats, staring in front of them at a dark puddle.

In the dim charcoal drawing of the street scene *Pogrom in Düsseldorf* (see illus. 16), which was frequently put on show – as No. 187 in the catalogue of the Rheinische Sezession in 1946, where Pankok displayed ten pictures concerning the history of the Jews;[55] in the catalogue of the 1946–7 Düsseldorf collective exhibition under No. 211;[56] and under No. 10 in the Hamburg catalogue – the Jews are portrayed as not fully dressed, having been dragged out of their beds. *Pogrom with ss Officer* from 1940 (illus. 23) reveals the people as being 'helplessly abandoned and exposed to a Gestapo officer who is

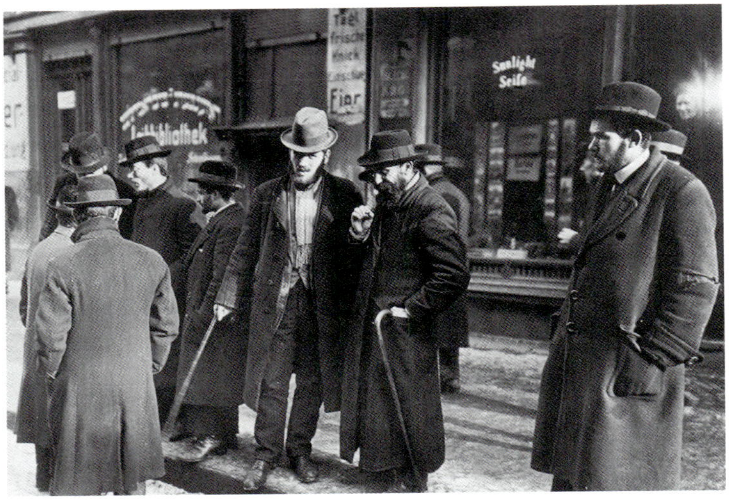

21 Walter Gircke, *Berlin Scheunenviertel*, 1928, photograph.

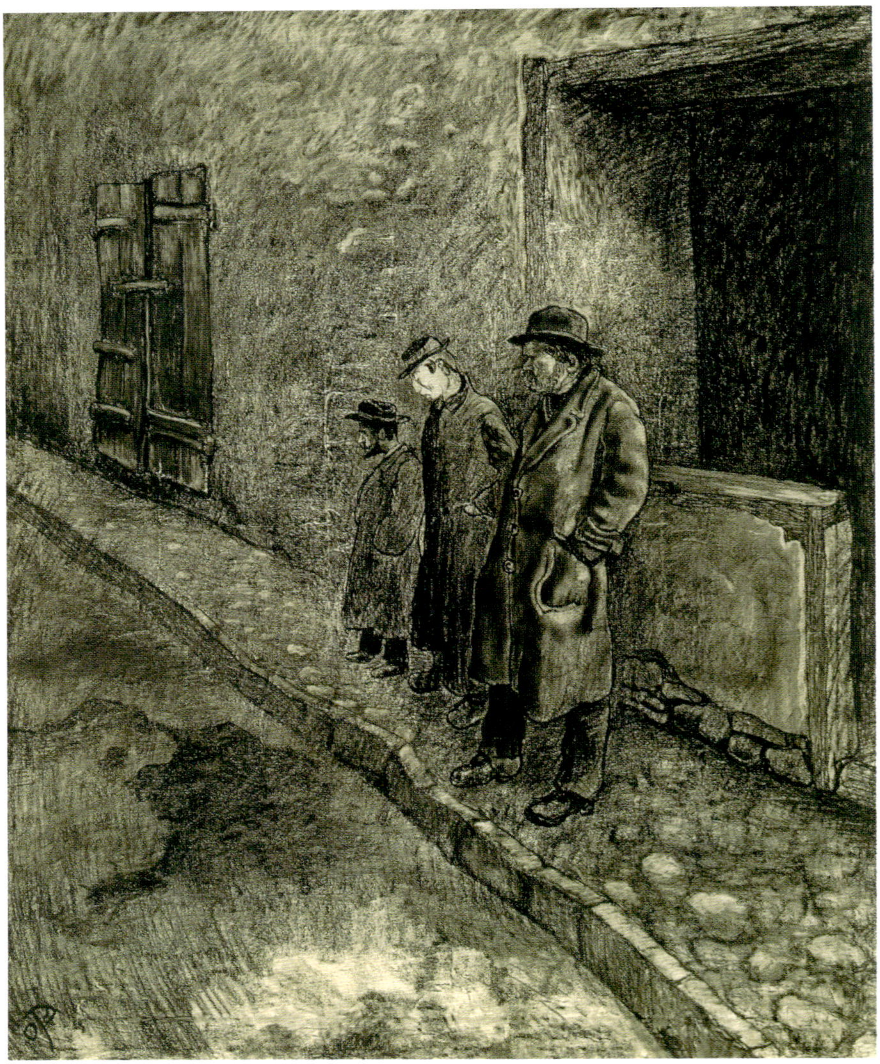

22 Otto Pankok, *Men Waiting (Ghetto)*, 1939, charcoal on paper.

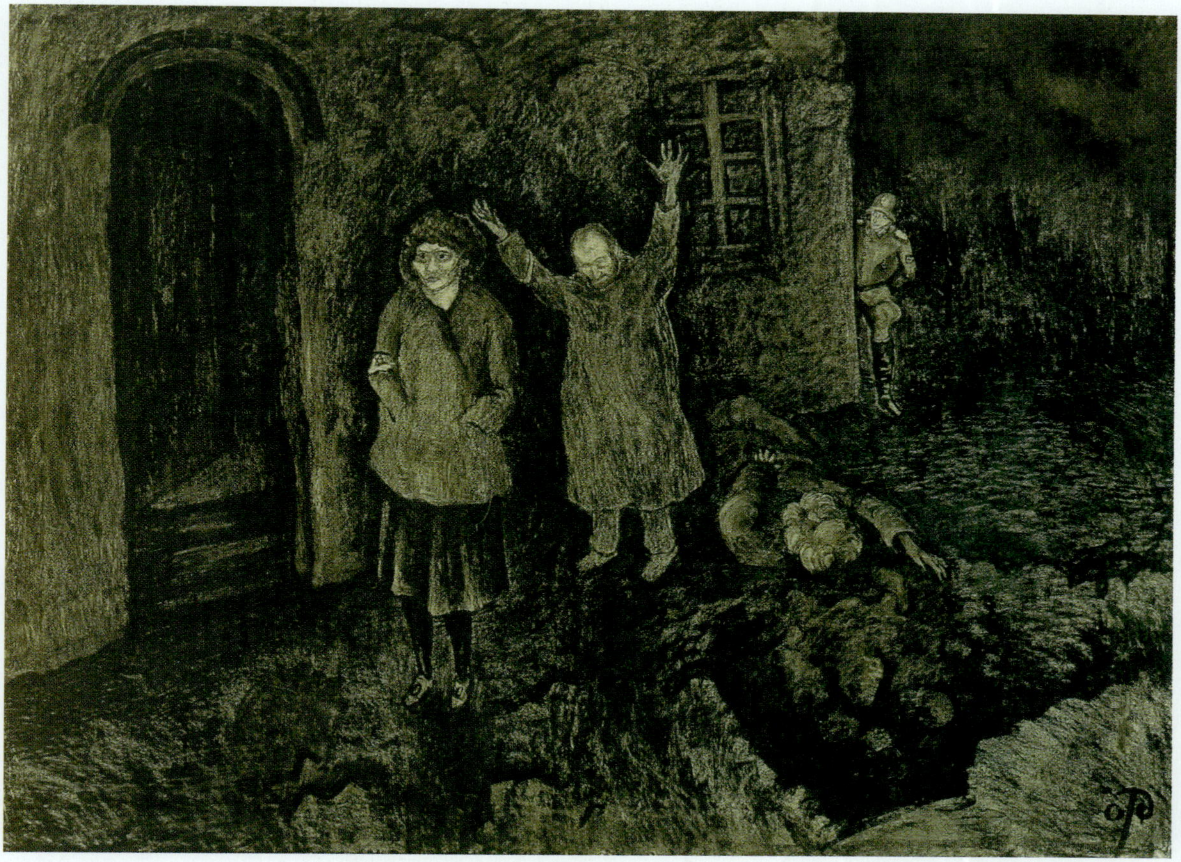

23 Otto Pankok, *Pogrom with* SS *Officer*, 1940, charcoal on paper.

eyeing them'.[57] Pankok turned the viewers of his painting into witnesses; they are the only ones who can see the Gestapo man coming round the corner. The slightly raised perspective suggests that this is being observed from a house opposite. Some visitors to the exhibition in Düsseldorf must still have remembered being in such a position as bystanders to acts of terror. In *House for the Jews* (illus. 24) the view is from the street. In 1945 Pankok painted these first assembly camps for Jewish citizens within each city[58] prior to their eventual deportation.[59] Terror and extreme anxiety are written on the faces of all the Jewish people looking out of the window, Jewish neighbours who had long since been deported – presumably in front of the very eyes of those now looking at them in a work of art in a museum – and were most probably no longer alive.

We learn from a letter of June 1948 to Pankok from a Danish teacher, in charge of a class of German schoolgirls whom she had taken to an exhibition by the artist, how little the younger generation knew about the persecution of the Jews. Together with the girls, she had looked at Pankok's 1943 picture *They Are Coming* (illus. 25), in which Jews fleeing their houses are shown, but the Nazi police taking them away to be transported are not. The way she described the discussion is significant as a reaction to how Pankok positioned the viewers as if they had witnessed the events and were still alive in 1945:

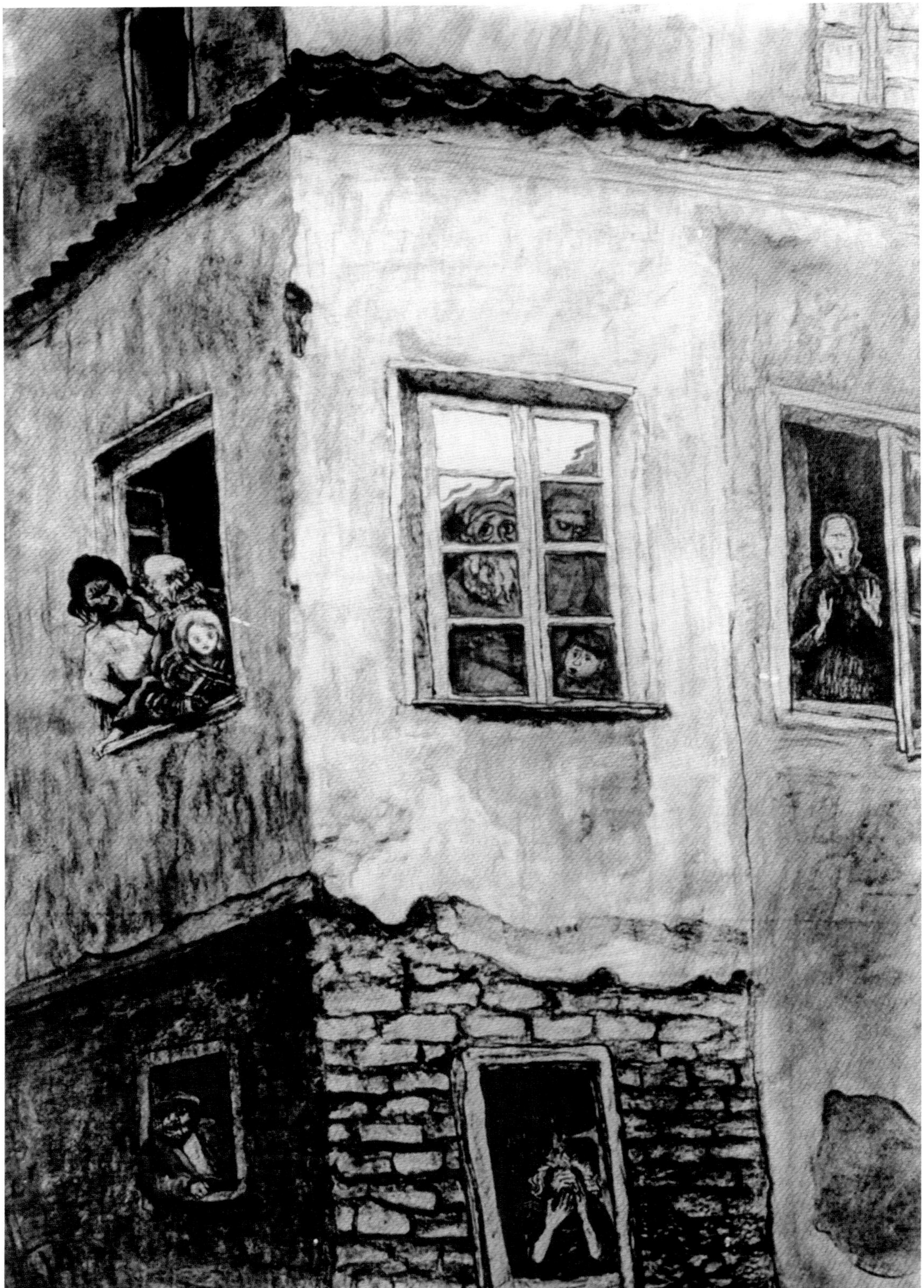

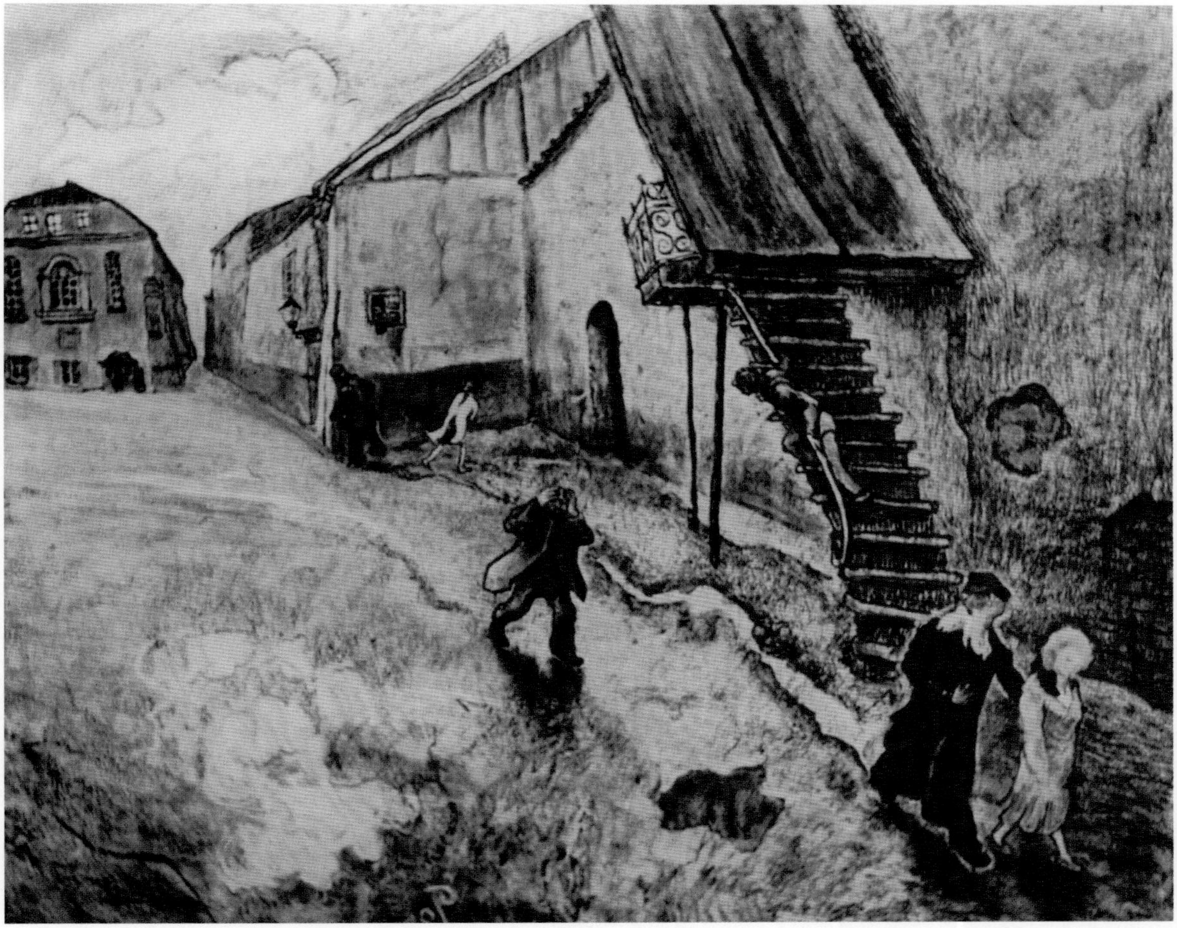

25 Otto Pankok, *They Are Coming*, 1943, charcoal on paper.

> I asked who 'they' were in the picture 'They Are Coming!' The pupils thought of the British, Americans, Russians or of air-raids. As a Dane, I thought straight away: these are Jews fleeing from their German persecutors. The girls also rejected any connection between the picture and the picture 'Progrom' [sic] next to it, compared with the way I saw it.

Right after this, she wrote about her overall impression of the way the Germans dealt with the crimes committed against the Jews:

> For 6 weeks now I have been looking for people in Germany who feel responsible for what happened to the Jews and were prepared to try and make up for it. I found only very few. One lady said, and this strikes me as typical: the Jews after the war have not understood how to gain the sympathy of the Germans![60]

24 Otto Pankok, *House for the Jews*, 1945, charcoal on paper.

During the Nazi period and afterwards, Pankok frequently dealt with the figure of the Jewish violinist,[61] such as in the 1947 etching WR 656, the

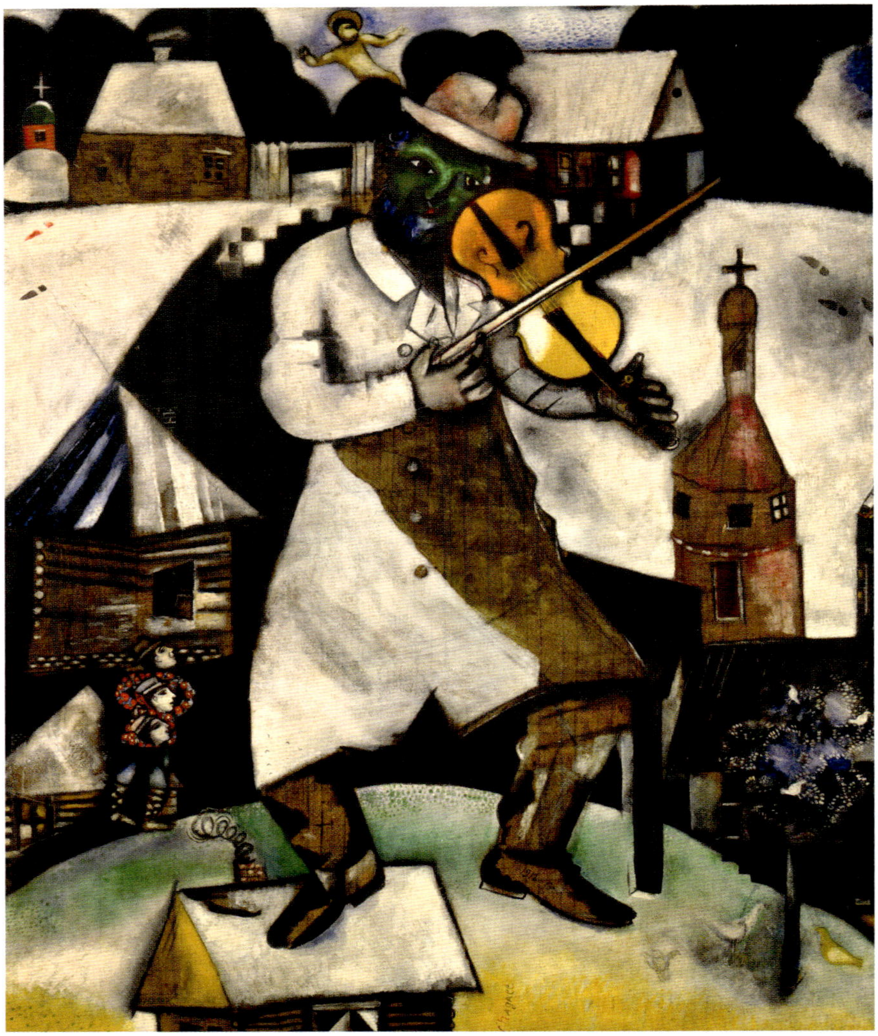

large 1954 monotype WM 216 and the 1949 bronze. This figure is seen almost life-size in the 1941 sketch *Old Violinist (Violinist in the Ghetto)* (illus. 27) measuring 150 × 97 cm,[62] whereas *Old Violinist at the Gate* of the same year[63] is still a small black figure, apparently playing a sad song in front of a cemetery. *Old Violinist (Violinist in the Ghetto)* comes across as a monument to the culture of the Jewish shtetl of Eastern Europe, both sounding a death knell and resounding with the joy of making music. The position of the body, with legs akimbo and knees slightly bent, is reminiscent of the *The Fiddler* by Marc Chagall (1924), who was much admired by Pankok (illus. 26). In one of the many variants by Chagall of the *Violinist* showing the Jewish settlement of Vitebsk, near the musician's head one can make out vibrating panes of glass in the wall at the back.[64] In Pankok's drawing one of the four panes is missing from the window frame. The black rectangle calls to mind the Writing on the Wall, indicating that the

26 Marc Chagall, *The Fiddler*, 1912–13, oil on canvas, 188 x 158.5 cm.

27 Otto Pankok, *Old Violinist (Violinist in the Ghetto)*, 1941, charcoal on paper, 150 x 97 cm.

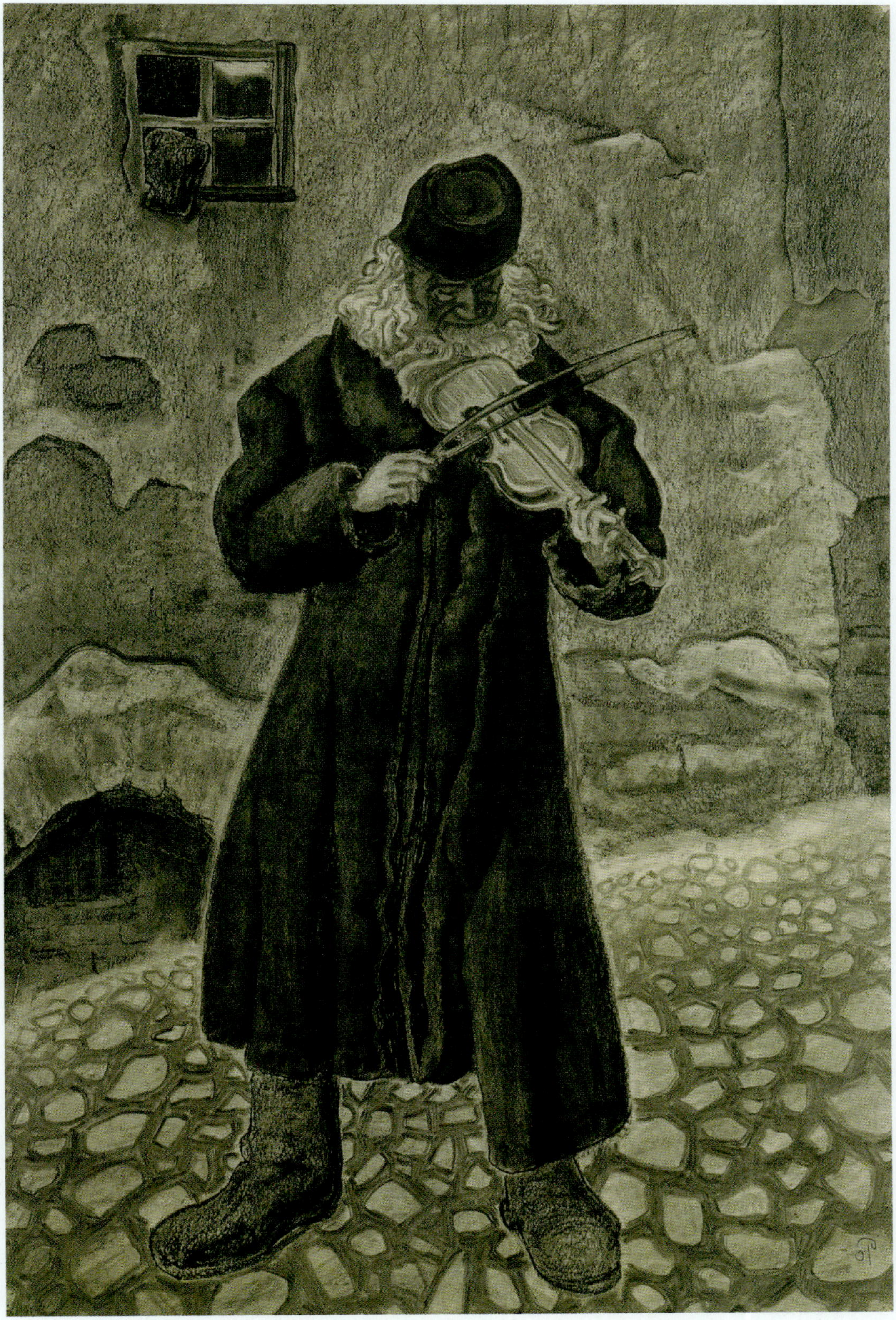

violinist is soon to be an absence himself, while the loose panel on one of the lower panes is in danger of falling out. The face looking down at the violin is again similar to Pankok's studies of the heads of Jewish characters, but with its luxuriant growth of hair and beard, it also seems to be given the features of the artist himself – Else Lasker-Schüler referred to him as 'the man in the beard'[65] – in which there is a hint of an identification of the painter threatened by the Nazis with the persecuted musician in the ghetto.[66]

From the 1930s until his death in 1966, in his graphic works – charcoal paintings, as they are referred to by common agreement in the literature, and in sculptures – Pankok devoted his work to excluded and persecuted social groups, including both the Jews and the Sinti[67] as well as street children. He did not forget them, either during the Nazi period or afterwards, and he not only produced pictures of them but helped them to survive as much as he could.[68] He never joined any political party but, without being imprisoned, he survived the Nazi period as an artist sympathizing with the critical Left in spite of being banned several times. He even dared in those times to reveal the crimes against the Jews in his pictures. And even though his cycle on the Passion, produced immediately after 1933, brought him a Nazi ban from exhibiting for its clear allusions to the present, he continued to paint.

Sinti and Homeless People

Pankok dedicated work to the Sinti as early as 1929, when he returned from Spain with the opinion that he had discovered in them, as with the rural population of Cadaqués, people who were still living in touch with nature. He set up his studio in the high-unemployment district of Heinefeld near Düsseldorf and became friendly with the Sinti settled there.[69] For someone like him who shunned urban civilization, regarding it with complete scepticism, they represented freedom and joie de vivre to a great extent.[70] In 1932 he started on his detailed studies of adults and children that he was to exhibit immediately after 1945 and published as early as 1947 in his own book *Zigeuner* (Gypsies).[71] None of the drawings and sculptures reproduced in it were dated in the texts; only in the case of a few of the works is it possible to identify the year. And it is not difficult to make out from the foreword that, with these images of their former life, Pankok wanted to reflect on the extermination of the Sinti:

> so let us look back at those unforgettable years that seem to us now like a blessed gift . . . I want to attempt to throw light upon them and, as far as I can, to capture the fleeting moment, so that this portion of life, this my island in a sea of madness and in the storms of hell will not sink for ever into the depths of oblivion.[72]

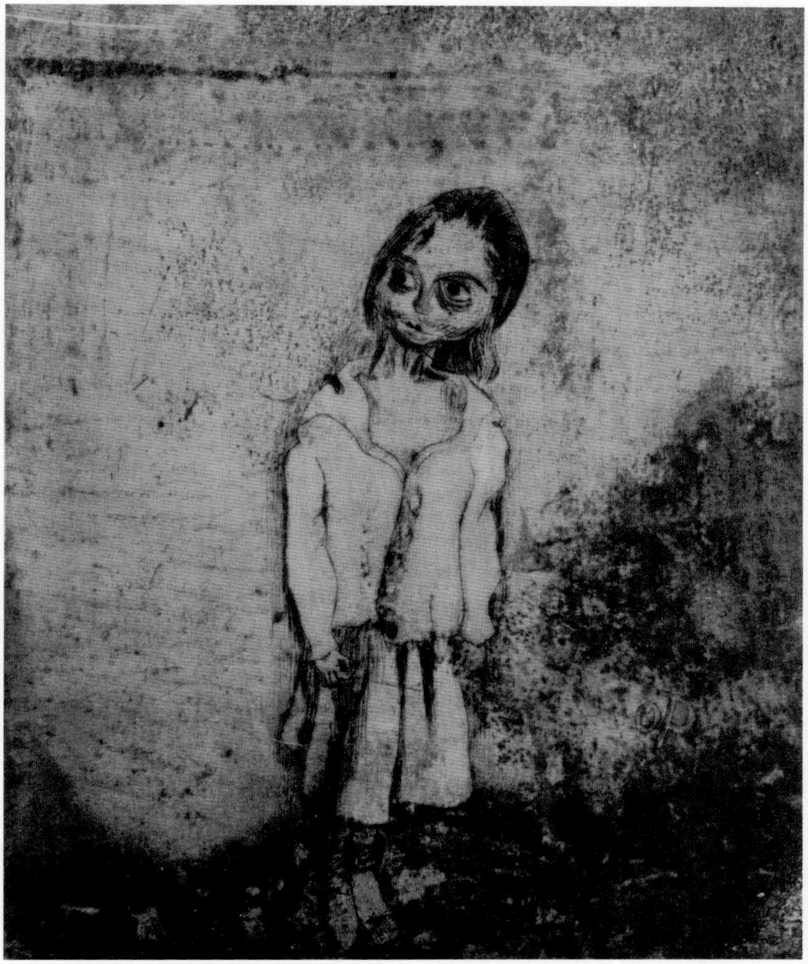

28 Otto Pankok, *Blume*, 1947, etching.

In the foreword he described the destruction of his 'island' and put his finger, unusually clearly for the period, on the fact that the German population had been witnesses to the crimes:

> They were dragged off into the death camps and the Eastern slaughter houses. We heard the cries of the children and their mothers sobbing under the Nazi henchmen's whips. We saw in the streets the dying having their poor faces smashed in to make them clean the pavements with the very last of their strength for those uniformed brutes.[73]

At the beginning of his book, full of hope for the future of the Sinti and their freedom, he dedicated the drawings and sculptures to their families:[74]

> These images are meant to be greetings to the free people, to those who were banished and humiliated and are now returning, to those who were made prisoners and are now emerging from their dark cellars and feeling

> the heat of the midday sun once again upon them . . . to those who are arising from the ruins and the corpse-strewn fields of Europe and are once again looking up at the star-spangled heavens. I address those few who are still alive and have never forgotten what freedom is, those who have not been forcibly silenced and who look life in the face and risk everything for the moment of freedom.[75]

He was not content with just the images produced pre-war but sought out the few people surviving in the huts of a former Nazi assembly camp on the Höherweg in Düsseldorf,[76] producing for example in 1947 several etchings of the child Blume (illus. 28), and in 1948 he made a portrait of Gaisa, whom he had drawn and modelled several times before 1933 in his studies of 'gypsies' near Düsseldorf and who had now returned from the camps as the only survivor of her large family.[77] The large-scale charcoal drawing has the title *Back from Auschwitz*[78] (illus. 29). In this nameless female figure, looking in terror and confusion, is summed up all the horror of the concentration camp. In the image, Pankok did not portray the violence that Gaisa had experienced, but in an essay of 1950 he put into words his description of her deportation to Birkenau[79] and her return from there in the company of an ss man who continually beat her and who boasted to the surviving Sinti about using gypsies as shooting targets in a German camp in Poland.[80] In the image, Pankok posed Gaisa as the only one of the Sinti he portrayed in front of a wall of children's drawings, making it possible to suggest both the dilapidated conditions in which she was living and also her lost youth and her desolation: a return that could no longer be a homecoming.[81]

References to Film Images: *Death Mills*; Fritz Koelle: *Inferno*; Peter Edel: *Mauthausen*

In the early 1920s within the artists' circle associated with the 'Junge Rheinland' (Young Rhineland), the group around the art dealer Johanna Ey, Pankok had spoken in favour of 'Klee and Dada',[82] so he was kindly disposed towards changes in the way human figures are represented. In his works, however, he continued to seek for a way of creating an image of the human being as an intact whole, in the style and with the same social engagement as van Gogh and Barlach. Pankok was not the only one who aimed to further develop this long European tradition. Peter Edel and Horst Strempel also – despite the latter's borrowing from Cubist styles of representation – remained true to this idea, which sculptors of the first memorials kept to in portraying human figures. Fritz Koelle, for example, intentionally followed a realistic model of representation with the first design, *Inferno* (illus. 30), for the Dachau concentration camp in 1946,[83] in which one figure is presenting another, like the text on the postcard demanding amendment: 'Your Victims

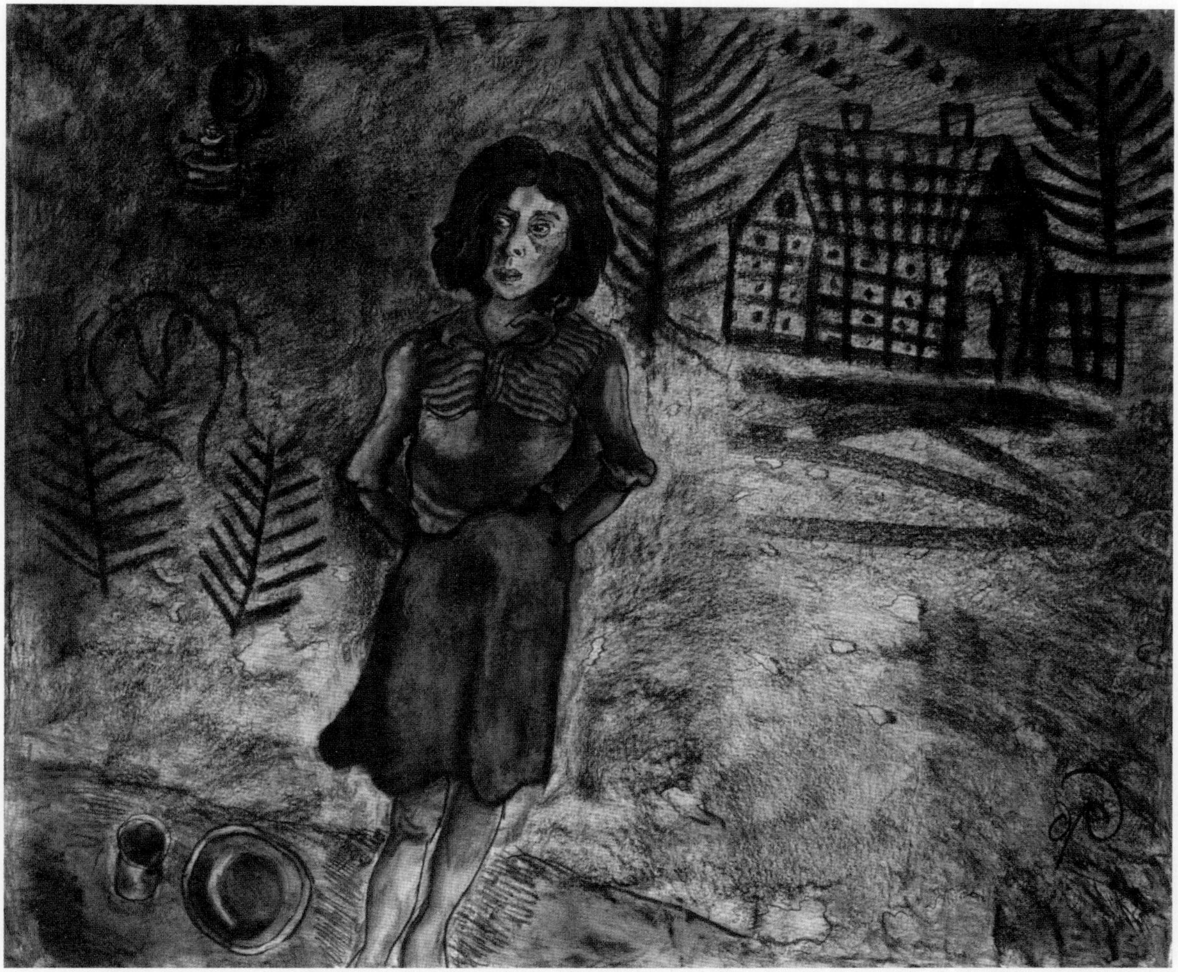

29 Otto Pankok, *Back from Auschwitz, or Gaisa against the Wall*, 1948, charcoal.

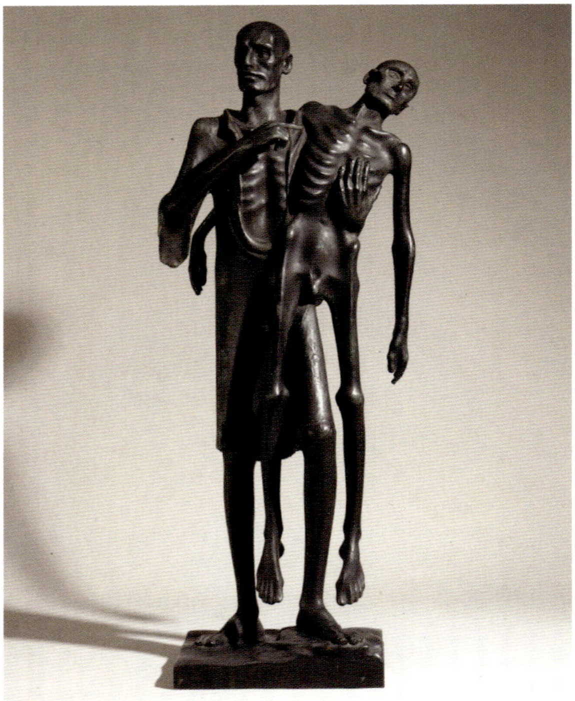

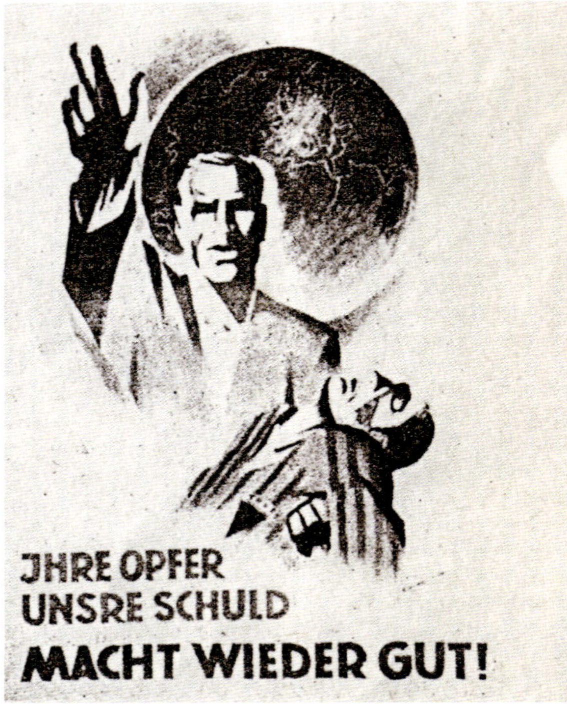

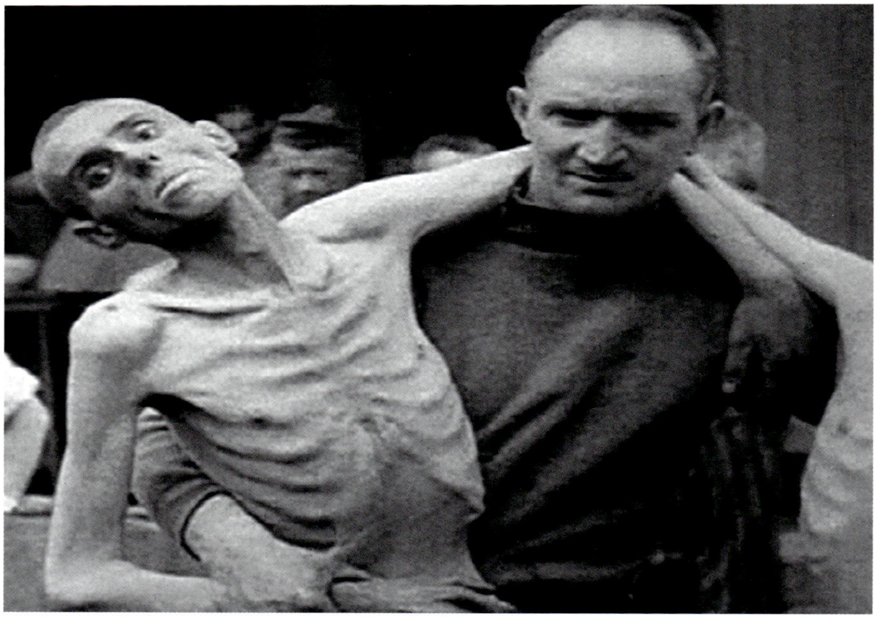

top left 30 Fritz Koelle, *Inferno*, 1946, bronze.

top right 31 Postcard from album *Conc. Camp Dachau*, 1946.

bottom 32 Scene from *Death Mills*, dir. Hanuš Burger, abridged version by Billy Wilder (1945).

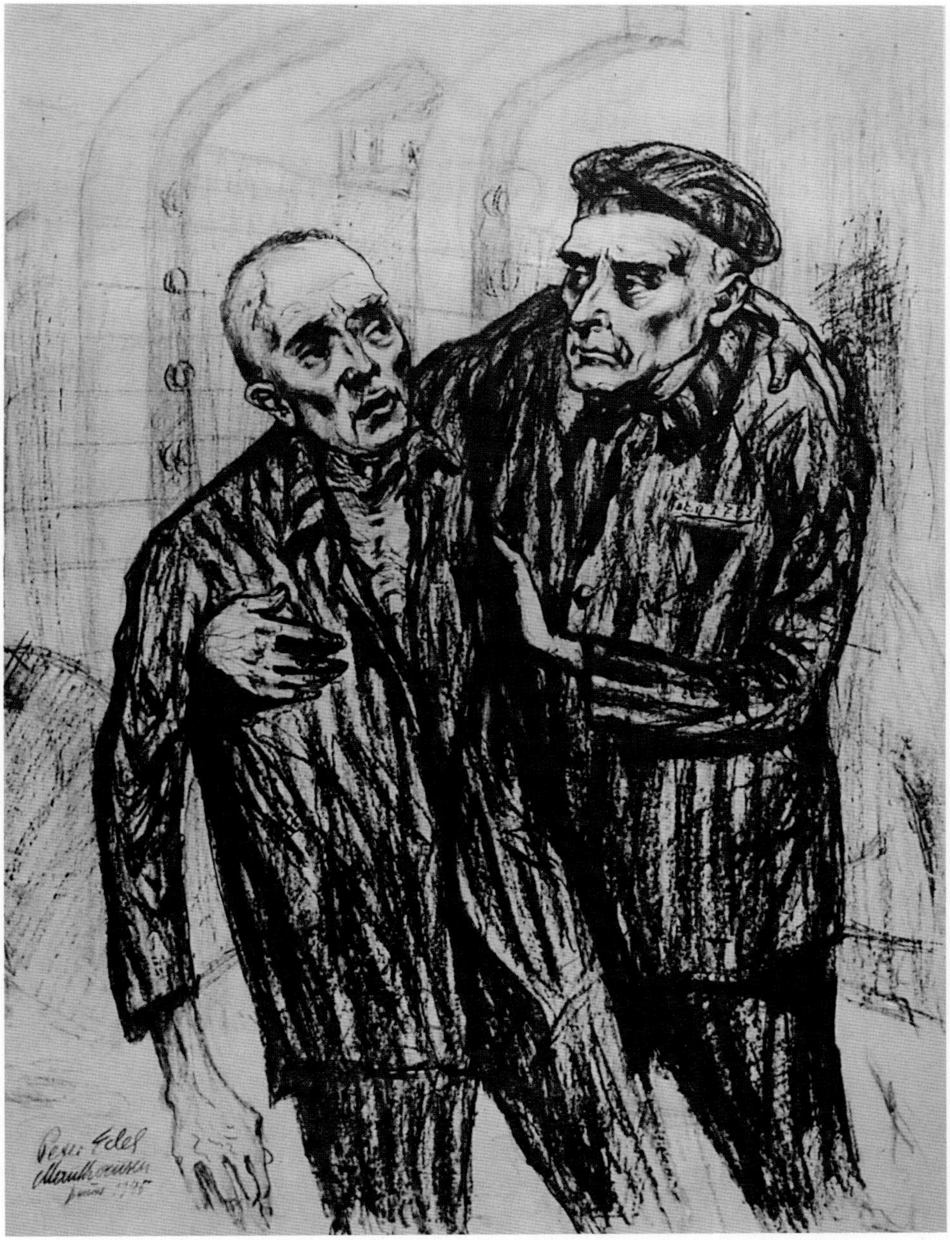

33 Peter Edel, *Mauthausen*, January 1945, fol. 15 from the series *Wenn es ans Leben geht. 20 Zeichnungen zu seiner Autobiographie* (Berlin, 1983).

/ Our Guilt / Make up for it!' (illus. 31).[84] Peter Edel illustrated his biography with a similar scene, indeed with people dressed in prison clothing, and gave it the same date as his own time in the camp, that is, *Mauthausen* (illus. 33). In the documentary film *Death Mills* (illus. 32) by Hanuš Burger and Billy Wilder, there is a long scene with prisoners from Ebensee concentration camp, likewise intended to confirm the solidarity between healthy prisoners and those close to death that made it possible to survive even during the Nazi period. As in a mirror image, an extremely emaciated human body in Fritz Koelle's *Inferno* in particular reveals a reference to the image in the film. Artists, as well as film-makers, were aware in their compositions of the history of Christian religious imagery around God the Father's Mercy Seat directing the faithful towards salvation in the shape of Christ's body.[85] They were following the iconographic tradition, even if they no longer held out any hope of salvation from the murdered son of God.[86] Koelle's design came in for criticism[87] on account of its 'naturalistic' representation and was finally replaced by the bronze statue of the full-length so-called unknown prisoner, no longer showing any bodies from the concentration camps, but only indicating his attitude of determination and resistance by having his hands in his trouser pockets.[88]

Sculptors like Koelle, Fritz Cremer, Herbert Volwahsen, Georg Kolbe, Waldemar Grzimek, Gustav Seitz, Will Lammert and others, in their representations after 1945 of the human figure current since the Renaissance, were not any different from the above-mentioned painters.[89] At the same time, however, there were other artists radically questioning this tradition.

Deconstructed Likeness: Wols, Gerhard Altenbourg, Eugen Schönebeck

Wolfgang Schulze, known as Wols, a German living in France during the Nazi period, countered this idea of an autonomous subject with existentialist negation (illus. 34). His concept of art, which can also be read as an answer to the Nazi dictatorship and its control over language and imagery, becomes apparent in his radical questioning of the relationship between the world and its depiction. If his images do remind one of human faces, then these are to be seen in a shape that comes across as being in a permanent state of mutation, capable of promising liberation through the creation of what is not open to interpretation.[90]

Gerhard Altenbourg, who was living in the Soviet occupation zone, on the other hand, bypassed the dominant requirement of Socialist Realism for the portrayal of intact and powerful bodies by presenting his human figures and their faces in all their mutilation and transience. Thus two of his grotesque drawings from 1949 have the titles *My Brother, the Greedy Pig* and *My Brother, the Greedy Pig, is Still Feeding His Face* (illus. 35 and 36).

34 Wols, *Composition*, 1947, oil and grattage on canvas.

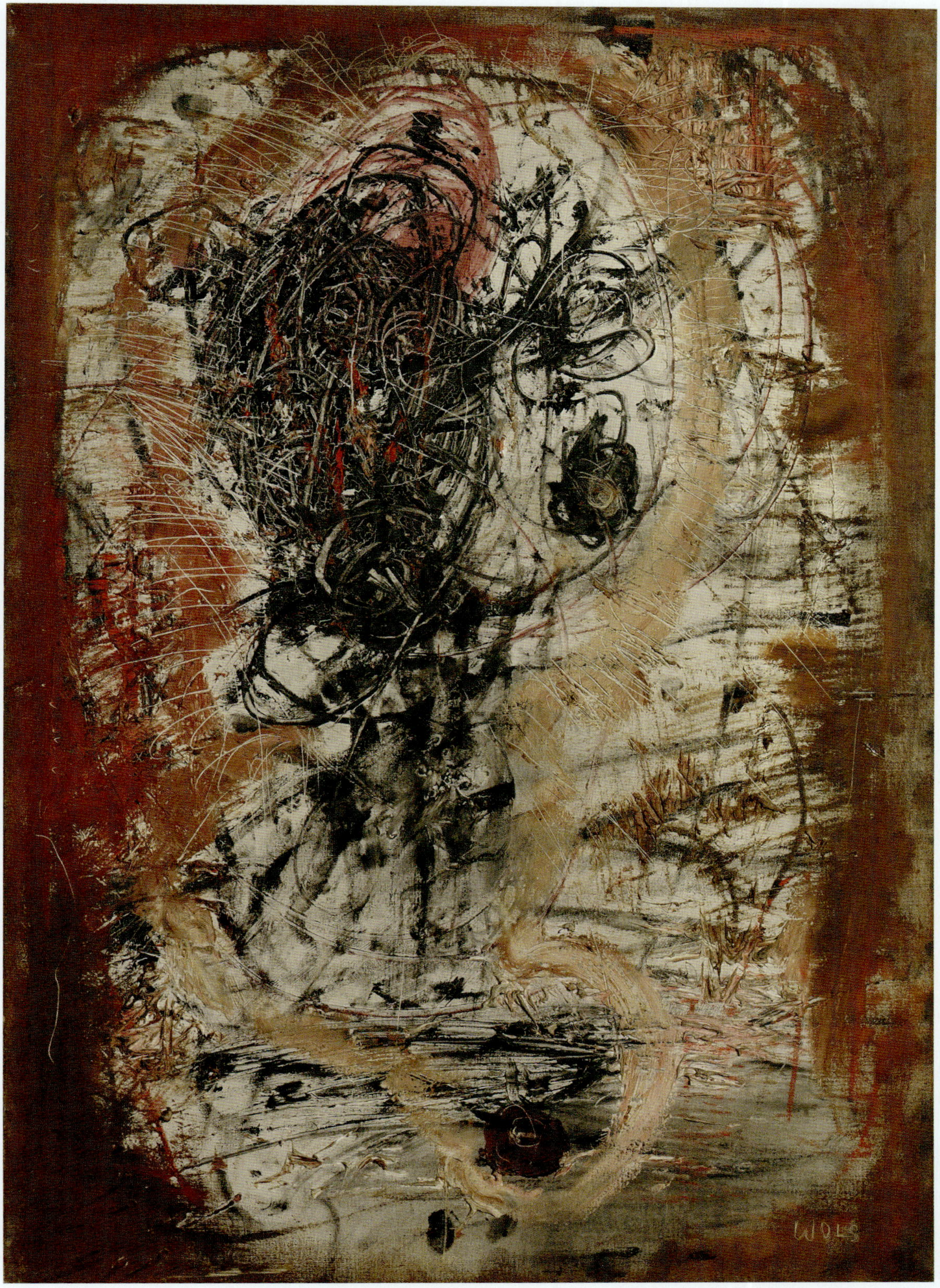
WOLS

At the start of the 1960s Eugen Schönebeck (illus. 37), who emigrated from East to West Berlin in the course of his art studies, struggled with the problem of the representation of the human being after the Second World War. What he painted owed much to Francis Bacon, abused, tortured and executed bodies, representing what Grosz called a 'pandemonium' of the human animal.

Body-Image-Writing: Pinkhes Shvarts, *Helft Schriiben!* (Help with the Writing!)

Pinkhes Shvarts, a young artist from Lodz, campaigned for retaining the bodies of those murdered in the form of writing. He had belonged to the former Polish avant-garde led by the Yiddish poet and writer Moshe Broderson. He was himself a Jew and was resident in Munich at the time he produced the poster in 1947 for the competition 'Collect and Record!' (see also illus. 9) that was awarded the first prize.[91] The poster, which was presumably hung in all 150 of the DP camps in the American zone of Germany, appealed for the recording of history and the actual memories of every single surviving Jew (illus. 38). The writing on it in large, white Hebrew letters under an ink pot with a quill pen reads in Yiddish: 'Helft Schriiben' (Help with the Writing) and then again underneath in smaller, blue writing: 'Die Geschichte fun letsten khurbn' (the history of the latest destruction).[92]

In the appeal there is a connection made between the scrolls of the Bible and a reference to the modern visual medium of photography.[93] The image shows, seen frontally from below, the upper half of a naked corpse whose trunk is obscured by the scroll and who is flung back against a barbed wire fence. As Laura Jockusch discovered, for the body of the *Katsetler*, the Yiddish term for the concentration camp inmates, Shvarts was exactly copying the photo of a Jew murdered in the Lodz Ghetto.[94] He serves here as a representative for all those who were murdered. His upper body is covered by the unwound beginning of a scroll of scripture; it is to be taken as a reference to the Esther scroll, familiar within Judaism, bearing the first words of the Book of Esther in red Hebrew letters in Yiddish: 'and so it happened in those days'.

Presumably the Book of Esther in the poster is presented to the viewer as an instruction, because it describes the successful struggle of the Jews and is the basis of Purim, the festival commemorating their salvation. The prospect of joy, however, is not portrayed by Shvarts. In the form of the two fighters on the right-hand side of the poster, proportionally much smaller than the dead man, he is indicating the act of retribution, specifically dealt with in Esther, by the Jews against their enemies. They were the first to be victorious 'in all the lands of King Ahasuerus'. But it is not the bloody deeds of the past from the Hebrew Bible that are revealed but gunmen with modern weapons. The fighter on the left is aiming a gun while the one on the right, looking back over his shoulder, is advancing holding a hand grenade or an anti-tank

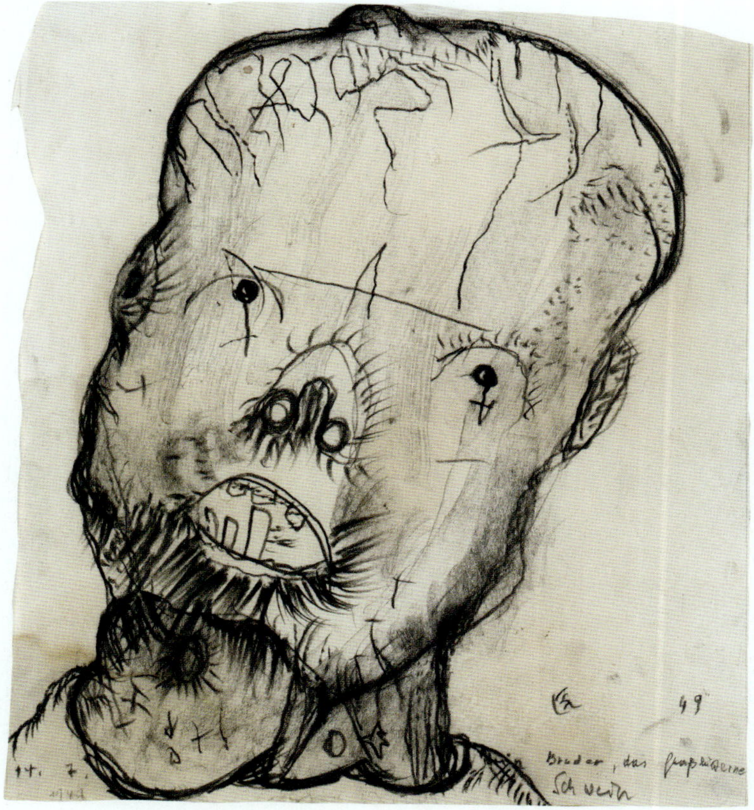

35 Gerhard Altenbourg, *My Brother, the Greedy Pig*, 1949, pastel on paper.

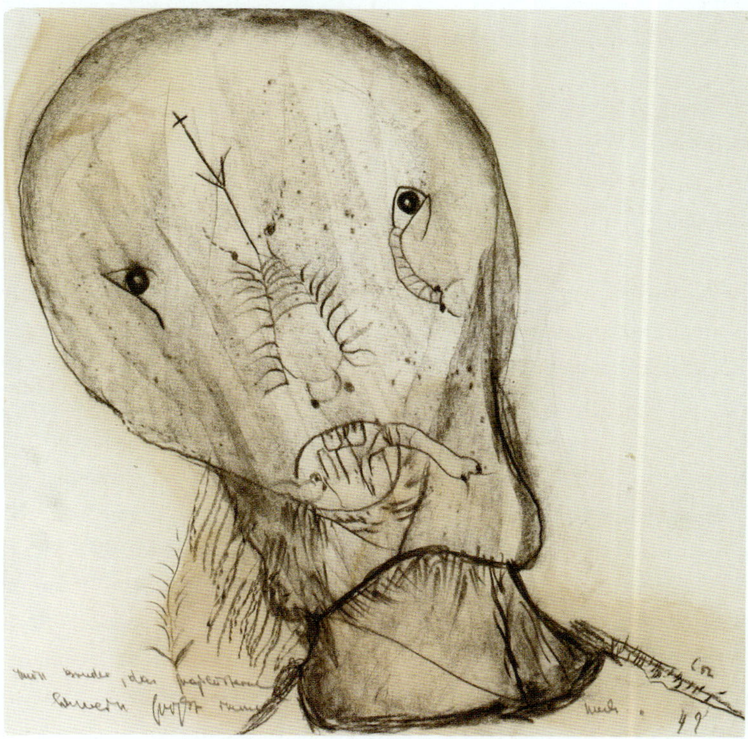

36 Gerhard Altenbourg, *My Brother, the Greedy Pig, is Still Feeding his Face*, 1949, pastel and stabilo pen on paper.

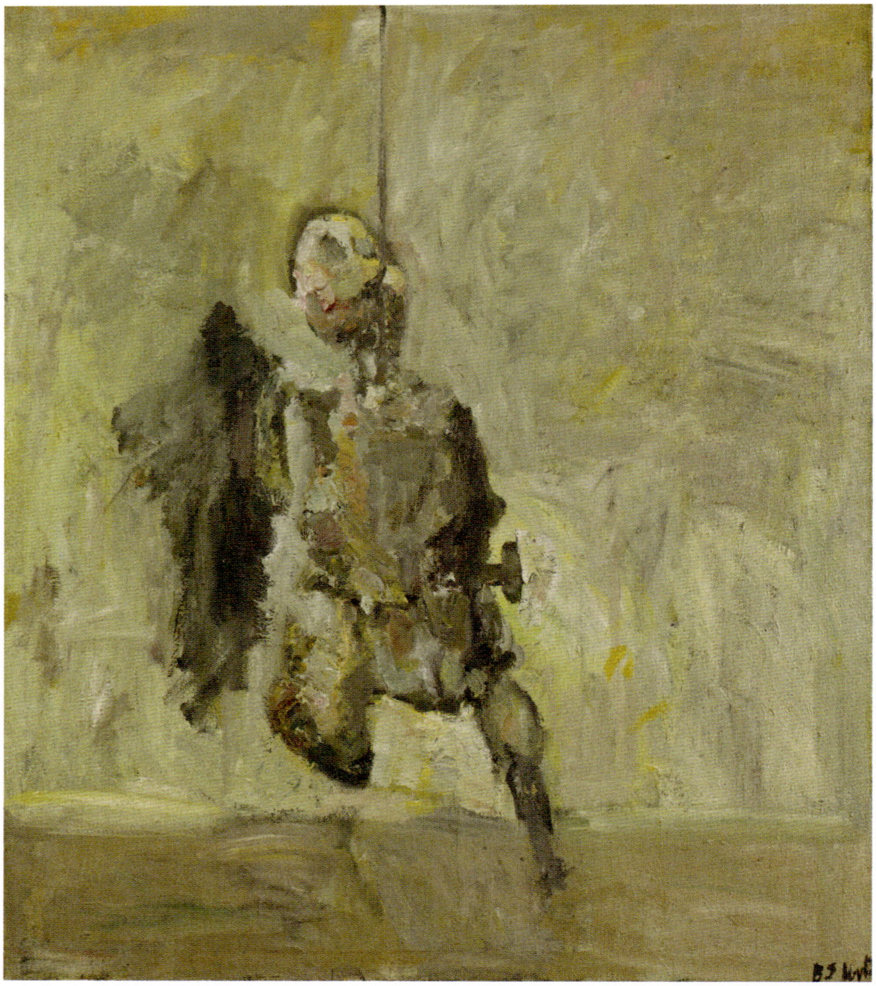

weapon in his right hand. It is impossible to say here whether this is intended to represent fighters during the Uprising in the Warsaw Ghetto or those taking part in a future and eventually successful struggle by the Jews. Only the way the advancing man with a bloodstained head cloth is looking back makes it clear and directs one's attention back to the dead man and the scroll of scripture lying in front of him, which has need of the hands of the living to record the history of the Nazi terror. The 'catastrophe' should be captured in writing within the Jewish tradition and thus, as an appeal of the time put it, 'eternalized', but not without indicating the ongoing struggle against the enemy. The memories still to be written down are again referred to in the text by an image, that of a stone placed on graves or left by those who visit them: 'The only gravestone which we are able to place on the unknown graves of our murdered fathers, mothers, brothers, sisters, and children.'[95] The displaced persons in the camps were called upon to bear written testimony in place of those who could bear witness only with their dead bodies.

37 Eugen Schönebeck, *Dead Man*, 1962, oil on canvas.

38 Pinkhes Shvarts, *Help with the Writing! The History of the Latest Destruction*, poster for the competition 'Collect and Record!', Munich, 1947.

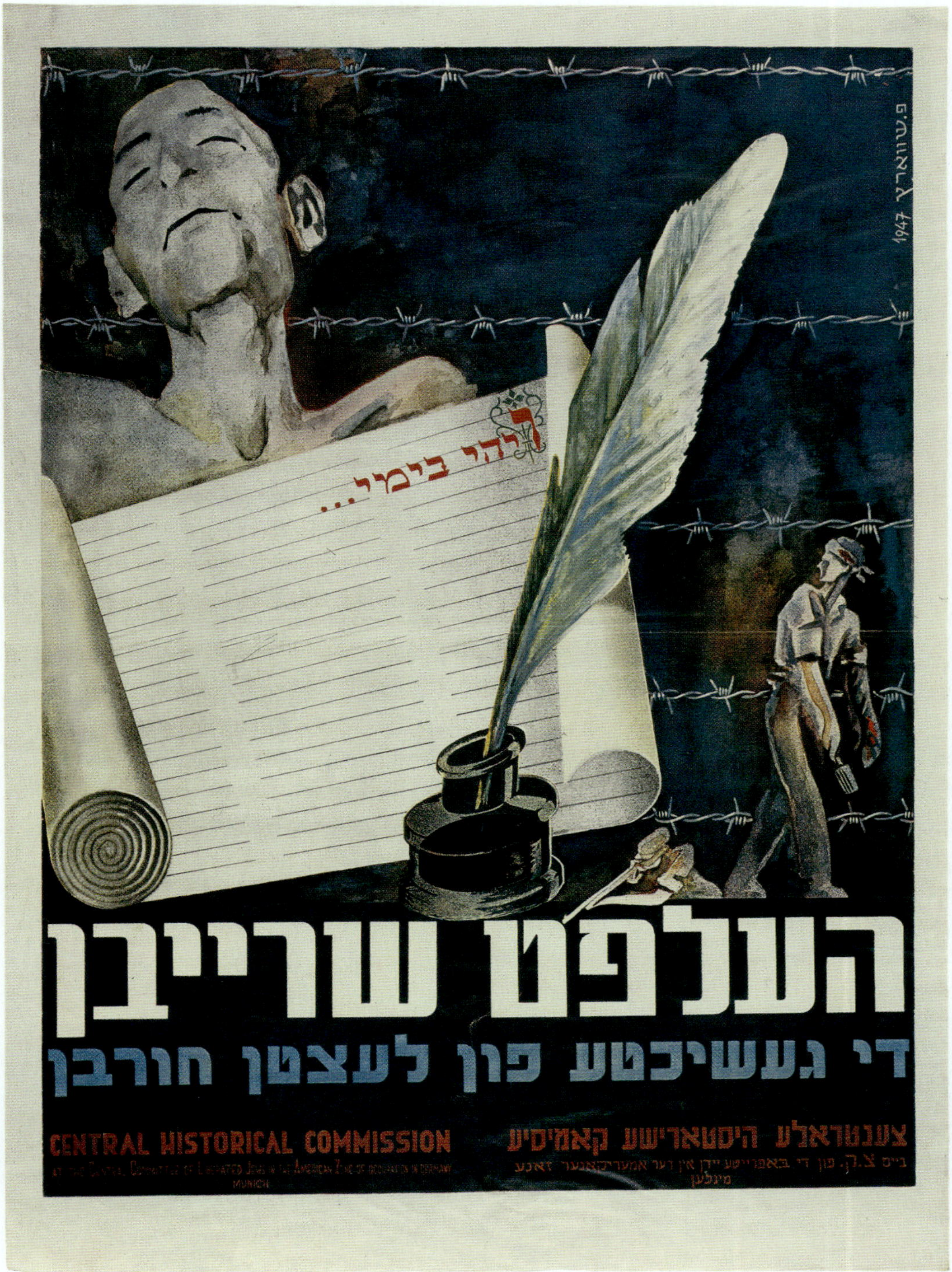
ויהי בימי...
העלפט שרייבן
די געשיכטע פון לעצטן חורבן
CENTRAL HISTORICAL COMMISSION
AT THE CENTRAL COMMITTEE OF LIBERATED JEWS IN THE AMERICAN ZONE OF OCCUPATION IN GERMANY
MUNICH
צענטראלע היסטארישע קאמיסיע
ביים צ.ק. פון די באפרייטע יידן אין דער אמעריקאנער זאנע
מינכען

3 Early Series

The 'brutalization of the human being', Maximilian Feuerring[1] wrote in his commentary on Zielezinski's graphic art in the *Kunstausstellung der Displaced Persons* (Exhibition of Art by Displaced Persons) put on in Munich in 1947, has changed the image of man. The human being has been revealed as 'having a different face and a different shape. The resemblance of the human being to a skeleton has become the norm, replacing the human figure as a figurative element of the composition.'[2] Feuerring did not mention that Jerzy Zielezinski, 'putting on record' such emaciated forms, was already part of a tradition begun by prisoners during their internment and continued by some of them, such as Leo Haas, even after 1945. These representations of the atrocities carried out by the perpetrators, however, were not nearly as widely known as the photographs taken by the liberators.[3]

Artistic production in the second half of the 1940s was bound up with the broad debate about the preceding twelve years. Newspapers, magazines and films reported on the crimes of the Nazis and were important forums for discussion of guilt. In cinemas, it was not just pre-war films or ones that had fallen foul of fascist censorship that were shown, but documentaries about the liberation of the camps. The film of the liberation of Majdanek[4] was shown at the Berlin Marmorhaus in August 1945.[5] By September a German version of the documentary *Auschwitz*[6] was on release in thirty Berlin cinemas.[7] And after the Nuremberg trials both the American production *Death Mills*, based on the pictures from the liberated camps also shown in the trials, and the Soviet documentary film *Sud Narodov* (Nuremberg Trials; 1947) reached the cinemas, intercutting between pictures from the courtroom and material derived from Nazi newsreels and the liberated camps.[8] The German occupation of Ukraine and the massacres of the Jews of Babi Yar is related in *Nepokorennye* (The Unvanquished),[9] a Russian film that was shown in German cinemas and received international acclaim. The SMAD (Soviet Military Administration in Germany) had given Deutsche Film AG (DEFA) the task of the 'democratic reconstruction of Germany' and the 'eradication of the remnants of Nazism and militarism from the consciousness of every single German'[10] and, in two of the first productions in line with this remit, the subject was also the fate of the Jews. Wolfgang Staudte's *Die Mörder sind unter uns* (The Murderers Are Among Us; 1946) at least touches on the fate of the Jews; in *Ehe im Schatten* (Love in the Shadows; 1947) by Kurt Maetzig it was the main theme. The film describes the story of a married couple categorized by the Nazis as 'mixed race', ending in the double suicide. It was given the award of best German film of 1948.

In art exhibitions, on the other hand, which were at first organized purely on a local or regional level owing to restrictions on travel and transport, as Jutta Held concluded, 'at first "everything" was exhibited that had had to be painted on the quiet and kept secret during the Nazi period.'[11] These were by no means just works critical of the period but mainly 'still-lifes of flowers and delicious fruit, nudes and charming landscapes . . . traditionally tasteful gold frames', as Adolf Behne described the character of the first exhibition of the Kammer der Kunstschaffenden (Chamber of Art Producers) in Berlin in the late summer of 1945. Here he was asking the rhetorical question whether the public would have preferred 'oil paintings of ruined landscapes, watercolours or sepia views of piles of corpses'.[12] Representations of war, terror and mass murder were also rare in sculpture, as public competitions for memorials, possibly confronting people with the past, were organized by only a few localities.[13]

Printed works by former prisoners in books and in album form nevertheless became an invaluable artistic source of insight into the brutal tyranny of the previous twelve years.[14] Survivors of the concentration camps like Jerzy Zielezinski and Leo Haas made as much use of this medium as those Jewish artists did who had been able to emigrate in time, such as Lea Grundig and Ludwig Meidner.[15] Only recently, research by Christmut Präger has revealed that in the period immediately after the war, whole cycles of graphic representations of the Nazis' crimes were also produced and published by artists in all four occupation zones who had not themselves been in the camps. They are 'inextricably bound up with' the sufferings of the population during and after the war.[16] We are dealing here with a record of the genocide on the part of non-Jews as well. This is a subject which, according to Hajo Hahn,[17] you do not find so clearly outlined in any of the novels by non-Jewish writers in German in the period just after the war. Whereas Strempel's triptych *Night over Germany* (see illus. 10) was limited to display in a museum exhibition, a series of drawings could reach a wider public and was readily available for private consumption.

Individual drawings often date from some years before they were first published and reveal how much information about the atrocities had already become public knowledge even before May 1945. The Jewish press had been reporting on the process of persecution since 1939. From the middle of 1942, news of the extermination had been increasing in volume, circulating via the non-Jewish media.[18] German Communists exiled in Moscow published the journal *Internationale Literatur*,[19] providing information to be taken up by other media outlets. After the uprising in the Warsaw Ghetto, *The Black Book of Polish Jewry*[20] was published as early as 1943 in New York and a report in the U.S. magazine *Life* carried photographs of the memorial ceremony at Majdanek, which was liberated by the Soviet Army in 1944. Meanwhile the trial held in Lublin against the guards there was open to worldwide scrutiny. Like Auschwitz later on, Lublin became a symbol for the Nazi extermination camps.[21] Sometimes in works by Ludwig Meidner, Lea Grundig and Teo Otto one can identify which news items their images were based on. However, one can only conjecture how Willi Geiger, living in seclusion in Bavaria, came to know about it.

Thanks to these cycles of pictures, it became possible to visualize recent experiences in different circumstances of violence, on the part of individuals and whole structures, that did not simply fall into pre-established categories of heroism and the sharing of grief. Unlike a painting, cycles do not aim to sum everything up in a single image but are able to convey a multitude of differing aspects of horror. What they represent are situations devoid of any coherent narrative, leaving nothing to live for but death. Unlike a film, the order in which one looks at the individual drawings and the time to be devoted to each one is up to the viewer. These cycles of prints were the source of those pictorial elements that later became key symbols in the collective memory: yellow stars, railway trains packed with human beings, stacked rows of wooden bunks, emaciated, twisted bodies and chimneys which, after they have been destroyed, can be shown to have had smoke coming out of them only in written descriptions, drawings and oil paintings.[22]

There is a close association of words and images in the volumes of poems by Nelly Sachs and Paul Celan that were published along with drawings by Rudi Stern and Edgar Jené. The way in which the spoken word places even surrealistic images squarely within the recent history is illustrated by Celan's reading of Edgar Jené's images.

Lea Grundig

In the Valley of Slaughter

Lea Grundig, a Jew and a Communist, narrowly escaped the Nazi tyranny and lived in a refugee camp in Palestine for almost a year after having survived a perilous Mediterranean crossing, then in Haifa and Tel Aviv.[23] As early as 1943 she began to record the recent history of the Jewish people in the cycle *In the Valley of Slaughter*, making her known to an international public. The

39 Lea Grundig, CURSED BE THE ONE WHO CLOSES HIS EYES AS NOT TO SEE! / CURSED BE THE ONE WHO SHUTS HIS EARS AS NOT TO HEAR! / CURSED BE THE ONE WHO REFUSES TO HELP, fol. 1 from the series *In the Valley of Slaughter*, Tel Aviv, 1944.

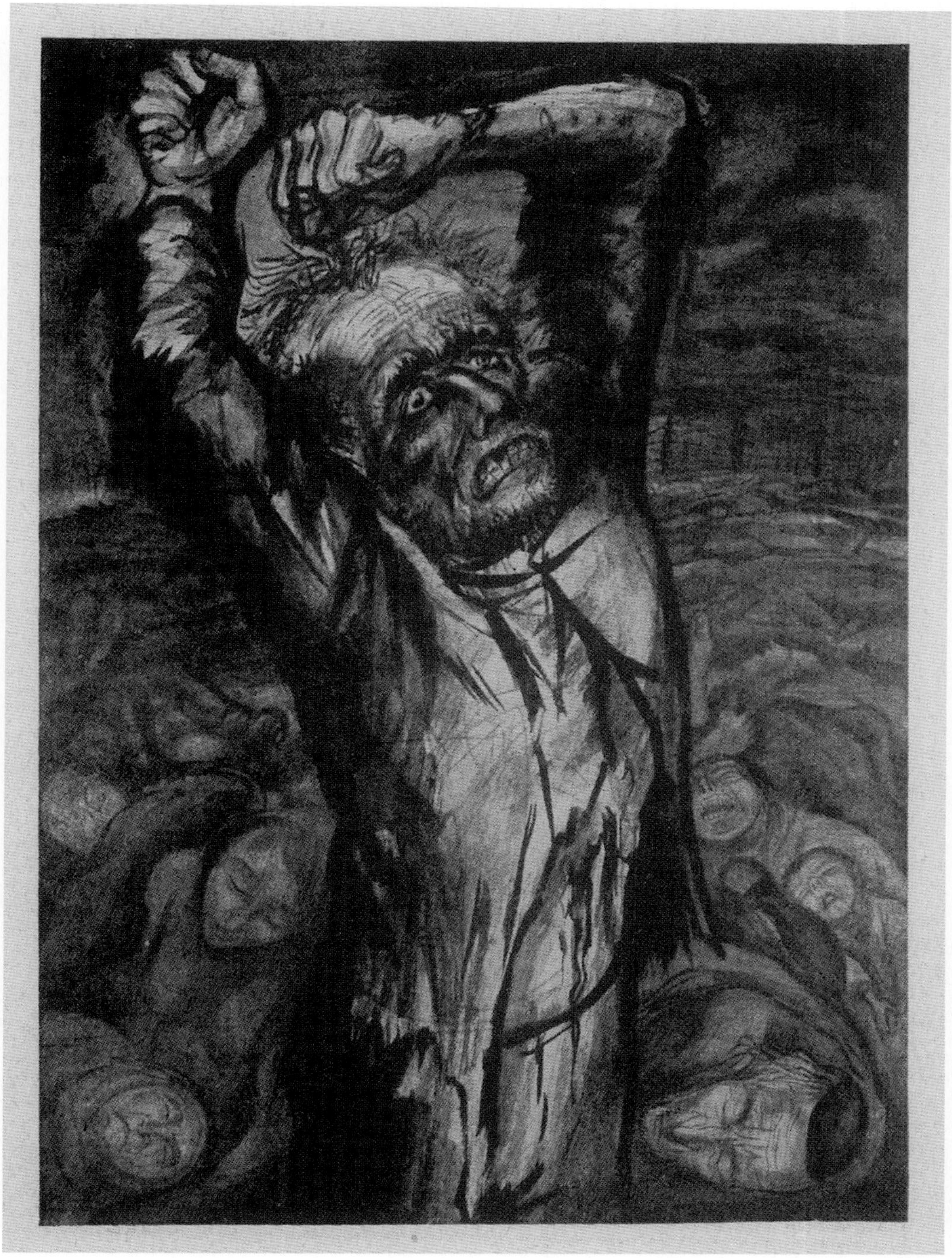

seventeen drawings (brush, ink washed) appeared in Tel Aviv in 1944, published with the title *In the Valley of Slaughter*[24] with Hebrew and English text, and in German in 1947, even before she returned to Dresden.[25] In the GDR this was the only cycle by this 'political artist', as the foreword refers to her, to have a separate publication devoted to it in the first number of the series of the journal *Zeit im Bild* published by Sachsenverlag with the title *Im Tal des Todes*.[26] Each of the seventeen reproductions on the recto pages has the title on the verso followed by an explanatory text by Kurt Liebmann.[27] The exhibition of these pictures was welcomed by Oskar Kokoschka and Arnold Zweig, as Kurt Liebmann noted in the German foreword.[28] They were also exhibited in the Pierpont Morgan Library in New York, and one of her drawings was printed in the *New York Times*[29] along with an etching by Picasso. The epigraph placed at the beginning of the volume is from Isaiah 33:1, proclaiming destruction of the enemy. Writing, after the end of the war, his comments on the drawings Grundig had made before 1945, Liebmann described the fate of the Jews in the Nazi period: 'Today we know that around 6 million Jews were exterminated in the Nazi "death factories". 6 million living, breathing creatures. Among these were 3½ million Jews from the East.'[30]

Liebmann continued to refer to the historical division between the assimilated Jews of Western Europe and Eastern European Jews but stressed the religious piety of the inhabitants of the shtetls as devout 'People of the Old Testament' who had been a repository of 'knowledge about the religious dimension of humanity'. According to him, they were passive victims of the persecution, because they believed that they had sinned. Lea Grundig, on the other hand, Liebmann argued, showed in her drawings 'people liberated from the problem, dating back a millennium, of Jewish self-hatred and self-accusation. People who can see socialism and want it.' Looking at the end of the cycle, he wrote that it shows 'the determination, not to leave revenge up to God but to take it into your own hands'.

As Amishai-Maisels explained, in contrast to various other artistic works dealing with the persecution, Grundig's work was based not just on the iconography of the Hebrew Bible and on the representations of pogroms from the start of the twentieth century[31] but on the photos taken by the Soviet Army of the mass murders carried out by the Germans, which had already been available during the war.[32] Rosamunde Neugebauer agreed with Amishai-Maisels in concluding that 'all Grundig's anti-fascist cycles of graphic art' should be seen 'as a significant contribution to the development of an iconography of the Holocaust based on the pictorial tradition of the Jewish diaspora'.[33] The title of the book, according to Amishai-Maisels, is a variation on a poem by C. N. Bialik[34] and refers to the description in Jeremiah 7:32 of the destruction of the cities of Judah. The first plate, *CURSED BE THE ONE . . .* (illus. 39), employs the iconography of the Hebrew Bible prophet's complaint,[35] the way the artist uses the brush making it look like a woodcut. Its precision and the chiaroscuro modelling of the bodies, creating

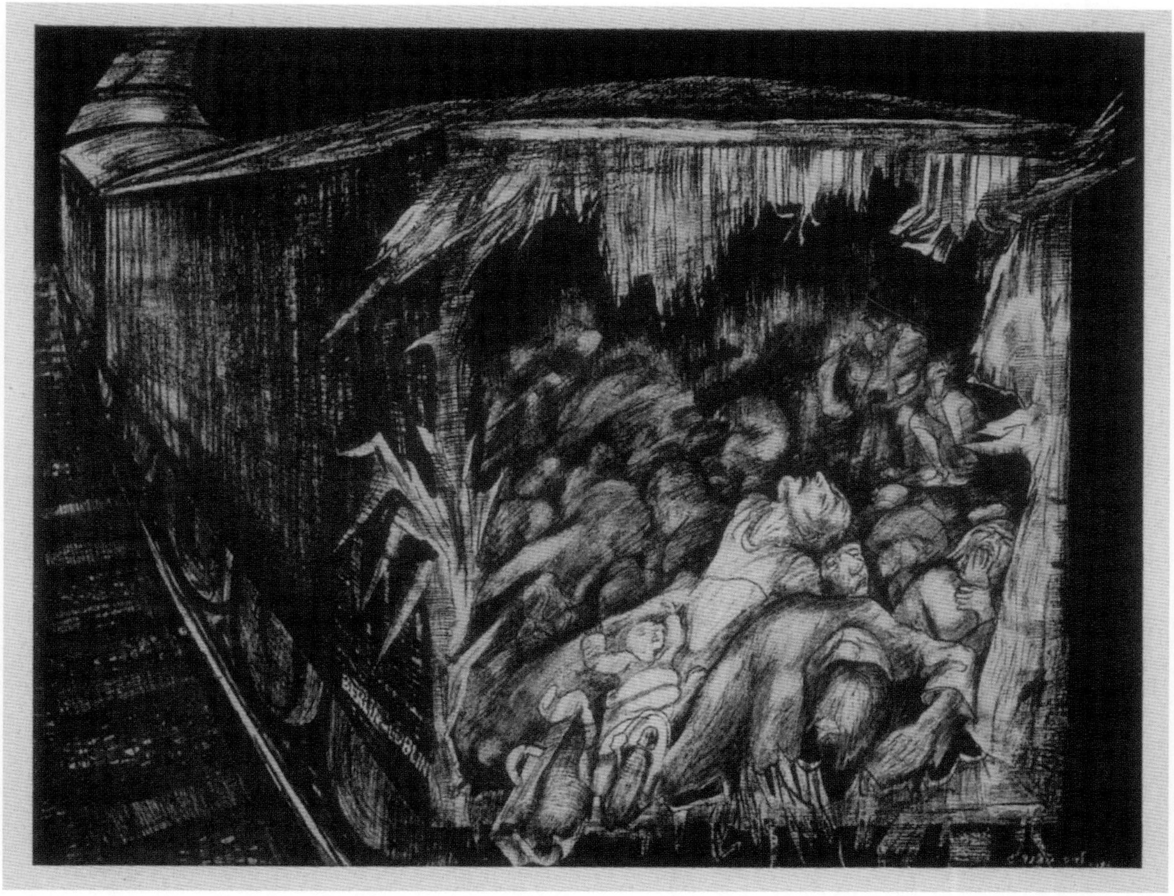

40 Lea Grundig, IN THE DEATH WAGONS, fol. 4 from the series *In the Valley of Slaughter*, Tel Aviv, 1944.

extreme contrasts, are paralleled only by the drawing *HOPELESS* showing the desperate mother with two children. The dead bodies scattered around the Cursing One, Amishai-Maisels argues, are reminiscent at the same time of those in the earlier iconography of the pogroms and in the photographs of those who were actually murdered. Grundig's concern to give the dead individual faces and to characterize them as Jews by their style of hair or the men's kippahs is evident throughout the cycle. In the opened-up railway wagon in *IN THE DEATH WAGONS* (illus. 40), she appears to have studied photographs showing the piles of corpses that had possibly already been published by that time.[36] By using the name Lublin, Liebmann was identifying the geographical place as Majdanek concentration camp where, after liberation by the Soviet Army in 1944, it had become clear for the first time that mass murder had taken place in this 'death factory' on a greater scale than had been previously known.[37]

In the print *TREBLIANCA* (illus. 41), on the other hand, she did not carry the horrific piling-up of bodies to the extreme but, despite the painful contortion of the bodies, showed their human faces and attempts to protect themselves.[38] Far away from the concentration camps, the émigrée Grundig

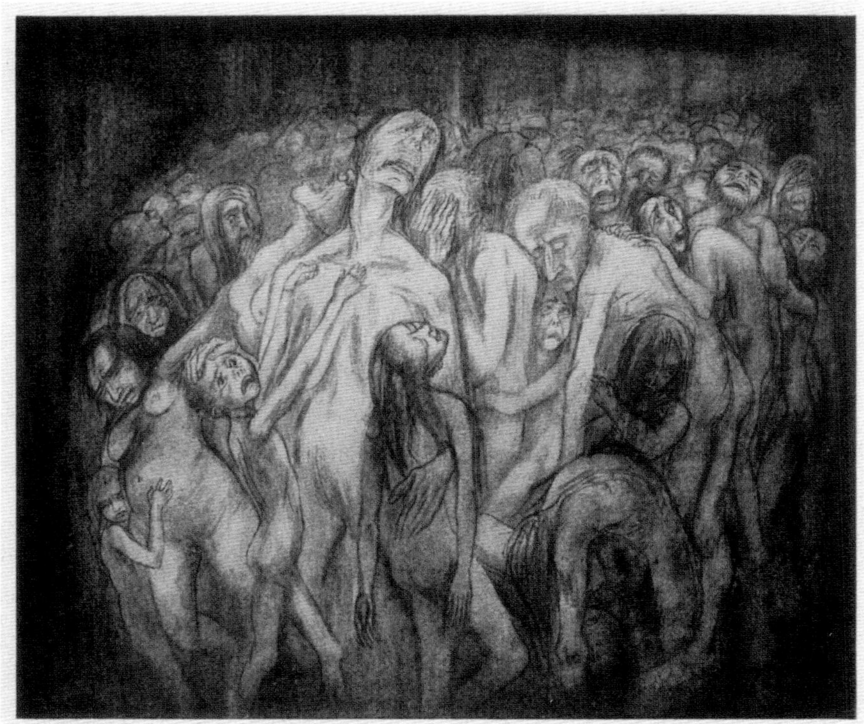

41 Lea Grundig, TREBLIANCA, fol. 11 from the series *In the Valley of Slaughter*, Tel Aviv, 1944.

42 Ludwig Meidner, *Gas Chamber*, from the series *Massacres in Poland*, 1942–53, charcoal on paper.

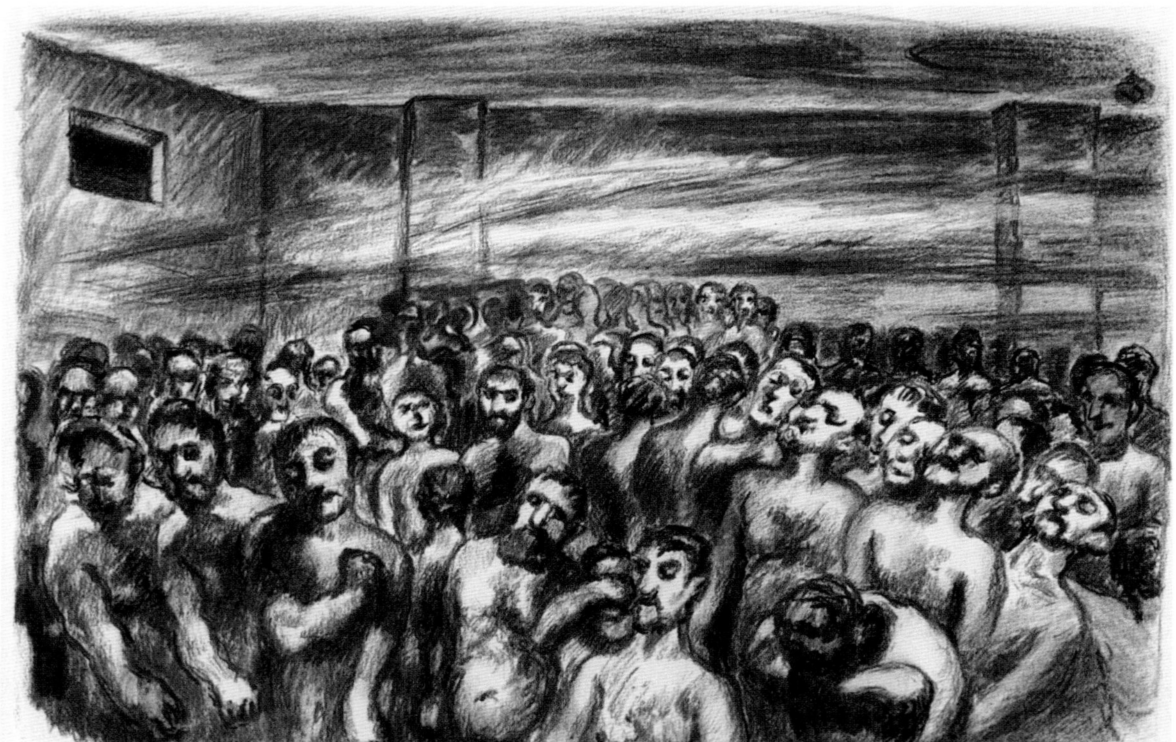

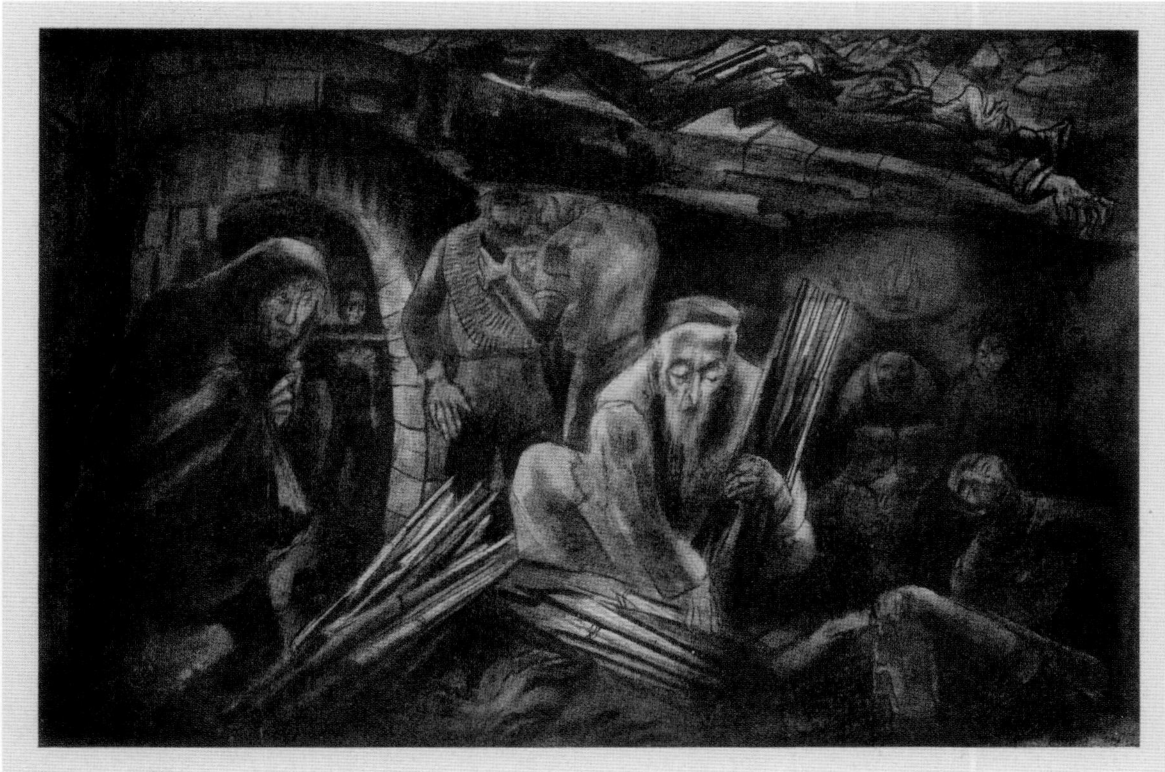

43 Lea Grundig, UNDERGROUND, fol. 14 from the series *In the Valley of Slaughter*, Tel Aviv, 1944.

imagined the deadly minutes in the gas chamber of which, as Alfred Kantor described, the inmates of the camps, facing death, continually suppressed their certain knowledge,[39] and which were portrayed by hardly any of the survivors.[40] Grundig showed the dying in pale white appearing out of the dark, a pregnant woman with children clinging to her, at any other time a guarantee for the future of the Jewish people, in the moment of collapse towering above all the other men and women. Liebmann began his commentary on this drawing by saying: 'The cries are frozen. The naked creatures have cried their souls out of their bodies.' One of the few who also drew this mass murder by poison gas at approximately the same period is Ludwig Meidner (illus. 42), who was not an inmate of a concentration camp either but an émigré in England.

Grundig continued the cycle *In the Valley of Slaughter* with the drawing *INTO ABYSS*, whose Christian iconography of the Fall of the Damned was altered by Liebmann to the Fall of the Saints,[41] also followed by the *REVOLT IN THE GHETTO* and the struggle of the *PARTISANS*. *UNDERGROUND* (illus. 43) shows, in nightmarish darkness, a rabbi collecting guns surrounded by women and armed fighters, arranged with the dead body on the roof above them in a way that might have been a model for the underground hideout in *Morituri* of 1948,[42] the first German film dealing with the persecution of the Jews and their survival underground.

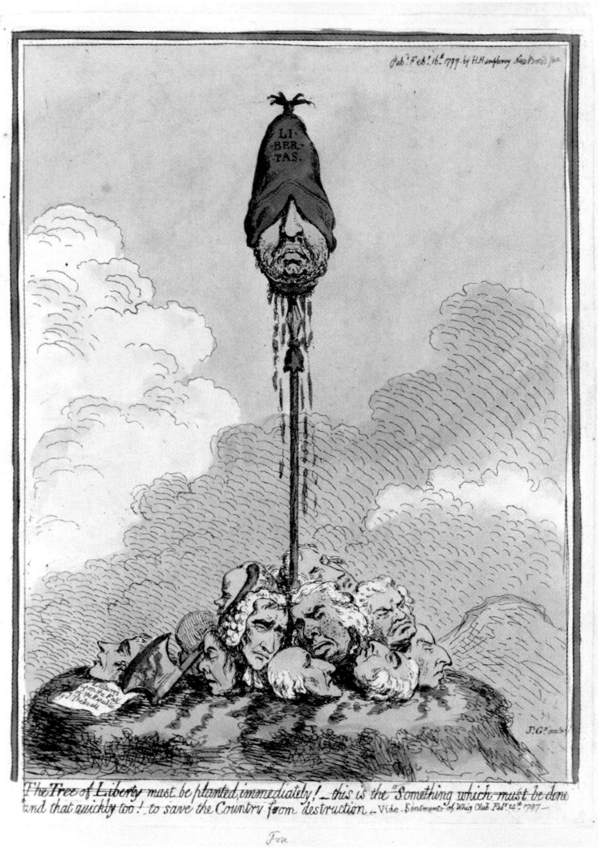

44 James Gillray, *The Tree of Liberty Must be Planted, Immediately!*, 1797, etching.

In the last of the seventeen plates, *ETERNAL SHAME* (illus. 45), as Amishai-Maisels emphasizes, Lea Grundig, by her use of the Golgotha-like pile of corpses, was recalling photographs made by the Soviet Army of German atrocities. Below four of the photographs taken of mass shootings and piles of corpses,[43] there is the caption: 'This photograph was found on the body of a German soldier' or 'officer'.[44] Grundig's composition refers to the cynical caricature by James Gillray calling for the beheading of Charles James Fox, the British politician who was one of the few to support the French Revolution (illus. 44). Grundig must have known this print, showing the Briton's head below the bloody Phrygian cap, a symbol of freedom that had fallen into disrepute as a result of the Terror under the Jacobins. She presented a variation on that ancient symbol of humiliation, a head on a pole. In her version the tyrant is not beheaded, but Hitler is shown as a wretched figure struggling within a flag with a swastika on a pole. When Grundig was doing the drawing, the desire to see Adolf Hitler hanged was still a vague hope. Liebmann in 1947, on the other hand, was able to use the images to counter any attempt to forget the murder of the Jews, at a time when Walter Ulbricht, the East German leader, was to publicly declare only a few months later that concern with emigration and the Nazi past was unprogressive.[45]

45 Lea Grundig, ETERNAL SHAME, fol. 17 from the series *In the Valley of Slaughter*, Tel Aviv, 1944.

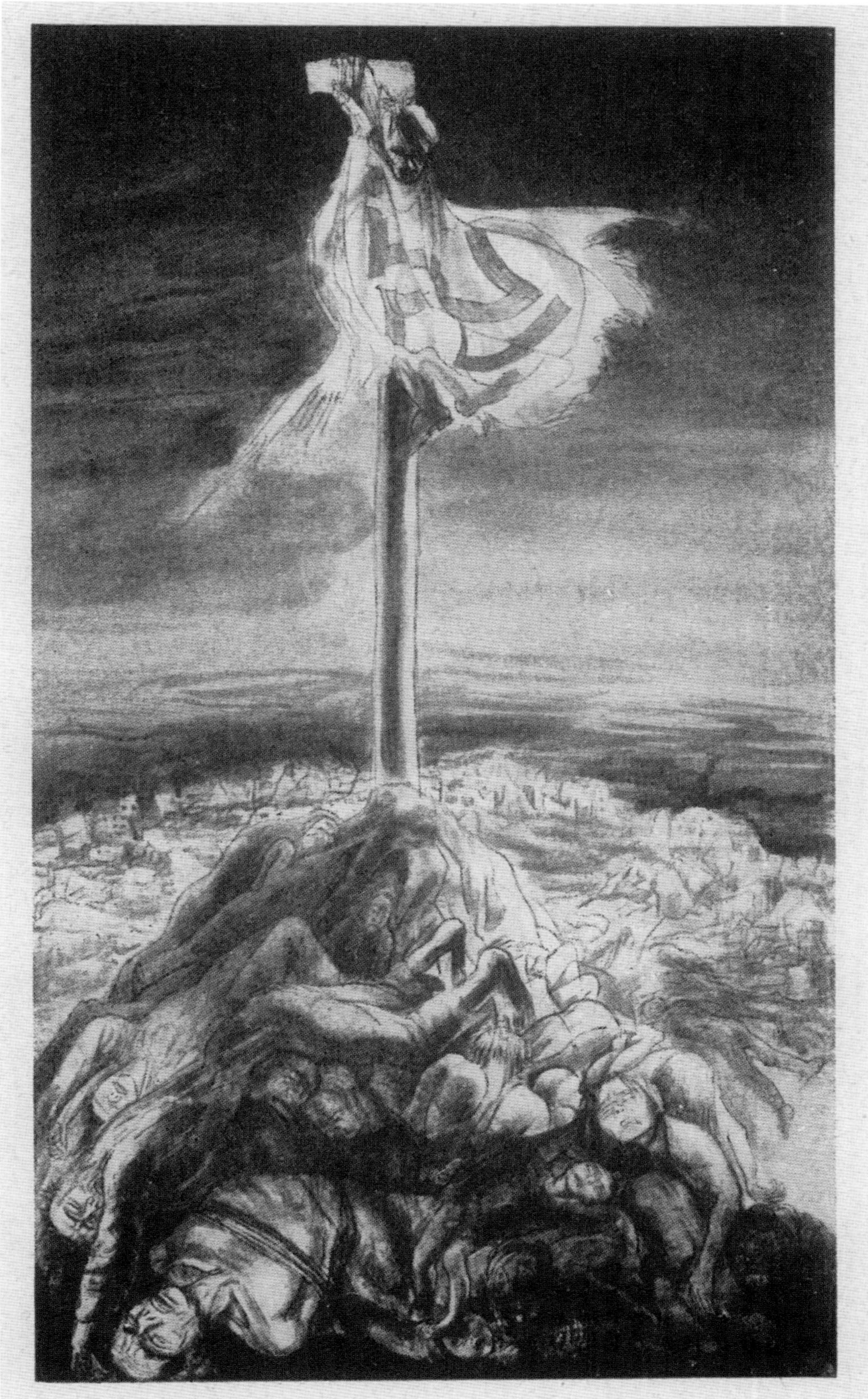

Liebmann, writing about Grundig's images, spoke out against this suppression of the past:

> Truly, what was done by that man hanging on his tattered standard,
> never forget, never forget . . .
> Hanging from the wretched pole is the exterminator.
> Exterminating everything about him and himself.
> To be remembered for ever. In eternal shame.

When the decision was taken in the Soviet occupation zone to focus above all on building socialism, Liebmann was concerned that Grundig's images should not be forgotten. His commentary does credit socialism with the desire to promote a change from passivity and putting up with things to activity, but there is in the end no victory, no view to the future, but a courageous exhortation to remember the eternal shame. The sequence in Grundig's cycle placing the struggle of the partisans as fol. 16 and the juxtaposition of the pile of corpses with Hitler on the gallows in one picture, fol. 17, the final one, made it possible in 1947 for the political utopia she had been longing for in the midst of war to be presented as having been achieved.

Amishai-Maisels, focusing her attention particularly on the 'Depiction and Interpretation' of the Holocaust, pointed out that only in a few of the drawings of *In the Valley of Slaughter* did Grundig attempt to copy the verism of published photographs and even in the last picture, as was always the case with her, she identified the dead as being Jewish by giving some of the men beards. Furthermore Amishai-Maisels argued that Grundig, like other Jewish artists who had not been in the concentration camps, after the cycle *In the Valley of Slaughter* 'did not continue to work from the documents' but employed the tradition of pogrom imagery even more,[46] whereas Christian artists, according to Amishai-Maisels, did not refrain from using photographic sources as models for the dead. Her explanation, using the artist Hyman Bloom's statement about his non-Jewish fellow-artists that 'the corpses were not "theirs"',[47] can also explain the possibilities and limits to Lea Grundig's representations of the persecution and murder of the Jews. As Grundig wrote in the account of her life about a newspaper photograph of a bearded Jewish man looking out of a transport wagon: 'I know that I shall die and the image will stay with me until the end.'[48] She identified with the fate of the murdered Jews and recognized her own escape as being fraught with danger. That is why she experienced her visit to the gas chamber at Majdanek in 1951 'as a re-entering'.[49] Her visual concepts, only rarely bearing any relation to what is called 'atrocity photography', can even be seen as attempts to create a distance[50] from the photographic record and from the threat to herself. 'I was so depressed, and haunted by horrific images. They continued to haunt me, day and night. I had to get them out of my system. So I painted them.'[51] As will become clear later in the analysis of Lea Grundig's work, in her lonely quest for forms of representation for the unparalleled extent of the murder, she made reference not just to the photographs taken by the victors and now available, but to Christian iconography and images of the pogroms, graphic art from the labour movement and even Nazi sources.

Ghetto Uprising

Before her return to Germany in 1949, Grundig produced another two cycles of drawings in ink between 1946 and 1948 – *Ghetto*, created as a book illustration, and *Ghetto Uprising*[52] – and in 1950 she completed a third cycle that she had already begun in 1943, *Never Again!*,[53] a confrontation with the persecution of the Jews which was, like the other cycles, to serve as an example for further representations by other artists.[54] Her *Ghetto Uprising*, also referred to as the *Great Ghetto Cycle*, was exhibited in Warsaw in 1949,[55] shortly after the inauguration of the memorial there by Nathan Rapoport.[56] Neither Grundig nor Rapoport had been in a concentration camp, and Grundig seldom referred to any event recorded in the photographs. Rapoport for his part was following the tradition of staging the victorious struggle in the style of Socialist Realism and the relief known as *La Marseillaise* by François Rude on the Arc de Triomphe in Paris. Grundig meanwhile, in drawing fol. 2, *Uprising* (illus. 46), of the first mentioned cycle, made use of the left-wing iconography of workers' demonstrations of Théophile Steinlen (see illus. 90) and Käthe Kollwitz (illus. 47) and the continuation of their style by Max Lingner in France in the 1930s. The way in which Grundig placed the leaders of the Uprising in a row is worth noting, as is the addition of the woman throwing the hand grenade,[57] who is here occupying the role of allegory of a nation, always cast as feminine, and in whose facial features Amishai-Maisels says she can identify those of Lea Grundig. It is not just here that she was transposing a well-known Nazi image of a hand grenade thrower and using it against the Nazis. By representing herself in line with the troop,[58] here not identified as being Jewish, she declared the Ghetto Uprising part of the anti-fascist struggle thought of as continuing into the present. The way the resistance of the Jews in the Warsaw Ghetto, almost all of whom were murdered, is represented was subsumed within the overarching idea of the continuing struggle of Communism of which Lea Grundig saw herself as a part.

For *The Situation in the Ghetto* (illus. 48), the first drawing in the *Ghetto Uprising* cycle, she alluded – in addition to recent oral and written reports translated into the narrative style of *In the Valley of Slaughter* using small-scale figures – to a very ancient type of image. She adopted a multi-perspective arrangement known since medieval times for an enclosed area, such as a town,[59] to show the interior and exterior view of a walled space, that is, the Ghetto, in one and the same drawing. Not only does it show in detail the various things going on in the Ghetto, involving the Torah scroll, coffins, a group of workers, rabbis and many desperate people, but on the left-hand side of the wall you can see bartering with the outside world taking place: a piece

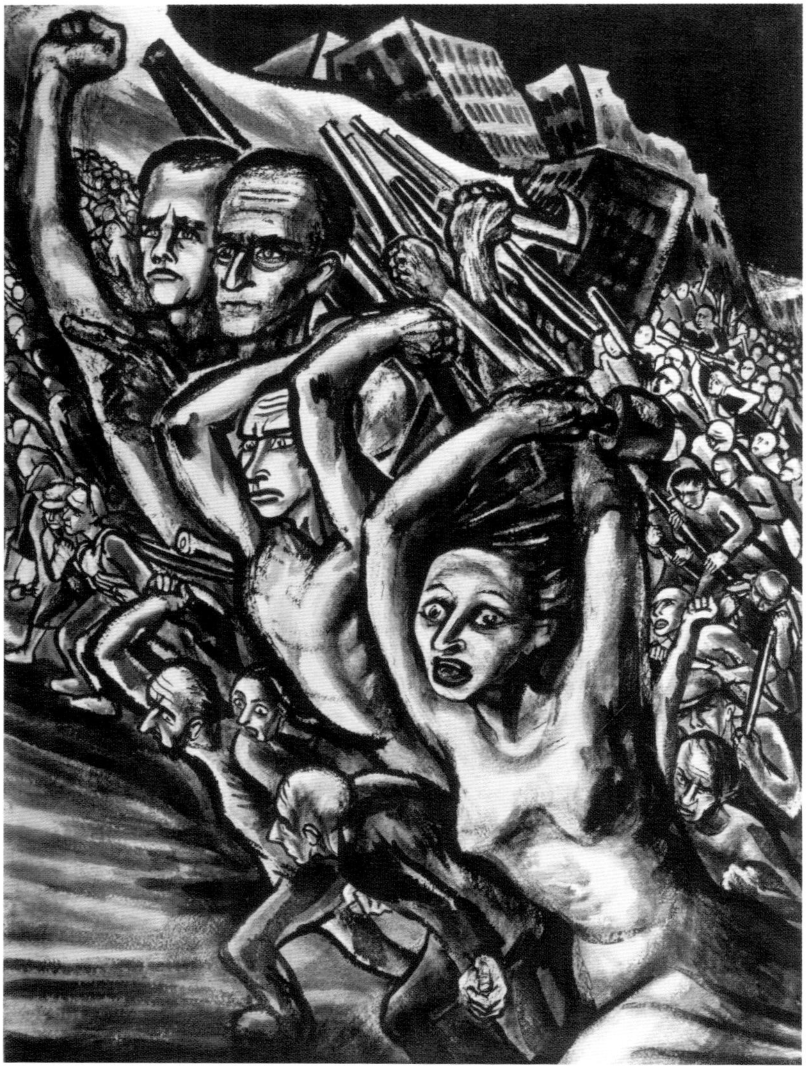

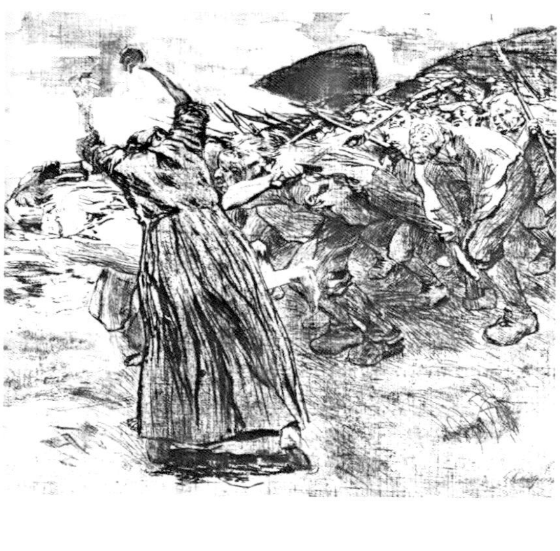

46 Lea Grundig, *Uprising*, 1946, fol. 2 from the series *Ghetto Uprising*, brush and black ink.

47 Käthe Kollwitz, *Outbreak*, fol. 5 from the series *Peasants' War*, 1903, etching.

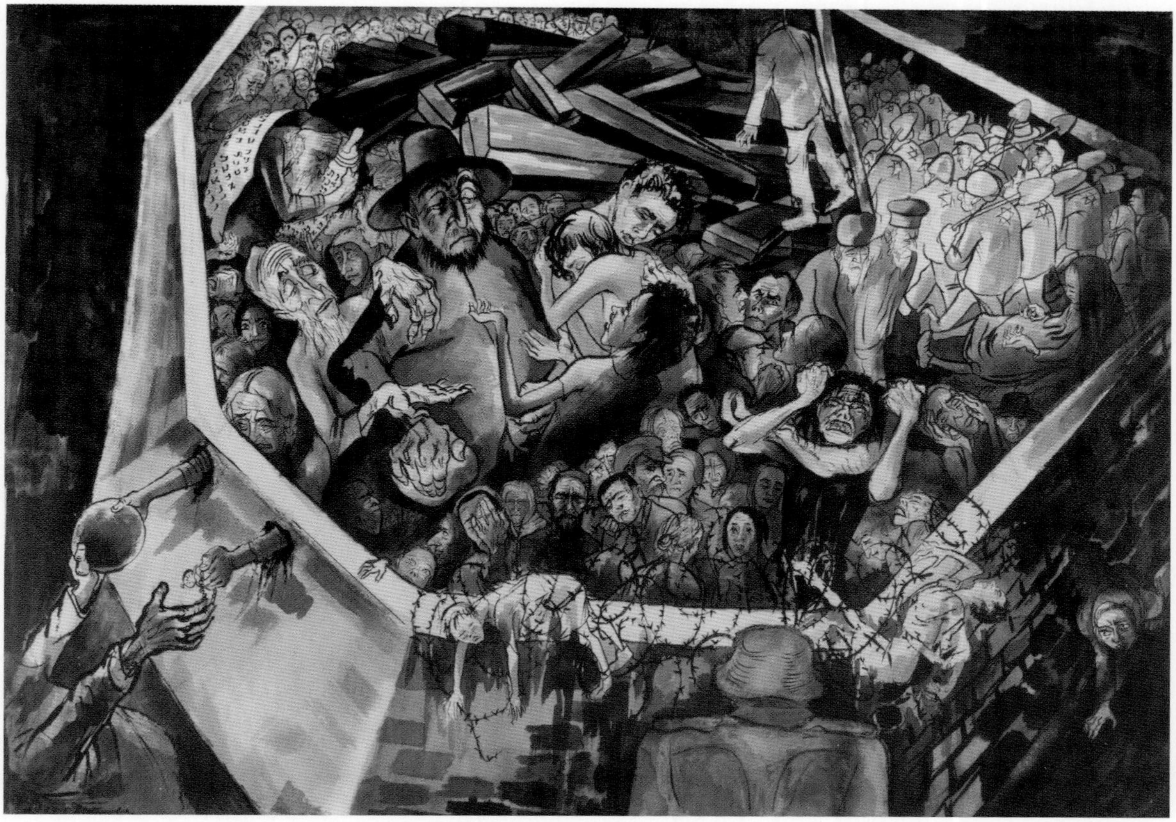

48 Lea Grundig, *The Situation in the Ghetto*, 1946, fol. 1 from the series *Ghetto Uprising*, pen, brush and black ink and wash (partially scratched out) over graphite.

of jewellery, maybe a wristwatch, for a loaf of bread. Children are shown dying in the foreground, having tried to cross the wall to run errands, which was forbidden, and on the right-hand side of the wall they are caught on the barbed wire. The whole scene is watched over by a German soldier with his back to us, wearing a steel helmet.

In *Requiem* (illus. 49), the last drawing, Grundig returned to her earlier composition *Imprisoned Sleepers* from her cycle of 1936, *Under the Swastika*,[60] now transformed into a memorial to the dead. Yet again, we find Grundig's inversion of the mainly Christian iconography. Whereas the imprisoned sleepers appear to be illuminated by the hopeful beam of daylight behind bars, in *Requiem* we see instead, among the dark ruins, a child wrapped in swaddling clothes as in an image of Christ in the manger,[61] in this case not bathed in splendour but in a perverted scene of child murder.

The three cycles that Lea Grundig produced after *In the Valley of Slaughter* dealing with the persecution of the Jews were never printed in the GDR, or in the FRG in their entirety either, for that matter; they were and are only available to the East and West German public in individual drawings in publications and exhibitions devoted to Grundig. Despite most of them having been made publicly available by the Ladengalerie (the gallery for realist art in Berlin) in 1996, art history has yet to come up with a comprehensive study of these cycles of drawings. The same works are reproduced again and again, whereas this present analysis of the published oeuvre and of the contents of the archive in the Academy of Arts in Berlin reveals an exceedingly rich variety of subject-matter and application of styles.

Ghetto

The representations in the *Ghetto* cycle were originally illustrations for the book by Reuben Ben Shem (Ruben Feldschu), *Between the Walls of the Ghetto*,[62] published in Hebrew in Palestine in 1947, which describes the bond between the Jewish children within and outside the Warsaw Ghetto right up until their violent deaths. The 132-page text contains twelve illustrations and is intended for young people.[63] The author, forgotten even in Israel today, studied under Sigmund Freud, received a doctorate in Vienna, in 1923 was ordained as a rabbi at what counted for traditional East European Jewry as a modern teaching institute and was nevertheless seen in the period between the wars as a well-known member of the revisionist Zionists. He took part in the preparations for the Warsaw Ghetto Uprising and was the only surviving Jew to keep a journal in the Ghetto. His gifted daughter, the pianist Yosima, to whom the book is dedicated, died of tuberculosis at the start of the Uprising while in hiding outside the Ghetto, after which her mother Prina Richter took her own life.[64] Feldschu described the moving friendships of the children, Yosima and Monik, through a catastrophic everyday life; in the course of the narrative, the girl Pnina and her brother Yosi are added. In the first two illustrations, which were displayed as pen-and-ink drawings in exhibitions in Germany, Lea Grundig made it clear how communication was defined by hunger. First she drew a girl searching through a rubbish bin (illus. 50). In the second scene (illus. 51), from the top to the bottom of the picture, faces getting bigger and older appear as in a sudden lightning flash, a shaft of light in a film, revealing the state of the feelings of the inhabitants, ranging from mutual aggression to extreme despair. Grundig has here extended Feldschu's description of children to the inhabitants of the Ghetto of any age.

The Joker in the Ghetto (illus. 52) may have motivated Roberto Benigni's last appearance as a comedian in his 1997 film *Life is Beautiful*[65] and, like all Lea Grundig's ink drawings, seems to be following in Goya's footsteps. It is a satire on the speaker appealing to the public with his arms raised. In a caricature of the image of the orator, he is clicking his right-hand thumb and index finger, his face distorted into a grin, and he stands at the bottom of the drawing, attired in his hat and baggy jacket, an extremely precarious figure in front of laughing and serious listeners. The story printed along with it, entitled *Jews Are Being Hunted Down and Hounded Out*, reveals the relief provided by the joke. The people hidden in the attic with Yosima and her father recover from their panic when they recognize the man climbing up towards them as one of their own. In reply to the question how, as an old man, he has managed to avoid Nazi forced labour, he describes a German in uniform

49 Lea Grundig, *Requiem*, 1948, fol. 4 from the series *Ghetto Uprising*, pen, brush and black ink and wash (partially scratched out) over graphite.

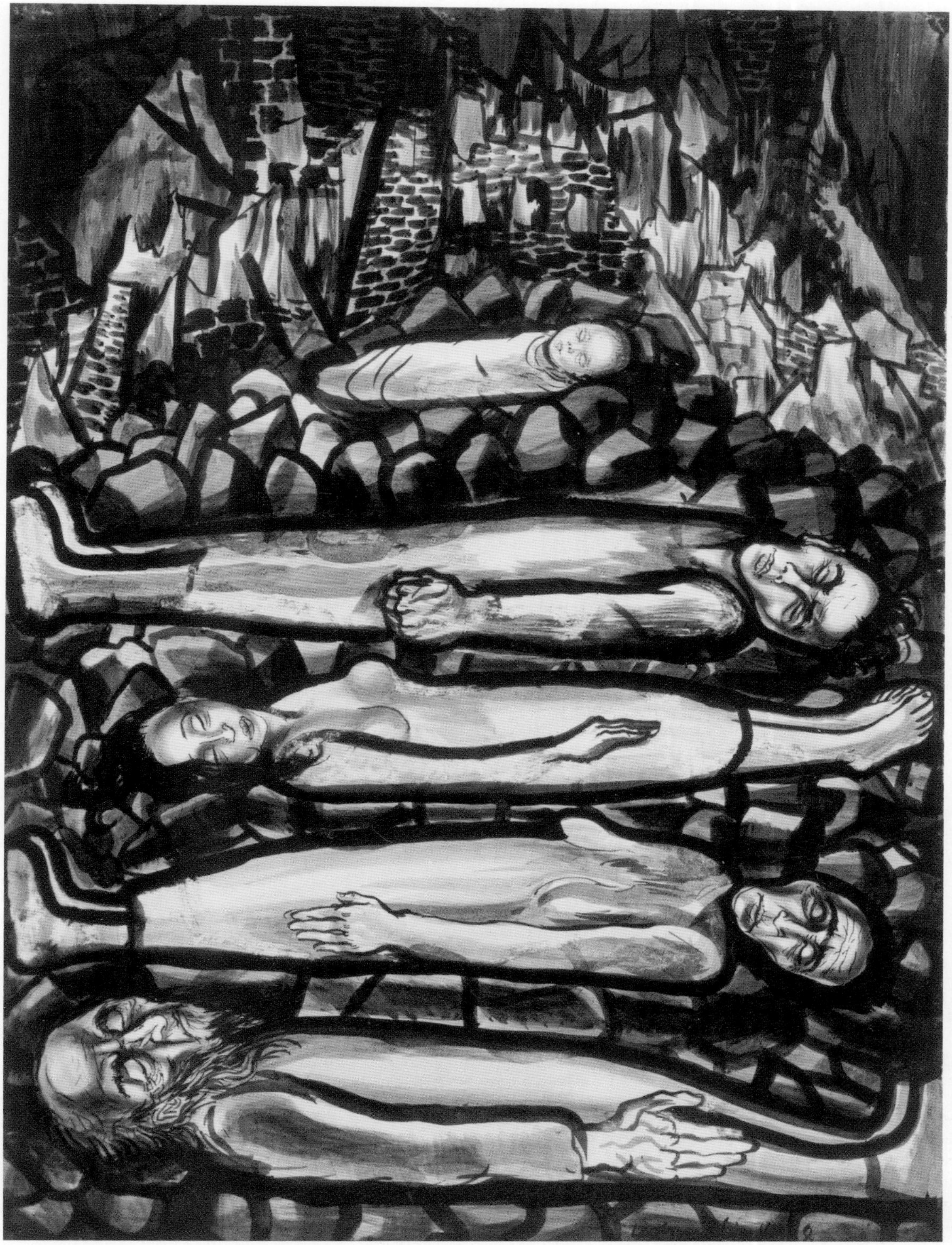

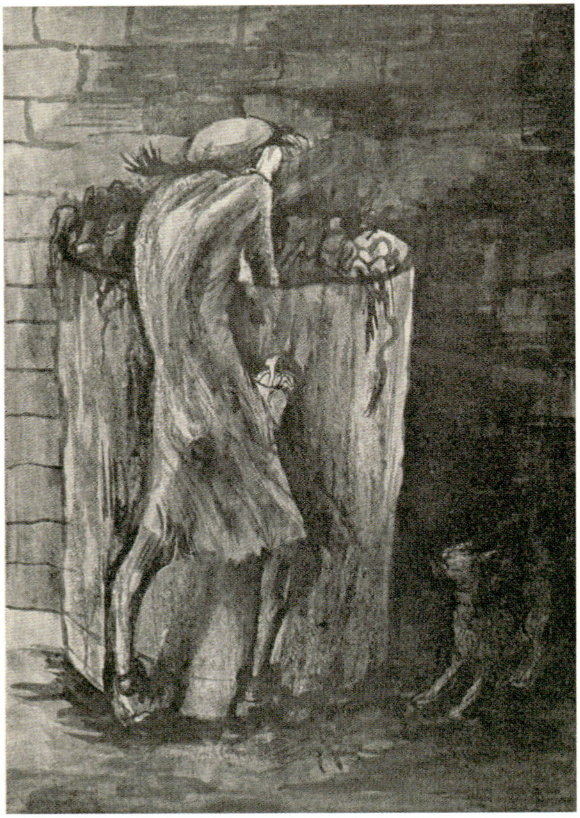

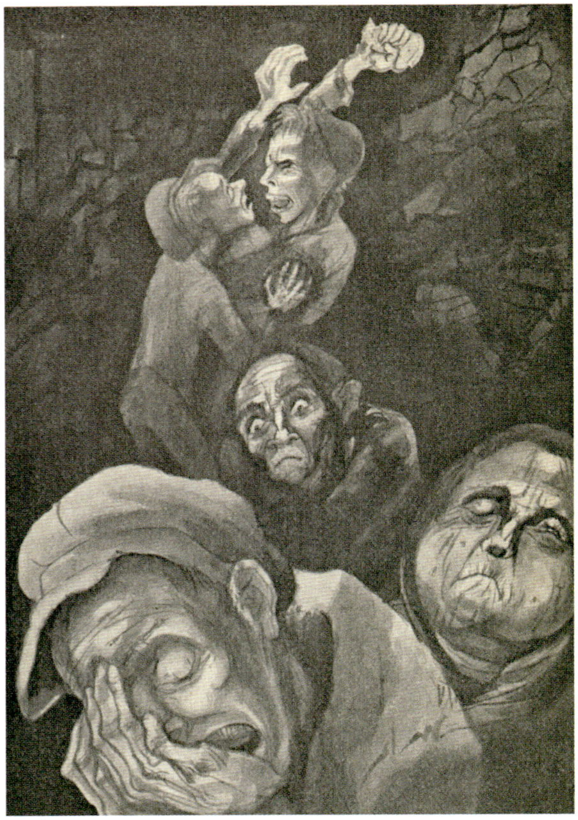

50 Lea Grundig, *Hunger in the Ghetto* I, illustration for Reuben Ben-Shem, *Between the Walls of the Ghetto* (Tel Aviv, 1947).

51 Lea Grundig, *Hunger in the Ghetto* II, illustration for Reuben Ben Shem, *Between the Walls of the Ghetto* (Tel Aviv, 1947).

and with a helmet on his head asking him why he is trembling and ordering him to work: 'Work won't do you any harm; work makes life sweet!' He answers this by saying: 'Jawohl, that's true, Colonel, but I haven't a sweet tooth, I don't like sweet things.' Fear dissolves into laughter, and they can now face holding out in their hiding place. The drawing only received the name *The Joker* outside of the Feldschu context in exhibitions in the GDR. The mortal danger that the joker is exposed to in the context of the story indicates how closely life-threatening danger and laughter are related in the specific culture of the Jewish joke. The joke, Katja Petrowskaja writes, is 'the weapon of the powerless'.[66]

Together with the exceptional image of the Jewish *Joker in the Ghetto*, a rare picture of one of the perpetrators, *The Female Commandant*, was probably also displayed in Potsdam in 1956 at an exhibition of works by Grundig (illus. 53).[67]

In the middle of the book, as a response to the previous chapter heading 'The Angel of Death Has Fallen Asleep', it now reads: 'And If He Has Awoken'. After the song about death, applying equally to rich and poor, by a man called Rubinstein described as *meschugge* (mad), the story focuses on the children, who spend their day trying to escape the Ghetto in order to beg for food, returning in the evening. Suddenly a German woman in a uniform

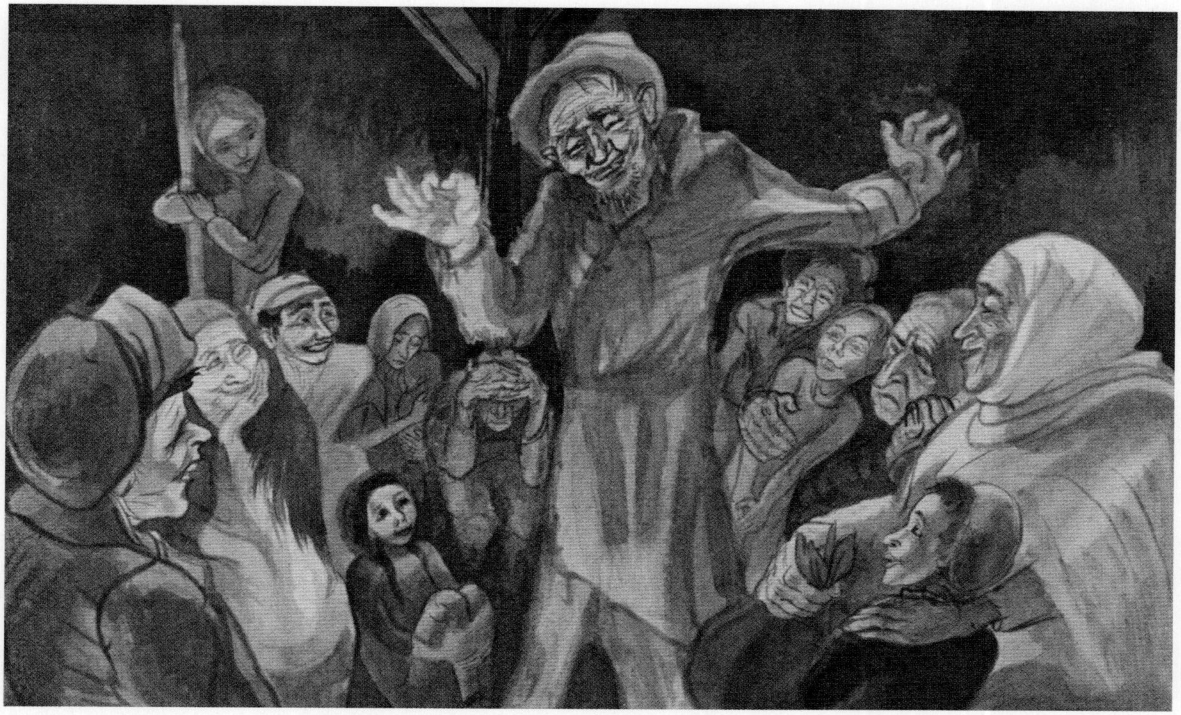

52 Lea Grundig, *The Joker in the Ghetto*, illustration for Reuben Ben Shem, *Between the Walls of the Ghetto* (Tel Aviv, 1947).

catches two children, brutally hitting one of them and shouting 'Shoot!' The child fights like a lion but suddenly becomes quiet, so the woman lets go of him, thinking he is dead. The boy Yosi, Prina's brother, is lying in a pool of blood but is still breathing and is taken to hospital.

What is more, in her drawing Grundig showed a female guard looking towards the viewer. With her right hand raised, she is about to hit out at the boy standing at the front of the composition as though both the child and the viewer might be struck. But there again, from the viewer's perspective – the film technique of shot reverse shot is here recycled for a drawing on paper – the answer to the command 'shoot' may also refer to the viewer him- or herself. Grundig knew how to make use not just of the usual film techniques but of documentary photography for her drawing. The origin of the artist's unusual drawing of a *Kommandeuse* hitting out was presumably a photo enabling her to portray German brutality with evidence of women also being involved. The face of the *Kommandeuse*, her thick lips cynically distorted, her eyes unevenly screwed up and her long fair hair, resemble those of the guard, the first from the right in the fairly well-known photo of female concentration camp guards from Bergen-Belsen that was also printed in a newspaper in Palestine as early as 11 May 1945 (illus. 54). The film *Death Mills* employs the same exposure of brutal women and shows the parade of female wardens, which this photograph is part of, while the masculine ones are to be seen at work only and hardly identifiable.[68] There is a hint at the cause of the maltreatment given by the piece of bread on the ground on the left of the picture.

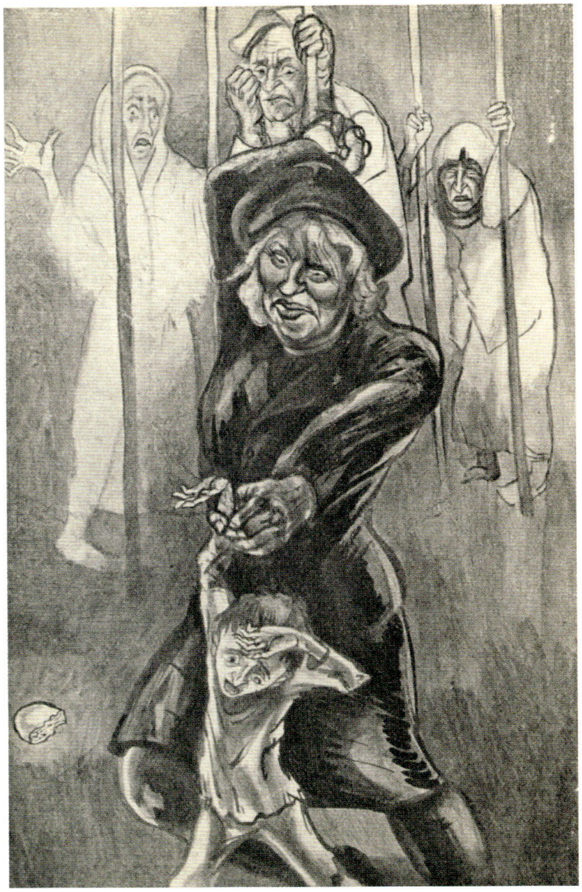

53 Lea Grundig, *The Female Commandant*, illustration for Reuben Ben Shem, *Between the Walls of the Ghetto* (Tel Aviv 1947).

54 Sergeant H. Oakes, *Female Concentration Camp Guards from Bergen-Belsen*, May 1945, photograph publ. in Schoenberner 1960.

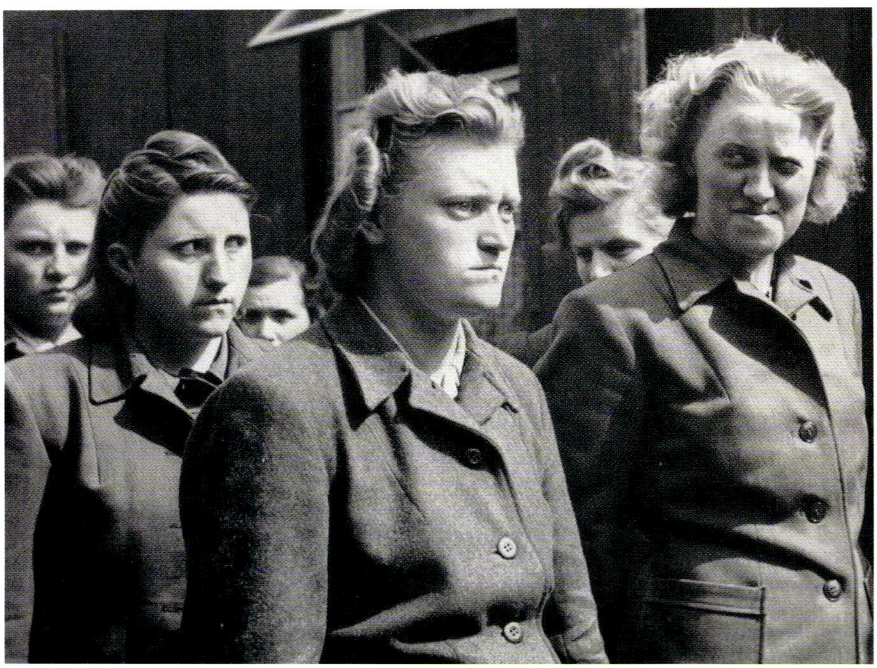

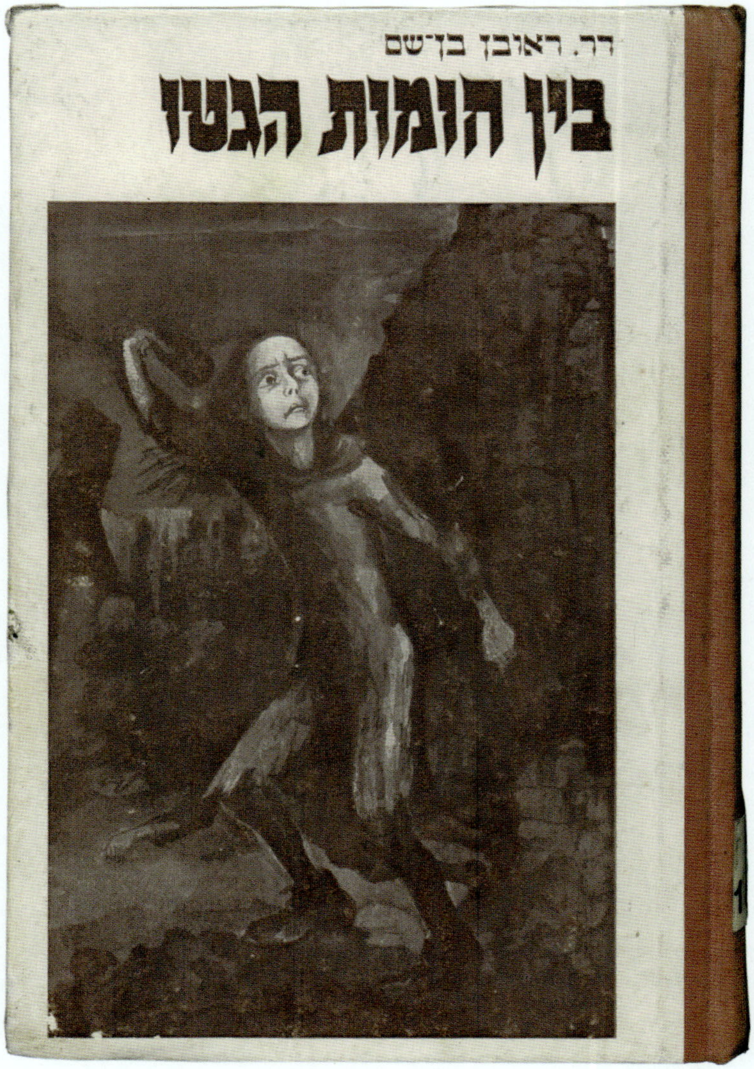

55 Lea Grundig, cover illustration for Reuben Ben Shem, *Between the Walls of the Ghetto*, (Tel Aviv, 1947).

The stance of the guard is similar to one in a snapshot – and calls to mind the order just given to shoot. But the one to be aimed at is not the child but the *Kommandeuse*. The artist's commentary on her action shows her being accused by the ghostly figures behind the bars. An act by the ss guard which is not visible in the photo is imagined in the style of portrait photographs. Grundig made use of Allied photo documentary and of photographs by the ss in order to make her art seem realistic and she recycled it for the portrayal of the crimes of the ss, calling for punishment.[69]

The *Kommandeuse* hitting out marks a turning point in Feldschu's narrative. It motivates the desire of the remaining children to stand by one another and seek revenge. They throw Molotov cocktails and start the Ghetto Uprising. Death, defence of the people and retribution, which the children are willing to take on for the sake of their dead parents and friends, dominate the last part of the book. Lea Grundig's last image (illus. 55), which is also on the cover of the book, is an embodiment of the dedication:

> To Yosima the י״ד
> My daughter for all eternity.

The girl, the attitude of her body resembling that of the 'eternal Jew',[70] is looking up out of the darkness. Leaning back, her face alone is illuminated and she is running forwards towards the left, but she is not throwing any of the Molotov cocktails frequently mentioned in the narrative. Instead, in her raised right hand, she is holding a catapult ready to throw a stone, familiar from the representations of David's battle with Goliath. Here Grundig was harking back to the ambiguous meaning of the Hebrew י״ד, which can mean both the fourteenth, thus giving the age of the author's dead daughter, and also 'Vengeance is mine; I will repay, saith the Lord.'

Never Again!

The 29 brush drawings belonging to the cycle *Never Again!*, like the previous cycle, have as their subject both the sufferings of the Jewish people during the Nazi period and the perpetrators: *Army and Generals at Stalingrad*,[71] *War Criminals*,[72] *National Militia*,[73] a commentary on *Thomas Mann's speech 'On Human Guilt'*,[74] a forward-looking *Pietà*[75] which probably inspired Will Lammert's memorial for Ravensbrück,[76] and her ink drawings for Bertolt Brecht's *O Germany, Pale Mother*,[77] which was to become a model around fifteen years later for the bronze head with the mark of Cain by Fritz Cremer for Mauthausen.[78] Out of the broad range of themes relating to the immediate post-war history of Germany, up for discussion here are four of the seven drawings[79] from the series, which was only partly published. These are directly related to the Judenmord and, with the exception of the drawing *The White Flag* (illus. 56), they became known to a wider readership through illustrations via the first publication of a book about Grundig in 1958.[80] The cycle was not completed by Grundig until after her return to Dresden.[81] Contrary to what Amishai-Maisels presumed, there is also in this cycle another image that reveals Grundig's preoccupation with press photography, or the study of documentary material, as Amishai-Maisels terms it. Lea Grundig produced her drawings intending what Hans Grundig summarized in relation to a work of art as opposed to a photograph: that 'even though it may just focus on one small part of the whole, nevertheless it contains all past and future incidents.'[82] The very fact that Grundig was referring back to a number of photographs, showing the military as well as focusing on the various gestures of sympathy, illustrates her aim. This went beyond simply making a documentary record to concentrate within one single image several events happening at different times, as described by Hans Grundig, and to develop a pictorial narrative made up of references visualizing how

56 Lea Grundig, *The White Flag. Germany Faced by the World – Collective Guilt*, signed and dated 1945, fol. 24 from the series *Never Again!*, brush, pen and brownish-black ink, graphite.

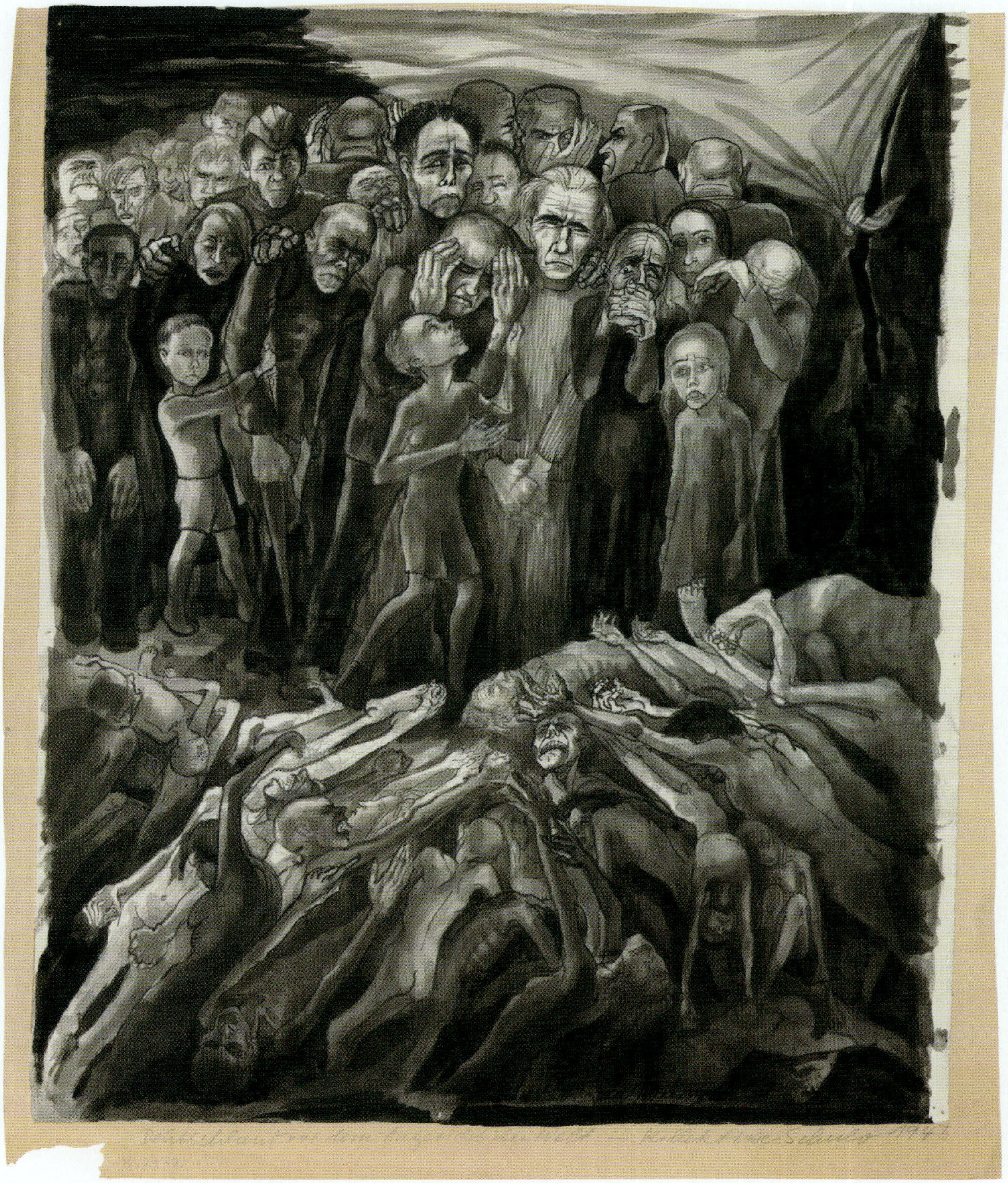
Deutschland vor dem Angesicht der Welt – Kollektive Schuld 1945

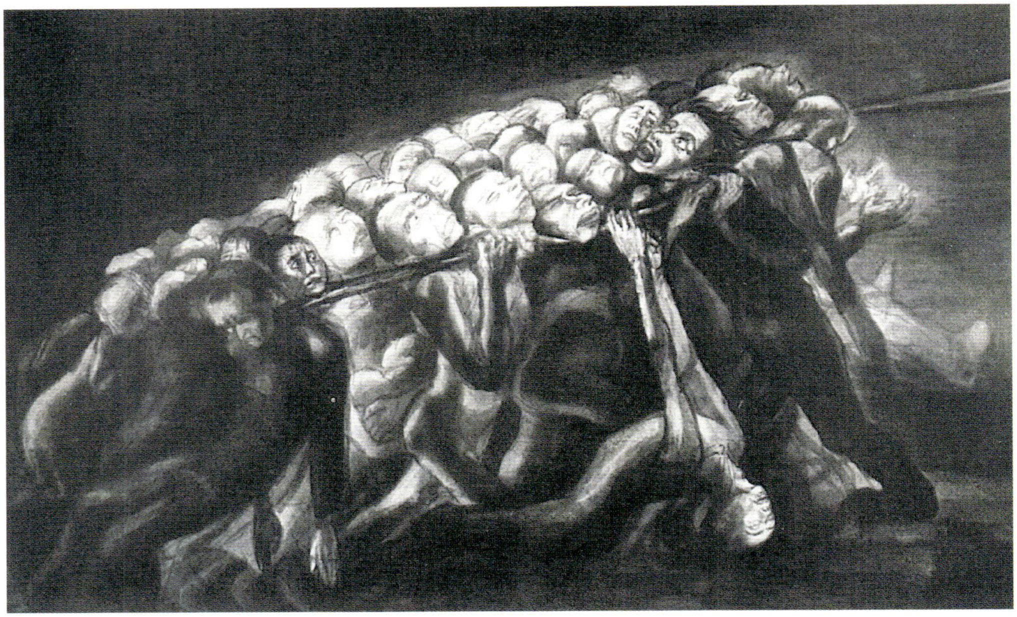

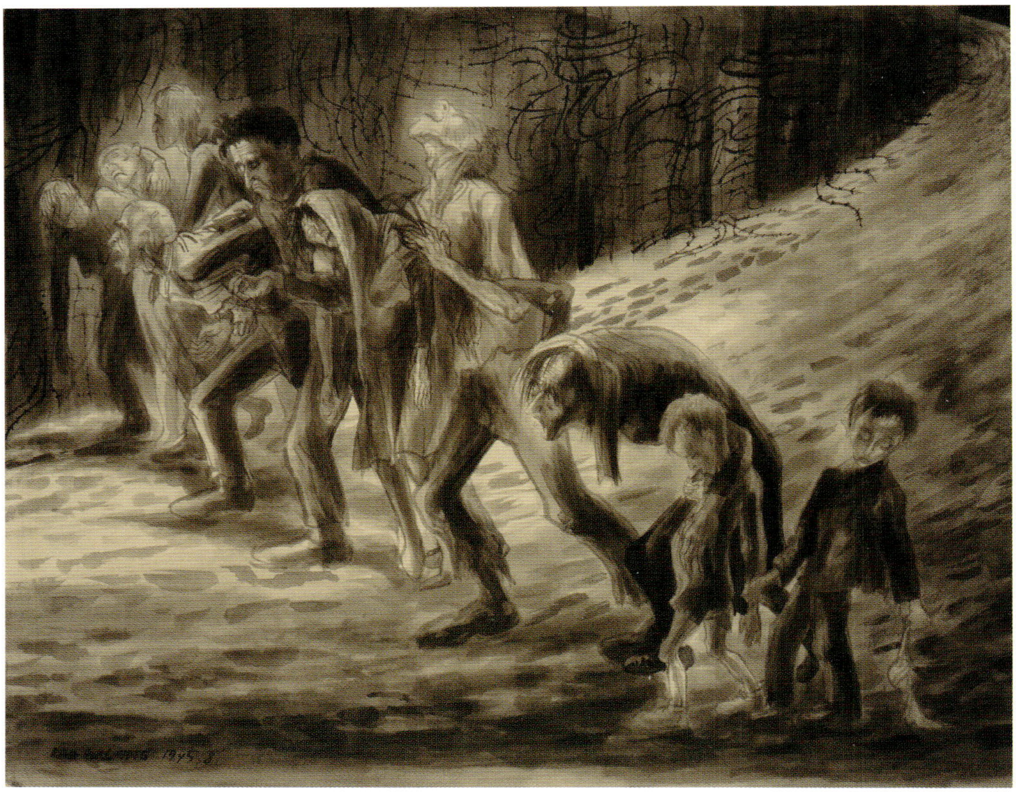

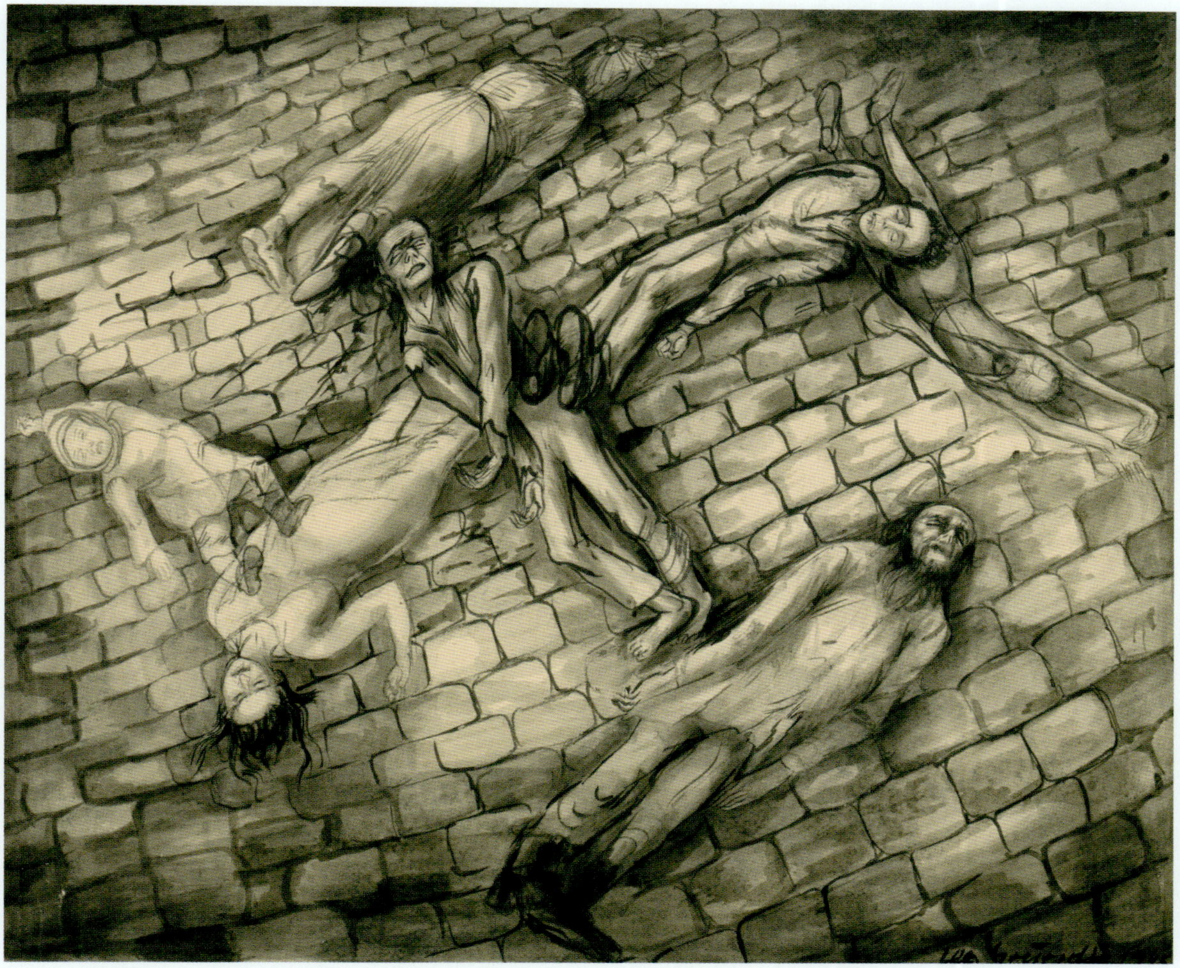

opposite top 57
Lea Grundig, *Terror*, 1946, from the series *Never Again!*, brush, pen and brownish black ink.

opposite bottom 58
Lea Grundig, *The Way into the Gas*, 1945, from the series *Never Again!*, brush, pen and brownish black ink.

above 59 Lea Grundig, *In the Streets of Poland*, 1944, from the series *Never Again!*, sign. and inscr., brush and pen in brownish black ink on yellow cardboard.

right 60 'Young Victims of Starvation', photograph, from *The Black Book of Polish Jewry*, American Federation of Polish Jews, 1943, appendix.

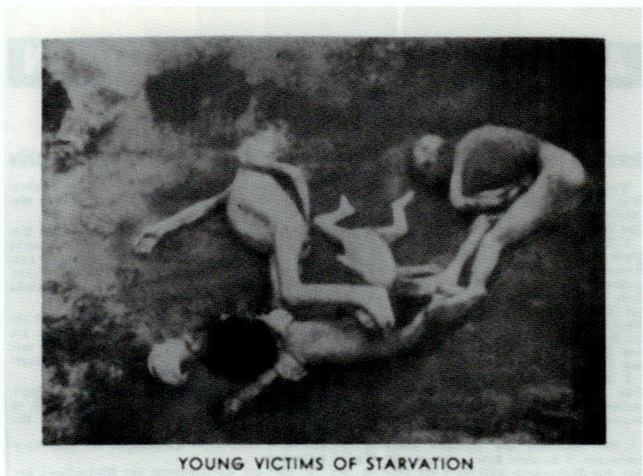

they should be interpreted. The photographs on which *The White Flag – Germany Faced by the World – Collective Guilt* is based come from the documentary photographs taken by the U.S. Army under General Eisenhower who, surrounded by the military, witnessed the sight of dead bodies lying in prison clothing in the camp at Ohrdruf,[83] and the photos that Margaret Bourke-White took, among other things, of the inhabitants of Weimar being forced to look at the dead bodies in Buchenwald.[84] In her drawing, Grundig highlighted their guilt even further by arranging the shiny arms and legs of the bodies, unlike those in the photographs, as if they are pointing accusingly at the men, women and children standing in front of them in their dark clothes and calling the attention of all the Germans to their responsibility, irrespective of whether they are looking on in grief or turning their faces away.

The drawing *Terror* (illus. 57) portrays this Nazi instrument of governance with people bound together, their faces distorted with terror pressed together; meanwhile in the foreground a figure is hanging head downwards with his hands caught in the rope. All the faces stand out shining bright against the otherwise all-pervading darkness and remind one of the terrified grimaces in Goya's drawing *Nothing: The Event Will Tell* from *The Disasters of War* and of *Saturn*, one of the so-called Black Paintings.[85] Grundig's image is a vision of terror, and as in Goya's drawing encompasses the whole human race, and it therefore appeared in Frommhold's 1958 selection that did not otherwise include any other representation identifiable as being Jewish, let alone a ghetto image. In *The Way into the Gas* (illus. 58) the artist avoided any identification of the miserable figures seen running, but as the line includes children, presumably Grundig wanted to record the act of murder based on race. This murder of families and a whole people is symbolized in the shape of a swastika on the cobbled pavement in *In the Streets of Poland* (illus. 59). Grundig's image reminds one of a photograph that had appeared as early as 1943 in *The Black Book of Polish Jewry*[86] showing starving children and young people (illus. 60). Above all, however, for the image she was harking back to Nazi symbolism, whose significance is revealed by the transformation of the reference. So-called 'living swastikas', formed by the bodies of schoolchildren or torch-bearers at Nazi mass rallies in the 1930s and published in the media,[87] were used by Grundig, in an aerial view with crude paralleling of imagery and dramatic Expressionism,[88] as a symbol of murder. It is not the human being who is tormented and tortured by the wheel of the Nazi party, as in John Heartfield's famous 1934 AIZ (Workers' Illustrated Newspaper) collage *As It Was in the Middle Ages . . . So It Is in the Third Reich*;[89] rather it is Nazi brutality that has entered into the human bodies, has tortured them to death Nazi-style. The murdered group of Jews turns into Nazi insignia.

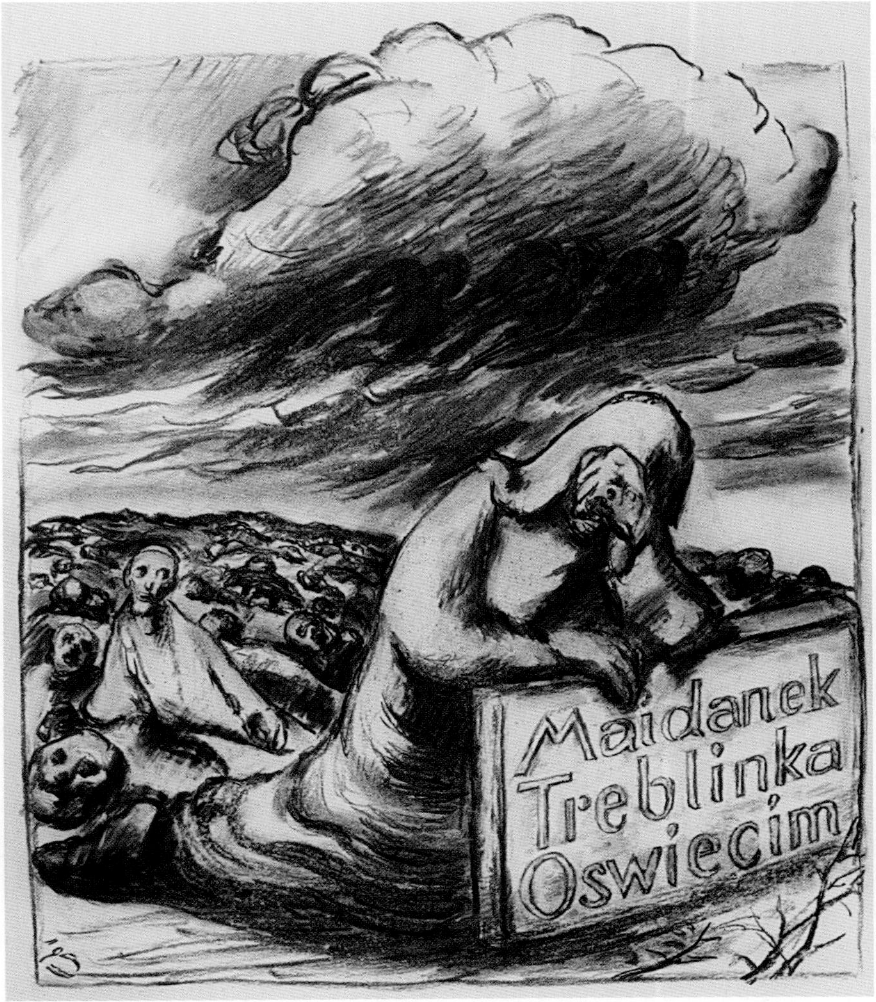

61 Ludwig Meidner, memorial page from the series *Massacres in Poland*, 1942–53, charcoal on paper.

Ludwig Meidner: *Massacres in Poland*

Even though in the GDR of the 1950s the works of Hans (see below) and Lea Grundig, as well as of Horst Strempel and Teo Otto, were subject to fierce criticism on the part of Party officials and denounced as 'ugly' by the press,[90] the Grundigs, unlike Strempel, were able to continue earning a living from their art, whereas the émigré Meidner, not a Communist and isolated in London, found it difficult to re-establish himself professionally even after his return to Germany.[91] Not until after his death were some of the drawings from *Massacres in Poland* (illus. 61) shown at a 1978 exhibition in Darmstadt,[92] and even Amishai-Maisels apparently did not know about this series.[93]

The cycle also called *Sufferings of the Jews in Poland*[94] was produced between 1942 and 1945 in England.[95] Meidner gives a figure[96] varying between 42 and fifty drawings. Forty drawings are documented, 26 of which are in the

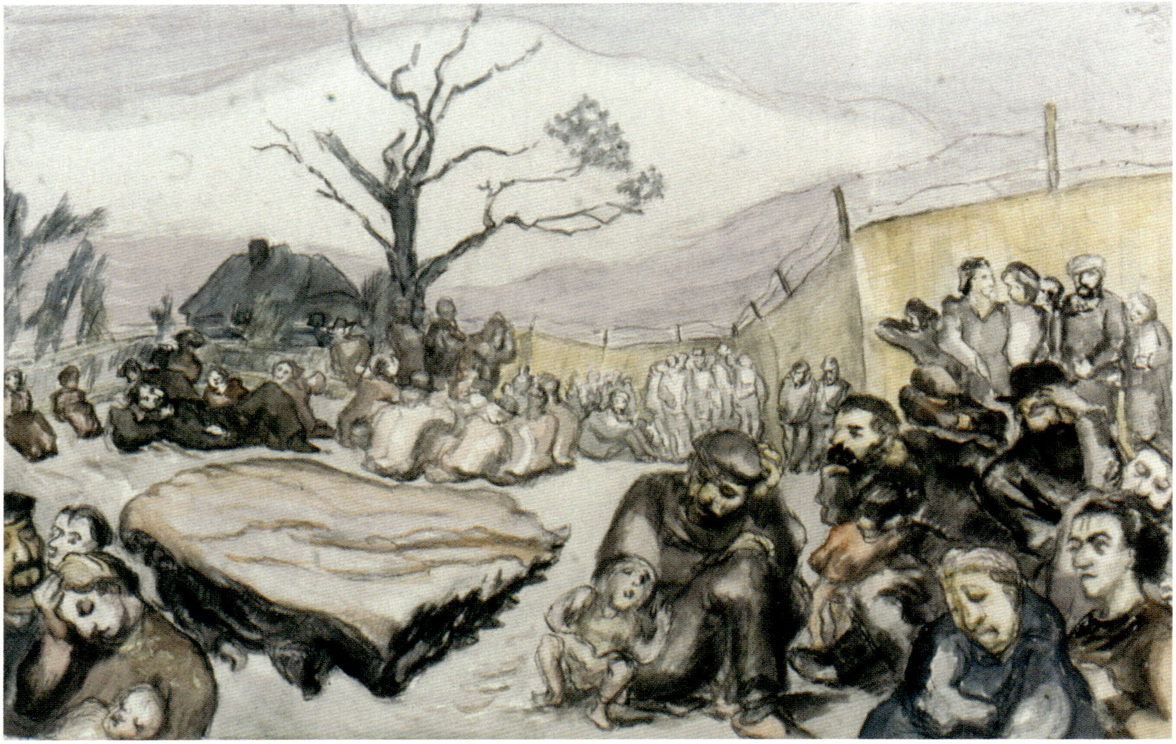

62 Ludwig Meidner, *Camp*, from the series *Massacres in Poland*, 1942–53, watercolour over charcoal.

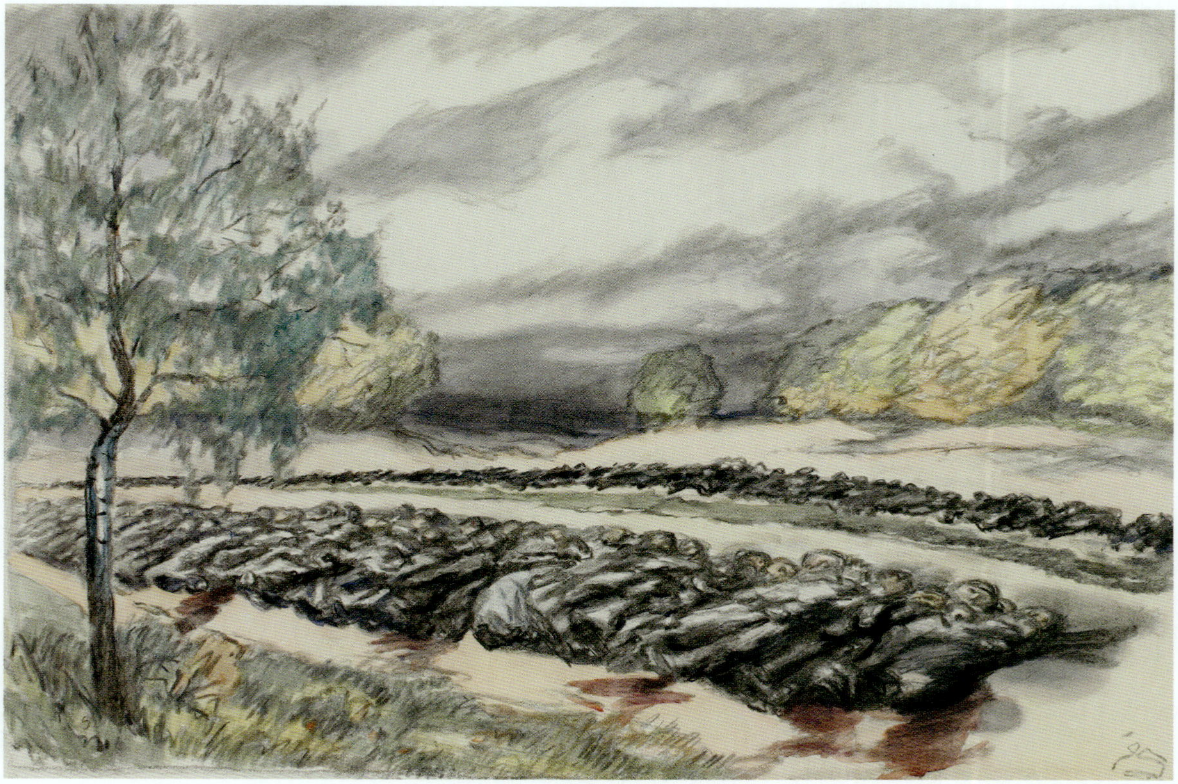

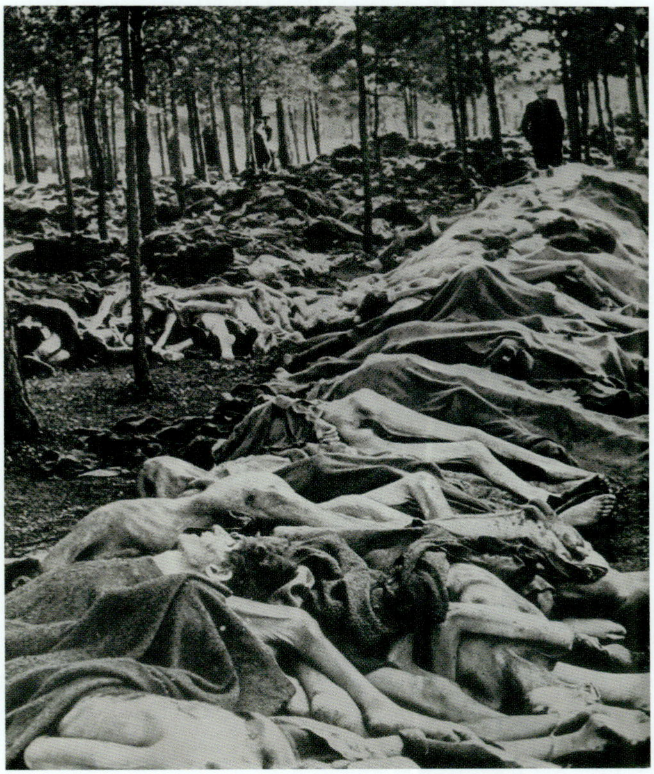

63 Ludwig Meidner, *Corpses*, from the series *Massacres in Poland,* 1942–53, watercolour over charcoal.

64 Sergeant Oakes, 'A Wood of Death ... Belsen, April 1945', from *Lest We Forget*, published in the *Daily Mail* (London, 1945).

Ludwig Meidner Archive in the Jewish Museum in Frankfurt am Main.[97] In January 1943 Meidner wrote in London:

> For weeks I have been working on a cycle of water-colour drawings, 'Sufferings of the Jews in Poland'. So that's how I am obliged constantly, constantly to think about the fate of my brothers. These drawings are illustrations, clear, without putting a gloss on anything; nevertheless neither sentimental nor overly crude. Kept within bounds . . . They capture the tragedy quite realistically. These works are free of mysticism.[98]

Nevertheless, against his will Meidner put a gloss on the position of the Jews. The events went beyond his power of imagination. He did not suspect that the Germans were about to leave no survivors behind for the mourning of the dead, portrayed in many of his drawings. As Amishai-Maisels noted in the case of Lea Grundig and other exiled Jews, Meidner referred to pogrom motifs from earlier representations of the history of the Jews of Eastern Europe to project himself into the contemporary situation of the Jews. In the 1943 coloured charcoal drawing *Camp* (illus. 62) Jewish men, women and children are positioned on the ground in front of a wall topped by barbed wire round three sides, bewailing the dead who are covered by a sheet. Behind the encamped figures the view is blocked by an old house. The tree standing next to it and towering over everything reveals bare branches on the left; on the right are three smaller branches with leaves at their tips. Meidner, who often made use of allegory, was here harking back to the emblem of the tree, half bare and half leafy, as a symbol of death and life respectively.[99] He was presumably drawing a reminder, in the shape of the three branches with leaves on the end, of the prayer for reading in the synagogue with the Torah scroll opened up that the Torah promises to be a tree of life to those who take heed.[100]

Another charcoal drawing goes under the title of *Corpses* (illus. 63) but has not been exhibited up until now and has only recently been made available on the Internet. With its unusual piling up of dead bodies in a landscape, it is clear that Meidner produced it under the influence of the pictures in the reports about the liberation of the Bergen-Belsen camp by the British, that is, after April 1945. For the representation of those who had been murdered, Meidner was presumably affected both by George Rodger's photograph of rows of corpses by the roadside, with a small boy walking past (see illus. 156),[101] and by the picture of Bergen-Belsen by the British photographer Sergeant Oakes (illus. 64). This photo presents, starkly viewed from above, the bodies of the concentration camp inmates arranged in rows, continuing into the distance in the shadow of a light-coloured pine wood as far away as where a man in black appears.[102] Meidner copied the exact arrangement of the endless number of dead bodies but not their nakedness, and placed them at a considerable distance from the viewer. Instead of the brief moment of a boy walking or a single living creature standing upright, he included a tree in the picture. The artist avoided taking a snapshot of the horror as captured unsparingly by the press photographs. With his charcoal, he instead revealed the extent of the persecution referred to by the Nazis as the 'final solution of the Jewish question'. A flat, light-coloured field is dissected by two parallel dark rows of corpses laid out in series, with the horizon in the middle charred, black and smoky. The tree on the left of the drawing and occupying the whole height of it, despite being in full leaf, does not represent an allegory of life; instead it frames a death camp. In place of the pines in Oakes's photo, Meidner chose a single, slightly bent tree with white bark, a *Birke*, a birch.[103] Meidner positioned the tree on a small meadow, the old-fashioned German word for this being *Aue*, to suggest the big Nazi extermination camp for Jews: Birkenau.

The photographs by Rodgers and Oakes and Meidner's charcoal drawing all capture the scene of mass murder in a landscape, but up to now only the photograph has been widely known. The alleged reality of the moment in the photograph goes beyond the imagination of the artist. Through the indexical character of the photograph, it promises greater credibility than other images. Only in the photograph, so it appears, can the 'unbelievable' acts no longer be denied.

When Meidner returned to Germany in 1953, he painted mainly portraits and views of nature,[104] subjects that, as remarkable as it may seem, the painter as well as his formerly Nazi public in Germany preferred, continuing to favour objectivity in painting. With Meidner's return to Germany, Amishai-Maisels acknowledged a decrease in his previously emphasized Jewish identity the more he achieved fame as a leading German Expressionist and found himself accepted once more.[105]

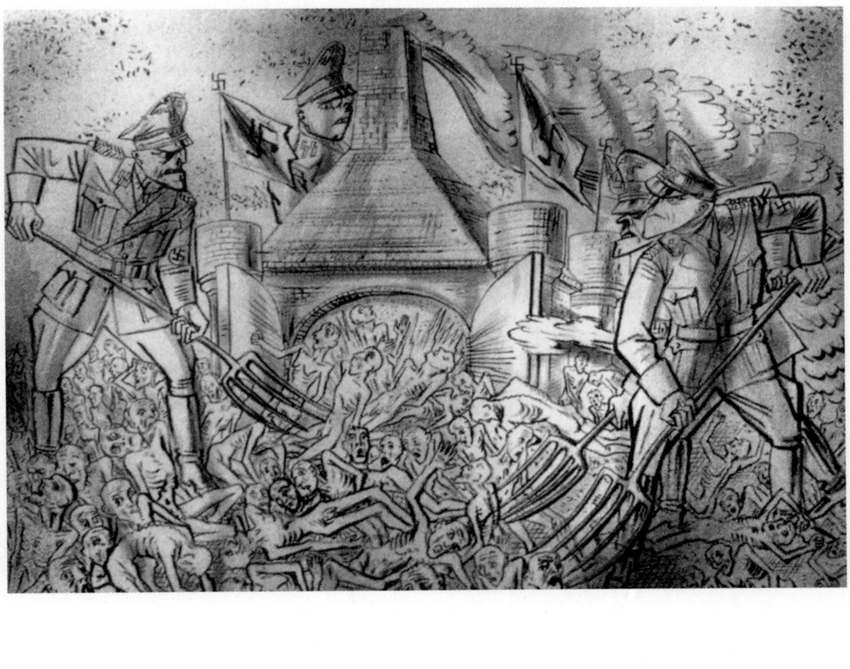

65 Karl Hubbuch, *An* SS *Model Industry*, 1945–6, drawing.

Karl Hubbuch: *Anti-fascist Information Panels*

As Präger described,[106] the artist Karl Hubbuch, a member of the anti-fascist movement who had been a left-wing realist during the Weimar Republic, started working on information about the Nazi tyranny immediately after 1945 in his art, continuing with critical drawings as in the 1920s. In 1945–6 he drew *An ss Model Industry* (illus. 65) in one of his *Aufklärungstafeln der Antifa* (Anti-fascist information panels) using pen, brush and ink on cardboard. A mass of naked, emaciated and shrieking people are being shovelled by men in uniforms into the open door of an oven, transformed here into the entrance gate of a Nazi fortress where swastikas are flying on the four towers. Only the oven doors of the crematorium are shown exactly as they had been,[107] whereas the fortress blends together what looks like the 'old German-style' hearth beloved of the Nazis and the Reichstag in Berlin. The ss men are recognizable from the runes on their lapels and armbands. They are huge figures, agents of the system, stoking endless numbers of little people in an image of the everyday task of shovelling coal. The burning of corpses, carried out here by the ss instead of the *Sonderkommandos* (special units) of the extermination camps, admittedly reminds one of the idea of a 'death factory', but Hubbuch's drawing goes beyond the mere depiction of an efficient machinery of murder operating on an industrial scale. As a 'model industry', not just the concentration camps but the whole system of the Third Reich is identified by the insignia of authority, a system which gains its power through the exclusion and consequent extermination of people. Presumably this image was displayed, along with others, at the Badischer Kunstverein in Karlsruhe as early as 1946, demonstrating how clearly right from the start the permanent opponents of the Nazis, even in the West, were able to express their concern with the past. But who wanted to look at it? It was not long before such works of art were rejected as being ideological and were no longer considered, and the debate about art as being non-political dominated the scene in contrast to the former usage of art by the Nazis.[108]

Willi Geiger: *12 Years – 20 Drawings*

During his 'internal emigration' in Munich[109] while the war was still on, Willi Geiger drew the sufferings and dying of the many victims of war[110] in his cycle *12 Years – 20 Drawings* which, according to a 1946 newspaper report, was intended at the time to be called *The Shame*. In three of the drawings, without specifically referring to those murdered as Jews, he addressed events that can be put under the heading of the murder of the Jews. Drawing fol. 11, in which the murder of the Jews is described as *The Last Journey*, carries the

66 Willi Geiger, *The Last Journey*, 1944, fol. 11 from the series *12 Years – 20 Drawings* (Wiesbaden, 1946).

67 Willi Geiger, *Death March*, fol. 12 from the series *12 Years – 20 Drawings* (Wiesbaden, 1946).

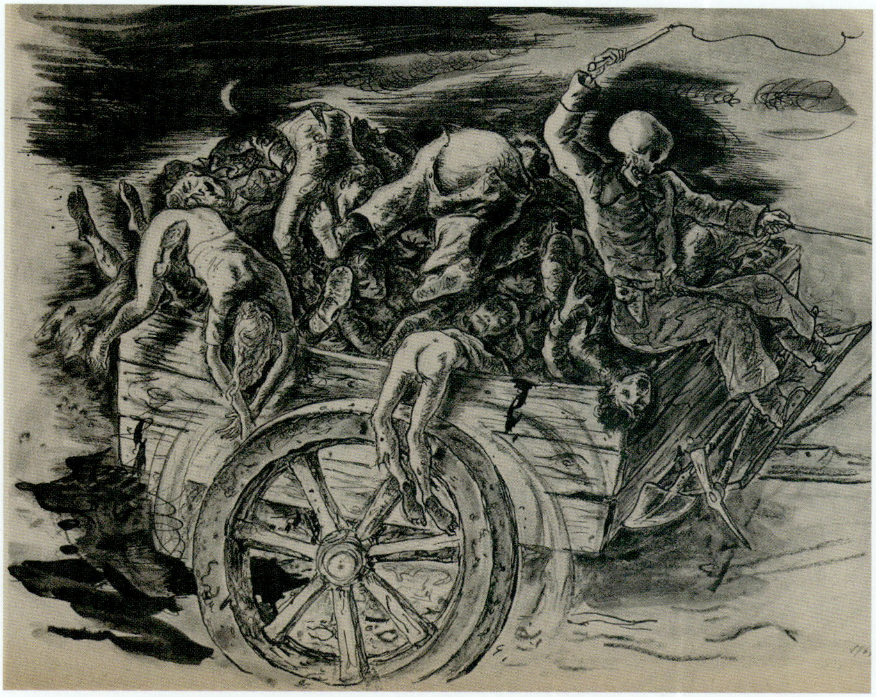

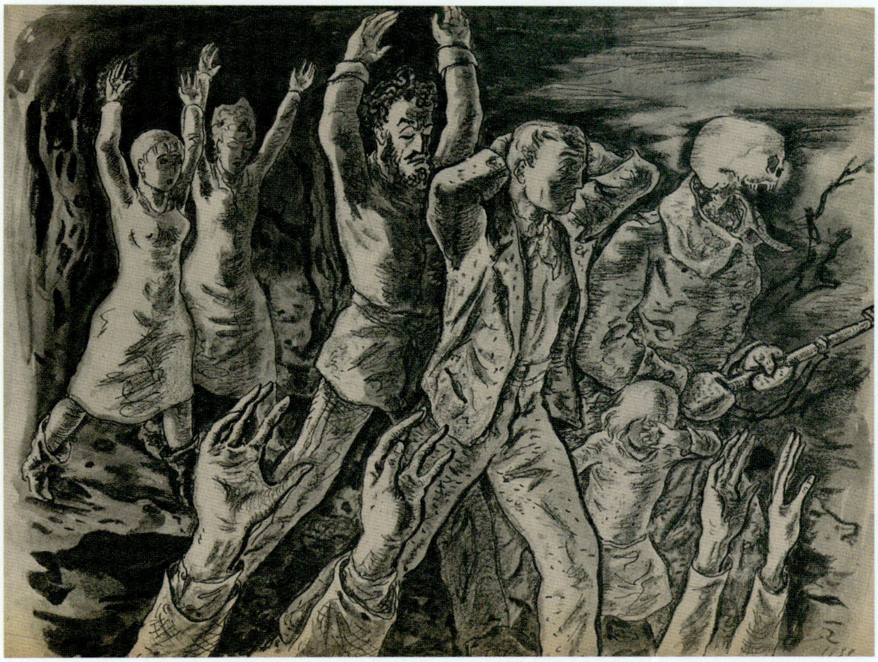

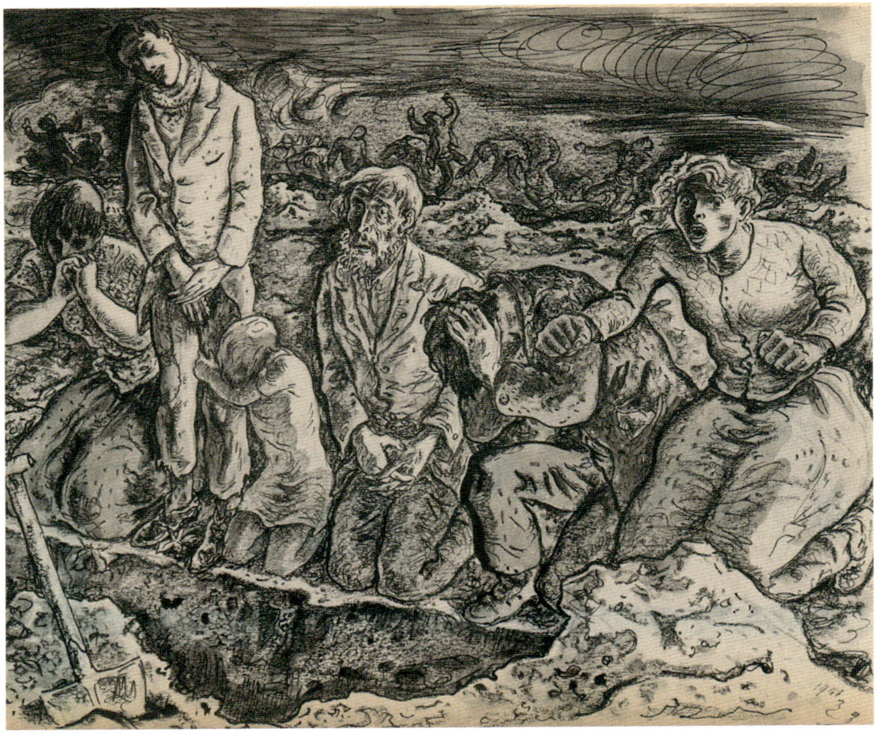

68 Willi Geiger, *When Will It Be My Turn?*, fol. 10 from the series *12 Years – 20 Drawings* (Wiesbaden, 1946).

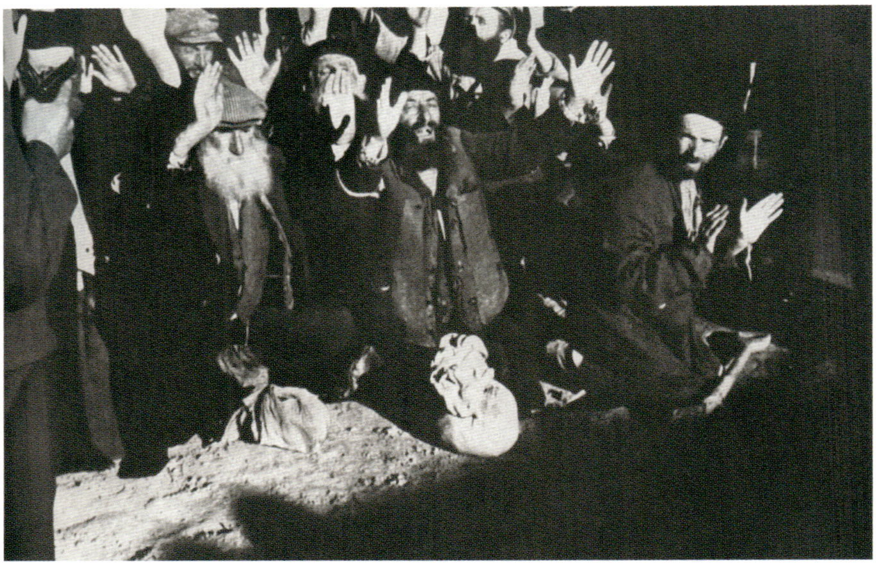

69 Photograph of Polish Jews, publ. in Schoenberner 1960.

date 1944 (illus. 66). The drawing, with the cart driven by the Grim Reaper, clearly preempts the images of horrific cartloads of corpses from the liberated concentration camps that, after 1945, were inseparably associated with the image of mass murder.

In 1939 Geiger drew fol. 12, published under the title *Death March* (illus. 67). It shows men, women and children tramping through a bleak, storm-ridden landscape with their arms raised. The campaign against Poland in 1939 was already a campaign against the Jews, the beginning of the deportations. With its title, which after the war was associated with the march of concentration camp prisoners towards the West, Geiger was linking both events.

Drawing fol. 10 in the cycle, *When Will It Be My Turn?* (illus. 68), is in addition headed '1941', making it possible not just to date it but to see it as a reminder of the mass shootings at Babi Yar in Ukraine in 1941. The death of more than 30,000 people in two days[111] is represented schematically by the figures in different positions of desperation forming the background to the picture. In the foreground, people are kneeling on the edge of a freshly dug grave; the shovel is still visible at the bottom left-hand corner of the picture. Geiger shows the men, women and children with individualized expressions on their faces and different gestures in expectation of being shot (illus. 69).

Franz Roh, an art critic and advocate of modernism, in his foreword clearly made a difference between this whose subject was a time when 'murder, violence and the threat of death drowned out everything else' and the 'utterly tranquil water colours' normally produced by Geiger. He regarded them as signs 'of an inhuman late capitalism, idolatrous nationalism, cruel racism, a brutal revolutionary hysteria . . . a fearsome symphony of disease, destruction and chaos for life as a whole'. Roh, however, was not just addressing racism in all its forms but noted the differing reactions of those viewing the drawings. Roughly speaking, they could be divided into those who turned away, not willing 'to look at anything so terrible any more', and others who were 'captivated by everything represented, these people we call art connoisseurs'. Already in 1946 Roh's further differentiation between kinds of 'art connoisseurs' illustrates the two sides in the future politics of art: whereas the 'ultra modernists' would have preferred the style of representation 'to be even more abstract', the conservatives found the style 'superb, bold, daring and not shrinking from telling the truth'. Roh himself in his article argued for refraining from such decisions, wishing that 'the drawings might inspire in us the feeling that even the most terrible can be represented'.[112]

Eduard Winkler: *Brown Death*

Winkler, like Geiger (see illus. 66), also made use of the image of death as a skeleton for his album *Brown* (that is, Nazi) *Death* in 1946, which carried the printed note 'In memory of the liberation of Munich from *Brown Death* by the entry of the Americans on 1 May 1945'.[113] He wanted to make a memorial 'of horror' to the 'Grim Reaper'. Like Joseph Beuys (see illus. 142), he took up the old theme of the Dance of Death and adapted this iconography to the murderous racists in the Nazi period in a number of drawings: *Death as a Direct Hit* (fol. 4) and *Death as a Member of the Master Race* (fol. 8). At the beginning of the series, after the drawing *Brown Death is Dancing*, he

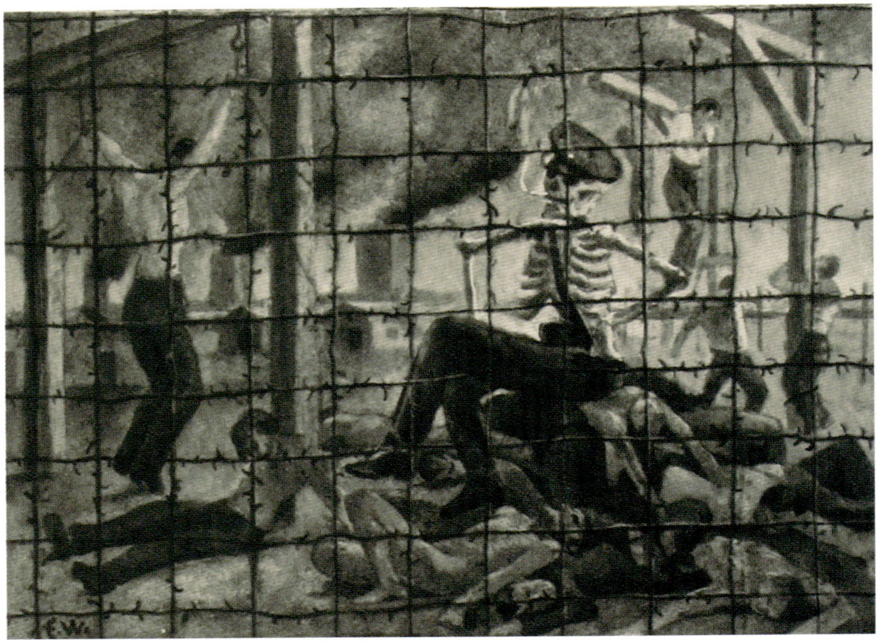

70 Eduard Winkler, *Death in the Concentration Camp*, fol. 2 from the series *Brown Death*, 1946, heliogravure.

placed the photogravure *Death in the Concentration Camp* (illus. 70) as fol. 2. Behind a square grid made of barbed wire, Winkler reveals Death smoking and in uniform, sitting on a pile of corpses between those who have been hanged and the smoking crematorium chimneys in the background. In the foreword by publisher Heinrich Graf, Winkler was referred to as 'one of the most steadfast opponents of National Socialism'. In his 'accompanying remarks' he addressed the work 'to the Germans for them to remember for all eternity', writing: 'It is to remind them of the shameful 12 years of tyranny they themselves brought about – in good faith to be sure – but recklessly abandoning that which constitutes the values of a nation: *freedom of conscience* and the *law*.'[114] The fact that such a series of images would not exactly be welcome one year after the liberation of Munich is illustrated by the afterword. This begins: 'The publication of this work might cause outrage on the part of many Germans, because our Fatherland and thus the German people could be blackened by criticism of the degeneration of Germany.' Instead, 'everyone who feels in a really German way' should, faced with the atrocities documented here, make a 'clear distinction' between themselves and the 'criminals subscribing to German barbarism'.[115]

Jerzy Zielezinski: *K.Z.Album* and *24 Drawings From the Concentration Camps in Germany*

As early as 1946 Jerzy/George Szwede, editor of the *DP Express*, wrote in the preface to the first publication in Munich of Jerzy Zielezinski's eighteen

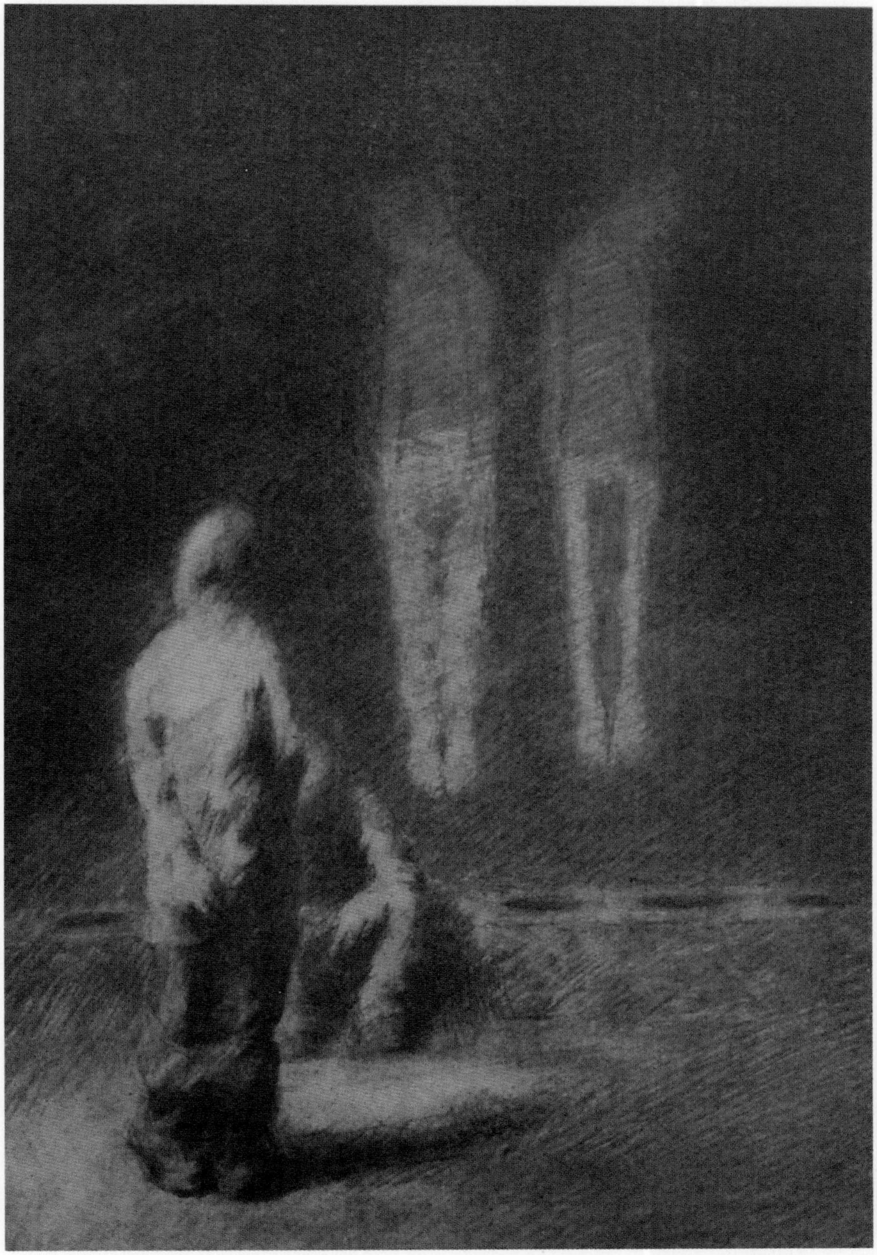

71 Jerzy (George) Zielezinski, *Those Strangled in the* WC *– Everybody Can't Die on a Battle-field*, fol. 10 from the series K.Z.*Album*, Munich, 1946, rotogravure.

drawings in book form as the K.Z. (Concentration Camp) *Album*[116] that they, unlike the many photographs, films and reports about death, would show the life of concentration camp inmates.[117] 'The real life, without any make-up, more than primitive, stripped of all sentimentality – the life of a camp prisoner, stronger than any idea and any imagination.' Zielezinski was born to a Catholic family in Poland in 1914; after his father's murder by the National Socialists he was interned in the Warsaw Ghetto, and later on at Auschwitz, Flossenbürg and Dachau. He was married to a Jewish woman doing forced labour in Germany, who died in a bomb attack. After emigrating to the U.S. he became a celebrated book illustrator under the name George Ziel, particularly of detective novels. Zielezinski died in 1982.[118] It must have been immediately after liberation and still in hospital, and then in a camp for displaced persons, that he started to make a record in charcoal of the memories of his time in captivity. Despite the attention that his cycles attracted when they first appeared, his work was soon forgotten.[119] Some of the drawings in the first album, such as *Those Strangled in the WC – Everybody Can't Die on a Battlefield* (illus. 71), portray the everyday life of the camp unsparingly, others reveal memories of another life and the longing for it. Zielezinski included many of them in the second album, *24 Drawings from Concentration Camps*, and added more from a collection of yet unknown dimensions.[120]

24 Drawings from the Concentration Camps in Germany contains many of the drawings from the *K.Z.Album* and exists in two versions printed in rotogravure by the publisher Bruckmann in Munich in 1946 and 1948.[121] The accompanying English text of the 1946 edition reveals how closely linked the recorded memories of the former political prisoner and artist are to the debate about art and how much they were subject to competition from photographs. The unidentified author L. G. forcefully introduced the accompanying text by expressing his initial resistance to seeing in an exhibition images of a concentration camp by a Polish artist. 'We have seen photographs and heard accounts. We know enough, I thought . . . We know the truth.' After viewing the images on display, however, he reveals his total change of heart: 'The photographs rouse us to fury and disgust, our reactions to them are simple and obvious; ultimately they leave a bitter taste in the mouth.[122] But the effect of these drawings is in no way comparable, and this is their secret and proves that they are not mere documents "humains". They are real art.' In the course of the text, this idea of 'real art' is developed in other terms and described as 'macabre magic', 'a bleak pattern of eternity' and 'terrible beauty' and as an 'ultimate truth' distinguishable not just from the photographs, but from the miserable everyday life of the camp. Despite these euphoric expressions, we become aware of the attitudes that the former prisoners had to struggle against to start a new life after the camps. Jerzy Zielezinski in the end decided to give up on the struggle with the art market and against judgements of taste. As an immigrant to the U.S., he successfully continued to turn violence into images, if only on the covers of detective novels.

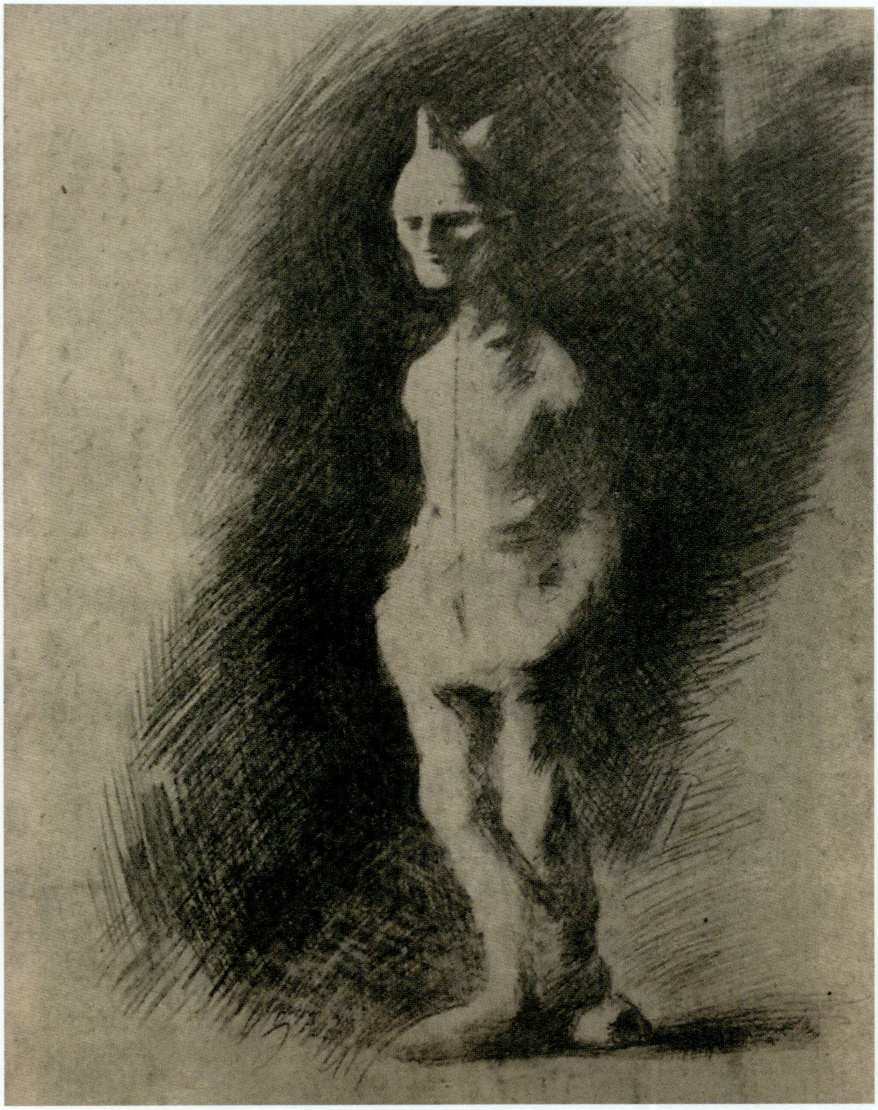

72 Jerzy (George) Zielezinski, *The New Inmate – I don't know what I should fear more, death or life in the camp*, fol. 2 from the series K.Z.*Album*, Munich, 1946, rotogravure.

Szwede, the former concentration camp inmate, did not distinguish in his text for the 1946 K.Z.*Album* between that which was represented and the style of representation; he expressed its meaning for society using the very traditional analogy of the artist as an anatomist, in this case of the psyche:

> the section of the human soul could, stripped as it was in the concentration camps, just as well furnish an immense new material for studies showing mankind the true way to its destination . . . We believe that Democracy alone is competent to interpret the symptoms of that diseas [sic] which has penetrated *the whole* of humanity and which appeared in all it's [sic] virulence inside the concentration camps.[123]

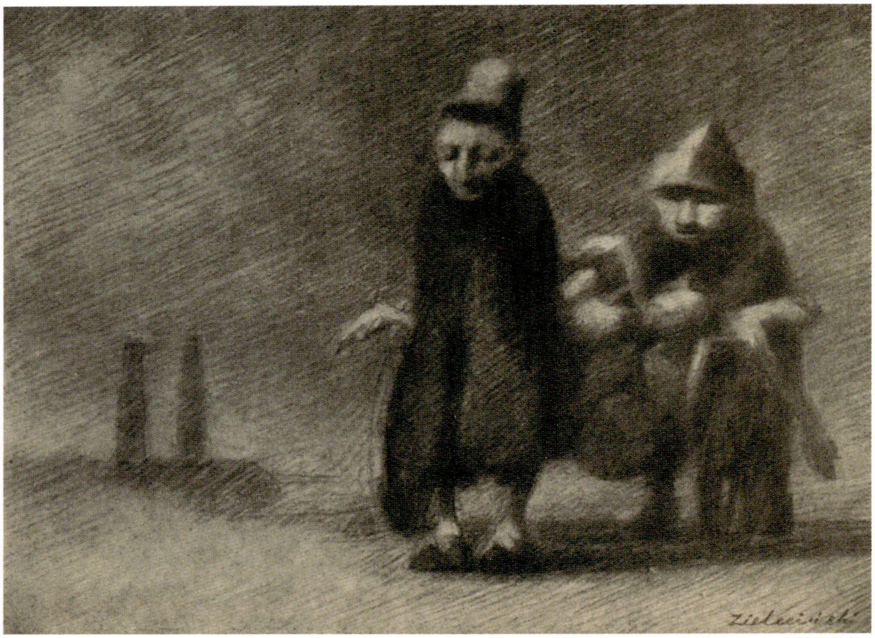

73 Jerzy (George) Zielezinski, *Special Mission – The one lying at the bottom of the cart is very fat, that's why it is so heavy to pull today*, fol. 7 from the series K.Z.*Album*, Munich, 1946, rotogravure.

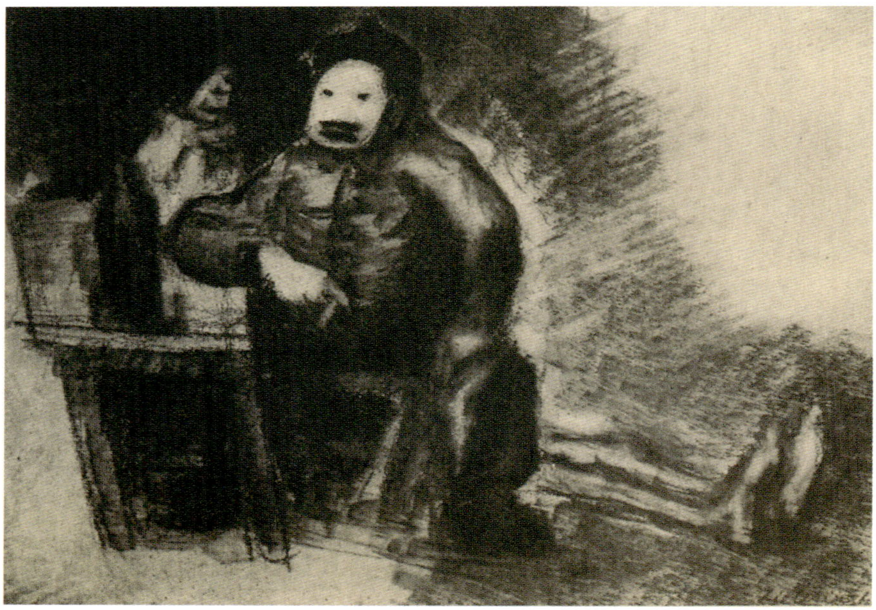

74 Jerzy (George) Zielezinski, *Meditation – He is breathing deeply and quietly, his glance roves over the heads of the 'Muselmans'. There are several slices of bread and margarine in his stomach*, fol. 9 from the series K.Z.*Album*, Munich, 1946, rotogravure.

There is at Princeton, in a volume of the 1948 edition, a German foreword by the conservative writer Ernst Wiechert, who had shortly before published an account of his experiences in Buchenwald,[124] written as early as 1944.[125] He said that Zielezinski approached him with the request 'that I write a few words on what he had recorded visually'. Under the title *Die Tafeln des Grauens* (The Plates of Horror), Wiechert set out his belief that now we know that the face of the Devil is not that of a beast but that of man.

> So this is what was recorded here visually, the horror surrounding the human being. Invented by the human brain and inflicted upon the human being by human hand. And this is the most horrific thing about this horror. Nothing to do with so-called fate, nothing to do with the so-called devil, but with man himself . . . I put the plates aside, and my hand is shaking a bit. Like it was at the time when I saw the first dead body hanging on the barbed wire or the guard dogs attacking someone who was bleeding. Not because it was death that I was seeing but because I saw the horror that I had only seen in dreams. But there it was now in broad daylight, everyday, and the nights weren't any different to the days and the dream to the reality.

The display of images to which the author of the English foreword is referring is probably the exhibition that had been shown to the public in the rooms of the Neue Sammlung at the Bayrisches Nationalmuseum in Munich in 1946. In this large exhibition of the work of 71 artists from the U.S. zone there were printed drawings by Zielezinski from the *K.Z.Album* and works from an album about the Warsaw Ghetto that it has been impossible to identify up to now, as an article by the Polish artist Maximilian Feuerring reported in 1947 in the magazine *Prisma*. The display took place on the initiative of the UN organization for the repatriation of deported refugees (UNRRA)[126] and showed 336 works by 'Poles, Lithuanians, Latvians, Estonians, Russians, Yugoslavs, stateless people and a relatively large group of Ukrainians'.[127] At the exhibition a year later at the castle of Ansbach, organized again by UNRRA, the artists represented were mainly from the Baltic States and Ukraine. On show were drawings and paintings, including many portraits and landscapes showing Franconia and the artists' homelands, in addition to handicrafts made of wood and textiles; the public were invited to recognize and appreciate national differences.[128] None of the artists mentioned in the catalogue confronted them with the horror that Zielezinski did.

His eighteen drawings in the *K.Z.Album*, as indicated in the forewords, show everyday life in the camps from beginning to end, the perspective in the process altering in line with the actions ordered by the camp officials: bathing, roll-call, work, torture, murder, evacuation, the various groups without badges for their identification according to the Nazi system of classification: men, women, children, Special Command Units, *Kapos* (prisoners

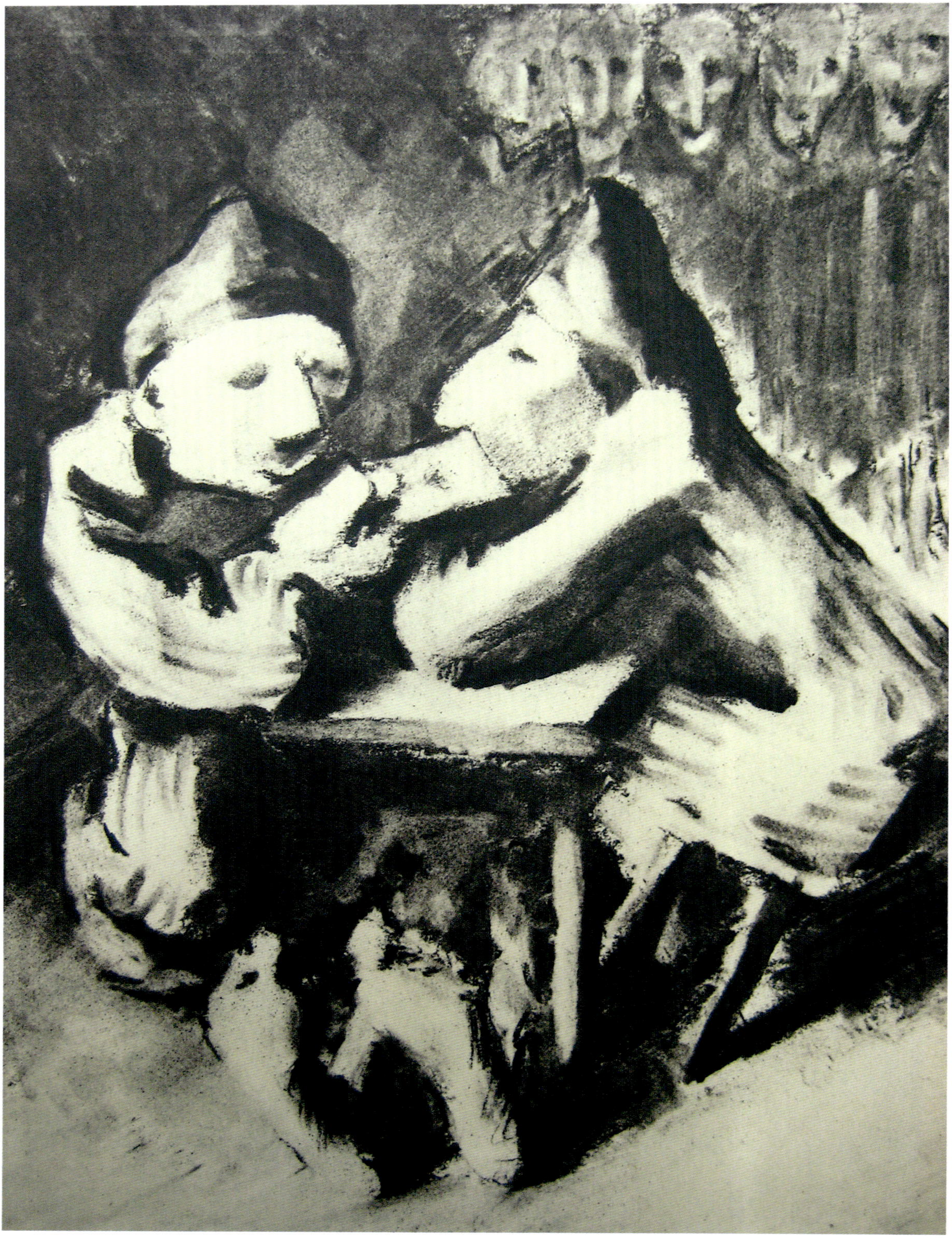

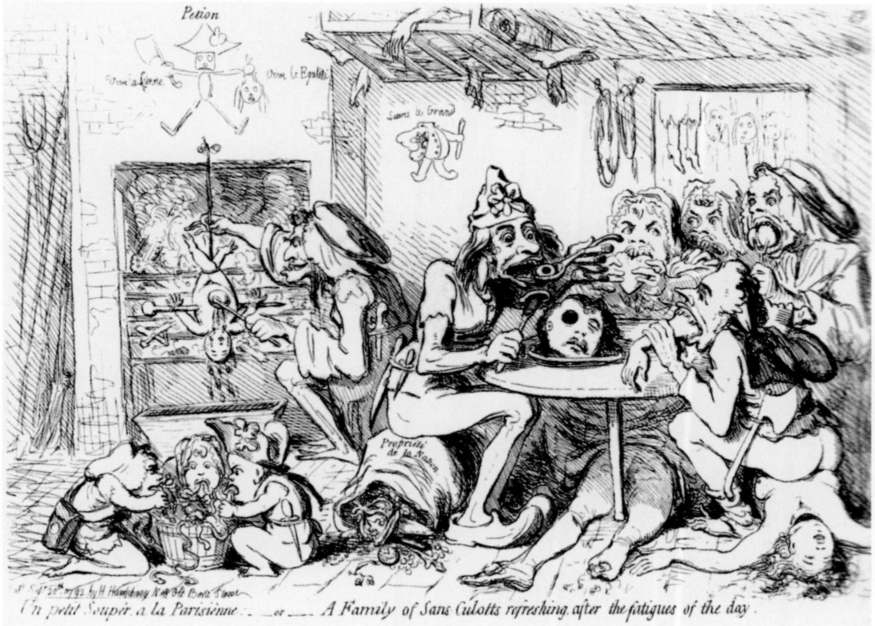

76 James Gillray, *Un petit Soupér, a la Parisienne – or – A Family of Sans Culottes Refreshing, after the fatigues of the day*, 1792, etching.

in charge of work units) and *Prominente* (privileged persons). The prisoners' thoughts are given by titles and, only in the 1946 *K.Z.Album*, by added statements: 'I am cold', 'Spleen' or 'I would have longed to walk across that lawn – far, far away . . .', Yet despite explanations and the indicated dissection of the psyche of the inmates, every image leaves one with questions: what are the horns that the person is wearing who appears in the pale light against a dark shaded background in the drawing *The New Inmate* (illus. 72), which was also published in *24 Drawings* with the title *The New Arrival* as fol. 2. With his Harlequin cap and the contrasting white suit, is he being represented as a melancholy Pierrot? And consequently, is the mood of the whole series that of what one can only call the most macabre and grotesque reality imaginable, as in the drawings for the various horrific visions Alfred Kubin created in Munich around 1900?[129] Is it not the case that in 1946 the phantasmagorias that the young Kubin produced in Munich for psychoanalysis were being acted out for Zielezinski in the concrete everyday life of the camp? As the figure, sketched in the drawing on the cover of the 1946 edition in the Marquard Library at Princeton carrying his signature, is likewise wearing this sort of fool's cap,[130] resembling those in Daumier's oil paintings and drawings,[131] it is likely that Zielezinski was even aiming to portray himself in line with the usual artist's self-image as a homeless and tragic figure on the margin of society inside and outside the camp.

75 Jerzy (George) Zielezinski, *The Prominents*, fol. 20 from the series *24 Drawings from the Concentration Camps in Germany*, Munich, 1946, rotogravure.

In the drawing *Special Mission* (illus. 73), two miserable figures, wearing headgear like something out of a second-rate children's film or pantomime, are shown dragging a cartload of corpses amid the desolate twilight near two chimneys (see also the chimneys in the central and the right-hand panels in

Strempel (illus. 10) and the illustration by Rudi Stern (illus. 100) on the left of the horizon). Only one sketch, *Meditation* (illus. 74), deviates from the style of drawing that is otherwise accurately done using parallel hachures, evoking as it does the sinister effects of artificial light. Here, exceptionally, the sun's rays break through into the dark room in the camp, as it were, from a white expanse. Taking into account the various comments on the hierarchy of prisoners in the camps Zielezinski made so ironically with titles and texts it can be presumed that neither the drawing *Meditation* nor *The Prominents* (illus. 75) should portray a 'Prominent' according to the Nazi signification for distinguished inmates who's fate was observed by a lot of people worldwide. Instead, he applied the term sarcastically to a *Kapo*, an inmate functioning as foreman, who was never to be find within the gang of workers, but gained his privilege by extreme brutality.[132] The overweight person is sitting right in front of the viewer, his legs apart like those of a monster, with his right arm leaning on a table drawn askew and in rough. Behind him on the right are the emaciated legs of a prisoner lying on the floor and on the left the deathly form of another *Muselman* can be seen, reminding one of the foolish Auguste figure in a clowning routine. Meanwhile, the face of the figure, sitting next to a bottle and holding a cigar between his fingers, is shown as a mask-like white space with two holes for eyes and two thick parallel lines for a mouth. The juxtaposition enacts the roles shared by the sad white clown and the Auguste, who admittedly was allowed to caricature the events and parody everybody, the director of ceremonies even, but was still only a clown.

In the second version of *The Prominents* in the enlarged series *24 Drawings*, the brutal pecking order of the inmates is represented more dramatically. In a scene referring back to the cannibalistic meal in Paris that Gillray used to caricature the French *sans-culottes* (illus. 76), two stocky figures in prisoners' clothing and caps are sitting opposite one another at a table playing cards. Both of the players are excitedly rocking their stools and are stepping on a dead body lying under the table, of which only the soles of the feet are visible. Meanwhile, on the right-hand side behind the players, in another reference to Gillray's etching, five ambiguous figures, resembling starving onlookers, skulls or masks, are arranged in the background.

The way in which Zielezinski distinguished his art from photography and the reason he was compared to Goya and Rembrandt by both Feuerring and Szwede becomes clear from the drawing *When Will It Be My Turn?* (illus. 77), newly added to the album *24 Drawings*. The artist presumably based his drawing not just on his own sketches, made secretly while still in the camp, but on the then well-known Allied photographs showing the liberation of Dachau concentration camp, which were displayed on street posters (illus. 78).[133] From above, in an unsparing but monumental fashion, the photographer, who is not named, showed a prisoner with a determined look and his trousers pulled down. Considering the way values were overturned in the concentration camp, the photo shows heroic dignity even amid the most dire misery in

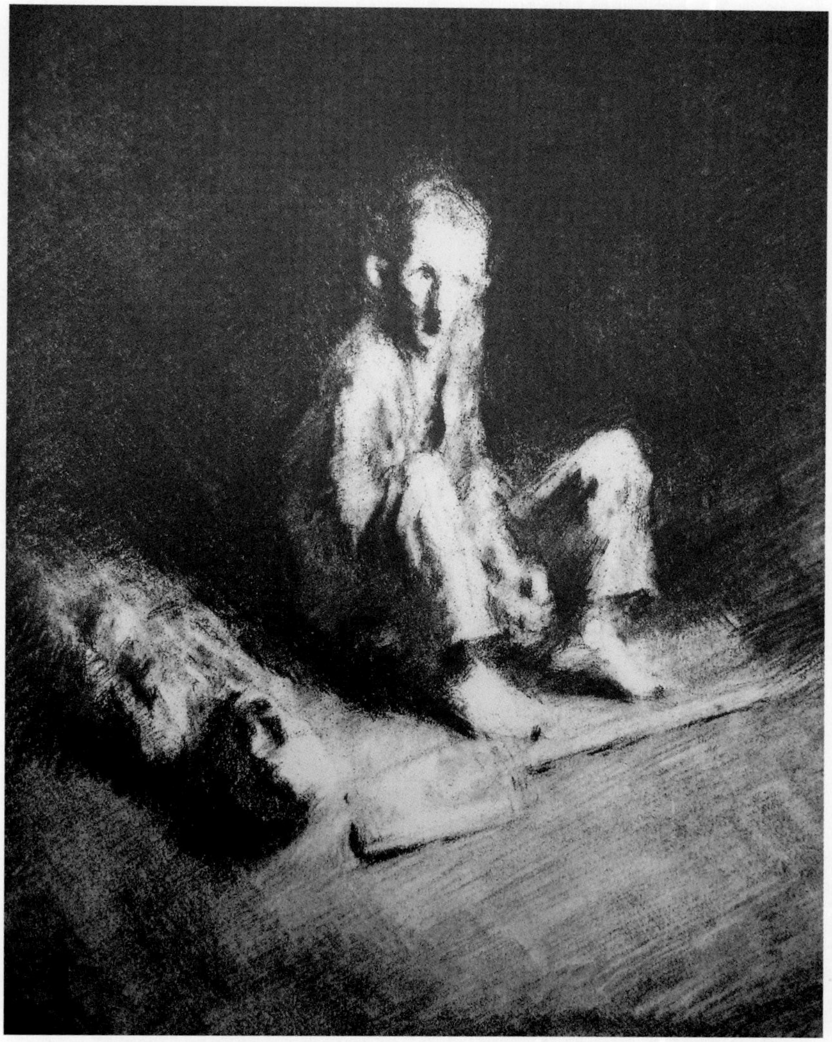

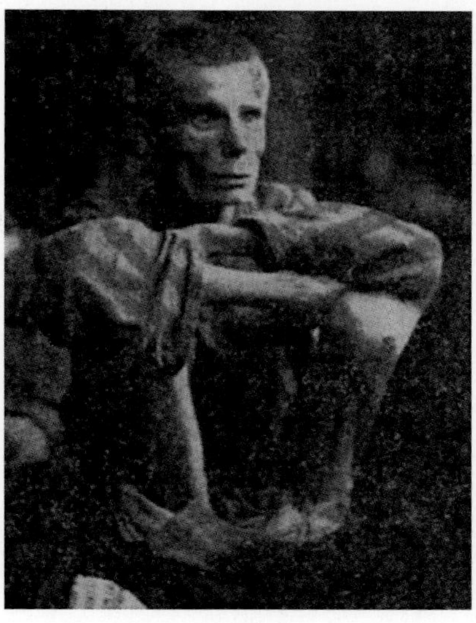

77 Jerzy (George) Zielezinski, *When Will It Be My Turn?*, fol. 6 from the series *24 Drawings from the Concentration Camps in Germany*, Munich, 1946, rotogravure.

78 *Starving KZ-Inmate*, from *Mitteilungen*, published by 12. Amerikanische Heeresgruppe, 5 May 1945.

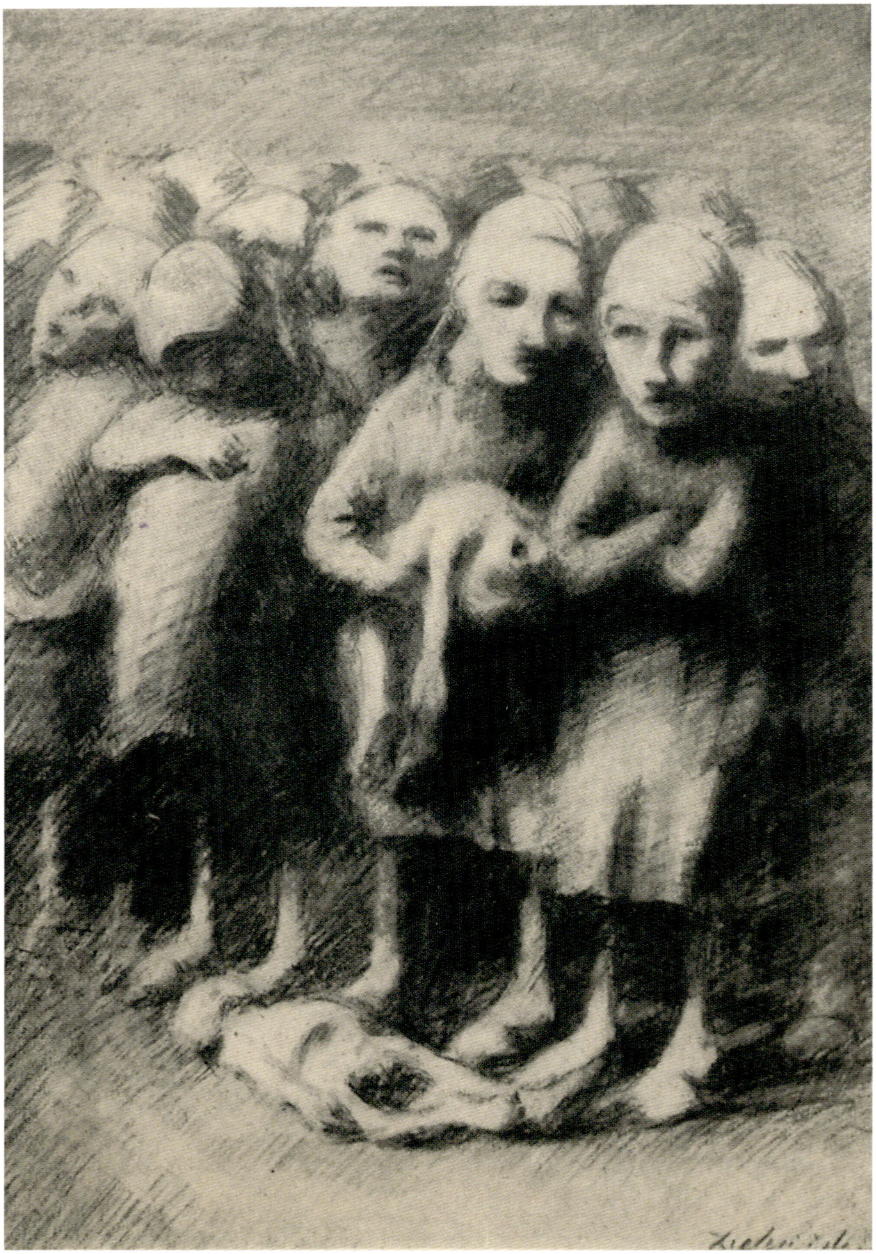

79 Jerzy (George) Zielezinski, *Roll-call in the Women's Camp. – There are Women Inside the Barbed Wire, They are all There, – Some of them Holding their Suckling Babies, and Those who Lost their Children Last Night*, fol. 5 from the series K.Z.*Album*, Munich, 1946, rotogravure.

which the process of survival constituted an act of resistance providing evidence of 'hidden greatness' even in the 'seemingly most undignified forms of behaviour'.[134] Zielezinski attempted to bring his record of the misery of the concentration camps into line with the prevailing ideas of art. His drawing reveals the slow evolution in the 'dirty' memories one year after the end of the war. The drawing *When Will It Be My Turn?* takes up the theme of the crouching prisoner, though by means of the pathos, borrowed from Rembrandt and Redon, of chiaroscuro drawing and the scene viewed from above, Zielezinski

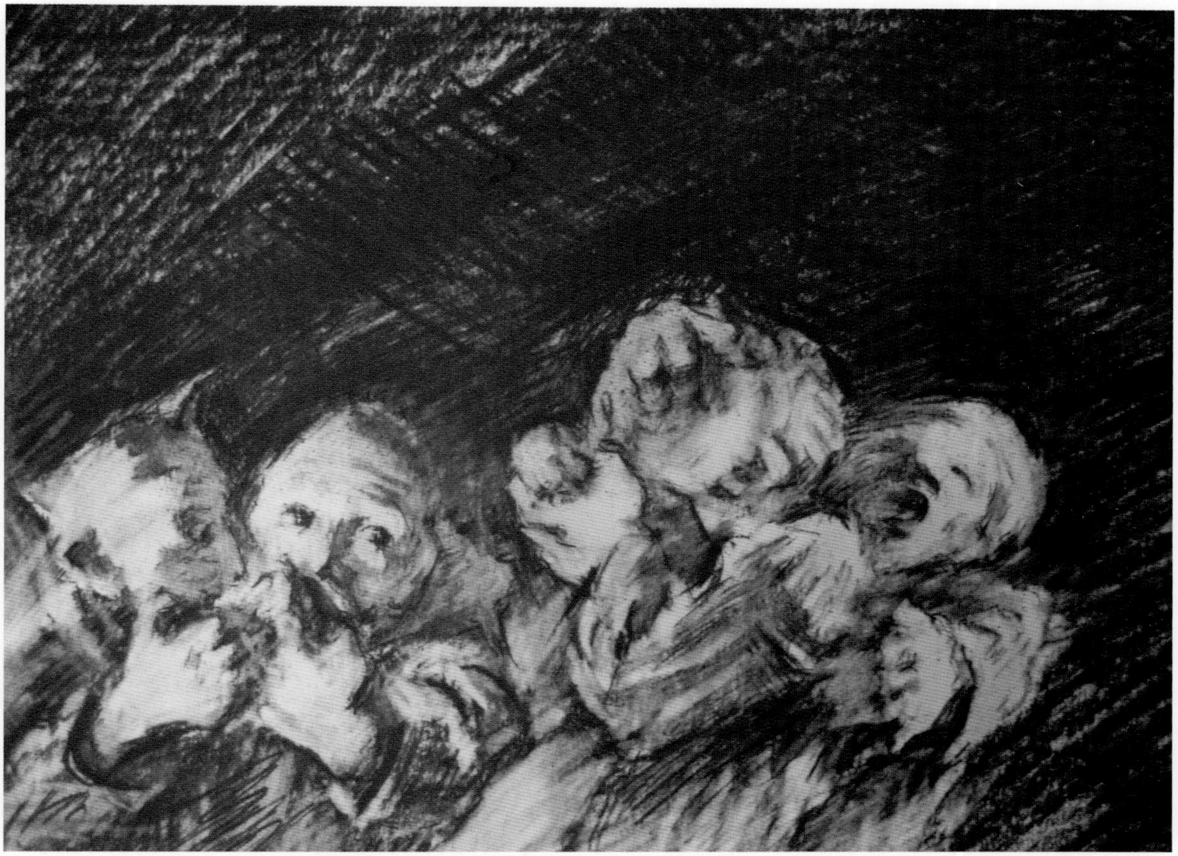

80 Jerzy (George) Zielezinski, *I Am Hungry*, fol. 4 from the series *24 Drawings from the Concentration Camps in Germany*, Munich, 1946, rotogravure.

suggests a distance in contrast to the crude record by the photographer that robbed the prisoner of any private space. His illustration, done with a pen, was directed at the mortal fear on the part of the crouching man looking at the corpse next to him and the shovel in front of him. In this work, by means of traditional, anatomically exact life drawing,[135] Zielezinski raised the view of the tortured soul to an artistic level that could combine the methods of fine art with suggestions of the events. The image does not reveal whether the figure who is still alive or the one who is already dead are political prisoners or Jews. As in all Zielezinski's representations known to me, no indications of the Nazi classification of prisoners are shown from any of the angles taken.

Zielezinski used his ability in different areas in dealing with shading, blurring outlines and different chiaroscuro effects in particular to represent scenes from the camp which no photographer could capture and which, like *I Am Hungry* (illus. 80), reveal themselves to the eye only gradually in their full horror. The head on the left of the drawing, again with two unequal horns, sticking-out ears and an animal-like skull profile, comes remarkably close to that of a predatory beast. *Roll-call in the Women's Camp*, printed in both editions, is shown by Zielezinski with women as well as children appearing

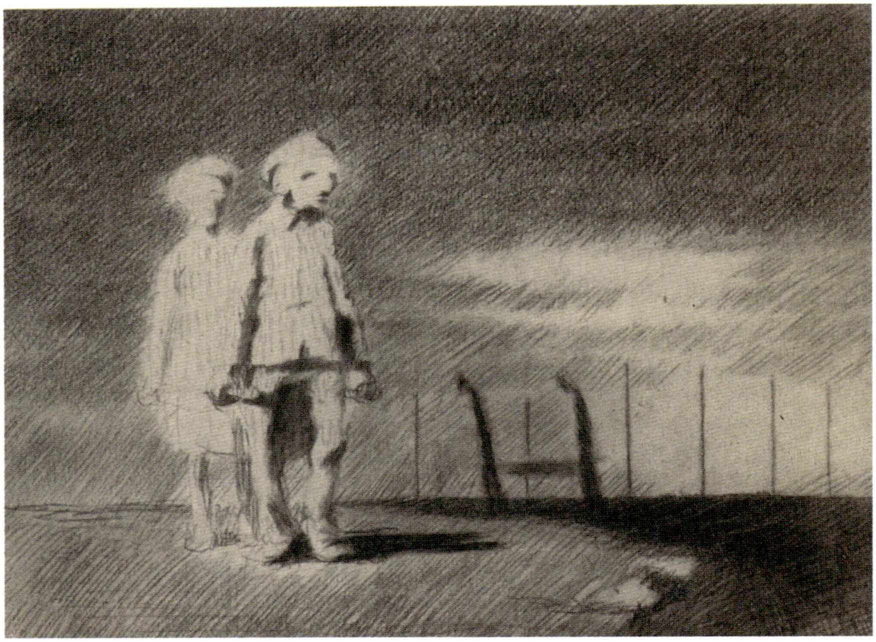

81 Jerzy (George) Zielezinski, *Work is Freedom – One More Loading and I'll Have Done Twenty-eight Until Noon. And in the Afternoon?*, fol. 4 from the series *24 Drawings from the Concentration Camps in Germany*, Munich, 1946, rotogravure.

82 Jerzy (George) Zielezinski, *Work is Liberty*, fol. 11 from the series *24 Drawings from the Concentration Camps in Germany*, Munich 1946, rotogravure.

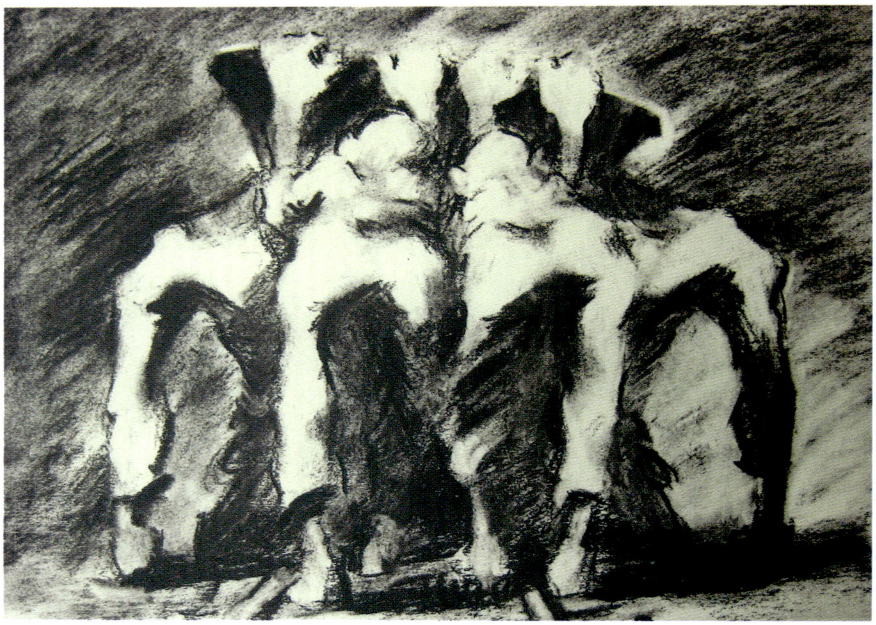

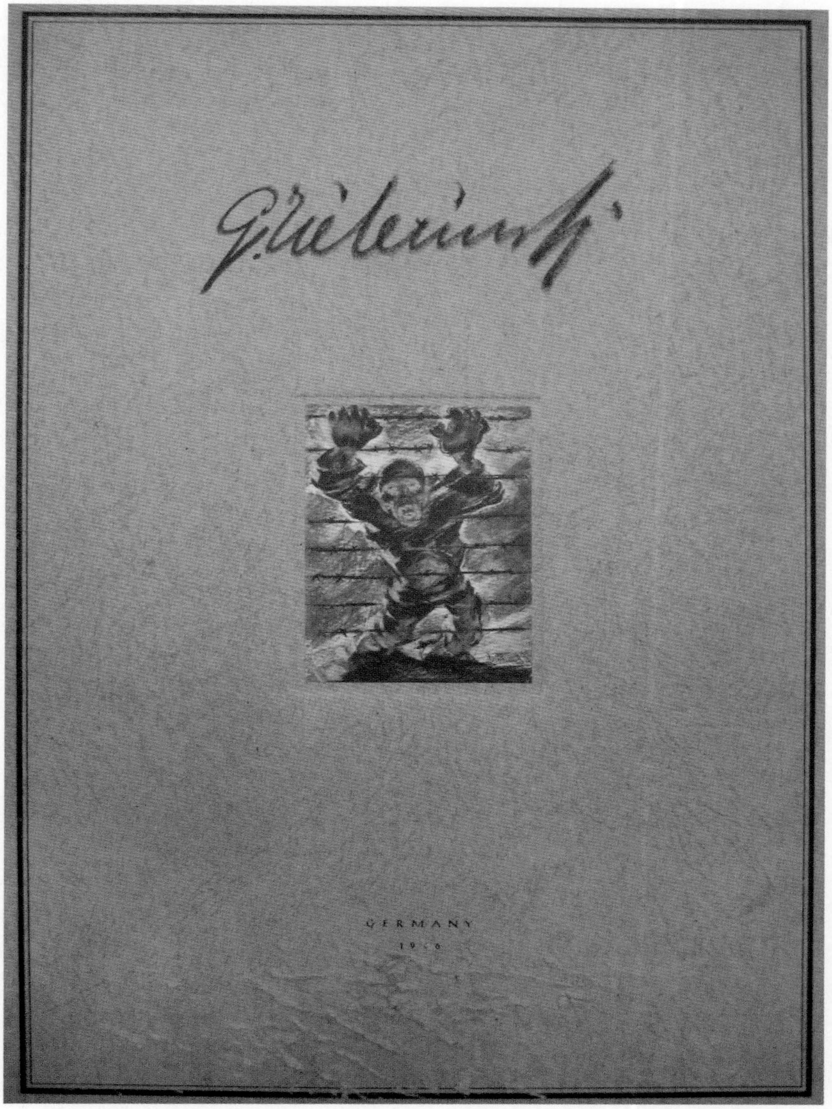

83 Jerzy (George) Zielezinski, cover of the series *24 Drawings from the Concentration Camps in Germany*, after fol. 22, *To the Wire!*, Munich, 1946, rotogravure.

in a false light that is excessively bright and washed-out (illus. 79). This is happening despite the fact that they are drawn as being pregnant, one of them presumably carrying her own dead child and another one with – difficult to recognize – a tiny corpse lying on the ground at her feet.

The twelve drawings that Zielezinski added to the second album of 1946–8,[136] in contrast to those from the *K.Z.Album*, generally show a more dramatic representation of individual figures using sharply defined chiaroscuro contrasts. The accompanying attempt to do without printed commentary in the form of text can be illustrated by the contrast between the two drawings that Zielezinski produced, one from each of the two series, both headed by a different translation of the motto at the entrance to the camps at Dachau and Auschwitz, 'Arbeit macht frei', and its unsparingly captured cynicism illustrated by him in the images. Drawing fol. 4, *Work is Freedom* (illus. 81), from the *K.Z.Album*, shows two prisoners, lit up against a grey background, one standing one behind the other in the obligatory clothing, who appear to be transporting a stretcher towards the front right in the picture. On the right in the background, behind metal bars, there are likewise a couple of stretcher bearers drawn only in dark grey side-on outline, revealing, however, that like the two in front of them they are carrying a stretcher with a dead body. The commentary reads: 'One more loading and I'll have done 28 before noon. And this afternoon . . .?' The work does not make the prisoners free, but death does, just as the title of the drawing of the corpses in front of the barbed wire fence (*K.Z.Album*, fol. 17) reads: *These Are Free*.

The other drawing on 'Arbeit macht frei', *Work is Liberty*, fol. 11 (illus. 82) of *24 Drawings*, shows, in stark black-and-white contrast and from an unusual rear view,[137] the lower bodies of four prisoners pushing a truck, so that it is almost impossible to see the difference between the arched pillars made up of human bodies and the moving container. The prisoners are replacing the traction machine; their work does not make them free but forces them into making superhuman efforts. Zielezinski drew a monumental image of people being worked to death in the concentration camps. The author Eljott commented on the series overall in the 1946 album: 'Et le résultat en fut une oeuvre d'art, vécue, vue, soufferte, une chef-d'oeuvre d'horreur' (and the result became a piece of art, lived, viewed, suffered, a masterpiece of horror).

In contrast to documentary photography, Zielezinski drew again and again what one can call 'macabre magic', for example in the image *To the Wire!* which is also printed on the cover of the 1946 album[138] below his signature (illus. 83): a large, black man without striped prisoners' clothing, resembling the 1933 film monster King Kong, hangs on the barbed wire with enormous hands, looking at us out of the far beyond, a suicide, a ghost, a nightmare and yet, there again, not.

Leo Haas: *From German Concentration Camps*

Leo Haas, a Jew persecuted by the Nazis for being a Communist, produced more than five hundred drawings while he was imprisoned at Theresienstadt/ Terezin, which he hid and then rediscovered there after 1945,[139] and published partly in cycles.[140] They unsparingly portray the sufferings of the inmates; it was only in a Theresienstadt trial, however, that they were used as evidence.[141] Even though they were consciously composed, something that applies also to the photographs, they are highly revealing visual documents of the history of the murder of the Jews and record scenes in the camp that no photo could capture (see illus. 1). It was not until the 1960s that Haas worked these drawings up into twenty aquatints that have very rarely been exhibited and, as Schulenburg noted, 'never in their entirety'.[142] As early as 1947, Haas published

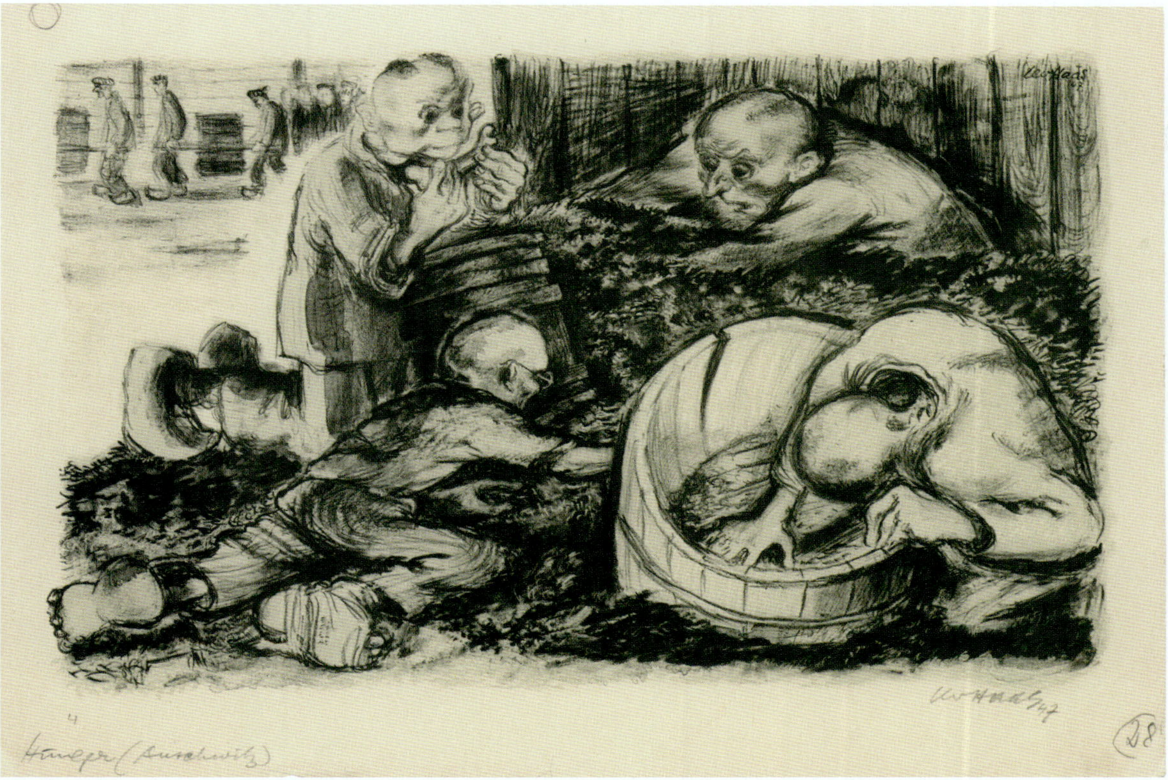

84 Leo Haas, *Hunger (Auschwitz)*, fol. 4 from the series *From German Concentration Camps*, 1947, colour lithograph.

in Prague twelve lithographs *From German Concentration Camps* with texts in Russian, English and French and a foreword and texts by Czech authors, of which the drawing *From Theresienstadt into the Gas* at least was shown in a Berlin exhibition in 1949.[143] In 1965 the Deutsche Akademie der Künste[144] in Berlin acquired all twelve drawings from the artist; unlike the album, they are signed 'Leo Haas' by hand, dated '47' and supplied with the following titles: 1. *Roll-call in Sachsenhausen*; 2. *From Theresienstadt into the Gas* (see illus. 86); 3. *Arbeit macht frei (Small Fortress at Terezin)*; 4. *Hunger (Auschwitz)* (see illus. 84); 5. *Auschwitz* (see illus. 87); 6. *Kapo* (prisoners in charge of work units) *(Sachsenhausen)*; 7. *Women's Block (Mauthausen)*; 8. *In the Bunker*; 9. *Concentration Camp in the Forest (Ebensee)*; 10. *Waiting . . . Waiting . . . (Mauthausen)*; 11. *Death March* (see illus. 85); 12. *Facing the Crematorium*.

'For lack of anything else, hatred could fill the emptiness; only hatefulness and abuse could distract them from their hunger. We sought targets for them just as assiduously as we hunted for a bit of potato amidst the peelings. We were obsessed,' wrote Robert Antelme in one of the many passages about hunger in his report on his time in the camp.[145] Leo Haas dared to draw this obsession with food in drawing fol. 4 (illus. 84) in a way that neither the former prisoner Peter Edel drawing a prisoner politely sitting at a table with an empty bowl,[146] nor Lea Grundig from a distance (see illus. 50 and 51), were able to do. Even Haas's own studies in ink and watercolour from 1944–5[147]

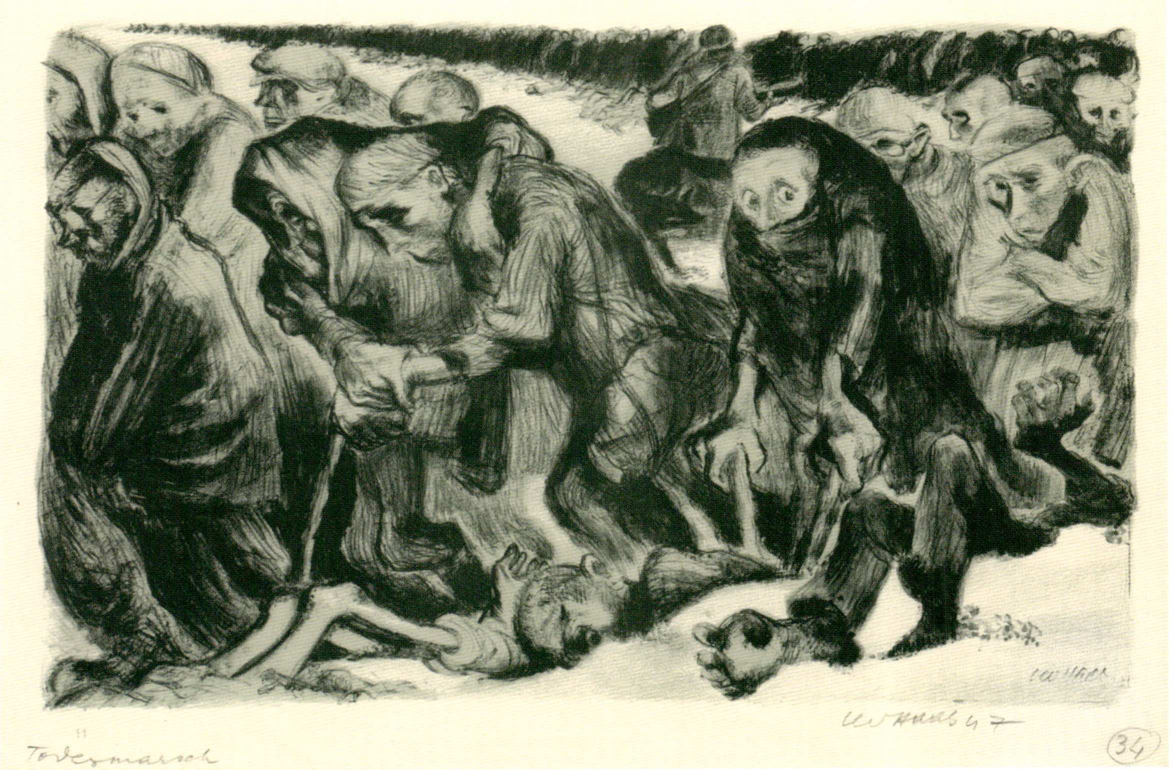
Todesmarsch
34

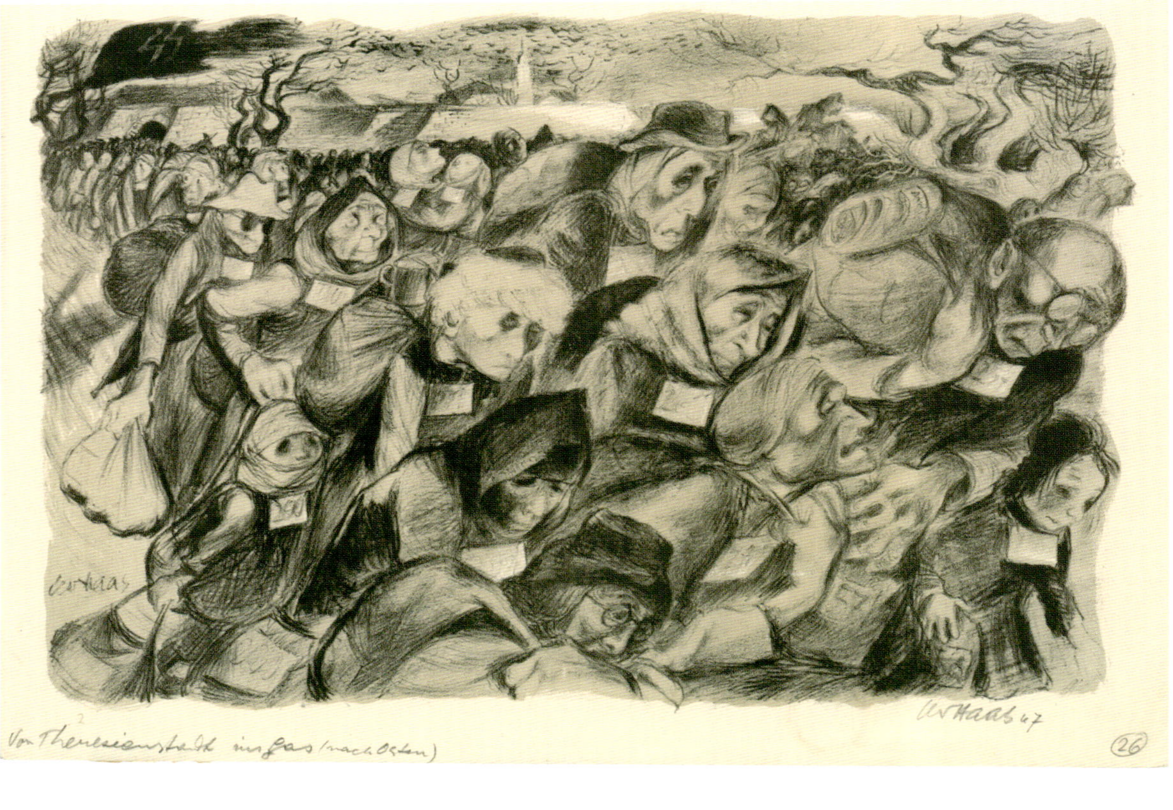
Von Theresienstadt ins Gas (nach Osten)
26

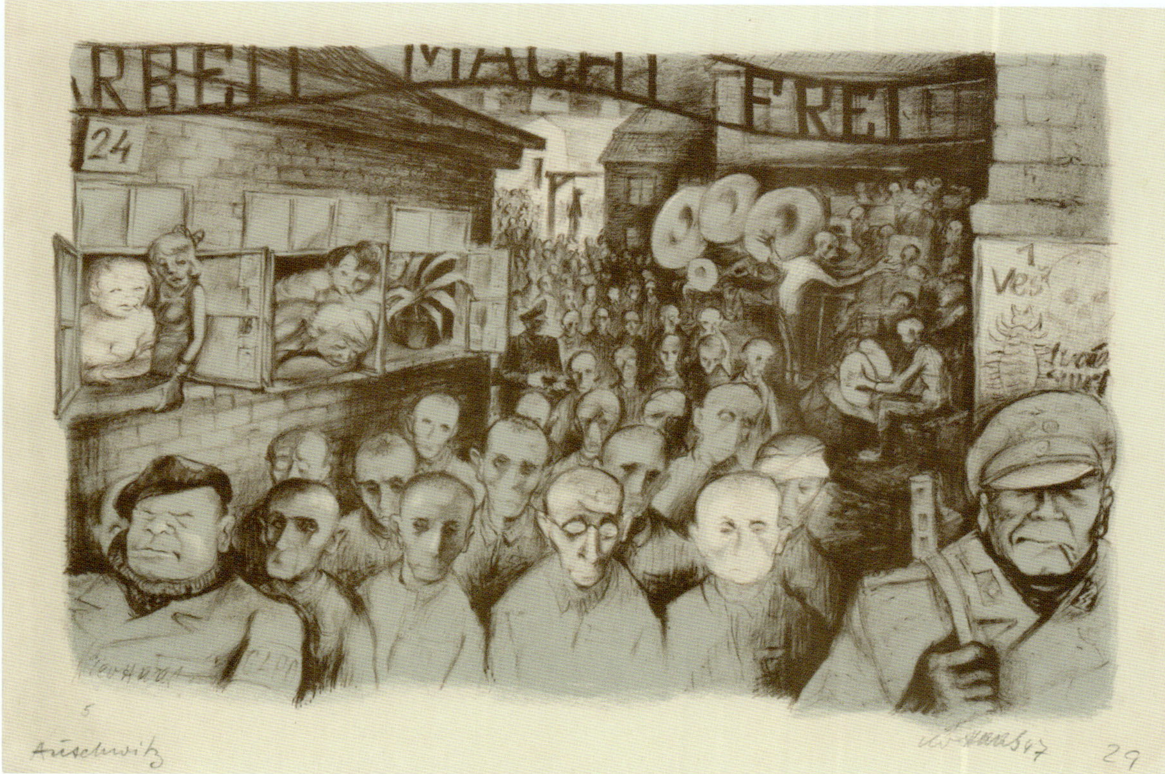

87 Leo Haas, *Auschwitz*, 1947, fol. 5 from the series *From German Concentration Camps*, colour lithograph.

on this physical torture on the part of all the concentration camp inmates do not have anything quite as infantile and deformed into a skull representing a human face as that of the kneeling prisoner top-left gnawing on a bone. Two other concentration camp inmates are grubbing in the rubbish tip, a third is scouring the bottom of a tub, while in the background presumably two containers of food are being carried in by a work column. The greedy search for something to eat shows the struggle for survival which every single person is engaged in and against all the others, turning the competition for sustenance into a threat. This 'animal-like hunger' was also drawn by Jerzy Zielezinski (see illus. 80). A generation later Art Spiegelman, the son of a survivor, telling his father's story in 1991 in the comic book *Maus*, touched on this comparison to animals: 'Like wild animals they would fight until there was blood. You can't know what it is, to be hungry.'[148]

85 Leo Haas, *Death March*, 1947, fol. 11 from the series *From German Concentration Camps*, colour lithograph.

86 Leo Haas, *From Terezin into the Gas*, 1947, fol. 2 from the series *From German Concentration Camps*, colour lithograph.

In the two lithographs showing the procession of people to their deaths (illus. 85 and 86), Haas employs the same crude style in his portrayal of those being persecuted, distorting the human proportions. Whereas Hermann Bruse emphasized the heroic resistance of individual men despite extreme physical suffering (see illus. 110), Haas portrayed in the main frail women and children, exhausted, abused, driven together. In *Death March* there they are, right before the viewer's eyes, even more hounded and terrified than their predecessors were in the images of the escape from a pogrom by Jacob

Weinles or in *Black Banner* by Samuel Hirzsenberg before the First World War.[149] In the procession *From Theresienstadt into the Gas*, the individual faces are in a scene, lined up alongside and in front of one another, reminiscent of the way George Grosz illustrated the crush of the city. The sample of the hounded procession of human beings without a beginning or an end, being driven onwards, reminds one also of *Christ Carrying the Cross*, the painting in Ghent by Hieronymus Bosch, who was being rediscovered at the time.[150] Comparing Haas's earlier forms of imagery, his new interpretation becomes readable. He could not, like Bosch, be providing any hope of salvation with the portrayal of the smooth face of a Redeemer amid a crowd of grotesque faces, distinguishing between good and evil, any more than he could distance himself through sarcastic caricature like Grosz. He was attempting, admittedly in a way similar to Grosz, to confront the public with a view of human beings, showing them in drawing fol. 2 (illus. 86) in sharp and graphic profile, using a slightly raised perspective looking down at the people as they are being driven on. The man's head at top right could also be that of the writer Max Herrmann-Neisse just as Grosz painted him. Haas, however, made use of these caricature character studies to show the violence distorting the faces of those being hounded to their deaths,[151] and nevertheless was able to give them individual, human faces. The artist had lived through such a transport 'from Theresienstadt into the gas', to Auschwitz, along with his mortally ill friend Bedřich Fritta in the winter of 1944. Fritta had died shortly after arrival in Auschwitz. Haas only had to bear being there for a few weeks; his artistic abilities were then put to use in the money-forging workshop at Sachsenhausen concentration camp.

When Haas produced the lithographs, he was familiar with the situation in several of the camps.[152] For his representation of *Auschwitz*, which he placed as fol. 5 (illus. 87) in the series after the image of *Hunger*, he selected the view of the Stammlager (main camp) from the entrance gate. The camp inmates, framed on the left by a *Kapo* and on the right by an SS officer, appear to be approaching the viewer like workers coming out of a factory at the end of the day. Haas represented the situation of the entrance topographically accurately with, on the left side of the entrance, Block 24, which had been converted at the end of 1943 into a camp brothel[153] for privileged prisoners. The windows divided into six glass areas in the brick building are copied exactly, with their lower panes wide open, framing the women, who were forced into prostitution, looking out of them. On the left, a window pane extending out of the image is invitingly open. With low-cut blouses, bows in their hair, of variable corpulence and belonging to different age groups, the forced prostitutes are presented much as in the pictures by Otto Dix or Jeanne Mammen[154] in the 1920s as images of the enticements of the big city, a temptation that was now more than unrealistic in this situation and highlights the absurdity of the perverse forms of degradation in the camp. Haas placed them on the left-hand side opposite a poster warning of the deadly effects of lice.[155] Right in front of this, however, he positioned the smoking ss officer, summoning up quite different connotations of the word 'deadly'. The cigarette not only reveals how casually the guard is carrying out his work but points to the connection between his work and the numberless dead people going up in smoke in the crematoria. Beyond the row of brothel windows, the image of the camp band is dominated by three gigantic horns of the brass band, and the view into the bells of the brass instruments extends the reference to sexual desire.[156] As the conductor of the camp orchestra on the right in the background is indicating the striking up of the band, going by the daily camp routine, Haas was showing here the prisoners marching to work in the morning. By the sign at the entrance to the camp, 'Arbeit macht frei', occupying almost the whole of the top border of the drawing, Haas illustrated the compulsion that all three groups of prisoners were subject to, and emphasized this even more by positioning the armed ss guard in front of the outside of the wall, but with his right shoulder still under the motto; to present-day readers that may indicate that even he is not free. Above the heads of the prisoners, against a light background, one can see in the way through the camp a body hanging on the gallows; it forms the vanishing point for the viewer's eye. By selecting this view of the entrance, it provides a realistic collage of what is going on in the concentration camp, combining slavery, torture and murder amid the bedlam of music and sexual desire under the shadow of the gallows. Haas did not refrain from showing the perversity of the system in the camps with their brothels which, except for Otto Schubert, neither in art nor in photography, had become part of the canon of the growing iconography of the camps and forced sexual labour only again became a subject of debate as a result of feminist research.[157]

Carl Lauterbach: *Ghetto Album*

The Düsseldorf artist Carl Lauterbach, like Karl Schwesig, Otto Pankok, Gert Wollheim,[158] Julo Levin, Peter Ludwigs and Matthias Barz, was a member of the Junge Rheinland movement and likewise belonged to the group of friends in the 1920s around 'Mutter Ey'.[159] He secretly put on record the fate of the Jews under the Nazi regime,[160] and these drawings were already being displayed shortly after the end of the war in art exhibitions in Düsseldorf. In 1981 Edgar Koenig wrote about Lauterbach's secret works:

> Up to 1945 there were series of drawings being produced showing the fears and sufferings of the people of Düsseldorf and all those affected in such a powerful way, the like of which I have never seen in any Düsseldorf artist of the period. In addition, after the Germans marched into Poland, Lauterbach worked on a 'Ghetto Album' expressing his sympathy with the Jews.[161]

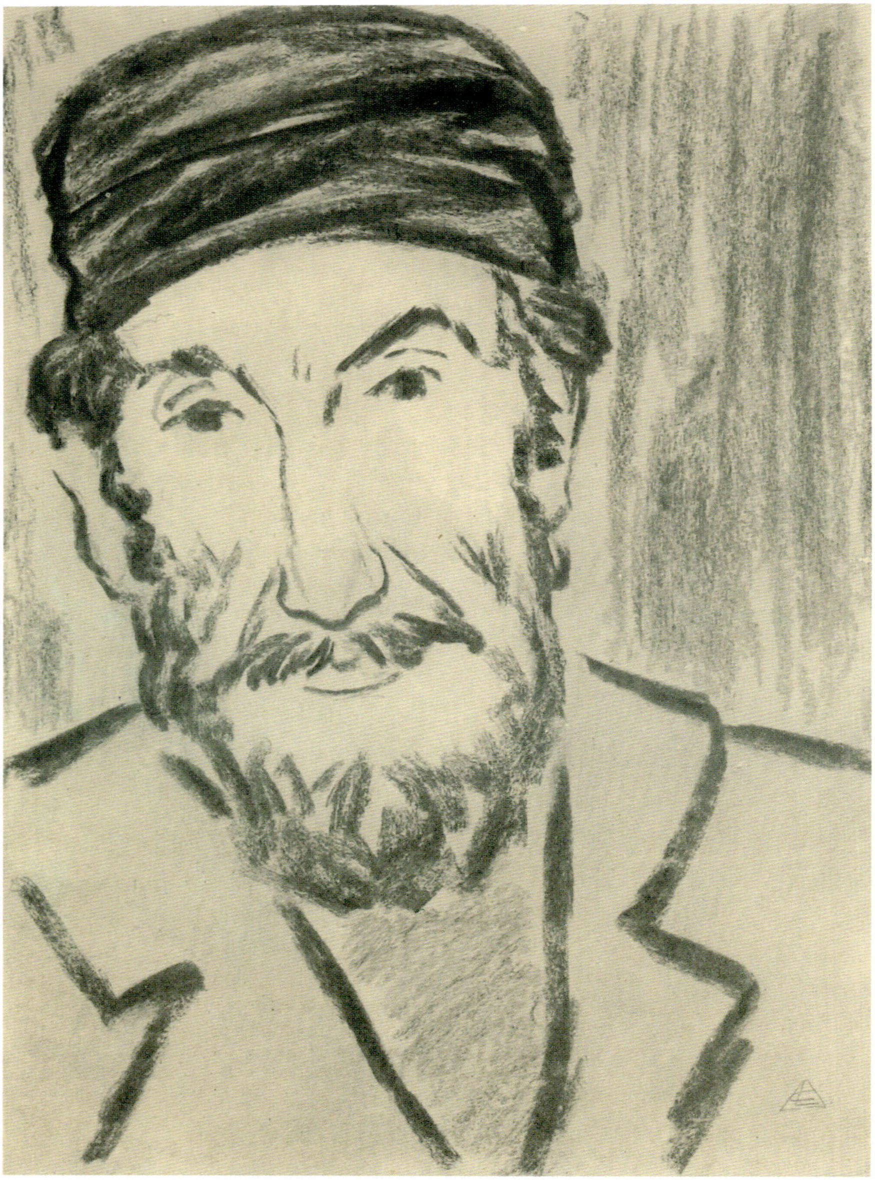

88 Carl Lauterbach, *From the Ghetto Album*, 1940, charcoal, from *Carl Lauterbach Zeichnungen* (Solingen-Ohligs, 1948).

It has not yet been possible for academics to establish the exact arrangement of what is often referred to as the *Ghetto Album*.[162] The artist himself also contributed to the uncertainty as to the order when, in his first big solo exhibition at the Kulturbund in 1947, he put 53 numbered works under the heading 'Ghetto', whereas he put the note 'From the Ghetto Album' under only one number (fol. 2).[163] Besides, it is presumed that Lauterbach made changes up to 1991, the year he died.[164] From the multiplicity of drawings showing mainly men or women – mostly in front of a wall and all of them without the Jewish star – we shall take three examples that were definitely available to a wider public in the immediate post-war period. They record

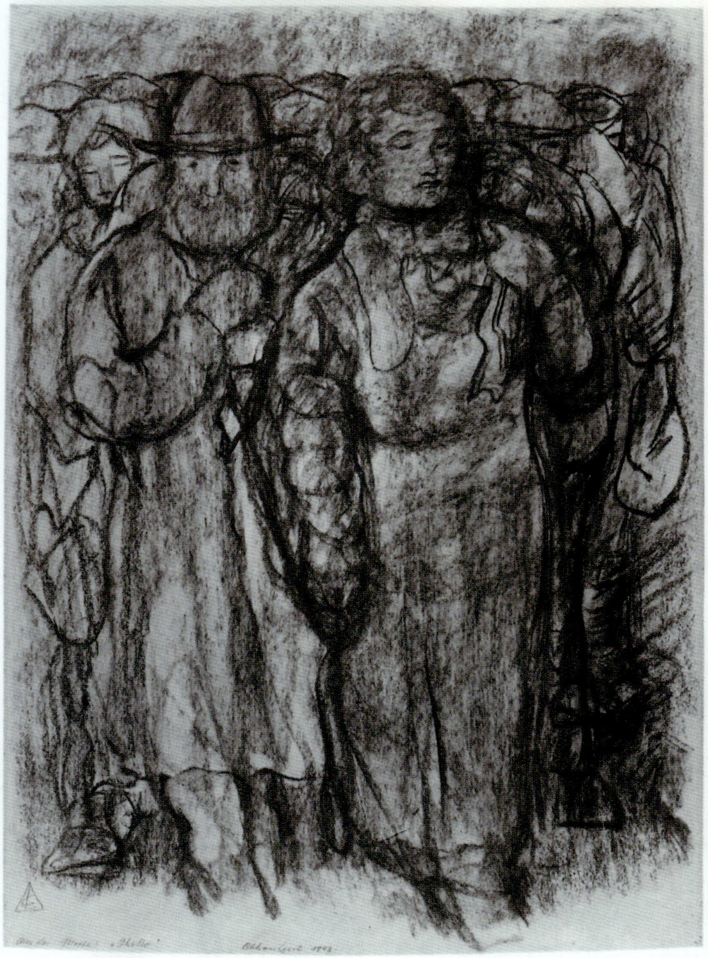

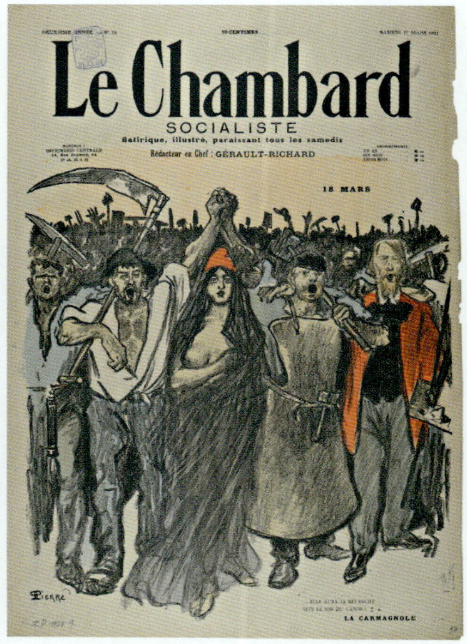

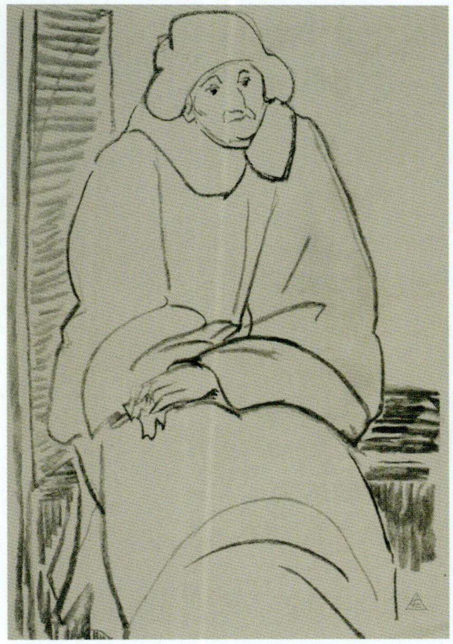

top left 89 Carl Lauterbach, *Deportation, From the Ghetto Album*, 1943, charcoal.

top right 90 Théophile Alexandre Steinlen, cover illustration, *Le chambard socialiste*, 14 (17 April 1894).

bottom right 91 Carl Lauterbach, *Jewish Mother*, 1940, charcoal, from *Carl Lauterbach Zeichnungen* (Solingen-Ohligs, 1948).

sympathy with the persecuted Jews on the part of this left-wing Düsseldorf artist. Along with the inhabitants of the ghetto illustrated by him, some of his sketches are distinguished by the perspective, shared only by Pankok, of a citizen who did not overlook the Jews still living in his neighbourhood.

In the volume with twenty drawings by Lauterbach that Anna Klapheck selected in 1948 'from nearly twenty years of creative work',[165] the second of the ten that go under the heading *From 'Drawings of the Period'* has the title *From the Ghetto Album* (illus. 88). As often in the *Ghetto Albums* now in the Düsseldorf City Museum, it portrays the face of a man with a beard and a cap on his head. Both are unusual for the male fashion of the time and mark him out as an inhabitant of the ghetto. The appearance is not caricatured in the distorted way that was so noticeable in the Nazi period, but what one sees is his bright elongated face looking straight at the viewer.[166]

The page following on from the portrait of the man, given as fol. 12 in the 1948 publication, shows *en face* a seated woman with the caption *Jewish Mother* (illus. 91). Her lined silhouette represents her in respectable middle-class clothing consisting of a coat and hat and a handkerchief in her left hand, while her raised eyebrows and the set of her mouth betray her worried look directed towards the right.[167] The drawings belong to a series of oil paintings of mothers produced by his artist friends, Peter Ludwigs and Julo Levin around 1940.[168] (See also the subject in Schwesig, illus. 117 and 118.) What is noticeable is the more frequent representation of middle-aged or elderly women in that period, compared with the greater variety of what was thought of as desirable in images of females in the art of the Weimar Republic. The turn towards mothers who are not able to offer any protection but are shown alone, worried and anxious illustrated to the art public of the post-war period the hopeless position of the mothers and of those who painted them.

The 1943 charcoal painting *Deportation* (illus. 89) was certainly shown to the public at the Düsseldorf exhibition in 1947.[169] In the foreground, a woman is running towards the viewer, gazing sideways lost in thought; next to her is an elderly bearded man with a hat. They are surrounded by a large crowd of people at the rear. This is not a united front of advancing demonstrators, as in earlier images of this type,[170] but uses broad charcoal strokes and dark blurred outlines, as in the representation of demonstrators by Théophile Steinlen (illus. 90).[171] It represents the procession of Jews towards their transportation to be exterminated, in marching columns that many of the citizens of Düsseldorf also would have seen.[172]

Fritz Ketz

This artist, who was not called up for war service for health reasons, had survived the period up to 1945 with great difficulty, carrying with him a suitcase with pictures on his trek via many addresses. If these had been discovered,

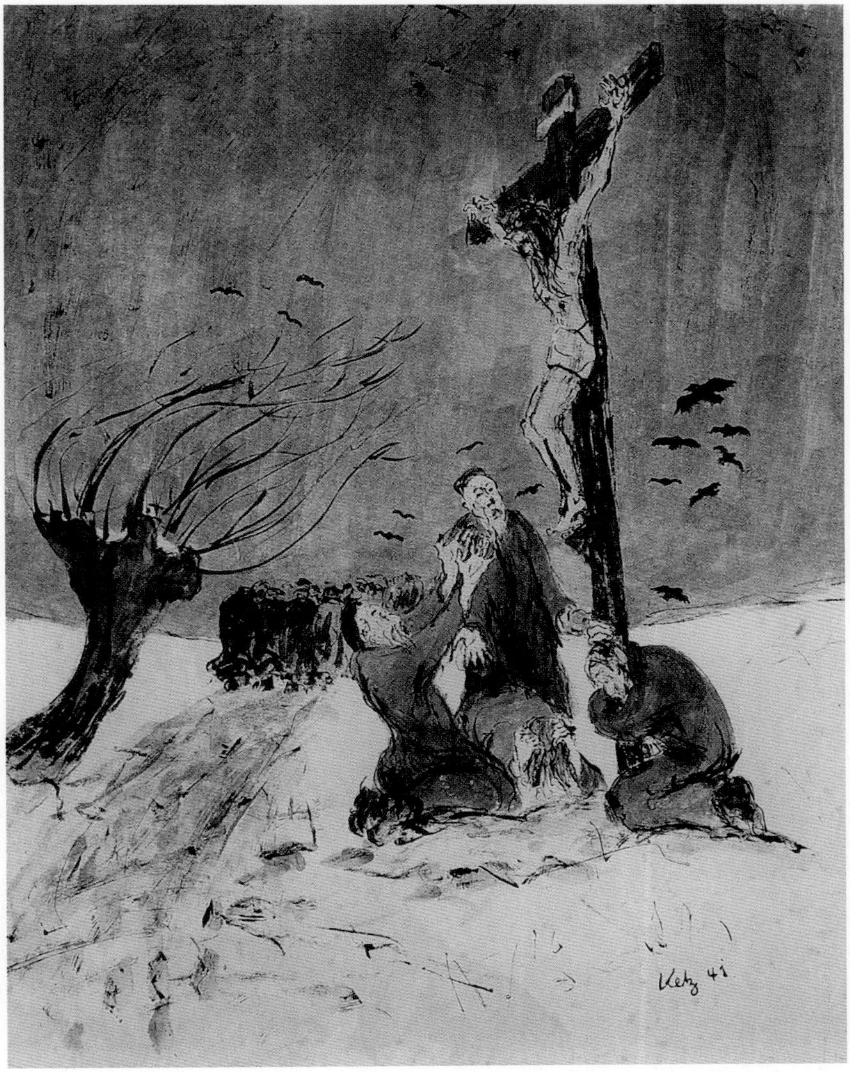

92 Fritz Ketz, *The Ones Pleading*, 1941, from the album *Figures and Images* (Reutlingen, 1947).

he would probably have been hauled before the court for propaganda hostile to the Reich.[173] In 1947 at a bookshop in Reutlingen, he published the album *Figures and Images*[174] as 'reproductions from hand drawings faithful to the originals' and with the considerable number of 10,000 copies. The eight drawings he selected from the few that were in fact saved from the bombs[175] and from the works produced in the following years include a self-portrait from 1946, and most of them recall the horrendous events of the war: *War-blinded Man* (1942), *People Lost* (1942) and *Missing Person* (1942). Apart from the drawings of a *Boy Partisan* (1942)[176] and the Jews pleading at a crucifix (see illus. 92), they include a Nazi death court judge and the last one, Hitler as Death, surrounded by skulls and applying instruments of torture to skeletons, with the title *Villain* (1945). In his 'introductory remarks', the publisher Jakob Witsch does not hide what the viewer looking for artistic enjoyment must be prepared for: 'Such manifestations of unsparing seriousness are not always pleasing to the eye of the beholder. Is that any reason to avoid them? That would mean that the job of art is to shield the eye from anything unpleasant.'

The Ones Pleading

The drawing *The Ones Pleading* (illus. 92), dated 1941, which up until now has only been discussed in terms of its 'Christian religious background',[177] represents people calling upon Christ on the Cross. The supplicants are identified as Jews by their kippahs, beards and long black clothing. The fact that Ketz does not leave any doubt in his iconography that he is intending to portray Jews is supported by the comparison to the drawing of Ahasver (illus. 94), which is just as identifiable as *The Ones Pleading* and was produced in the same period of systematic mass murder. In the drawing *The Ones Pleading*, Ketz did not portray the ridicule and putting to death of the Jews but recalled their futile appeals for Christian mercy. Four Jews are portrayed with dramatic gestures of despair set against a snowy landscape with a crucifix, as in Doré's *Ahasverus*, placed side-on. On the path to the side, a dark huddle of people is shown heading into the unknown. For the viewer of the time it was not hard to see this as a human column being led towards a camp or a mass transport. The image is framed on the left by a twisted weeping willow with wavy branches like a threatening scourge above the procession of people scurrying towards the horizon; the group of marching people, the pleading Jews and the one being crucified are surrounded by black crows in the winter sky. Jewish artists before and during the Nazi period, in strong opposition to anti-Semitism, had represented Christ as a crucified Jew.[178] Now this non-Jew Ketz, even though he made Christ's beard resemble those of the pleading ones, represented the despair of the Jews under the symbol of Christian belief. Ketz continued his visual commentary on the 1941 deportation of the Jews in the first post-war publication of his drawings. In juxtaposition with the other illustrations, he commented on the structure of the legal system based on violence that the judges administered. He portrays them in the fifth drawing of the series as judges with skulls and in the last drawing he shows Hitler as a villain, playing with skulls.

The Ones Eradicated

After 1945 Ketz did not participate in the demonization of the Nazi past,[179] or in attempts to keep quiet about it, but published his portrayals of the crimes. In 1946, in another ink drawing, he reminded people about *The Ones Eradicated* (illus. 93). By means of the black background out of which appears the bright circle with the agonized faces of the living dead, an impression is given of the medieval image of the mouth of Hell and Schedel's burnings of Jews (see illus. 2), now overwritten with the vision of a gas chamber in the extermination camps.

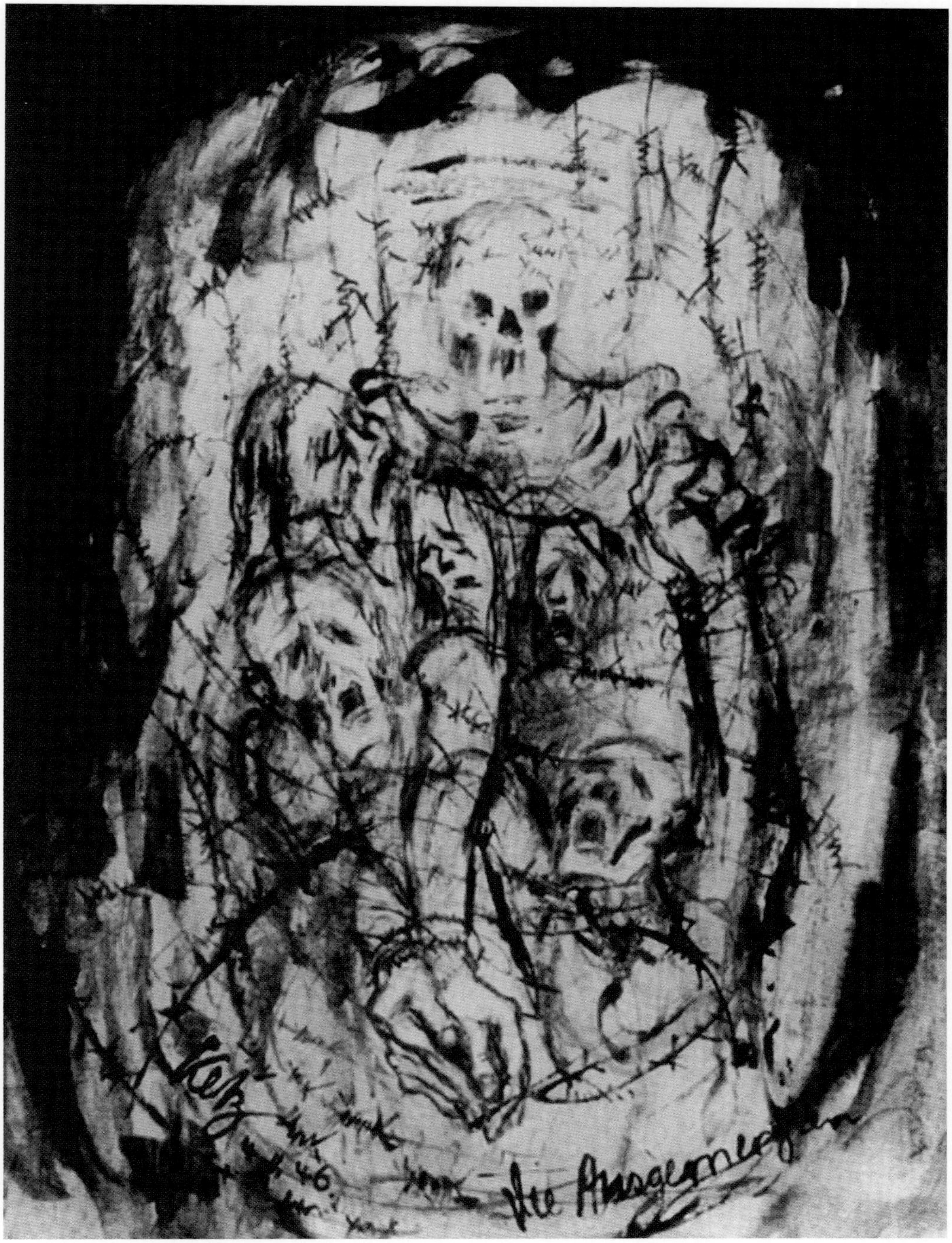

93 Fritz Ketz, *The Ones Eradicated*, 1946, pen, brush and ink, wash.

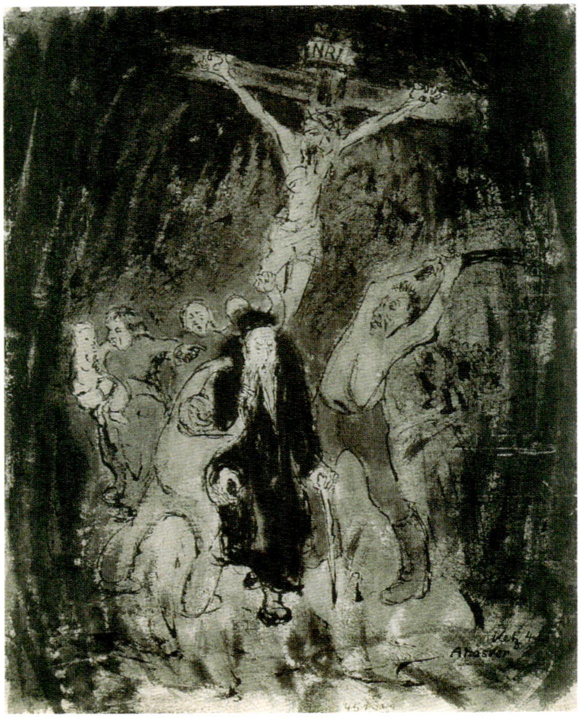

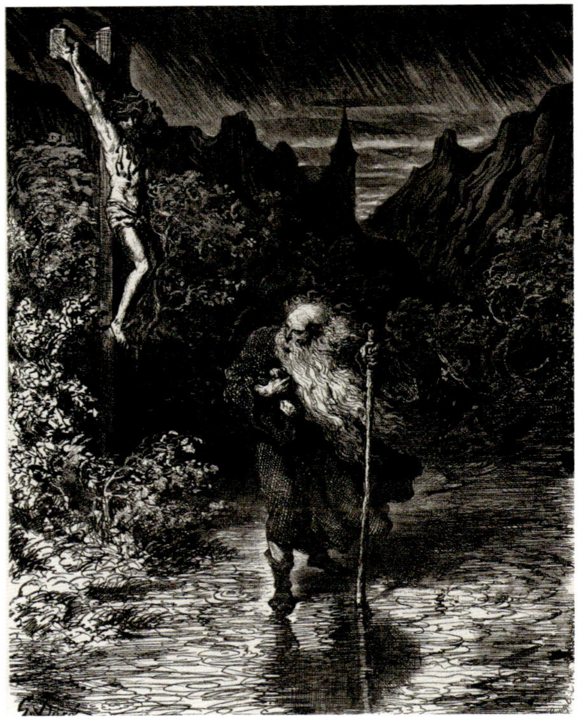

94 Fritz Ketz, *Ahasver*, 1941, pen, brush and ink, wash.

95 Gustave Doré, *Ahasverus*, woodcut for *La légende du juif errant, 12 compositions* (Paris, 1856).

Ahasver

It is more than likely that Ketz was influenced in the drawing by Gustave Doré's *Ahasverus* of 1856 (illus. 95).[180] His version (illus. 94) displays similar characteristics to Doré's bearded Jew, walking towards the viewer with the long stick in his left hand and the money bag in his right. Ketz, however, completely changed the surroundings. Ahasver, Ahasverus, the 'eternal' Jew, is not walking on past the crucifix but is represented as a tormented man suffering in front of Christ, again a reference to the Passion story. Not only is a figure behind, in the same position as the viewer as it were, cutting the Jew's beard – an act of amusement captured on Nazi photos – but on the right of the picture a tormentor is about to scourge Ahasverus, as in the mocking of Christ, while a mother with a child on her arm is pointing at the Jew with a dismissive gesture. Certainly the position of Ahasverus's right hand resembles that of Doré's Jew, but the money bag has been transformed into a bundle which, like the gnarled stick, reminds one of the meagre baggage of wandering journeymen. Already by the end of the nineteenth century, Jewish artists had engaged in a new interpretation of the Christian narrative and had turned Ahasverus into a figure for Jewish artists to identify with,[181] whose suffering Christianity is responsible for. Ketz takes on a somewhat less drastic version of this reinterpretation, but his figures are likewise attacking the Wandering Jew under the sign of the Cross. As Rosamunde Neugebauer concluded about drawings made in exile, for other artists too who had been

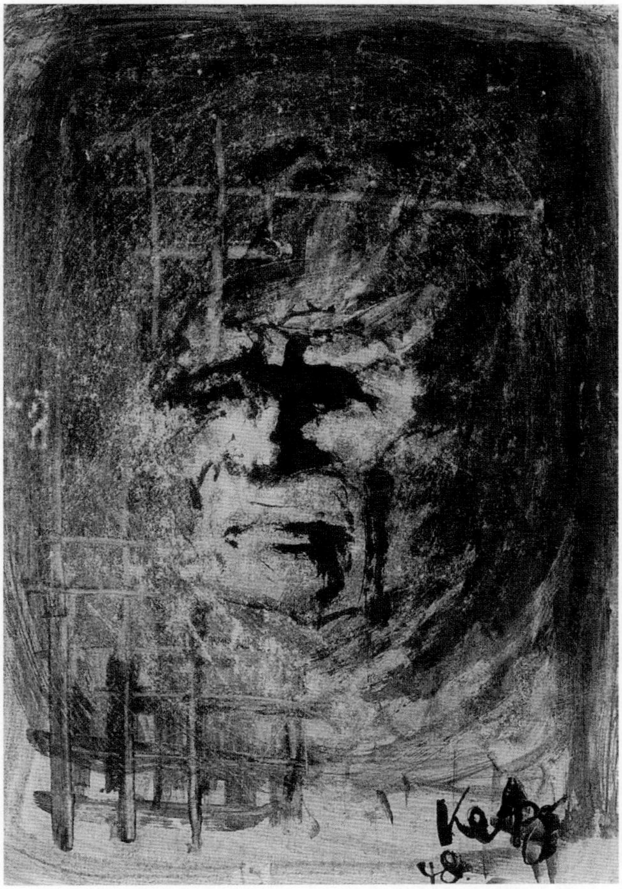

96 Fritz Ketz, *Self-portrait*, 1948, brush and ink.

forced to flee by fascist regimes, the Wandering Jew became a figure that did not just encapsulate the suffering of the Jews but with whom they themselves could identify in their longing to return to their homeland.[182] Though Ketz did not go into exile, during the Nazi period he had no fixed abode in Germany; in his drawings compassion and self-questioning are closely linked.

Self-portrait

At the same time Ketz was working on sixteen charcoal drawings of the Passion, so it is reasonable to presume that the artist was intensely concerned with the question of guilt about the crimes of the Nazis. This could possibly also relate to undeniable self-questioning, explaining why his 1948 *Self-portrait* in ink (illus. 96), unlike the traditional one in the 1947 album, appears so much darker and at the same time more lacking in outline. It shows the bars of a cell by way of a ghostly warning, the shadow of a swastika across his face and a U-shaped crown of thorns above. The left side of his mouth and a wound on his left cheek seem to be oozing blood, so that the self-portrait reveals both the deliberately added signs of his participation in the period and his sufferings of it as a result.

Teo Otto: *Never Again*

In his *Nie Wieder: Tagebuch in Bildern* (Never Again: Journal in Images),[183] Teo Otto displayed 75 ink drawings about memories, feelings, violence, political events and places, using spontaneous-looking brushstrokes and powerful combinations of words and images. With their free use of illustration, they are clearly distinguishable from the publications by those who had stayed in the country. This stage designer had emigrated to Switzerland for political reasons in 1933 and had this series of figural sketches of human suffering published by the Berlin publisher Volk & Welt in 1949, frequently contrasting them with the Nazi claims from the various theatres of war. The tripartite division of title, image and text on many pages corresponds to the emblematic one between lemma, icon and epigram, though they extend over two pages, with the title and commentary always placed on the verso. The book is unpaginated. Many of the representations refer directly to the sufferings and murder of the Jews. Otto prefaced the series by the following statements:

> Long before Hitler started the war against the world, he had declared war on the German people. Long before Oradour, Treblinka, Auschwitz filled the world with horror, the signposts to death were pointing right towards the middle of Germany: Dachau, Börgermoor, Oranienburg.

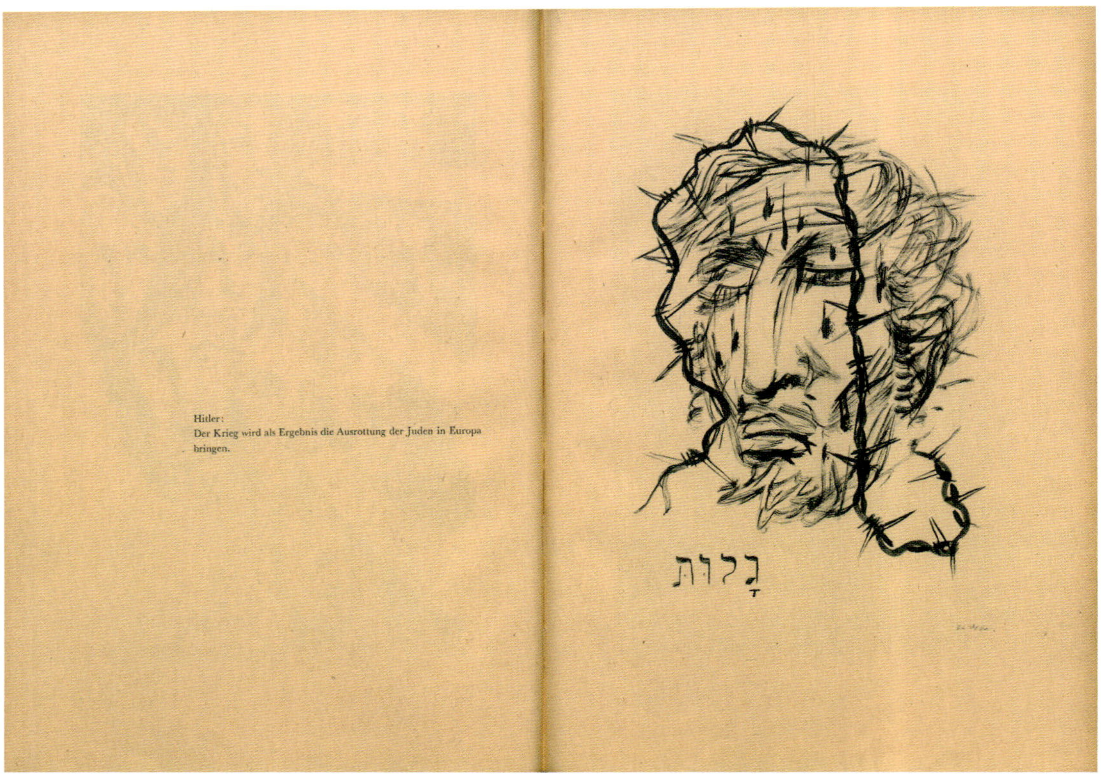

97 Teo Otto, *Hitler: The war will have the result of bringing about the eradication of the Jews of Europe*, from *Nie wieder. Tagebuch in Bildern* (Berlin, 1949), photo lithograph.

98 Teo Otto, *If only stones could speak*, from *Nie wieder. Tagebuch in Bildern* (Berlin, 1949), photo lithograph.

99 Teo Otto, *Deported to the Extermination Camp*, from *Nie wieder. Tagebuch in Bildern* (Berlin, 1949), photo lithograph.

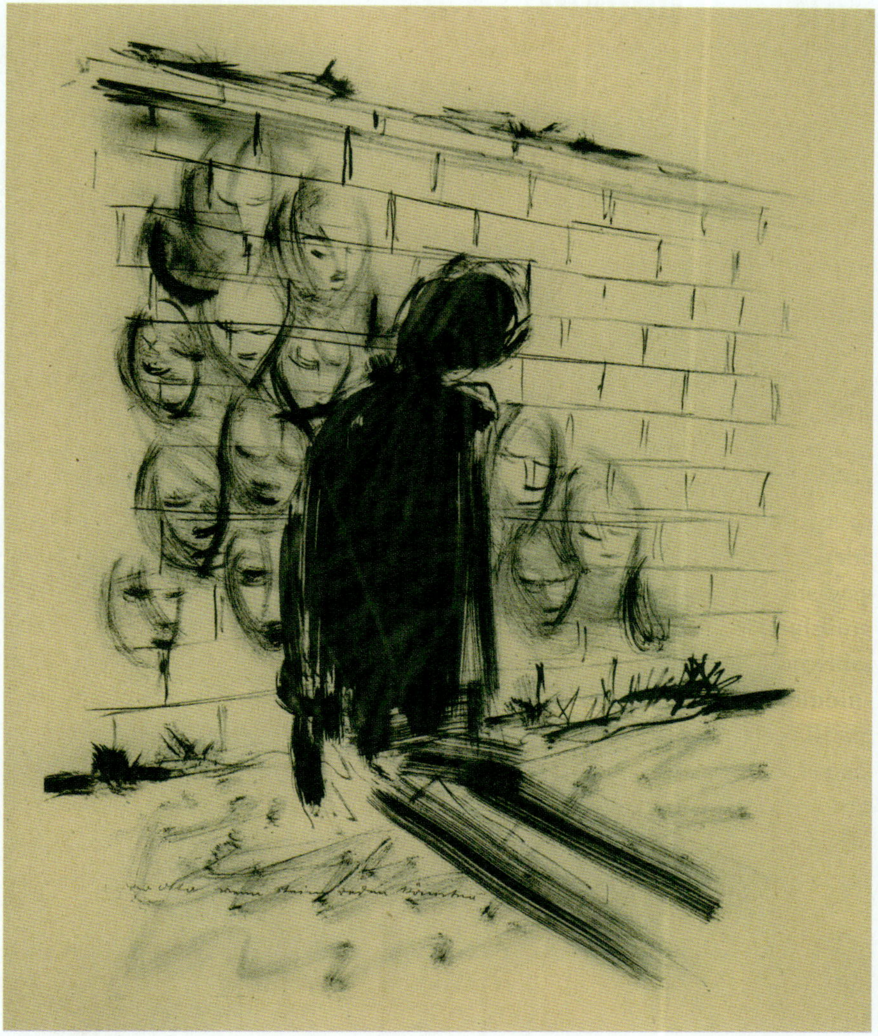

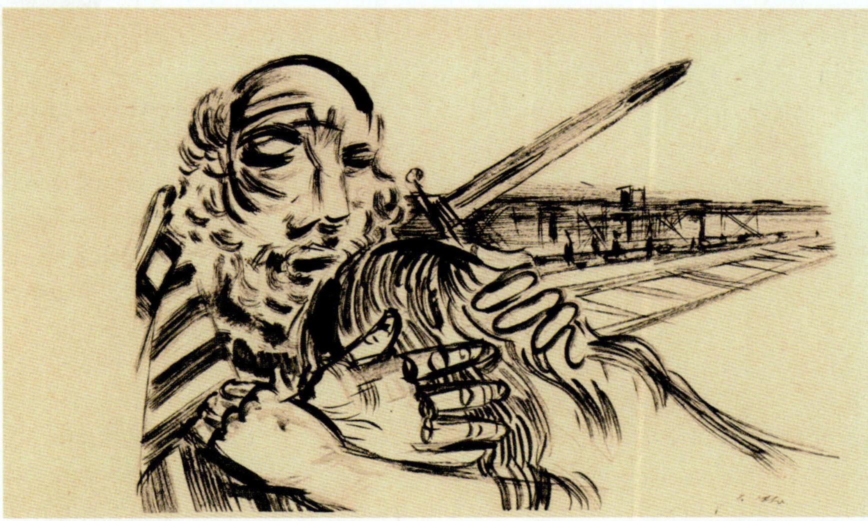

He began the series of brush drawings in black ink with the portrayal of someone hanging on the electric wire *Before the Break of Day* by commenting: 'For years and years thousands have been suffering and dying in the jails and concentration camps, without a name, hardly noticed by the world.'

Among his representations of the war and its effects on the population, time and again mention is made of how control was maintained by means of internment, for example in *Night in the Camp*, which names the innumerable concentration camps, prison camps, internment camps, youth camps, training camps and transfer camps, and the sleeping, emaciated faces crammed together, a hand hanging down from the bunk bed above them.

In the first quarter of the series of images, Otto drew the injured face of a man, surrounded by barbed wire, resembling Christ with the crown of thorns (illus. 97). Only this drawing carries a caption in Hebrew which, according to Präger, means 'made manifest' or 'made equal to man';[184] it confronts Christians with their involvement with the Jewish children of God, which is starkly spelled out by Hitler's statement on the left-hand side that the war would bring about 'the eradication of the Jews from Europe'.

The fourth page selected here (illus. 98) stands as a testament to the endless murders that were carried out, not by industrial methods, but by man against man. It suggests the body of a prisoner who has been shot, his head hanging down, and having been in addition hanged against a wall which in its turn reveals the shadows of many heads. Otto places against this portrayal the well-known saying 'if only stones could speak . . .' The reader of the time might have associated this with Christ's statement in Luke 19:40: 'I tell you that, if these should remain silent, the stones would immediately cry out.'

The drawing *Deported to the extermination camp* (illus. 99) gains its particular force from the sight of an old man with a prayer shawl and kippah, with both hands protecting a girl from the threat of a dagger with a bloody tip, and cattle wagons in the background, the viewer knowing all the while how hopeless this protection was. Otto's commentary just explains the history behind this image of deportation. 'Gleichschaltung (elimination of opposition) in Hungary: concentration of the Jews in ghettos.'

The foreword to this journal was written by Bertolt Brecht, who used the various drawings by Otto about the suffering of human beings to illustrate the political attitude that the spirit of war is 'the spirit of business', drawing the conclusion: 'Struggle for peace is the struggle against capitalism.'[185] On the last page there is the announcement that Brecht's *Kriegsfibel* (War Primer) was 'shortly' to be published by the same publisher. It was another six years before the publishing house Eulenspiegel printed it.[186] Again Brecht was to use the emblematic arrangement of words and images, but in his case he used images from press photography with the didactic aim of deciphering the 'hieroglyphic tablets' of the illustrations 'for the unsuspecting reader'.[187] Unlike Otto's *Journal in Images*, this *War Primer*, criticizing war and fascism from a Marxist perspective, contains only one photo relating to

Jewish history during the fascist period. It is a variation on the theme of the ancient Christian story of the eternal Wandering of the Jews for the present day. *Refugees without Refuge* (pp. 58f. in the English edition) shows the motif of a mother and child, often used for refugees after the war,[188] in this case one rescued from the water who had been aboard a stranded ship bound for Palestine on the Sea of Marmara. The text asks the question: 'Where can they go, these 7,000,000 European Jews?'

Rudi Stern: Illustration for Nelly Sachs's *In the Habitations of Death*

In den Wohnungen des Todes (In the Habitations of Death), the first edition of the poems of Nelly Sachs after the war, published in Germany by Aufbau in East Berlin in 1947 (with copyright note from 1946), was illustrated by Rudi Stern. The artist makes use of references from Jewish iconography and elements from the photographs of the concentration camps applied to the poet's words. His sketchy portrayals of landscape still hark back to the illustrations of Max Slevogt and paintings by van Gogh and Menzel, but there is a break in this tradition. A darkened sky and smoke predominate throughout his eleven pages accompanying the poems.

The volume starts with the dedication by this Jewish author who had fled from Berlin to Sweden:

> To my dead brothers and sisters

Followed on the next right-hand page by:

> *Dein Leib im Rauch durch die Luft.*

> Your body as smoke through the air.[189]

Sachs returns to this heading in the final line of the first poem and refers to the body as that of the Jewish people:

> *Und Israels Leib im Rauch durch die Luft!*

> And Israel's body as smoke through the air!

The correspondence between Sachs's words and Stern's image of smoke deserves to be examined more closely because of the meaning that is attached to this symbol in memories of the Nazi genocide. Stern's first drawing, two smoking chimneys above two buildings behind barbed wire, is printed immediately after the line quoted here, which can be interpreted both as a separate poem

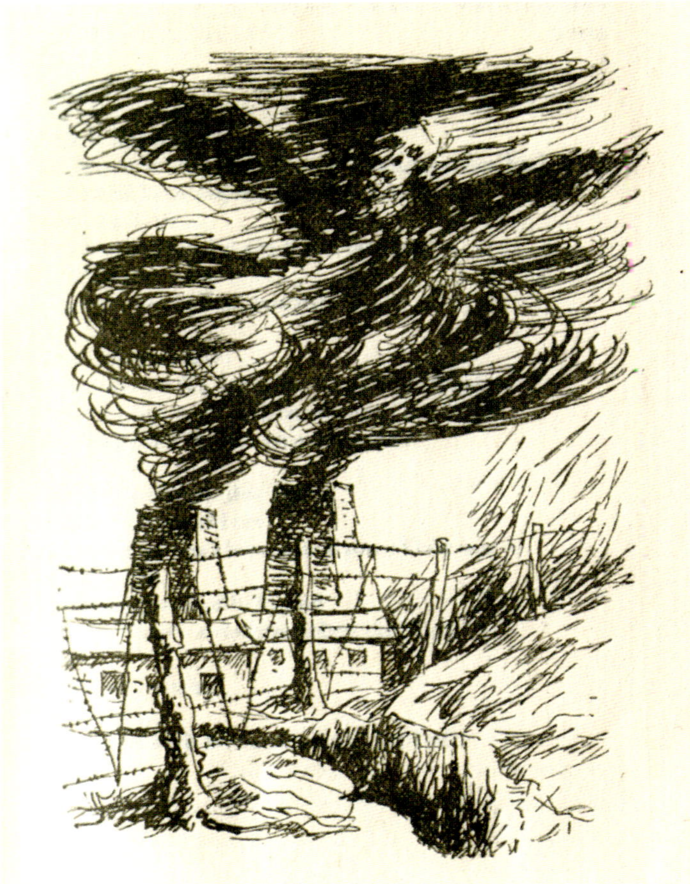

100 Rudi Stern, illustration for Nelly Sachs, 'Your Body Dissolves as Smoke Through the Air', from *In den Wohnungen des Todes* (Berlin, 1947).

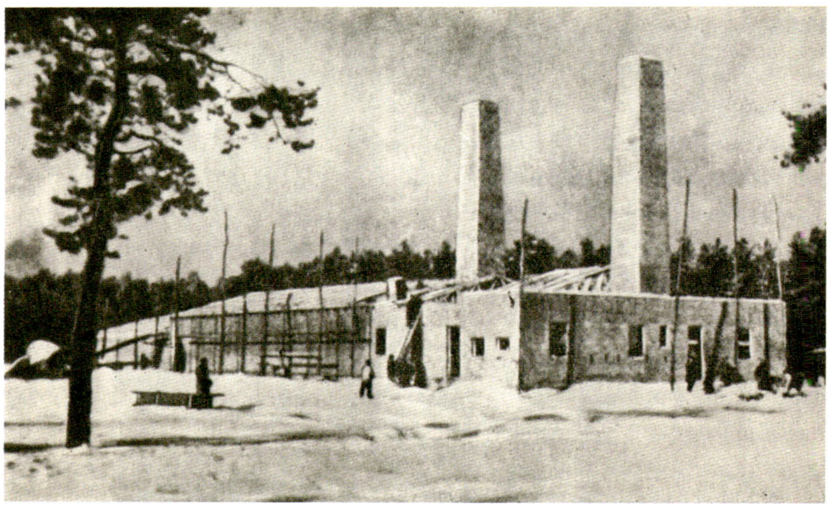

101 Auschwitz-Birkenau, Crematorium III under construction in 1943, photograph publ. in Sehn 1957.

and as the title of the first of the four cycles in this volume (illus. 100). It is placed there to be read before the page with Sachs's poem:

O die Schornsteine
Auf den sinnreich erdachten Wohnungen des Todes,

O the chimneys
On the ingeniously devised habitations of death,

The poet headed this with a verse from the Book of Job (19:26):

Und wenn diese, meine Haut zerschlagen
sein wird, so werde ich ohne mein Fleisch
Gott schauen.

And though after my skin worms destroy this body,
yet in my flesh shall I see God.

Rudi Stern, political artist, illustrator and caricaturist,[190] was presumably basing his image on the brick buildings of the crematoria as shown in photographs (illus. 101). He must have known them from how they were shown in Nazi photos, as they were the only ones showing the complete buildings, which were blown up in 1944 when the SS were retreating.[191] He put together parts of buildings comprising crematorium III and crematorium IV in his drawing and took over the barbed wire and the squat shape of the chimney of crematorium III, but duplicating it, as in the case of crematorium IV. In addition he shortened it in comparison with the surrounding buildings. In the seventh illustration to the poem 'Grave Inscriptions Written in the Air', both of the buildings are there with the same chimneys; the function of the crematoria in this drawing intensifies the image of the mouth of Hell, often depicted in Bible illustrations since the Middle Ages, into which crowds of people are driven. The smoke from two chimneys forms the background to this, whereas in the first drawing he devoted the majority of the picture to the dark smoke.[192] Stern added to the chimneys the smoke that the photographs don't show, attempting to echo the poet's words:

O die Schornsteine!
Freiheitswege für Jeremias und Hiobs Staub –
Wer erdachte euch und baute Stein auf Stein
Den Weg für Flüchtlinge aus Rauch?

O the chimneys!
Freedomway for Jeremiah and Job's dust –
Who devised you and laid stone upon stone
The road for refugees of smoke?

But presumably it seemed to Rudi Stern as if these two smoking chimneys did not do sufficient justice to the poem. Perhaps he realized that the sketch of the chimneys still did not give the public of the time enough indication as to their function, or an unambiguous symbol of the extermination of the Jews. In any case Stern inserted a skull into the clouds of smoke that are revolving like the sails of a windmill. The suggestion of a cross in the middle under the chin of the skull remains an enigma.

Words and images in this slim, inexpensive and yet elegantly formed volume of poems published in an edition numbering as many as 20,000 copies[193] give voice to the now easily readable signifiers for mass murder in the camp, coinciding almost exactly, though probably independently, with Paul Celan's 'Death Fugue' (see below) and the *Buch des Alfred Kantor* (The Book of Alfred Kantor).[194] If, despite the many clear references to the crematorium chimneys in Sachs's poem, Stern thought he ought to add familiar symbols of death to the smoke from the chimneys, for Art Spiegelman they did not need a skull added to represent the standard symbol of Auschwitz. Nevertheless, just like Strempel, Stern and Zielezinski (see illus. 10, 100 and 73) before him, he drew the two chimneys[195] shown on the 1943 photo of the crematorium. In the case of Stern's felt need to make the significance of the two smoking chimneys more obvious by adding a skull and the mouth of Hell, one can see at work the process by which symbols are formed, then just getting underway, that Spiegelman in his turn was trying to move on from forty years later. In his graphic novel *Maus II*, he returned to the image of the smoking chimneys at Auschwitz but developed their meaning, including them as a repetition of the sign of the deadly threat to the prisoners in the everyday life of the camp.

Paul Celan, Edgar Jené

'Death Fugue'

Paul Celan's poem 'Todesfuge' (Death Fugue), which is now quite well-known, appeared for the first time in German in 1948 in the volume *Der Sand aus den Urnen* (Sand from the Urns), published in Vienna.[196] 'Death Fugue' was preceded by a drawing by Edgar Jené that is also included under this title in Celan's publication on Jené's images in the same year.[197] Celan's poem and Jené's lithographically reproduced drawing have identical titles, but it is not known exactly when these originated. Certainly, both artists met in the course of the first half of 1948, remaining in close contact with one another, and Celan took part in the first exhibition of Surrealist art initiated by Jené at the Agathon Gallery in Vienna.[198] Celan had just arrived from Bucharest and even recited his poem in Jené's studio, where the celebrated representative of Surrealism living there at the time invited people for discussions and readings and where Celan and Ingeborg Bachmann became acquainted.[199] Jené, who had already fled from Saarbrücken to Vienna in order to escape the Nazis in 1935, in 1980 recalled the occasion, still deeply impressed:

> This evening has remained an unforgettable event. Particularly *Death Fugue*, which he finished with, moved me most deeply. None of the innumerable more harrowing accounts of the concentration camps brought home to me so vividly as this poem the terror of this inhuman time. And not just me either.[200]

He did not, however, at the same time mention his own drawing *Death Fugue*. Certainly, Celan had already published his poem in Romanian in Bucharest translated by his friend Petre Solomon, but there it had come out under the title *Tangoul mortii* – in German *Todestango* (Death Tango).[201] Solomon wrote that he owned a manuscript by Celan, also entitled *Todestango*.[202]

The Saarland Museum in Saarbrücken[203] has an album containing the drawing *Death Fugue* (illus. 102), done in pen and ink,[204] signed and dated 'Jené 44', although it is nevertheless generally given in the literature as being

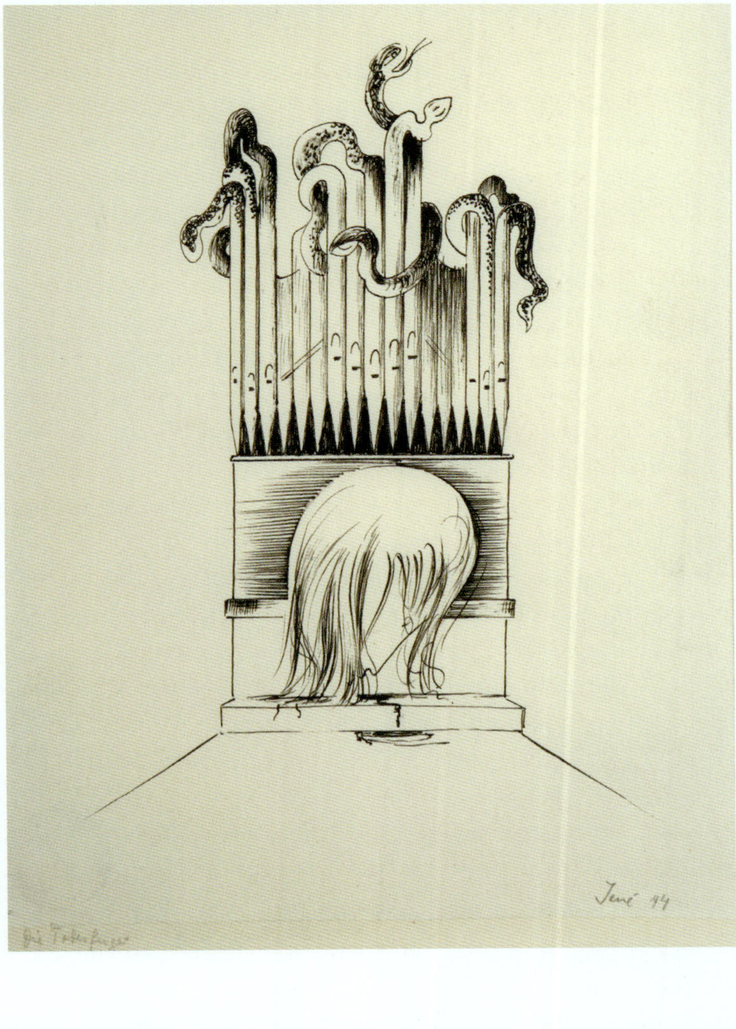

102 Edgar Jené, *Death Fugue*, 1944, pen and ink, signed 'Jené 44'.

from 1947.[205] In addition, Jené's drawing is taken to be a response to Celan's poem. The discrepancy between the dates begs the question of what these details are based on. Doubtless the drawing was published with minimal alterations twice altogether with texts by Celan. It is now included in an album, announcing on the cover 'TODESFUGE Drawings from the War Years', referring to 1939–45. The file was acquired by the museum in 1952, at the time not yet part of the Federal Republic of Germany, and contains 35 drawings that had been partly published by Otto Basil in 1945; *Death Fugue* was not among them.[206] In Celan's 1948 volume of poetry it was placed immediately before the poem (p. 57); another drawing, *O Blume der Zeit* (Oh Flower of the Time),[207] whose title refers to the last line of the poem, 'Umsonst malst du Herzen ans Fenster' (In vain do you paint hearts onto the window), is placed at the beginning of the volume. Both illustrations were published in the same year under these titles as independent works, the third and fourth in the series of eight original lithographs. The publication was edited by Celan who dedicated to his friend and supporter in Vienna an essay of four and a half pages in the form of a dialogue that is now seen as a basic text for his theory of poetics: *Edgar Jené und der Traum vom Traume* (Edgar Jené and the Dream of a Dream).[208]

It is also known that Celan had his volume of poems *Der Sand aus den Urnen* pulped because of the large number of printing errors; it was not published until 1948, after his departure for Paris. In addition, towards the end of the same year, when Jené appeared in Paris for the exhibition of his own pictures at Galerie La Dragonne, Celan spoke disparagingly of the painter, 'who had not refrained from providing my book with two examples of the most extreme tastelessness'.[209] Celan planned to tear out the now rejected drawings from his own author's copy, something he carried out at least in the surviving copy in the German literary archive at Marbach.[210] His distancing himself from the illustrations to his first volume of poems may be explained by Celan's sudden change of taste, presumably also due to his break with Surrealism, already hinted at in the text about Jené's drawings. It can also be seen as the poet's rejection of the related subject-matter in the drawings that were for him no longer convincing.

Jené, the Francophile native of the Saarland, who had embraced Surrealism in 1930 after reading Max Ernst's 1929 collage novel *La Femme 100 têtes*, chose for his drawing the view of the monumental instrument used for music in church. The drawing reminds one of the collage *The Immaculate Conception*, which Max Ernst had published as the last drawing in the first chapter of the novel (illus. 103).[211] The powerful and rectangular arrangement of the organ pipes is juxtaposed with a female nude suggesting a virginal St Cecilia, the patron saint of organ music. Jené's drawing, however, is not an illustration of the purity of music, but of its power, in the way Heinrich von Kleist described it in his novella *Die heilige Cäcilie oder die Gewalt der Musik* (St Cecilia or the Power of Music).[212] There, music drives one to madness, whereas for Jené it

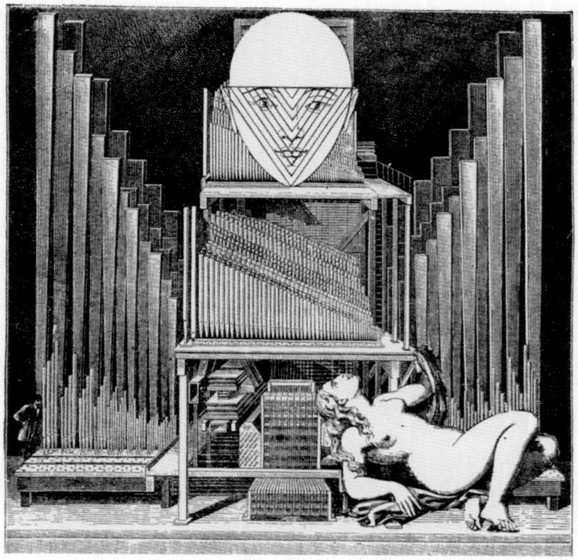

103 Max Ernst, *The Immaculate Conception*, 1929, collage, from *La Femme 100 têtes* (Paris, 1929).

leads to death, as suggested by the liquid seeping out of Jené's organ console – is it blood? Or, to use Celan's words, 'black milk'?

Jené's view of the organ dominating the image can be associated with the poem, whose whole linguistic development reminds one of the composition of a fugue,[213] frequently played on the organ. Celan's *Death Fugue* refers to the strictest of musical structures in its title and form. Wiedemann has analyzed the 'enormously artificial character' of it, which refers to traditional lyric but distances itself from it through interruption and paradox, finding the tradition to be no longer adequate. The function of the poem's form itself 'might be seen as a mirror for an industry of killing exactly thought through and brought to perfection', as a rejection of 'literary tradition' and 'musical music'.[214] Wiedemann indicates in addition that Celan included in *Death Fugue* contemporary reports from the Russian newspapers *Izvestia* and *Pravda*, closely relating the lines

> *er pfeift seine Juden hervor läßt schaufeln ein Grab in der Erde*
> *er befiehlt uns spielt auf nun zum Tanz*
>
> he whistles his Jews out in earth has them dig for a grave
> he commands us strike up the dance

to reports of Jews in the ghetto and the prisoners' orchestra in the camp of Janowska near Lemberg (Lviv).[215]

The intentionally ambiguous imagery of Celan's language, demonstrating the perversion of language by the Nazis, has a possible equivalent in the Surrealist transformation of the organ pipes into snakes. Snakes that Jené on his mask of Medusa in his 1943 pen drawing *Veil of Veronica* likened to curly hair.[216] Snakes that the man and concentration camp guard in Celan's *Death Fugue* 'plays with'. The poet was reminded at the same time of pigtails, as can be seen from his notes.[217] These can only be identified symbolically with the figure of Gretchen in Goethe's masterpiece *Faust* who, by way of a counterpoint to the other women's names in terms of feminine allegory, can be interpreted at the same time as the figure of Germania for the Nazis.[218] Celan distinguishes between her 'golden hair' and the 'ashen hair' of the Jewess 'Shulamith' (Song of Solomon 7:1). Jené on the other hand emphasizes the difference between the thick, black, squirming snakes and the few pale and smooth strands of hair on the chalky white skull in front of the console. One can make out the profile of a girl's head leaning over,[219] in Jené's images most often a sign of mourning,[220] which can now be taken, together with the poem, as an allegorical personification of the persecuted Jews. For both authors, snakes and hair are in opposition and yet nevertheless related to one another in a deadly association, on which there is a variation in Jené's version of the organ console: the ends of the shining organ pipes, sharpened like assault weapons against a dark background, point down to meet the frame of the wall behind the keyboard right above the head, which is leaning over towards the black puddle at the base of the ranks of pipes.

Jené's drawing evokes the impression of an epitaph, similar to what Celan refers to as a 'tombeau', a 'funerary monument' or the 'inscription on a grave'.[221] The silent image of the deadly sounds on the organ, in addition, calls to mind Celan's ideas about the Dance of Death.

The association between the poetic imagery and that of the drawing is unavoidable. Meanwhile, the question of the origin of the title *Death Fugue* cannot be settled unequivocally. According to the date given by Jené and his account, it could be that, under the influence of Celan's poems, he reviewed some of his ink drawings from the end of the war, since the prototype of the other drawing, *O Blume der Zeit* (Oh Flower of the Time), in Celan's volume of poems, did not originally have a title in 1945.[222] He made alterations, left out the right-hand half, and added a title using this line of the poem from the volume *Der Sand aus den Urnen*. Whether Celan helped select these two drawings that he later rejected is not clear. In any case he knew about the inclusion of a lithograph by Jené before it went to press.[223]

In his meeting with the poet, the painter may have associated his works from the previous years with Celan's poem. Did Celan at first consider that placing the drawing before *Death Fugue* was appropriate? Did he see himself as confirmed in changing the name from *Death Tango* to *Death Fugue*? Or did he want his work not to be associated with the Nazi dance culture but with serious music? It is reasonable to think that only after getting to know the poem did Jené make the drawing and that he later backdated it; one argument in favour of this is that its style is distinguishable from the other drawings in the album by the precise silhouetting of the view of the organ. This is, however, something again that can be explained in terms of a homage

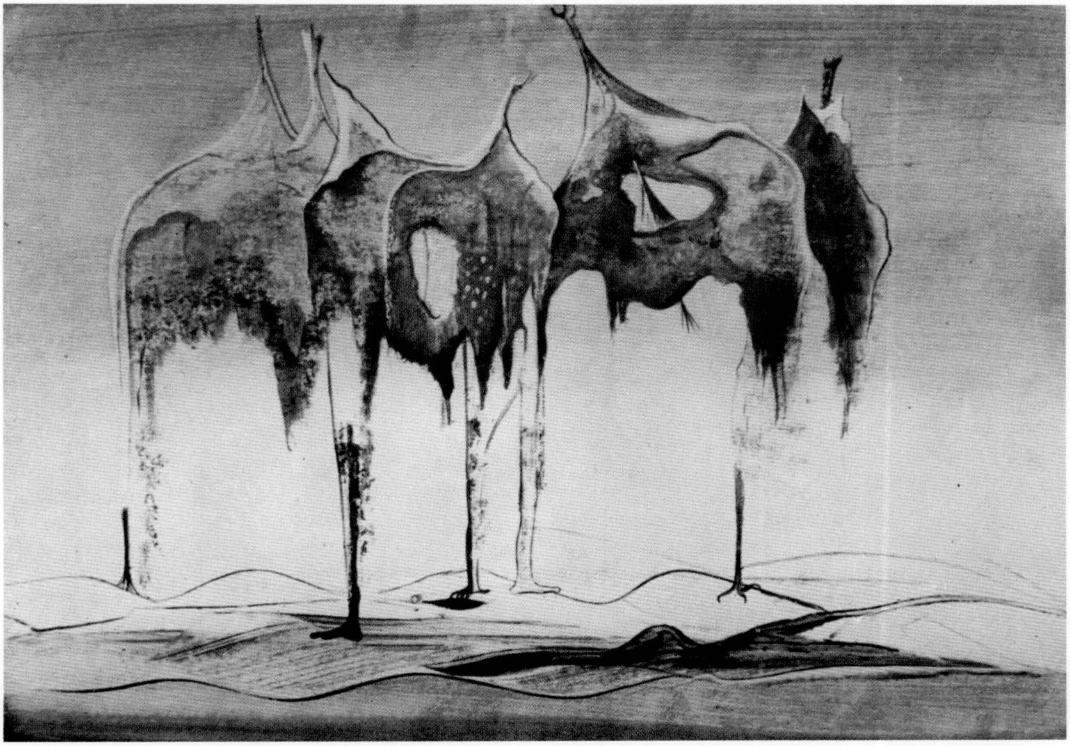

104 Edgar Jené, *The Red Sea Passes Over the Land*, 1949, painting (missing), from Paul Celan, *Edgar Jené* (Vienna, 1948).

to Max Ernst's collage novel. Quite apart from who decided and when, the dialogue between the two authors, celebrated for different reasons, led in 1948 within the short space of half a year in Vienna to the production of synaesthetic images referring to music while comprising texts, drawings and paintings about the murder of the Jews.

The Red Sea Passes Over the Land

In the volume he published with Jené's images, Celan commented on Jené's 1947 picture *The Red Sea Passes Over the Land* as the third of the four paintings (illus. 104).[224] The sea, which in the Jewish tradition had parted, making possible the exodus of the children of Israel out of Egypt, is shown as dangerous: it is flooding the land, leaving no hope of salvation. Celan, who must presumably have known the paintings as coloured originals, referred to it as 'The sea of blood passes over the land'. In his commentary he went on to say: 'The ghost of war haunts the lands on bare feet. It has talons like birds of prey or toes like a human being!' He continued his train of thought, sparked off by the surrealistic image with variations on a tent of blood, walls of blood and rags of blood, and finally a fountain of blood, 'which we can see our own reflections in, we the lost'.[225] Celan referred to the surrealistic shapes, situated the image in the context of the war that had just taken place and by the closing statement 'Edgar Jené's images know more' acknowledged the unending dialogue with the images.

4 Captured in One Picture

After the war, framed paintings in oils continued to enjoy a high status in the hierarchy of art. Unlike works in album format published in large numbers and mostly at a reasonable price, the framed oil painting needs a space in which to be publicly available. Painters fulfilled the requirements for concentrating artistically on a single rectangle by using motifs from other visual narratives such as barbed wire, chimneys and the representation of tormented people. They amplified these, however, by means of pictorial composition, choice of colour and, like Horst Strempel (see illus. 10) and Hans Grundig (see illus. 114), suggestions of the tradition of religious painting on panels. This sort of art in its various stylistic formulations was not free from political interference. From the start, the Soviet occupying power saw art policy as an essential part of their re-education of the Germans; one week after the end of the war, the Soviet governor of Berlin, General Berzarin, invited two hundred representatives of culture to his residence,[1] and the Kulturbund, licensed by the Soviet Military Administration (SMAD) to bring about a democratic renewal of Germany, was founded on 3 July 1945, one day before the Western Allies arrived in their sectors of the city.[2] The *Allgemeine Deutsche Kunstausstellung* (General German Art Exhibition) organized by the SMAD in October 1946 in Dresden still displayed art in various styles from the whole of Germany. The enquiry carried out into the public reaction to this, however, documented enraged responses to Expressionist and abstract art, providing a basis for the heated debate about Formalism and establishing the doctrine of Socialist Realism.[3]

Re-education through art was, for all those taking part, quite a straightforward undertaking, since modernism and everything associated with it was seen as controversial, not just by the Soviets. American congressmen in Washington too were opposed to their own contemporary art, regarding it as too left-wing.[4] The way it was received was also problematic: German young people, it was reported, responded particularly negatively to modernist figurative art and non-objective painting.[5]

The American military administration OMGUS[6] did not initially take art into account in relation to the 're-education' and 're-orientation' of the population. They concentrated on the mass media of press, radio and film. It was only spurred by competition with their communist adversaries in the Cold War and as a result of appeals by the German-born American Hellmut Lehmann-Haupt and the director of the Art Collecting Point in Wiesbaden Edith Appleton Standen, warning against the dangers of fascist organizations in the West, that the American occupying forces discovered fine art as an instrument of control in post-war German society.[7] By way of cautious invitation, a private group called 'Prolog' was discreetly set up in the American sector, to which Karl Hartung, Bernhard Heiliger, Carl Hofer, Gerhard Marcks, Margarethe Moll, Karl Schmidt-Rottluff and René Sintenis belonged, among others. In March 1947, with *Henry Koerner USA 1945–1947*, the first OMGUS-sponsored exhibition 'of American modernism' was mounted in post-war Germany.[8] While in Vienna Edgar Jené, the artist from the Saarland, attempted, with the short-lived support of Paul Celan, to promote Surrealism with a first exhibition in 1948,[9] Hilla Rebay, with the authority of OMGUS, put on the first exhibition of abstract art *Zeitgenòssische Kunst und Kunstpflese in den USA* (Contemporary Art and Art Cultivation in the USA) at the Kunsthalle in Karlsruhe.[10] This subtle continuation of American military policy by means of cultural exchange, prizes, bursaries and 'Care' packages can be seen as preempting ideas also pursued later by the CIA.

In April 1947 *Time* magazine wrote: 'Cheaper and easier to find than movies, galleries have become popular entertainment in Berlin.'[11] What was on display, however, was mainly the sort of thing that also appealed to public taste already before and during the Nazi period: still-lifes, landscapes, nudes and portraits in a naturalistic style. In the political environment of the occupation and the rebuilding of Germany, pictures produced about the murder of the Jews were few and far between. If we survey the works assembled here from the period 1945 to 1949, it is noticeable that apart from the Jewish Communist Lea Grundig, who was forced to live in Palestine between 1940 and 1948, and Dore Meyer-Vax, male artists especially made contributions and only left-wing ones engaged in portraying the subject-matter in the sense of showing what crimes had been committed. Düsseldorf in particular, with the exhibitions initiated by Werner Doede,[12] became a place where, alongside popular subjects like landscapes and portrait art and even within these genres, the public were made aware of the murder of the Jews. Otto Pankok and his surviving friends from the Junge Rheinland group, the Rheinische Sezession and the circle around 'Mutter Ey' exhibited their pictures on the persecution of the Jews and Sinti. These were focused on the perspective of the citizens of Düsseldorf towards their persecuted fellow human beings from that earlier time and were directed at the exhibition public of the present.

As people who had resisted the Nazi tyranny from right back in the 1930s, they were free after the end of the war, unlike the extremely vast number of opponents, to affirm only in retrospect their political views, to portray the crimes and – even if much less often – to comment on the murder of the Jews.

Edgar Jené: *The Camp, The Prisoners*

Jené had served as a translator in a POW camp. In his 1945 oil painting *The Camp* (illus. 106) he differentiated himself in Vienna from the critical realism of most of his contemporaries in Germany who turned their back on memories of the Nazi tyranny. It becomes clear, not just in comparison with his painting *The Prisoners* (illus. 105), dated 1941, that in his dream-like associations he was referring to the painful history physically encapsulated in the two pictures by the watchtowers and railway lines. Zoomorphic figures are advancing towards the viewer in isolation from one another, looking like nothing so much as skeletal scarecrows. The comparison between the two pictures related thematically and compositionally is revealing about the use of figures mutated into phantoms of terror, something Max Ernst had introduced in his 1937 painting of *The Angel of the Home or the Triumph of Surrealism*.[13] In this surreal way, Jené was able to emphasize the dehumanized treatment of the prisoners.

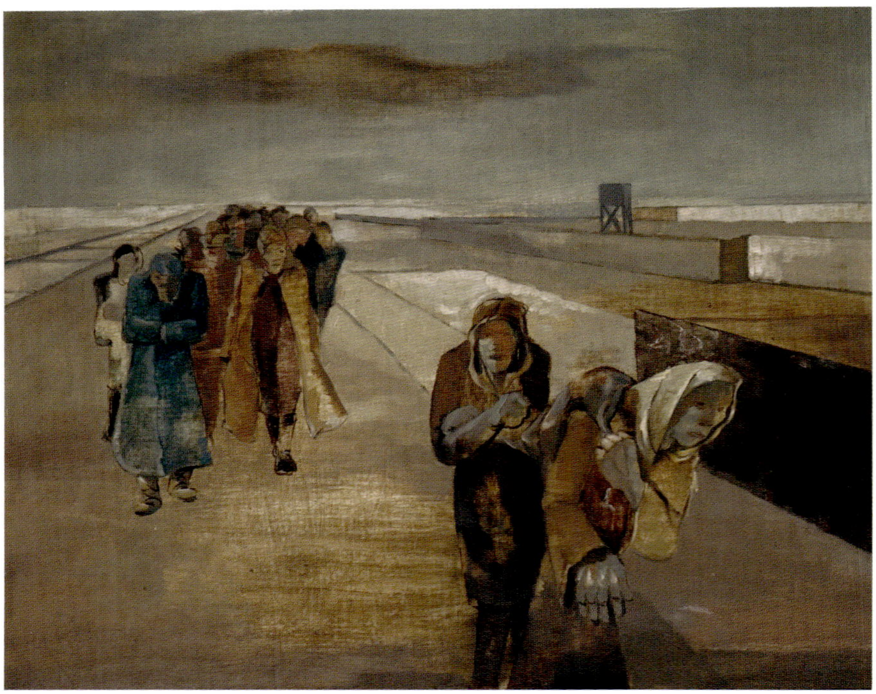

105 Edgar Jené, *The Prisoners*, 1941, oil on wood.

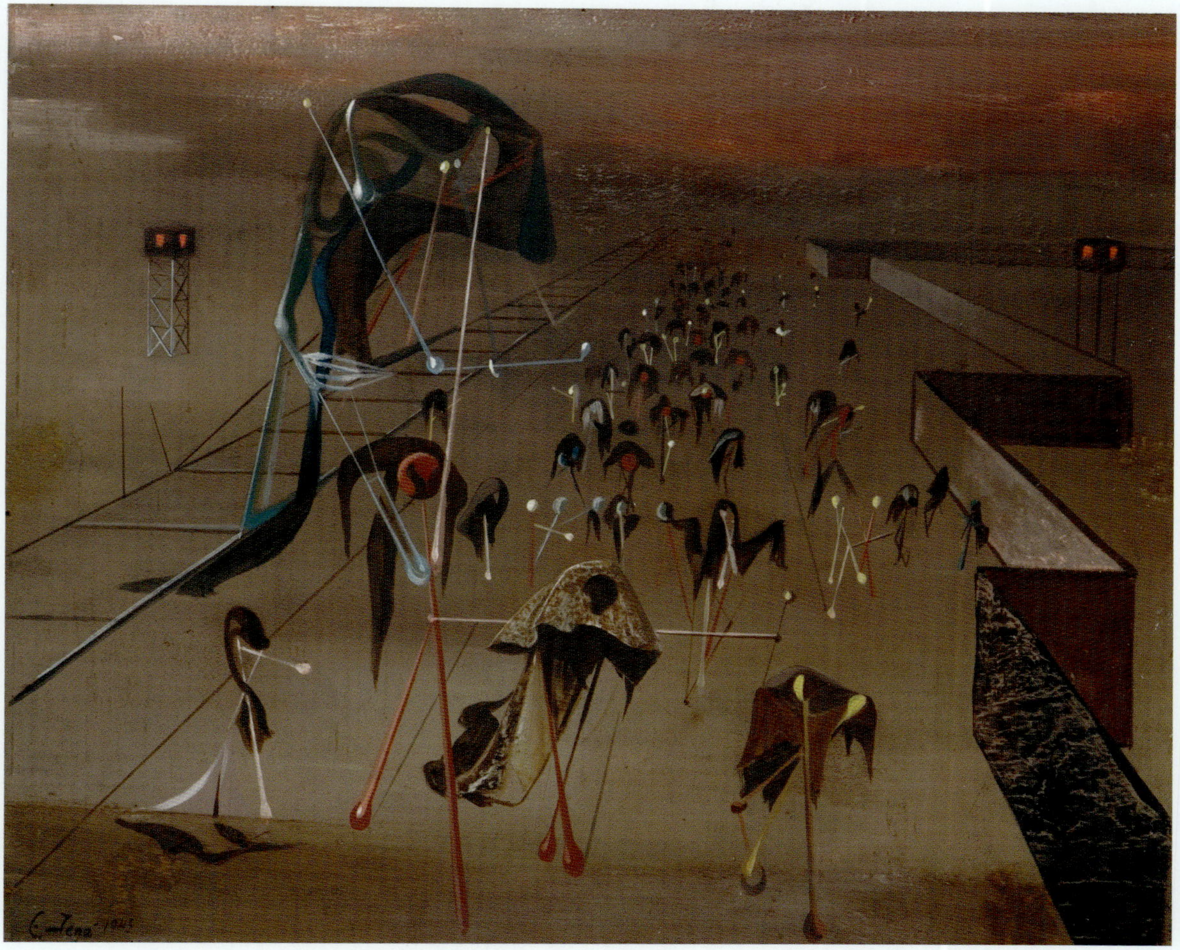

106 Edgar Jené,
The Camp, 1945,
oil on wood.

Otto Pankok: *Max and Alice Stern*

As he had done already in his memorial to the Sinti and homeless people (see illus. 128), in 1945 Otto Pankok produced a reminder of the dead Max and Alice Stern in a charcoal painting of the couple when alive (illus. 107), an ancient theme in the history of remembrance of the dead.[14] In the charcoal drawing, he was honouring his older friend and colleague. The Impressionist painter from Düsseldorf came from a Jewish family, took part in the First World War[15] and married the 'Aryan' Helene Burnier after the introduction of the (Nuremberg) Race Laws. She stood by him during the Nazi period despite hostility, and when he was killed in a cellar in a bombing raid on Düsseldorf in 1943, having been refused admittance to an air-raid shelter as he was a Jew, she took her own life the very same year. For his drawing of the deceased, Pankok made use of a photograph of them from 1930 (illus. 108). While he depicted the carpet and the pictures on the walls – presumably the painter's own – he altered the atmosphere of the sitting room considerably. This is certainly in line with his statement, in the foreword to the first exhibition in Düsseldorf of his work in 1946, that he could no longer bring himself to paint a normal citizen: 'He has no background any more, just scenery.'[16] In the drawing after the photo, Pankok reduced the number of chairs with expensively carved backs, made the table emptier and flattened it out. He isolated Alice Stern and showed her as being older and more emaciated and looking into space, and placed Max Stern like an isolated monument in the foreground, his left leg visible instead of hers. Both of them are sitting in the middle of nowhere, behind and between an armchair and the round table. Max Stern has put his lower arm on top of the table. Upon it, next to a blank sheet of paper, is lying just one closed book with a star on it, the black family album. By drawing the star on it, Pankok was once more indicating that he was not going along with the Nazis' murderous use of this sign but employing it to expose the malice at the heart of the system. By transforming the photograph into the charcoal drawing, Pankok suspended the passing moment, death itself in photography, through the act of painting and captured those depicted at that moment in time in the sitting room for all time in his drawing: a memorial for their friends and a testament to the deadly violence inflicted on one's neighbours.

Mathias Barz: *Inferno*

Together with his friend Pankok, who exhibited nine charcoal drawings on the persecution of the Jews, Mathias Barz displayed his large oil painting *Inferno*[17] (illus. 109) in 1946 at the newly founded Rheinische Sezession in Düsseldorf. It was only a year since he had been identified by the Nazis as a

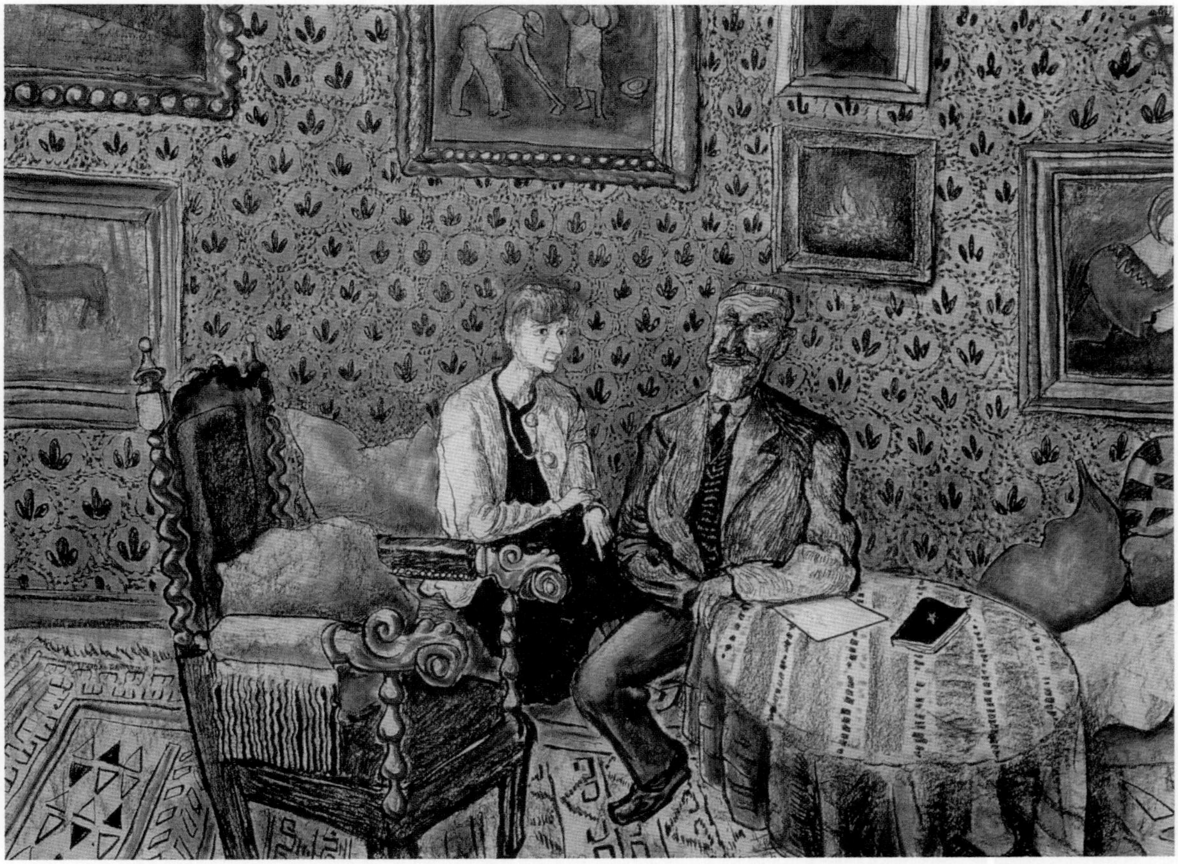

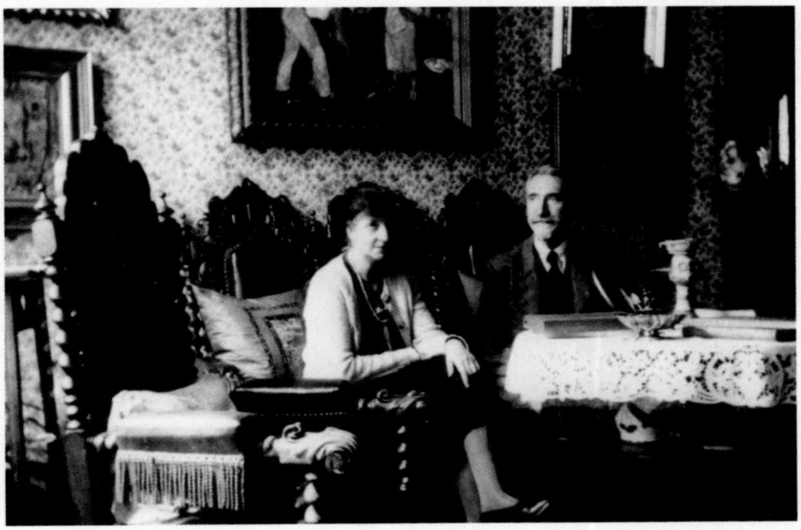

107 Otto Pankok, *Max and Alice Stern*, 1945, charcoal on paper.

108 *Max and Alice Stern*, c. 1930, photograph.

member of the Communist Party, along with his Jewish wife, the actress and singer Brunhilde Stein. Having been banned from performing, she survived maltreatment at the hands of the Nazi tyranny, and the dangers of living in hiding and had returned to Düsseldorf.[18] Barz's painting may have been completed in 1946 despite the overpainting mentioned several times in the literature; one thing that is certain is that it is signed and dated. It was exhibited in the Kunstverein für die Rheinlande und Westfalen in Düsseldorf along with other works by him and those of his painter friend Karl Schwesig, and it was on sale for 2,000 Deutschmarks.[19] It was finally acquired sometime between 1982 and 1985 by the Düsseldorf City Museum after an exhibition of his works there.[20]

What we are confronted with in the painting is a procession of people belonging to all age groups and wearing the yellow Jewish star, moving from top left towards bottom right.[21] Beneath Christ on the Cross, drawn larger than life, they are walking towards the viewer. With this direct confrontation between the crowd of human beings in the image and the viewing public faced with it, Barz seems to be making reference to the 1889 painting *The Entry of Christ into Brussels*[22] by the Belgian James Ensor and even more to his 1896 etching *Death Pursuing the Human Herd*,[23] even if Barz is not holding up a mirror to the art public with any masked faces. Much more, he was trying through his representation to draw attention to those who had been condemned to extermination. Across the full extent of the picture Barz painted reddish-blue flecks in the style of late Impressionism[24] which, along with the darting brushstrokes for the clothing of the figures at the front, seem to suggest that they are passing through a sea of flames, an *Inferno*. On the right-hand side of the picture above a collection of skulls we again see the Nazis' Jewish star, transparent here, however, and particularly large, like an official stamp applied to the whole painting. The way it is silhouetted in black corresponds to that of Christ looming over everything. With his arms bent upright it is reminiscent of the artist's sketch for the destroyed 1922–3 picture *The XV Station*,[25] and the charcoal drawing by his friend Otto Pankok[26] from the 1933 cycle about the Passion, the title of which repeats the last words of Christ (Mark 15:34): 'My God, my God, why hast thou forsaken me?' The more pronounced this pictorial reference to Pankok's portrayal of Christ as accusatory becomes in the final version, the stronger the suggestion of the association between the sufferings of the Jewish people and the crucified 'King of the Jews' (Mark 15:12). This comparison is probably not to be seen in opposition, as in the case of Ketz, but as the representation of Christ's compassion, with the Jews. In the 1980 Düsseldorf catalogue on Barz, the relevant interpretation reads: 'The procession of tormented Jews, above them, as one of them and suffering like them, Christ on the Cross', while the *Westdeutsche Zeitung* of 27 July 1955 described it as a 'Crucifixion procession'.

Barz's attempt to link the crucified Christ to the suffering of the Jews, even if noticeably altered, continues the viewpoint of the left-wing avant-garde

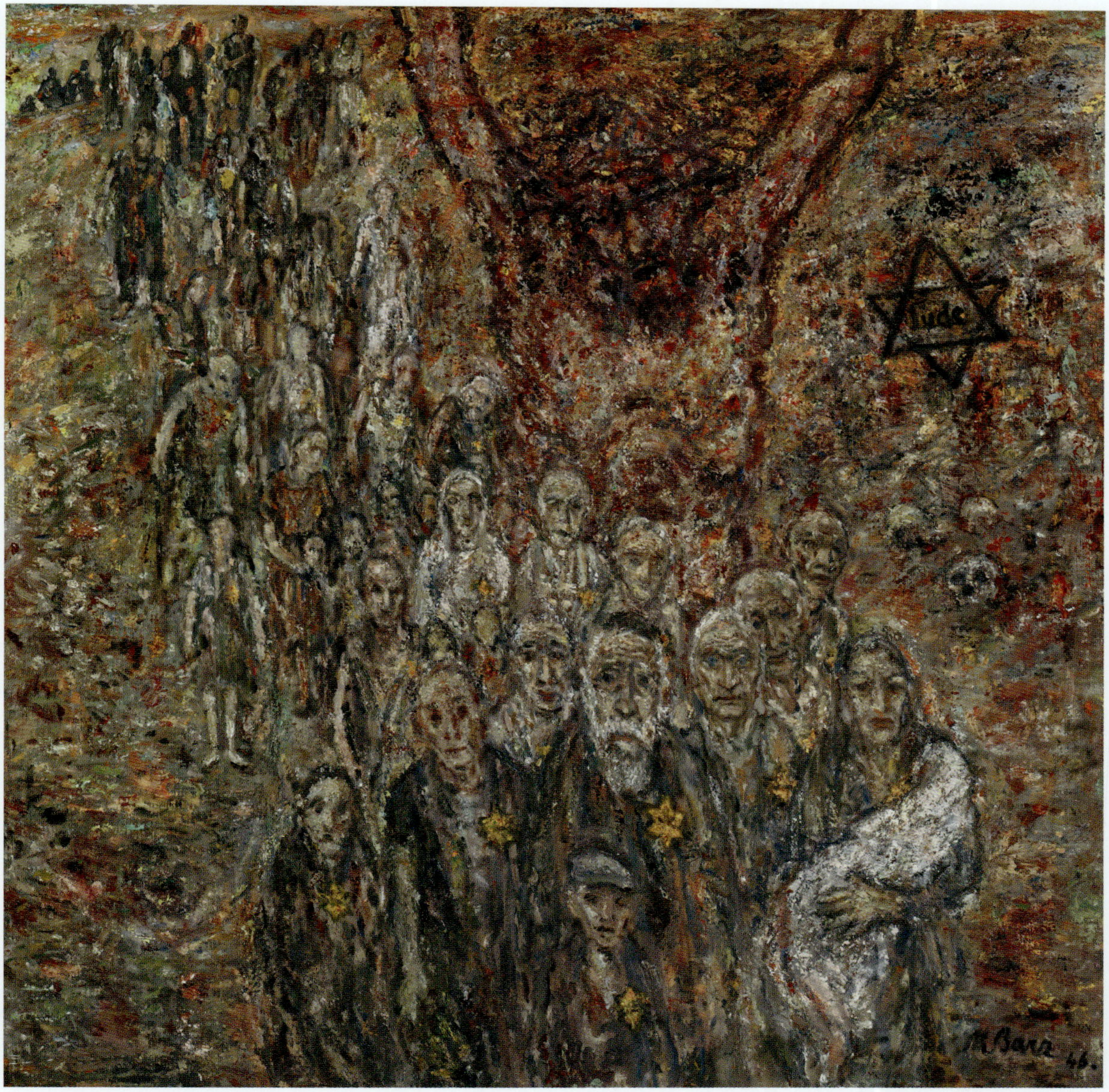

109 Mathias Barz, *Inferno*,
1946, oil on wood.

of the 1920s Junge Rheinland[27] movement after 1945. In the earlier period Barz, who came from a strictly religious family, had painted *The XV Station* as a warning after the First World War. It was intended to show 'Christ on the Cross in the trenches'. 'In front of him a soldier who has been shot, in the background tied to a stake, one who has been officially shot as a conscientious objector. Soldiers exercising on a barrack square, a black, white and red flag, a malnourished child and a brothel scene.'[28] The Nazis had confiscated the picture in 1933 and publicly burned it on the Town Hall square in Düsseldorf. In the new *Inferno*, Barz now put the crucifix into the picture, not as a general warning against military violence, but as an accusation of the murder of the Jews in the war of extermination.

Hermann Bruse

Hunger March

Hunger March (illus. 110), which Hermann Bruse[29] painted between 1945 and 1946, portrays those who had been punished for their convictions with torture, imprisonment in camps and death during the Nazi period. Bruse had joined the German Communist Party in 1932 and after it was banned in 1933 his studio in Magdeburg became an important centre for the Party gone underground for a year; as a result he was condemned to two years in the state prison at Luckau. As a member of the Saefkow resistance group,[30] he was rearrested in 1944, and it was only the ending of the war that saved him from certain death. The column of exhausted figures who are barely managing to keep upright accords with the socialist ideas of art that Bruse later represented as a lecturer at the Pädagogische Hochschule of the Humboldt University in Berlin. Art had to serve the base and continually ask itself the question how it could help 'to really shape our age'.[31] In the first few years after the liberation, he commented accusingly on the process of law during the Nazi period and showed the consequences of the crimes and the war in images of ruins, grief, madness and hunger.[32] With the paintings *Hunger March* and *Ecce Homo*, he reminded the world of the maltreatment and death in the camps.

The picture *Hunger March* does not exactly reveal whether here it is a variation on the theme of a labour column in the camp,[33] or is intended to illustrate to the public once more the experience of the death marches[34] from the camp. One thing is clear, however: it testifies to the constantly present solidarity of the prisoners, which also included the dying (see the text from the competition for the memorial at Auschwitz, pp. 187–9.). None of the prisoners is wearing a yellow star; all one can see on the clothing of the two figures in the front row are red patches identifying them as so-called 'Politicals'. The claim to leadership advanced by the communist resistance is clearly evident. Bruse did not refer to other groups of prisoners. In his discussion of the exhibition *150 Jahre soziale Strömungen in der bildenden Kunst*

110 Hermann Bruse, *Hunger March*, 1945–6, oil on hardboard.

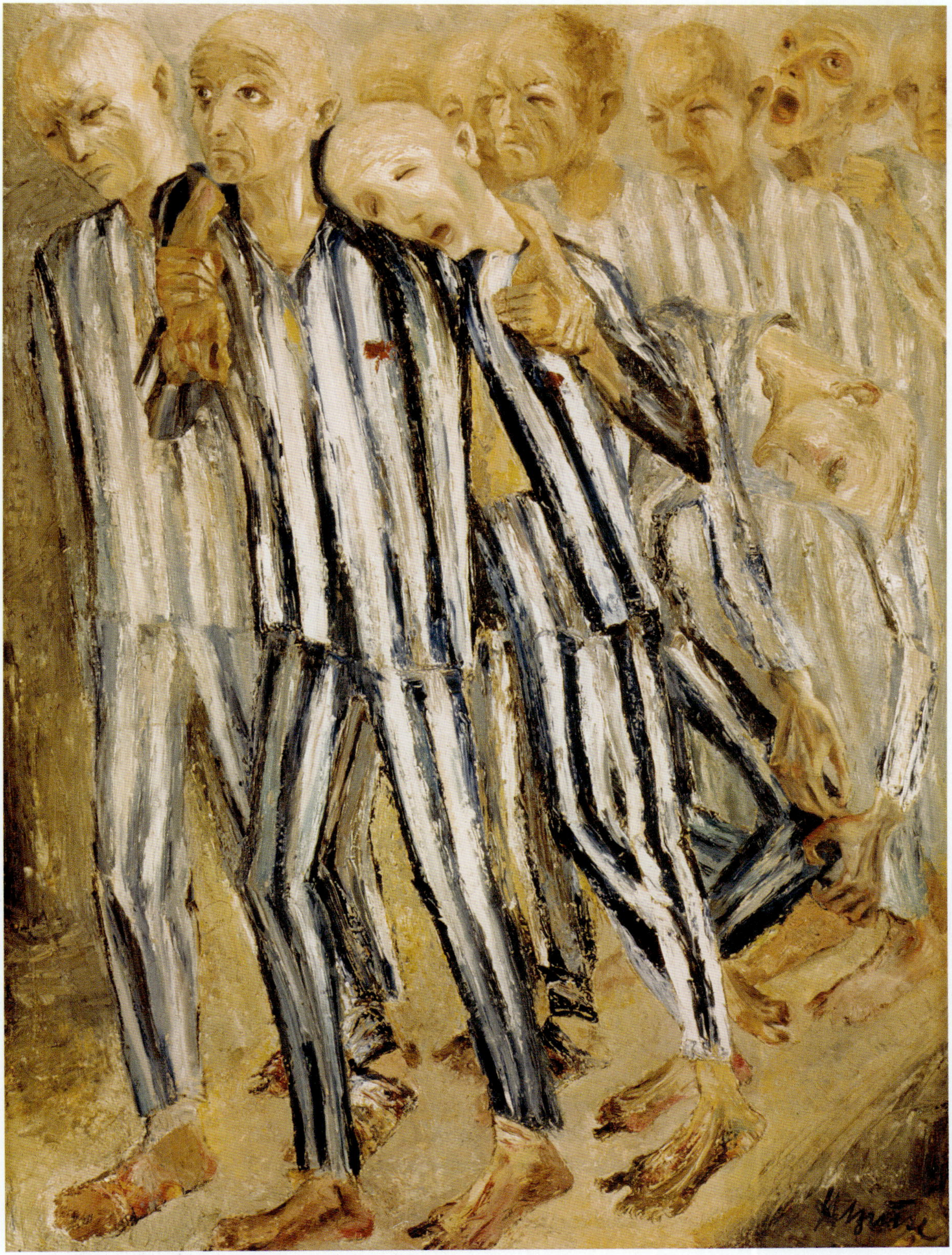

(150 Years of Social Trends in the Fine Arts) organized by the Freie Deutsche Gewerkschaftsbund (FDGB: Free German Trades Union Association) in 1947, under the heading 'Do current affairs harm art?', Heinz Lüdecke called it 'a convincing and direct indictment'.[35]

Ecce Homo

Bruse was even clearer in his accusation against the Nazis in his painting *Ecce Homo* (illus. 111). An emaciated corpse lying with its legs drawn up fixes in the memory the torments of those who died in the camps. Bruse's painting closely resembles the photographs of the dead in the liberated camps.[36] Here, however, the dead man is shown from a perspective of extraordinary humility, seen presumably on one's knees from ground level. Behind his head, Bruse made the barbed wire look like a gloriole of stars across the horizon, adding to the impression of a sacred image.

Henry Koerner: *My Parents II*

The 'first and the last time that OMGUS[37] organized an art show that dealt in some way with the Holocaust', Cora C. Goldstein stated in her discussion of 'American Visual Propaganda in Occupied Germany',[38] was the exhibition of the paintings and drawings by the Jewish artist from Vienna Henry Koerner, held in Berlin at the Haus am Waldsee in 1947.[39] Koerner had fled to the U.S. in 1939, continued to work there as a trained graphic artist, was drafted into the U.S. Army in 1943 and, via this draft, he was naturalized as a U.S. citizen in 1944. Only when he returned to Europe did he become aware that, apart from two members, his entire family had been murdered in the German extermination camps. After drawing at the Nuremberg trials in his capacity as officer in the Office of Strategic Services, the American military government delegated him to their Berlin HQ where, in his spare time, he not only made drawings but produced oil paintings about his history and showed his actual impression of the city to the Berlin public. His pictures, including his painting *My Parents II*[40] (illus. 112), attracted considerable attention.[41] The exhibition had been prompted by the HQ finding itself in competition with the cultural policy that the Soviets were already promoting in Germany[42] and by its aim of encouraging artists to turn their backs on Nazi painting.

Koerner had trained in the Graphische Lehr- und Versuchsanstalt in Vienna in order to be employed in the studio of Viktor Theodor Slama, who had specialized in political posters for the Social Democrats and Communists. In New York, while acting as a poster-designer and then in the military, he met socially critical artists like Ben Shahn and Bernard Perlin, representatives of precisely the kind of art that, in the exhibition travelling around Europe *Advancing American Art*, Republican congressmen had banned as being too socially critical and left-wing. But Koerner did not just get to

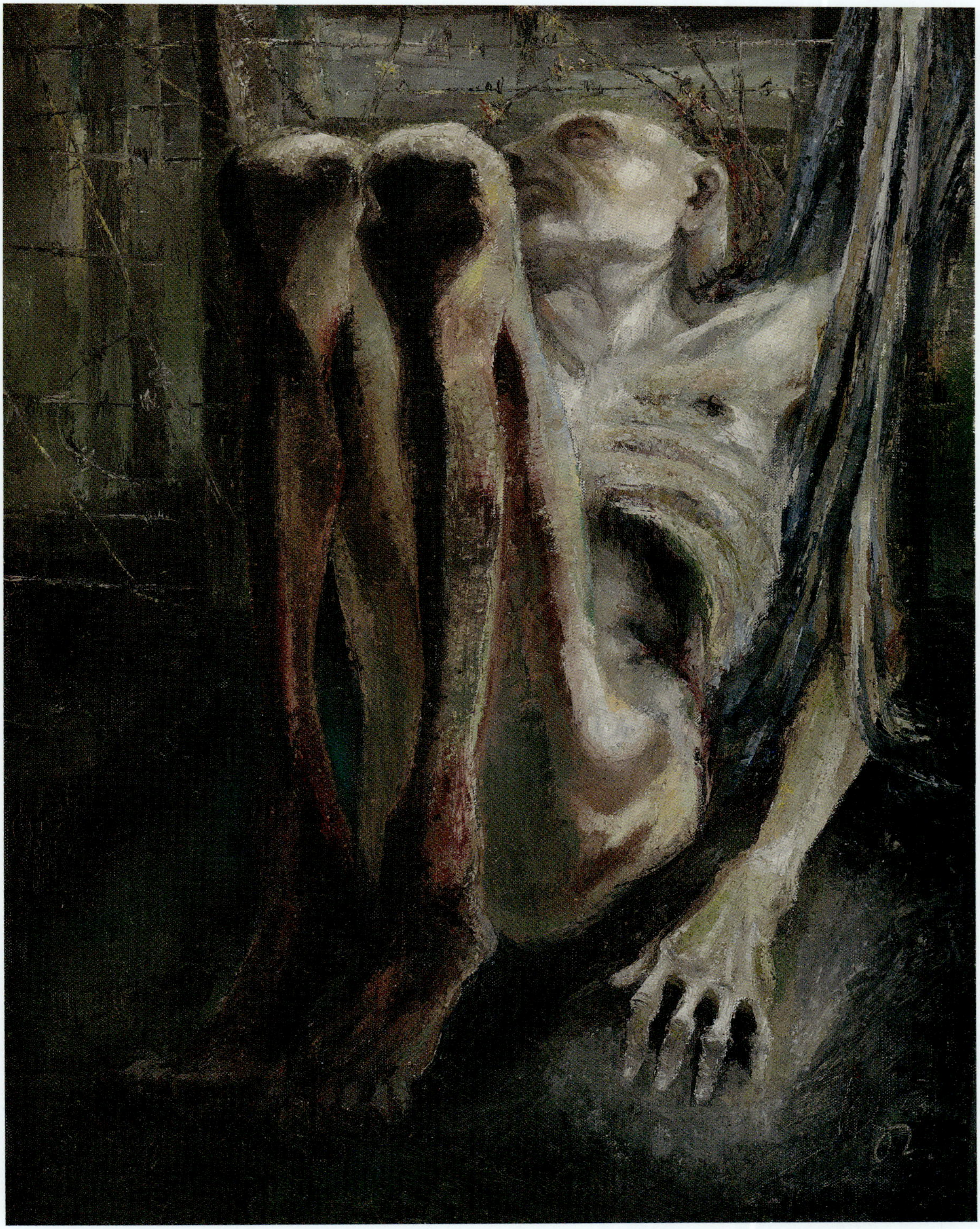

111 Hermann Bruse, *Ecce Homo*, 1948, oil on canvas.

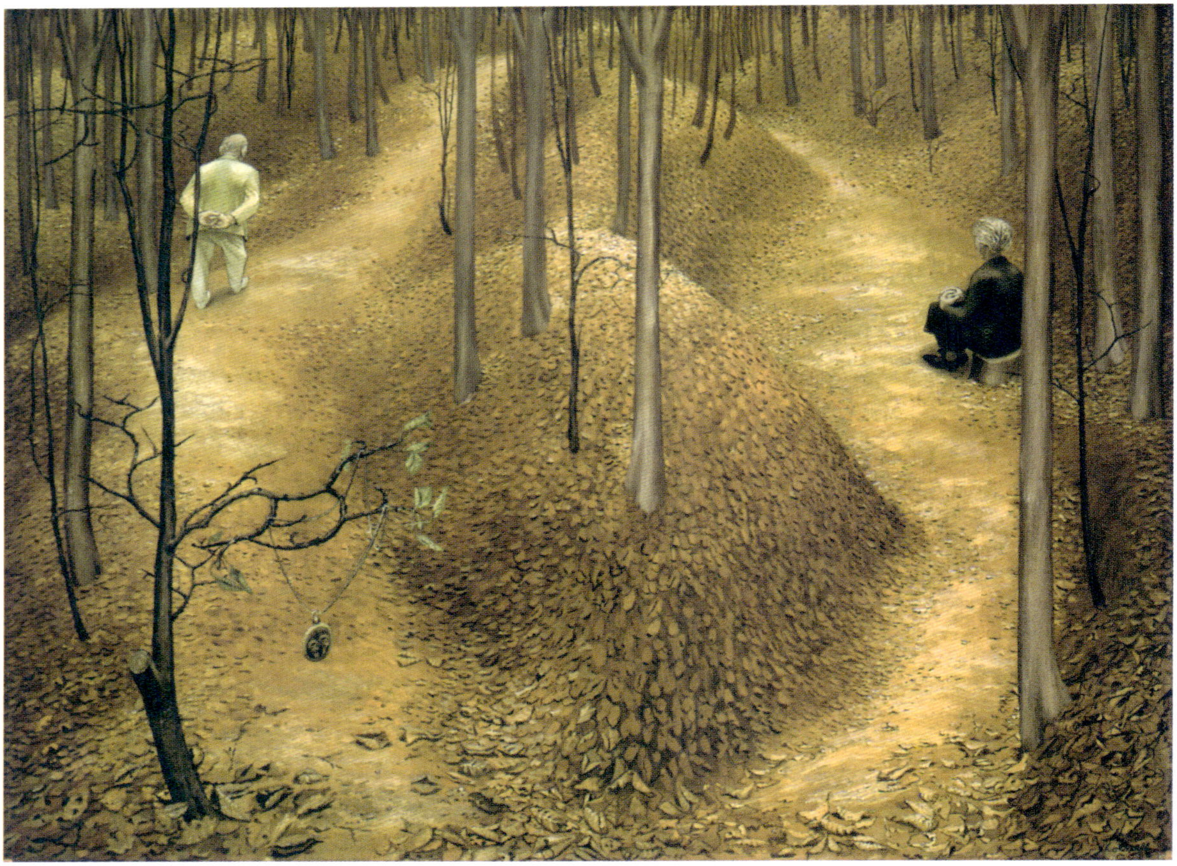

112 Henry Koerner, *My Parents* II, 1946, oil on hardboard.

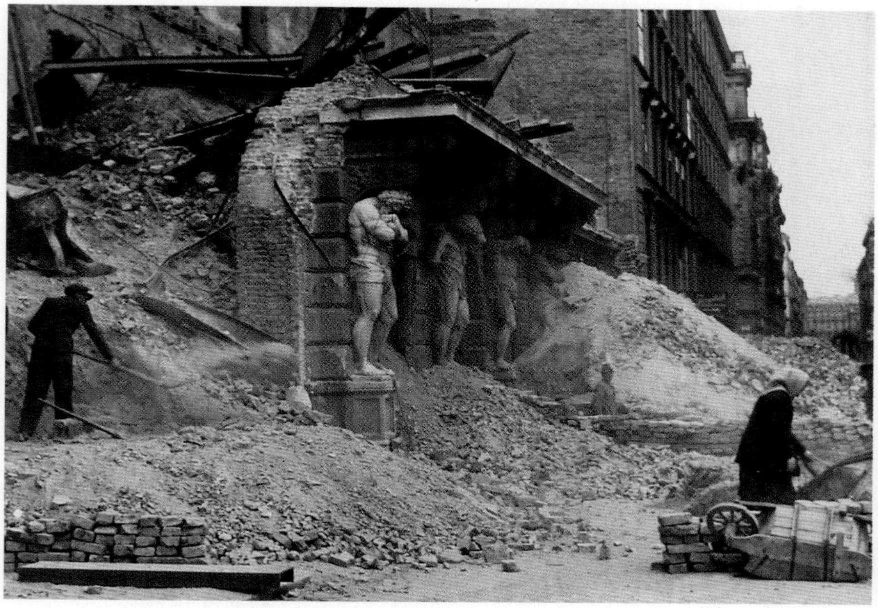

113 Henry Koerner, *Ruins on Schillerplatz*, Vienna, 1946, photograph.

know these artists. His style of painting, with his figures appearing rather stocky in a landscape shown as through a fish-eye lens, also reveals his study of the American regional painters such as Thomas Hart Benton, who had devoted himself during the world economic crisis to recording the values of life on the land in the Midwest of America. Some of them, who tended towards Surrealism in the way they represented figures, are said to belong to the so-called Magic Realists,[43] a description that has also been applied to Koerner. In the picture of his parents, Koerner used his artistic knowledge of narrative figurative painting from the American art scene to recall his family, who were murdered by the Nazis in the landscape of the country of his birth. His statement about it was quoted, not in the Berlin catalogue, but in a two-page article in *Life* magazine on 10 May 1948 along with three colour illustrations: 'I helped my parents to walk once more in the beloved Vienna woods. And I hung the locket with its photo of their children on a tree where their ways parted.'

In the painting, Koerner tried to breathe life back into his parents on their diverging paths through the brown woods of autumn with all the leaves lying on the ground.[44] At the same time, with the piles of leaves reminding one of the piles of rubbish in a photo of the Schillerplatz in Vienna (illus. 113), suggesting a burial mound, this fictional scene evokes the memories of the murder of two generations of the Koerner family. This is particularly noticeable owing to the separated parents being turned away from one another and the medallion, hanging on a branch at the front on the left, with the images of the artist and his murdered brother.

Unlike American reviews of Koerner's exhibition, the German-language catalogue contains no personal details about the artist. As Goldstein discovered through research, art criticism in the German press too, for example Edwin Redslob in *Der Tagesspiegel*,[45] did not mention his family history.[46] Therefore most of the visitors to the exhibition were unaware of the cause of the melancholy autumnal mood in this picture. Only those who knew from the weekly magazine *Der Spiegel*[47] that Koerner's parents 'had been killed for "racial" reasons', could recognize this painting in the exhibition as the bringing to life of the dead Jews. This is comparable to what Pankok had done in another way in a charcoal painting of the married couple Stern (see illus. 107). *Neues Deutschland* of 7 May 1947 had nevertheless mentioned Koerner's painting of his parents, admittedly ignoring the remembrance of the dead and instead interpreting it as 'the loneliness . . . to which people condemn one another today'.

Even on the occasions when reminders of the murder of the Jews appeared in the art scene, it was possible to overlook them, pass them by or say nothing about them. The author C. L.[48] had already succeeded in doing, in his art-historically learned article printed in the catalogue, what Redslob managed to do in his review, that is, to avoid any mention of recent German history. C. L. wrote from a purely artistic point of view about the problem of abstract or objective painting, praising the 'power of the objects' in Koerner's painting and comparing his involvement with the 'uncannily dramatic' to films and literature, without saying a single word about *My Parents* and the many other pictures that by their very titles can be taken as referring to the present.[49]

Hans Grundig: *To the Victims of Fascism 2*

Hans Grundig was imprisoned for five years in a concentration camp. In *To the Victims of Fascism 2* of 1946 (illus. 114), he most definitely wanted to honour the dead, using the traditional technique of fine art painting, a sacramental gold background and the emotional form of the predella of an altar painting, calling to mind the way Grünewald painted the recumbent body of Christ in the Isenheim Altar. Grundig wrote in 1947:

> I wanted to paint it as wonderfully and beautifully as I was able to do. I wanted to paint it so impressively that everyone would be moved by the power of the silent face, by the situation of the poor tormented body . . . I wanted to encompass this shattered wonderful humanity with all the splendour we humans are capable of. I decided it had to be in pure gold, so that is what I did. This is how they now come over in their impressive solemnity, linked to the raw beauty of the force of nature that is Death. I do not know whether I am right to have done it like that.[50]

With the framed lateral format of the painting, Hans Grundig lent traditional dignity to the epitaph in memory of those lying dead, unlike for

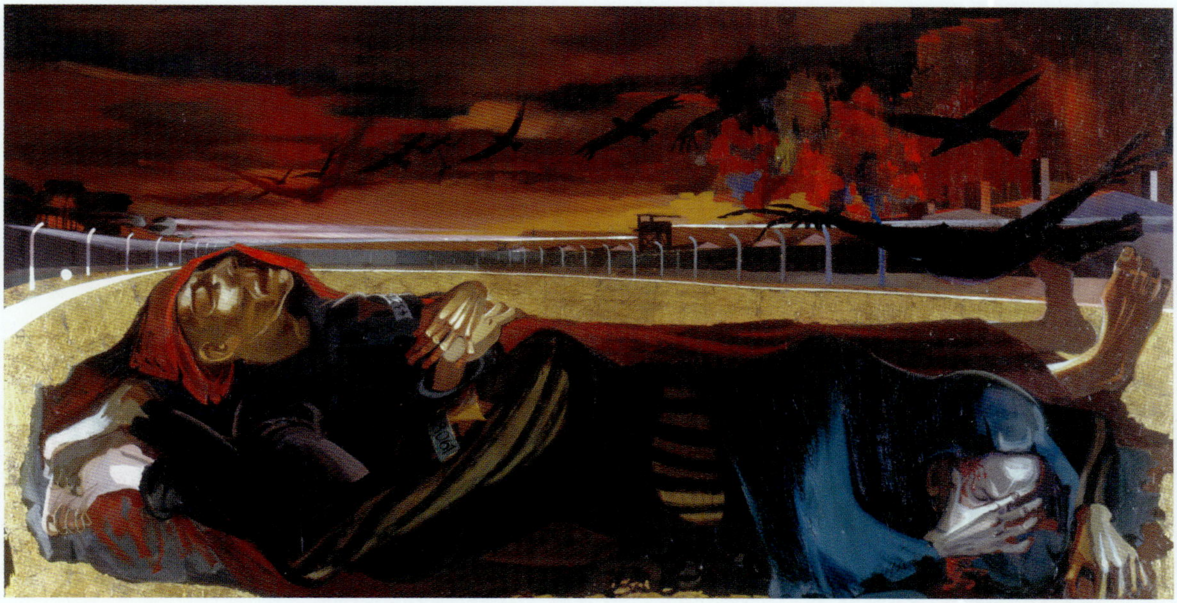

114 Hans Grundig, *To the Victims of Fascism 2*, 1947, oil on hardboard.

example the 1945 drawing by Zoran Music from Dachau.[51] In the second version,[52] above the red angle of the upper thigh of the nearer of the two dead bodies, he painted a yellow triangle, the badge of the Jewish political prisoners of the concentration camp until the middle of 1944.[53] Below this is placed the concentration camp number that Grundig had to wear as a prisoner at Sachsenhausen.[54] Fortress walls and barbed wire surround the dead prisoners, who are shown larger than life and slightly bowed. The one nearer the front, as an 'imprisoned fighter',[55] is wearing prison clothing and the one at the back is highlighted by a red cloth around his head against the gold background. A large crow from a black flock against a fiery red sky appears to be swooping down onto the dead body on the right of the picture. Grundig in the oil painting heightened the record of death in the concentration camp into a modern devotional image that does not render grief visible as an allegory like war memorials in the West,[56] but leaves mourning up to the viewer. The picture is dedicated at the bottom to his three friends who were likewise active in the communist resistance: Christel Beham and Fritz Schulze,[57] who were murdered by the Nazis, and the artist Helen Ernst.[58] Associating himself with the group of the dead by the use of his own number can be likened to bearing witness, as Giorgio Agamben defined it, 'to the taking up, in one's own language, of the position of the one who has lost it'.[59] The painting fulfils Grundig's role of bearing witness by the (im)possible association of the surviving painter with those who can no longer bear witness, because they are murdered witnesses. Even if Grundig talks of the 'force of nature' that is Death and of raw 'Beauty', his picture shows that those being honoured did not die a natural death but were victims of the murderous system of German fascism.

Dore Meyer-Vax: *Death Mosaic*

One artist who formed an extension to Hans Grundig's group of those who had been maltreated in the concentration camps was Dore Meyer-Vax, with her 1947–51 oil painting *Death Mosaic* (illus. 115), showing a dead mother with her dead children. Even though Meyer-Vax placed the dead bodies into an urban landscape of destruction, she was nevertheless making a direct reference to Grundig's imagery with the positioning of the dead bodies, the dominant blue of the clothing and the red cloth around the woman's head.

The work illustrates the close association between Meyer-Vax and Hans Grundig, whom she knew from her study under Carl Hofer in Berlin. It is a homage to her friend, feeding into the many works in which the female artist described the suffering of women and children as a result of fascism,[60] something that she committed herself to opposing for the whole of her life. It is not possible to say whether Meyer-Vax, in her works indicating that they take Nazism as their subject,[61] was referring to the persecution of the Jews. As a woman and a left-wing artist, she did not belong to the canon of West German art history, and only the East German Verband der bildenden Künste, the Union of Fine Artists, according to its president Lea Grundig, gave her as the first West German female artist the opportunity to display her work in a retrospective.[62] Her friendship with Felix Nussbaum,[63] which lasted all through the war, will therefore have to stand as sufficient evidence that she had not forgotten the suffering of the Jews. *Death Mosaic* is nevertheless a contribution to the generalization in West Germany of the victims in the figure of the dead mother and child.

Karl Schwesig

As a Communist, a member of the Junge Rheinland group and a co-founder of the Rheinische Sezession, Karl Schwesig found himself subject to persecution by the SA (Storm Troopers) immediately after the Nazis' seizure of power. In a number of cycles, he illustrated his maltreatment in the 1933 *Schlegelkeller*[64] and his internment between 1940 and 1943 in the camps at St Cyprien, Gurs, Noé and Nexon in France after his escape from Düsseldorf to Belgium. In Gurs he drew his own series of postage stamps on the white borders of sheets of French postage stamps. These formed a contrast to the nationalist slogans on the stamps, such as *Liberté* showing a view through the barbed wire of the camp huts,[65] or changed the allegory of Liberty into 'an old Jewish woman with a staff in her hand'.[66] In the tiny waistcoast pocket notebooks which he invented and which he managed to smuggle out of the camp to Switzerland, he drew for example the series *The Geneva Non-intervention*, which survived in his later, 1948 drawing[67] with the handwritten explanation:

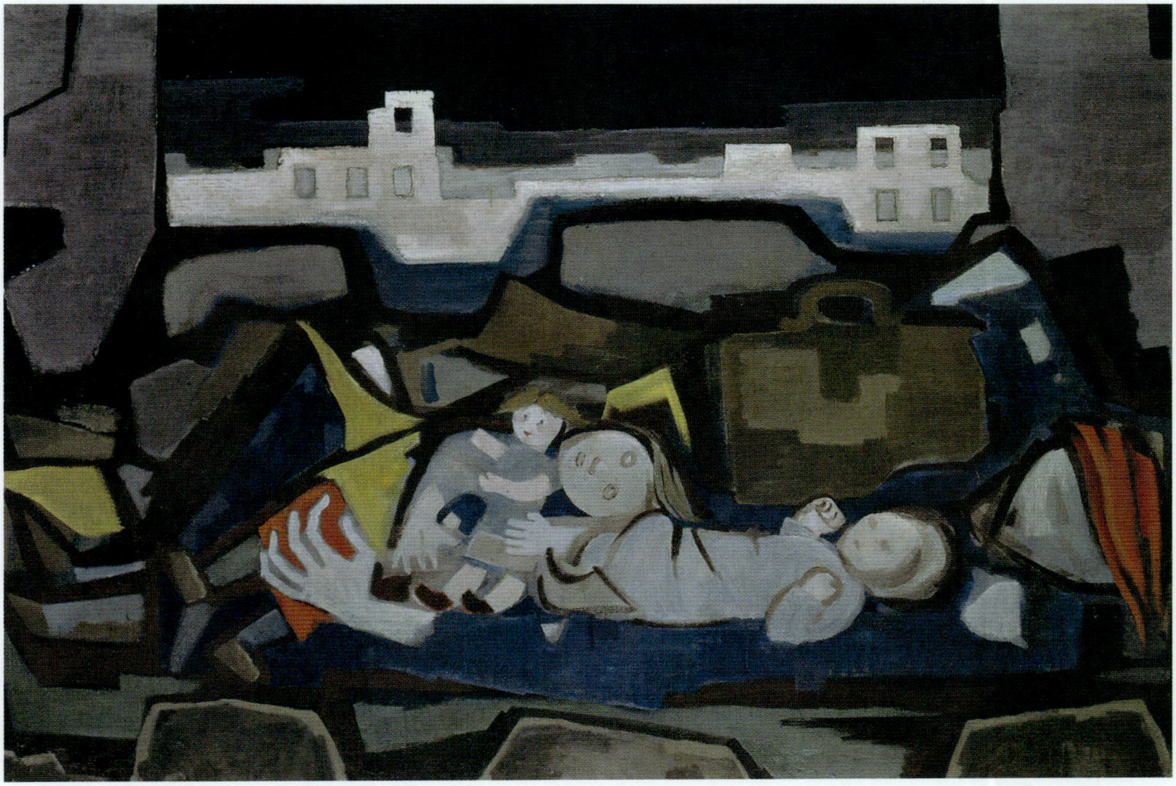

115 Dore Meyer-Vax, *Death Mosaic*, 1947–51, oil on hardboard.

> Camp Noé (Haute Garonne) concentration camp of the Vichy government. Along with the frail old Jewish people from Baden, those vegetating here included Spaniards mutilated in the war defending their republic against Hitler, Mussolini and Franco. I shared their fate from 1940–43.

Twenty-eight miniatures with Spanish captions illustrate the everyday struggle of the Spanish fighters, while the 29th drawing, REPUBLICA ESPANOLA, shows the torso of the Venus de Milo among the miserable figures, 'as she hasn't any arms', as he himself explained (p. 96). He illustrated the lives of these 'freedom fighters without legs'[68] once more in 1948–9 in etchings based on drawings the size of a matchbox, as the cycle *Les Inutiles*, which had to wait until 1981 to be edited by Galerie Remmert and Barth from the work he left behind after his death.[69]

Jewish Infirmary at Noé

When, in the winter of 1948, Schwesig had over 200 missing drawings and watercolours returned to him from his time in the camps, he also planned to develop the small drawings into twelve large paintings, along with the etchings for the *Inutiles*. It is not clear whether they were to be grouped under a common heading. Four pictures have survived: *At Work (Noé Camp)*, *Men Mutilated in War at Noé Camp*, *Grabbing for Bread (Noé Camp)*[70] and *Jews in*

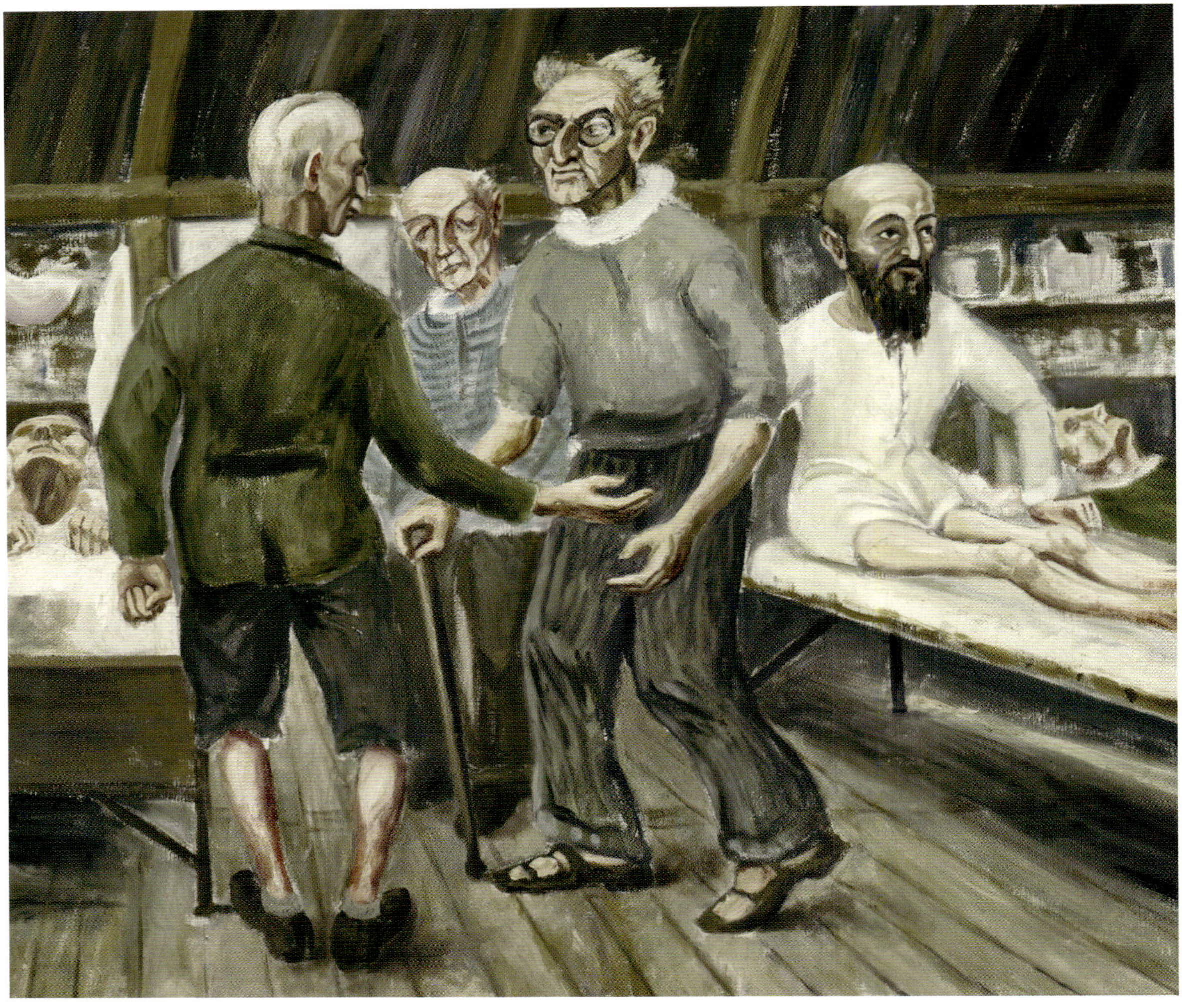

116 Karl Schwesig, *Jewish Infirmary at Noé*, 1947–8, oil on canvas.

Conversation (Noé Camp). In the literature this painting is also referred to under the much more accurate title *Jewish Infirmary at Noé* (illus. 116).[71] With crude brushstrokes, it shows in the middle a group of three elderly men in conversation in a camp hut made of wooden planks, surrounded on the left and right by old fellow prisoners in bed. While the sick man with his eyes closed on the left appears to be already dead, the man on the right is sitting upright in bed and is a lot less close to death than the one lying flat. In these 'sickness' images of the men in various states, this oil painting captures the dying of the old Jews in Noé.

Jewish Women

Fairly unusually in the way art has dealt with Jewish history, Schwesig also took notice of old Jewish women.[72] Attached to the collection of his drawings about the camps,[73] the literature includes two illustrations of ink brush drawings: *Jewish Women from Baden in Noé Camp* (illus. 117) and *Jewish Women with a Child in the Camp* (illus. 118). Schwesig produced them after the end of the war 'around 1948'. It is unclear whether they represent preparatory images for a later picture in the planned cycle of paintings and were therefore to be seen as being on the same level as the oil painting of the men in the *Jewish Infirmary*, or as individual studies intended to document his observations in the camp for the post-war public. With almost the accuracy of caricatures, he shows four Jewish women of varying ages who appear to be promenading in civilian clothing, with a stick and an umbrella, in front of barbed wire and a guard keeping watch. They are, however, going round in circles in the camp yard with extreme frailty, and the barrel of the soldier's rifle is pointed at the back of the head of the emaciated-looking woman at the front. The second ink drawing seems to be directed more at the life that female figures have symbolized since time immemorial. In front of a brick wall and a window, the sick bay perhaps, two women are shown in profile; the one at the front with the headscarf is lifting a small child up to her face,

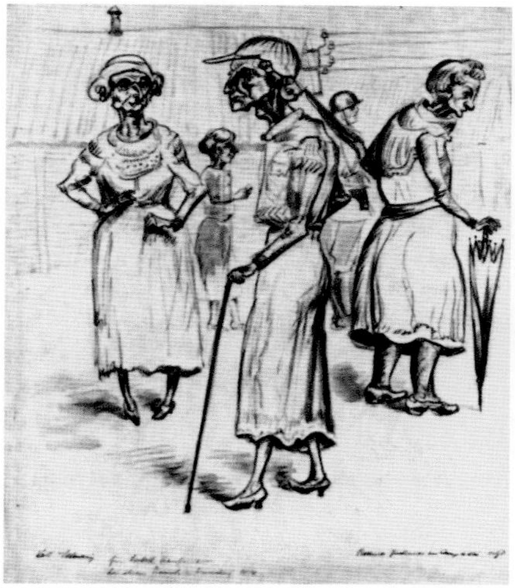

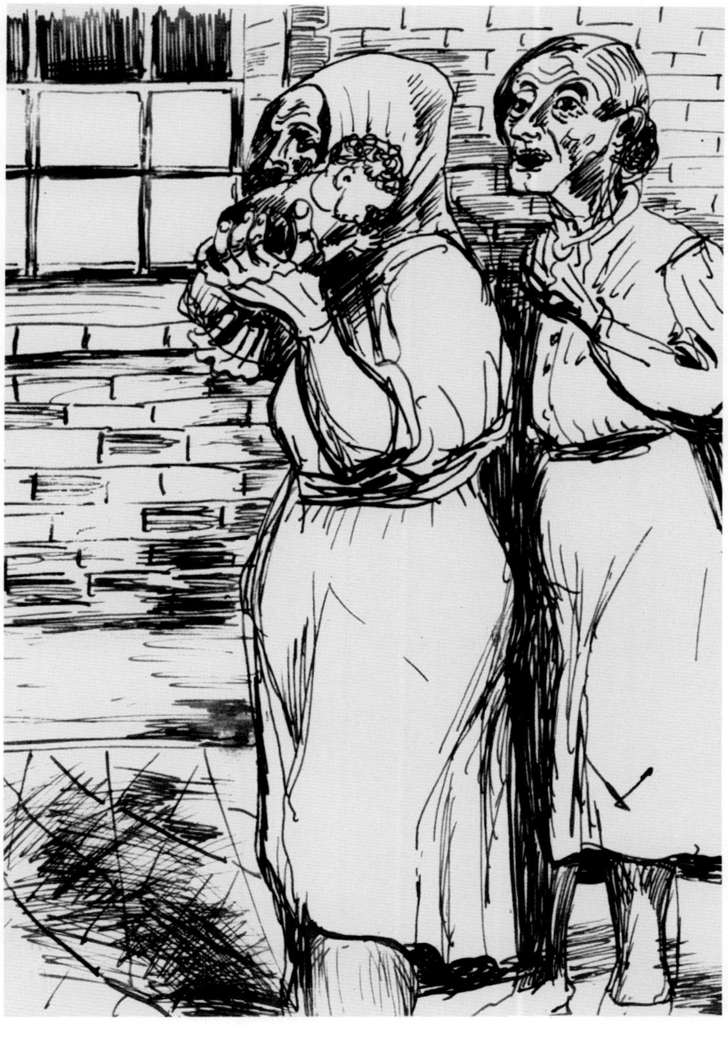

117 Karl Schwesig, *Jewish Women from Baden in Noé Camp*, c. 1948, brush and ink.

118 Karl Schwesig, *Jewish Women with a Child in the Camp*, c. 1948, brush and ink.

while the middle-aged one behind is looking at the baby with curiosity, well aware that death threatened at any moment to overtake such a young life in the camp.

The One Murdered is Guilty

Schwesig liked to caricature well-known standard images from art history in order to make the art connoisseur, as well as the general public who were interested in art, aware of the contemporary social situation. In 1949 he found himself more and more confronted with a situation in which his criticism of the former Nazis was not accepted but was even prosecuted because of his criticism of the new officials, who were often the same as the former ones.[74] He made use of the famous lithograph by Honoré Daumier of a massacre by the French authorities carried out against innocent Paris home-owners. Schwesig's accusation was directed at the guilty supporters of the contemporary legal system. For his etching, he took the body of the murdered man from Daumier's lithograph *Rue Transnonain, 15 April 1834* (illus. 119) without showing his face, and surrounded him on the right by a group of jurists in their robes, making the former raised-arm 'Hitler salute' and probably shouting 'Heil Hitler' in the direction of the policeman doing the same salute on the left. His comment on West German society expresses extreme cynicism at the way they put more and more effort into integrating the former Party members rather than caring for those persecuted by the Nazi regime: *The One Murdered Is Guilty* (illus. 120).

Harlan's Groschen

Another trial, one that drew a lot of official attention, provoked Schwesig's criticism of the treatment of the Nazi past and concern with the Jews in particular. He reacted to the acquittal of Veit Harlan that took place in April

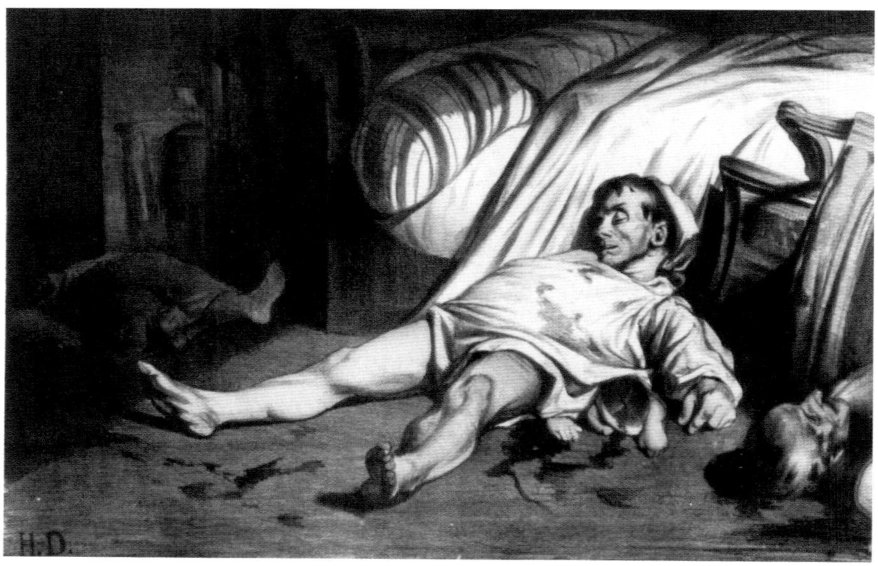

119 Honoré Daumier, *Rue Transnonain, 15 April 1834*, 1834, lithograph.

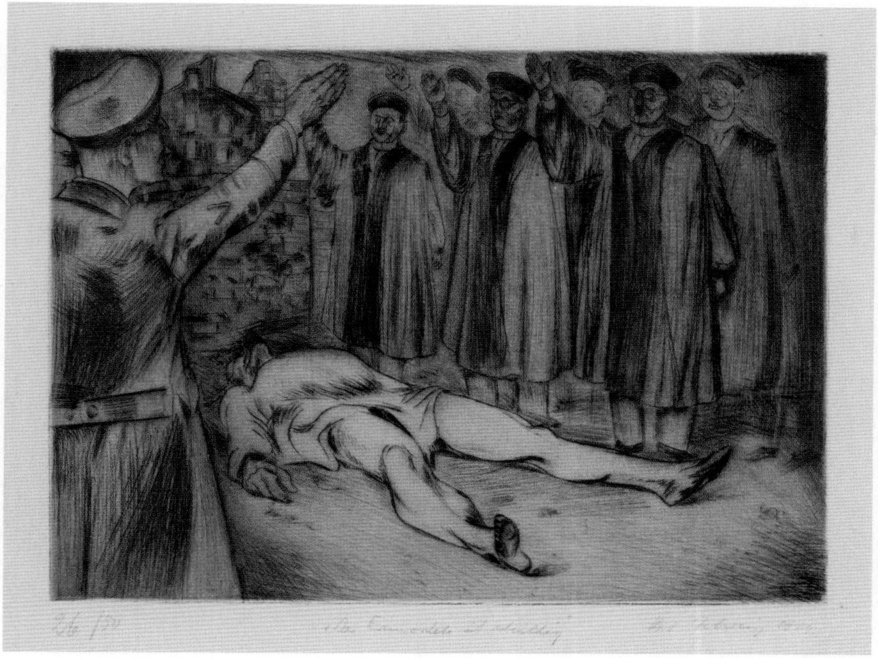

120 Karl Schwesig, *The One Murdered is Guilty*, 1948–9, etching.

1949. Harlan was the director of the anti-Jewish propaganda film *Jud Süss* (Jew Süss), which had been commissioned by the state, and was acquitted of the charge of having aided the persecution. Schwesig's reaction to this was the etching *Harlan's Groschen* (illus. 121). Schwesig was here appropriating Titian's composition showing Christ in discussion with the Pharisee – 'Render therefore unto Caesar the things that are Caesar's' (Matthew 22:21) – in the famous painting *The Tribute Money* (illus. 122).[75] Schwesig turned this into an attempted handing over of money from Harlan to an old man identifiable as a Jew and made use of Titian's anti-Jewish view of the Pharisee to expose Harlan as having been a servant of the Nazi state. The religious Jew seen *en face*, in a bright halo with a kippah and dreadlocks, points like Christ at the tribute money, while Harlan – now with the Pharisee's beard, as in the Titian – displays a coin with a swastika stamped on it. In place of Christ, the Jew is handing over the tribute money for the Nazis' Reich. Schwesig's reinterpretation of Titian's painting can be taken as saying that the Jews, as in *Jud Süss*, rendered 'unto God the things that are God's' (Matthew 22:21) and had paid for Veit Harlan's successes with the tribute of their lives.

In this cynical alteration of the meaning of Titian's *Zins-* (that is, interest paid) to Schwesig's *Harlan's Groschen* there is also the element of an allusion to Judas's tribute money. It highlights Harlan's position as that of a corrupt opportunist – but not without slipping back into an anti-Jewish stereotype.

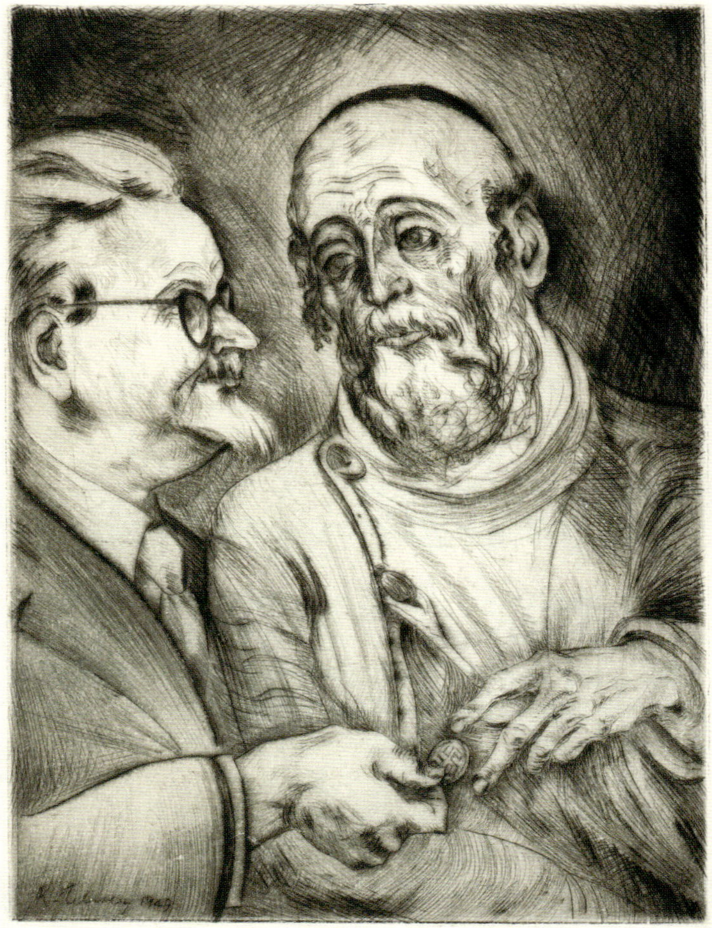

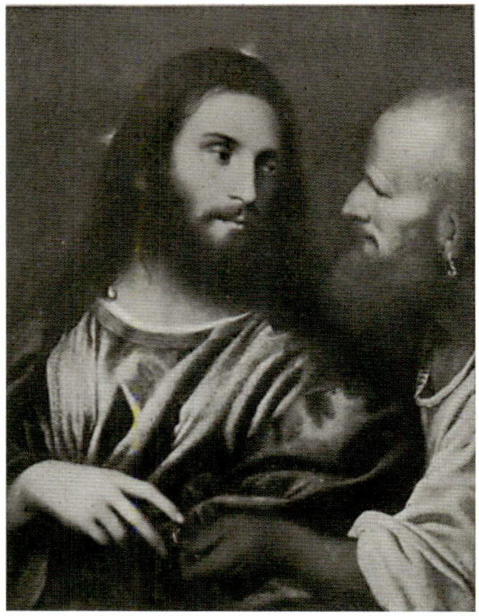

121 Karl Schwesig, *The Harlan's Groschen*, 1949, etching.

122 Engraving after Titian, *The Tribute Money*, c. 1516, from *Katalog der Vereinigung der Kunstfreunde* (Berlin, 1912).

Heinrich Ehmsen: *Auschwitz*

Heinrich Ehmsen, an artist in 1948 still living in the Western sector of Berlin, chose a different view of the concentration camp for his painting *Auschwitz* (illus. 123) than Hans Grundig had done two years before. He had already been a Communist in the Weimar Republic. After being arrested by the Nazis, he came to terms with the regime. After the end of the war he was a founder member of the Kulturbund and a co-founder of the Hochschule für Bildende Künste, the Academy of Fine Arts, in Berlin where he was in charge of the painting class. As a photograph of his studio and catalogues testify, he dealt in a number of pictures with both the *End of the War* (1945) and with the present *In the Ruins* (1945) as well as with the camps in *Street of Horror* (1948).[76] Turning aside from small-format works, in the 1948 monumental oil painting *Auschwitz* he embarked on the extraordinary attempt to portray the 'factories of death', as the camps were often described after the trial in Lublin in 1944.[77] The concept of the image certainly originated, not only

123 Heinrich Ehmsen, *Auschwitz*, 1948, oil on plywood.

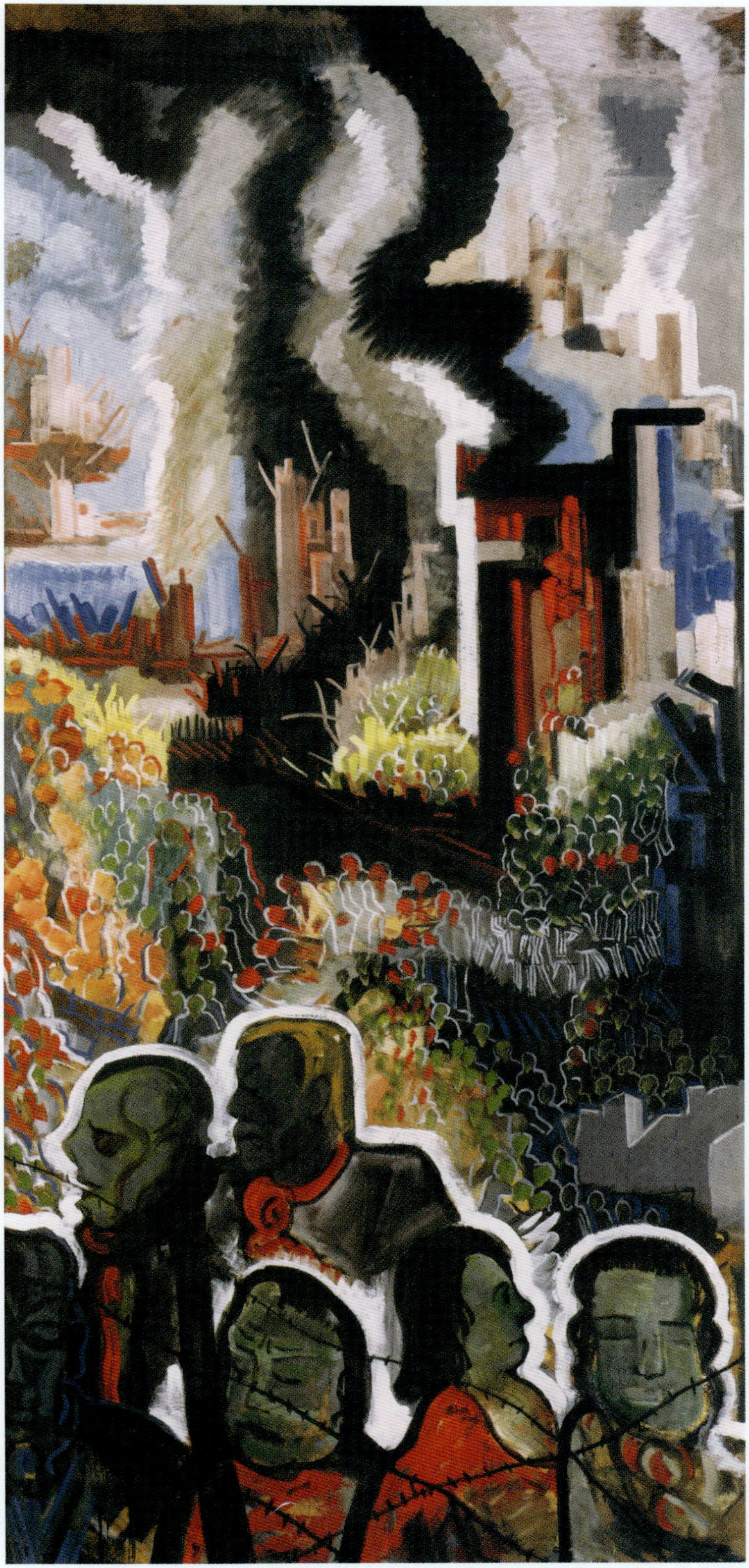

as a reminder of the IG Farben factory that had been built in Auschwitz to exploit the labour of the camp inmates, but in order to explain the political and economic sources of fascism, with its inhumane machinery of extermination being an extreme case of capitalism. Smoke, black alternating with grey, rising up into the sky, can be made out behind and between indefinable ruins, and in the middle distance brightly painted streams of people in prison clothing are arriving at a tower glowing red. In the foreground, the anonymity of the many individual figures is eclipsed by the white bordered portraits of six prisoners with red scarves or vests behind barbed wire. One cannot be certain whether Ehmsen, by the use of the title *Auschwitz*, and the German public of the time had in mind the overwhelming majority of Jews that had been murdered there. That is because at the time, one year after the inauguration of the memorial site at Auschwitz, this place was still associated above all with the struggle and heroism of the Polish people.[78] The yellow patches, however, that remained exposed in the picture after the overpainting of the yellow layer of paint underneath and which are visible on the chests of several of the prisoners could be a reminder of the Jewish star in a hidden suggestion similar to that in the case of Strempel.

Carl Buchheister: *Composition with Brutal Opposites (Concentration Camp Picture)*

An abstract material picture dealing with the Nazi past was produced by the artist Carl Buchheister. He had already done abstract paintings in the Weimar Republic, but during the Nazi period he found himself forced in the direction of figurative painting in order to survive. His *Composition with Brutal Opposites (Concentration Camp Picture)* (illus. 124) was created as early as 1949. The date and the subtitle have not been questioned up to the present.[79] The abstract colour composition which, it is claimed, does not aim at any obvious depiction or any figurative association, nevertheless – not the least on the basis of the title of the image – summons up an association with blood by the use of colour for the *Brutal Opposites*. For example, the red stream of paint covering the picture on the left can be imagined as being washed over by the pale white from bottom right. Another panel, an enlargement as it were, is placed onto the picture surface that the red paint seems to continue flowing over, even though it has started to snake dark sandy brown in some places, reminding one of spilt blood. A yellow stick is placed across the two picture surfaces from bottom right against the flow of paint and overlying it in the middle is the knot of a grey piece of twine. The physical materials suggest a direct attack and heighten the associations set in train by the blood-red and pale white colouring, particularly given the recurring hints of yellow and the appearance of the colour symbolism relating to the German past. The pictorial space presented to the viewer, extending beyond

124 Carl Buchheister, *Composition with Brutal Opposites (Concentration Camp Picture)*, 1949, material picture.

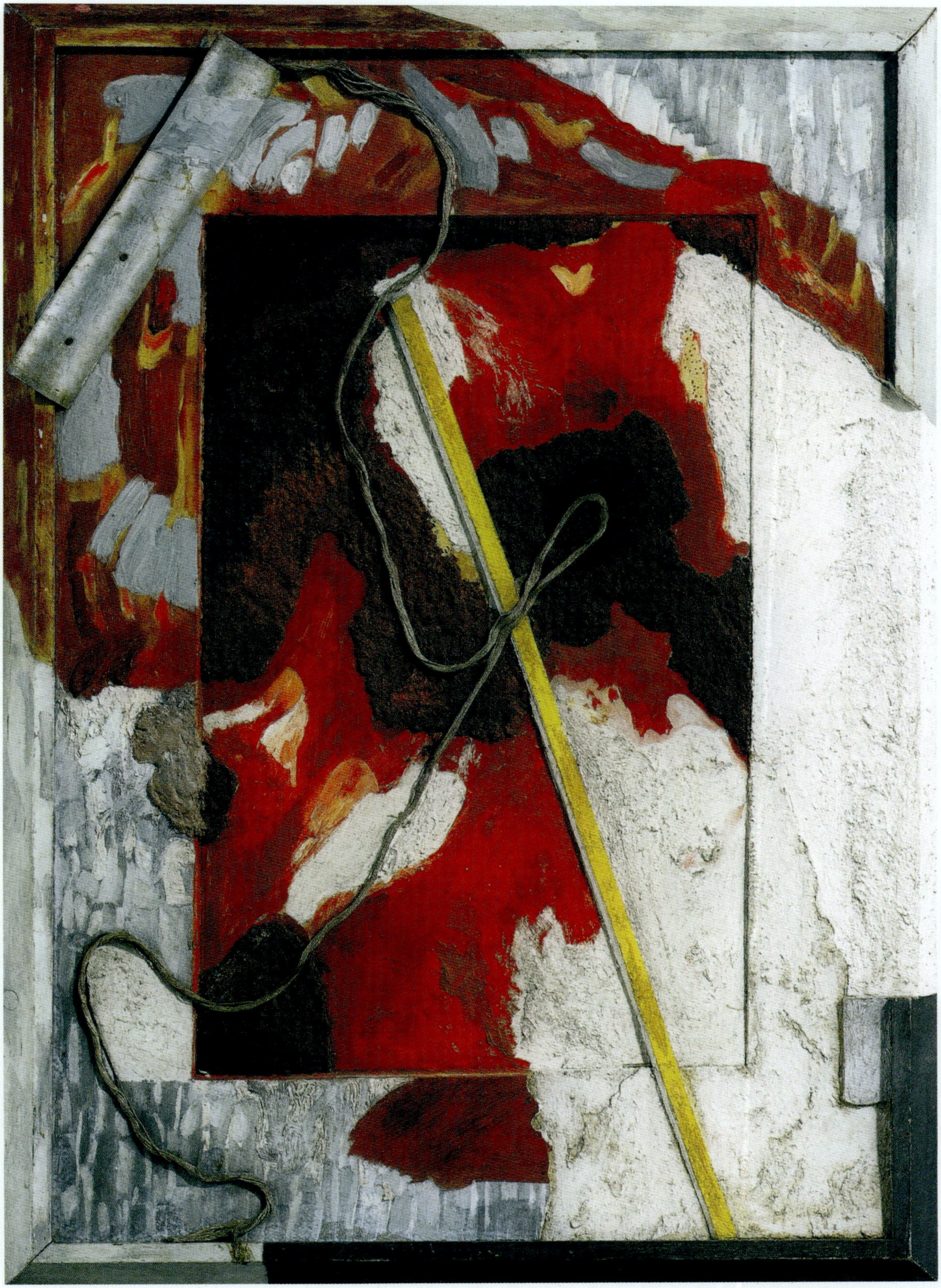

the discontinuous frame, and the title point towards the fact that what has happened has not yet ended. The arrangement and the materials were at the time capable of rousing suppressed memories without confronting people with what was claimed to be the incontrovertible evidence of photographs.

Max Lachnit: *Auschwitz Groups*

Lachnit, a sculptor and architect from Dresden, gave the title *Auschwitz* to a small sculpture of three figures 30 cm tall (illus. 125) and a second sculpture of two figures (illus. 126), encapsulating the feelings of grief, lamentation and despair.[80]

Only a few years after his painter colleague Ehmsen, Lachnit made use of a totally different visual repertoire for Auschwitz. Today it is a record of the fact that, quite unlike Adorno in his statement[81] formulated at the same period, he was coming to terms with knowledge about this camp which was becoming a symbol for concentration camps in general.[82] Lachnit did not visualize the system of industrialized mass murder; instead he formulated emotional reactions to the events at Auschwitz by means of unusual variations on extreme gestures of the body expressing despair that were only given the title *Auschwitz* later on, presumably in the 1950s.[83] Although grief at the deaths was mostly represented by female figures, Lachnit left the gender of the three figures unclear. In the group of three, two of them are standing close together; bending deeply forwards, they form one block with a hollow in the middle, while the larger figure on the left stands aloof with the material sweep of its long garment like a sickle and turning its back sideways on them. It is holding its arms back at an angle, with both hands clenched and its head withdrawn. Its body is stretched to the maximum extent and represents a defiant rearing up against the body position of the group of two sunk in grief. The contrast between the different body gestures also characterizes the *Auschwitz Group II* and presents the official GDR interpretation by the fact that the figures rising up are larger than the others and the one in the second group even has its head raised looking into the distance – the future.

In the Weimar Republic even the representation of female figures on war memorials had come to be associated with the political risk of giving rise, not just to an outpouring of grief, but to a protest against war.[84] Walter Ulbricht, the most powerful man in the GDR, began to see the danger of passivity resulting from backward-looking expressions of grief. Already in 1948, he demanded that people should not dwell on grief about the past but look towards the future and drive forward with the task of building socialism.[85] Lachnit's brother Wilhelm had already set out in this direction in painting with his 1945 picture *To the Victims of Fascism (The Death of Dresden)* and with the 1948 pastel *Dynamic Awakening*.[86] Admittedly, in both paintings there are seated figures bending over, but in the first one a child is looking

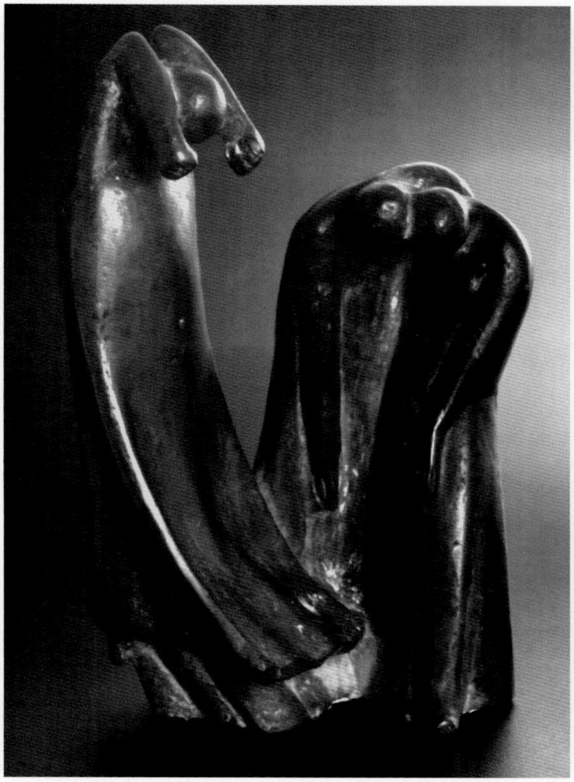

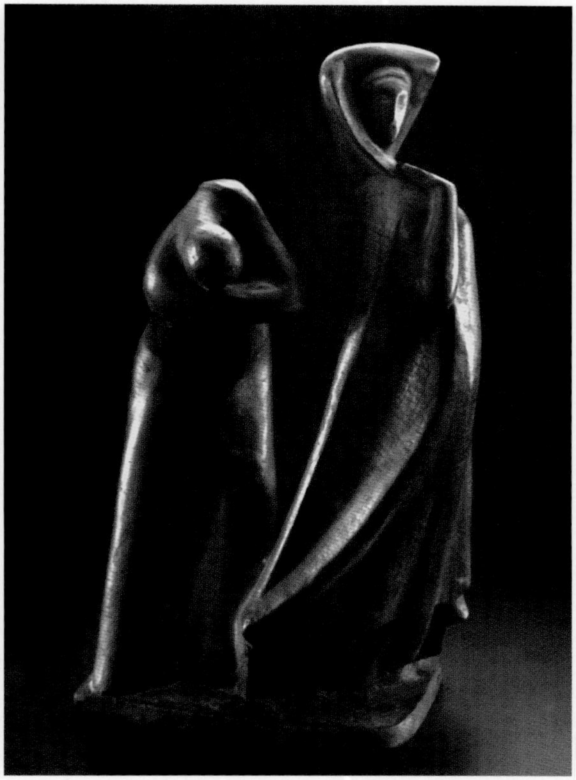

125 Max Lachnit, *Auschwitz Group I*, 1949–52, bronze.

126 Max Lachnit, *Auschwitz Group II (Fleeing Angel)*, 1949–52, bronze.

up, and the second is dominated by a man, above the grieving people, climbing ever upwards and carrying a plank on his shoulders.[87] Koelle also changed his first model of *Inferno* (see illus. 30) for the Dachau memorial, showing an abused concentration camp inmate, into an 'Unknown Prisoner' looking directly forwards.[88] In his small Auschwitz figures that never became public memorials, Max Lachnit linked the agonizing grief at the murder carried out by the Germans with their 'coming to terms' with this. In the smaller figures he represented grief as the start of this process and in the larger ones, the politically formed wish to begin anew and work on the task of reconstruction. The title, added later, signifies that it was not possible after all to forget the despair about Auschwitz.

5 A Confession

Hanns Georgi: *Vision (Persecution of Bloodstained Hands)*

For the perpetrators, the revelation of memories was a precarious business and the attribution of guilt was therefore limited to the legal process. A remarkable exception is provided by the artist Hanns Georgi, who is almost unknown today. He was born in Dresden where he lived until his death, then in the GDR. He had joined the NSDAP in 1933[1] and, after the war, he continued with his late Impressionist style of portraying nature. Between 1946 and 1948, he found a way of achieving some distance by the use of energetic brushstrokes. His picture does not present a record of the murders carried out by the Nazis such as the ones politically motivated artists engaged in, but more an angst-ridden nightmare for the post-war period, a *Vision (Persecution of Bloodstained Hands)* (illus. 127). Presumably the latent fear of revenge[2] visualized here affected immense numbers of people, but so far this is the only painting to show any sign of it.[3]

Advancing from the right, an endless procession of gesticulating figures in bare feet are portrayed. At the front, moving along with them, is a figure made of skin and bone, shown as patchy yellow, naked and barefoot, reminiscent of the corpses in Allied photographs of concentration camps. As one, they are attempting from behind to grab hold of an isolated figure in a brown SA uniform. This figure, bowed over and identifiable by his uniform and cap as a Nazi, is dragging himself leftwards out of the picture with bloodstained hands and feet. A figure at the side, identifiable by his crutches and brown rags as a war cripple, is looking on at the scene in the position of the viewer of the image; his feet too are standing in blood. Georgi's picture shows a

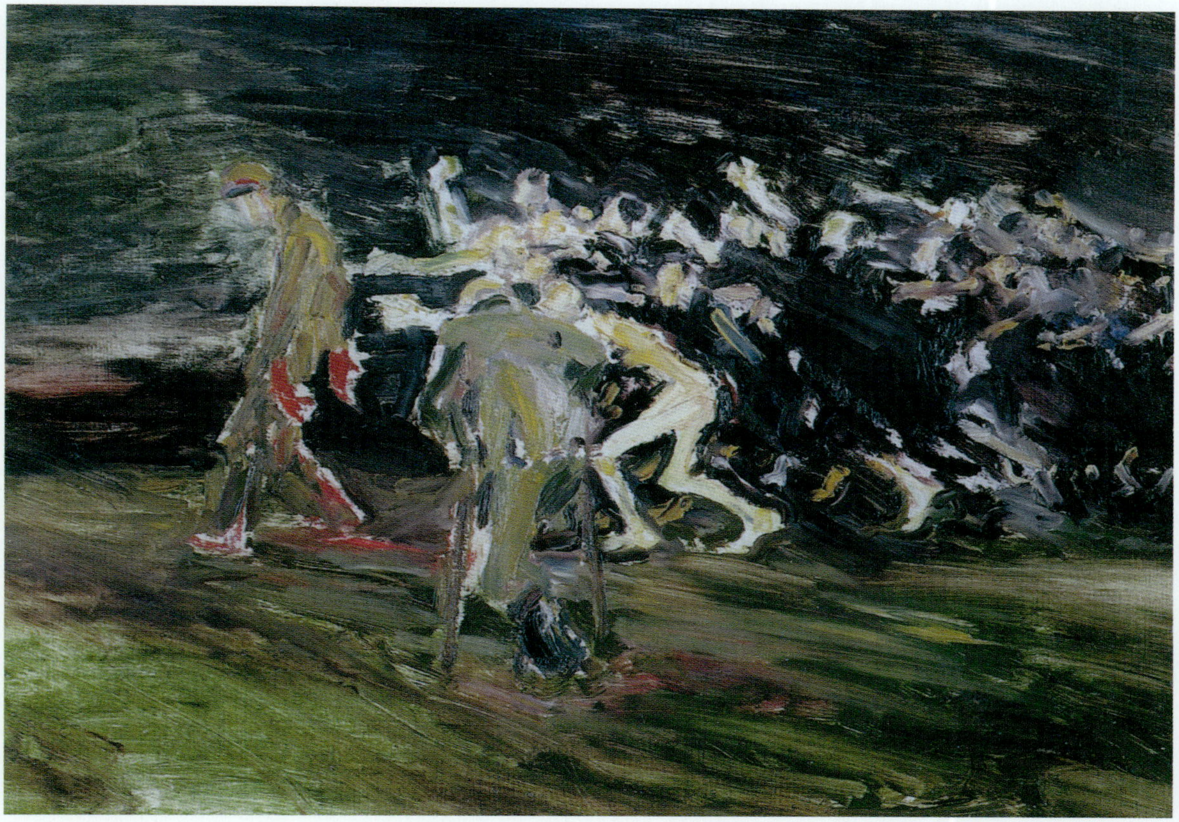

127 Hanns Georgi, *Vision (Persecution of Bloodstained Hands)*, c. 1946–8, oil on hardboard.

perpetrator being caught red-handed by ghostly persecutors, thus revealing the Nazi soldier's guilt in the vision of revenge by the victims. In the narrative of the image by this former Party member, transformed into the unreal world of nightmare, the Jews are still there: as the undead.

6 Remembering in the 1950s

After the founding of the two German states in 1949 and until the end of the 1950s, there were even fewer commentaries on the murder of the Jews in paintings and drawings than we were able to discuss here for the earlier period. This is in line with the findings from research into other media. In his retrospective survey, Harald Schmid concluded that between 1945 and 1947 there were numerous exhibitions on the atrocities, but after that it was not until 1958, twenty years after the pogroms of Kristallnacht in November 1938, that the subject was returned to.[1] In West Germany, neither the press nor the radio nor television can point to any notable contributions on the murder of the Jews until the middle of the 1950s, the broadcasting organizations only putting the subject on their agenda again in 1958.[2]

The leading politicians in the GDR founded their state on the victory over fascism, and to that extent remembering the Nazi period in memorials was part of the obligations of the state, which it took on board much earlier than did West Germany. The national memorial site at Buchenwald was inaugurated as early as 1958 after years of preparations; the one at the former women's concentration camp at Ravensbrück in 1959. In Western Federal Republic, by contrast, it was only after 1964 that a bronze plaque was installed in the Hofgarten in Bonn, the federal capital, in commemoration of the past. It simply read: 'To the Victims of the Wars and of Tyranny'.[3] Jews were not mentioned at any of the sites referred to.[4] In Eastern Europe, the focus in all the cultural commentaries about the Nazi period was directed towards the anti-fascist resistance. The Jews ranked second in the hierarchy of victims. Between 1950 and 1953, their situation again became precarious, as the power struggles within the socialist SED Party made use of anti-Jewish stereotypes. Jewish Communists and the boards of Jewish communities were denounced as bourgeois cosmopolitans and were arrested and not released until after the death of Stalin. Many Jews fled to the West; for many years afterwards, they remained almost invisible in the GDR.[5] Yet despite the prevailing need to present the future in the style of Socialist Realism, from the middle of the 1950s, there were opportunities to remind the public about the murder of the Jews. Lea Grundig's works were continually shown at exhibitions, and Konrad Wolf's film *Sterne* (Stars) of 1959[6] made the persecution and extermination of the Jews its main subject.[7]

The conservative government of the Christian Democratic Union (CDU) in the early Federal Republic was presented with the task of integrating millions of former Nazi supporters into a democracy, in the process of which it seemed useful to forget their individual crimes so as to be able to govern the new state. This resulted in denazification being in effect brought to an end in the middle of the 1950s by the amnesty law[8] and the reintegration of the civil service. Given the plans for rearmament, there was hardly any public discussion of such issues as remembering the crimes committed by the Wehrmacht and in particular the murder of the Jews. Whenever the subject of the past came up, the main issue was the experience of the war, and with it, the possibility of identifying with the community of victims in West Germany and distancing oneself from the small number of condemned criminals and the politically suspect fellow travellers of the Nazi tyranny.

It is all the more surprising then that the documentary film *Nuit et Brouillard* (Night and Fog) by Alain Resnais[9] created so much interest among broad sections of the West German population.[10] And this was despite, and possibly also as a result of, the initial fuss caused by Vollrath von Maltzan, the German ambassador in Paris, who pointed to the rule of the Cannes Festival about not upsetting the feelings of other nations, which led to the film not being shown in the official programme of the 1956 festival. This set off such widespread protest that the West German government found themselves forced to distribute the film. They bought the rights, and on the recommendation of the French poet and writer Jean Cayrol, who had written the text for *Night and Fog*, Paul Celan translated the French version into German. The film was then on release in West Germany from 1957. It was not often shown in the GDR, where it was presented with a different, more extensive and, what was claimed to be a more literal translation. In a second attempt at making it more German, the way it was presented addressed in no uncertain terms both the lack of emphasis on the tendency of capitalism to move towards fascism and solidarity among the prisoners, and the closing scene of the film was not accepted.[11] By contrast, in West Germany the film was available from the Federal Office of Home Affairs and from the media organizations of the various Länder for showing in cinemas and schools and by trade unions. Presumably the reason why it struck such a chord with the population had something to do with the fact that a new generation had grown up after the war and that this film carefully questioned the uniqueness of the events, made people aware of the continuing possibility of such violent measures and portrayed the German audience as not being the only guilty ones. Resnais' documentary, showing the genocide in the camps and at the same time becoming involved with the ongoing Algerian War,[12] included frequent visual references to the deportation of the many Jews, with their clearly visible Stars of David; apart from the mention of one Jewish female student, reference was made exclusively to *déportés* in a universalizing sense. In the German version, Paul Celan referred to them as 'concentration camp prisoners' but at the end of the film he put it more clearly by characterizing the system, which Jean Cayrol had described with the image of the 'monstre concentrationnaire', and called it 'racist madness'.[13] Even if the word 'Jew' is not audible in the text of the film, the connection was obvious to the West and East German cinema-going public.

Most Western Germans had been officially denazified by the 1950s and many of the curators who had been heads of museums during the Nazi period had got back their positions and public recognition. Being modern meant going by what the U.S. did and promoting abstract art. In so doing, it was that much easier to keep quiet about how closely associated it was with recent Jewish history and Jewish artists. Mark Godfrey recognized that in the development of modernism by the Jewish art critic Clement Greenberg, the great champion and advocate of abstract art, modernism acted 'as a protective barrier, a wall against the threat of history'.[14] Greenberg, he argued, had not seen Abstract Expressionism in relation to Nazi genocide in his many writings. According to Godfrey, he had wished to keep it out of this problematic area; this was probably due to a worry about the downgrading of the artists and their works by 'chauvinists', as Godfrey for his part now euphemistically describes anti-Semitism. Greenberg, however, himself a committed Jew, declined to draw any parallels, the reason being that, if it had become known that the movement was represented by many Jewish artists (mention may be made here of Barnett Newman, Mark Rothko, Adolph Gottlieb and Morris Louis), it could undermine the development of modernism.[15] In the art scene appeared the phenomenon noticeable in the post-war period that both the former advocates of National Socialism and the Jews kept silent about the past. The reasons why modernism proved such a shelter are fundamentally varied, but they can throw some light on the overwhelming acceptance of Abstract Expressionism and 'art informel' in the West.

There were also, however, artists in the 1950s who did not remain silent about the past. Participation in the competition for a memorial at Auschwitz shows that, even before the date frequently quoted by historians of the trials beginning in Ulm in 1958 against the *Einsatzgruppen* (special units functioning mostly as death squads), the Nazi past was not swept under the carpet. The fact that there is little evidence of this in public statements, let alone a wide debate about the murder of the Jews, makes the artworks from the 1950s listed here and the history of their reception particularly revealing, since most of the few works presented here for a long time remained or are still in the possession of the artists. Otto Pankok gave the *Memorial* that he had been working on for a long time to the Museum in Gelsenkirchen, and the *Jew Walking*, purchased notably by the Deutsche Akademie der Künste in East Berlin, is his last work on the subject. As far as is known, Gerd Baukhage worked only on the two drawings exhibited, after which his canvases 'locked away' the memory. Sitte suffered as a result of the subject-matter of *Lidice* and his criticism at the hands of the cultural policy of the GDR. Carl-Friedrich Claus, who had taken an interest in matters relating to the Jews since his childhood, worked in apparent isolation; Goral first developed his portrayal of violence in opposition to post-war society in Hamburg. And without receiving any commissions, Gerhard Richter in Dresden began a confrontation with the past that is still ongoing. In the discourse about the Buchenwald memorial Lea Grundig extended the official perspective on the prisoners there and included the Jews. The pictures are as varied as the biographies, there was no debate about the persecution of the Jews in the society that they were confronting, and Sitte was the only one able to imagine a public and a locale where his painting could be hung.

Otto Pankok

Memorial to the Jewish People

In the immediate post-war years, one single memorial was erected for the Jews – and also for the Sinti, Stateless Persons and Russians (illus. 128). It is not on show in any public square but as a collection of ten bronze statues on a round base made of stone in the museum at Gelsenkirchen, where it has been since 1955. Uniquely, the artist Otto Pankok added to the five Jewish figures – the Jewish violinist, the three seated Jews and the reclining one – sculptures of other minorities and ethnic groups. These included the reflective Ringela, a young 'gypsy' who had been murdered,[16] the girl with ringlets reminiscent also of the girl wearing a dress with a ringed pattern; a boy reclining, possibly the stateless Raklo;[17] and a *Russian Listening*. Otto Pankok assembled the *Memorial to the Jewish People*, as it was referred to in the 1955 exhibition catalogue,[18] based on studies and models from the period between 1932 and 1950 and sold it to what was then the local museum in Gelsenkirchen.[19] The way Pankok conceived of the honouring of the dead with the sculptural monument made up of a fictional genre scene, people listening around the bronze of the *Jewish Violinist II*,[20] can be seen in the context of his whole oeuvre. The book about the *Gypsies* and the charcoal painting of the Stern married couple (see illus. 107) clearly demonstrate Pankok's idea of remembering those murdered by portraying them alive. For the *Memorial to the Jewish People*, Pankok assembled in a circle around the ghetto violinist nine figures in the reflective poses of those who

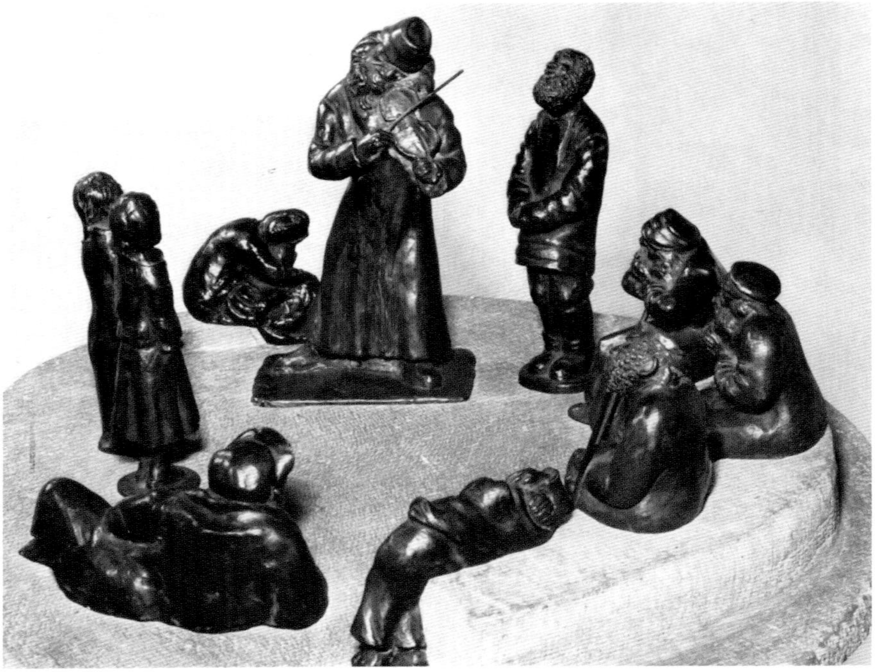

128 Otto Pankok, *Memorial to the Jewish People*, 1932–50, 10 sculptures in bronze on stone, up to 40 cm high.

had been persecuted, permanently cast in bronze. In the foreword to the municipal art exhibition in Gelsenkirchen in the spring of 1955 in which the memorial was presented to the public, Hulda Pankok described the collection of figures:

> These moving images of the Jews and their burning synagogues were thus created in complete secrecy during a time of persecution. All these images were protests out of love. The memorial, which will capture for ever what happened, was a response to the fact that, for no reason at all, people here were killed and persecuted. On the monument there is the old violinist, engrossed in his playing, behind him a man listening carried away by the music; some others seated and reclining dreamily around him. On the wall there are old people sitting enjoying a good rest. Such innocent old people, this noble violinist, these people full of goodwill and faith and these dear, dear children were senselessly maltreated and persecuted. This is what the artist is intending to portray and make sure it is never forgotten. And he hopes that people will not be able to stand in front of it without feeling emotion.[21]

The figures of the memorial are shown dressed like the former shtetl inhabitants and the Sinti. They remind one of what Pankok referred to as 'unverbildete Menschen' (unspoilt people) who were not to be allowed any future. The inherent Romanticism does not attract him towards any new formal language. As a left-wing person adhering to no party, he disassociated himself from the Nazis in his circumstances and founded a 'new association of artists'.[22] As he spoke out against abstract art,[23] the creation of this memorial was also his response to the many non-figurative or semi-abstract concepts for a *Monument to the Unknown Political Prisoner* in 1953.[24] He reacted to the memorials erected in many places for the war dead[25] by the official German war graves commission in the 1950s by dedicating his memorial to the Jews.

The fact that Pankok's reminder of the genocide was widely understood is confirmed by a review in the *Westfälische Rundschau* of 7 March 1955.[26] Taking its cue from the 'Jewish memorial', it gives expression, carefully worded and in brackets, to the way in which the deeds of the Germans were being swept under the carpet:

> How he manages to convey pity for the suffering of the human being! How he has been moved by the via dolorosa of Jewry (in the memorial to the Jews)! (Almost with astonishment one asks oneself: who is concerned any more with 'such topics'! We left all that behind long ago! Didn't we?)

The *Neue Volkszeitung* of 12 March 1955 praised Pankok as an artistic 'master' and explained his political attitude towards his fellow creatures, not without mentioning the absence of his pictures referring to the violence against Jews:

> With some unease what we miss in the selection are the pictures, secretly produced by Pankok while being persecuted during the Nazi period, about the persecution of the Jews. For us, the human and artistic focus of the exhibition was the moving group of bronzes *Memorial to the Jewish People* (which is unfortunately not displayed in a place totally accessible to the viewer); these Jewish men and women of the ghetto in front of a venerable old Jewish violinist, created by a passionate heart full of humane feeling and by the hand of a master, are the embodiment of total despair, but also an outcry against inhumanity that cannot be ignored.

A third person, this time commenting in the *Buersche Zeitung* of 7 March 1955, wrote: 'A memorial to the Jewish dead appeals to one just as much through its realism as through its irrational interpretation of the way the Jews have lived and suffered.' In another five reviews of the exhibition, the *Memorial to the Jewish People* was not mentioned, but the fact that only a few 'official and unofficial guests' attended the opening was.[27]

Jew Walking

After the *Memorial to the Jewish People*, Pankok only produced one more sculpture of a Jew, a single male figure in 1957: *Jew Walking* (illus. 133). Here one can see just how important for him once again Walter Gircke's photograph of Jews in the Grenadierstrasse was (see illus. 21). One thing for sure is that this street scene showing Eastern European Jews in the Scheunenviertel

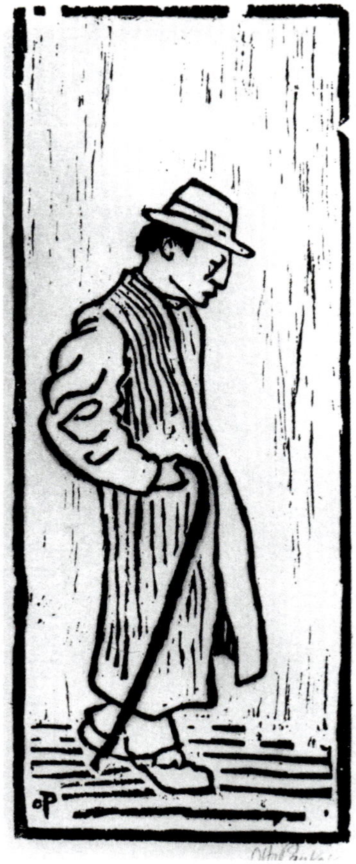

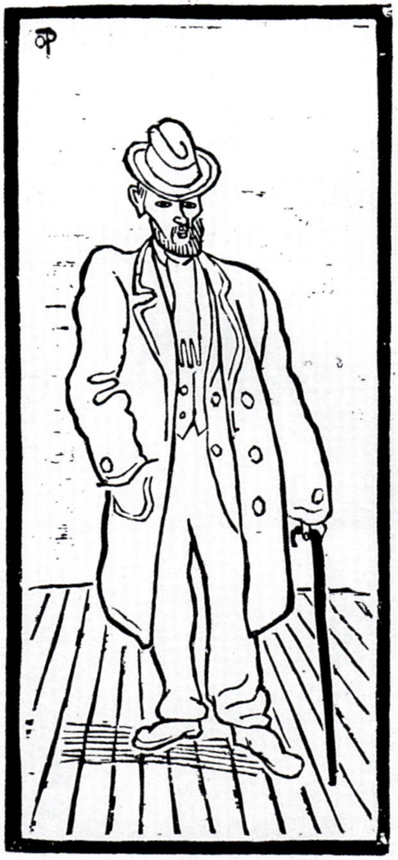

top left 129 Otto Pankok, *Jew Walking*, 1942, woodcut.

top right 130 Otto Pankok, *Jew Standing*, 1942, woodcut.

bottom left 131 Wlodzimierz Kuhn, *A Perfect Man in the Newspaper*, 1922, lithograph.

bottom right 132 Caricature, 'A Student of the Imperial University in Approved Clothing, publ. in Pluvium 1906', from Eduard Fuchs, *Die Juden in der Karikatur, ein Beitrag zur Kulturgeschichte* (Munich, 1921).

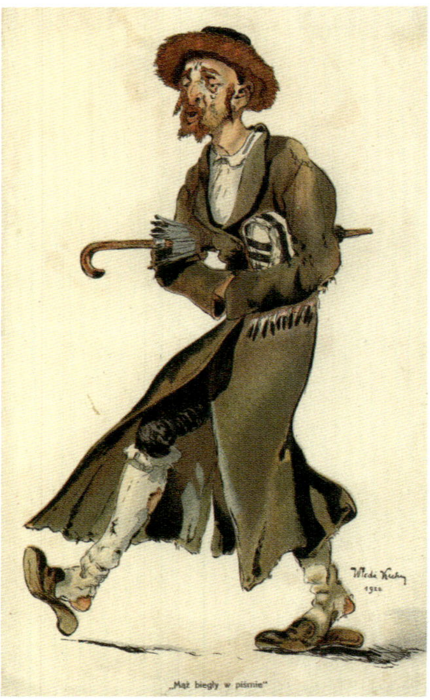

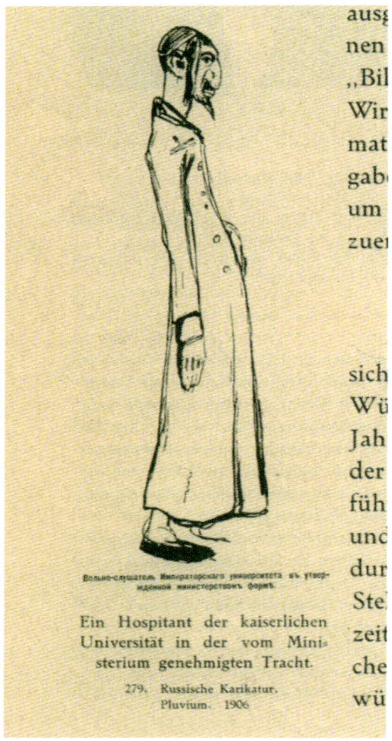

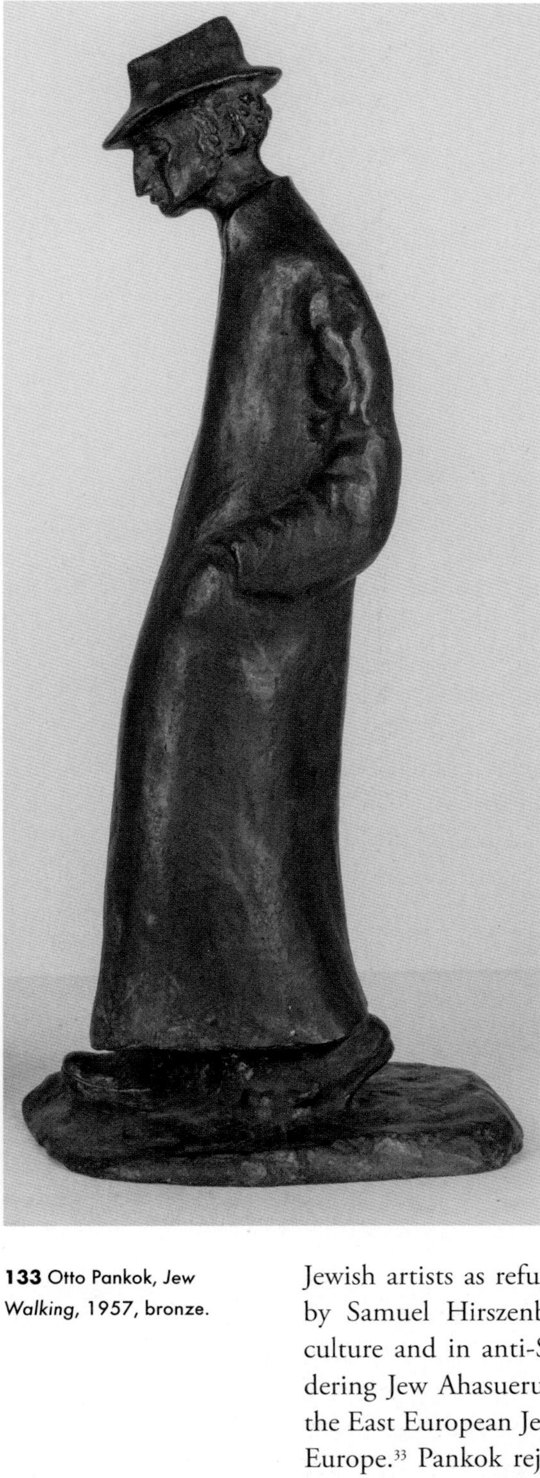

133 Otto Pankok, *Jew Walking*, 1957, bronze.

in Berlin during the Nazi period, which Pankok took as a model, was a subject intended to be viewed with contempt in the same way as the collection of photographs shown in the Nazi propaganda publication *Der Untermensch*[28] (see illus. 17) was. This did not stop Pankok carefully studying it and basing on it images of Jews other than those that were intended. His sympathy for the creativity of excluded ethnic groups and his vision of humanity, running counter to the malignant stereotyping on the part of the Nazis, meant that again and again, as was already the case with his drawings of the ghetto, he looked anew with favour upon the Jews. Among the works published up to now, the figure of the *Jew Walking* first appears in 1941 in his charcoal drawing *Men Waiting (Ghetto)* (see illus. 22) as the middle one of the three. In 1942 Pankok made a woodcut of him as a single figure[29] (illus. 129), already calling it *Jew Walking*. His head and hat are taken from the fifth person from the right in Walter Gircke's photograph (see illus. 21). His stick and long coat are also borrowed from the same photograph, this time from the second person from the right. In the same year Pankok also made a woodcut, *Jew Standing* (illus. 130),[30] from the third man from the right, the only figure in the photograph standing in the light and facing the camera. In 1947 Pankok made a slightly caricatured version of three Jews from the Grenadierstrasse on a metal plate for the drypoint etching WR 627.[31] In 1957 he worked on his last sculpture of a Jew.

The 44-cm-tall bronze shows a Jew in a long coat with his hands in his coat pockets carefully placing one foot in front of another; his eyes, slightly shaded by his hat, are looking at the ground. Images of Jews walking are portrayed by Jewish artists as refugees scurrying by, as in the well-known painting *Exile* by Samuel Hirszenberg from around 1904 (see illus. 3).[32] In Christian culture and in anti-Semitic caricatures, they represent the eternal or wandering Jew Ahasuerus, and in the twentieth century, also the caricature of the East European Jew (illus. 131) who had fled from the pogroms in Eastern Europe.[33] Pankok rejected the negative image of such people and took the main figure in Hirszenberg's *Exile* as his model for the way the man in his sculpture is walking and holding himself. The Jew, shown by Pankok as slightly bowed, looking thoughtfully, with the corners of his mouth turned down, without a beard or a hooked nose, is making his way along, admittedly not without betraying a touch of earlier caricatures of a scrawny figure (illus. 132).[34] The eternal wanderer has become the one going on his melancholy way. Pankok's friend the painter Otto Nagel made sure that in 1961, in connection with a one-man exhibition of his friend from the Rhineland, two castings of this sculpture were produced in East Berlin for the Deutsche Akademie der Künste. One of these was for a travelling exhibition of Pankok's works that was on display at nine museums in the GDR between 1961 and 1963.[35]

Willi Sitte: *Massacre II*

Willi Sitte was born in Kratzau in what is now the Czech Republic and lived in the GDR. At the end of the war he deserted to the Italian resistance and in the 1950s, though he was not yet in accord with the type of art approved by the SED, the East German Socialist Party, he continually addressed the crimes of the Nazi regime. Dedicated to figural representation, he chose allegories of death in his early drawings and, as early as 1951 when the GDR was putting leading Jewish comrades on trial,[36] he dared to take up the biblical story of the slaughter of the children of Bethlehem.[37] Without wraping it up in any allegorical or biblical allusions, in many drawings after 1956[38] he set out to represent the massacre at Lidice. The large 12-m^2 tritych was intended to be the official state offering by the GDR for the twentieth anniversary of Lidice; however, it became the subject of dispute as to cultural policy over the aesthetic bounds of Socialist Realism. After being exhibited at Moritzburg Castle in 1962, it is thought to have disappeared; where exactly it vanished on the journey between Halle and Lidice is still not quite clear.[39]

A number of sketches, drawings and smaller paintings indicate just how intensively Sitte was working towards a new form of historical imagery.[40] One of his great models was Picasso's *Guernica*, but in addition he was also able to refer back to the work *Lidice* by his fellow artist Strempel who, in a 1949 oil painting, had represented the shooting of the population by a band of German soldiers.[41] Sitte kept to the representation of the perpetrators and the victims, but developed the scenario even further. In 1949 he had visited the site of the massacre near Prague, after a memorial had been erected for the murder of those taken hostage by the Germans in June 1942, commemorating the act of revenge for the shooting of Reinhard Heydrich, the Reich 'protector' for Bohemia and Moravia. All young boys over the age of fifteen and all the men living there were shot and the women and children were taken to various concentration camps or, if 'capable of becoming Germanized', were to be brought up by SS families. Most of them died in the process. The place was destroyed. The attempt to completely eradicate Lidice immediately set off an international wave of solidarity to such an extent that whole localities were renamed 'Lidice'.[42]

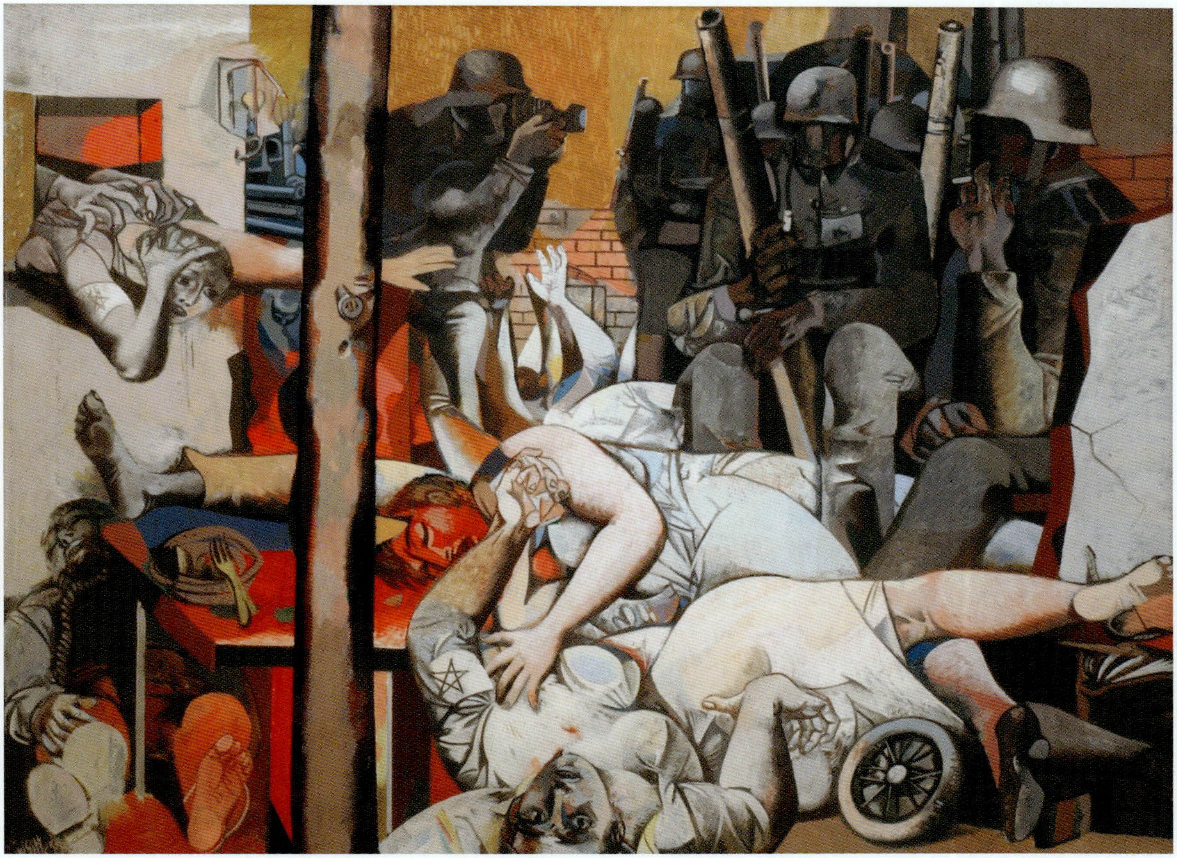

134 Willi Sitte, *Massacre II*, 1959, oil on hardboard.

The horrific crime committed against the innocent villagers, even though there were probably no Jews among the inhabitants,[43] was associated by Sitte in his 1959 study *Massacre II*[44] (illus. 134) with the history of their persecution. In this oil painting he admittedly did not portray the moment of the shooting in the way shown in historical paintings from Goya's 1814 *The Third of May, 1808* up to Picasso's 1951 *Massacre in Korea*. Nevertheless, like Werner Tübke (see illus. 159), he referred to these works by the three gun barrels looming into the picture from behind the wall on the right, indicating the continuity of injustice and cruelty. Sitte juxtaposed the dark grey wall of the uniformed perpetrators after they have done the murdering with the bright white and red bodies of women, even though only the male inhabitants had actually been murdered at Lidice.[45] This fact was only suggested on the left of the picture by the one dead man lying in the shadow under the table with a rope around his neck. Like Picasso, Sitte was here keeping to traditional gender roles in the representation of violence – signified as being male – in an image of the abused female body.

For the representation of the massacre, Sitte made use of the existing film material[46] about Lidice since the German death squads had taken pictures of their actions. He reported with disgust on the Nazi films[47] and employed artistic means to attack this use of documentary photography. Using the traditional medium of fine art, like Fritta with his drawing (see illus. 1), he showed the production of the film images of the massacre by the soldier on the left-hand side, and captured in oil on canvas the brutality and sadistic scopophilia of the German soldiers. Even though their faces were known to Sitte from the film, he represented them as faceless men in uniform.[48] Two female figures are wearing armbands with a pentagram. In addition, in the case of the one belonging to the woman, who appears to be falling desperately gesticulating out of the window to escape the clutches of an attacker, the word Jew can be read, even if it cannot be seen clearly. In the painting *Massacre II*, the sign of the star occurs twice in a five-pointed style by analogy with the Soviet Star, but neither red nor yellow and only in the internal structure resembling the Star of David. The interpretation of this pentagram as a 'yellow star' by Hütt[49] is lent support by Sitte's statement that, out of ignorance, he was at the time still using a combination of the Soviet Star and the Star of David.[50] In the 1967 picture *The Warsaw Pair*,[51] he painted the Star of David exactly as a yellow hexagram. Even without knowing the later statement by the artist, the upshot of the association of the Soviet Star and the hexagram is that, by the massacre of the women, Sitte intended to remind us of the millions of Soviet and Jewish victims of the countless pogroms. And in addition, off to the left-hand side, shown indistinctly in grey, he was nevertheless referring in particular to the persecuted Jews. The abused female figures can be taken as feminine allegory pointing beyond Lidice to the fact that in Eastern Europe a large proportion of the murdered Jewish and non-Jewish population, if not the majority, had been shot in cold blood[52] or beaten to death, as at Kowno in Lithuania in 1941.[53]

Gerd Baukhage: *The Hanged Jew with a Hat On*

In 1957, a year after West Germany had begun rebuilding its army as the Bundeswehr, and former members of the Wehrmacht were once again permitted to wear their medals and honours, though without Nazi insignia, the painter Gerd Baukhage exhibited his drawings *Memories of the War* in a one-man exhibition at the local library in Oer-Erkenschwick.[54] Presumably on display there was the series of twelve large watercolours, all approximately the same size, that he had created at almost the same time in 1956–7 with this general theme and which, according to Becker, were to be the only images in his oeuvre produced on the subject.[55] Baukhage had been a soldier in the war from 1939, fighting on the Russian campaign, being taken a prisoner of war and returning to Cologne from imprisonment in Russia in 1949. In the series of watercolours with lines across them in black ink, he partly addressed the subjects that 'the Wehrmacht war artists' had dealt with, following the tradition of war painting, such as the corpses of horses, ruins and tanks.[56]

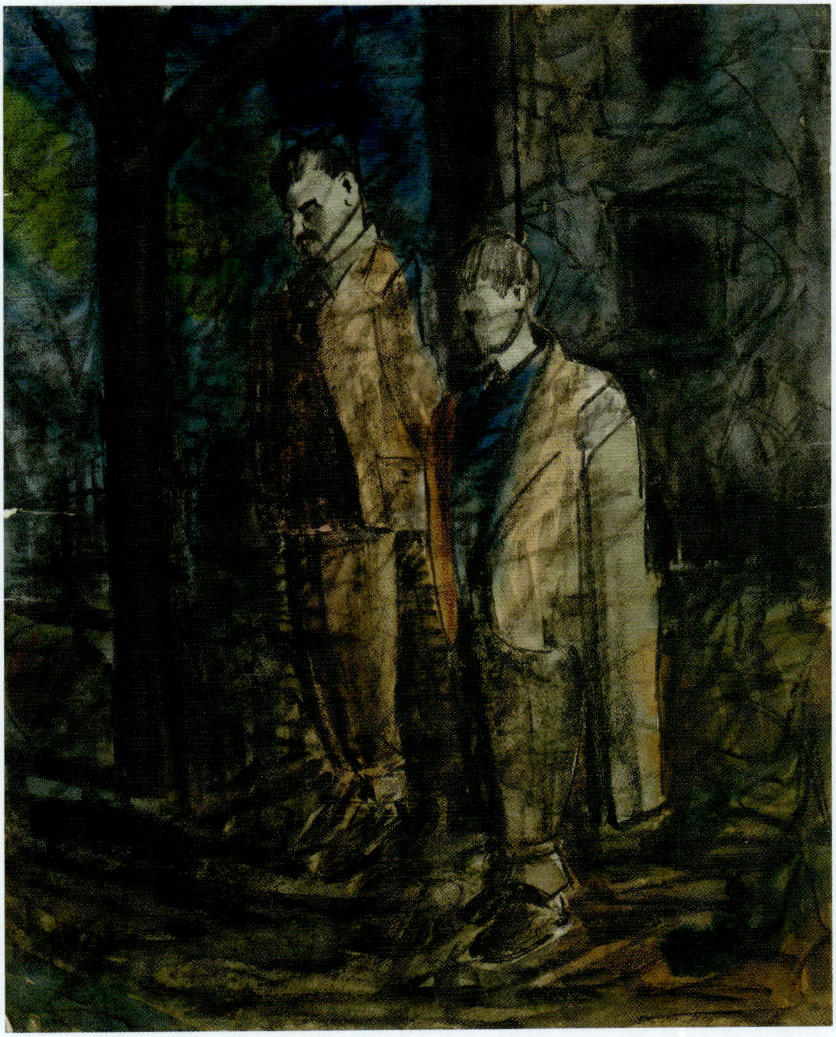

135 Gerd Baukhage, *The Ones Hanged*, 1957, charcoal on watercolour on paper.

Baukhage, however, dramatized the range of imagery by the personification of death, the representation of dead bodies. This series of war memories includes two drawings showing people being hanged in which Baukhage dealt with the crimes of the Wehrmacht that were still a subject of controversy in the 1990s. Summary justice and lynch law were not shown in the official Nazi war painting but were to be found as photographs in the soldiers' breast pockets.[57] In the oil painting on paper by the French painter Georges Rouault entitled *Homo homini lupus ou Le Pendu* from the years 1944 to 1948, the figure of a body hanging became an emblem for the horrors of war.[58]

In one drawing Baukhage drew *The Ones Hanged* (illus. 135), in another drawing a single figure is highlighted face-on; it is entitled *Hanged Jew With a Hat On* (illus. 136).[59] In the bluey-green-tinted watercolour, unlike in the case of the other two, whose clothes are hanging loose, he is shown with a well-fitting coat and hat. His long coat following the shape of his body, his shackled feet in parallel with one another, and above all, the uprights of the gallows encompassing him on both sides, its construction framing the hanged man more than bearing him, all suggest an intentionally dignified memorial to the murdered Jew. Baukhage added to some of the drawings in the series a lot of black lines criss-crossing; they may evoke the impression of flying shrapnel in the course of battle or, as in the drawings shown here, paint over the memories of war.

The images of war were to prove exceptional in Baukhage's output. From then on,' as it says in Becker's monograph, 'Baukhage made sure with iron discipline that he didn't give in once more to emotion.'[60] More often, in the following years he covered the white picture surfaces with painted *Versperrungen* (blockages or obstructions).[61]

Gerhard Richter: *Anne Frank*

In 1957 in Dresden Gerhard Richter produced a series of ink drawings for the possible publication of an edition of *The Diary of Anne Frank*. According to his biographer Dietmar Elgar, he is supposed to have created twelve drawings for it;[62] the Gerhard Richter archive contains four originals; four others are on view there as photos from Richter's Dresden photo album. As he later explained, even during his student days, beginning in 1951, Richter had concerned himself with the 'cruelty' of the Nazis.[63] It is something that he is still working on right up until today. The freelance certificated mural painter qualified in 1956 at the Kunsthochschule in Dresden, and was then promoted as a promising young artist by the institution.

Even though he was experimenting with a large number of media at the time, he chose to use an ink pen for his artistic engagement with these very personal diary entries. All eight of the drawings show face-on or in profile the head of a young woman, displaying a vague similarity in general with the photos of Anne Frank as available in the edition produced by the publisher Lambert Schneider in Heidelberg in 1950.[64] Likewise they also bear a certain stylistic similarity to Picasso's girls' heads of the same period[65] and ones by Jean Cocteau.[66] Richter does not appear to have aimed for an as exact as possible likeness of Anne Frank. Instead, he produced different aspects of a female face that correlate with the quotations from the diary that he has written underneath them.

A harsh, face-on view has the caption: 'Evening after evening the green and grey army lorries trundle past and collect Jews. The Germans ring at every front door to inquire if there are any Jews living in the house. If they find one they take . . .' (*The Diary of Anne Frank*, Thursday, 19 November 1942)[67] (illus. 137). A fleetingly drawn left profile – with the suggestion of a melancholy gesture, a hand up to her cheek – carries the caption: 'I get frightened when I . . .'[68] (*The Diary of Anne Frank*, Thursday, 19 November 1942).[69] A stark profile with one eye

136 Gerd Baukhage, *Hanged Jew With a Hat On*, 1957, charcoal on watercolour on paper.

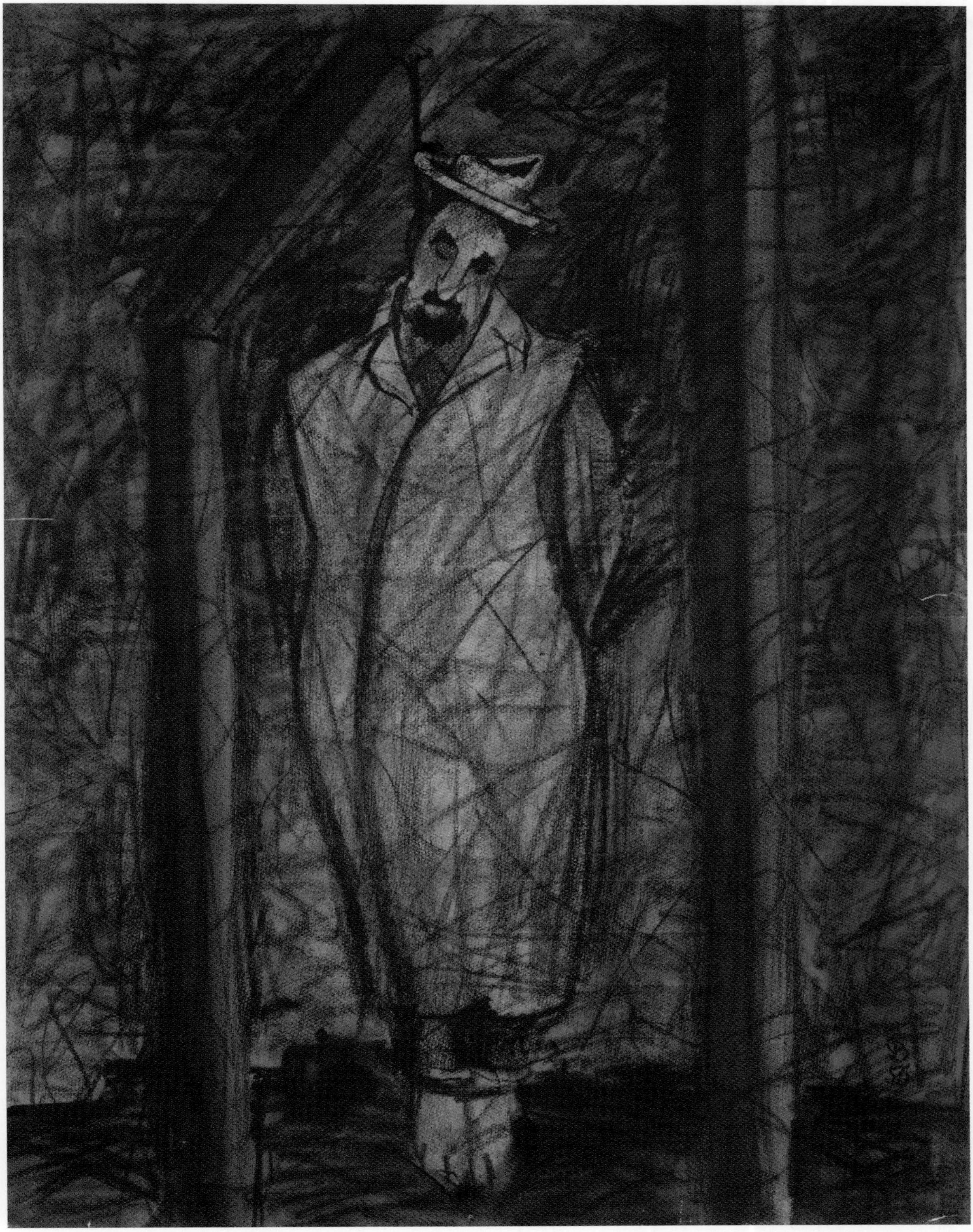

directed towards the viewer is captioned: 'Is it possible that we will ever laugh again and tease each other, when these horrors have faded a bit in our minds . . . if I want to laugh about something' (*The Diary of Anne Frank*, Friday, 20 November 1942) (illus. 138).[70] A face full on, but leaning slightly backwards as if with laughter, and a text reads, after the first, illegible line: 'Cycling, dancing, whistling, looking out into the world, feeling young, to know that I'm free – that's what I long for'[71] (*The Diary of Anne Frank*, Friday, 24 December 1943).[72]

Going by the only information available up until now on the drawings given in Elger, Richter envisaged an illustrated edition of Anne Frank's diary. This would also have been possible given that the first edition of 1957, the same year as Richter's studies appeared in the GDR published by Union Verlag, was published without illustrations, unlike the Heidelberg edition of 1950. It was distinguished by a fine layout: silver lettering and borders on cloth binding.[73]

The official GDR reception of Anne Frank had already begun by 1 October 1956,[74] when the play by the American authors Frances Goodrich and Albert Hackett based on Frank's diary had its German-language premiere simultaneously in Dresden and at seven other theatres in West Berlin, Konstanz, Düsseldorf, Hamburg, Karlsruhe, Vienna and Zurich.[75] None of the GDR press reports showed a photograph of the twelve-year-old girl; instead they included those of the main performers,[76] although the actress Ruth Schroeder reported how much attention in the first performances was given to the

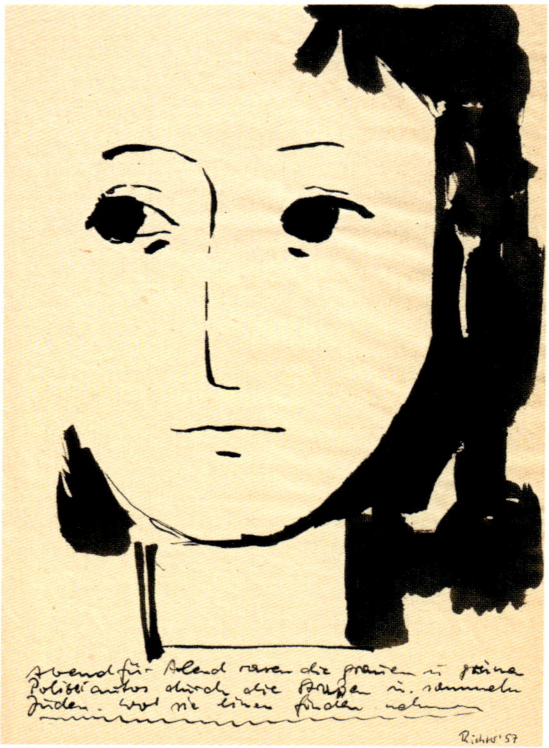

137 Gerhard Richter, *Anne Frank*, 1957, brush and black ink on paper.

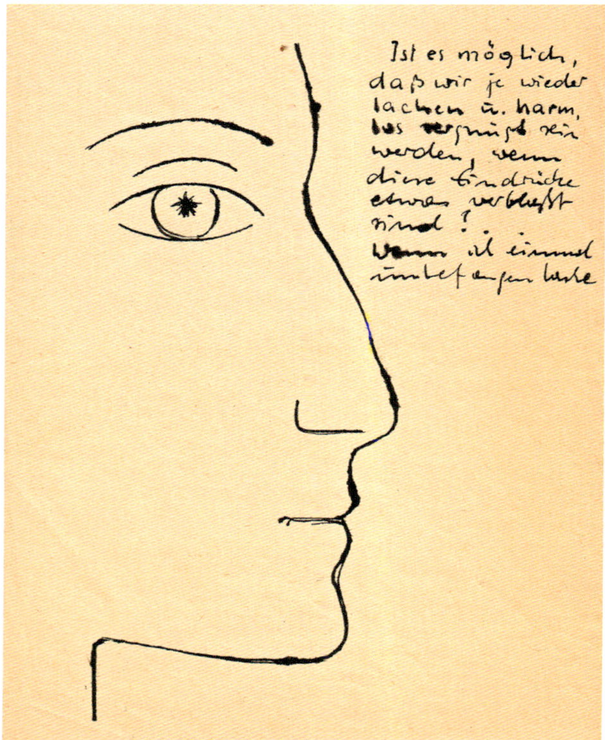

138 Gerhard Richter, *Anne Frank*, 1957, brush and black ink on paper.

similarity between the actress playing the main role and the photos of Anne Frank available at the time.[77] It is not clear whether the reason was just the lack of reproduction rights or whether one can deduce a certain attitude as regards contemporary relevance from the fact that in 1959 in the competing political volume *Ein Tagebuch für Anne Frank* (A Diary for Anne Frank), only photographic portraits of Kati Székely, the actress who played Anne Frank in the theatre and in the documentary film, were given full-page reproductions.[78] Possibly, however, the way it was received ran counter to Richter's idea of focusing on the differences in facial expressions rather than on any individual likeness, a subject which very much occupied him in the drawings made in the same period of the head of his girlfriend, Marianne Eufinger, whom he married that year.[79] In the aspects of the female face and the quotations from the text, he captured the particular fears, cares and longings of the adolescent girl by whom the reading public felt moved, but he also directed the reader's attention towards her observations on the mortal danger for the Jews in the Netherlands. As he was not making a portrait of Anne Frank, he was less concerned with the usual identification on the part of the reading public with the author than with a general perspective on the persecution of the Jews that can be seen as an allegory for the whole of the Jewish people.[80]

Lea Grundig: *Roll-call in the Concentration Camp*

In the 1950s, Lea Grundig contributed to the building of socialism by producing images from working life and illustrated books of fairy tales and writing travel reports. In 1956, however, with the etching *Roll-call in the Concentration Camp*, she reminded people once more of the fact that it was not just communist resistance fighters that belonged to the victims of fascism (illus. 139). She exhibited the drawing in a number of places in the following years.[81] It shows two prisoners in a concentration camp with the features of her husband Hans Grundig and those of her murdered friend Christel Beham, honoured also by Hans Grundig in *To the Victims of Fascism 2* (see illus. 114). The two men, who had been imprisoned for resistance against the Nazis, are carrying a weakened comrade like medical orderlies supporting him under the left and right shoulders. The motif of solidarity between prisoners that Peter Edel had pictured in his 1944 drawing *Going to the Infirmary*[82] in the concentration camp at Sachsenhausen, shown at many exhibitions, also influenced the painting *Hunger March* by Hermann Bruse, much referred to in the GDR (see illus. 110). In Edel's etching two hefty inmates identifiable by their clothing are carrying a third, emaciated one in a shirt; none of them has any of the distinguishing marks that are obligatory in the camp. By the red stripe on the prison uniform, Bruse closely associated solidarity with the political prisoners. Lea Grundig admittedly took as a subject the solidarity of the fighters and Communists standing up defiantly with a fellow prisoner on

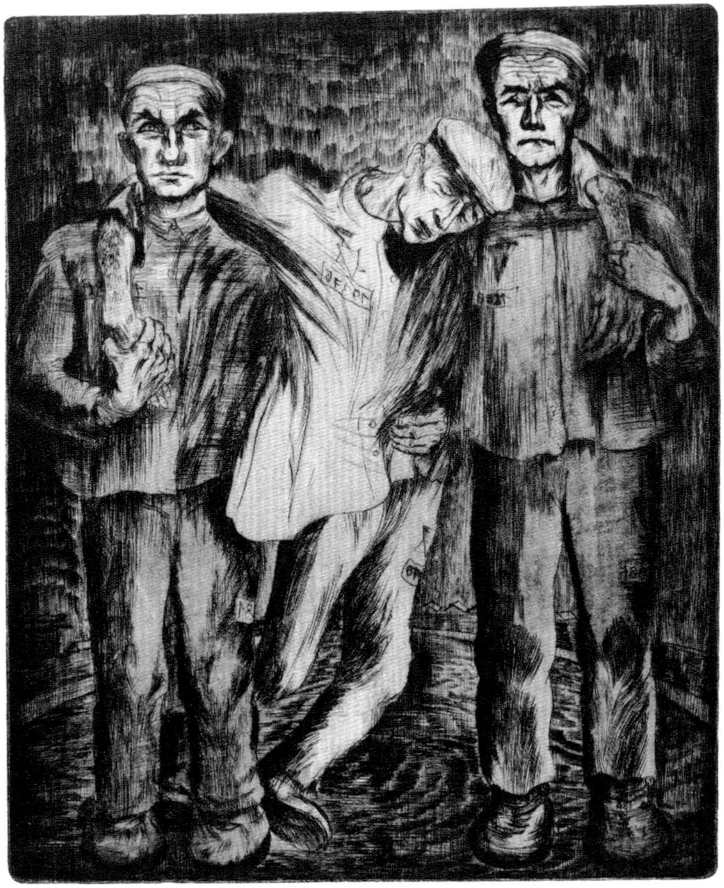

139 Lea Grundig, *Roll-call in the Concentration Camp*, 1956.

the verge of collapse, but she identified the one being carried as a Jew by the Star of David.[83] Even though she kept to the hierarchy of victims in the division of roles, prevailing in the GDR, as being resistance fighters first and then those 'who during the Nazi period only ranked among the persecuted such as Jehovah's Witnesses, gypsies, Jewish people',[84] shortly before the inauguration of the National Memorial Site at Buchenwald she was making reference to the largely forgotten group of Jewish victims.[85]

Lea Grundig had kept exactly to the process by which memory was reduced to the 'trio: resistance fighter – victim – victory'.[86] Along with many others, she had supported the first proposal by Fritz Cremer for the memorial that did not yet correspond to this pattern but showed a group, based on Rodin's *Burghers of Calais*, of reflective, disoriented, suffering human beings.[87] Thus he would no doubt have provided a more accurate history of the camp in which not just 'politicals' but many Jews were murdered. Grundig published the drawing *Roll-call in the Concentration Camp* when, after many years of debate, the foundation stone for the bell tower was laid, in front of which the concentration camp was simply represented by a group of fighters assembled under the flag.

Competition for an International Memorial at Auschwitz

Given the few artistic statements from the 1950s that were available for consideration in this study, it is worth noting that the second largest group of participants in the competition in 1957–8 for an 'international memorial' at the German concentration camp of Auschwitz came from Germany. All the same, there was no question of support for this project by the West German parliament such as that agreed unanimously by the Assemblée Nationale in France.[88] Twenty-nine artists from the GDR and 95 from the FRG out of a total of 618 from around the world applied, and in the end 22 from East Germany and 39 from West Germany submitted models.[89] The fact that the same year the autobiography of Rudolf Höss, the former commandant at Auschwitz, was published in German and became 'by far the most widely sold and discussed book about Auschwitz'[90] illustrates the increased interest in the history during these years.

The debate about a memorial went back to 1944. A prisoner, Jerzy Brandhuber, later to become an employee at the state museum there, had been secretly given the task of planning a memorial by a resistance group, already consisting of all the elements that are now associated with Auschwitz. He planned a 50- to 60-m-tall chimney on a square base and an eternal flame in the middle of a large rectangular parade ground to the west of the camp at Birkenau. Arranged in rows of ten, just as in the roll-call, six million stones for six million prisoners were to be placed around the chimney. There was to be no grass and no trees between them, just fencing posts with guns and lights, and former SS men were to weed the ground right up until the end of their lives.[91] This act of planning based on immediate experience envisaged the chimney as the central architectural feature of the extermination camp and made it a symbol for Auschwitz.

In the 1957 international competition of the International Auschwitz Committee (IAC),[92] the former prisoners of the camp did not want to be involved in directing the artistic process. The participants in the 1957 competition were issued on request with the eleven-page booklet *Programm und Bestimmungen* (Programme and Guidelines) for the competition,[93] 'plans and photographs for the erection of the memorial' and a 'documentary publication about the camp at Auschwitz' produced by Dr Jan Sehn, the former judge in the trial in Warsaw against Höss,[94] and they were advised to watch the documentary film *Night and Fog* (see p. 171). The text of the competition reads as follows:

> We [the International Auschwitz Committee] who were ourselves years ago prisoners of Auschwitz concentration camp and belong to the few who came away from Auschwitz alive feel duty bound to help in this great, arduous task . . . We are helping then by informing you about the

> experience of Auschwitz. Auschwitz is a place of martyrdom for the Polish people. Auschwitz is the site that has become for the whole world a symbol of all the unspeakable crimes committed by German Nazism in the pursuit of their 'racial policy'. *In Auschwitz 4 million people had to die in just 4½ years. In the whole history of mankind nowhere else were so many defenceless people murdered in such a short space of a time.* Millions of Jews, tens of thousands of gipsies became victims in Auschwitz of the 'racial policy'. People belonging to 22 nations were murdered here. (p. 2)

All the applicants had been informed about the mass murder and in particular about the Jews and the Sinti and Roma. In Germany during the following period, more than fifty architects, landscape planners and artists from West Germany and the GDR engaged closely with the issue of the crimes committed by the Germans at Auschwitz.

After the introductory information on the IAC and the mass killings, this majority communist committee highlighted the resistance and international solidarity and those who read it were given the following words by way of consolation:

> In Auschwitz there was not only hunger, disease, beatings, barrack huts and death. Even in Auschwitz – and there in particular – humanity triumphed over the inhumanity of German Nazism. This began with the help given to comrades which brought the helpers themselves into the greatest danger. This finally led in Spring 1943 to the formation of an international resistance organization, the 'Auschwitz group of fighters'. Here, where human life in the truest sense of the word counted for nothing, was revealed – strictly in secret and by no means a mere gesture – a true heroism. (p. 3)

The actual conditions of the competition begin by characterizing Auschwitz-Birkenau as:

> A bastion of human suffering, where Nazism brought to perfection, with the most extreme precision, the machinery of extermination of those whom they did not consider worthy of living . . . Every square inch of earth is soaked with the blood of prisoners from 22 countries – men, women and children . . . The message of those who survived must be passed down the centuries, even when there are no more people left with tattooed forearms to carry out this duty. (p. 4)

Jews or even 'gypsies' are no longer mentioned in the brief for the memorial that was to remind people for ever of 'what Auschwitz was, encapsulate it and pass it on to the world'. There is a specific plea for a memorial 'that is as far as possible free of symbols identifying individual societies and communities. The memorial should be a meeting point of all peoples and not speak in any particular language with words that only this group or that group understand or even want to hear.'[95]

As regards the positioning of the memorial, the competition organizers recommended

> the site between the ruins of the large crematoria at the end of the railway line – the so-called 'ramp' . . . In this place also in Spring 1955, a memorial was erected to commemorate the 11th anniversary of the liberation of the camp, intended to be the foundation stone for the actual memorial. It contains earth from different concentration camps and extermination sites from the Nazi period. It is not necessary that this memorial stone be kept in its present form . . . The artists must, however, never forget that this memorial is intended not just to remind people of martyrdom and struggle but also of the companionship that arose through common suffering and struggle, that fraternity whose flame burns more brightly than the fire of the crematoria. (p. 4)

The recommendation for this site was reinforced by issuing a 'Special Plan of the Area'. And as regards the language of the information supplied, there is a comment in the information:

> The poet who could describe Auschwitz has not yet begun his work. We must limit ourselves to a sober and strictly objective explanation of the conditions in the camp and the reasons behind why we are holding our competition. Were we to go beyond this sober language – we should have to fall silent. (p. 2)

The poignant remark at the end suggests that the secretary of the IAC had been involved in writing the text. This was Hermann Langbein,[96] under whom the committee had earned respect and importance in both East and West in just three years. A former actor whose judgement was clear, scrupulous and no doubt strict, but above all harsh in respect to himself, Langbein went unrecognized as a 'half Jew' during the Nazi period and had as a Communist been a prisoner in Gurs and a 'privileged prisoner' in Dachau, Auschwitz and Neuengamme, and had gained a knowledge of the functioning of the camps that even some members of the SS did not possess.[97] He refused to bow down to Party discipline, and his work with the IAC failed in the end as a result of the sharpening East-West conflict.[98] As early as 1944 and 1949, in his written statements he described his particular experience in the camps; he never spoke about his nine weeks in the bunker, and insisted on the fact that most of those exterminated in Auschwitz had been Jews.[99] Nevertheless, in his role as secretary of the IAC he did not emphasize any differences between the groups of prisoners,[100] and consequently this intentional strategy[101] fitted in with the communist demand for internationalism in the class struggle.

It is typical of the post-war tendency in East and West that no distinction was made between those who were persecuted for different reasons. In the talk of brotherhood and humanity in the information supplied, only the 'Polish martyrs' are mentioned and otherwise discussion was on a general level, leaving out the fate of those sections of the population – such as women and children, Jews, Sinti and Roma, Jehovah's Witnesses and homosexuals – who were underprivileged anyway and who were the first to be murdered.

Study of the entries included in Spielmann's variable-quality record (without illustrations) of 426 projects points to a similar conclusion. The overwhelming majority of the submitted proposals in the areas of architecture and sculpture, or combinations of both, address the issues of suffering, fraternity and survival or victory. Only three clearly highlight Jewish history. Two of these models were submitted from West Germany.[102] They will be dealt with first. Following them, the contributions by Helmuth Wolff and Joseph Beuys will be analysed, having become known to a wider public, at least in West Germany.[103]

Joseph Henry Lonas

Joseph Henry Lonas, who was born in the U.S. and received his training as an artist there, was a graduate student of the Hochschule der Künste in Berlin in 1958.[104] For Auschwitz-Birkenau he submitted a project in which he proposed 37-m-high geometric forms made of steel, one for each direction of the compass, symbolizing the four years and the four million people murdered there. At a height of 12 m the plan was to have four containers preserving the ashes of those murdered. Lonas integrated the trees already growing there into the memorial which, as recommended for the competition, was to be placed between the two crematoria and the intention was to place diagonally opposite them a bronze sculpture of a 'prophetic figure'. The reference to Judaism was emphasized in the installation by undefined verses of the Hebrew Bible prophets set into one of the two walls pointing south and east.[105]

Lidy von Lüttwitz

She was the only German artist who managed, with the subject of the model she submitted, to do justice to the complex task of building an international memorial of fraternity and, at the same time, reminding people of God's support for the Jews in the Hebrew Bible as well as remembering their suffering in Auschwitz. Lüttwitz had planned to set up at the place recommended by the committee an 11-m group of figures made

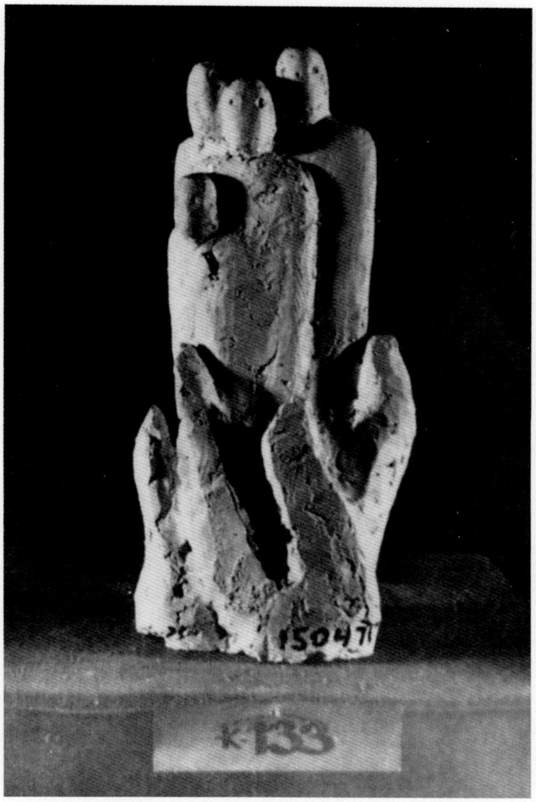

140 Lidy von Lüttwitz, *Model for an International Memorial in Auschwitz-Birkenau*, 1958.

of bronze that was to be surrounded by flames. A 5 × 5-m-high space, intended to preserve the urn from the memorial stone, served as a base.[106] Four heads can be made out on the photograph K133 of the group of people in the fire (illus. 140), reminding the Jews and also the Christians of the three men in the Fiery Furnace according to Daniel 3,[107] and of the illustration of the burning of the Jews in Schedel's Nuremberg *Chronicle of the World* of 1493 (see illus. 2). The fourth person whose head appears to be placed lower than the other three is, according to the account of King Nebuchadnezzar (Daniel 3:25), identified as 'the Son of God': 'Lo, I see four men loose, walking in the midst of the fire, and they have no hurt; and the form of the fourth is like the Son of God.' Possibly the sculptress had even read about the modern electronic music *The Fiery Furnace* by Karlheinz Stockhausen, composed in 1955 and premiered in Cologne in 1956.

The sculptress, who established herself after the war[108] – in 1955 she created a figurative memorial warning of violence for the Town Hall in Berlin-Reinickendorf[109] – emphasized with the towering stele the solid block of the men coming out of the fire. Her favourite sculptural idea, the steep striving upward and growth using vegetable-like or curved forms, she carried over into dynamic blocks representing tongues of fire that the men in the sculpture appear to be resisting, and she explained this: 'By leaning upon one another human beings can succeed in staying upright.'[110]

Helmut Wolff

The architectural design by the young sculptor from Berlin belongs to the seven entries that the prize jury chose from out of 426 in the first round of the process.[111] This led to it being exhibited at Auschwitz, where all the submitted models were intended to be on display for thirty days. Wolff's work was in addition shown afterwards with the six others at UNESCO in Paris. It was also published in the journal *Bauwelt*, which gave the layout, a geographical map showing the various concentration camps in the whole of Europe and a plan of Auschwitz-Birkenau.[112]

Wolff had chosen an unusual concept for the time for his proposed memorial. He had complied with the wishes of the committee, who had announced in the introduction that what they were aiming at was to make the artists very much aware of 'the experience of Auschwitz' (illus. 141). He had

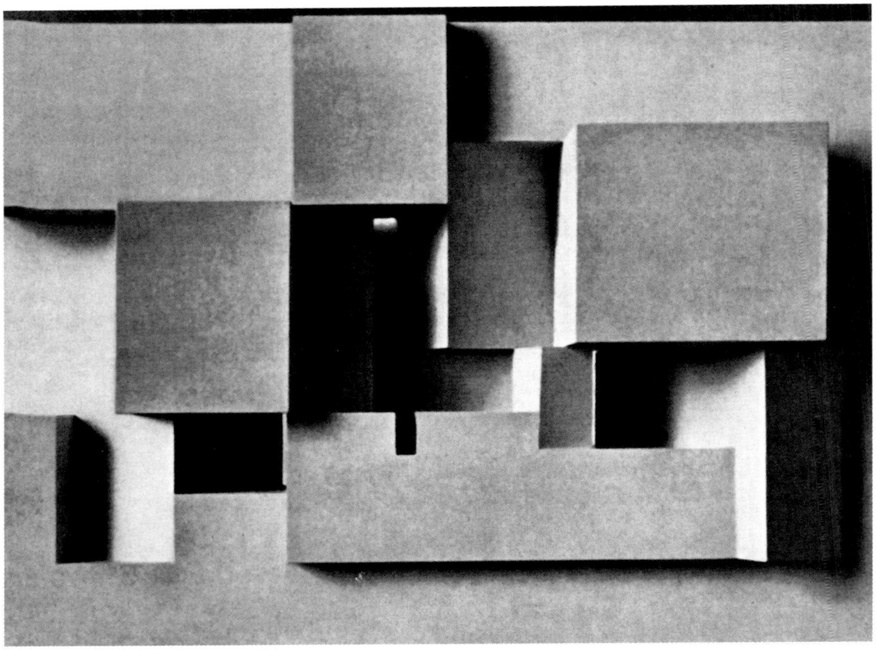

141 Helmut Wolff, *Model for an International Memorial in Auschwitz-Birkenau*, 1958.

proposed a 'gate-like construction' 26 m long, 18 m high and 6 m wide, composed of heavy concrete blocks jutting out in front and behind. It had the shape of a Cubist-structured wall as a sopraporta relief, first developed by Josef Hoffmann in the modernist style in the Vienna of 1900,[113] and was now intended to represent coercion and violence.[114] He too again proposed the position between the two crematoria at the end of the railway track, placing the accessible frontage of the architectural feature opposite them. 'Hollows inset on the front side, ending by narrowing conically into a crack just allowing one person to get through. The experience consists in the movement of passing through.' The visitors were intended to end by passing through and on to the memorial stone behind the projected memorial. Wolff wrote in the commentary on his design: 'I started with the intention of representing suffering by means of tangible material in order to make the horror palpable, to impose an experience upon the visitor, forcing him or her to take part in it. The way the victims went should be trod once again symbolically.'[115]

The obligation of reliving that Wolff wanted to impose upon visitors reminds one of the way in which the Allies forced the inhabitants to view the concentration camps at Buchenwald and Bergen-Belsen. The criticism of the prize jury, however, focused on the unwanted contrast between the camp situation and the memorial standing right opposite. In addition, they expressed concern that the experience of the architecture was at the same time inappropriate for many visitors and would distract them from viewing the camp. In the second round of the prize jury Wolff's work was eliminated.

For Eduard Trier the use of symbolism was what particularly distinguished Wolff's entry for the competition; in 1962 he considered this submission for the competition to be the most important because it 'is not designed for viewing but for re-living'.[116] Heinz Ladendorf, a professor of art history from Cologne, in light of contemporary events,[117] only referred in 1963 to the 'subject of the Wall'[118] while Adolf Rieth, in the first German publication on 'Concentration Camp Memorials to the European Peoples', in 1968 mentioned Wolff's proposal as the only one from Germany in the competition, emphasizing once more the intention of a reliving of experience: the memorial 'was in addition intended to bring home over and over again to the viewer the path the prisoners trod as victims, and thus serve as a warning to the future'.[119] The concept that Wolff aimed for, involving the experience of history through the experience of space, is also the basis of the concrete pillars and their arrangement in the *Memorial for the Murdered Jews of Europe*,[120] inaugurated in Berlin on 10 May 2005.

Joseph Beuys

At the start of the 1950s Joseph Beuys suffered from serious depression, which he later described: 'this crisis' was no doubt due to the after-effect of 'memories of the war'.[121] The contribution for the competition at Auschwitz-Birkenau was the first large-scale work he began after that. Beuys had taken part in the war, including a crash in 1944 over the Crimea as an aircraft gunner.[122] He dealt with the Nazi past[123] through various stages of recovery that are important for his artistic production. In 'Joseph Beuys Lebenslauf Werklauf' (Joseph Beuys Curriculum Vitae and Oeuvre), a text first published in 1964,[124] the artist writes about his birth in 1921 as 'the exhibition of a wound covered by a plaster'. His aeroplane crash, turned in 1980 into the mythical story of being rescued by Tatars, is not mentioned. This interpretation of his own life story as an artistic production corresponds, on the one hand, to Beuys's (art-)theoretical concept of 'social sculpture'; on the other, it enabled him to distance himself from his own war experiences and – following Mark Rosenthal's observation[125] – therefore perhaps also from his own guilt.[126]

He demonstrates this concept also in his contribution for Auschwitz and, as one could conclude from looking back over his whole oeuvre, he appears to have developed it only in the course of this work. Before that, as a pupil of Ewald Mataré, he had collaborated on another memorial site in Cologne, a 'war memorial'.[127] It consisted of a copy of *The Grieving Parents* by Käthe Kollwitz at the war cemetery of Roggeveld Eesen in Flanders from 1931, and in 1959 it was set up in the ruins of the church of St Alban in Cologne. Its 'expression of suffering', according to the *Kölner Stadtanzeiger* on its inauguration, was intended 'to remind people of all the dead that the Second World War carried off'.[128] Indeed, Mataré had received the commission but had delegated the execution of the sculpture to his pupils. Between 1953 and

1954 Beuys made the sculpture of the father, enlarged by 10 per cent, and Erwin Heerich that of the mother. Beuys himself had been selected to produce the *Memorial for the Dead of the Two World Wars* at Meerbusch-Büderich inaugurated in May 1959. The 3-m-high oakwood form, hanging freely in an old church tower and appearing to be related both to a crucifix and an angel, Beuys wanted to be taken as a 'general symbol of resurrection'.[129] In recording his memories of the Second World War, Beuys did not make any distinction between the dead perpetrators and the war dead and those who had been murdered. Beuys was to hold to this view of those killed in the Second World War.

Death and the Maiden

A watercolour of 1957 documents Beuys's artistic engagement with the dying in the camp at Auschwitz. On the back of a yellowing package stamped with the address of the awarding body of the competition, the Comité International d'Auschwitz, and its general secretary at the time, Hermann Langbein, he painted *Death and the Maiden*[130] (illus. 142) in watercolours. In doing this, he did not refer to the photographs of the events in the camps that had been supplied to him with the documentation by Jan Sehn from the IAC, but on the stamped cover of the package[131] he painted a scene widely known particularly in Germany from the vanitas images reminding people of the mortality of human beings.[132] Beuys answered the letter from a survivor of Auschwitz by using the image of the traditional metaphor for death itself as the deadly union of the sexes, the seducing and seduced maiden.[133] Along with its carrier, the image of the allegory of mortality emphasizes an exonerating change of perspective from those who had been murdered to that of human beings as a whole.[134]

Model for a Memorial at Auschwitz-Birkenau

Beuys's competition entry for Auschwitz-Birkenau is more revealing than the questionable memento mori for the camp at Auschwitz of his artistic statement that he is unable and unwilling to illustrate the events themselves.[135] As he engaged with this project towards the end of his psychological crisis, it probably contributed to his own healing process by enabling him to work through the past.

According to the records of the competition, two monumental gates[136] were to consist of irregular building blocks based on two reinforced concrete supports, the first of which would tower above the camp gate. At a distance of several hundred metres, they would lead up to a memorial (illus. 143 and 144). The memorial was to be made of silver and would reflect the sunlight in an irregular crystal-like shape.

As Beuys explained to the committee:

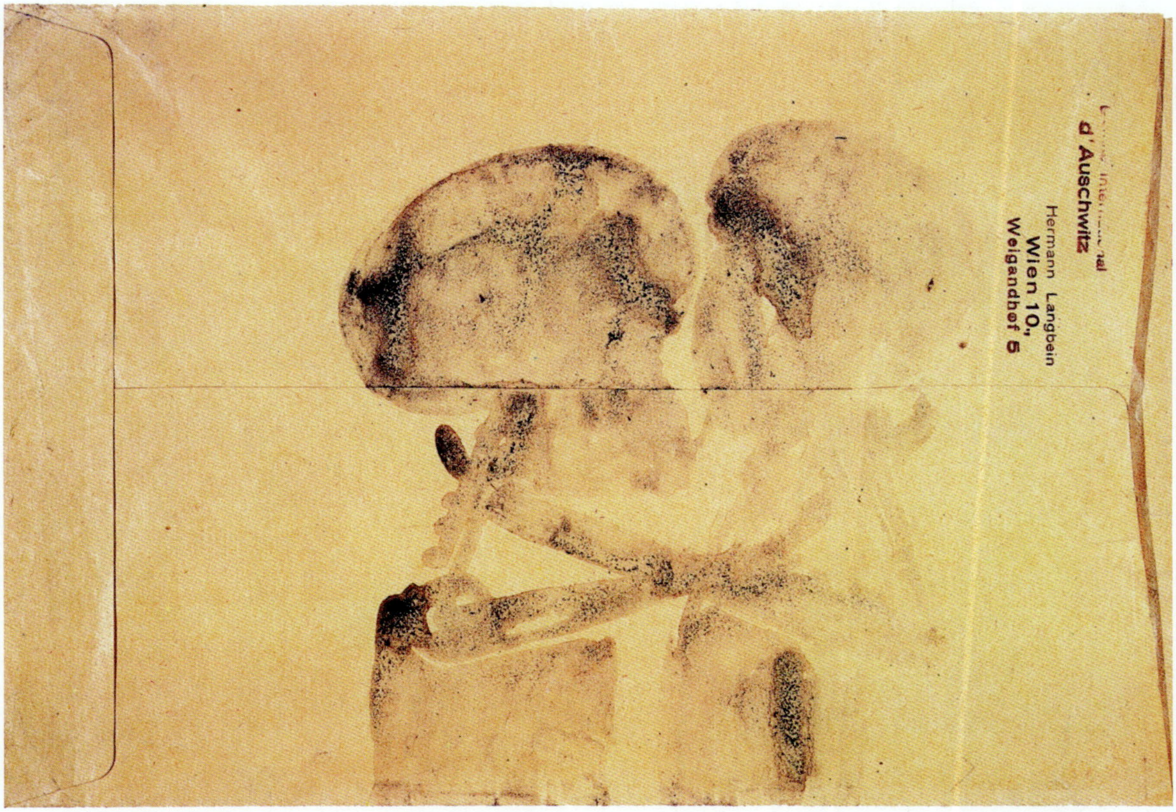

142 Joseph Beuys, *Death and the Maiden*, 1957, brush and ink on an envelope.

The concept consists of three sculptural elements within the camp at Auschwitz. They are to be erected along the whole length of railway line between the main gate and the termination of the ramp. The three sculptural elements are divided into:

Two preparatory symbols made of reinforced concrete;

The actual memorial which is intended to stand in place of the former temporary urn . . . It will be cast in polished solid silver according to the enclosed lead model. At its zenith it will reach a height of 2.30 m, and a width of approximately 6.50 m. The memorial will have its open side pointing in an easterly direction. What has been a plinth up until now should be completely removed so that it can stand flat on the ground . . . The first symbol is to be visible from a long way off, therefore to a considerable extent towering above the watchtower. Its height and projecting surface make it shine out. The second, smaller upstanding feature has the job of conveying the expression of the large symbol into the interior of the camp, also pointing in the direction of the memorial. Both concrete symbols should emphasize, heighten and encapsulate the atmosphere of the camp . . .

In the case of the memorial, the important thing was the search for a metaphor to do justice to the many layers of significance. The sculpture

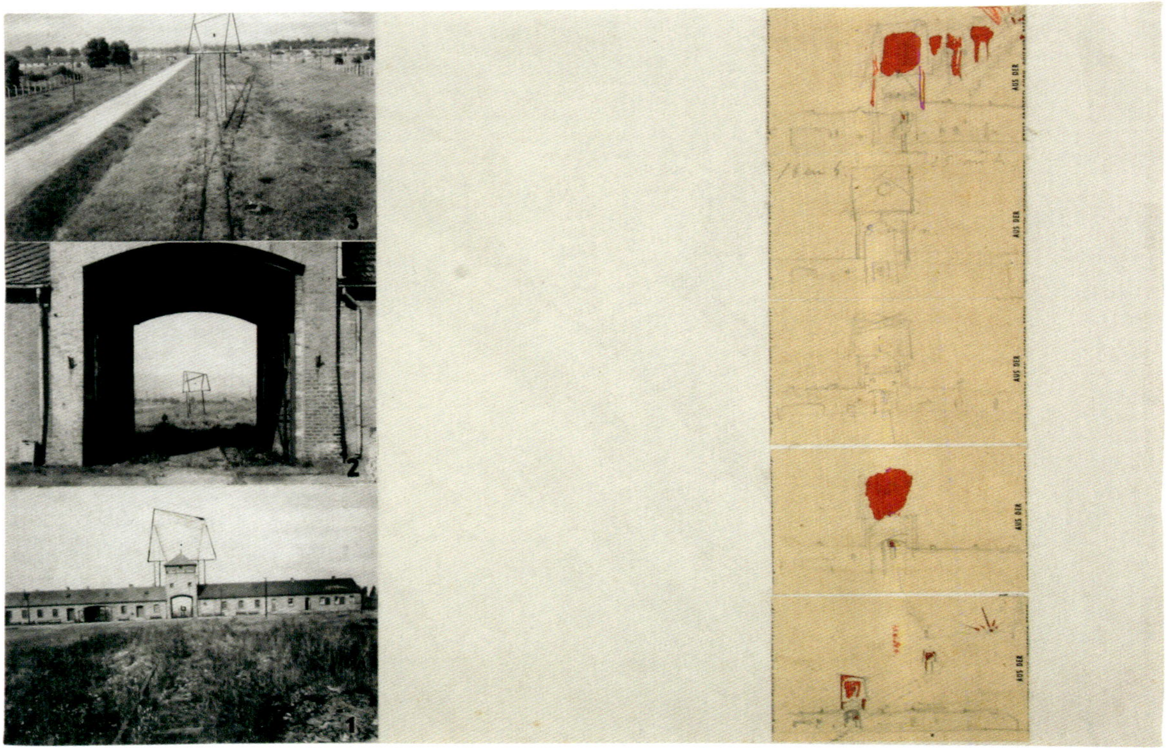

143 Joseph Beuys, *Sketches for the Auschwitz Memorial*, 1957, collage on book paper, with two photographs and a picture.

> is a beacon, a bowl, a crystal, a flower, a chalice. The rays of morning sun should be reflected there in all their variety, shining out of the polished silver.[137]

Mario Kramer indeed thinks, in the working out of the designs of Beuys's project for a memorial, the 'drawings have more the character of a track left by a wounded animal', but his ambition, to create a monument towering over the remains of the camp at Auschwitz-Birkenau, 10 m high, with its gate at the start and ending at the level of the crematoria, is not negligible.[138] Like most of the participants, Beuys followed the recommendations of the competition organizers, including the choice of the location for the installation of the 'actual memorial'. Another sketch[139] indicates that the course of the path marked by the 'symbols' was to lead from the entrance building up to the memorial by crossing the railway line. This drawing also shows the reconstructed crematoria.

In his explanation of the actual memorial, the crystal form, Beuys emphasized its being rooted to the ground without making use of the memorial stone already erected there.[140] Along with the 'the polished silver shining' in the morning sun, the draft for the memorial is intended to suggest the familiar idea of darkness into light and, in Beuys's variation influenced by Rudolf Steiner,[141] a transformation from the realm of the earth into light from the East. The crystal form fits in with this concept since, in Beuys's view, it symbolizes

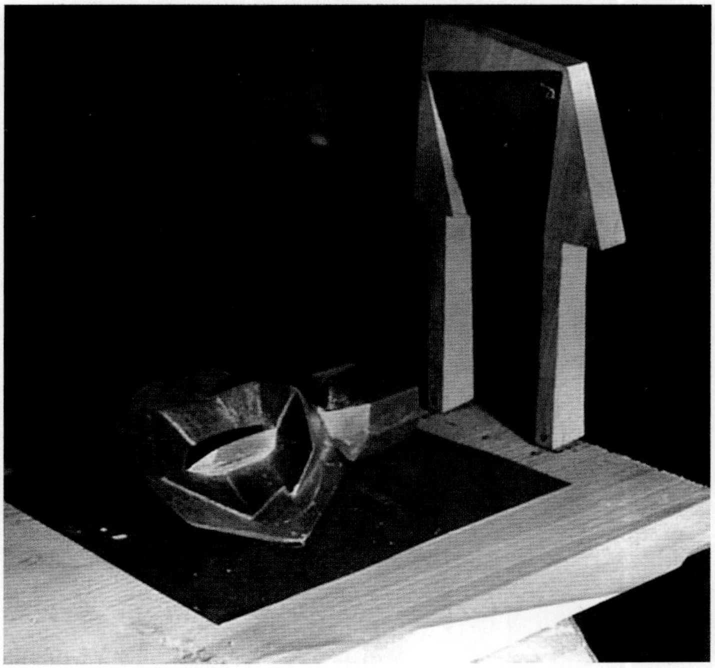

144 Joseph Beuys, *Model for an International Memorial in Auschwitz-Birkenau*, 1958, photograph.

both the realm of death, earth-bound material hardened into mineral,[142] and the process of transformation into the spiritual realm; it corresponds to his use of metaphor 'for a resurrection through death'.[143] In addition, it resembles the watercolours and sculptures of lamps in other sketches by Beuys from this period which he positioned in precisely spaced pentagons and hexagons in a circle.[144] As Beuys was reading James Joyce's *Ulysses* at the same time as the competition and after his recovery and was trying to create graphics based on this work in six notebooks,[145] they also include sketches on these ideas for the memorial layout at Auschwitz. To judge from a pencil drawing in Book 2, p. 3 of the *Ulysses* notebooks (illus. 145), he was as concerned with the light and the (re)interpretation of it as he was with symbolically reflecting the burial places of the vanished Celts.[146] Against a background of two corbelled arches from Irish megalithic graves of the Neolithic period, projecting from their ends the two 'symbols' conceived by Beuys for the memorial viewed side-on, two of the characteristic concrete posts of the concentration camp are visible.[147] One of the lamps frequently used there appears to be shining from one of them while on the bent end of the other a single, large electric bulb is attached, sending beams in all directions. Beuys covered almost the whole page with two towers of different heights. Their resemblance to the chimneys of Crematoria II and IV at Birkenau can be seen just by comparing them with the photographs published by Sehn. From there it is clear that Beuys studied them and used the documentation here and in other works.[148] He incorporated into this sketch two chimneys from the photograph that had been taken during the building of Crematorium III (see illus. 101). The way they dominate the buildings, being more than twice their height, is a development by Beuys in line with the relation in size of the various elements of the photograph. On the left of the drawing, the pencil lines of the beams of Beuys's crystal extend over the block that is seemingly made of stone.

The literature interpreting the concept talks about another source of inspiration for the form of the two 'symbols'. Both Dieter Koepplin[149] and Franz Joef van der Grinten[150] refer to the 1953 drawing *Dwarves' Graves* (illus. 146)[151] and other drawings of this subject from the period before work on the Auschwitz memorial. On display there are various forms reminiscent of what were then still referred to in German as *Hünengräber* (Giants' Graves) and, like the disorderly arches in Paul Klee's *Revolution of the Viaduct* of 1937[152] (illus. 147), spread out over the drawing. The use of this basic motif, however, for the Auschwitz memorial is 'not to be taken lightly';[153] both commentators are keen to explain the forces devoted to dwarves in Beuys's cosmology in terms of the 'mythical power over the forces of nature . . . the secret force that endures',[154] dwarves acting on the earth 'in their own way' from the inside.[155]

The two gates with the irregular rectangles as sopraportas, which Kramer, following Franz Joseph van der Grinten, describes as 'scaffold-like',[156] can in addition be taken to be reflections of the crystal form of the memorial as well as belonging to the anthroposophical tradition of avoiding a right angle. Beuys added a personal note, only visible on the model of the smaller gate,

145 Joseph Beuys, sketch from the notebook *Joseph Beuys Extends Ulysses by 2 Chapters on the Order of James Joyce*, 1957.

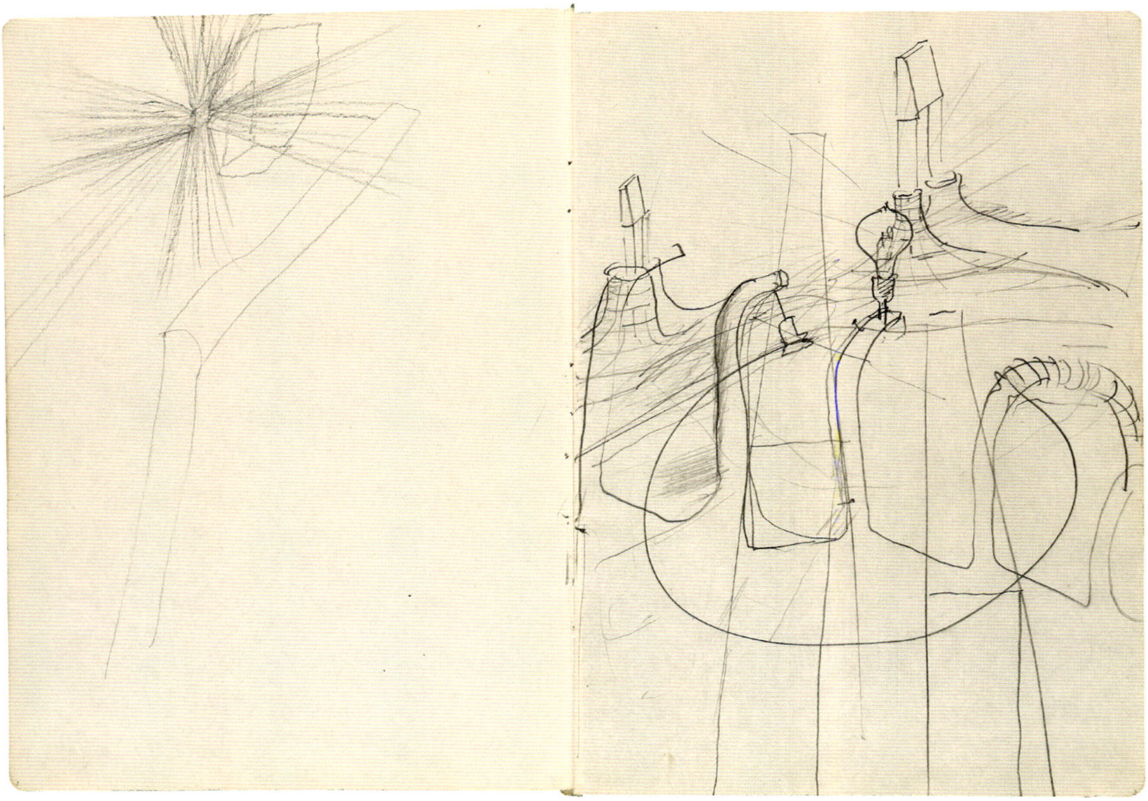

146 Joseph Beuys, *Dwarves' Graves*, 1953–4, pencil and opaque white on paper.

147 Paul Klee, *Revolution of the Viaduct*, 1937, oil on cotton.

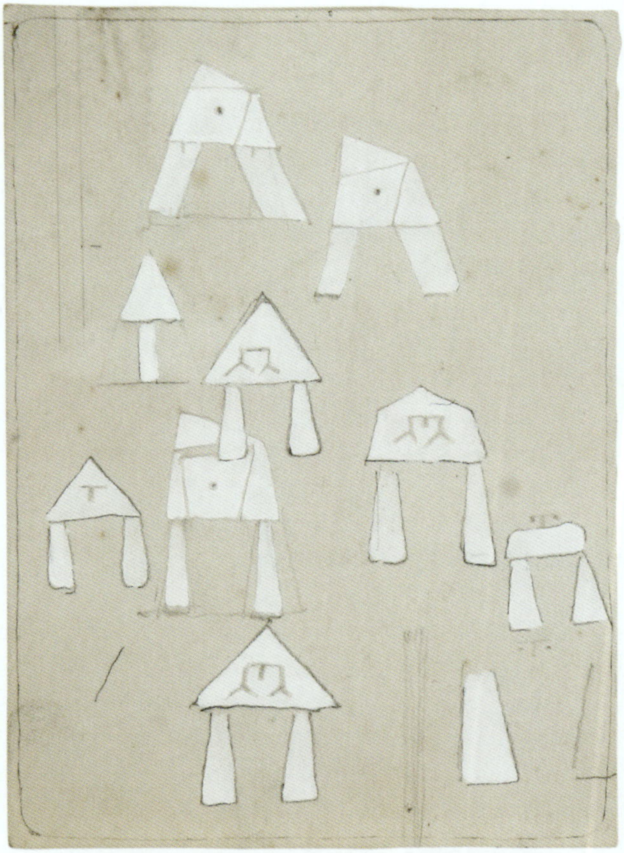

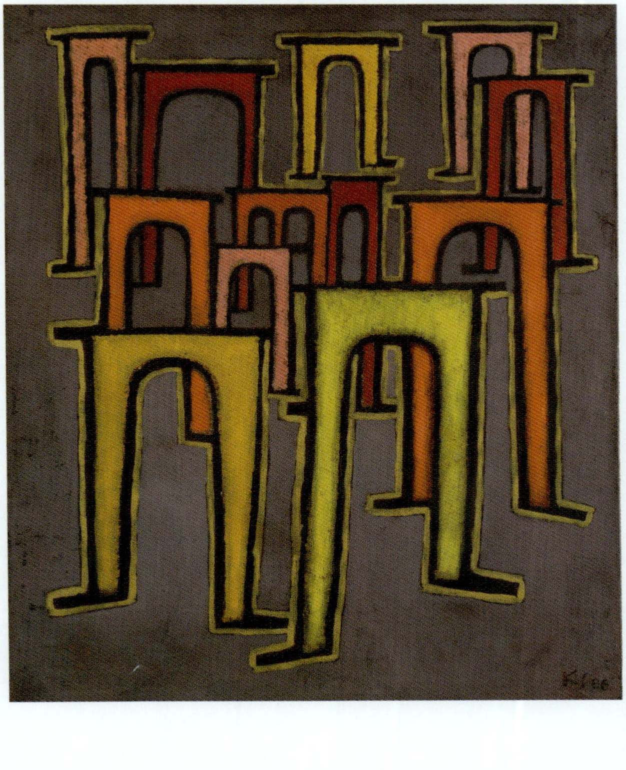

by stencilling the numerals of his date of birth but leaving the millennium numbers out. Kramer remarked that Beuys was using these numbers as a reminder of the tattoos on the prisoners' bodies.[157] Beuys fits into the German debate about victimization that lumped together those murdered and persecuted by the Nazis with all those affected by the war, as in the case of St Alban in Cologne. However, the artist-author, not himself a witness like Hans Grundig, sought to identify himself with those killed in the camps and was making an appeal for sympathy.

His proposal was also eliminated, like many of the others, probably on account of the tall 'symbols' since, for the short list, the jury excluded any concept with a monumental vertical element.[158] For Beuys, however, this did not mean an end to his engagement with the Auschwitz model, Jan Sehn's book[159] and the plans supplied with the competition information.

Arie Goral: *Sacrificial Animal and Boatman*

For Arie Goral, the Hamburg-born emigrant returned from Israel, previously Walter Sternheim, integrating into the post-war society of West Germany was a problem for the whole of his life; nevertheless he remained there. In his varied engagement as a Jewish intellectual, writer, gallery owner, political activist, teacher and painter, he reflected on his situation as a Jew in Germany after 1945, by no means taking this to mean only his personal fate.[160] After the end of the Jewish-Arab War in 1948 at the age of 39 in Israel, he had himself begun to paint while painting with children, continuing his training from 1951 at the Academy in Florence. There he specialized mainly in the world of the 'Orient' and the Israeli landscape, for which he had a great longing. In 1953 he returned to his native city, giving speeches there and giving free instruction on art to children and young people. The happiness of what he once called his painted 'World-Dream-Pictures', initially under Chagall's influence displaying colourful memories back to southern climes,[161] gave way to his increasingly hardening criticism of the suppression of the Nazi past in his environment. Outraged at the stance of the Federal Government over the case of Government Minister Oberländer in 1962 (see p. 224), he even considered emigrating once again.[162] His views on the German situation, along with a large number of political interventions, formed the background to the 1959 picture *Sacrificial Animal and Boatman* (illus. 148), which was thereafter to become a frequent subject with slight variations.[163]

The carcass of an animal of a disproportionately large size, painted blood-red and skinned, is hanging by a back leg from a grey sky down into the city between the two turquoise-coloured spires of the Hamburg churches of St Peter and St Jacob.[164] The skipper of one of the typical Hamburg boats, the man steering the lighter, appears at the bottom left of the picture and, to judge from his stance, is looking up at the animal carcass, the dripping blood

148 Arie Goral, *Sacrificial Animal and Boatman (Sacrificial Animal Hanging Above the Lake Alster in Hamburg)*, 1959, oil on hardboard.

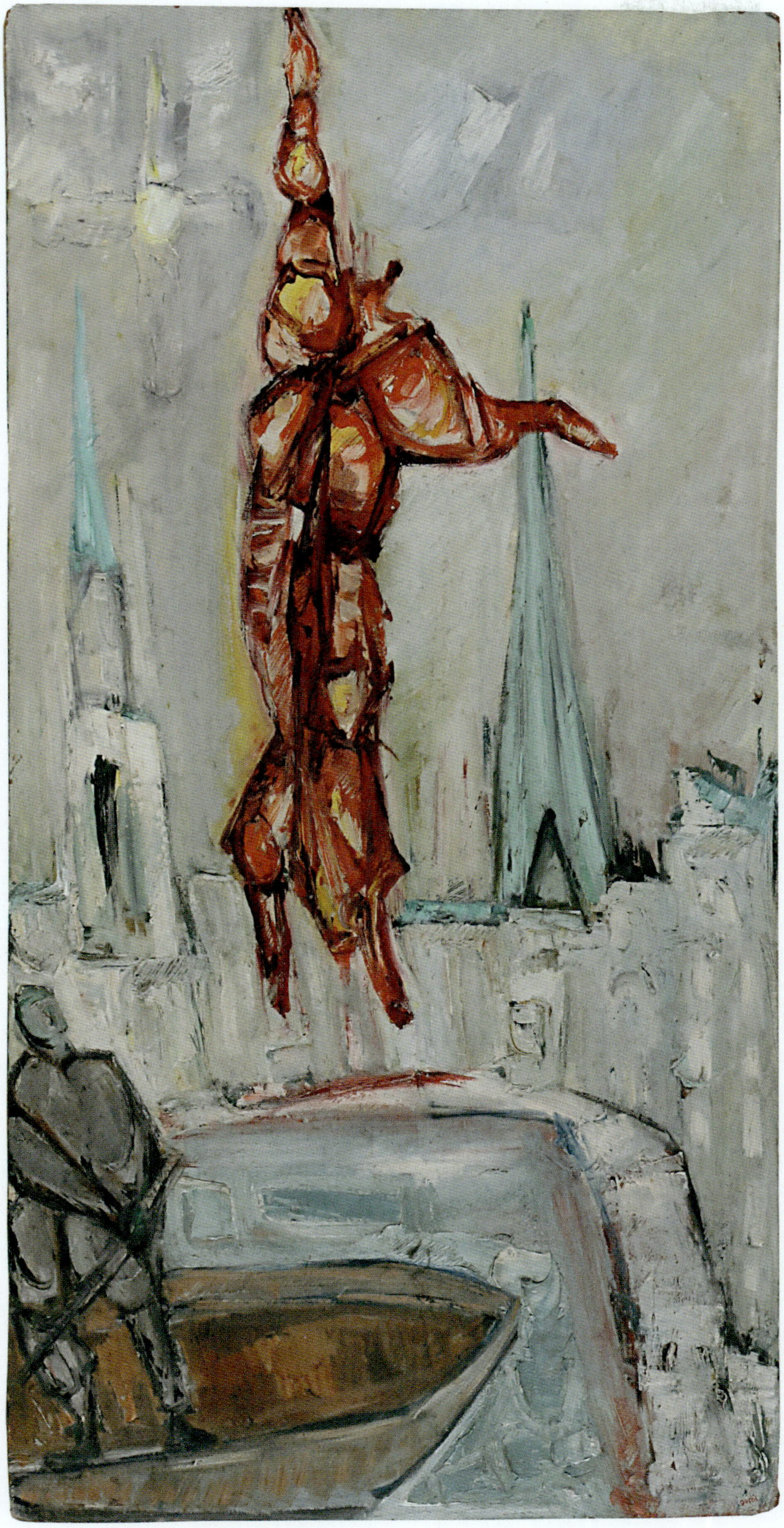

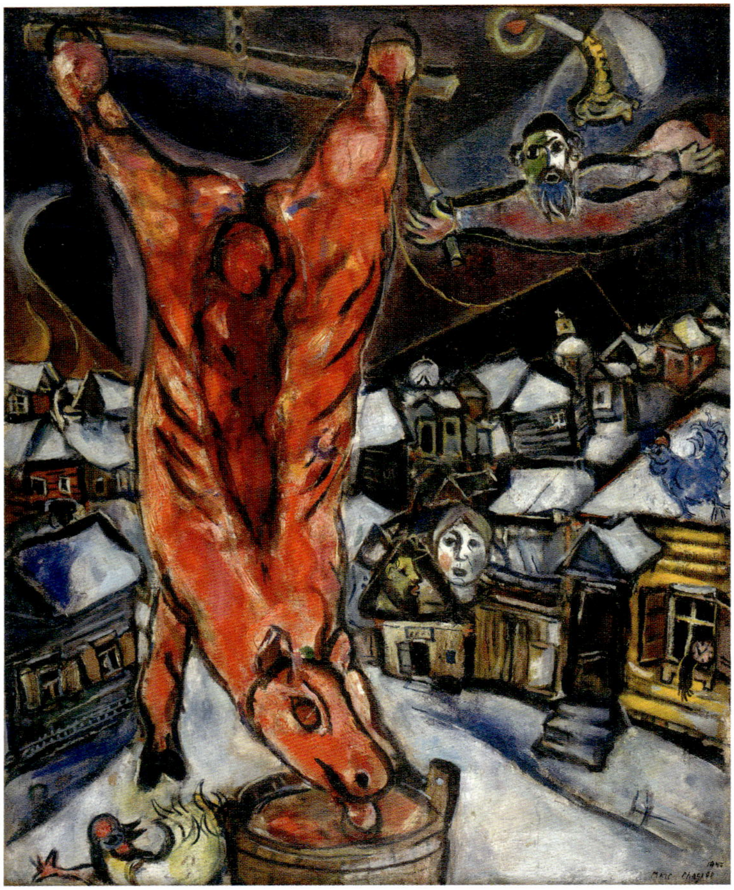

149 Marc Chagall, *Flayed Ox*, 1947, oil on canvas.

of which is colouring red parts of the bank of the Binnenalster, the inner-city lake in Hamburg. In the top left-hand corner of the oil painting, Goral has inscribed a cross into the grey sky, something that does not show up well in reproductions. Its crossing point consists of a round, white disc with a certain resemblance to Chagall's white discs and the use of light in the picture *White Crucifixion*[165] and a lithograph of 1950.[166]

Choosing Marc Chagall's painting *Flayed Ox* (illus. 149) as a model signifies Goral's wish to paint a reminder of the bloody past and the murdered Jews with the bloody stigma hanging above his native city.[167] Goral admired the celebrated painter, who was like himself a Jew and an emigrant. It is fairly safe to assume that he saw Chagall's big retrospective exhibition at the Hamburg Kunstverein in 1959 since that is the year in which Goral created *Sacrificial Animal and Boatman*. Goral could at the same time have seen pictures from the same period as *Flayed Ox*[168] about the murder of the Jews, such as *The Falling Angel* and *Résistance (Ghetto)*, but also the earlier pictures such as *White Crucifixion*, *The Martyr* and *The Yellow Crucifixion*, and may have read the surrounding narratives which contextualize the monumental centre of the images, typical of Chagall.[169] Chagall was probably remembering old

Vitebsk with its mixed populations of Russians, White Russians, Lithuanians and Poles, a corresponding variety of religious affiliation, and its snow-coloured log-huts while he was painting the picture as an emigrant in the U.S., portraying the catastrophe of this town, which represented the town of his Jewish youth. The ox hanging from a crossbeam over the whole extent of the picture is not shown as a headless slaughtered animal carcass as Chaim Soutine and Rembrandt[170] portrayed it in *Slaughtered Ox* before him, but as a flayed ox, skinned and blood-red with a large open wound. The way it is portrayed can be interpreted both as a gash in the carcass ready for gutting and also as a mortal wound in the animal's back. The head with the tongue hanging out above a wooden barrel full of red-stained water indicates that the animal is being bled and is possibly still attempting to lap up water. Chagall's childhood memories of kosher slaughter at the house of his grandfather, who was a rabbi and a butcher, are heightened in this painting into an image of passion of the animal, gigantic in relation to the houses, signalling the suffering that is befalling the whole town. Into the picture of the flayed ox, there appears an old bearded Jew out of the sky at top right, his eyes, open mouth and extended arms expressing his horror at the scene. With the knife in his right hand, he reminds one of his grandfather's occupation, but the broken-off candelabra above him, the hints of flames above the houses on the left and the black glove next to the clock in the window of the yellow log house at bottom right with the blue cockerel on the roof[171] suggest a slaughter going far beyond the usual butchery. The representation of animals and human beings living together, displayed as an example in the 1911 *I and the Village* on the cover of the catalogue for the Hamburg Chagall exhibition, has become in the painting *Flayed Ox* a symbol of the deadly violence committed by the Nazis in the town. Chagall selected a favourite subject of painting, its close connection with slaughter and violent death, in order to make use of it as a symbol of Jewish martyrdom – by analogy with his images of the Jewish Christ and the mother and child.[172]

Goral transposed the basic image of the hanging, bleeding ox above Vitebsk to the German Hanseatic city, whose many churches show it to be Christian. The result was an allegorical image of slaughter against a Hamburg background intended to remind people of the extermination of the Jews of that city.[173] Goral painted the port city against the symbol of the flayed animal next to the crucifix and between the church spires of the city in several versions, which were probably exhibited in Hamburg in December of the same year.[174] In the 1960s he did not abandon the symbolism of a sacrifice using a hanging animal, but made his omen even clearer by representing human beings hanging by their legs.[175] In one of these pictures from 1968–9 he added his name right next to the mouth of the one hanging.[176]

Carlfriedrich Claus

Remembered Poem of a Jewish Girl

The draughtsman, philosopher and linguistic theorist Carlfriedrich Claus refused to be incorporated either artistically or politically; as a pacifist Communist living in the GDR and watched by the STASI, he created quite individual representations based on his engagement with the Jews since childhood days.[177] Towards the start of his artistic activity he made a collage and, using a brush and washed ink, painted the 1959 drawing *Remembered Poem of a Jewish Girl*,[178] the title of which is given, according to the information in his list of works, as *Ashes Her Hand Rain Her Eye Looks Out From Auschwitz Rain Always Ashes* (illus. 150). An ink drawing, washed and watery like rain, covers a page on the back of which is written:

Erinnertes Gedicht eines jüdischen Mädchens
Asche ihre Hand, Regen.
  Ihr Auge blickt her aus Auschwitz   ⊑*Regen immer, Asche.*
  Carlfriedrich Claus, 1959/60   *: Asche.*

Remembered poem of a Jewish girl
Ashes her hand, Rain.
  Her eye looks out from Auschwitz   ⊑Rain always, ashes.
  Carlfriedrich Claus, 1959/60   : ashes.

With its rhythmic repetition of the word 'ashes', the words 'eye' and 'rain' it sounds like a response to Paul Celan's poems *Todesfuge* (see pp. 134–8). More than that, however, it reminds one of his poem 'Engführung' ('Stretto' or 'The Straitening')[179] that was published in Frankfurt am Main in the same year in the collection *Sprachgitter* (Language Mesh):

Asche.
Asche, Asche.
Nacht.
Nacht-und-Nacht. – Zum
Aug geh, zum feuchten.

Ash
Ash, ash.
Night.
Night-and-night. – Go
to the eye, the moist eye.[180]

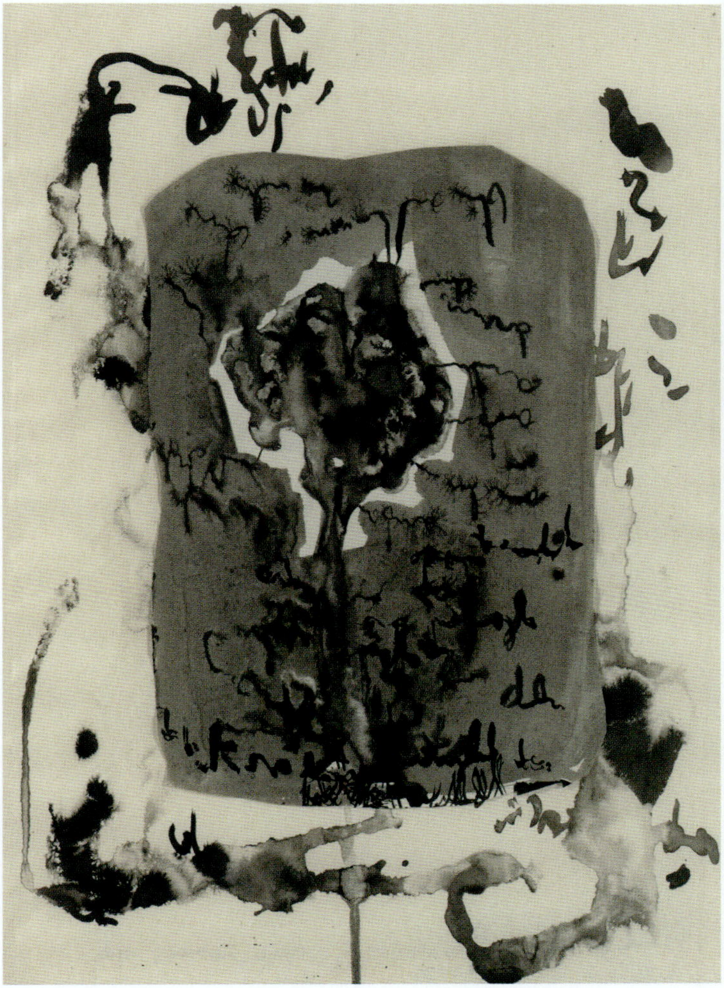

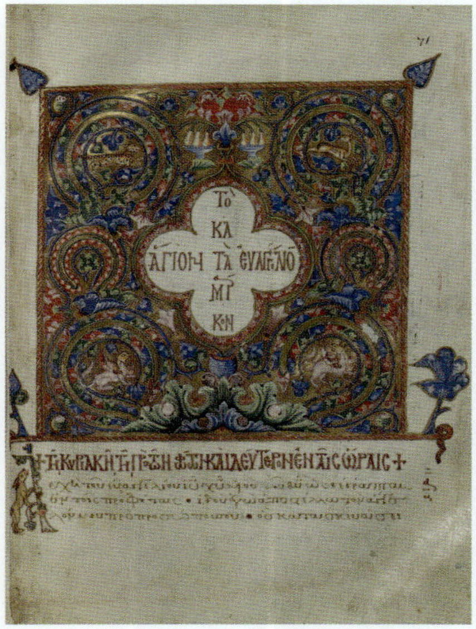

150 Carlfriedrich Claus, *Remembered Poem of a Jewish Girl*, 1959, collage on writing paper, brush and black ink, wash.

151 Folio 71r of the Greek Gospel grec. 71, illuminated parchment, Byzantium, 12th century.

Celan did not specify who is speaking. Claus by contrast gave this task to an anonymous girl who, by use of the word 'Auschwitz', becomes an allegory for the genocide of the Jews.

The picture–text collage consists of an irregular top sheet with a drawing in ink applied wet on wet and leaving the middle uncovered for a central figure that is glued onto another piece of writing paper. It reminds one of precious written and painted works of art such as Byzantine book illuminations (illus. 151) that frequently show rectangular miniatures on bright parchment, whose ornaments highlight a biblical text or symbol in the middle surrounded by drôleries in the corners.[181] The shape in the middle which Claus placed on the lower paper, possibly reminiscent of a young girl's face, is very similar to Wols's faces – and is blurred and gently fading along with the signs of writing. Out of the washed ink, the *Poem* and the face appear and disappear.

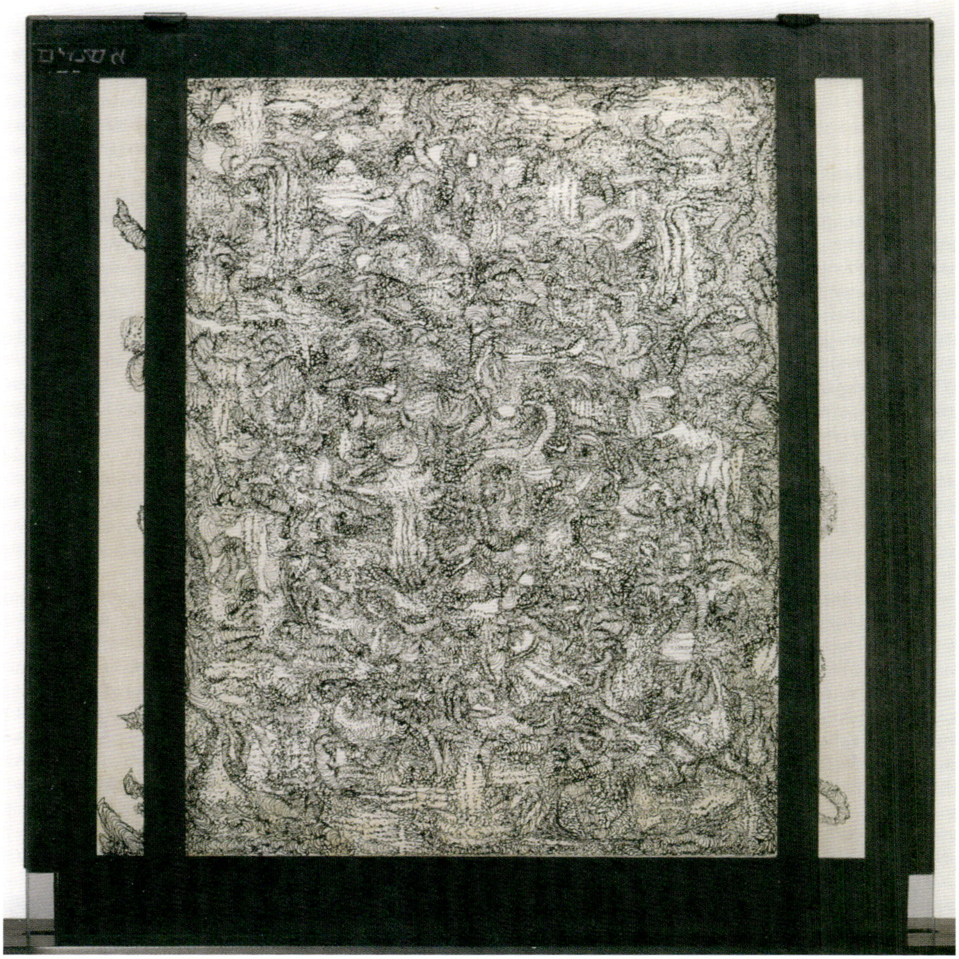

Memory-al for the Rabbi Jizchok Leib Safra

Once more, Claus remembered the murder of the Jews in the camps; his immensely vibrant, intricate drawing of 1961, however, was not devoted to an anonymous femininity serving to represent all the murdered Jews, but to an individual male.[182] The title written on the reverse, *Memory-al for the Rabbi Jizchok Leib Safra (Murdered at Auschwitz in 1944)*, reveals that it is dedicated to a rabbi conversant with the Kabbalah, something that Claus was also interested in (illus. 152). It is neither in the familiar tradition of portraying rabbis[183] nor takes death as its subject. Instead, it consists of three drawings with lines like handwritten characters, the middle of which is four times as wide as the margins and reminds one of the open Torah scroll with the text continuing over the rods. The delicate lines seem to abolish borders. The drawings of movements of language enter into a dialogue with the respected rabbi beyond his death, a personal honouring of the dead as a discourse about language, writing and their 'reception', the Kabbalah, carried on synaesthetically.[184]

152 Carlfriedrich Claus, *Memory-al for the Rabbi Jizchok Leib Safra (Murdered at Auschwitz in 1944)*, 1961–2, pen and ink on white paper, in three pieces attached to black paper.

7 Remembering Again: The Early 1960s

Given the trial in Ulm in 1958 concerning the *Einsatzgruppen*,[1] the lead-up to the Eichmann trial in Jerusalem and the trials against the West German politicians Theodor Oberländer[2] and Hans Globke[3] in the GDR, the generation growing up after the war were confronted with the extermination of the Jews. They had to consider the fact that mass murder had been committed by Germans within and outside concentration camps. During the years towards the end of the Adenauer era, there were renewed calls for investigations into the relationship between the present and the past. Although those accused in Ulm were not charged with murder but only with having been accessories to it, the perpetrators found themselves catapulted by the trial out of their cosy seclusion within West German society.

Unlike the 1950s, when works of art about the genocide went largely unnoticed, they were now drawn into an ongoing debate about the extent of the murders. In 1960 Erwin Leiser's film *Mein Kampf*[4] rekindled the debate concerning what had been known about the plans and activities of the Nazis before and during their period of rule. In it Leiser, a German Jew, who lived in exile in Sweden after the pogroms of 1938, not only showed the rise of Adolf Hitler within the Nazi Party but, unlike *Night and Fog*, he referred to the politicians and industrialists who financed and supported Hitler. The policy of extermination in Poland is traced using archive material, representative of the atrocities in other countries, such as the unfinished film *Asien in Europa*.[5] Leiser contrasted these pictures of 'everyday life' in the Warsaw Ghetto, of the suppression of the uprisings and the destroyed city, with material from newsreels, Leni Riefenstahl's *Triumph des Willens* (Triumph of the Will)[6] and the anti-Jewish propaganda films *Jud Süss*[7] as well as *Der Ewige Jude* (The Eternal Jew).[8] In the GDR the film was indeed praised, but it was not allowed to go on release. In West Germany it was shown in cinemas and used in schoolteaching.[9]

The world premiere of the Hollywood film *Judgement at Nuremberg* about the jurists involved with the Nazis took place the following year in Berlin.[10] In the West it was seen in the context of the Wall, which had been built only a few months previously. It was taken by some to be anti-German and by others as a means of identifying with those who are in the clear, in the figure of the guilt-ridden judge Janning.[11]

The GDR media followed, and commented on, both the Eichmann trial and the trial in Ulm. Lea Grundig, Peter Edel,[12] Leo Haas and other artists who since the first post-war years had continually reminded the world of the crimes of the German Nazis in exhibitions now again received more attention. Werner Tübke began to study the subject and devoted part of his cycle on the *History of the Workers' Movement* to the murder of the Jews (see illus. 159). The realism of the paintings and drawings, however, represented also by Lea Grundig and Dore Meyer-Vax, now lumped in all together with the German Communist Party, banned in the West since 1956 and under suspicion of still being supported by the GDR, met with politically motivated opposition in West Germany, becoming part and parcel of the debate about quality in the art business.

In the way the murder of Jewish men, women and children was viewed in West Germany, the main emphasis was placed once more on photography as the basis of remembrance. Bazon Brock started his public installations and Wolf Vostell addressed the topic but his works, as far as one can make out, became known to the public only after 1963. Both refer to the photographs that had become available once more with the public revelations in the course of these years.

Photo Books

As early as 1945 booklets in several languages had been distributed to the Germans and those forced to move to Germany, aimed at revealing the extent of the crimes. The one published in 1945 – *Bildbericht aus 5 Konzentrationslagern* (Pictorial Record from 5 Concentration Camps)[13] – reports on the camps at Buchenwald, Bergen-Belsen, Gardelegen, Nordhausen and Ohrdruf. The fact that the Jews were the largest of the persecuted groups is not mentioned in it. Likewise the pictorial record at the end of the war in *Life* on 7 May 1945, p. 33, only talks about 'political prisoners', 'slave laborers' and the 'living and the dead'. It is a similar story, as Schulze describes, in the case of how the history of Bergen-Belsen is viewed.[14] Although the British military knew that the dead and surviving prisoners were mostly Jews, 'the extent to which Jews were involved at Bergen-Belsen was generally played down in the publicly circulated reports, photos and films, filtered out or not even commented upon.'[15]

Three years after Jan Sehn's documentation of the concentration camp at Auschwitz-Birkenau which had been recommended to the participants in the competition for the memorial there, in Warsaw the album *We Have Not Forgotten* appeared. Its photographs of the sufferings of the Polish people under the Nazis were used in works by Bazon Brock (see illus. 154), Wolf Vostell (see illus. 168) and Werner Tübke (see illus. 207). In the text it mainly talks about the Polish nation as a whole, but in the captions to the photographs on the murders in the ghettos mention is made of the Jews. Whereas in the foreword to the first edition the debate about the rearmament of West Germany with atomic weapons is given as a reason for the publication,[16] the second edition refers to anti-Semitism rearing its ugly head again.[17]

Gerhard Schoenberner: *The Yellow Star*

The first photo book in West Germany on the *Judenverfolgung in Europa 1933 bis 1945* (Persecution of the Jews in Europe from 1933 to 1945), still now enjoying some public success, was published by Gerhard Schoenberner in 1960 under the title *Der gelbe Stern* (The Yellow Star) by the publishing house of Rütten & Loening in Hamburg. At the same time, the exhibition *Die Vergangenheit mahnt* (The Past is a Warning), for which Schoenberner had done the research along with Hanno Kremer and written the texts, opened at the Kongresshalle in West Berlin.[18] The poster for the exhibition (illus. 153), with its 'compromise between the exhibition organizers and the state subsidizing it',[19] illustrates the situation at the time as regards how far the public had come to terms with the murder of the Jews. A photograph of the ss taking

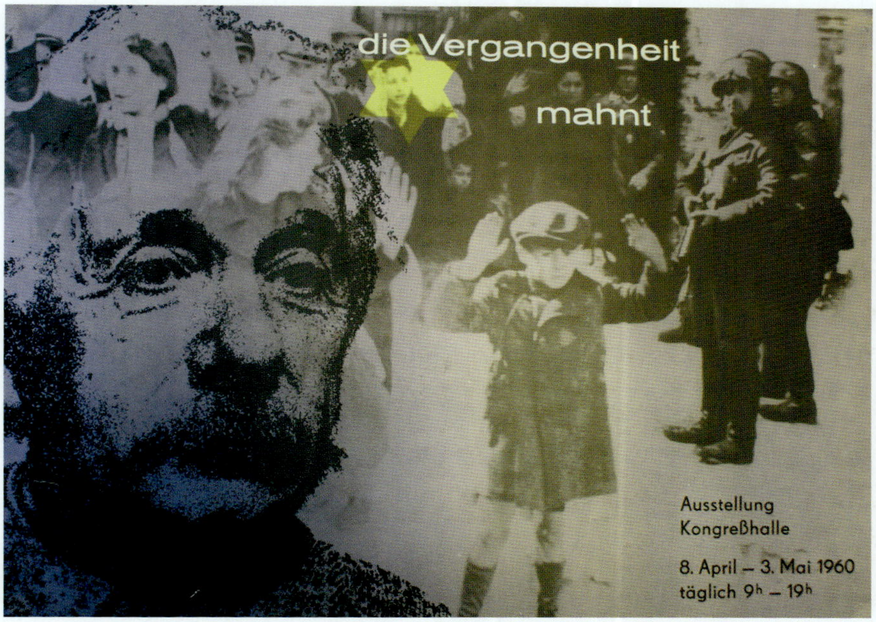

153 *The Past is a Warning*, exhibition poster, Berlin, 1960.

Jewish women and children prisoner during the Uprising in the Warsaw Ghetto, with the image of the boy with his hands raised that became so widely known,[20] had to be overshadowed under pressure from the committee by a photo of Albert Einstein. However, the request by Joachim Tiburtius, the cultural senator of the conservative CDU, to edit out the Waffen-SS insignia 'so that the men in uniform would not be seen as German'[21] was not adhered to by the exhibition organizers. The hypocritical way things were given a positive gloss through the use of montage is apparent, as can be seen, albeit in a more dramatic context, from a remark by Hannah Arendt in her book *Eichmann in Jerusalem*, which came out in German in 1964: 'There are more than a few people, especially among the cultural élite, who still publicly regret the fact that Germany sent Einstein packing, without realizing that it was a much greater crime to kill little Hans Cohn from around the corner, even though he was no genius.'[22]

Schoenberner's book is unlike volumes published earlier[23] in that, using brief texts and striking photographs, the author developed a continuous narrative about the different SS strategies for excluding, torturing and killing the Jews. The book presented a dramatization using a modern layout, with the help of commentaries on the images and the text, and the order of chapters: 'In Hitler's Germany, Poland Experimental Field, In the Ghettos, Mass Executions, The Deportations, The Extermination Camps, Resistance, Liberation'.[24] It formed the basis for the pictorial narrative about the murder of the Jews in Germany for some time to come. Its popularity was not affected by the fact that, in the foreword, Schoenberner had spoken in no uncertain terms about the pictorial material adopting the viewpoint of the photographers as well as about what they showed: 'It is the murderers themselves who photographed their handiwork' (1969, p. xii). As regards his publication, he wrote: 'Belated moral condemnation and humane regret are not enough. The historical facts must be known, the social causes that made them possible must be understood, and we must become aware of our own responsibility for what goes on around us' (1969, p. xv). Historians in 2007 declared Schoenberner's book to be one of the *50 Klassiker der Zeitgeschichte* (50 Classics of Contemporary History).[25]

In the artworks commented on here, attention will be drawn particularly to Schoenberner's compassionate view of the 'victims' while they were still alive, such as the prisoners looking into the camera in the barrack of the dying at Buchenwald photographed by Private Harry Miller in April 1945 (see illus. 213).[26] They establish eye contact with the viewer, demanding that he or she identify with those suffering. The image became well-known through frequent reproduction and, as one can see in the works of Wolf Vostell, Josef Beuys, Werner Tübke and Gerhard Richter, it has become a symbol of starvation and murder.

Jürgen Stroop

The Jewish Quarter of Warsaw No Longer Exists

Schoenberner had borrowed from a large number of photographs in *Es gibt keinen jüdischen Wohnbezirk Warschau mehr,*[27] the report by Jürgen Stroop, who as the leader of an SS brigade and a *Generalmajor* (brigadier general) of police under Heinrich Himmler had been responsible in 1943 for putting down the Warsaw Ghetto and had meticulously documented the murders carried out under the orders of Friedrich Wilhelm Krüger, the senior SS and police commander for the Eastern Sector.[28] According to Stroop, Krüger, his direct superior, had given the order to photograph 'every single thing'.[29] In 1960, at almost the same time as Schoenberner's *Der Gelbe Stern*, the whole report was published by Luchterhand,[30] but it did not meet with anything like the same popularity despite the fact that senior judge Robert H. Jackson had already particularly highlighted Stroop's report in his opening statement at the Nuremberg trials in November 1945 and five photos from it had been projected onto a screen during the course of the trial.[31] Also receiving very little notice was Josef Wulf's book *Das Dritte Reich und seine Vollstrecker* (The Third Reich and Its Executors),[32] which, along with selected images and the actual text on the liquidation of the Ghetto, also documents in detail the resistance against it and describes the perpetrators.

Stroop had won praise for his report from Heinrich Himmler, the Reichsführer of the SS and head of the German police, who had especially given him the task of liquidating the Ghetto since General von Sammern-Frankenegg, the one responsible for carrying it out, was according to Stroop 'a weakling, an Austrian intellectual from the Tyrol',[33] who had not completely carried out Himmler's long-standing order. Then, once the Uprising was finally put down, Stroop was also appointed as the senior SS and police chief for Warsaw. After pages of remembrance of the troops killed and wounded 'for the Führer and the Vaterland', the whole report contains a twelve-page summary of the fighting, said to have been sparked off by the enforcement of Himmler's order 'to transport the armaments and matériel located in the Ghetto along with the workforce and machinery to Lublin'.[34] There follow 57 pages of 'daily reports'; then a 48-page 'pictorial report', some of which is made up of photos, taken in isolation from the SS's original specific intention of collecting material to tell their own heroic history,[35] that were to become widely circulated 'symbols of the events in the Warsaw Ghetto'.[36] According to Joachim Jahn, the photographer is probably Franz Konrad, head of the 'Werterfassungsstelle' (Valuation Office) in occupied Warsaw. Because of his exact knowledge of the place, Konrad was given the order to accompany Stroop the whole time, and in the trial against him and Stroop he stated that he had taken the photographs.[37]

Richard Errell: *Picture Book for Those Who Forget*

In the run-up to the Eichmann trial, Richard Errell, whose original name was Richard Loewy and who had managed to reach to Palestine in 1937, documented the 'barbarity' of the Nazi regime. Between the 'Beginning' and the 'End', he juxtaposed the pro and contra, each on one side of a double-page spread.[38] Under the title *Bilderbuch für Vergessliche* (Picture Book for Those Who Forget), he addressed the subject of the way the murder of the Jews had been dealt with since the end of the war. As early as December 1945, the Dresden artist Otto Griebel had produced collages for a *Bilderbuch für Vergessliche Deutsche. Aus authentischem Bildmaterial* (Picture Book for Those Germans Who Forget: From Authentic Pictorial Material), the drawings of which were, however, published only in part.[39]

When Errell's work appeared, the generation born in the war years started to ask questions of their own parents as to what they knew and were forgetting, concealing and repressing, and dealing with the subject was to become a considerable motivating factor in the culture of protest in West Germany. In the newly revived debates, arguments based on the documentary quality of photographs predominated over any evidence from painting or drawing.

In West Germany the younger generation of creative artists likewise started to be interested in the subject. They were not demonstrating what they had witnessed any more but were preoccupied with a variety of set pieces based around memory and copied photographs as evidence.

Bazon Brock

The Hamburg Line

In 1959 Bazon Brock used photographs of concentration camps for an art installation with the *Line* at the Hamburg Hochschule der Künste at Lerchenfeld. It was, as the 'artist without a work' wrote in the text of the concertina fold stuck onto the poster of the installation, 'the first of the great non-works that Brock was to foist upon himself in the course of his life'.[40] He had planned the event together with Friedensreich Hundertwasser, then a visiting lecturer in Hamburg, as a several-day-long project with students. Only when the propitious moment had been determined with the help of an astrologer was an announcement made to the press; the institutional authorities, however, ruled that the public should be excluded. In the painter's studio, in the company of all those present day and night for the whole of the time available, Hundertwasser and Brock planned an unbroken line to be drawn in a spiral using black and red paint over the white walls. The act of painting itself was also to be executed in one go and by taking it in turns, with two people carrying it out in each case and another pair of students assisting.

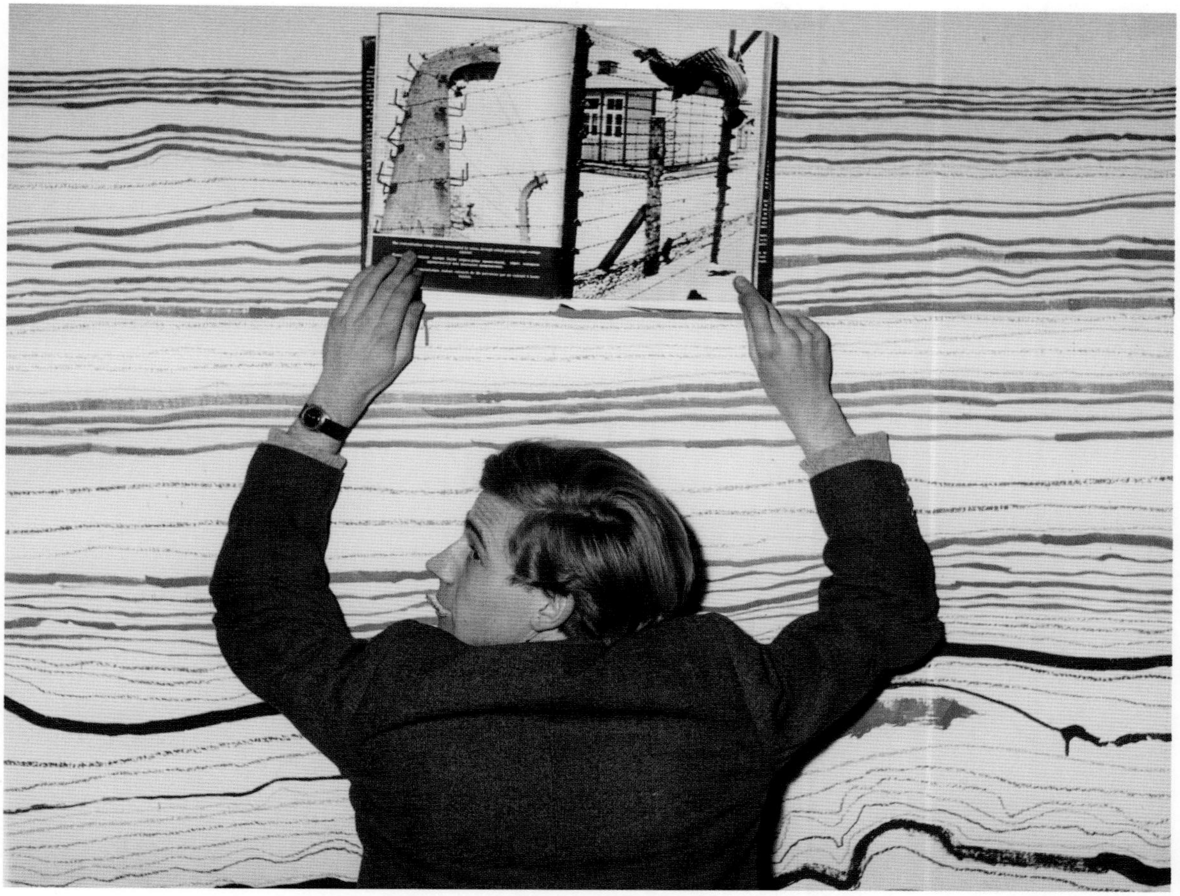

154 *The Hamburg Line*, performance by Bazon Brock and Friedensreich Hundertwasser at the Hochschule für Bildende Künste Hamburg, 18–20 December 1959, photograph.

It was planned to continue the line out of the studio into the Hochschule and on into the city 'through the parks, streets and beyond the Alster'.[41] The installation, which was intended to bring together art and life, drew a lot of attention from the press but caused some disquiet among some of the lecturers at the Hochschule and was brought to a premature end by the artists fearing that they might be violently ejected.[42]

Rejecting Tachisme and turning against the suppression of ornamentation, 'a SPIRALOID going beyond the slough of Tachisme'[43] was to be created. With the line, the two people behind the event had chosen the sign for the individuality of the male artist and his handwriting since the Renaissance. They had above all wanted to develop a formula pointing in the direction of different social formations and combine art and life in a spatial experience. Hundertwasser already wrote as early as 1954: 'I dare to say that the line I trace with my foot going into the museum is more important than the lines made on the pictures you see hanging inside the museum.'[44] Among the hints of meaning Brock put on the poster for the installation, one finds ironical references to everyday life mixed in with politically loaded statements. The following points to the history of fascism: 'In life and action one should always / keep to the big LINE: because the Führer / and the Duce never lose sight / of the big line, they are entitled / to take on the reforming of Europe.' One is reminded of the Jews with the statement 'Even the / Jewish / nation / strayed / at every moment over / the narrow / difficult-to- / maintain / line'.[45] There was another reference to the history of the Jewish people, on the concertina fold mentioned before, in the form of an excerpt from the Books of Moses recording only the exodus and some of the stops on the way out of Egypt but not the miracles, predictions and laws and not ending with the death of Moses in Jordan but stopping at Kadesh in the Sinai Desert. As in the two texts appearing before this installation, Brock in his review published in 2012 of the painted installation and the accompanying 'Exercitien' (spiritual exercises) also drew the attention of participants and readers to the uncertain but thoroughly politically motivated area, as it had to be made clear which key 'areas of meaning' were being addressed: 'the lifelines, the threads of the Fates, the track across the desert, the camp ringed with barbed wire, the patterns made by the wind and the waves on the shore, the furrows made by a plough, the lines of notes, the zebra's stripes, the stripes on prisoners' clothing, the combinations of lines as kinaesthetic forms, walking the line (alluding to walking the streets)'[46] In producing the lines on the walls, Brock was aiming to give the students 'effective instruction using readings, projections, demonstrations on the board and choral repetitions'.[47]

These 'spiritual exercises' on art and life included ones on art and German history. Brock placed pages 76–9 from the volume just published in Warsaw, *Wir haben nicht vergessen* (We Have Not Forgotten),[48] up against a wall covered with painted lines, thus clearly associating the line, referred to in the text, with barbed wire and the camps (illus. 154). The illustrations on the left reproduce a concrete post with electrified barbed wire from the camp at Auschwitz-Birkenau, and on the right, a human figure bent double and hanging over the barrier. The photo on the right is not identified in the book but originates from the SS records department at Mauthausen.[49] Brock was thus making use of the half-forgotten Dada montage technique in which both the installation and the photograph of it are meant to be works of art.[50] His discovery and display of illustrated documents about the Nazi crimes identifies him as a young representative of the post-war generation that was beginning to campaign against the silence surrounding the murder of the Jews.

D.A.S.E.R.S.C.H.R.E.C.K.E.N.A.M.S: 1. wheel of life of brazon brock, prime mover

In 1960 in a collector's edition produced with Bernhard Childs[51] et al., Brock also described his profession, among others, as being a 'line maker'. On one of the first pages in the unpaginated volume with the title *D.A.S.E.R.S.C.H.R.E.C.K.E.N.A.M.S* (with full stops removed and spoken aloud: *Das Erschrecken am es*, that is, 'The horror of it'), he aimed at the reception of the Nazi period in his own time. Associating the Freudian Unconscious with Martin Heidegger's

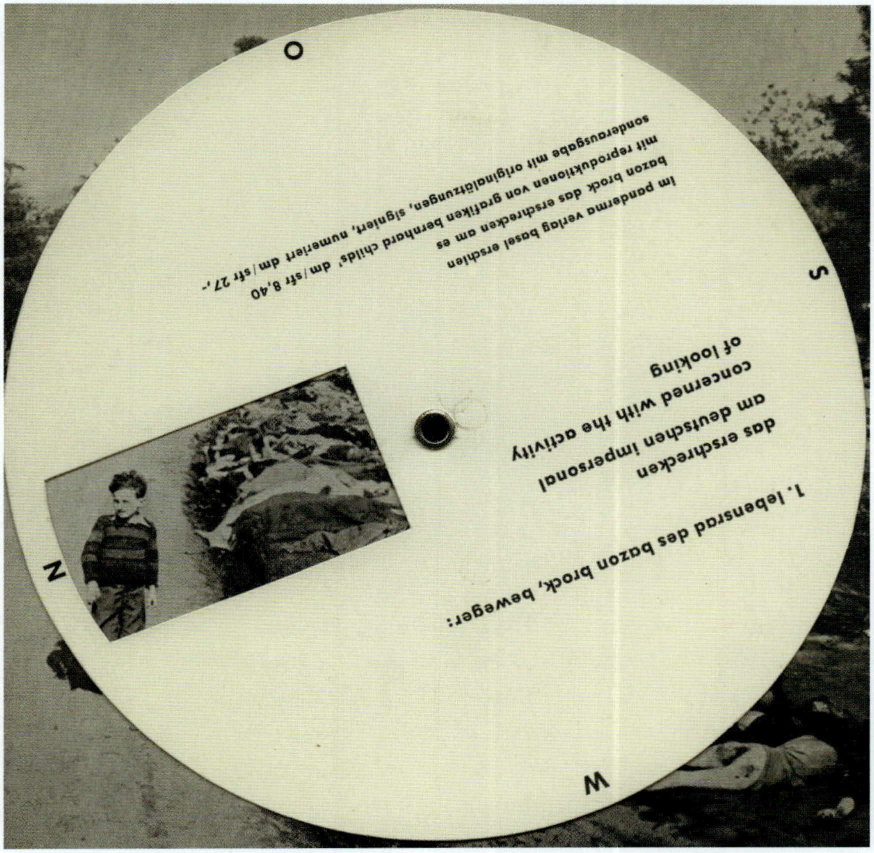

155 Bazon Brock, *1. wheel of Life of bazon brock, prime mover*, paper object for D.A.S.E.R.S.C.H.R.E.C.K.E.N.A.M.S.

description of 'Sein' ('Being'),[52] under the heading 'woher s kommt' ('where "s" = "it/id" comes from'), he was putting together references suggesting different aspects of 'Being' under the Nazis. Brock quoted a commentary from the summer of 1942 on the legitimation and nobility the Reich received from German poetry[53] written by Heinz Otto Burger,[54] who was still teaching as a professor of German Studies at the University of Erlangen in 1960 and a former member of various Nazi organizations. Brock added this to the words of the Nazi-sympathizing philosopher Martin Heidegger and those written in 1947 by Rudolf Höss, the former camp commandant at Auschwitz, about his idyllic family life at Auschwitz.[55] Between Burger's and Heidegger's statements, there is a West German directive on the import of fresh meat, allowing this only with the heads still present, even if they have been removed. One can't help thinking of the well-known film of the time *Night and Fog* and the sequences where human bodies appear with their heads mutilated.

For the publication of the book, he produced a paper object with the title *1. lebensrad des bazon brock, beweger* (1. wheel of life of bazon brock, prime mover) and down at the bottom: 'das erschrecken / am deutschen impersonal / concerned with the activity / of looking' (the horror / in the German impersonal / concerned with the activity / of looking), and the last four lines

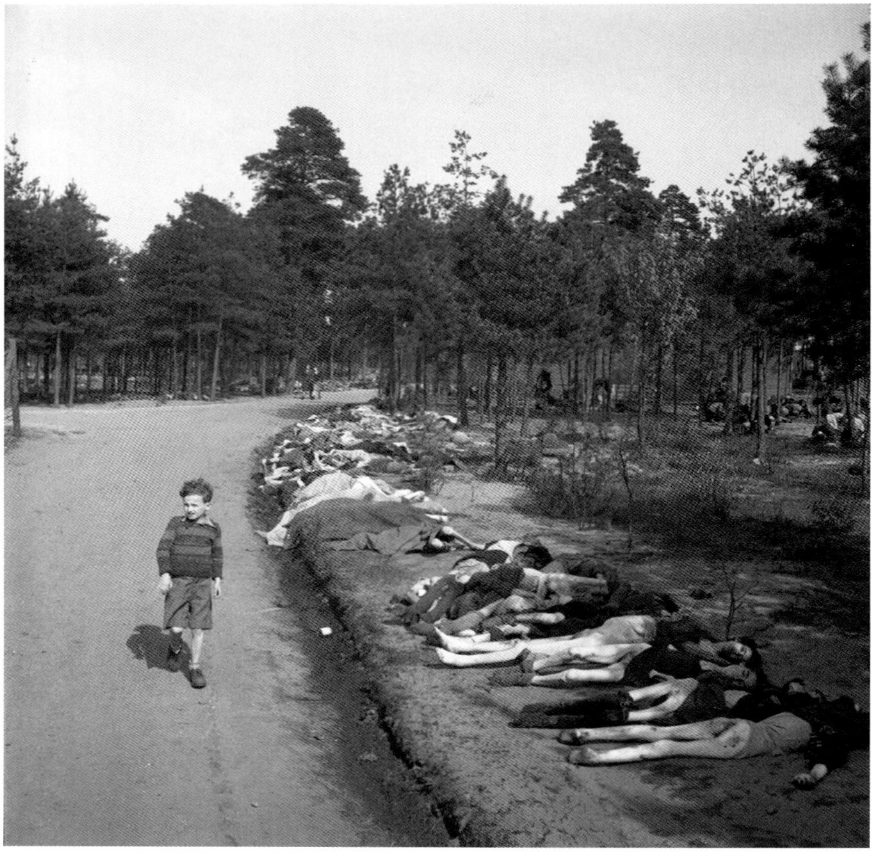

156 George Rodger, 'Belsen 1945', photograph, first published in *Life* (7 May 1945).

advertise the publication 'das erschrecken am es' (illus. 155).[56] Underneath the round and rotatable 'wheel of life', with a window revealing the image below, he had placed the rectangular photo from April 1945 by George Rodger published first as a cropped version in the American magazine *Life* on 7 May 1945 (illus. 156). The British journalist had photographed a boy walking past a row of bodies piled up on the side of the path at Bergen-Belsen concentration camp, his face turned away.[57] The way Brock presented this as open to multiple interpretation, along with the photo only just visible in places, illustrates the horror both at the impersonal perspective of the Germans and at their horror felt in the activity of looking at it. Rotating the disc reveals the image either of the boy walking or of the piled-up bodies. It demonstrates that Brock, who had been a child at the end of the war, like the boy in the photo,[58] was basing the course of his life – whatever direction it might take – on the murder of concentration camp prisoners.

Gallows Humour

Before the many political postcards Klaus Staeck became famous for in the 1970s, in 1962 Brock produced a postcard in connection with his installations *Thursday Manifestos*[59] in Frankfurt am Main (illus. 157). On it he had combined adapted instructions for the game 'Galgenschwengel' (Hangman)[60] with a photograph from the publication already used for the *Hamburger Linie* from Warsaw on the Nazi regime.[61] The game for children and adults and the photograph together form a cynical combination because, instead of the usual stick figure on the gallows, seven hanged men are shown with children and adults watching, taken from the documentary photograph. The borderline between the instructions for the game and the Nazi past becomes blurred. According to the rules of the game, every mistake leads to another element of the gallows being drawn, on which those choosing the wrong letters are symbolically hanging at the end of the game. As an example of this, the word used in the instructions is 'Kolibri' (hummingbird); Brock replaced this with 'Rechtsstaat' (Constitutional State) which even in 1962 was no doubt something that needed to be learned in Germany.[62] He was thus making a spectacle not only of the German crimes, but of the continuation of a system of education which still traded in images of deadly violence in

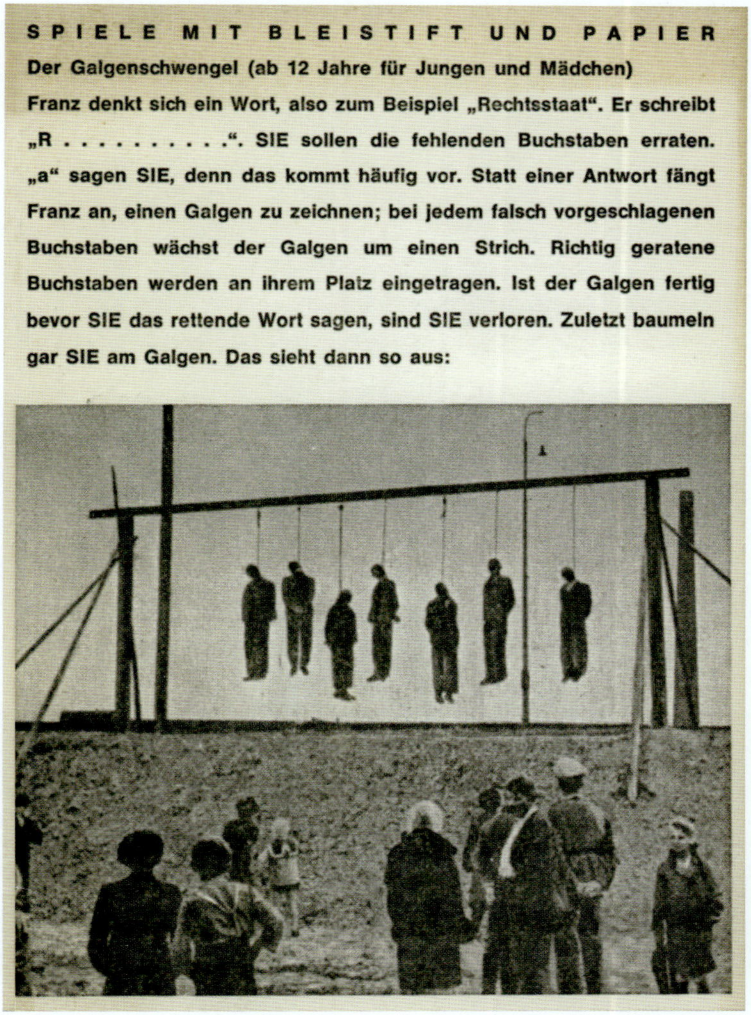

157 Bazon Brock, *Gallows Humour – A Game Using Pencil and Paper*, 1962, postcard.

supposedly harmless children's games. In a description of himself in 1964, he included the postcard within his 'documentation on the decay of the German consciousness' of 1962[63] under the title: 'Wollt Ihr das totale Leben?' (Do you want total life?)[64] This adaptation of the quotation from the notorious speech to the German people by the Nazi propaganda minister Josef Goebbels[65] was to become a battle cry for installation art and Pop art in the following years.[66]

Otto Schubert: *Auschwitz*

It was presumably under the influence of the Auschwitz trial that Otto Schubert, a former member of the Dresdner Sezession, devoted himself to representing Auschwitz (illus. 158), something no one had dared to do in oil painting since Ehmsen's painting (see illus. 123). The triptych, over 3 m wide (illus. 158), cannot be dated exactly; it was not purchased by any of the museums in the GDR and is now in the collection of Gerhard Schneider. The rare example of an artwork dealing with this key site of the crimes committed by the Germans consists of three scenarios in Schubert's particular style similar to that of Expressionism and Max Beckmann. Three canvases represent the whole process of murder, starting with abuse and ending with gassing. The foreground of the central picture is covered with many young, eroticized female nudes; on the right-hand side, towering over everything, a male figure with a beard and a long robe is raising his hands, reminiscent of the painting *The Prophet* by Jakob Steinhardt[67] and Lea Grundig's cursing figure (see illus. 39). Facing him are an armed SS killer with a sword and – long before the travelling exhibition *Verbrechen der Wehrmacht* (Crimes of the Wehrmacht)[68] publicized their being accessories to the crimes – an ordinary soldier assisting him and an Alsatian dog, all three of them in a triumphant pose over a woman's dead body. On the extreme right-hand side of the picture is the haggard figure of an elderly man with a beard turning slightly away to the left and looking on blankly. He has his hands in the pockets of his ragged clothing – an attitude symbolizing resistance and strictly forbidden by the SS guards.[69] A model for this attitude may have been the central figure in Boris Taslitzky's monumental painting (3 × 5 m) *The Small Camp in Buchenwald* from 1945, who Schubert's figure resembles as regards the direction of his head with his cloth cap and his concealed hands.[70] Against a background showing burning, the camp band in prisoners' clothing are in position below the shrouded sun. A semi-naked man bearing a whip in the middle of the picture threatens to torment people before they are murdered. Schubert's piling up of scenes of gruesome death is reminiscent of the model of Crematorium II at Auschwitz by Mieczyslaw Stobierski with its many figures, which he produced in 1947 for the memorial site there,[71] and the apocalyptic vision of the end of the world in Pieter Brueghel the Elder's *Triumph of Death*.[72]

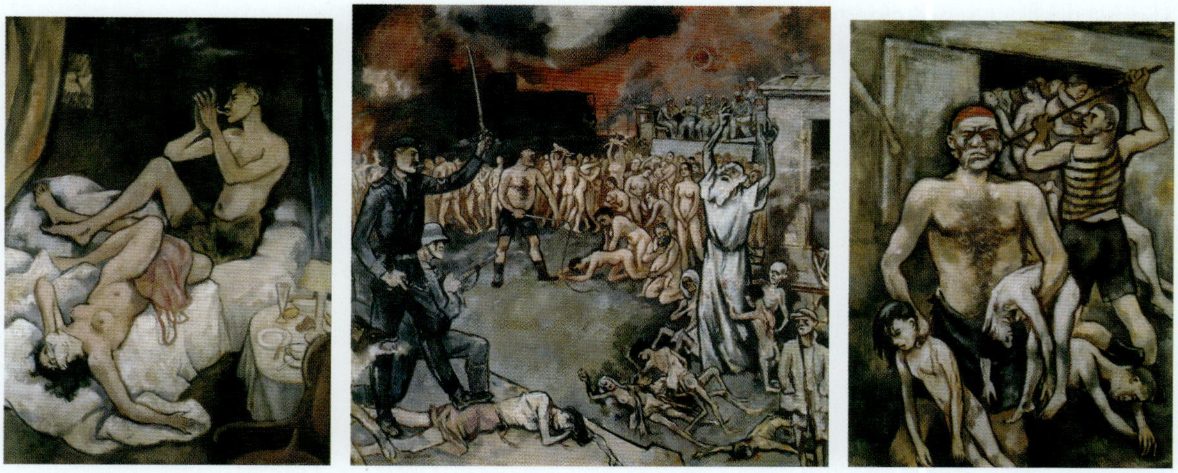

158 Otto Schubert, *Auschwitz*, 1960, oil on canvas.

The right-hand panel represents the work of the *Sonderkommando* (special units), something not shown in any of the photos. Two men are shown handling dead bodies in front of an open gas chamber. In the left-hand panel, there are a similarly naked man and a female nude lying head first with her face hidden on a bedstead. The skirt between the woman's legs resembles the one of the corpse in the central panel lying like a slaughtered animal at the soldiers' feet. The arrangement of the armchair, the glass of champagne and the curtain heightens the impression of lust and luxury in the private life of an SS man or in a brothel, not hiding the forced nature of the prostitution. The exceptional highlighting of the perpetrators' sexuality is captured visually in the neatly symmetrical composition of the images showing a scene of bedding and gassing as an act of sexual violence. The scenes in the three canvases that appear to be so far apart are linked together in a trivial way by the lighting of the cigarette devoured after sex or murder. In documenting the events, Schubert was able to refer back to drawings by former prisoners, showing them in an overall panorama familiar from historical painting. He did not, however, take as a model photographs of the selection process on the 'ramp' such as those that frequently featured in images of mass murder in the photographic publications at the time. Though Auschwitz had already by then been turned into a symbol, he represented the camp and the use of physical violence in detail. Possibly for us today, however, this fictional illustration of the camp, together with its display involving idealized nudes in the form of unharmed female figures, strikes a discordant note, making it difficult for us to continue looking at the picture. Knowledge of the photos of the camps showing emaciated, starving, naked figures has radically altered the aesthetic terms in which we remember the extermination of human beings during the Nazi period.[73]

By emphasizing the size of the main figures, Schubert aimed at generalizing the information the picture conveys. Yet whereas Leo Haas only shows the camp brothel from the outside (see illus. 87), Schubert reveals the details of the abuse undergone by the female prisoners. Showing the intimate sphere of the perpetrator,[74] his picture of Auschwitz can therefore be seen as pornification of Nazism, a subject of fantasy after 1945 when women survivors were accused of having only escaped death through prostitution.[75] The sexual fantasies revealed behind such perverse accusations became common in novels, comics and films.[76] Schubert, who in the 1920s had pictured sexual activity in the style of Cézanne and a sexual murder,[77] returned to the social critical debate of that time about the representation of sexual pleasures on the part of the ones in charge, with his reference, aimed at deterrence, to obscene acts of lust and murder carried out on naked female figures portraying the rape of the Jewish people.

Werner Tübke: *History of the German Workers' Movement* IV

Werner Tübke turned to historical painting as being what the art historian Meissner calls the 'genre dominating the style of the future',[78] and in the course of the cycle of pictures *On the History of the Workers' Movement* he recalled the murder of the Jews. In a contract for the work made between the Bezirksauftragskommission, the Regional State Committee who commissioned fine art for the Leipzig Regional Council, and the painter on 22 June 1959, the work was planned to adorn two rooms in the basement of the Andersen Nexö rest home in Leipzig in a traditional German style consisting of 'painting on wood panelling in the bar'. According to Tübke's diary, in April 1960 the Nexö home took delivery of the drawings for the design. Tübke then started work on four triptychs.[79]

He had chosen for himself[80] this series of images relating the history of the workers' movement, undertaking this task after thoroughly studying the literature on the subject,[81] and he divided it up into a total of twelve panels in four triptychs. The first triptych shows events from the November Revolution in 1918; the second, inflation, the uprising in Hamburg and the suppression of the Kapp Putsch; the third, the beginnings of the Nazi tyranny with the Reichstag fire, Communist Party demonstrations and the Burning of the Books; and finally the fourth, concentration camps, Stalingrad and the Battle for Berlin (illus. 159). The fifth triptych, which in the predella was intended to illustrate the start of rule by the people in the form of the nationalization of private firms, land reform and the Nuremberg trials, exists only as a design in two pencil studies.

The left-hand wing of the fourth triptych, not explicitly planned from the start as a reminder of the murdered Jews and at first intended to show the resistance group led by Anton Saefkow,[82] Tübke devoted to the executions in the concentration camps. Given the context of the subject and the initially intended portrayal of the communist resistance to the Nazis, it is surprising that Tübke drew the Star of David on the clothing of two of the people in the painting that he finished. Behind a watchtower on the right of the picture and above a red cloth, a red flag, one can make out white smoke on the ground coming out of several light-coloured gun-barrels aimed at the tormented prisoners – compare Sitte (see illus. 134), Goya and Picasso. Every one of those destined to be killed is individually characterized and both the prisoner placed at the front facing the guns and a dead body lying in the foreground are indicated by Jewish stars. Other prisoners have numbers on their backs. At the bottom of the wing, the barbed wire is not drawn as he first intended,[83] but now the concrete posts typical of the camps are shown and another guard with a steel helmet and a baton is positioned behind the wooden support of the watchtower on the right. What Eckhardt Gillen, looking back at the official criticism of the time, now may see as a trivializing of the historical events,[84] then presented the public of the time,[85] 'unmonumentally', in a familiar 'traditional German style', with an unusual historical painting of the execution of groups of human beings in the camps. Sitte, in the case of those murdered at Lidice in *Massacre II* (see illus. 134), had suggested only killings with gun barrels in the background, whereas Tübke, like Edward Manet and Fransisco Goya before him, by the white smoke coming out of the gun barrels on the right of the picture, captured the very moment of the deadly shots aimed at the shackled prisoners, the fact of the murder. At that time no artist in West Germany and, in East Germany, only Sitte in *Massacre II* and Lea Grundig in her drawing *Roll-call in the Concentration Camp* (see illus. 139) had identified and highlighted the Jews clearly by the Star of David. Showing the exact details allowed the viewer standing close to the picture to follow the process of the events happening to individual figures, likewise to all the people in the picture. Thus it provided an alternative to the anti-fascist heroic version of history as shown in Cremer's Buchenwald Memorial, for example.[86] His following in the tradition of the multi-figured paintings of Pieter Brueghel and his school,[87] able to combine communal scenes with recounting the fate of individuals, typifies Tübke's life-long attempt to influence the reception of the artistic heritage by appropriating the history of art against the grain of contemporary taste and towards what were still seen as 'ongoing periods of dramatic change'.[88] This included recording continuities in the use of violence against the people on the part of the state from the early modern period right up to the present day.

Admittedly, Tübke's gift as a painter was recognized at the time in the GDR. The fourth triptych in particular, by its differentiated use of oil painting on hardboard, stands out from the other pictures in the cycle; nevertheless the artist was criticized on account of the rather gloomy subject-matter for the residents of the old people's home,[89] and also a friend of his, Alfred Kurella, head of the cultural commission of the Politburo of the central committee of the SED, was concerned about his 'stylizing in an archaizing way', which he considered a 'serious objection'.[90] In 1962 the 'form constructed as being

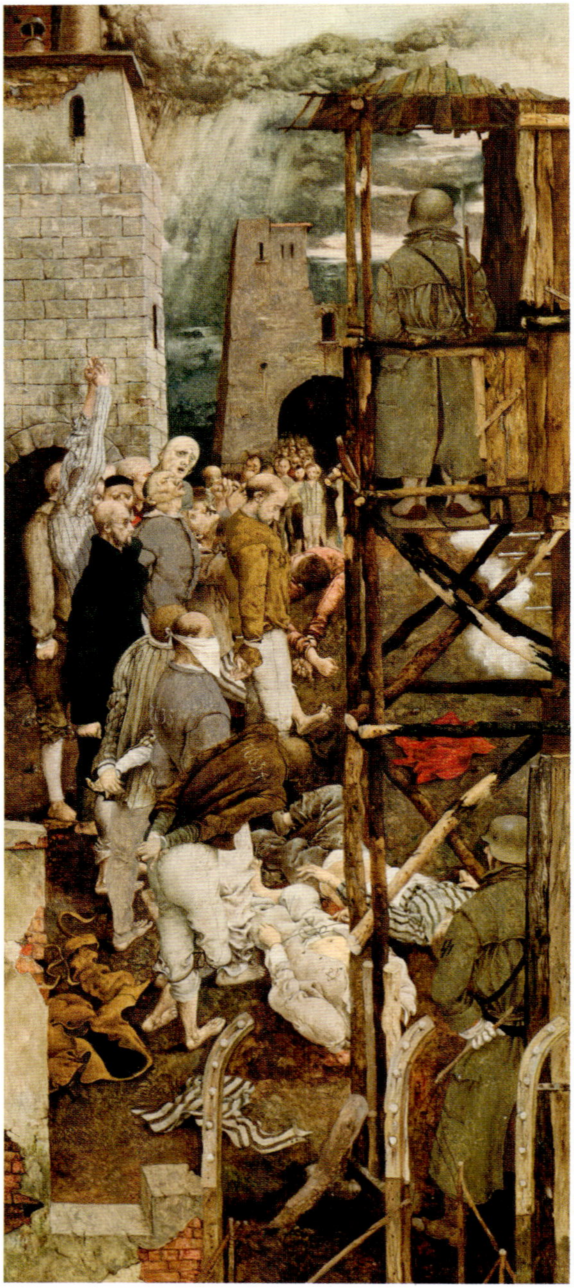

159 Werner Tübke, *History of the German Workers' Movement* IV, 1961, oil on hardboard.

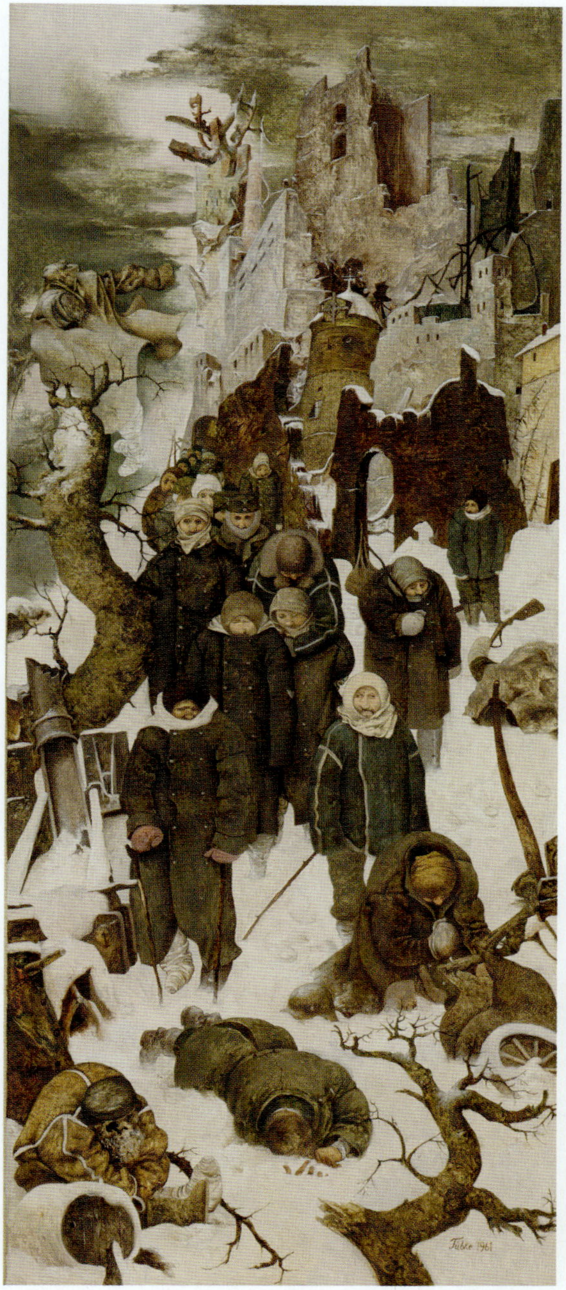
Tübke 1961

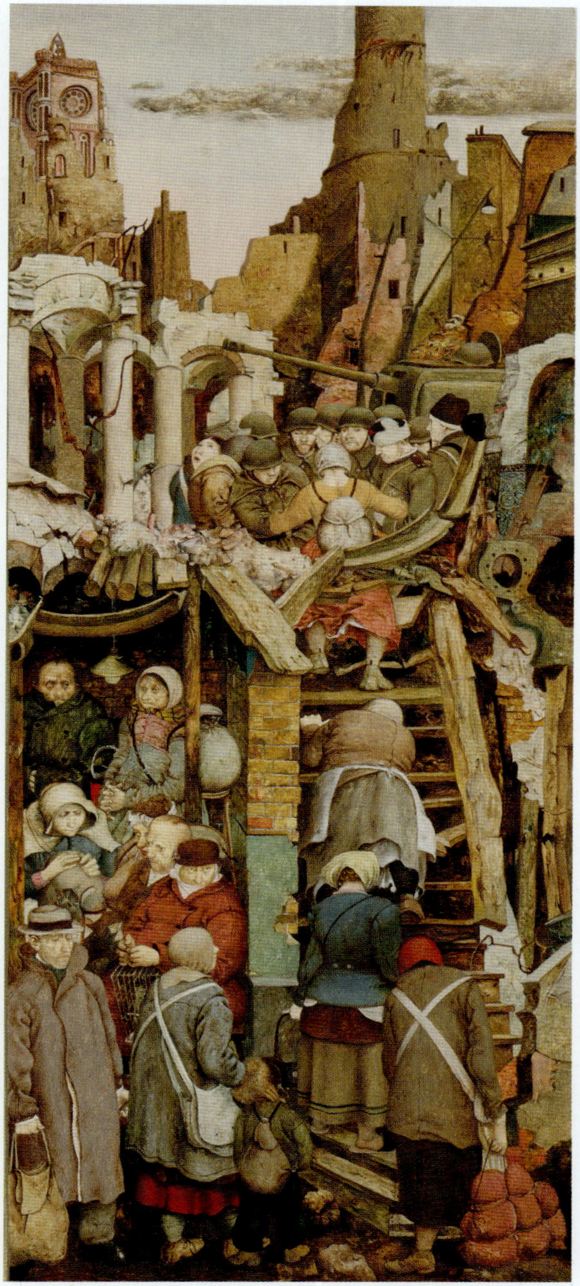

reminiscent of old German paintings' was also questioned.[91] The old people in the rest home did not appreciate Tübke's images, as we learn from the record of a visit by the IG Bildende Kunst (Association of Artists) to Tübke's studio on 29 April 1965,[92] which notes the artist's complaint about the 'downright unworthy position' the painting was hanging in at the home. The home then approached the Leipzig Museum with a view to making an exchange of its wall decor and this was duly carried out.[93]

Exhibitions in the GDR against Theodor Oberländer and Hans Globke

The trials against these two West German CDU politicians were discussed and reported on by much of the media in the GDR and supported by many well-known artists. Walter Heynowski's 1960 film *Mord in Lwow – Archive sagen aus* (Murder in Lviv – The Archives Speak) was shown in cinemas and on television, where images of Nazi crimes carried out in Eastern Europe were intercut with quotations from the writings of the once-devoted Nazi Oberländer and his current political views. With the repeat showing of the 1947 documentary film *Sud Narodov* (Nuremberg Trials)[94] in the GDR cinemas in 1962, there was a call for a reopening of legal proceedings in view of the resurgence of fascism in West Germany.[95] The graphic artist John Heartfield, speaking for the Klub der Kulturschaffenden Johannes R. Becher (Johannes R. Becher Club of Cultural Workers), issued an invitation to its members for an exhibition 'to take a stand against the reappearance of fascism and racial hatred' in West Germany;[96] it was opened by him in February 1960[97] and

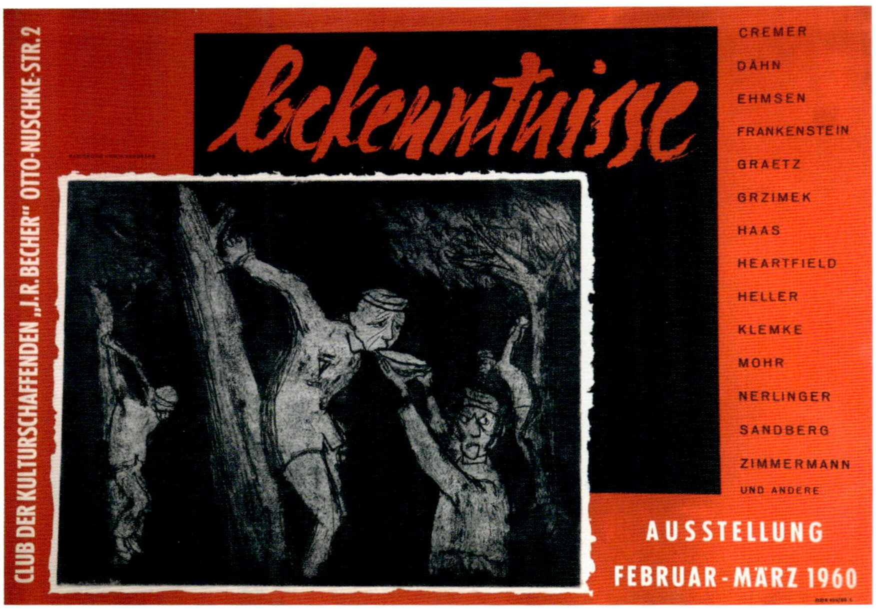

160 Poster for the exhibition *Confessions*, Klub der Kulturschaffenden, Johannes R. Becher, with the motif *Heroes* by Herbert Sandberg, Berlin (East) 1960.

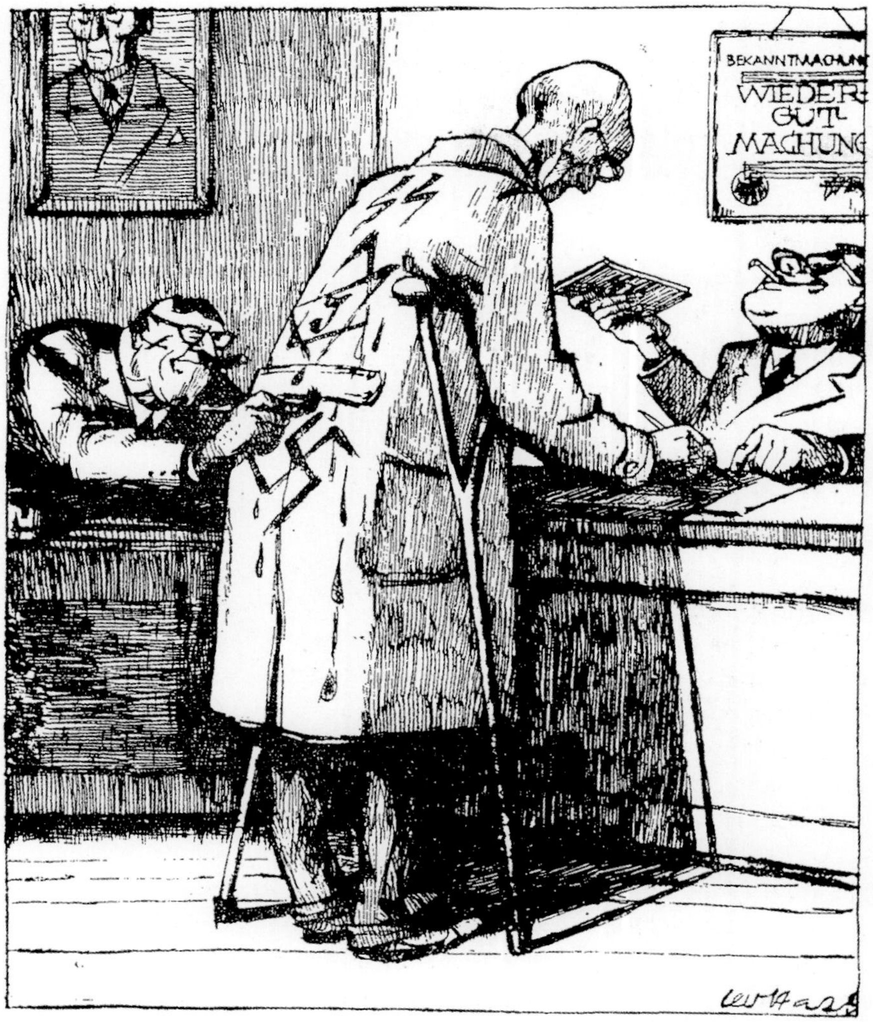

161 Leo Haas, *All Made Up For*, 1960, caricature commenting on the trial of Hans Globke, from *Bildende Kunst*, 5 (1960).

even displayed works by him from the 1930s. A poster (illus. 160) was provided by the motif *Heroes* from Herbert Sandberg's autobiographical cycle *The Way* made between 1958 and 1964.[98] Three prisoners are shown hanging from trees reminiscent of Golgotha; one of them is being offered not a sponge of vinegar but a drinking bowl by a fellow prisoner. This act of – strictly forbidden – solidarity is one of heroism. In the poster the aquatint etching is framed by a jagged white border typical of snapshots of the period. This addition illustrates the hierarchy of the visual arts, as the reference to the medium of photography is intended to prove the authenticity of the graphic artwork.

Along with Heartfield and Sandberg, those taking part in the exhibition included famous artists who had portrayed the Nazi policy of extermination in other works, such as Fritz Cremer, Walter Grzimek,[99] Wolfgang Frankenstein and Leo Haas,[100] who exhibited drawings of his time in concentration camps (see pp. 114–19), published a biting caricature. In the etching *All Made Up For* (illus. 161) he used an applicant's back with SS runes, the

'Jewish star' (of David), so abused by the Nazis, and the swastika to attack the specific Western German policy of *Wiedergutmachung* (Making up for it), legible in the top right of the poster. The Adenauer government, identifiable by the chancellor's portrait in the top left, granted compensation to German refugees and German Jewish survivors, and pensions not only to war veterans but to former members of the ss as well.

As in many previous exhibitions, Lea Grundig clearly reminded the world of the persecution of the Jews. She lent the exhibition organizers[101] *Roll-call in the Concentration Camp* (see illus. 139) and three drawings from the 1935 series *The Jew is Guilty*.[102] Grundig's correspondence with the club reveals that the exhibition was so well received that it was also shown at a convalescent centre and in Czechoslovakia.[103]

Lea Grundig

During the show trial against Adenauer's State Secretary Hans Globke, Lea Grundig, along with Peter Edel, was involved in another exhibition against fascism and anti-Semitism. The display put on at the Internationales Ausstellungszentrum Berlin in Friedrichstrasse was intended to support the prosecution with evidence using photocopied documents and exhibited drawings by Peter Edel, who appeared as a witness in this trial, from his time in the camps (see illus. 13, 14, 15 and 33).

Since the start of the Eichmann trial, Lea Grundig had worked on new drawings about the murder of the Jews that she now exhibited, along with other works, as the series *The Globkes*. The East German newspaper *Neues Deutschland* welcomed the news that Lea Grundig had 'produced them as a result of the coming trial'.[104] This series, which had not previously been seen as a cycle, was intended to be made up of seven drawings, as can be proved by the fact that she wrote the number 7 in several places in the sections she allotted in the plan for the work and for going on loan, with the provisional title 'Eichmann'. She apparently presented the first designs in Berlin in March 1963, having noted '7 Eichmann' under the heading 'to Berlin'. Starting in July 1963, that is, after the announcement of the 'Eichmann Series', she drew up a precise plan for the work to be done on the drawings up until the opening of the exhibition. She now put the titles of the pictures together under the name *Globke Cycle*. She continued to work on the drawings even after the exhibition, noting in April 1965 under the title *Globke Series* the drawings *Children*, *Final Solution*, *The Living and the Dead*, *Earth of Auschwitz* and *Globke*, with another title that is illegible. In a later note, with the addition of *Globke Cycle* for September 1965 as a continuation of the work, *Prosecutor* and *Court* are mentioned, in December she wrote 'finished 2 crosses (Globke)'.[105] The seven drawings in the series – *Ghetto 1*, *Globke 2*, *Globke Final Solution*, *3. Coloured*, *Footprints*, *4. Court Judgement*, *5. Past is Present* and *Children* – are

162 Lea Grundig, *The Earth of Auschwitz*, 1962–6, at first attributed to the *Globke Series*, later on to *That a Good Germany Might Blossom*, brush and black ink, opaque white over watercolour.

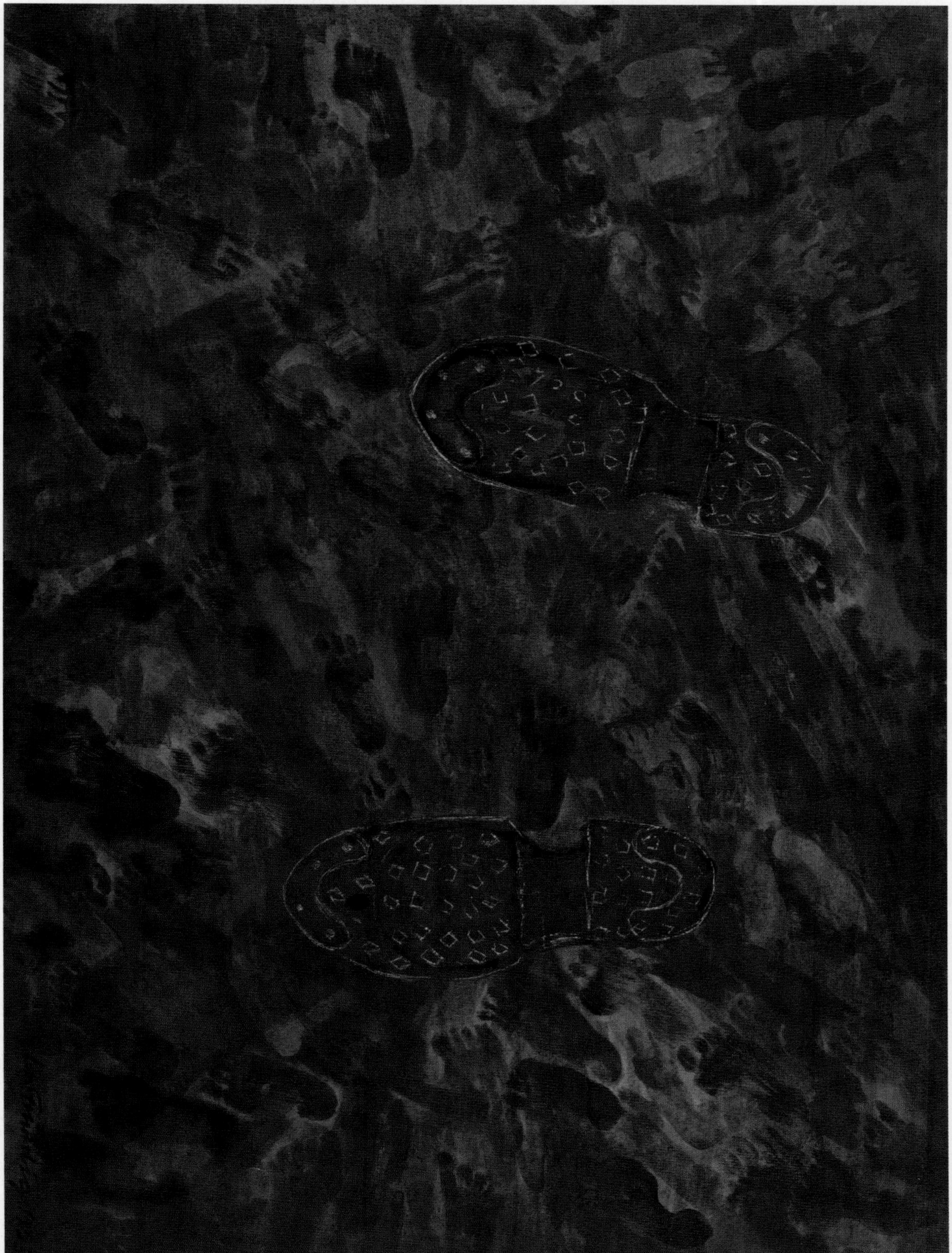

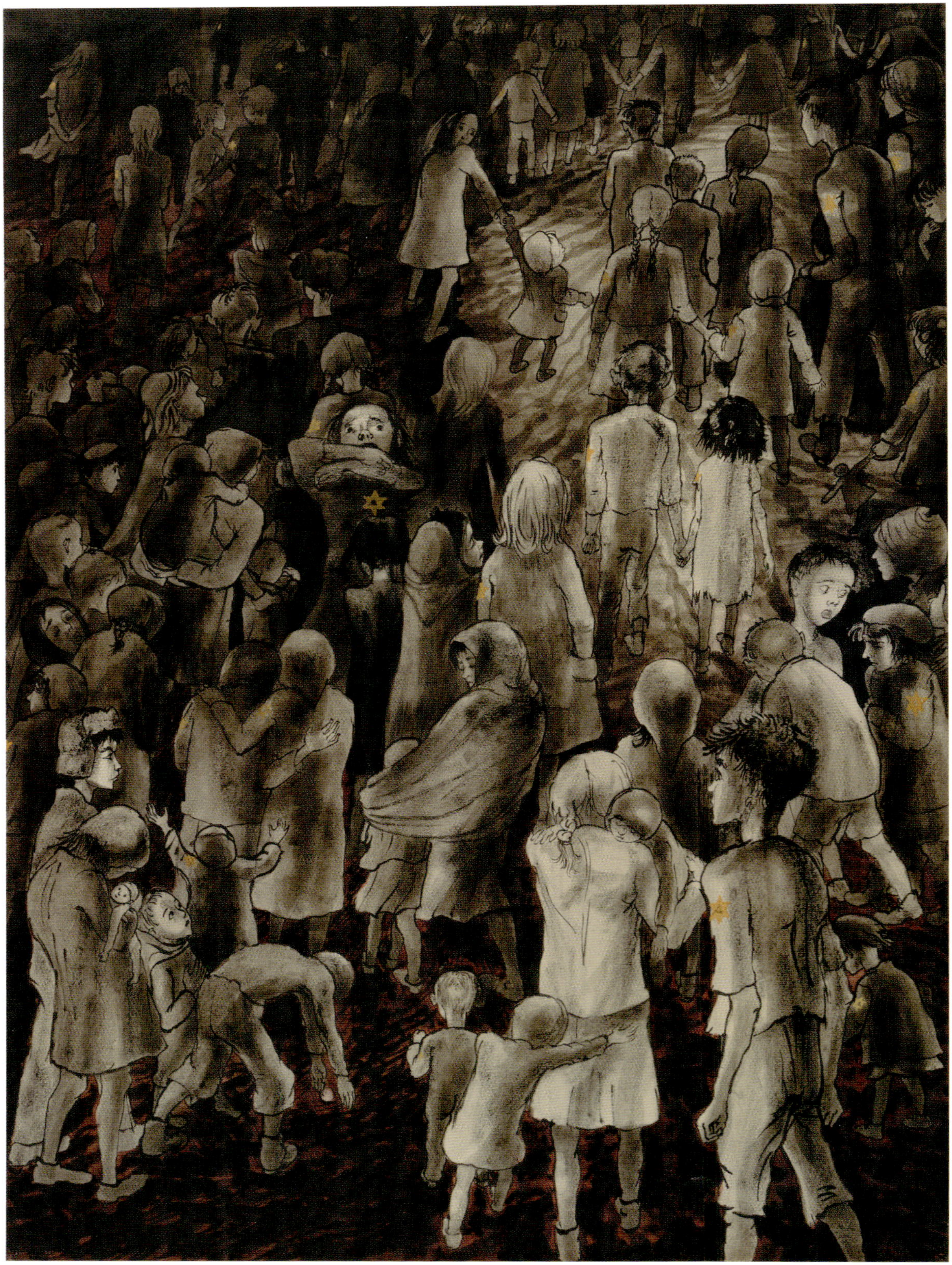

now attributed to the series *That a Good Germany Might Blossom*, which now belongs to the State Hermitage, St Petersburg.[106]

Earth of Auschwitz

In the drawing *Earth of Auschwitz*, formally named *Footprints* (illus. 162) Grundig returned to a motif that she had already worked on in the 1930s in the etching *This Is How It Will Be II*, with its premonition of the future.[107] She shows the many footprints made in the ground by naked feet in an image illustrating the state of 'having walked away'.[108] The footprints of those walking barefoot become the only thing they have left behind to prove they have ever lived, signifying both their contact and their loss.[109] The drawings *The Way into the Gas* (see illus. 58) and *Street of No Return*[110] had the same relics of the presence and disappearance of human beings. Only once before did Grundig choose footprints from the rough soles of shoes, a feature of the 1941 ink drawing *Footprints*; in her silhouettes corpses are piled up as in mass graves.[111] In the last drawing showing these footprints, she created a new variation on the representation of the murder of the Jews reminiscent of a frequently reproduced photograph from Bergen-Belsen (see illus. 200), in which numberless outlines are impressed in the sand next to dead bodies. Without conventional representation of perspective, the surface of the painting becomes the ground on which the footprints of the bare soles are captured in ink and watercolour. The chaos of the footprints is on the one hand quite realistic; on the other it reminds one of the informal painting dominant at the time in the West. The view of the surface of the painting is sharply interrupted by the imprints from the soles of two nailed shoes which being so concrete – again rather like Pop art or Neo-Dada – appear to stand out from the footprints. It is not obvious whether they were the ones that caused the feet to be walking about in the first place, driving them on, or are intended to bring to mind objectified memories of the Nazis' brutal violence that naked human beings struggled against in vain.

1,200,000 Children Were Gassed

Lea Grundig had initially created the ink drawing *1,200,000 Children Were Gassed*,[112] just like *Earth of Auschwitz*, under the title *Eichmann Cycle* (illus. 163). She portrayed the almost unimaginable number of children as a large group of human figures, some of them with armbands on which a Star of David can be seen. Footprints are vaguely suggested by red paint. Almost all of the children, big and small, on their way up a hill, have their backs turned to the viewer. Only one girl,[113] standing out a little in the middle, is shown face-on, terrified, her arms folded in front of her mouth. At about heart height, the child is wearing a Jewish star on a dark shirt – a sign of the death sentence that all Jewish children were subject to.

163 Lea Grundig, *1,200,000 Children Were Gassed*, 1962–6, at first attributed to the series *Globke*, later on to *That a Good Germany Might Blossom*, coloured ink.

Dore Meyer-Vax: *Knight, Death and Devil*

The Nuremberg artist Dore Meyer-Vax was a life-long campaigner against war and West German rearmament, including nuclear arms. 'In the government, the administration, the law and the military the old Nazis or the sons of the Nazis have regained control,' and the chance of a new start in 1945 had been 'woefully missed', she wrote in the catalogue of the exhibition mounted in East Berlin in 1965 and in Frankfurt an der Oder in 1966.[114] For several years during this period she worked to portray the 'barbarity of the Hitler regime', 'the criminal shedding of blood and the related madness'[115] associated with the military since the Wilhelminian period and the suffering of women and children.

The monumental linocut *Knight, Death and Devil (in the 20th Century)* (illus. 164) is composed like an instruction board and to be read from left to right. It shows in the upper level, to be imagined as being in the background, a group of people being corralled by a man with a gun and in a uniform reminiscent of the early twentieth century. In the centre of the background Meyer-Vax uses a motif made familiar from the images of the extermination camps current in the post-war period and in the reports of the trials. She makes reference to the Nazi mass murders by depicting a seemingly isolated cart loaded with dead bodies. She reminds us of the imprisonment and torture in the notorious Gestapo cellars with two seemingly dead bodies and a female figure gesturing in despair in front of windows placed high above them. Like a mirror image of the scene on the left, on the right-hand side of the picture, there are people with their arms raised being threatened by an unidentified person. In front of these scenes, intended to present a panorama of twentieth-century

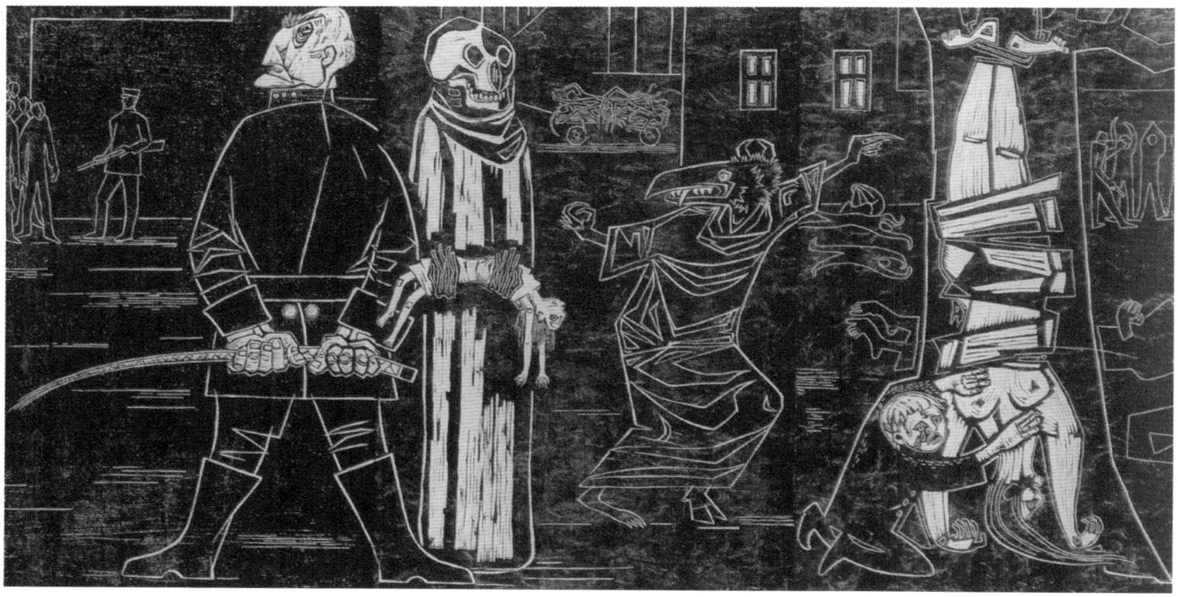

164 Dore Meyer-Vax, *Knight, Death and Devil (in the 20th Century)*, 1963–71, linocut, printed by hand on Japan paper.

acts of violence, Meyer-Vax placed the eponymous figures: a three-star general represents the knight, preparing to inflict punishment; his gaze is turned away, not looking at any of the dead. It is not clear whether he is holding a riding crop or an unsheathed sword. His face, like that of a bird of prey, refers to the caricatures by Th. Th. Heine about the First World War; his stance, with his legs wide apart, reminds one of the SS officer that Antelme describes as a guard in charge of forced labour in the camps: 'With legs spread out and knees bent, his riding crop in his hand, his helmet with the death's-head over his eyes.'[116] In the form of this knight, reminding one equally of the supervision of recruits being drilled and of people in the camps, the author sums up the history of German militarism; in both cases this general is in charge of an army of those condemned to death. Standing close by him is Death in a long cloak, holding the dead body of a child or a woman in both hands. The third of the figures mentioned in the title, the Devil, portrayed as having a bird's head with horns and a cloven hoof, Meyer-Vax places slightly behind, attributing to him the crimes of the Nazis signalled as being works of the Devil. His right hand seems to be drawing the attention of the general and of Death from the left-hand towards the right-hand side of the picture, pointing the claws of his left hand in that direction and making a connection between historical events and present and future acts of violence. The knight, Death and Devil, threatening and killing people in the background of the picture, also inflict violence on a female figure hanging from a tree by her feet, who forms a contrast to this group. Behind her there is another dead body. The woman being hanged is also drawn as having been murdered, as her head is bent and turned away from a weeping child clinging to her. Through the large, white surfaces of the body of the abused, naked, female figure and Death's cowl, the artist was emphasizing the opposition of life and death. She devoted many of her pictures to the life and suffering of mothers and children, portraying them as representative of all the dead of the war in *Death Mosaic* (see illus. 115). In the bloody panorama of persecution and murder, the abused female also becomes an allegory for war crimes.

As a basis for this print, the artist borrowed the characters and the title from Dürer's Christian knight riding into death,[117] which has been reinterpreted since the nineteenth century as his victory over Death and the Devil,[118] but radically questions the heroism of soldiers by confronting them with the murders of people. In her instructive tale she sketched the history of German militarism and the two world wars caused by this as well as by elite troops of Nazis, who thought of themselves as being in the tradition of the Orders of Christian Knights, presenting their racist genocide as in the service of the future of the German people. She nevertheless called to mind the other tradition, of which she also considered herself a part, the one of resistance to war and violence. Thus the group of people herded into the back left-hand corner can be seen as a reference to the failed revolution of 1918–19 and the small group on the right as being oppressed, but continuing in their struggle. Meyer-Vax symbolized her unshakeable belief in a peaceful future, like Wilhelm Lachnit in *The Death of Dresden*,[119] by the orphaned, but surviving child.

Wolf Vostell

Wolf Vostell linked his work firmly in the relics that remind us of the murder of the Jews and with his own present-day political reality. He called his works *de-coll/age*, a term he used for a lot of different works. He was playing on the term *décollage* coined by the French affichistes Raymond Hains, Jacques le Villeglé and François Dufrène for assembling and tearing up, dividing and rubbing out. By dividing up the word, however, Vostell emphasized the de-constructive act of erasure, and separating off the letters *a g e* reminds one of the French word *âge*.

165 Wolf Vostell, *German View*, 1958–9, de-coll/age object, part of the environment *Black Room*, organic and industrially produced materials.

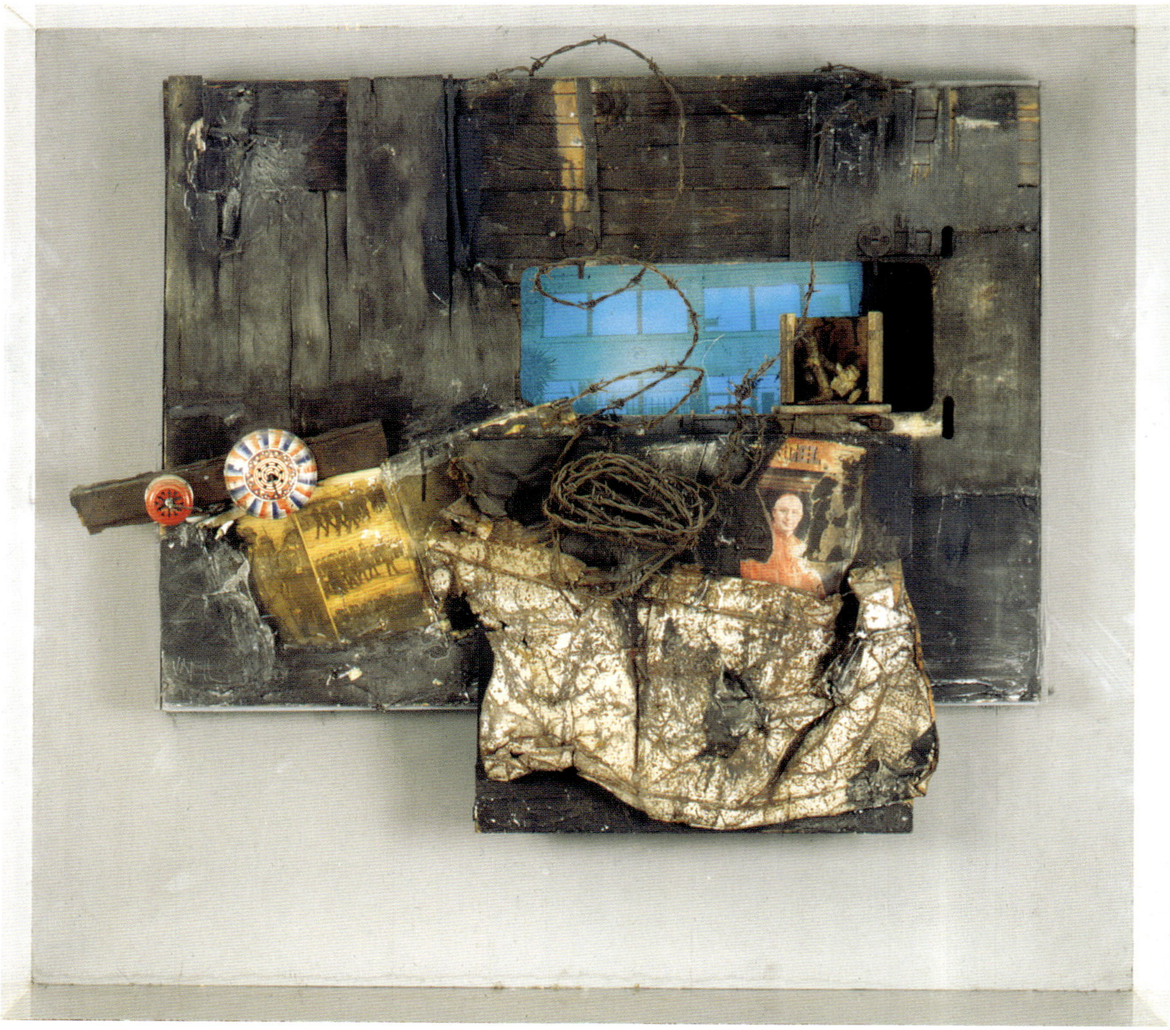

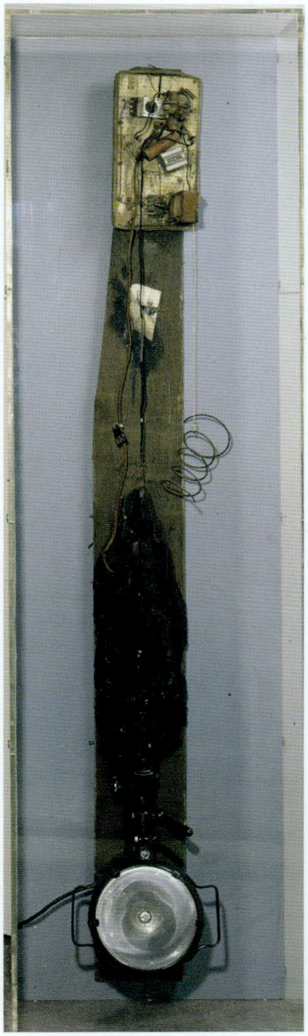

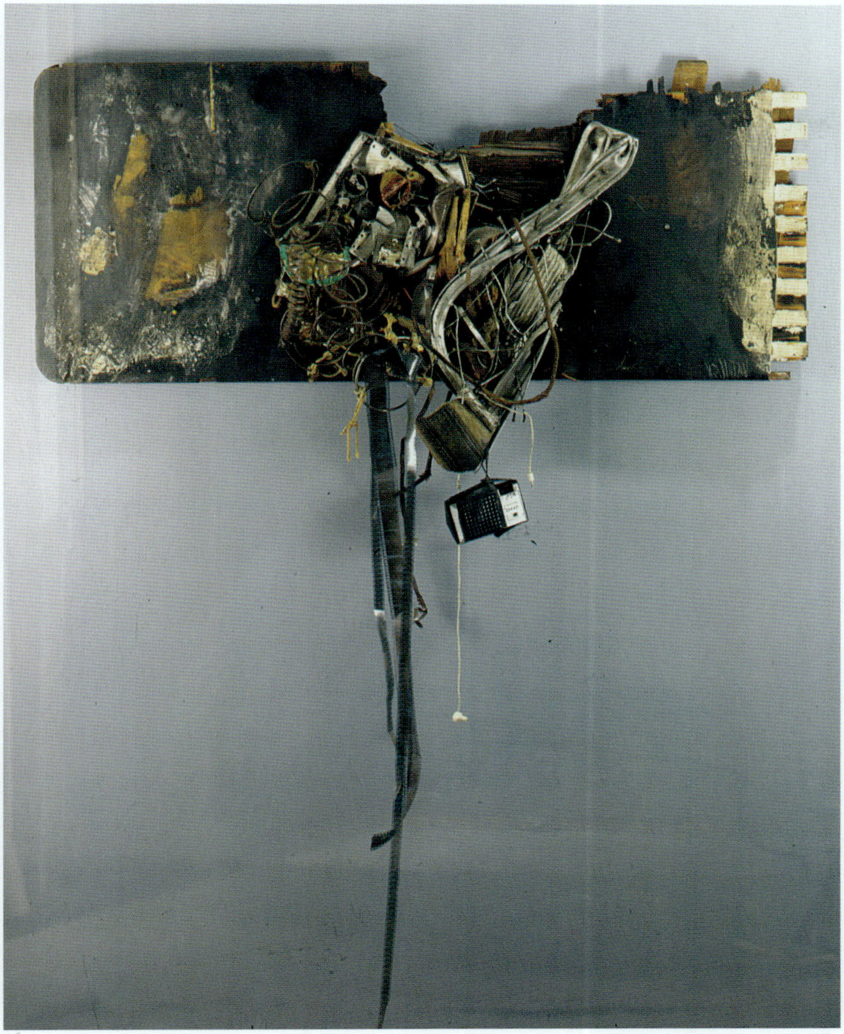

166 Wolf Vostell, *Auschwitz Searchlight 568*, 1958–9, *de-coll/age* object, part of the installation *Black Room*, organic and industrially produced materials.

167 Wolf Vostell, *Treblinka*, 1958–9, *de-coll/age* object, part of the installation *Black Room*, organic and industrially produced materials.

Black Room

His first environmental work, *Black Room*, dated up until now between 1958 and 1963,[120] represents precisely this combination of breaking off former bonds and attaching them to newly assembled found objects, tearing open the German past again. In the three assemblages making up this environmental work, *Auschwitz Searchlight 568* (illus. 166), *Treblinka* (illus. 167) and *German View* (illus. 168), there is none of the traditional iconographic encoding of violence and death in the camps but just the aesthetic of the material itself and its specific significance. Here Vostell was not going for an aesthetic transformation of what cannot be represented; rather he was showing the extermination from the perspective of the German present. In a period when there was a policy of renovation being carried out to aestheticize the memorial sites in Germany, he produced a composition consisting of junk: an old, demolished piece of wood, with long hair hanging from it, torn-up wires and a light bulb burning in the searchlight. The positioning of the searchlight with its harsh light at the bottom of the piece of wood is a reversal of lighting;[121] it illustrates the violent dark side of the Enlightenment. It is a reference to the round-the-clock control in the camps and places the public in the role of those being watched over. *Auschwitz Searchlight 568* and *Treblinka*, using modern rubbish, allude to the shattering, the total destruction, the process of extermination. As a third composition, Vostell added the assemblage *German View* to *Black Room*, the present added to Auschwitz and Treblinka. All three are related to one another and yet not the same. In the work *German View* there is a continuously flickering screen behind barbed wire. This television set is framed both by symbols of the Catholic Church – a crucifix and Curial Cardinal Fumasoni-Biondi[122] – and photographs of the military of the two German states, dressed again exactly in the style of the Wehrmacht,[123] and two children's spinning tops. The bottom right of the television screen is hidden by a container surrounded on three sides with the not entirely chewed bones from a pork chop. As the authentic remains of a non-artistic reality, Sebastian Hackenschmidt explained for the context of the 1960s, they were considered to be material evidence of the past – reminding one of the view into the open ovens in the crematoria. In the assemblage *Black Room* they function as metonymous signs for those who had been violently murdered by the Nazis; along with the barbed wire they overlay whatever might be reported on German television.[124]

A further reference to violence by the state appears at the top of the piece of wood in *Auschwitz Searchlight 568* in the form of a faded scrap of paper, on which one can see what is probably a traffic policeman with a whistle and his arm raised, someone – as Vostell believed – controlling murderous events on the streets[125] with a gesture reminiscent of the Hitler salute.

The quality of the material and its being originally left over and thrown away are, along with the unambiguous titles, reminiscent of the images from

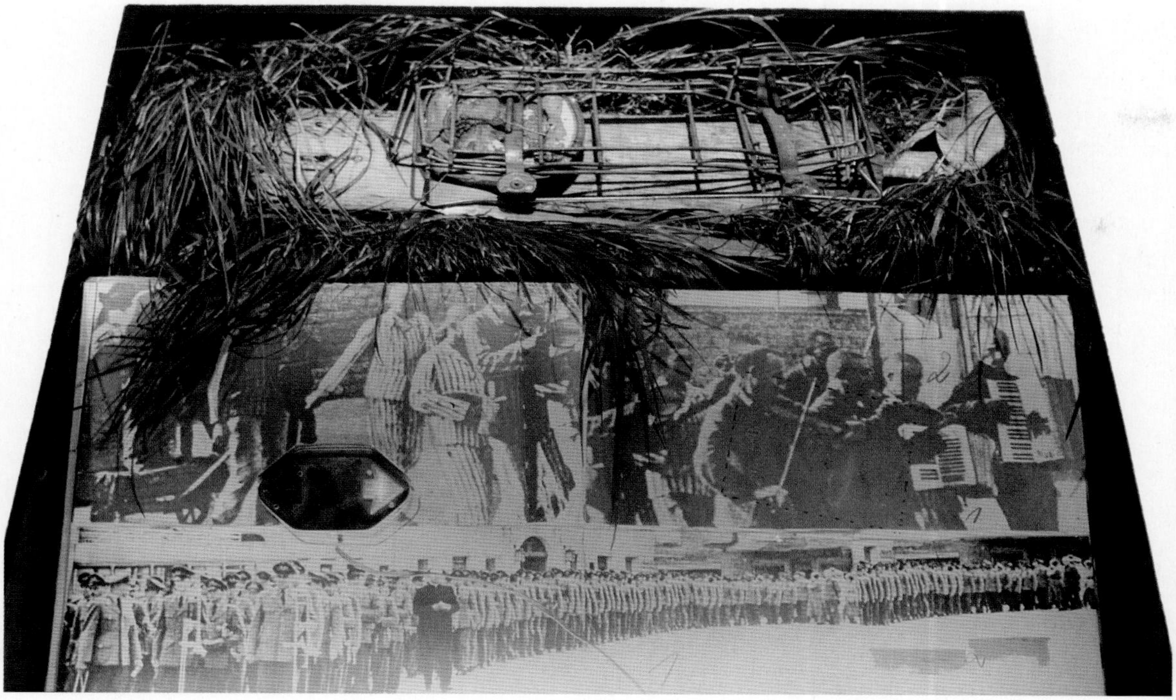

168 Wolf Vostell, *Treblinka*, 1958–61, object with a No-Book (1961), a book against violence, organic and industrially produced materials, photographs.

the museum in Auschwitz that Alain Resnais includes in *Night and Fog*. Vostell referred to the thesis, later to become popular, of the 'memory of objects'[126] and showed that things have to be called by name if they are not to be forgotten. By capturing the public in the light of *Auschwitz Searchlight 568*, the methods of supervision in the camps are identified, but one's gaze is distracted by the screen continuously flickering and surrounded by rubbish. The television placed behind barbed wire now presents the *German View*, and grabs the attention of the viewer.

Treblinka (No-Book)

Vostell chose the name of Treblinka extermination camp for a book of objects. It is kept in the store at the Staatsgalerie in Stuttgart. In February 2012 I was able to view it there only behind glass in a case and from the narrow side. Because of restoration work it was not possible to leaf through it 'for the foreseeable future',[127] so the important details of Vostell's work could only be gleaned from the catalogue to *documenta* in 1977.[128] Next to a photograph of a view of the open book, it says: '*Treblinka*, 1958–61; book of objects in a black wooden case, unique; Archive Sohm, Markgröningen. Child's shoe, metal grille, wood and grass above the "Nein-Buch" (No-Book) (1961), a book against violence. With a battery-operated indicator that flashes when the pages are turned over.'[129]

The photograph of the concentration camp – something not used by Vostell up to that time – the case, the metal grille, the squashed tin can

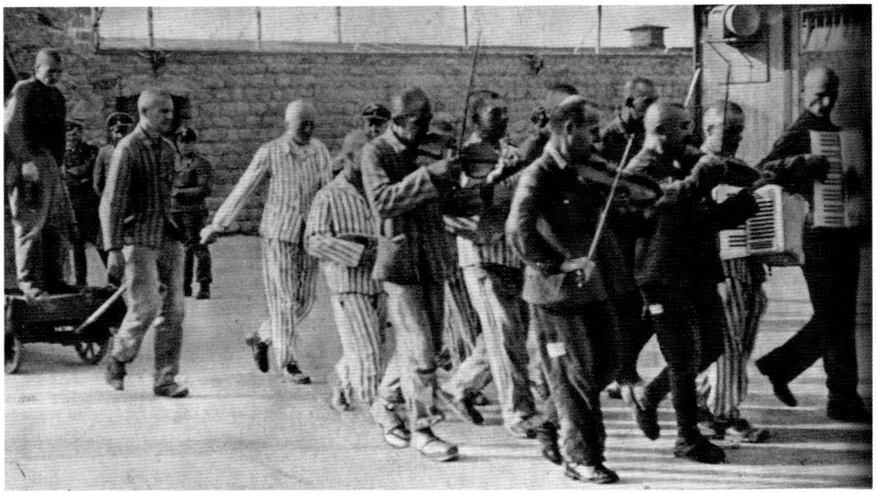

169 'The treachery and cruelty of the SS-men were without limit. Prisoners were forced to play while they accompanied their comrades to the execution site', from *We Have Not Forgotten* (Warsaw, 1959).

underneath, the child's shoe, along with the book's state of denial, indicate an association with the NO!art movement in New York.[130] Vostell must have got to know about it by 1963 at the latest when he first exhibited in New York.[131] The NO!art movement, founded in 1960, used materials Vostell placed into his book of objects. Boris Lurie and Sam Goodman in particular included the most graphic photographs of corpses in the camps liberated by the Allies, putting them into collages along with rubbish, newspaper cuttings of advertisements and pornographic pictures in opposition to the established New York art of Abstract Expressionism, Pop- and Op art. Vostell, however, aimed at different contrasts in the context of contemporary West Germany. He used the model of the photo books current at the time, and onto a photograph, enlarged into a double-paged illustration, of a concentration camp when it was still functioning (illus. 169) he stuck a composite photo showing an indefinable group of West German Bundeswehr soldiers marching. It is possible that with this he was even intentionally seeking to make reference to the layout of photos juxtaposed, without any breaks, such as those shown of various killings in *Der Gelbe Stern* covering four separate pages.[132] Even though the two photographs in the landscape format of the book of objects appear separate to one another, they together cover the double sides right up to the edges, so that the column of West German soldiers merges into one with the prisoners in the camp. Vostell placed the two columns in such a way they are moving in opposite directions and it is as though the band of doomed musicians is playing for the present-day military. In the No-Book both of them are marching to the same tune, a death march.

The fact that the photograph is of the gruesome event of the procession with the camp band on the way to the execution of Hans Bonarewitz on 30 July 1942 in Mauthausen, taken by SS-Oberscharführer Fritz Kornatz, which was used in the Nuremberg trials of 1946 to document the activity at the camp,[133] is not obvious, at least in the presentation of illustrations in the open book. And Vostell probably will not have known as he presumably took the photo from the book *We Have Not Forgotten*,[134] already used by Bazon Brock, which did not contain this information. Instead, the collage underlines the widespread concern and warnings about the rearmament of West Germany and its military. It is not clear to what extent Vostell, when making this provocative comparison, was aware of the particular photograph of the gruesome punishment, accompanied by music from the camp band, of a prisoner who had tried to escape. The public execution of the prisoner Bonarewitz is not shown in the photo, but Bonarewitz, standing on a cart on the extreme left, is covered by straw in Vostell's book and the artist made it difficult to identify the photo by giving it the title *Treblinka (No Book)*. Was this photo deliberately made anonymous and just simply stuck on as a sign of drill in the camps? We will not know for sure until, hopefully in the foreseeable future, those responsible at the Stuttgart Staatsgalerie are able to turn over the other pages.

As Vostell's 1967 colour series *Treblinka* suggests from a photograph,[135] which was identified by Schoenberner as being of Treblinka[136] and only recently has been shown to be of Jewish women from the ghetto at Mizoč forced to undress before execution,[137] the artist in his work did not just use the names of the extermination camps but researched into the associated photographic documentation. And finally in 1967 he was no doubt reacting to a public that was now better informed than it had been earlier.

8 The Past in the Present: Commenting on the Auschwitz Trial

As a result of the Auschwitz trial and the discussion of it in the media, in West Germany there was a belated change in the public memory of the murder of the Jews. More detailed reports on the proceedings were made available. Interest in the acts of cruelty and satisfaction at the punishment of the perpetrators made up one part of the public reaction, pleasure at the descriptions and the written accounts of torture and other extreme violence published in detail in the coverage was another one.[1] At the same time in West Germany there was now an effort being made to achieve a broad awareness of the crimes. Starting in 1963, after the beginning of the Auschwitz trial on 20 December in Frankfurt am Main, there were in fact several events held in Germany devoted to documenting the murder of the Jews from different political points of view. Public institutions now also engaged with the subject. The three years that had elapsed since the exhibition and the publication of the book by Schoenberner, the Eichmann trial in Jerusalem in 1961–2 and Hannah Arendt's book about it[2] saw an intensified public discussion of the genocide of the Jews. The trial in Jerusalem had caused the historical events and the political strategies leading to the murder of the Jews to become public knowledge worldwide, the spotlight now in Frankfurt fell above all on the particularly brutal and sadistic crimes committed by the individual accused, answerable to German justice.[3] What is more, the visitors to the galleries of the documentary exhibitions were confronted full-on with stark enlargements of photographs of the atrocities committed by the perpetrators.[4]

In West Berlin, Heinz Galinski, chairman of the Jewish Community there, opened the travelling exhibition *Leben, Kampf und Tod im Ghetto Warschau* (Life, Struggle and Death in the Warsaw Ghetto) on 18 April 1963, the eve of the twentieth anniversary of the Jewish uprising in the Warsaw Ghetto. It had been conceived by the Jewish Historical Institute in Warsaw; Galinski had the display sent to Berlin, where it opened on the occasion of the annual remembrance celebration in the Community Centre.[5]

In East Berlin on 19 April, the twentieth anniversary of the Uprising, the exhibition *Martyrium, Kampf, Ausrottung* (Martyrdom, Struggle, Eradication) opened in the Polish Cultural Centre with a formal ceremony. The *Berliner Zeitung* described the exhibited photos from the Stroop Report:

> Portraits of the heroes stare out at the viewer, young Jewesses shortly before being shot, dead bodies, women, men, children, workers, intellectuals. Even the tormentors of the Jews are seen in their shining SS boots, prepared to trample on the Humanity of the whole world. Their gestures speak of cold, naked sadism. The viewer is horrified, and he reflects upon it.[6]

At the remembrance event, the first Polish feature film about the Ghetto Uprising, Aleksander Ford's *Grenzstrasse*,[7] that is, *Ulica Graniczna*, was shown; it won a prize at the Venice Film Festival in 1948. The memorial speech was given by 'the Berlin publicist Peter Edel'. On the evening of 22 April, 'in honour of the victims', there was a performance of Yiddish songs and piano music.[8]

The large exhibition on cultural history *Monumenta Judaica 2000 Jahre Geschichte und Kultur der Juden am Rhein* (Monumenta Judaica: 2,000 Years of Jewish History and Culture in the Rhineland) ran from 15 October 1963 until 15 February 1964 in Cologne. It had been commissioned by the city after the anti-Semitic daubings around the turn of 1959–60, and attracted over 100,000 visitors. In the display, which contained more than 2,000 objects, maps, plans and diagrams under the headings of the political, legal, social and economic history of the Jews in Germany, No. XI was the section *Das Schicksal der Juden am Rhein im nationalsozialistischen Einheitsstaat. Die Jahre 1933–1945* (The Fate of the Jews in the Rhineland in the National Socialist-controlled State: The Years 1933–1945). After 61 written documents unsparingly revealed examples of the extent of the Nazi persecution, in the catalogue 27 large photos of the events of the period are illustrated, including five from Schoenberner's book. The contributions to the fine arts are limited to works from the Weimar Republic or were listed under *Denkmäler und Mahnmale seit 1945* (Memorials and Public Remembrance Since 1945).[9]

On the holy Day of Repentance and Prayer, 20 November, one month before the start of the Auschwitz trial, the exhibition *Warschauer Ghetto* (Warsaw Ghetto) opened at the Paulskirche in Frankfurt after considerable advance publicity in the press. The representations of the Warsaw Ghetto were planned as a counter exhibition to that of the Jewish Historical Institute in Warsaw, which Galinski in Berlin had not cancelled, despite objections from Bonn, and which had been shown in nine German towns by the end of 1964. In promoting the exhibition at the Paulskirche, the Federal Press Office as funder had responded, without themselves coming forward, to an initiative from the German embassy in London. The reason for this was that they wanted to respond to the feared accusations in the Polish presentation by putting on their own exhibition limited to the historical facts.[10] The decision, however, was acted upon only when the intention of the Jewish Historical Institute in Poland to stage their exhibition in Germany became known, making an improvement of the foreign affairs profile of West Germany a pressing concern. The Frankfurt exhibition was based on the collected pictorial material belonging to Alexander Bernfes, a survivor of the ghetto, son of the last rabbi in Warsaw. It had already been displayed in London in 1961 and it was enlarged for Frankfurt above all by documents from the Federal Archive. The exhibition impressed the visitors, particularly because of the many large-format photos. More than a thousand citizens were at the opening to hear representatives from the West German government, the Bundestag, the Federal Parliament, the state of Hessen and the city of Frankfurt, the president of the Verband für Freiheit und Menschenwürde (Association for Freedom and Human Dignity) on behalf of the Federal Press Office as organizers, the military representative of the Federal Republic and Franz Böhm, the CDU Member of Parliament and president of the Gesellschaft für Christlich-Judische Zusammenarbeit (Society for Christian–Jewish Co-operation). After the speeches, to conclude, an actress and an actor recited literary texts. The reading from the *Tagebücher der Verzweifelten* (Diaries of the Desperate),[11] the 'tale of the Ring' from Lessing's *Nathan der Weise* (Nathan the Wise) and the recitation of Johannes R. Becher's *Kinderschuhe aus Lublin* (Children's Shoes from Lublin)[12] had a 'thought-provoking and moving effect' on everyone present.[13] On the same day of remembrance, one year later, also at the Paulskirche, life-size copies of photos were put on display in the exhibition *Auschwitz – Bilder und Dokumente* (Auschwitz – Images and Documents).[14]

It was not the convention at such commemorations to show works from the fine arts. Some of the artists of the time, however, had begun to develop new forms of commemorative events, for example the widely known and scandalous installations shown on 20 July 1964 in the *Festival der neuen Kunst* (Festival of New Art) under the auspices of the student representatives at the Technische Hochschule in Aachen.[15]

Wolf Vostell

Early Happenings in Aachen, Wuppertal and Ulm

In the art movement FLUXUS, the rejection of the traditional concept of art also addressed the issue of other forms of established – and allegedly dishonest – bourgeois activity in the fields of culture and remembrance of the past.

In order to abolish the barriers between art and life as well as between the artist and the public, 'happenings' were staged for people to take part in and re-experience, even some in which latent aggressions were explored. Wolf Vostell's happenings in particular were frequently marked by clear references to the German past. In the directions for the happening *Skeletons Environmental Change De-Coll/age Theatre*, with which in 1954 Wolf Vostell sought to change a well-known part of the town of Wuppertal,[16] he wrote down nineteen instructions for what was to happen, clearly recalling the conditions in the Second World War and the persecution of the Jews:

> 1 100 skeletons of animals and human beings, also raw meat and innards to be placed in the river wupper without explanation
> . . .
> 11 the trams to go round with windows nailed up
> 12 every policeman to tell people about his past
> . . .
> 13 blood to be constantly flowing down the wall of a building
> 14 people dressed in yellow to be sitting on a busy square
> . . .
> 17 all Christians to wear a wooden cross sewn onto a piece of clothing
> 18 a train to be pulling a cattle wagon
> 19 people to be standing in front of a bank building saying NO.

Among these instructions, in which the request to wear a badge, the colour yellow, the cattle wagon and the skeletons were references to the images that had in the meantime become inseparably associated with the persecution and murder of the Jews, the addition of '100 washing machines' reminded people of the contemporary debate about the cleanliness of the Germans and of their need to 'wash themselves clean' in the metaphorical sense. The last instruction calls for resistance, which was now no longer to be directed at an over-mighty state, but was to take the form of criticism of capitalism and consumerism, against the power of the banks.

The spectacular event of 20 July 1964 at the Technische Hochschule in Aachen, which made FLUXUS notorious in Germany, did not have to be called off so much because of the blow from a fist received by Joseph Beuys, causing him to grab the crucifix that he then held up to the cameras, as in the picture often shown, like an exorcist.[17] It was more because the yellow paint dust, which those participating in Vostell's *de-coll/age* event *NEVER AGAIN* had to throw at one another, threatened to clog up the air-filtration system.[18] The title of this happening contains a demand originating with the resistance movement, becoming widely known once again due to the rearmament of West Germany and the Easter Marches (the equivalent of the Aldermaston Marches in the UK). In addition, it called to mind the contemporary peace movement on the very day when people were supposed to be thinking about

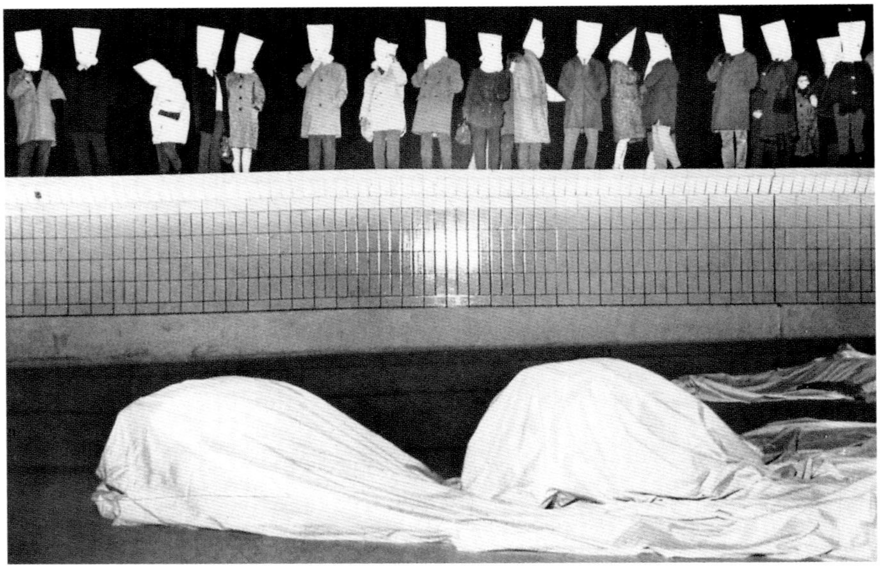

170 Wolf Vostell, *In Ulm and around Ulm and All around Ulm; Station 21: Calling Peace of Mind into Question – Or Where Were You 20 Years Ago?*, from *Das Kunstwerk*, XVIII/7 (January 1965).

the unsuccessful attempt on Adolf Hitler's life. Vostell had placed a radio typical of the 1950s on the edge of the stage, on which bones were lying, looking as though they had come straight from the slaughterhouse and, as Sebastian Hackenschmidt interpreted, reminding people of the crimes committed.[19] The radio played a permanent loop of the question by Joseph Goebbels, the former Reichspropagandaminister, in the Berlin Sportpalast, asking the public whether they wanted total war, and their fanatical reaction. In Aachen, to the question 'Do you want total life?', the new public enthusiastically yelled the earlier answer 'Ja' from 1943 in reply and soon took over control themselves of the event. The public's involvement was afterwards celebrated by the artists taking part as being their own act of resistance and thus the greatest success of the event.[20] While Bazon Brock, standing on his head, attempted to give a speech, Joseph Beuys played around like an alchemist with fat and other substances and Vostell was unmistakably calling for an activity. He had had whistles and handouts with instructions distributed, leaving it up to the public to whistle aggressively in reaction to the signal from a blue light, at which those participating had to fall into what was not by accident yellow dust, or to feel their heartbeat in sympathy. Vostell himself wore a gas mask while he attempted to direct the events on the stage and in the auditorium.[21] Admittedly, in this happening, he did not go as far as Stefan Wewerka who in 1961 at the Galerie Lauhus in Cologne 'gassed' the audience,[22] but the references here were just as clear as they were six months later in Ulm.

In the happening 'composed' for Studio f in Ulm under the title of a familiar tongue-twister, *In Ulm and around Ulm and All around Ulm*,[23] presented on 7 November 1964, gas masks were likewise employed in an underground car park, and '"corpses" lying around in blankets' had to be dragged away. 'For older people it sends shivers up their spine – for young people it's more of a joke,'[24] Jürgen Morschel, the reviewer of an art journal, described the public reaction. In addition there was the experience of having to watch with an empty stomach while other people were eating, and a ghostly scene in an empty swimming pool in which the public, along with actors, pulled paper bags over their heads and everyone was to sing a song of their choice. The title, location and set of this section 21, *Calling Peace of Mind into Question – Or Where Were You 20 Years Ago?*[25] (illus. 170), summoned up different associations, such as the Ku Klux Klan, gas chambers termed shower rooms or a firing squad on the side of a mass grave. The canonical Nazi anthem 'Es zittern die morschen Knochen' (The Rotting Bones Tremble) that the hooded spectators sang unmistakably linked the scene by its very sound to the Third Reich.[26] Morschel, who at the same time was in this event attempting to define what a 'happening' is, called the artist a 'moralist', for whom 'Auschwitz and Hiroshima' are always present and who takes the viewer of art out of the museum, 'in order to confront him or her with the banalities of the world of consumption and the allures of technology, above all, however, with the brutality and barbarism lying in wait everywhere concealed under the thin veil of aestheticism, indifference and forgetfulness of the past'.[27] He considered the happening as a whole, however, to be too long and too overloaded. One of the scenes intended to remind people of the concentration camps and gas chambers, it was discovered later, was thought to be of a sauna and for most people the toilets had been more important.

As a Neo-Dadaist, Vostell conceived and organized more happenings on the topic, controversial at the time in left-wing circles, of the continuation of Nazism in the present and, in the context of *24 Stunden* (24 Hours) in 1965 at the

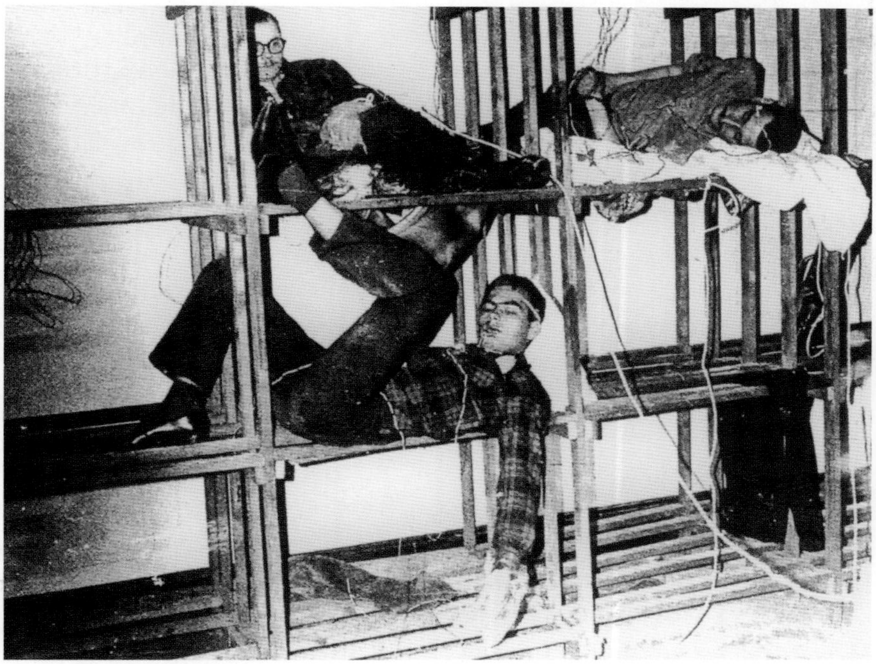

171 Wolf Vostell, *Consequences of the Emergency Laws*, happening with audience participation, *24 Hours*, 1965.

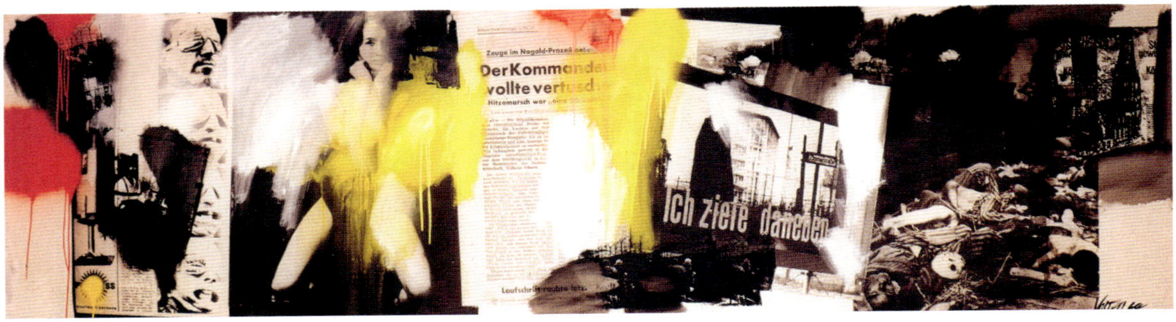

172 Wolf Vostell, *A Car Journey on the Crowded Autobahn Cologne–Frankfurt Takes More Out of You Than a Week of Hard Work*, 1964, screen printing and spray can colour on canvas.

Galerie Parnass in Wuppertal, he got the public to lie down on wooden shelves in the happening *Consequences of the Emergency Laws*.[28] (illus. 171) The arrangement, admittedly on the one hand intended to be critical of consumerism and highlighting the commodification of personal relations, also clearly suggested the huts in the camps, given that they are shown in the well-known images. Photographs such as that of the hut of the dying at Buchenwald (see illus. 213) had been seen by a broader public in exhibitions and publications on the trials in Düsseldorf and Frankfurt.

A Car Journey on the Crowded Autobahn Cologne–Frankfurt Takes More Out of You Than a Week of Hard Work

Vostell reacted directly to the Auschwitz trial using a newspaper cutting from the *Frankfurter Allgemeine Zeitung* which is part of his monumental wall of images and which he once more quoted in the title of this work: *We Were a Kind of Museum Object*.[29] In the equally large and subsequently more closely examined painting *A Car Journey* . . . of 1964 (illus. 172), the key position is now occupied by a newspaper article on the Nagold trial (dealing with a scandal over the training of recruits in the barracks there) which was drawing as much attention as the news about the torturers coming out of the Frankfurt courtroom.[30] For the monumental landscape format, Vostell copied from Schoenberner's book a photograph of dead prisoners and American soldiers in an open railway goods truck at Dachau[31] and combined it into a collage made up of events taking place at the same time as the trials: a photo of the English society girl Christine Keeler from the press reports about the Profumo Affair in Britain,[32] a photograph of experiments by the American military and the same photograph of the Berlin Wall over and over again. Cologne, the departure point of the car journey, is referred to on the extreme right-hand side by the article 'Steel raining down in the flak over Cologne', showing the silhouette of the cathedral in front of the ruins of the city. Vostell superimposes the illustration of the liberation of a camp so that the American soldiers can hardly be made out. Besides the city of Cologne, the disconcerting title also names Frankfurt, the destination of the journey, where the crimes shown in the photo were being investigated. Vostell not only made a causal connection between the murder of the Jews and the destruction of

German cities but presented his analysis of the present as a continuation of the Nazi period: the Berlin Wall and the wall of the truck can hardly be distinguished; the street sign of the Berlin Zimmerstrasse, where on 17 August 1962 Peter Fechter bled to death under the eyes of the public on both sides having attempted to cross the wall, with the headline 'Ich ziele daneben' (I aim close by), contradicting the deed, and the blurred bystanders in front of a wall topped with barbed wire could be those at the Berlin Wall as well as those outside a concentration camp. Analysis of the reality of the crimes committed and the linking of contemporary events to those of the past, and vice versa, are, as Wenzel described,[33] characteristic of the late 1960s and 1970s. In preparing the FLUXUS event of 20 July 1964, Tomas Schmit, the organizer, wrote: 'faced with the perfection of technology, the economy, armaments, culture and after the perfection of the murder of the Jews and before total annihilation', art is 'ANTIPERFECTIONISTIC'.[34]

Joseph Beuys

Auschwitz

Despite the presence of reproduced photographs from the Nazi period in books of photos and in exhibitions in the 1960s, Joseph Beuys's works commenting on Auschwitz lack any depiction of violence. When at the time of the

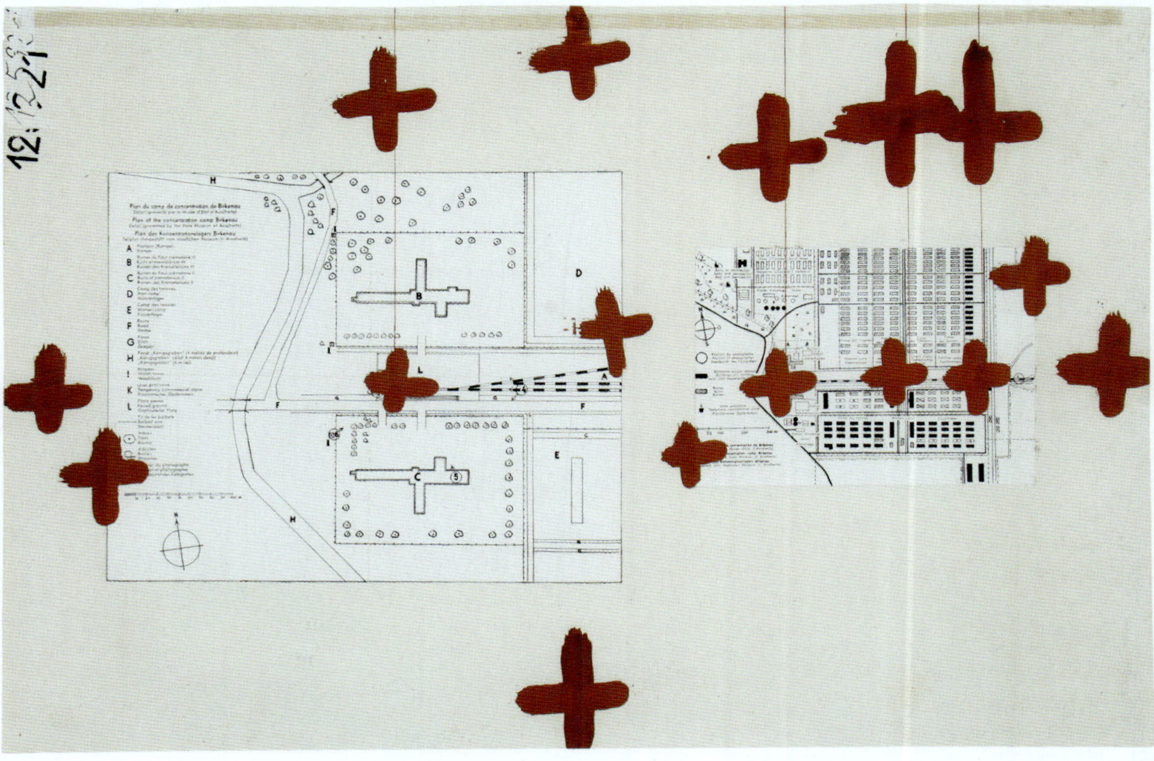

173 Joseph Beuys, *Auschwitz*, 1963, pen and ink, brush and oil (brown cross), brush and opaque white on map of Birkenau Concentration Camp on book paper.

Auschwitz trial he referred to the physical place, he made use of a photographic panorama of the whole of the site or the plans of the camp supplied with the information in 1957 on the competition for a monument at Auschwitz (see p. 187). Onto an undated drawing made of book paper[35] (illus. 173), he stuck two details from the plan of the camp at Birkenau – the ramp between the huts and the gas chambers, crematoria II and III on a much smaller scale. On the left-hand border, as in the design *Sketches for the Memorial* (see illus. 143), he stencilled the series of numerals with his date of birth, here too without giving the thousand, and again signed it by hand. Covering the whole paper Beuys painted sixteen large- and small-format 'Brown Crosses', as he called the emblem adapted by him as a universal symbol in a particular colour mix. As always in Beuys's works, his intended meaning, influenced by anthroposophy, is difficult to unravel. Mario Kramer's interpretation refers both to the usual numbering of the graveyard crosses and also to what he himself had witnessed with associations from Beuys's wartime experiences, starting with his talk of a 'flock of birds' flying away. Then: 'it makes you think of the view from an aeroplane, when a soldier is aiming the dropping of bombs using the cross hairs of a telescope.'[36] But it should also be borne in mind that the crosses, which Beuys used sixteen times, in his imagination symbolize not just death, that is, graveyard crosses, but like the Christian Cross are meant to point towards the overcoming of death. This supposition gains support from the trade name of the colour: caput mortuum.[37] Beuys attempted by a variety of mixtures to give this colour his own shade. It goes back to a synthetic paint pigment that the alchemists of the fifteenth century derived from what was left over from the production of sulphur. The name and the history of the type of paint can be found in Doerner's standard work on painting materials, which has been republished frequently since 1921. Beuys must have got from it the other term for the colour, colcothar, that Doerner describes: 'It reminds one of the place of the skulls, Golgatha, from the Hebrew "golgotha". And from there, Golgotha, the place of skulls to Kolkothar, the caput mortuum, the death's head, is not really so far.'[38] The covering colour is reminiscent of blood and soil, and Beuys is said to have occasionally added hare's blood to it.[39] By reason of its name and history, the colour is bound up with the strange world of alchemy that was to become increasingly more important in Beuys's work in the 1960s.

As a slight variation of the Red Cross, the Brown Cross, as well as transformation, indicates healing. In Beuys's way of thinking this would probably point to the overcoming of the death principle through life, the 'Christ impulse', as he understood it.[40]

KZ=Essen 1 and *2*

Beuys also drew Brown Crosses on his sculptural works *KZ=Essen 1* and *2* from 1963. In German 'Essen' does not just mean 'meal' or 'food' but is also the name of the German industrial city where the firm of Krupp, the most

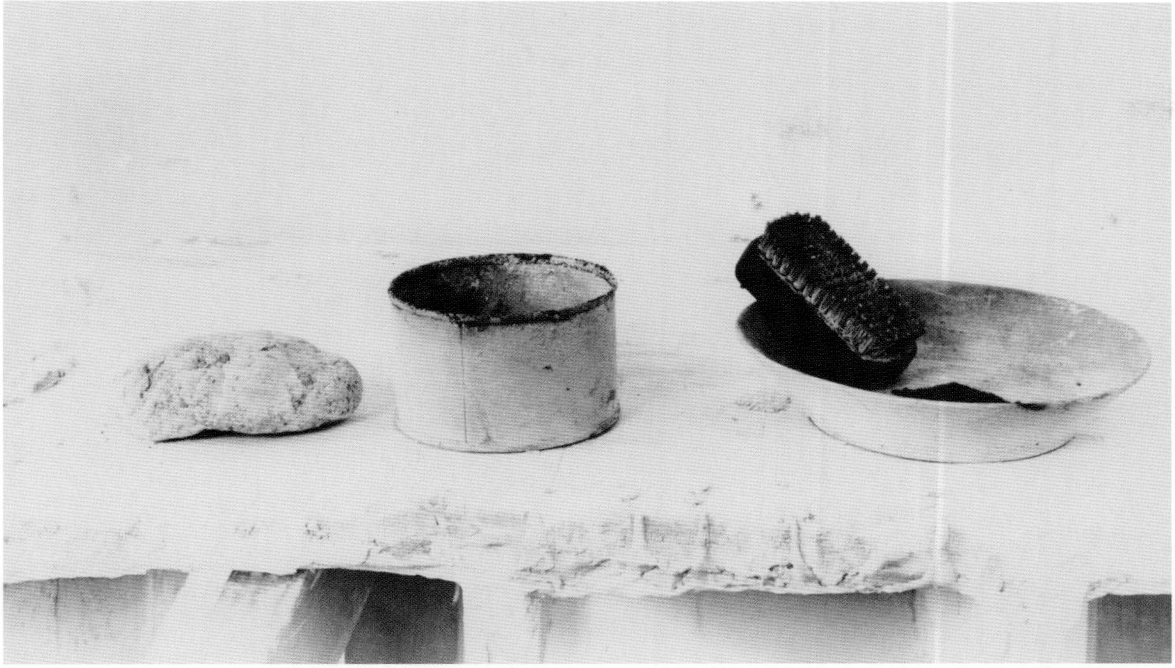

174 Joseph Beuys, *KZ=Essen 1 and 2*, 1963, part of the installation *Beuys Room*, box 3, china dish, painted white and with sinter, nail brush at the rim; open tin, painted; gypsum mortar.

important arms producer, was based. The people taken to become forced labourers for them were imprisoned in the camp at Essen-Humboldtstrasse, a satellite camp of Buchenwald. The city's name might also refer to the psychiatric clinic where Beuys stayed in the early 1950s. The assemblage (illus. 174) appears to convey the situation as regards food in the camps, reminiscent of the illustration of a prisoner's daily ration (illus. 175). In 1970 Beuys reused the works in an assemblage in a 'box' containing various other objects such as a sledge brake, a piece of wood with half a camembert, a *Sender* (transmitter), a paint brush, a block of paraffin, a camera and a *Wetterwart* (weatherman) shown in an exhibition at the Galerie art intermedia in Cologne.[41] Both of the works can most likely be dated to 1963 on the basis of the handwritten pencil signature 'Beuys 1963' on the porcelain bowl of *KZ=Essen 1*. Ute Klophaus,[42] whom Beuys rated highly and who photographed the development of his works and installations over a twenty-year period, only photographed the objects individually, which may justify the comments here being based on just what can immediately be seen.

In the period between the Eichmann and the Auschwitz trials, when everyday life in the camps once more impinged on the consciousness of the German population, Beuys presented discarded everyday objects, a tin can and a porcelain bowl as – evident from the title – relics of a camp, arranging them, as can be seen, as a contrast with the receiving of food. The open can is empty and what was before a malleable lump of not very appetizing plaster mortar is turned to stone next to it, nor does the nail brush in its empty bowl hold much promise of satisfying the permanent hunger that camp prisoners

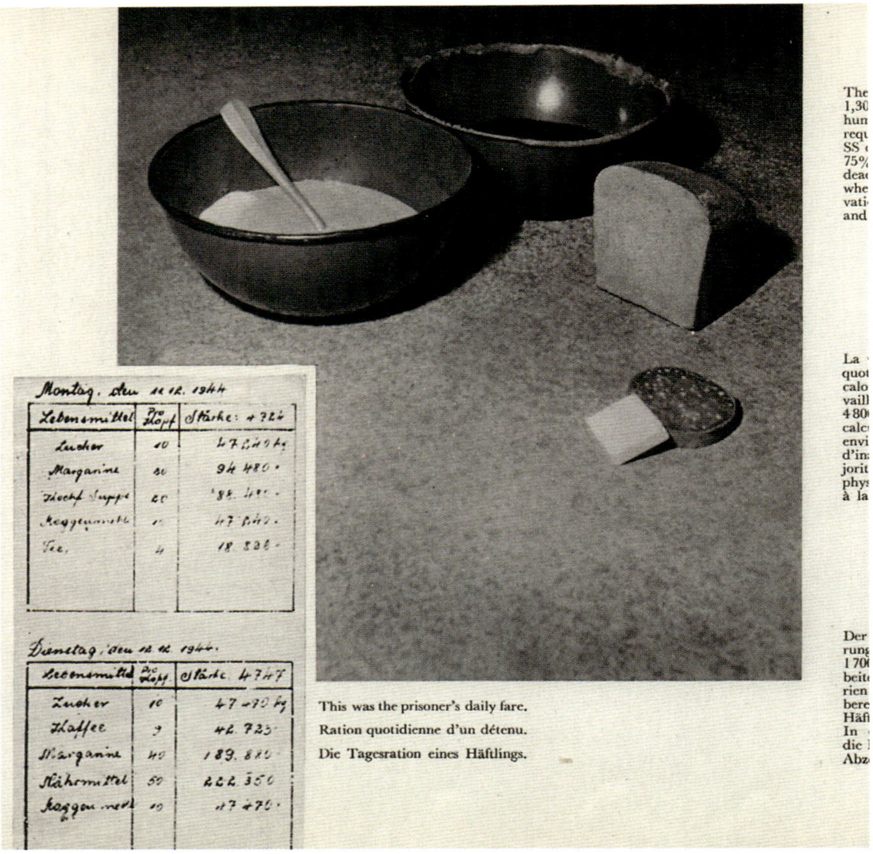

175 *Prisoner's Meal Ration*, publ. in Comité International d'Auschwitz, ed., *KL Auschwitz Krakau*, (c. 1963).

were subject to; its usual use is for cleaning.[43] With his three-dimensional works, Beuys moved away from the steel and steel-pipe sculptures appreciated at the time, such as those by Brigitte Meier-Denninghoff, Norbert Kricke and Hans Uhlmann, but also from the biomorphic works such as those by Henry Moore. He became an agent provocateur of the art scene in the modernist tradition as part of the so-called Neo-avant-garde[44] with his grubby everyday objects, assemblages of readymades standing out against the gleaming white walls of museums and galleries. Beuys did not stop at attributing new meaning to the readymades by changing the environment of the things and to the allegedly non-authoritarian dialogue between the artist and the viewer within the FLUXUS movement.[45] He loaded the objects with his esoteric philosophy and gave them titles using references to recent German history. As so often, he made use of his cipher of a Brown Cross and painted it both inside the white painted tin can and the white, encrusted porcelain bowl and also on the wooden part of the nail brush. Beuys made it into his signature on his objects, his works, thus simultaneously endowing them with the signs of transformation or healing, but without, however, claiming to be representing the catastrophic events:[46]

> I do not feel that these works were made to represent catastrophe, although the experience of catastrophe has certainly contributed to my awareness. But my interest was not in illustrating it, even when I used the title *Concentration Camp Essen.* This was not a description of the events in the camps but of the content and meaning of catastrophe. That must be the starting point – like a kind of substance – something that surmounts *Concentration Camp Essen.* Similia similibus curantur: heal like with like, that is the homeopathic healing process.
>
> The human condition is Auschwitz, and the principle of Auschwitz finds its perpetuation in our understanding of science and political systems, in the delegation of responsibility to groups of specialists and the silence of the intellectuals and artists. I have found myself in permanent struggle with this condition and its roots. I find for instance that we are now experiencing Auschwitz in its contemporary character.[47]

Drawing a parallel between Auschwitz and contemporary events, viewed with hindsight, brings home the misunderstanding at the time of the full extent of the Nazis' crimes.

The homeopathic ideas about healing quoted are directly related to the objects worked on in Kassel that are called 'Essen', that is, food, but are demonstrably not edible, such as the mortar, and illustrate emptiness and thus have hunger as an intended subject. More remarkable than the explanation for the finished work are the fundamental thoughts on the principle of Auschwitz and its universality, something that was not peculiar to Beuys in the West German debate.[48] For Beuys it highlighted the deadly dangers of

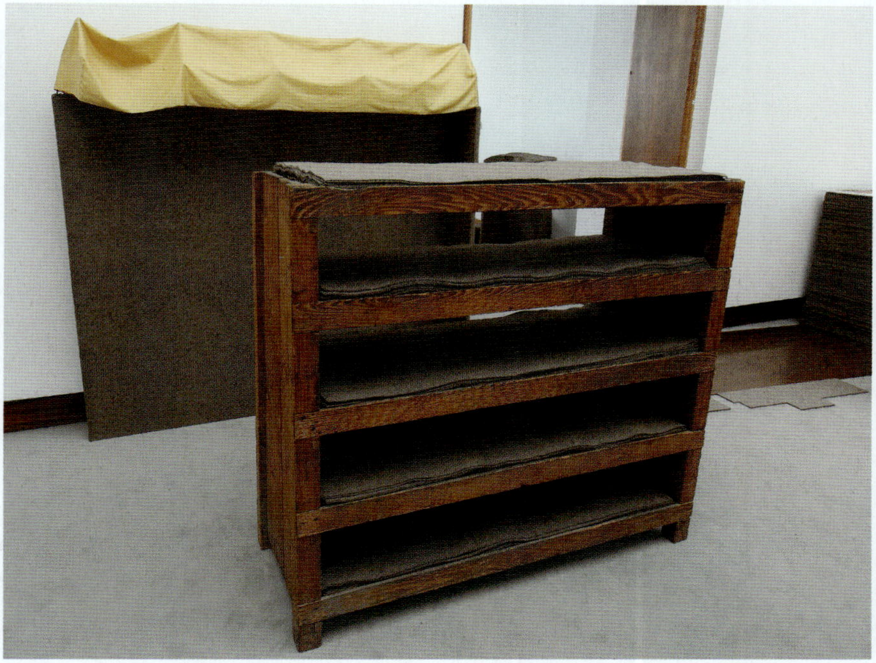

176 Joseph Beuys, *My and My Loved Ones' Abandoned Sleep*, 1965, part of *Block Beuys*, wooden shelf with felt.

simplistic materialist thinking and thus became a principle, bringing past and present closer together.[49] Such a paralleling, however, is only possible when mention of the name Auschwitz does not address the murder of the Jews by the Germans in the gas chambers there as the central and unique event characteristic of the Nazi period.

My and My Loved Ones' Abandoned Sleep

Representations of things from the camps are extremely rare with Beuys. The wooden shelf of 1965 entitled *My and My Loved Ones' Abandoned Sleep*[50] (illus. 176), which he developed for a performance and, as the record of the installation published posthumously reveals, in memory of his ancestors,[51] was covered with layers of felt and integrated in 1970 within the *Block Beuys* in Darmstadt. Only when it received academic attention was it associated with the wooden bunks for the prisoners in Auschwitz.[52] The memory expressed in it about the wooden bunks in the camp is given material form for Beuys in the long scenes in the film *Night and Fog* and the illustrations in Jan Sehn's book that the artist had been sent along with the competition information in 1957. Two full-page photographs reproduced there show the hard sleeping bunks with blankets lying or hanging around inside the living hut of the camp for men and women at Birkenau (illus. 177). For Beuys's works using felt, which was usually produced using animal hair (illus. 178), one can certainly see how much they contribute to the creation of a myth surrounding his own personality.[53] His involvement with Auschwitz does, however, lead one to conclude that covering with felt here is intended to suggest the memory of human hair that was used in Auschwitz to make felt,[54] and at the same time it exemplifies his idea of warmth and healing. Nearness to the camp victims suggested by 'My Loved Ones', without placing any historical distance between them and himself, is something Beuys had expressed ten years previously when he stencilled his signature with the numerals of his date of birth on the smaller gate model and a paper plan for the Auschwitz Memorial in imitation of the prisoners' tattoos.

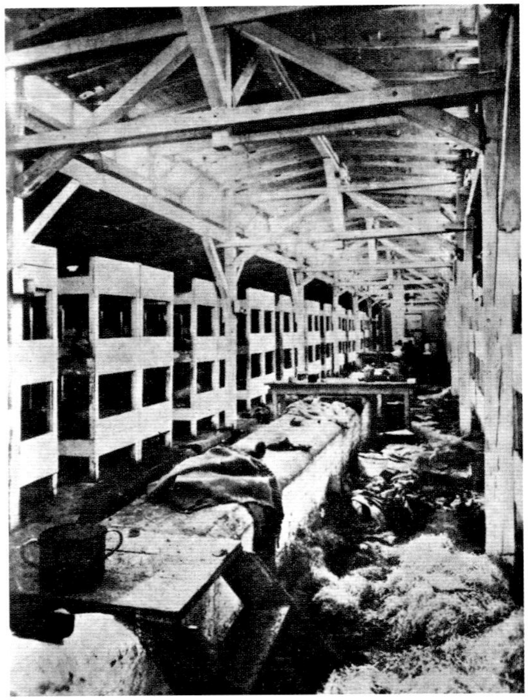

177 Stanislaw Mucha, *Inside of a Living Hut in the Brzezinska Men's Camp (Temporary Horse Stable Barrack Type 260/9)*, photograph, publ. in Sehn 1957.

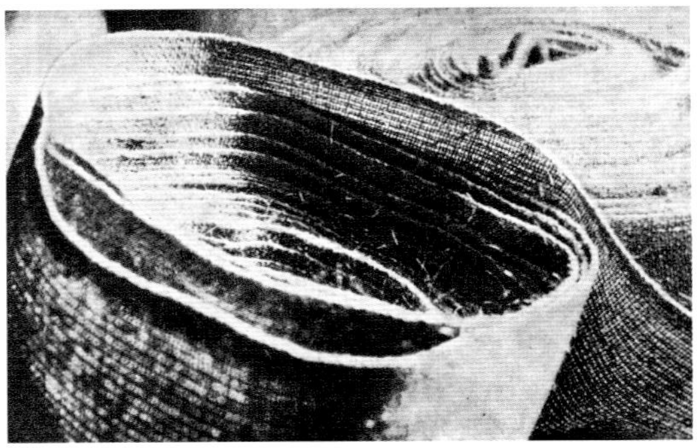

178 *Found After the Liberation: Bundles of Hair for Tailors, Manufactured on an Industrial Scale by the Nazis from the Hair of Women Gassed*, photograph publ. in Sehn 1957.

Gate Models for the *Auschwitz Memorial* in *Block Beuys*

When Beuys in 1970 collected together in the Darmstadt *Block Beuys*[55] as a sort of retrospective what remained from his many happenings and the three-dimensional works produced up until then,[56] he also used the two gate

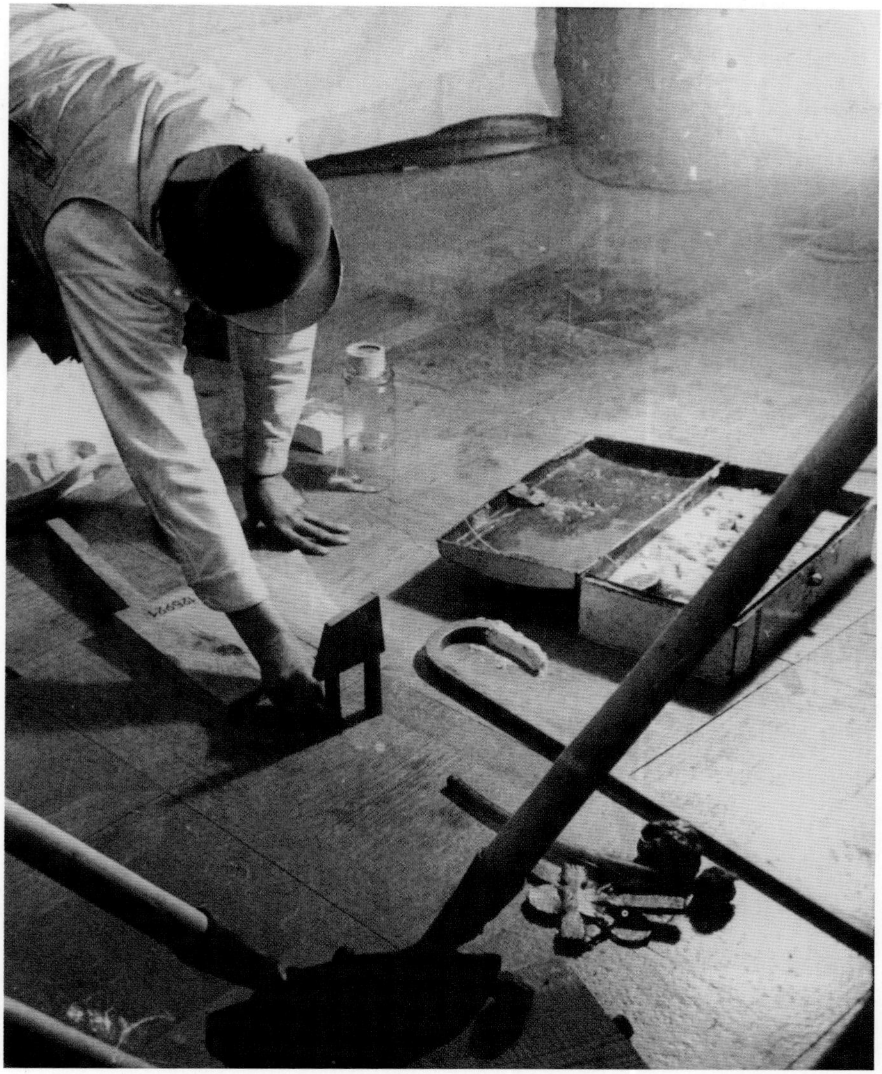

179 Joseph Beuys with the arches from his model for the Auschwitz Memorial, performance *And Inside Of Us . . . And Beneath Us . . . Everything Flooded*, happening with audience participation, *24 Hours*, 1965.

structures from his 1958 model design for a memorial at Auschwitz-Birkenau (see illus. 144). After getting them back from Auschwitz in July 1960,[57] he used them in 1965 in the installation *And Inside Of Us . . . And Beneath Us . . . Everything Flooded* in the happening *24 Hours* at the Galerie Parnass in Wuppertal[58] (illus. 179). Beuys distributed various objects about the room from an orange box, which he did not leave for the duration of the happening stated in the title. 'To the participants in Wuppertal,' Schneede summed it up, 'Beuys seemed to be a penitent and an ascetic.'[59] Probably for Beuys there was a connection between this act of contemplation and remembrance of Auschwitz; it is still an open question whether this was clear to the public.

In Darmstadt the smaller gate can be seen slightly hidden away on the right-hand side of the upper compartment second from the left in front of the chocolate hare on the motorcycle and next to many other everyday objects in Beuys's former tool cupboard from the Düsseldorf Academy.[60] Beuys called the cupboard object placed in Room 2 *Scene from the Stag Hunt*. This cupboard, with its numerous compartments and drawers, was part of the furniture of his studio and, as an artwork, its date is given as the year in which he started his professorship; it was not part of any particular installation but was a 'stage prop . . . an extra'[61] playing a part in all the happenings and any activity included within the artist's *Siberian Symphony*.[62] According to Stephan Malaka's detailed study of Beuys's way of thinking as manifested in the Darmstadt *Block*, the stag is intended to lead the viewer, as a soul mate, through the chaotic maze of materials in the 'cabinet of curiosities', into progressing out of himself and towards the occult possibilities of perception lying dormant within human beings.[63] Fritz, in her comparison of the motifs and connotations of the total oeuvre with the entries to the dictionary of German superstitions,[64] finds that equally represented alongside the pre-Christian significance is the Christian tradition in which the stag becomes a symbol of Christ, and Beuys uses it here 'to visualize spiritual processes of development anew'.[65] Within this symbolic world, the stag hunt is only referred to in the legend of St Hubertus, so the cupboard object and within it remembrance of Beuys's involvement with the subject of Auschwitz can also be seen as a biographical souvenir of his own intellectual development.[66]

In display case 1 in Room 5 of the Darmstadt Landesmuseum, given in Eva Beuys's publication as dating from the period 1957–67,[67] Beuys has reassembled the two supports from the former large gate model for Auschwitz in the form of a building facade and placed it on the base of the display case. In the 1990 publication they have the title *Signs of Transformation* and are dated 1957. The pointed end of them that could be referred to as a gable is fitted into two wooden boards above. Painted in a sort of red, the structure is exhibited there together with sixteen other 'materials' from the artist's symbol-like world of objects. A *Radio* from 1961, consisting of bones from cloven-hoofed animals tied together, is placed in an empty space surrounded by the two wooden supports; a bronze *Foot* from 1955 is at the bottom end of the left-hand rectangular pillar; next to them are sculptures made of fat from 1963 with a *U-shaped Double Lamp with Hare's Fat* from 1961, a bottle of mineral water as *Neptune* from 1967, an undated alarm-clock and a *Sheep in the Snow*[68] from 1952. If one can identify any overall sense in the composition of the individual found objects, sculptures, everyday objects and food leftovers, it seems to be to make the visitors to the museum alert to the failure of an overall perspective and instead to set them on a course of becoming involved with the things, and the secrets they contain, from the 'cabinet of curiosities' in the form of nine glass display cases.[69]

This impression is confirmed by Beuys's statement in an interview on the occasion of the exhibition of the Ströher Collection at the Neue Pinakothek in Munich in 1968. In reply to the question from the interviewer, Dr Müller, about the objects, he says: 'They are simply a result of my work, props from my happenings, which in that respect are very much like tools that have been used to give clues, about all sorts of things, about physical phenomena etc.' In the course of his explanations about the meaning attached to the objects he added: 'The way they are placed is perhaps not so important either. Except for one single display case. It is one thing I called Auschwitz Demonstration, and the History of the Concentration Camps, they have a certain meaning attached.'[70]

Auschwitz Demonstration

The fourth display case in Room 5 of the Darmstadt *Block Beuys*, entitled *Auschwitz Demonstration* (illus. 180), is displayed prominently in the space that Beuys arranged himself, as with all the other rooms and display cases. *Beuys* selected this display case as the only one from the Darmstadt *Block* for his exhibition at the Guggenheim Museum in New York. He placed it as No. 24 and the last position at the end of the spiral in the museum beside the work *Bathtub*, which he regarded as a sign of birth. Displaying a panorama photograph of Auschwitz-Birkenau, the display case, arranged together with eight others, clearly draws attention to the camp, this being in addition the only one Beuys gave any sort of title to. In Eva Beuys's publication it is dated to the period '1956–1964' with the subsequent line 'Auschwitz 1957'.[71] Next to a photo of the display case there is a transcript of an interview with Beuys by Max Reithmann in 1981, in which he commented on the impossibility of representing the events at Auschwitz and described his works in this respect as 'positive counter images', 'Spielzeug' (toys). In reply to Reithmann's question: 'Do you think that anything like what happened at Auschwitz or during the Third Reich can be portrayed?', he said:

> No, it can't. Of course not. All you can do, as I said, is try to make up a medical prescription. Remind people about it, and in combination with performances. In any case you have to say, it all belongs to performance art, this as well. With the ongoing things, just putting something together that is not a portrayal of this terrible image, something that cannot be portrayed in a picture but was portrayed in its actual progression while it was happening, so that it cannot be translated into an image. Something, let's say, people can be reminded of in its positive counter image, i.e. by really removing it from the world of human beings. So as what remains of all these inhumane acts can be overcome. To that extent then this Auschwitz display case is actually a toy. I don't claim to have conveyed – in these things – any of the horror of it.[72]

The *Auschwitz Demonstration* has one main perspective, and within it fourteen objects 'of equal value', as Kramer wrote,[73] are placed alongside one another; in the literature they are read from right to left. Next to the highly rectangular relief of a fish from 1956, *Fish*, there is a round disc with the end bits of a sausage, *Battery (Sausage)* from 1963,[74] and next to that the *Warming Sculpture* from the celebrated FLUXUS happening of 20 July 1964, a small electric cooker with two hot plates on which blocks of fat as big as bricks are placed as if for melting.[75] The left-hand side of the display case is enclosed by two cylindrical wooden barrels, in one of which is a mummified rat on dried grass, *Rat*, from 1957. In the other one, a foot-rule opened up in a zig-zag fashion, *Blitz* from 1964, is displayed, sawn off at 42 cm, now well known as the year in which the mass murder by gassing in Auschwitz began, painted brown at the bottom end and wrapped in felt. Next to *Blitz* and surrounded by the white electric wire of *Warming Sculpture*, is placed an old porcelain dish, dusty and stuck together. On it there is a crucifix made of brown modelling clay, *Cross* from 1957, and a dried-out biscuit is leant against its side. The object is also described in the literature as *The Crucifix on the Plate*,[76] which Beuys had included in the installation *Manresa* in which, using light and electricity, he sought 'to find a way out of the crisis and into a new consciousness'.[77] The plans of the camp placed next to it were for even longer in his collection *Tool*, as they belonged to the information material for the competition for a Memorial at Auschwitz. The opened-out concertina fold *Auschwitz* of 1957 from Jan Sehn's 1957 Auschwitz documentation[78] stands upright with a view presumably taken from the tower of the camp gate at Birkenau looking towards the ramp and the huts of the camp. On the back of this, the plan of the 'POW camp'[79] is shown. In the background the view of the camp dominates a pencil drawing by Beuys, leaning up against the glass of the display case, of a female nude (illus. 181) standing with bent knees in front of a stretcher and attempting to cover her genitals with her hands, *Sick Girl, Ambulance Behind* from 1957.[80] One cannot make out her face; here too, as in the watercolour *Death and the Maiden* (see illus. 142), she seems to represent an allegory of the feminine for all victims.[81] The drawing for which a photograph, likewise published in Sehn's book (illus. 182), of the victims of medical experiments might have served as a model, is the only representation in Beuys's work of a camp prisoner. The stretcher refers, on the one hand, to the deadly result of these experiments; on the other, it was intended to proclaim 'salvation using the motif of death'.[82] 'According to the homoeopathic *Similia similibus curantur*, death and catastrophe give birth to that healing "substance" which is the agent of a process of reversal, spiritual rebirth and recreation of man and the universe.'[83] Only in this representation did Beuys contradict his own statement that he could not and would not portray the catastrophe.

Between the drawing and the plan of Auschwitz there are four thick rings of black pudding next to one another right up to the side wall of the display case +– *Sausage*, dating from 1964,[84] that have had fat coming out of them, gradually dried out and partly covered by a white film.[85] Each of them has a brown-painted plus or a minus sign on its end. In the middle of the display case between the view of Auschwitz, *Battery (Sausage)* from 1963 and the *Warming Sculpture*, next to a *Non-identity Mark (Aluminium)* from 1960

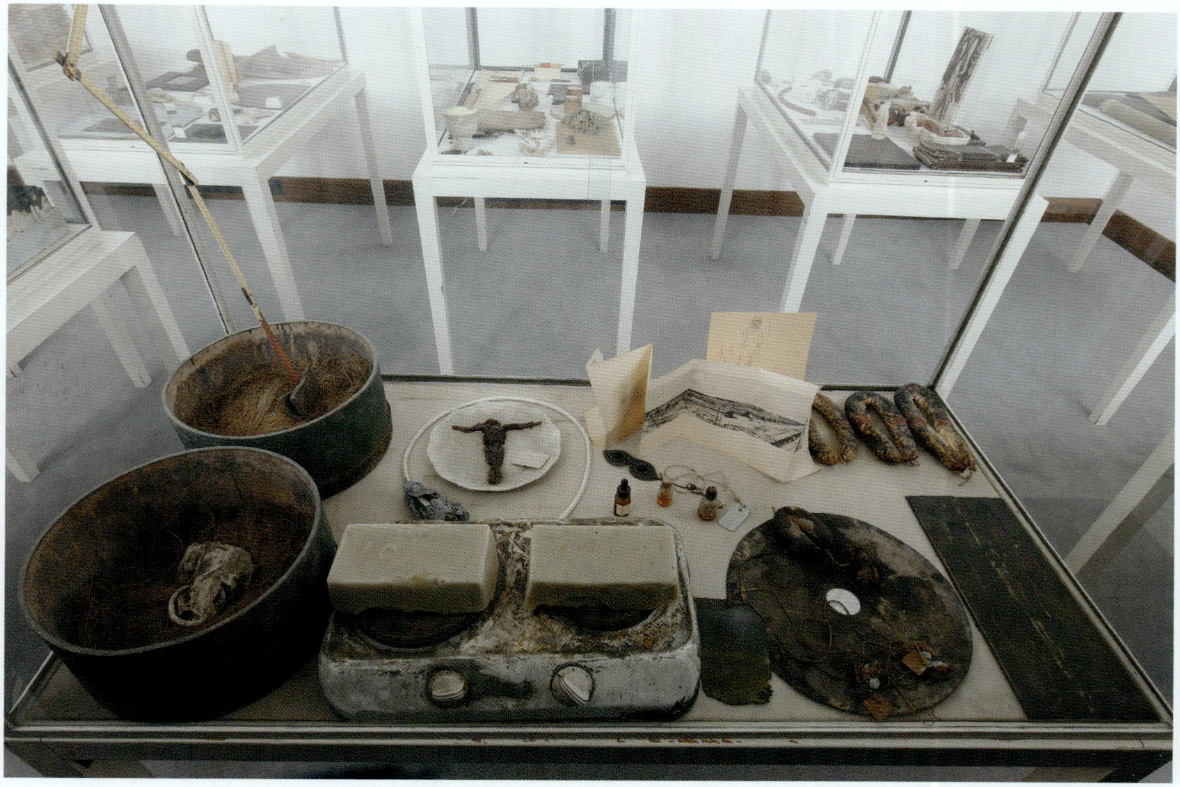

180 Joseph Beuys, display case *Auschwitz Demonstration*, part of *Block Beuys*, 1956–64, assemblage.

and a pair of mountain sunglasses from the Aachen happening of 20 July 1964, there are three small bottles: *Bottle with Fat (Solidified)*, *Bottle with Fat (Liquid)* and in the centre of the display case *Iodine (Bottle)*, all dated 1962.

The display case with the fourteen objects arranged in it has been closely examined by several art historians since 1997 in attempts to explain it, something that has rarely happened in the case of the artworks dealt with in this book. Remarkably all of the studies, mainly referring to Beuys's statements, hardly differ in their interpretation of the contents of the display case.

Mario Kramer was the first to do any basic research. This was in the 1997 Berlin catalogue *Deutschlandbilder* (Images of Germany) in the chapter 'Lebensmittel' (Groceries, that is, the means of sustaining life) under the title 'Josef Beuys: "Auschwitz Demonstration 1956–1964"' on Beuys's works for the competition for an Auschwitz Memorial in 1958. His contribution focuses simply on Beuys's work, without getting involved in the art scene of the period, with the aim of 'recording the relations of the individual pieces to one another, but also to other works and installations by Beuys' (p. 296). These become clearer and clearer in the course of his commentary on the expending of energy and warmth, on materialistic thinking and transformation, and on the material and the spiritual in Rudolf Steiner's sense. At the same time, looking at West German society, he thinks that Beuys's 'position on the historical events during the Third Reich is quite clear and unambiguous'

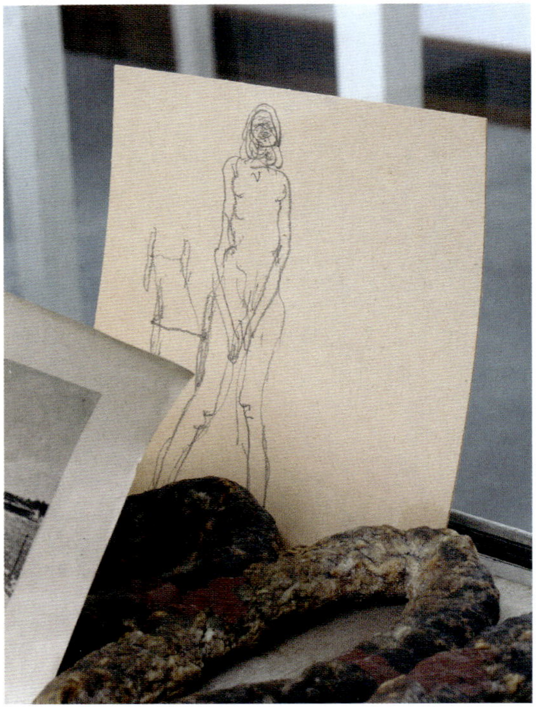

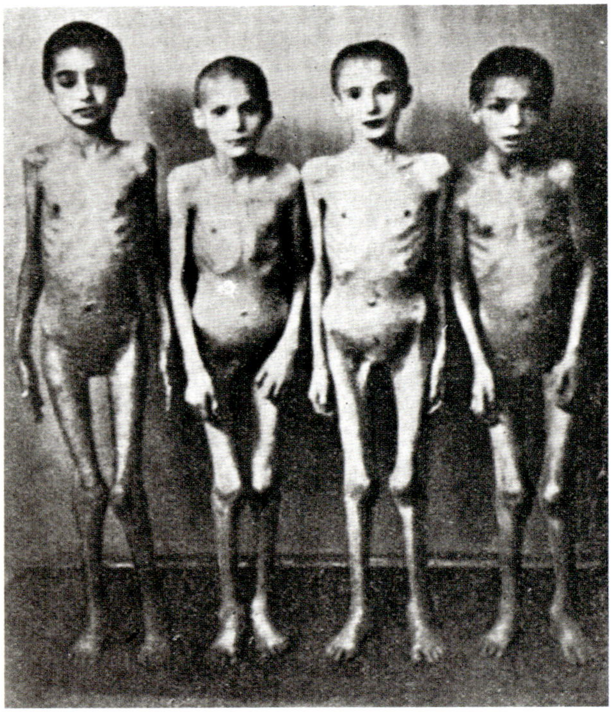

181 Joseph Beuys, *Sick Girl, Ambulance Behind*, 1957, from the display case *Auschwitz Demonstration*, part of the *Block Beuys*.

182 'Children in the Brzezinska Camp', photograph from the collection of Dr Mengele, SS physician, publ. in Sehn 1957.

(p. 303), that Beuys's work must be 'seen from the perspective of the repression of history in post-war Germany' (p. 302) and that one could go so far as to say that 'the whole of Joseph Beuys's early work can be described as a sort of catharsis – as freeing himself from spiritual conflicts by means of artistic expression' (p. 293). Kramer is careful about interpretation. However, Beuys's work cannot be seen just in the context of repression but it contributed to people in West Germany talking about 'all the victims' and 'all the dead' and not addressing the murder of the Jews.

Stephan Malaka deals with the display case *Auschwitz Demonstration* in his dissertation *Die Aktualisierung der Alchemie im Werk von Joseph Beuys* (The Revival of Alchemy in the Work of Joseph Beuys).[86] Malaka, who did not pay any regard to Kramer's work, concentrates just on interpreting the *Block Beuys* – and in particular *Auschwitz Demonstration* – as a definitive example, 'as an anthroposophical analogy' (pp. 61–6), of a revival of alchemy in line with the author's involvement with anthroposophy and the occult. He refers here to what he postulates as the 'fourfold historical link: Beuys – Steiner – Goethe – alchemy'.[87] In the, not hierarchically ordered, juxtaposition, according to Malaka, every single object in the display case is to be read following Beuys's knowledge of Steiner's teaching as a material sign for the secret significance of death and transformation, resurrection and renewal, as a manifestation of a world-view influenced by alchemy, aimed at bringing together 'once more' science, philosophy and gnosis within art.[88] Particular attention must, he says, be paid to the small iodine bottle placed in the centre of the display case which, as with this tincture acting as a medium of contrast in X-ray photographs, makes the invisible visible,[89] and the four rings of black pudding which, with reference to 'ouroboros', the serpent biting its tail, stand for wholeness, for a new beginning supplying endless energy and for 'unity in the ever-changing cosmos'.[90] Malaka's reinterpretation of *Auschwitz Demonstration* agrees with Kramer's insofar as both of them – just focusing on the artist's work – see Beuys's statements by analogy with the arrangement of the display case as the death principle to be overcome, as the transformation of the material, and associate his sculpture with transmutation. This, however, unlike in the case of FLUXUS, is intended to lead the human being, born again out of materialism, towards the fulfilment of a unity of mind, soul and body. Only Kramer talks of the artist 'liberating himself from spiritual conflicts'. These can, however, also be seen in relation to the artist's past and that of all Germans during the Nazi period.[91]

Nicole Fritz is the one who takes Beuys's ideas to their logical conclusion: 'Following the logic of Beuys's image of history', she analyses his interpretation of the 'materialistic death zone' and the 'historical event of Auschwitz' as a 'process of extinction', as a 'necessary situation of suffering', because he 'allows the possibility of spiritual development only in the course of history. The crimes committed during the Nazi period are therefore, however, seen by Beuys as an expression and necessary consequence of an internal law of history.'[92]

The anthroposophical and esoteric interpretations of the objects in line with Beuys's views are recognizable and comprehensible for a circle of 'initiates'; nevertheless Beuys became immensely popular with the German public in his role as an artist as well as through his works and performances.[93] Bunge 1998, p. 142, quotes an article by Hermann Pfütze on Beuys in the Kunstforum of 1989 which even expressed the supposition 'Perhaps his work is the first that can rightly be called "Art *after* Auschwitz".'[94] For Beuys and presumably not just for him, expectations of art as an enigmatic manifestation of the supernatural triumphing over materialism seem to have eclipsed memories of the Nazi period. His works are evidence of his consistently demonstrated efforts to remind people of the events in 'their positive counter image',[95] as he explains in the 1979 interview taking as an example the *Auschwitz Demonstration* and *KZ Essen*, and to set the forces of healing against the past. Little attention has been paid up to now to the connection between his works and the art scene of the time, seeing him in a historical context. This is what Buchloh early on complained about, arguing for him to be compared with Schwitters, the Surrealists and Arman's display cases[96] – and in addition to see them alongside the sculptures and drawings by Meret Oppenheim[97] as well as Joseph Cornell's *Boxes* and their mysterious objects behind glass.[98] The contrast with these works produced in other different situations, along with Beuys's theoretical borrowings from anthroposophy and homoeopathy, might underline the fact that he belongs to a West Germany characterized by a range of policies in relation to reparations and making up for the crimes of the past, euphemistically called 'mistakes'. His great popularity seems to be bound up with the heroic image of the artist as a healer.[99] Tomberger showed that, precisely in triumphing over his body marked by war, now as a victim and a mythic healer after the war, Beuys was able for the first time to risk a reformulation of the heroic status of the male artist, by claiming to shape society. The relation of his indirect reworking of the past to the persecution of the Jews is not immediately evident from his works despite the *Auschwitz Demonstration*. He was so absorbed in his multifaceted ideas of transformation, the expending of energy and the developing of sculpture that he did not consider it outrageous to place four black puddings – an 'impure' material for Jews (Genesis 9:4) – next to the concertina-fold plan of the camp installations at Auschwitz-Birkenau.

Hubert Berke

Hubert Berke, a well-known member of the post-war art scene in the Rhineland, worked from 1964–5 on a group of works whose subject was the sufferings of camp prisoners and memories of the perpetrators.[100] This is unusual in that he belonged to the war generation of artists like Willi Baumeister, Ernst Wilhelm Nay and Fritz Winter who, after their experiences during the Nazi period, avoided all directly political subject-matter in their pictures and devoted themselves exclusively to their abstract art. Berke did not directly address the question of the murder of the Jews in his works either, but his pictures in what is called the *Concentration Camp Series* have to be seen in the context of the Auschwitz trial as regards the period in which they were created and partly in the light of their detailed portrayal of the maltreatment of Jewish prisoners.

Berke had received his artistic training before the war under Paul Klee in Düsseldorf. Alienated by the Gleichschaltung of the Düsseldorf Academy and the way it was brought in line with Nazi ideas, he got by, based in Cologne from 1934–5, by producing everyday graphics and book illustrations.[101] At the same time as taking part in official exhibitions during the Nazi period, he drew in secret, among other things, a Passion cycle in ink (1936),[102] began the series *Masks in the Bog* (starting in 1941), painted a caricature of Hitler in 1943[103] and in 1944 the gouache *No Way Out Any More!*[104] Due to heart disease, he managed to avoid military service up until 1941; immediately after the war he went on to become a prize-winning representative of abstract painting.[105] With the emerging unrest of the 1960s and a definite politicization of pictorial works in West Germany, Berke worked more intensively on his never completely neglected studies of the suffering figure. Immediately after 1945 he completed a pen drawing on the subject, *Job in Ruins*,[106] the lamenting biblical figure Jewish artists referred to in the context of the Warsaw Ghetto.[107] Immediately after the war, along with Berke, other non-Jewish artists in

183 Hubert Berke, *The Ones Hanged (Concentration Camp Series)*, 1964, oil on canvas.

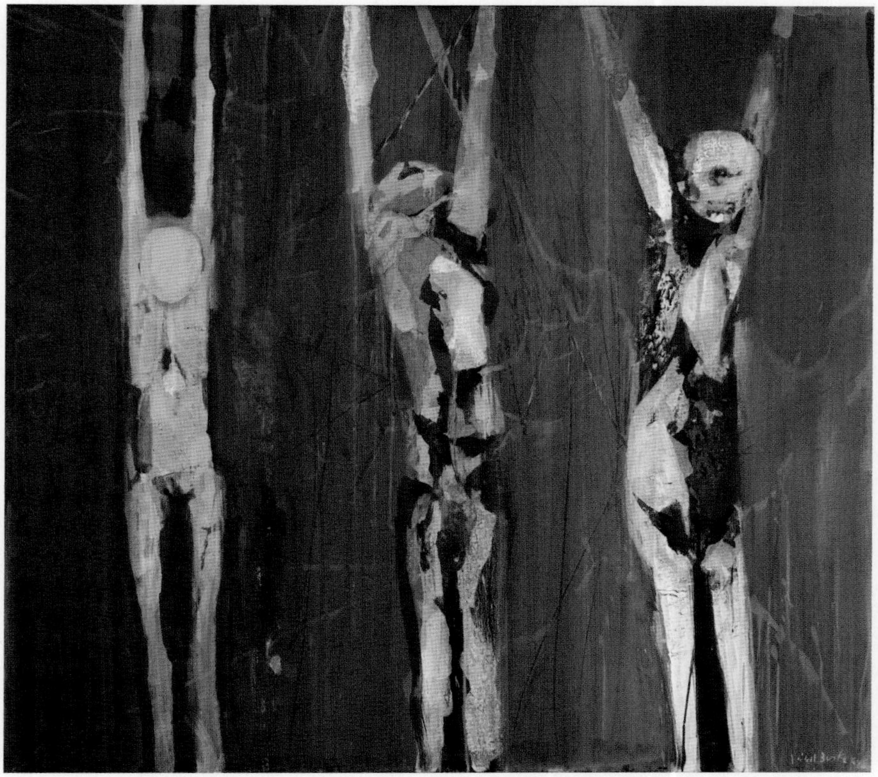

Germany such as Gerhard Marcks and Otto Dix reinterpreted this figure. Job was able to serve as a model for a community of the suffering without bringing up the question of who the perpetrators were.[108] Briefly before the *Concentration Camp Series*, Berke experimented with the series *Figurines of the Anteroom to Hell* (starting in 1961), and shortly afterwards with one on *Biafra* (starting in 1967).

Concentration Camp Series

What is called the *Concentration Camp Series* has so far not received any special public recognition. Up until 2014 it had still never been exhibited in context and is kept for the most part in Berke's archive in Cologne. It is not catalogued. Some of his pictures were illustrated individually in recent publications. The title *Concentration Camp Series* for the whole work was fixed by Kreidler in agreement with the artist's widow Brunhilde Berke shortly after Berke's death in 1979, based, despite Berke's casual use of signatures, titles and dates, on a number of definite works which are the only ones to be discussed here.[109] The series is characterized by two subjects, busts and skulls of the dead and the tortured, including many abused female bodies.

The Ones Hanged in this series are represented exclusively in oils on canvas. Even though Berke did not use the name and the symbol of the Cross – two of the paintings of the female figures hanged are shown with arms extended

overleaf

184 Hubert Berke, *Hanged Male Figure*, 1964, oil on canvas.

185 Hubert Berke, *Hanged Female Figure*, 1964, oil on canvas.

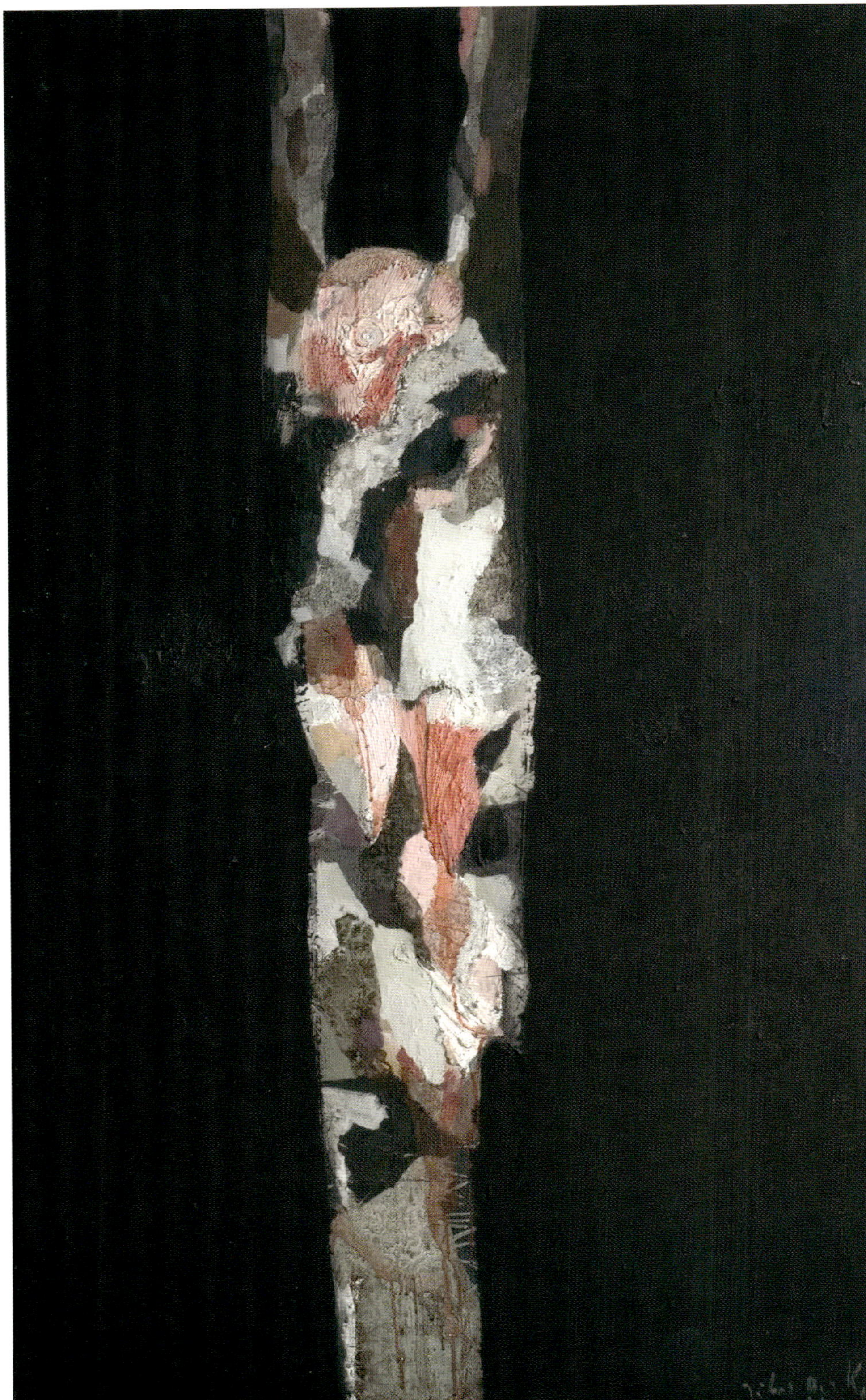

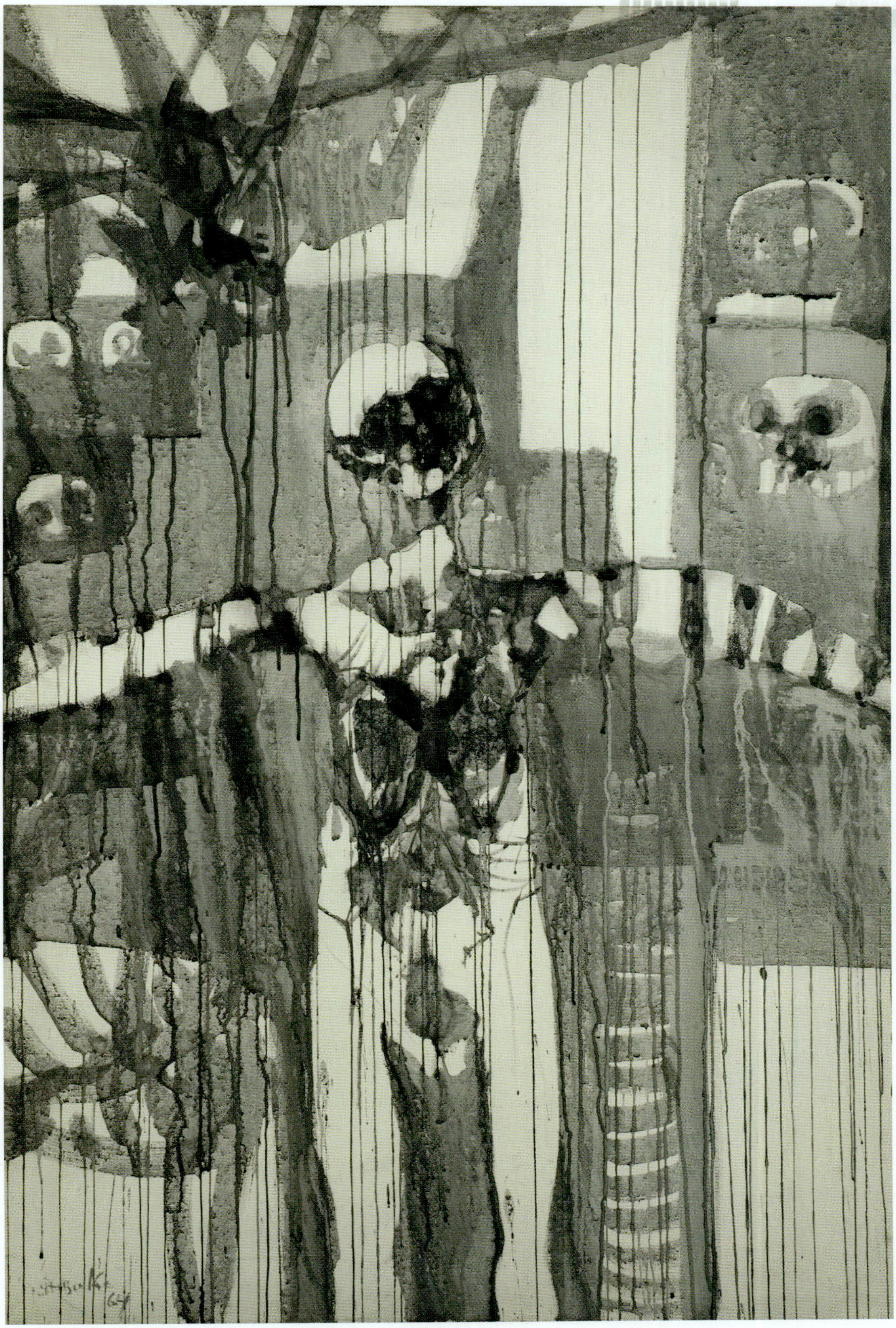

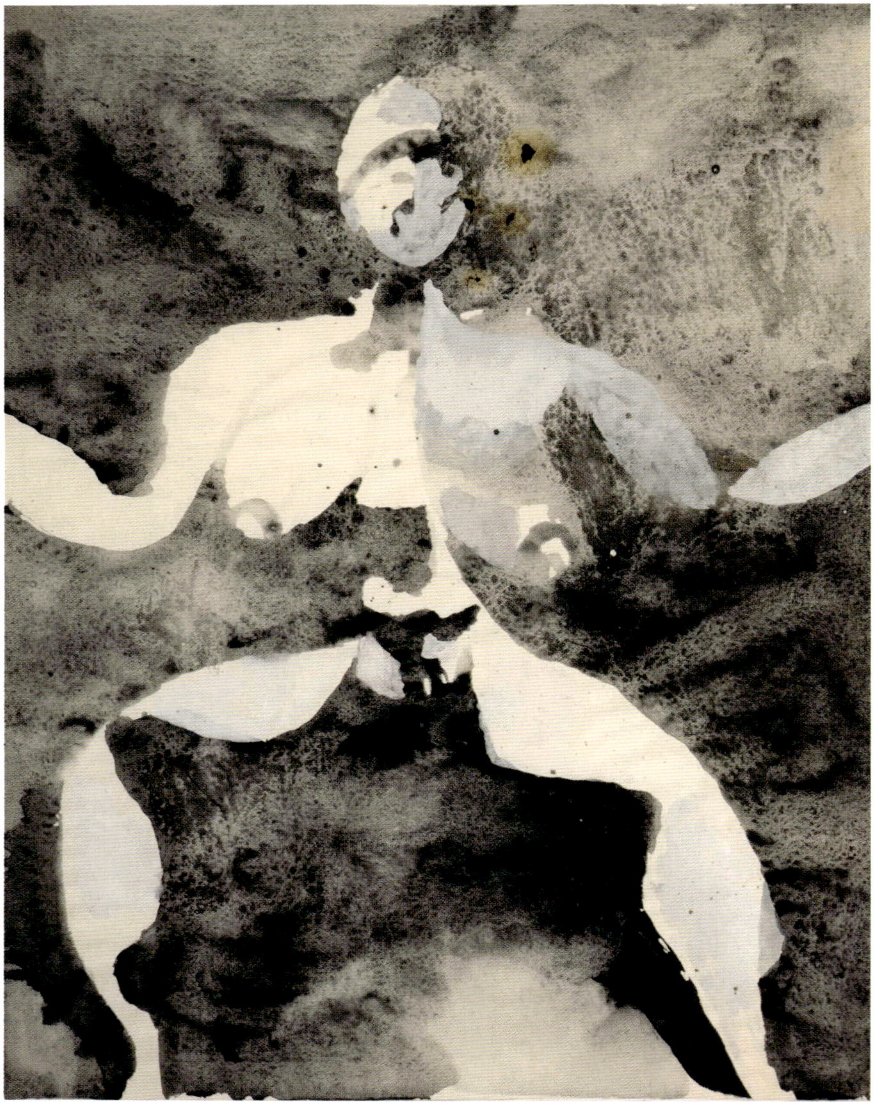

186 Hubert Berke, *Untitled (Concentration Camp Series)*, c. 1964, tempera on Ingres paper.

(illus. 183) – Kreidler saw in the tortured bodies, presented as vertical stripes in upright format, echoes of the late Gothic forked crucifixes traditional in the Rhineland.[110] In addition the composition particularly of the painting *Hanged Male Figure* (illus. 184) seems to point towards Berke's involvement with Barnett Newman's colour field painting, together with whom he had exhibited at *documenta 2* in 1959 in Kassel.[111] Newman, starting in 1948 with *onement 1*,[112] had defined the spatial structure using the vertical so-called 'zip', suggesting separation but also connection between the different elements, rather like a zip fastener. Newman kept to this rigid non-objectivity when, during the Eichmann trial at the start of the 1960s, he painted the cycle on the murder of the Jews *The Stations of the Cross: Lema Sabachtani* and, as was characteristic for his pictures, took into consideration the relevant position of the viewer in

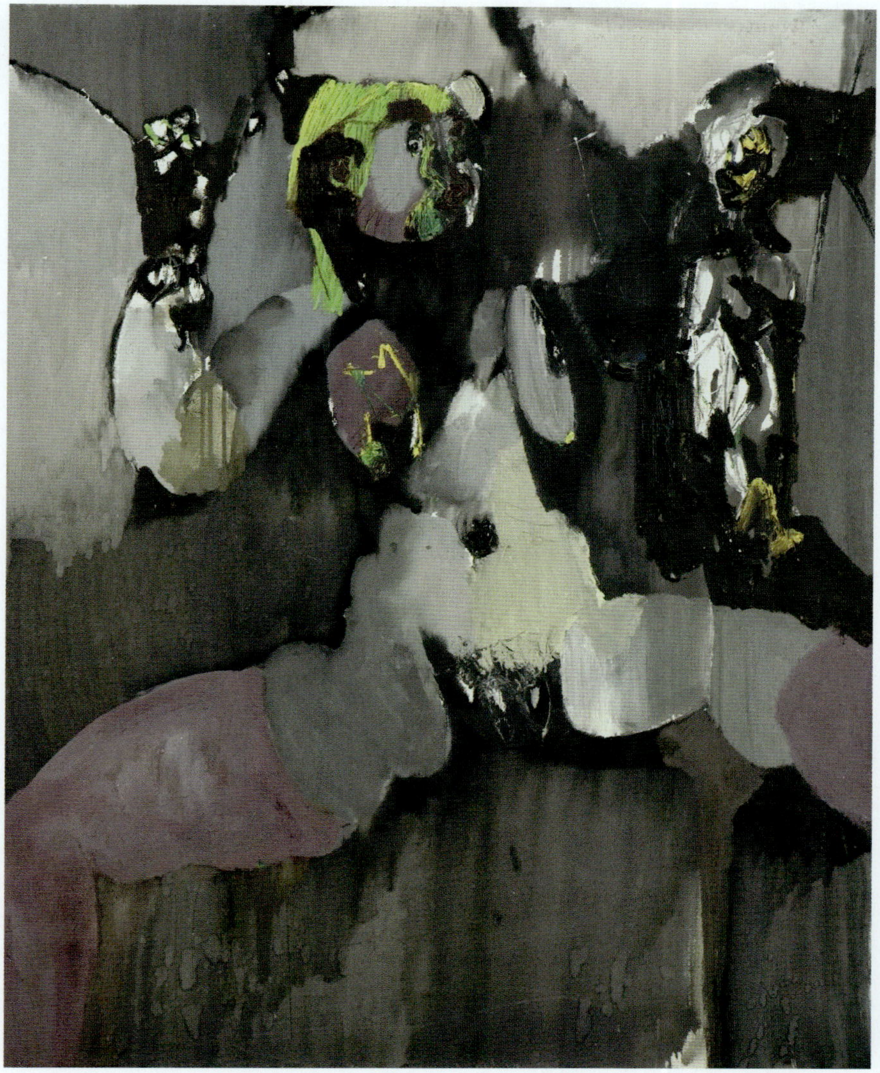

187 Hubert Berke, *Untitled (Concentration Camp Series)*, c. 1964, oil on canvas.

the surrounding space.[113] Berke, who presumably knew about the latest development by his well-known American colleague, exactly echoed his works,[114] in the emphasis on the narrow vertical stripes, but also in the extent to which he kept to Klee's motto, 'abstract with memories'. The vertical stripe covering the whole picture, not quite in the middle, reveals the individual irregular brush marks as also applied over and over again by Newman contrasting with the straight borders. However, in Berke's images of the hanged figures they simulate the three-dimensionality of the human body; at least the head and the arms thrust upwards seem to be recognizable. The black colour fields – comparable with Newman's white ones – become an indefinite background; the white, red and grey patches of paint appearing there, however, can be read figuratively as tortured bodies and in the traditional sense they are capable of evoking the compassion of the viewer[115] with the suffering of the tortured.

The other pictures of *The Ones Hanged* reveal even more clearly the agony of torture, also described by many of the witnesses in the Auschwitz trial; Berke collected the photos and stuck them onto cardboard.[116] The painter represented those being tortured as female bodies or ones whose sexual features remain unclear. The pair of dark patches bordered by almond shapes on the upper body of the figure in the oil painting *Hanged Female Figure* (illus. 185) could indicate female breasts, but they remind one also of pulmonary lobes in X-ray photos, and it is possible to make out suggestions of a vulva and/or penis between the legs of *The Ones Hanged*. As regards the attitude of the extended arms, he could have found models in the photos he kept of the bodies at Bergen-Belsen (see for example illus. 200). The techniques of modernism, such as distortion, painting over the face and letting the paint run, were employed by Berke as indicative of the destruction of the human body which is, nevertheless, left whole in silhouette. Berke shared with his contemporaries like Picasso the traditional concept of the female nude as the ideal for the artist's power of creation, particularly in the representation of war and violence.[117] The extent to which, however, Berke differed from the fragmented and deconstructive portrayals of the body current among his contemporaries and the deliberately deformed ones by Willem de Kooning and Jean Dubuffet can be seen from the ink drawing of a female figure with legs wide open which leaves the whole of the non-fragmented body as a white area on the paper (illus. 186). Berke, a member of the group Zen 49, seems to have been less concerned here with the modernist image of the body than with Oriental ink techniques and made use of tabooed positions of female figures only in order to express sadistic torture. They were also visible in the Bergen-Belsen photo mentioned that he owned. It is remarkable how he presents the viewer with the perspective of the observer or bystander, which according to Theweleit is the key element in torture,[118] by means of the faces looking on that appear in the upper half of the untitled picture looking like a rape (illus. 187), and in *The Ones Hanged* (see illus. 183).

Figurines of the Anteroom to Hell

Berke did not limit himself to representing the victims. In the series *Figurines of the Anteroom to Hell* he also portrayed the perpetrators, as in *The General* from 1961[119] and *The Bodyguard* from 1963.[120] And in the picture of the mass murderer Wilhelm Boger (illus. 188), singled out in the trial at Frankfurt for having been particularly sadistic, he accused the perpetrator of violence against the female body. The watercolour with ink wash from 1964 shows the stark view from below of a female figure lying with her legs spread out and a bleeding vagina above the head of the SS torturer. Against a bright background the name Boger can be deciphered in a slight arch ('Bogen' meaning 'bow' in German) using half-suggested squiggles with red marks. While in the Frankfurt trial it was Boger's shooting and torture of male prisoners that was mainly reported,[121] to Berke's way of thinking, however, the victim is

188 Hubert Berke, *Boger*, from the series *Figurines of the Anteroom to Hell*, 1964, brush and black ink, wash, yellow and red watercolour.

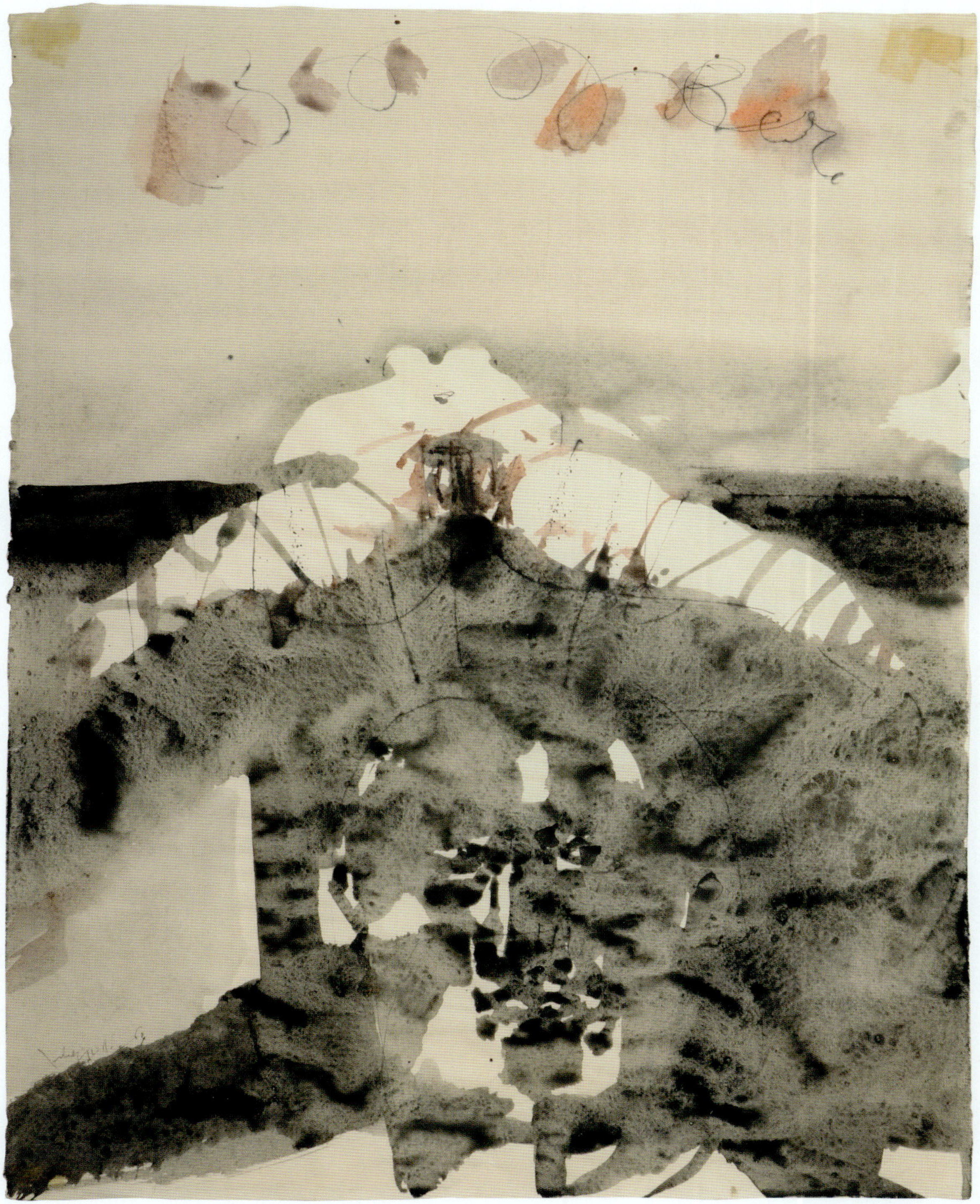

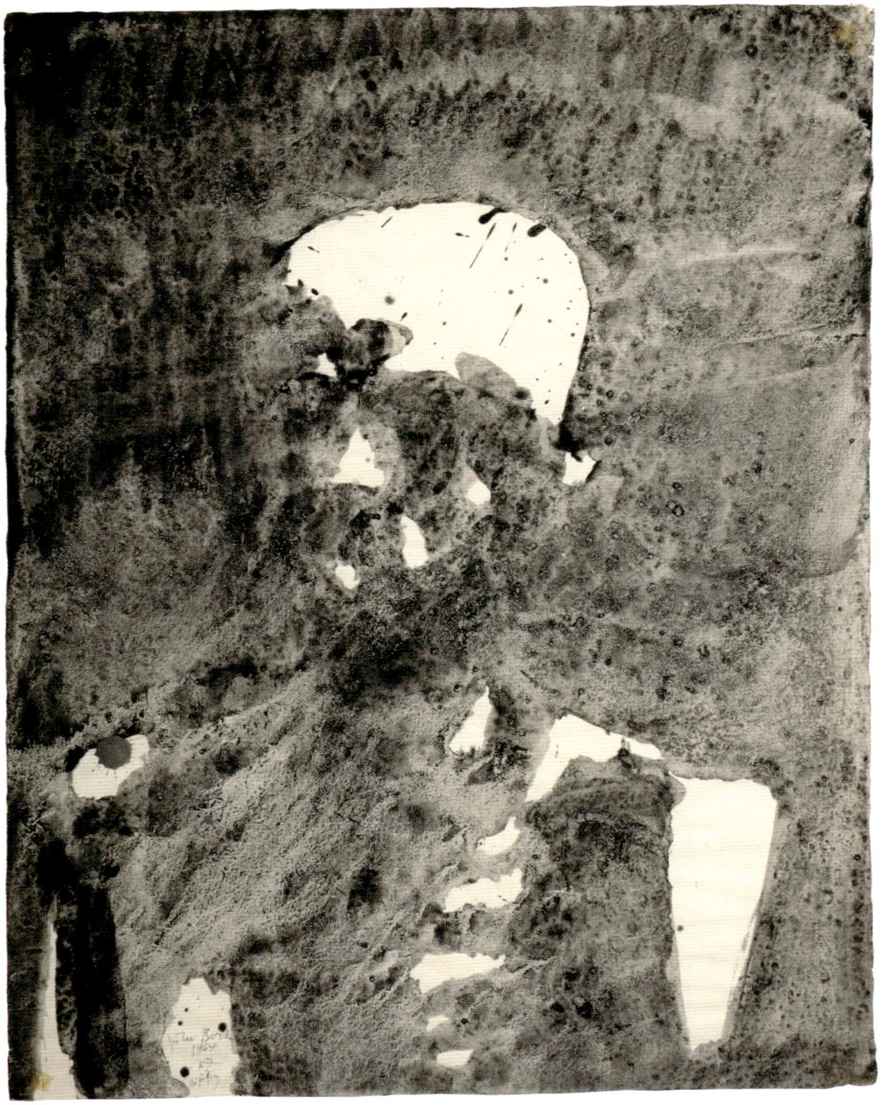

189 Hubert Berke, *Concentration Camp Prisoner*, from the series *Busts of the Dead*, 1964, ink wash and tempera.

also associated with the female, and the raped, female body, ever since Goya a symbol of the use of violence against the people, is spread out, reflecting the script. Boger's face appears underneath, blurry in black ink wash and yet recognizable in watercolour. The corpus delicti left as a white area on the paper looms out of the darkness, towering over the head of the perpetrator, who was known among the camp inmates as the 'beast of Auschwitz' or the 'Black Death' and leads the eye of the viewer towards the name smeared as if with blood at the top of the drawing.

Busts of the Dead

In the series *Busts of the Dead*, produced at the time of the Auschwitz trial, Berke only applied the name *Concentration Camp Prisoner* (illus. 189) to a

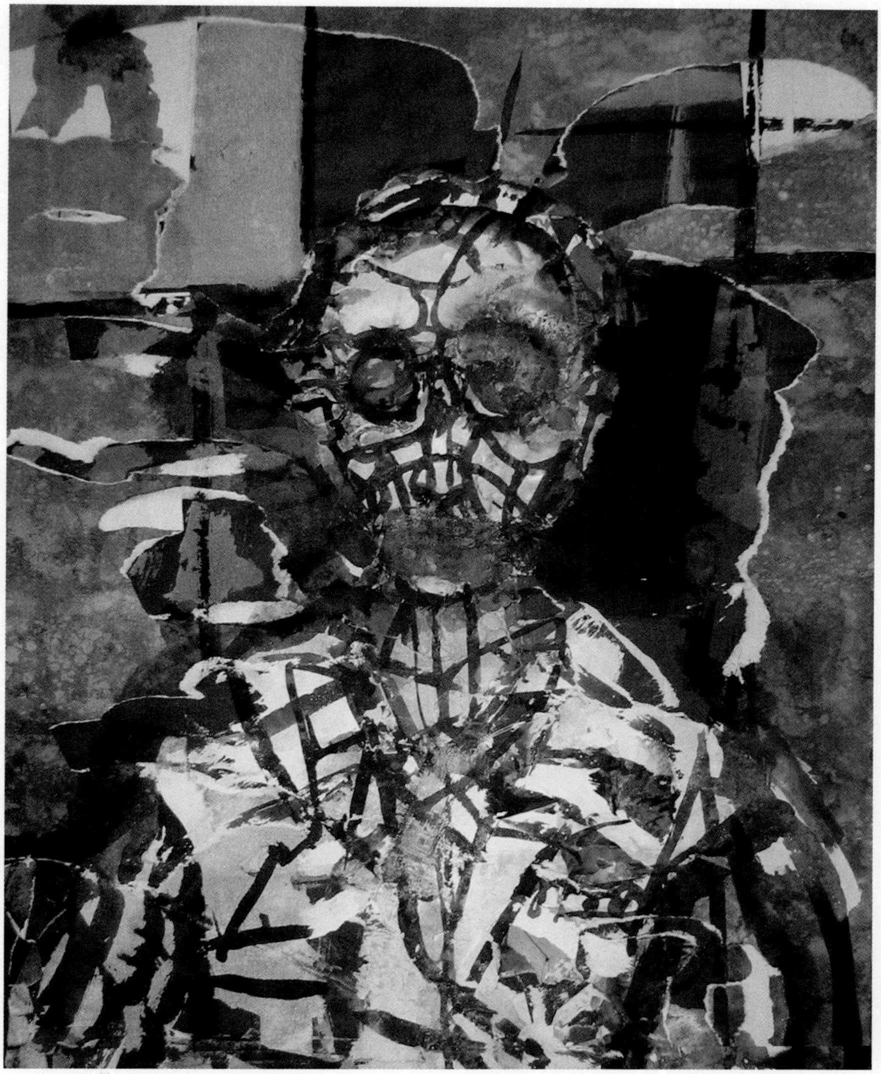

190 Hubert Berke, *Concentration Camp Prisoner*, from the series *Busts of the Dead*, c. 1963, ink wash and tempera.

few of the works. As there were detailed reports about the various witnesses appearing in the press at the time and he had in mind the persecuted inhabitants of the ghetto from the newspaper cutting he kept, it is likely that he did not wish to distinguish between the former camp inmates in his watercolours, ink drawings and oil paintings but was thinking of them all together. The drawing *Concentration Camp Prisoner* is particularly strongly ink washed, leaving certain areas of the paper white for the skull and the skeleton, and is suggestive of the prisoner's death. Painting over the face and letting the colour run emphasizes his extinction so that the white triangle – perhaps a camp insignia – on the left side of his face at eye-level appears like a death's head looking out of his eye socket and yet as though it is alive.

In the other drawings of death's heads and busts of the dead from the series,[122] most of them untitled, the eyes are much more emphasized, as for example in the single collage of the series, which can also be included in the series of representations of camp prisoners due to the suggestion of the striped clothing of the 'living dead' (illus. 190). In the image of a prisoner, Berke sought to render graphically the reality of the Nazi crimes in Auschwitz using torn materials and paint – two small reddish patches in the vicinity of the neck at the bottom right of the collage, only visible in the original – and placed a blackened bandage over his mouth and left eye. The way the large, dark eye sockets in the pale face are revealed appears to be related to a piece of imagery used just after the war by Marie Luise Kaschnitz in her essay *About Guilt*.[123] In 1946 Kaschnitz wrote about a secret witness observing a murder happening and making him part of what happened, 'about a pair of eyes whose gaze he can't evade, following him, fixing him, searingly staring out from a vacant face'. Hahn argues, convincingly based on her text,[124] that this 'conventional imagery', which he traces back to the myth of the Gorgons, is possibly intended to avert contemporary photographs and film clips of the Nazis' crimes and is presumably all the more pointedly aimed at portraying the agonies of conscience of the witnesses after the event. With the penetrating gaze from the dead eyes, in Berke's paintings of death's heads and busts of the dead, what is also called to mind is the representation of the prisoner observing, who is always already one being observed and who is in the unavoidable and possibly painfully involved position of a witness to the events on the part of those observing the picture as present-day bystanders.

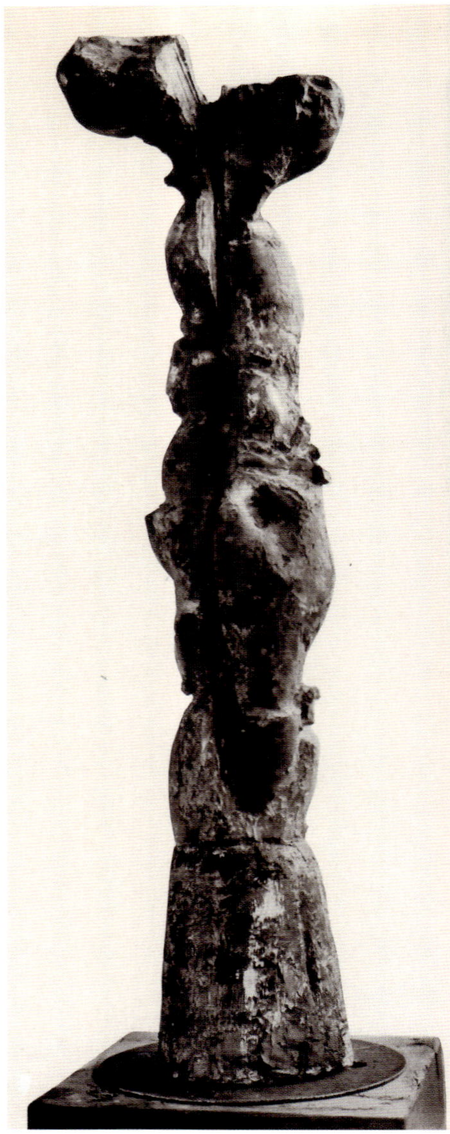

191 Rolf Szymanski, *Synagogue*, 1963, bronze, model for a sculpture.

Rolf Szymanski: *Synagogue*

For *documenta 3* in 1964, which took place in Kassel during the Auschwitz trial in Frankfurt, Werner Haftmann, as one of the main people responsible for the exhibition, stated as the 'guiding principle': 'That art is that which distinguished artists do.' It is all the more remarkable that, in this selection of works by what counted as the elite artists of the time, there was only one work on show that suggested a connection to the history of the Jews.[125] Rolf Szymanski, who had already in the 1950s moved over from the Leipzig Kunstgewerbeschule to Benhard Heiliger at the Berlin Hochschule der Künste, presented the sculpture *Synagogue* from 1963 (illus. 191) at the Museum Fridericianum and two other bronzes with the titles *Small Figurehead* from 1962 and *Lying Female (Negress)* from 1961.[126] All three female figures display swelling body shapes, disrupted by fragmentation and crumbling

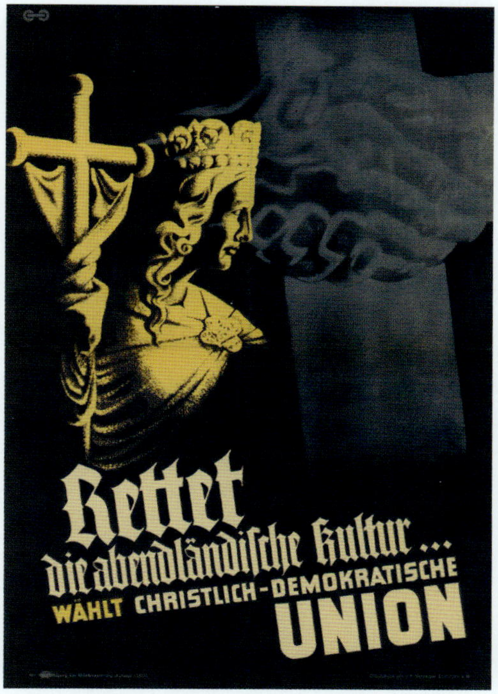

192 Poster for the Christian Democratic Union (CDU), elections for the State Parliament of Baden-Württemberg 1946: 'Save Western culture, Vote Christian Democrat Union'.

decomposition. Eberhard Roters called them 'tragic metaphors for the Sensual'.[127] *Synagogue* is 207 cm high and is an enlarged version of *Synagogue, Small Model*, which Szymanski produced in Rome in 1962 on a bursary from the Villa Massimo. He described the version of the *Synagogue* that he gave to the Pädagogische Hochschule in Reutlingen in 1962 in the 1975 catalogue of his works: 'The "seeing body", split lengthways and raised up, of a gigantic torso.'[128] It was in line with the aim he expressed apropos of a 1959 sketch of a figure: 'Standing or lying figures – mental image of the feminine principle, not of any particular individual.'[129] One can see the relationship of these works 'set to the rhythm of instinctive vitality'[130] to Henry Moore's female nude sculptures erected all over Europe, particularly after the war, as sculptural representations of life.[131] This is illustrated particularly by comparison with Moore's *Upright Motives* from 1955–6.[132] Both artists in their art worked on setting up the idea of the Feminine rather like a column, even if Szymanski never went in for smoothly flowing round forms in his sculptures, but rather emphasized the contrast between the curves and their disruption by fragmentation and the crumbling structure of the outer surface.

The titles of his works, he stated to Roters, 'are applied afterwards but they are important',[133] and the name *Synagogue* as an indication of the persecution of the Jews is meant to be taken seriously, particularly since Szymanski worked on different versions of *Synagogue* over quite a long period. Besides, he had wanted to take part in the competition in 1957 for a memorial for Auschwitz,[134] and 1961 saw the creation of the *Black Column*[135] that he associated with the dark force of Leviathan (Job 41:1–8). It is said that the stone figures of *Ecclesia and Synagoga* in Strasbourg Cathedral were the basis for his *Synagogue*.[136] However, whereas in the Middle Ages the personification of the Old Covenant always appears as an anti-type to the New Covenant, Szymanski dedicated his sculpture exclusively to an allegory of Jewry that had been despised more and more over the course of time. Representing the inferior alone, without a triumphant counterpart, was unusual, but an election poster for the conservative CDU as early as 1946 had advertised in favour of the salvation of Western culture using the victor, the Ecclesia, and her sign of the victory of Christianity over the Jewish faith, a banner on a cross (illus. 192). The Pädagogische Hochschule in Reutlingen did not take kindly to Szymanski setting up the abused torso. When it came up for discussion whether the state teaching institution should set up a 6-m-high version of the *Synagogue*, they rejected this art commission as 'not optimistic enough'.[137]

Werner Tübke

Four years after finishing the *History of the German Workers' Movement IV* (see illus. 159), Werner Tübke started on a new series of pictures about Nazi violence and the murder of the Jews. At that time the show trials had taken place in the GDR against West German 'Blutrichter' (that is, judges with blood on their hands)[138] and leading Bonn politicians, and the Auschwitz trial was ongoing in Frankfurt am Main. Certainly Nicole Thur proved that Tübke's recent involvement with the subject of genocide was based on a commission by the local management of the Deutscher Kulturbund in Leipzig dating from 12 October 1964[139] and should consequently be seen in the context of the campaign mentioned. Nevertheless, he was the one who identified the exact choice of subject-matter by the overall heading 'West German justice'.[140] On 28 October 1964 he wrote to the local management in Leipzig: 'I am keen to get started on the subject of the picture (chosen by myself) – in all likelihood there will be several – and it will fully occupy my time until July of next year. Possibly even longer quite apart from the commission.'[141] Three days later he wrote to them in clearer and more concrete terms:

> I have then chosen the commission myself and the project can perhaps be summed as follows: coming to terms with the past, prompted (not just) by the trials. An outwardly perfectly respectable gentleman (a pharmacist etc.) earlier employed on the 'Ramp', crimes against justice, terror, left-wing father of a family with a liking for a German Christmas, he also had a mother, is an intellectual, basically an outsider of society, how good someone can be under certain circumstances, what a swine he can be under other circumstances. But not everyone behaves like that 'under certain circumstances'. Bourgeois respectability and Nazi terror, a pleasant life. A work of history painting – if the term was not (justifiably) so abused. But still relevant today. No study of behaviour, no psychologising, no illusions arising from (established) theories of history, nothing but basic questions about existence. Archetypes, Judas, Cain–Abel, power and the misuse of it, the concrete historical situation yet: 'Third Reich' continuing into the Federal Republic – Just going on like that. But it is not my concern (of course it is also a possible one, but not mine just here and now): locking up West German patriots, arresting GDR citizens in West Germany.[142]

Tübke worked for more than two years, from 1964 to 1967, on eleven paintings, fifteen watercolours and approximately 65 drawings.[143] In conversation with Eduard Beaucamp, he explained that he had obtained material on the Auschwitz trial in Frankfurt am Main from the East Berlin lawyer Friedrich Karl Kaul,[144] which must also have included the book *Der Gelbe Stern*[145] that

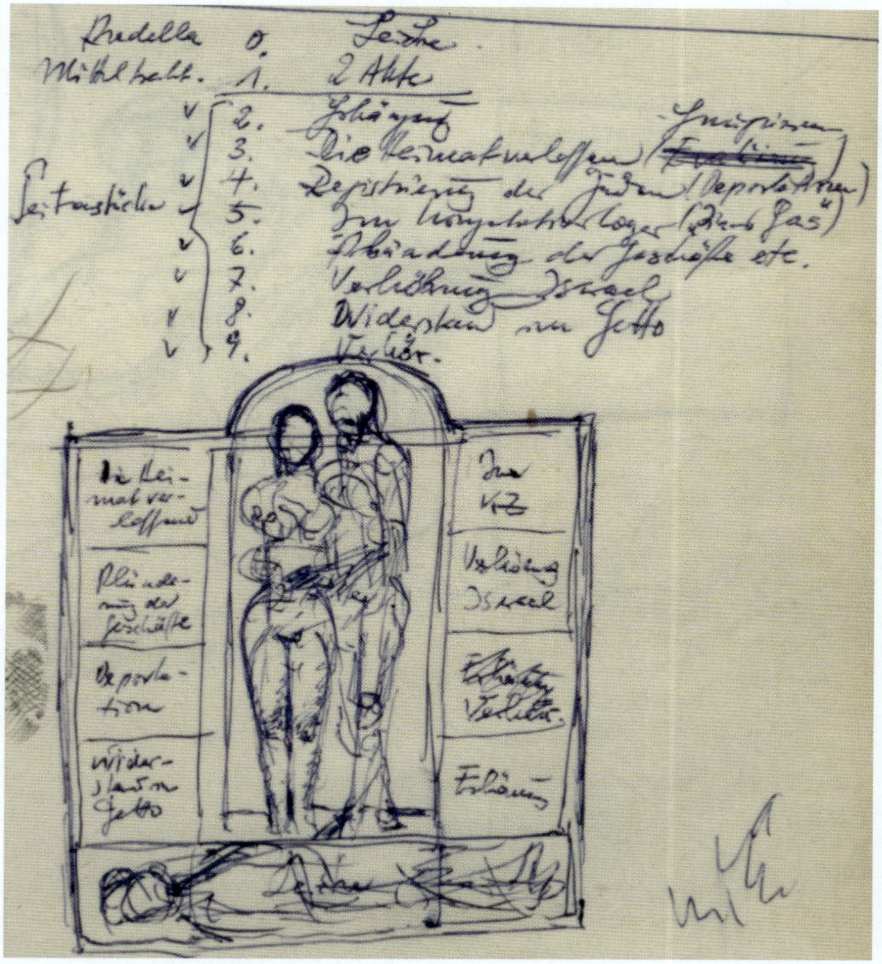

193 Werner Tübke, sketch for a triptych dedicated to the persecution of the Jews, Skizzenbuch, 1964.

appeared in West Germany in 1960, as will become clear from looking at the individual works on this subject.

Sketch for a Triptych

When setting out to plan his pictures, strict criticism of the way justice was being dominated was not the main element, as it was to be later in the cycle named *Dr. jur. Schulze*; nor was it the course of German history, as in the 1961 triptych *History of the German Workers' Movement* IV (see illus. 159). Tübke's first drafts in 1964 on the subject of West German legal justice in the still unpublished diaries reveal instead a picture consisting of three panels devoted entirely to the history of the persecution and murder of the Jews during the Nazi period.[146] Tübke sketched a triptych (illus. 193) with a semi-circular top section to the central panel, a predella showing a dead body lying and four areas in each of the two side wings, into which are inserted the stations of the persecution of the Jews.[147] Both above the triptych and on the side wings of it, Tübke noted in each case eight stages different to one another.

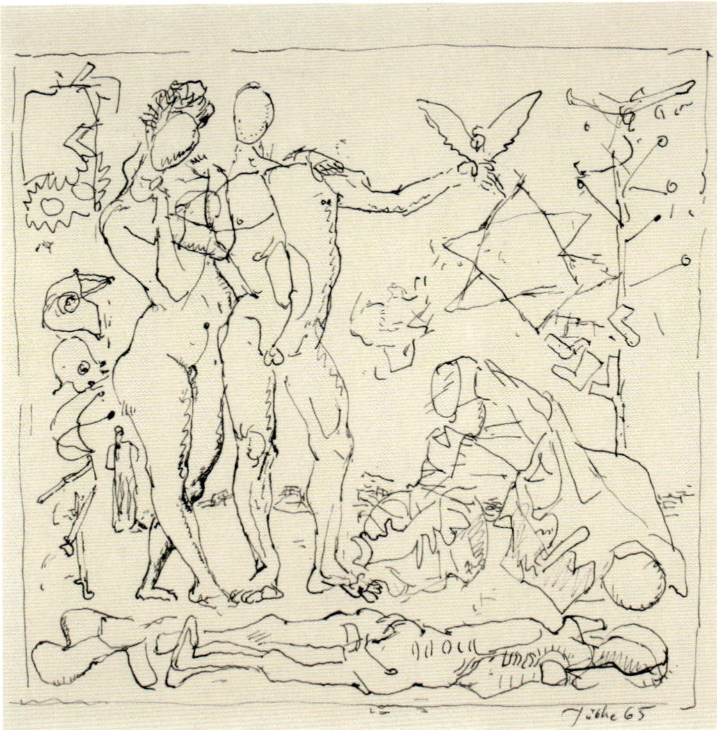

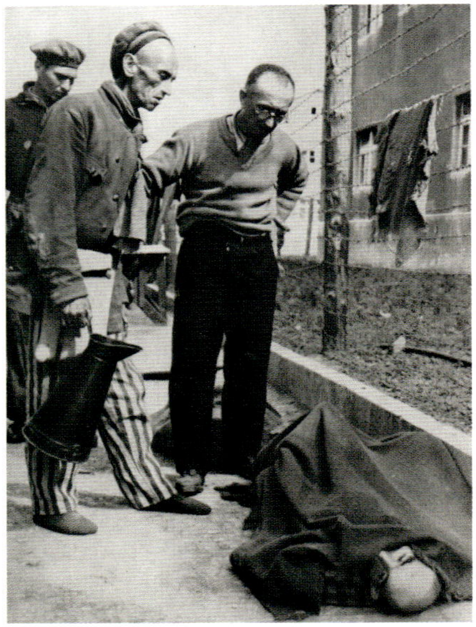

194 Werner Tübke, sketch for the series *Dr. jur. Schulze*, 1965, graphite.

195 *Buchenwald 1945*, photograph publ. in Schoenberner 1960.

On the left side wing he wrote: 'Leaving the Homeland / the Plundering of Shops / Deportation / Resistance in the Ghetto' and on the right side: 'In the Camp / Mocking of Israel / Interrogation/Hanging'. In the transcription of Tübke's notes, the last word could well be read more as Hanging than Salvation, at least presuming that Tübke forgot a downstroke for the middle 'g' in the German word 'Erhängung'. Tübke's list of the eight stations of Jewish persecution above the triptych are:

Predella:	0. Dead body
Middle section:	1. two nudes
Side pieces:	2. Hanging
	3. Leaving the Homeland Emigration ~~Evacuation~~
	4. Registration of the Jews (Deportations)
	5. In the Camp (Into the Gas)
	6. Plundering of the Shops etc.
	7. Mocking of Israel
	8. Resistance in the Ghetto
	9. Interrogation.

The row of writing at the top does not follow the historical sequence which the words inserted into the side wings sketched keep to, more or less. The way they are arranged into stations of the persecution also corresponds by and large to the eight shown in the *Der Gelbe Stern*. Unlike Schoenberner, however, Tübke planned not to record any coherent narrative of the history but instead the violence of the SS and Jewish resistance to it at each individual stage.

The side wings with the subdivisions into small pictorial areas remind one, in the similarity of their arrangement, of the stations of the life and suffering of Christ or Mary on the late medieval altars of Northern Europe. Christianity in its typology had at one time annexed the Jewish Bible as its own Old Testament and only seen it as a portent of its own history; Tübke now reinterpreted the history of Jesus's suffering into the Passion of the Jews[148] and used it to show the history of Christendom as murder of the Jews.

It is not wholly clear how we are to take the 'salvation' possibly laid out by Tübke, whether it is supposed to appear in the form of eight stations on the side wings or form the title of the central section. For the central panel 'two nudes' were intended, which Tübke included in the sketch as well as putting them into a separate drawing (illus. 194). In it, above a dead body lying there, two nudes are seen leaning against one another; the female one shows her hands crossed over her breast, while the male one is holding a dove in his left hand. On the right side of the picture, a ruined swastika can be made out on the skeleton of a tree; between this and the pair there appears a large, lightly drawn Star of David. Presumably here Tübke, by the use of the two naked figures, was again referring to the promise, much longed for after the war, of a new beginning for the reproduction of humankind. This promise had emerged in 1946 in the form of well-rounded female nudes on the designs for memorials – as for example in Halle in 1946 for the victims of fascism – and had since then become a favourite subject in the GDR[149] arising from the 'life-affirming repertoire of aspiration in socialist art commissions'.[150] In the seventh painting of the *Memoirs of Dr. jur. Schulze*, Tübke created out of this requirement two powerful female nudes among suggestions of the smashed remains of history.[151]

Already in this sketch Tübke made use of a photograph from *Der Gelbe Stern*, which he would refer to in many versions. From a photograph from the camp at Buchenwald (illus. 195) he copied the body lying on the ground that three bystanders are looking at. The prisoner on the left side is holding a can in his hand, as if he could perhaps still help his comrade by giving him water. It is not clear whether the one lying there is writhing in pain, struggling against death or already dead. Only a skull is projected out of the blanket thrown over him, his body drawn together, and his raised legs stand out in a jagged silhouette, as if he wanted to defy death. One can clearly distinguish him from the dead body lying at the bottom of the sketch. This ambiguous figure was placed by Tübke in a central position in the paintings *Schulze I, II* and *III* (see illus. 203 and 207) and in many of the drawings in the cycle, but not with the dead bodies in *Requiem* (see illus. 196). He also referred to the prisoner and the water can on several occasions. The man in civilian clothing, on the other hand, who occupies the position of the observer, he did not make use of in any version.

Tübke, however, rejected the initial idea of representing the course of the disastrous history of the Jews under the Nazis as a series of pictures in a late Gothic altar format. Only his notes in the green sketchbook document this fundamental linkage between Christian and Jewish suffering. No other artist captured this connection as systematically. Only Lea Grundig, in Tel Aviv during the war in 1942–3, drew in ink – admittedly without any Christian references – a cycle on the suffering of the Jewish people in eighteen drawings (see illus. 39–41, 43 and 45), which may have been known to Tübke, along with Leo Haas's drawings and Kantor's record of events.[152]

Instead of attempting a revision of Christian typology, Tübke sought to present, in a variety of pictorial formats, media and compositions, multi-fractured memories of violence and desire, of the persecuted and their persecutors, of the executioners and the executed, sometimes in aggressively bright colours and in the style of the Old Masters.

Requiem

The 1965 oil painting WVZ G 62 entitled *Requiem*[153] (illus. 196) was a sort of prologue to the series.[154] The perspective of individual dead bodies, which ever since Andrea Mantegna's *Lamentation of Christ* has been frequently foreshortened as leading into the picture from the soles of the feet,[155] now appears reversed. Tübke placed the dead bodies with their heads turned to the bottom of the picture. Seven bodies are seen on bare ground in front of a prison wall.[156] The surface, almost parallel with the picture, of the bare prison yard reminds one, with its negation of the rules of central perspective, of memorial tablets and late Gothic painting. Tübke commented on this medieval period: 'At this stage that is so interesting for the development of the history of form and subject-matter, in which the surface is still right and the space is already right, this is a treasure trove for the contemporary artist to be learning from. There are no references to formal logic.'[157]

Just as Tübke studied late medieval pictorial composition, he appropriated what had survived in the way of photographs of the murder of the Jews. For this painting he copied from the photo of a waterlogged area of the camp at Bergen-Belsen (illus. 197)[158] three of the dead bodies lying in the foreground. Tübke placed the one lying parallel to the edge of the picture with its naked pelvic bone on the top left side in his painting; the corpse on the left side of the photo he in turn placed in the centre, while keeping more or less the position of the dead body visible on the extreme right side of the photo. The stripes of the camp clothing were not copied; instead the pieces of cloth and the remains of clothing of all the dead are kept grey with slight colour variations. He copied the rough sheets of cloth belonging to the dead body with long hair at front left from the centre of another photo from Schoenberner's book showing a pile of bodies at Bergen-Belsen,[159] and the chasm-like folds

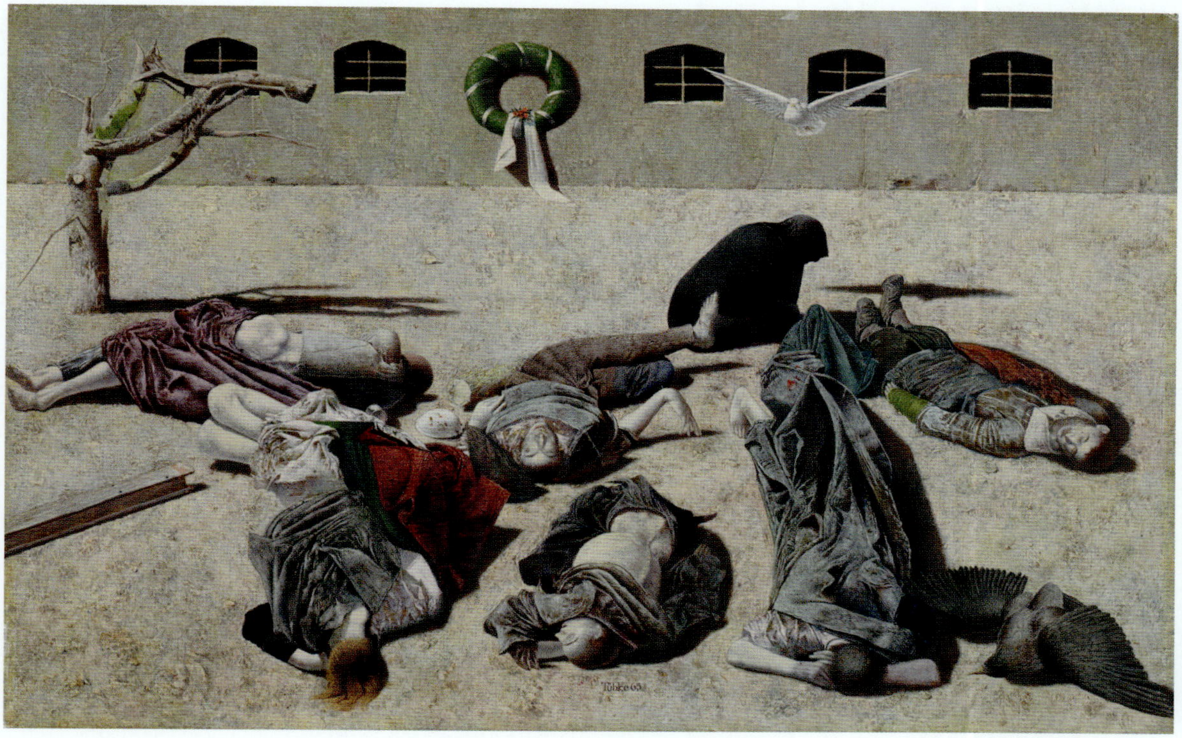

196 Werner Tübke, *Requiem*, 1965, oil on canvas on plywood.

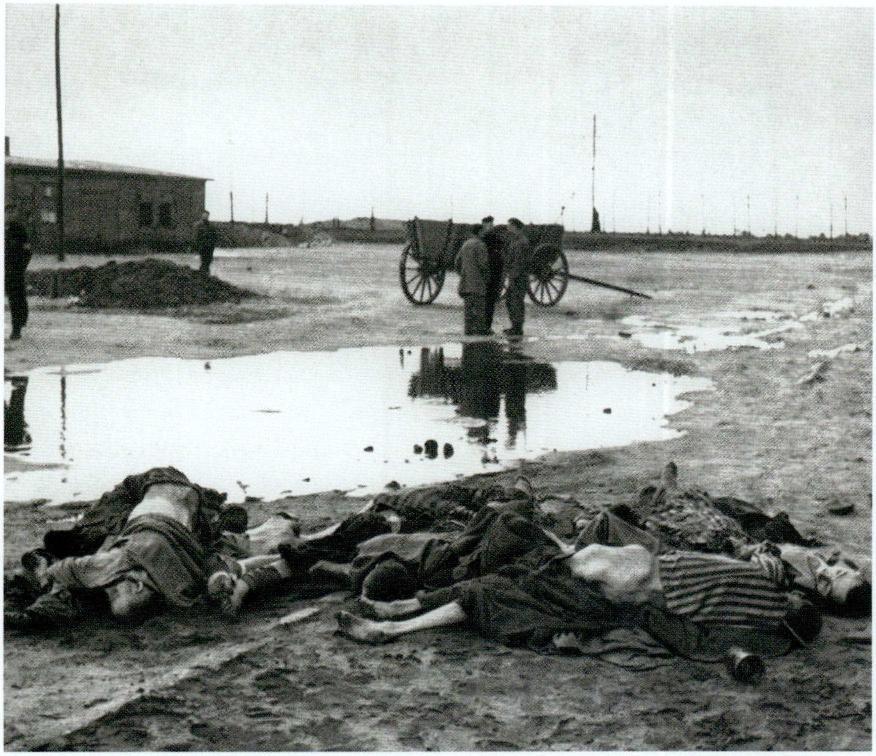

197 *Bergen-Belsen, May 1945*, photograph publ. in Schoenberner 1960.

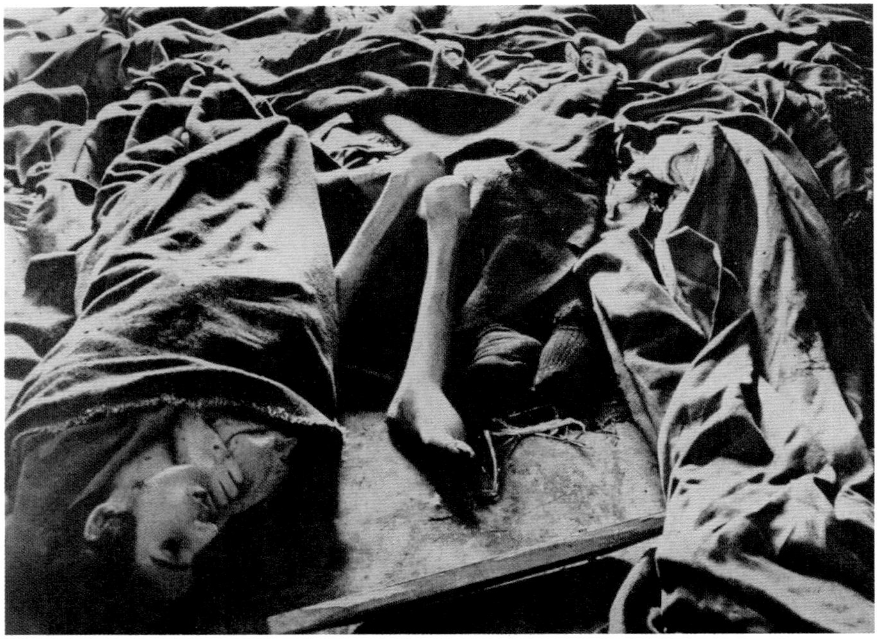

198 Stanislaw Mucha, *Corpses of the Prisoners in Block II in Auschwitz*, photograph publ. in Schoenberner 1960.

of the grey shroud for the dead body second from the right, forming the vertical dominating the picture and almost parallel with it, from an unidentified photo in Schoenberner's book of a hut full of dead bodies (illus. 198).[160] The naked arm with the hand bent in the centre of the picture is reminiscent of the dead body visible in a photo from Bergen-Belsen showing a pile of corpses bulldozed together.[161]

By tracing and reporting fairly exactly the dishevelled coverings, Tübke augmented the jagged profile of each of the seven bodies. He portrayed them individually struggling with death through the dramatic outlines of the folds of cloth and copied the state of rigor mortis showing through the wraps, which now look as though they are carved in stone. 'To give a contour to what has been seen': this statement by Peter Weiss about his method of writing in *Der Schatten des Körpers des Kutschers* (The Shadow of the Body of the Coachman)[162] also characterizes the way Tübke worked, having mentioned it in particular in an early text, not published until 1960, from his sketchbook, adding the comment 'Micro-novel, describing with relevance *and* immediate clarity'.[163]

It is worth comparing the painting to the ink pen drawing *Requiem*, fol. 2 in the cycle *Ghetto Uprising*, which Lea Grundig produced between 1946 and 1948 in Palestine (see illus. 49) and the drawing *In the Streets of Poland* from her cycle *Never Again!* from the same period (see illus. 59). Although pictures on this subject were not especially favoured in the GDR in the 1950s, Tübke was in a position to know them from an earlier publication.[164] Shortly after the end of the war Lea Grundig drew, using a broad brush on *Requiem*, five bodies one behind the other parallel to the picture, presumably of one family, and by their different facial features gave them back their own individuality. The crude aerial view of the flat surface in Lea Grundig's drawing *In the Streets of Poland* may have inspired him. In Tübke's *Requiem*, the faces of the dead are difficult to make out; twenty years after the war the artist had carefully studied the history in published photos and portrayed the violent death of each individual based on the traces they had left behind being 'immediately visible' in the animated folds of material around their rigid bodies. No narration is added pointing beyond the events in the photo. In this way, Tübke gave back individuality to the dead in the desperate photos of piled-up bodies of camp prisoners; for them, the innumerable murdered camp prisoners without names, he created a cenotaph in a two-dimensional painting. Next to a green wreath in honour of the dead against the prison wall, a white dove flies over the bare courtyard with the abused bodies. At their feet there is a black figure bending over – the incarnation of mourning. Its silhouette follows the angle of the branch of the barren tree over on the left side, leading the eye towards the outstretched wings of a dark grey bird on the extreme right-hand corner of the picture – a symbol of death, as in Hans Grundig's painting (see illus. 114) that Tübke in this *Requiem* had distanced himself from, as regards its similarity to the iconography of the lamentation of Christ.

Tübke devoted himself entirely in this period to Jewish history, and his works illustrate that the tendency to the fantastic so many times attributed to him often detracts from the sharpness of detail in his response to the visual evidence of history.[165] It may be due both to a premature categorization of Tübke's painting and a concern with his being ingenious that there has been no art-historical discussion up until now of how varied Tübke's use of Schoenberner's book of photos was. Tübke does not merely copy; the photos were documentation to him and beyond invention. He himself ignored questions about individual figures.[166]

Shot against the Wall

Whereas in *Requiem* Tübke took the subject of the dead bodies lying in the courtyard from Schoenberner with certain alterations, he did something different with the 1965 pen drawing with watercolour *Shot Against the Wall* (illus. 199). He did not make use of the photographic record of the shootings at the wall shown in *Der Gelbe Stern* (for example, the illustration on p. 99, bottom right), but for each of the figures in front of a wall, half the height of a man, he went back to a particular photograph. Only the man on the right with a beard and raised hands is picked out from a row of Jews who, as Schoenberner commented on the photo, had to dig their own graves (see illus. 69).[167] For the kneeling one on the left, Tübke took as a model the photo of a standing prisoner from Small Belsen[168] (illus. 200), and for the two lying with bullet holes, the photo of the 'Rebels who had been shot' (illus. 201) from the Stroop Report on the Warsaw Ghetto Uprising. The second one kneeling on the left positioned in profile above the waist, looking towards the one

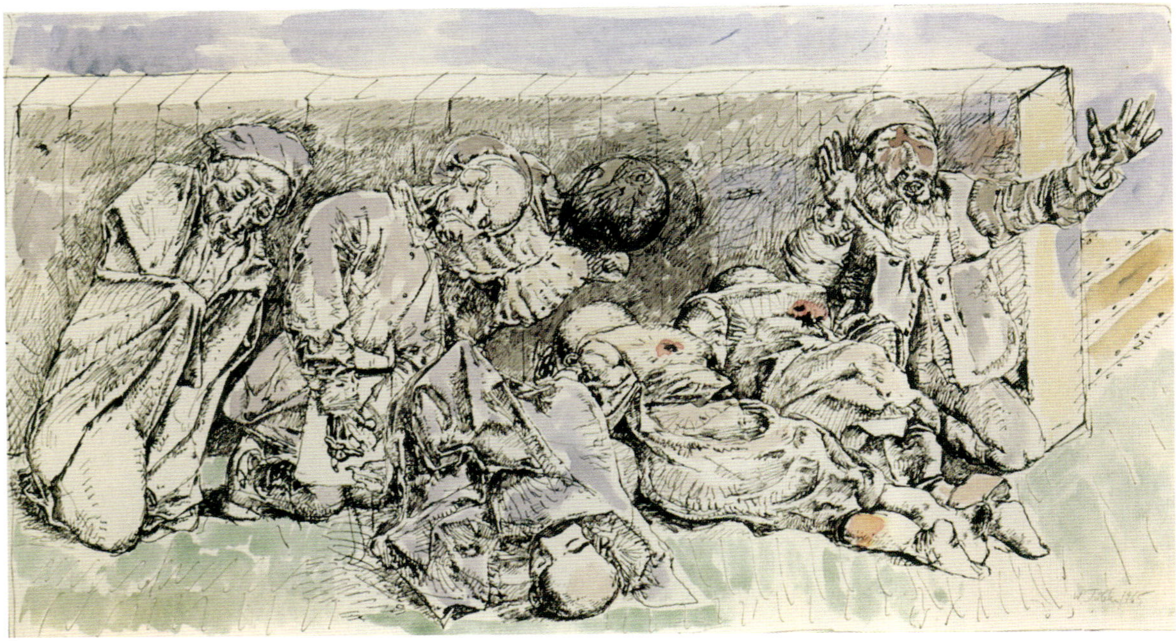

199 Werner Tübke, *Shot Against the Wall*, sketch for *Memoirs of Dr. jur. Schulze* III, 1965, watercolour over pen and black ink.

with the jagged sheet lying in front of him, is likewise taken from the photo already referred to from Buchenwald after the liberation (see illus. 195), though here he is not carrying a can but has his hands folded. In another motif of the drawing taken from the photograph, the very perspective of the photographer was imbued with traditional Christian iconography and the attempts to interpret these anew in wartime. The photograph (illus. 202) of the dead man as though crucified, seen obliquely from above, is perhaps reminiscent of Wilhelm Morgner's *Crucified One* from 1912, showing a naked torso of a figure who has been crucified from the side and in profile and not from the front as usual.[169] Tübke did variations of the thorax hanging diagonally in the centre in front of the wall in other drawings as well.[170] His pen drawing, which comes across as being from long ago, takes on a contemporary aspect through the collage of already published photo documents of the persecution of the Jews, even if it is not yet known who first came up with the title of the drawing and whether there was possibly even in addition some implied contemporary criticism of the inner German East–West border.[171] It is worth emphasizing how closely Tübke relied on pictorial documentation, not just of the anti-fascist fighters, but also of the murdered Jews for his studies of the *Memoirs of Dr. jur.Schulze*, and right from the very start.

Memoirs of Dr. jur. Schulze II

In the paintings on the *Memoirs of Dr. jur. Schulze* II (illus. 203) and III (illus. 207), the direct relation to the system of justice is evident in the figures seated in the centre; both of them belong to the 'court-like terms of the early discourse about the Holocaust' in the 1960s at the time of the Auschwitz trial

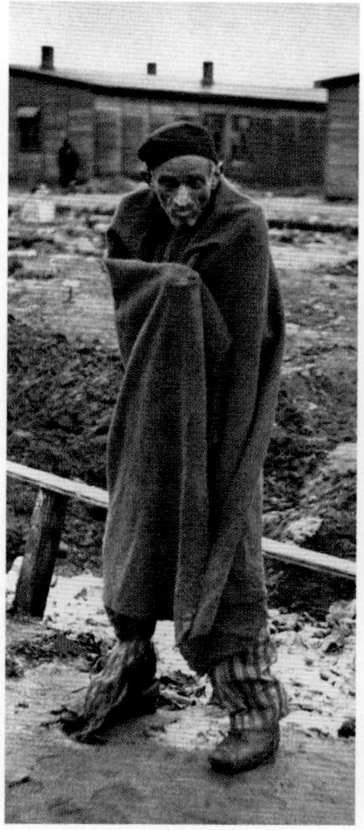

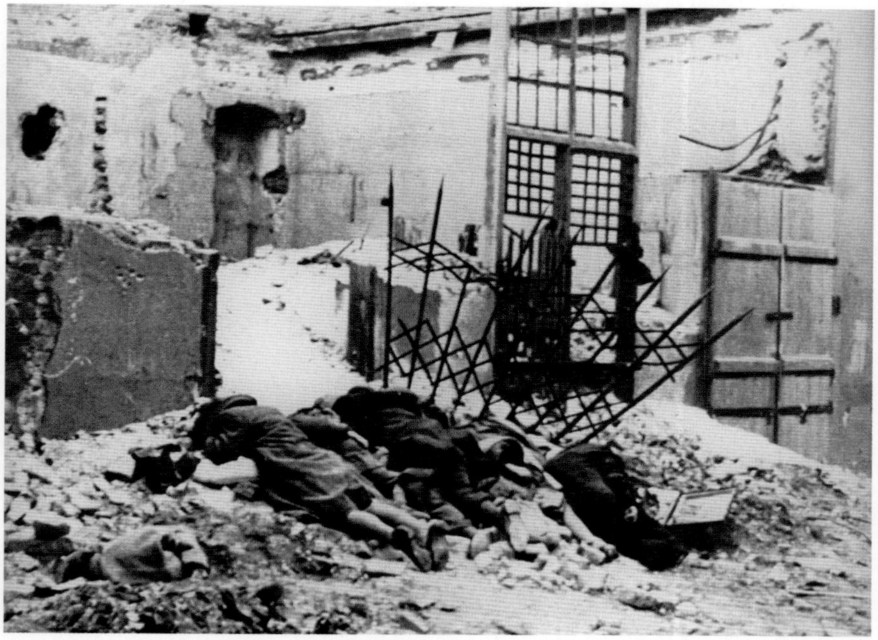

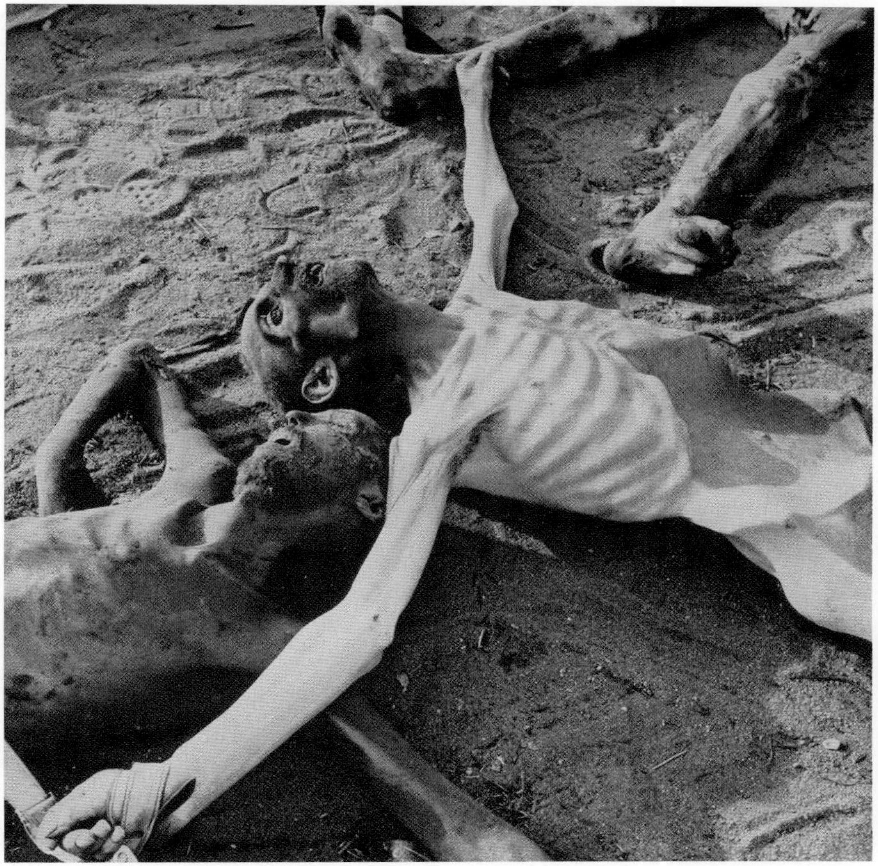

top left 200 *Small Belsen*, 1945, photograph publ. in Schoenberner 1960.

top right 201 'Rebels Who Had Been Shot, in the Warsaw Ghetto' (Stroop Report): *Bandits Eradicated in Battle*, photograph publ. in Schoenberner 1960.

right 202 Photograph, probably Bergen-Belsen, May 1945, publ. in Schoenberner 1960.

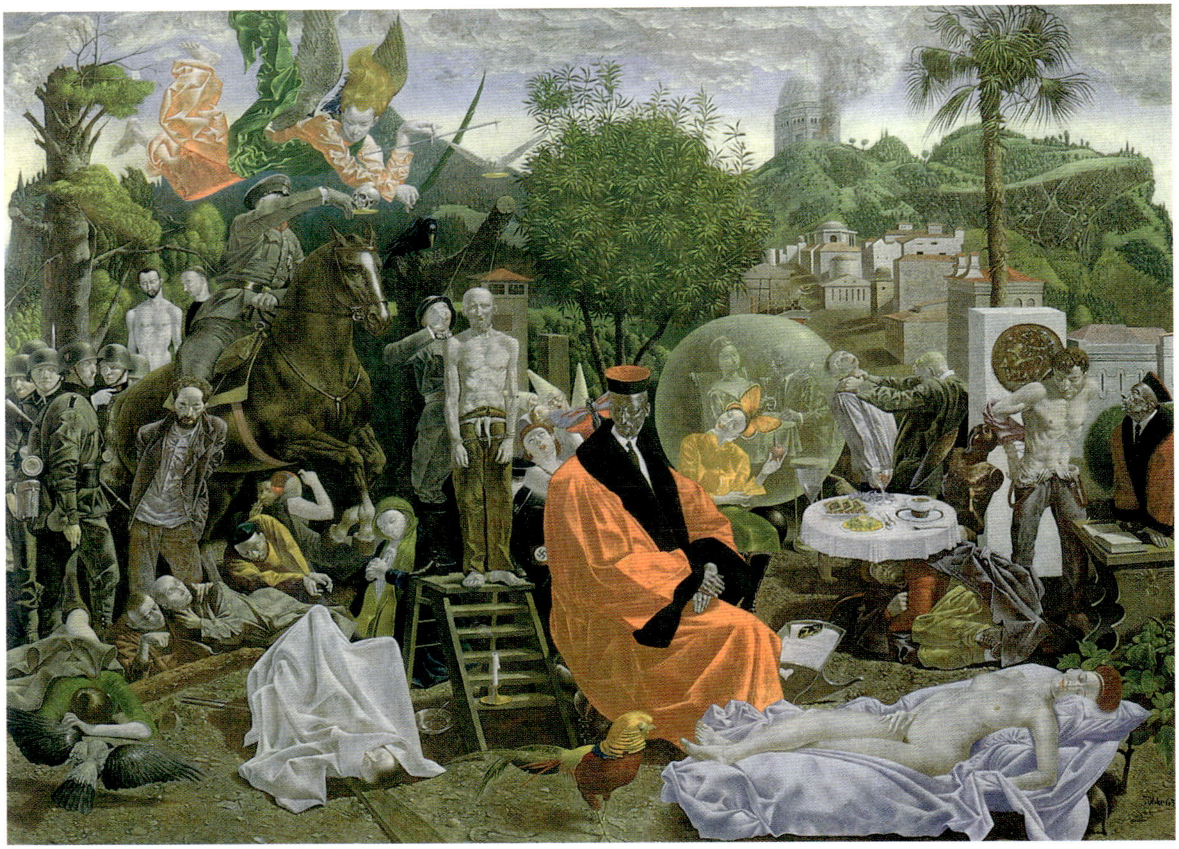

203 Werner Tübke, *Memoirs of Dr. jur. Schulze II*, 1965, technique of superimposing different colours on canvas on wood.

identified by Mirjam Wenzel.[172] Neither of the paintings shows a continuous series of historical events, as was recorded in the first sketch (see illus. 193); instead situations are presented from different perspectives and contexts as if to give evidence. There is no analysis, based on the theory of class struggle, of social developments but instead there is the almost postmodern attempt[173] to capture individual memories through the combination of relics and pictorial schemata from different eras and not pointing towards any utopias. Oriented as they are on the use of many figures, as in medieval painting, they call for a close reading faced with an original painting and they clearly differ from the large-scale eye-grabbing works of his contemporaries. Tübke outlined his intention in an interview at the first exhibition of the cycle as: 'It treats everything in more or less the same way: victims, terror, criminals . . . The whole thing shouts out, "painted against the grain".'[174]

Apart from the Frankfurt trial, it was, from the GDR perspective, the case of Hans Globke, commentator on the Nazi race laws and the man closest to Konrad Adenauer since 1949, which caused most outrage at the prosecution and conviction in West Germany. The news of it revealed to the artist and to observers, faced with the horrific representations, that it was possible to find the main culprits in West Germany and not to have to look for them in their own part of the country. *Schulze*, the everyday name Tübke chose for the cycle, points the finger at 'Everyman', and implicates each and every beholder in his memoirs.

The picture that used a technique of superimposing different paints onto canvas on wood and now goes under the name *Schulze II*, Tübke described on 31 December 1964 as the 'first panel', at the same time, however, not yet giving the main figure *Dr. jur XY* any name, and noted: 'It will represent an old legal official looking back at his past.'[175] In fact the judge's robe does not correspond as regards colour to that worn by members of the West German legal profession that the series of pictures was above all supposed to be about. By the way it is cut and the red colour, the judge's robe in *Schulze II* is made to look like that of the notorious Nazi *Volksgerichtshof* presided over by Roland Freisler, only the colour of the black velvet on the neck, sleeves and cap border being different and thus immediately suggesting the black robes of West German judges. Here again one can see how very keen Tübke was to distance himself from 'everyday political illustrations'[176] but nevertheless aimed to portray the 'concrete situation of historical events'.

One can agree with Emmrich, in her groundbreaking 1976 description of these pictures, when she talks about a 'pictorial narrative on four spatial layers parallel to the level pictured' and says that, despite different 'stages of the temporal sequence' and differently situated events, one can speak of 'a whole' due to the figural composition.[177] No unified narration is presented, yet the different memoirs of the judge looking sideways are shown which collide with one another in highly animated scenes. These are thoroughly interwoven with photographs of the persecution of the Jews from *Der Gelbe Stern*: an arrest

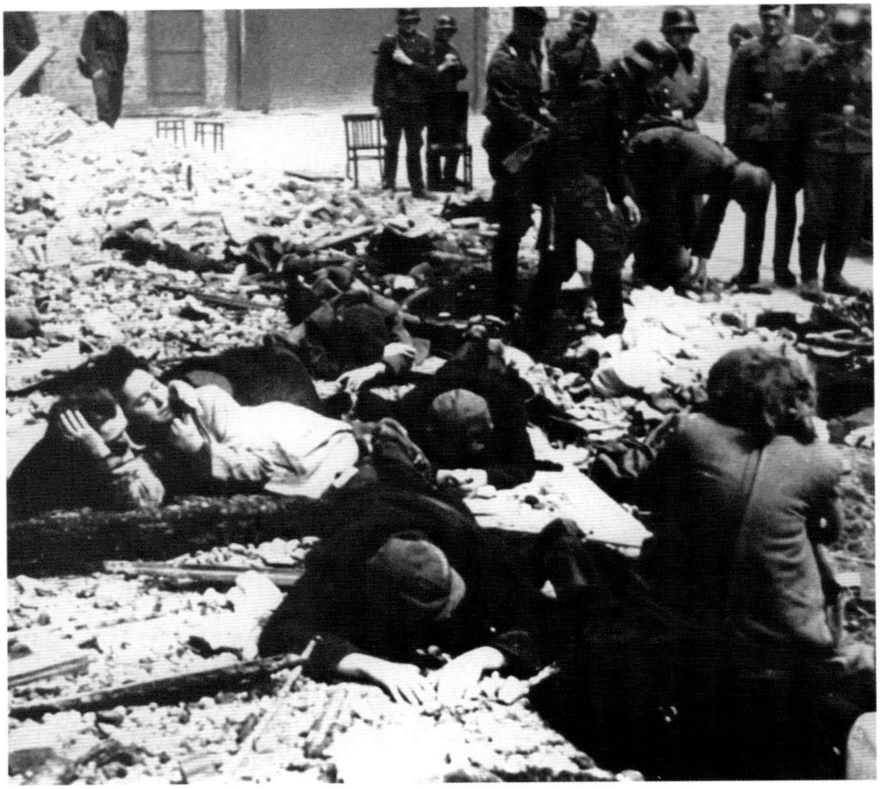

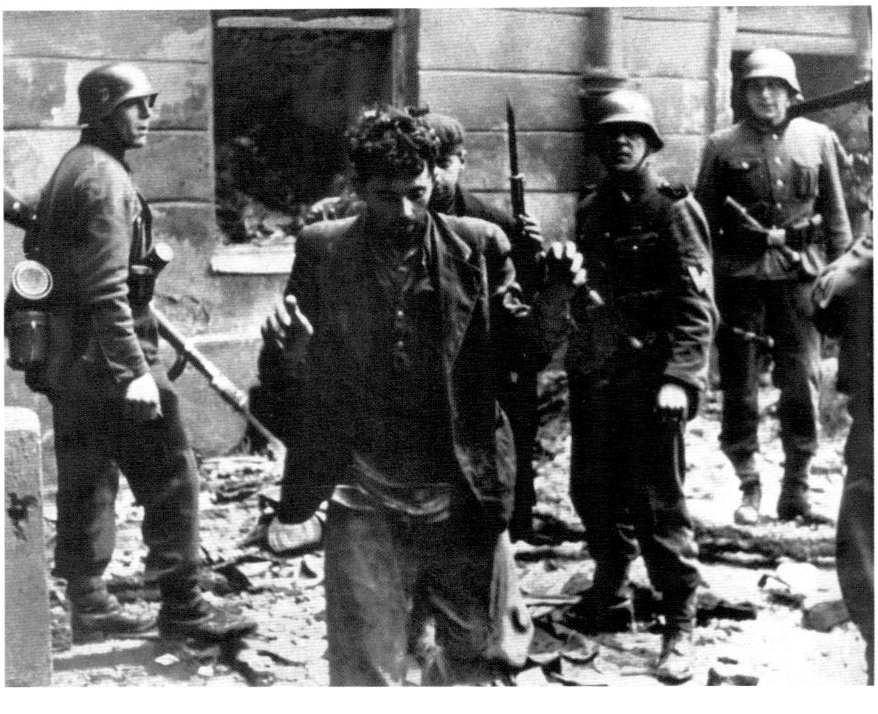

204 *Just Pulled from a Bunker*, Warsaw, 1943 (Stroop Report), photograph publ. in Schoenberner 1960.

205 *The Defenders of the Ghetto are Led Away to be Executed*, Warsaw, 1943 (Stroop Report), photograph publ. in Schoenberner 1960.

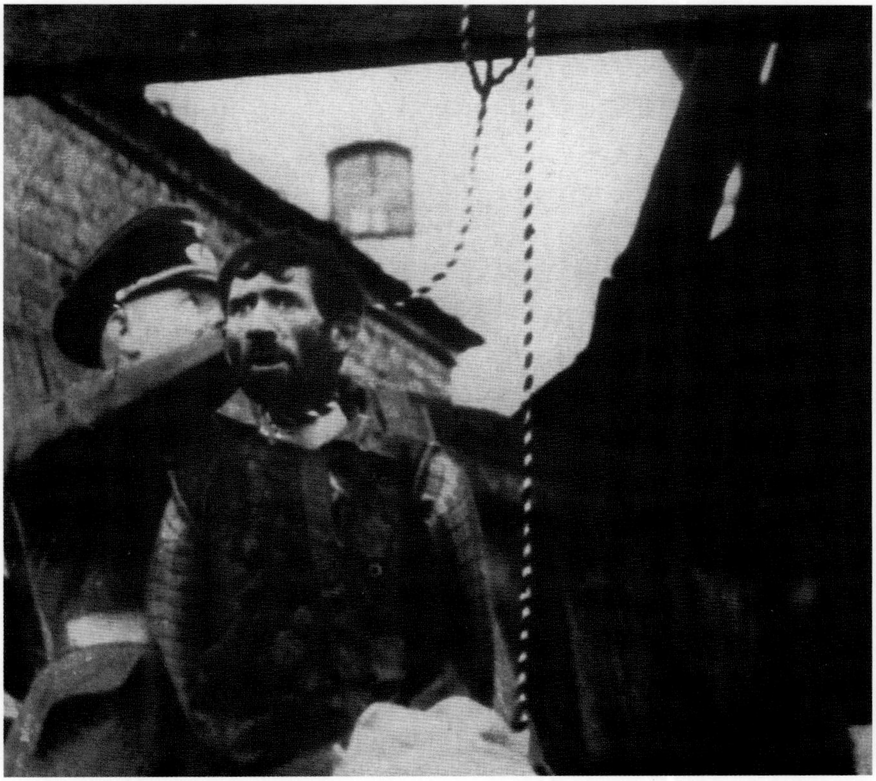

206 *Hanging of a Russian Peasant*, photograph publ. in Schoenberner 1960.

on the extreme left of the picture which, like the couple lying on the ground below (illus. 204), is based on the capture of Jews in the Warsaw Ghetto from the Stroop Report (illus. 205), as right from the first painting *Schulze I*,[178] a hanging based on the photograph of the execution of a Russian peasant (illus. 206) occupied the central position. Particularly clearly indicated is the person lying from Buchenwald (see illus. 195) with the distinct shroud, highlighted by its colour and jagged silhouette against its immediate surroundings and placed at almost a right angle to the sleeping female nude, displayed erotically on an artistically arranged white sheet. Tübke turns the judge's body towards the seductive nude, but he is looking at the ambiguous figure. The animated silhouette of the latter might be read as a warning that the dead camp prisoners have not been laid to rest.

As a reference to the 'brown [Nazi] terror and a nice life'[179] a golden pheasant, formerly the symbol of the Nazi elite,[180] is parading in the foreground at the feet of the judge and the beautiful woman lying there. The judge's past and his desires are once again displayed in the bubble next to his head. A female figure with a beautiful butterfly in her hair is visible in front of a couple, all of them enclosed in a bubble.

This is accompanied by a scene in which a prisoner is being strangled next to a stele, in front of which a man with a naked upper body is being harangued by the second representation of Judge Schulze – yelling like Freisler, who twisted the law presiding over the *Volksgerichtshof*. The bronze medallion set into the front of the stele captures for all eternity the features of the man with the naked upper body. Tübke, as Emmrich writes, was here raising the 'features of his face to the level of classicism in the monument'.[181] The fact that he included this stele in the picture shows his intended wish to remind people continually of the victims, the terror and the criminals.

The picture *Schulze II* resembles the brightly coloured painting of lives of the saints against a Southern landscape of the Italian early Renaissance,[182] immediately also revealing terror, however, either in the shape of the burning Berlin synagogue[183] on the horizon or the angel flying above the scene with an olive branch and scales; an SS horseman is placing a skull on the left-hand scale.[184] The effect of the image is heightened by repeating the spectacle of the persecuted five times over – Emmrich talks of a generalization of the aspects of the 'ecce homo' theme.[185] The firm resolution of the young men was captured by Tübke, despite the torments inflicted upon them; three of them are standing with their upper bodies naked, whereas the faces of the two men in uniform carrying out the acts are obscured. Like Sitte in *Massacre II*, Tübke did not here portray any individual perpetrators. His copying of those dressed as prisoners on the extreme left from the photo in Schoenberner 'The Defenders of the Ghetto are led away to be executed' (see illus. 205), turning the figure with the gesture of surrender, the raised arms, into a single resistance man standing though shackled with a bright face and an upright forehead, shows how he reworked the prisoner from the SS photo of their captives. The old principle of illustration, visualizing the lives of biblical characters, saints and martyrs in a series of several separate scenes, in which each main protagonist returns, was being used here by Tübke for the torture of those persecuted under the Nazis in a portrayal of the new/old terror. By means of the 'technique of addition' he aimed to 'paint' the history of the persecution as 'a list'.[186]

Memoirs of Dr. jur. Schulze III

In version III of the *Memoirs of Dr. jur. Schulze* (illus. 207) as well, Tübke was intensely concerned with the history of painting and with the maltreatment, resistance and murder of the Jews during the Nazi period. This monumental example of miniature painting, the only one in the cycle in an upright format, was displayed at the seventeenth regional exhibition in 1965 in Leipzig,[187] along with Bernhard Heisig's third version of the *Paris Commune* and Wolfgang Mattheuer's painting *Cain*,[188] and attracted some attention. All three artists themselves belonged to the 36-member jury for the selection.[189] Despite Alfred Kurella sharply criticizing Tübke for his departure from Socialist Realism in the newspaper *Neues Deutschland* in 1967,[190] *Schulze III* nevertheless made it into the Nationalgalerie in Berlin in 1965 as a loan from the Leipzig Regional Council, and was 'handed over' to them finally in 1987.[191] In 1971 the exhibition of the whole cycle on the *Memoirs* brought the artist international recognition

207 Werner Tübke, *Memoirs of Dr. jur. Schulze III*, 1965, tempera on canvas on wood.

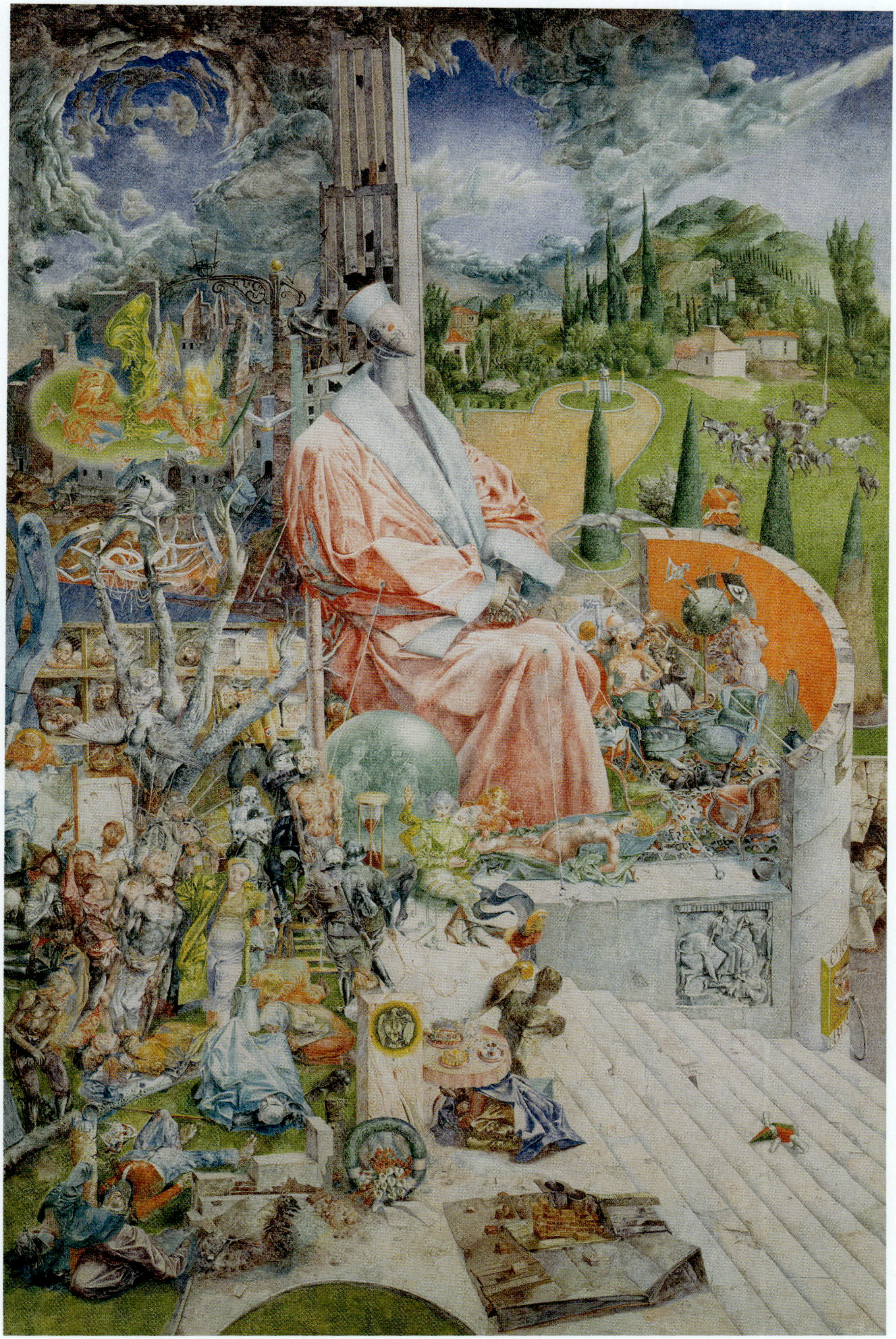

at Emilio Bertonati's Galleria del Levante in Italy and that of the *Frankfurter Allgemeine Zeitung* thanks to Eduard Beaucamp.[192] This reinforced Tübke's reputation in the GDR and led one year later to the painting being shown at the Nationalgalerie in Berlin within the first overall display in the GDR of the 'variations on the theme of the *Lebenserinnerungen des Dr. jur. Schulze*',[193] and in West Germany it was shown at *documenta 6* in 1977.[194] In the meantime it has become the most frequently published version of the cycle.

In version III in the left-hand half of the picture, Tübke brought together, in a way characteristic of himself and the Leipzig School, individual, originally separate figures from different pictorial sources for the scenes of violence during the persecution and murder of the Jews: references to memories, frequently based on SS photos of the Warsaw Ghetto, without any continuous narration. From the first glance at the multitude of people, one can see that Tübke was referring in general to fifteenth-century painting by the intricacy and the bright colours, even if they shout out in the manner of the Pop art of the time. In addition, the judge-puppet placed at the centre in three-quarter perspective as a figure dominating the picture, with its wooden head attached by wires to a tower-like neck and hands consisting of nothing but wired metal parts, reminds one of the bio-mechanical constructs of Hieronymus Bosch's diabolic figures.[195] It looks as though Tübke has realized Schoenberner's words in the introduction to the book of photos: 'The Biblical prophecies about the Last Judgement and the angst-ridden visions of a Kafka became reality. The monsters of Hieronymus Bosch arose in human shape. They no longer had the faces of toads, nor fangs or horse's hooves, but a smooth-shaven chin and a neat parting, they were respectable family men . . . Dante's *Inferno* came about in the modern world' (p. 5).[196] And even the motto of the publication 'Germany, you shall not forget the murdered nor the murderers. Klabund' (p. 5) was like a model for Tübke, as his 'reflections about working on Dr. jur. Schulze III' prove, which was published as a text for the exhibition of the cycle in 1972 in Berlin.[197]

Tübke's intention of showing the murdered and the murderers was, as

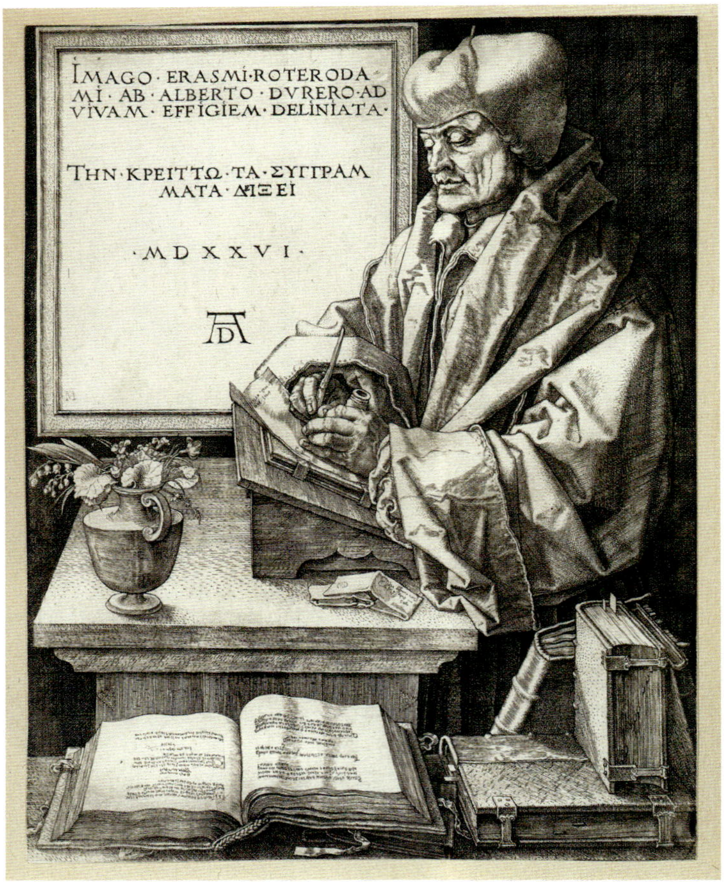

208 Albrecht Dürer, *Erasmus of Rotterdam*, 1526, copperplate engraving.

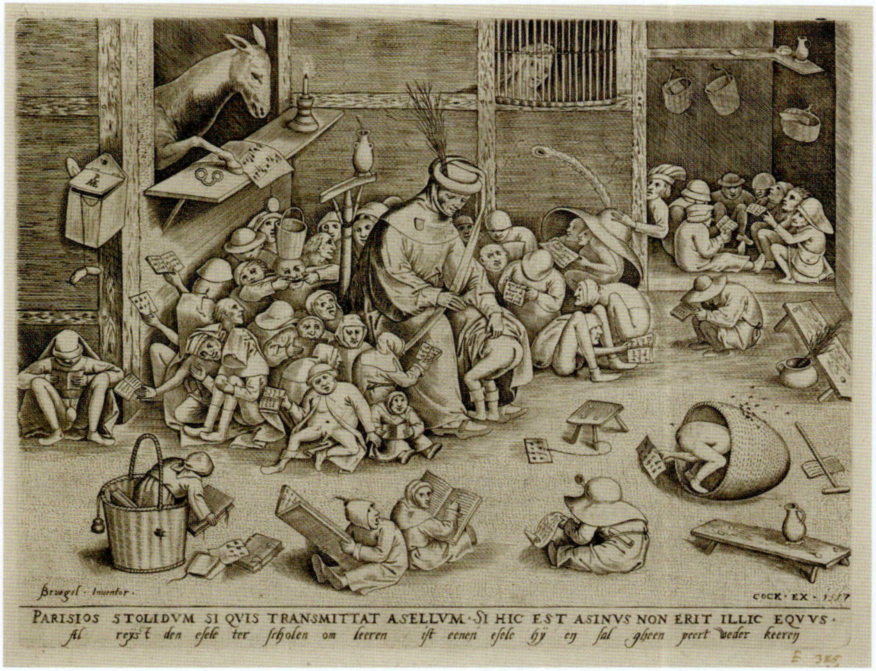

209 Pieter van der Heyden after Pieter Brueghel the Elder, *The Ass in the School*, 1556, etching and copperplate engraving.

in *Schulze II*, realized following the style of court proceedings. The central figure of the judge acknowledged purely as a function, Tübke described in the following terms: 'a complete neutral element, expressed as "It", seemed to me to be needed, couched in formal Latin, in order not to provoke any sympathy with Dr. jur. Schulze.'[198] Tübke placed it in the picture like the Judge of the World at the Last Judgement. Contrary to Christian representations, in this profane World Court he admittedly exchanged the places of the good and the damned. Whereas traditionally the torments of Hell are arranged on the left hand of God, that is, on the right of the picture, in *Schulze III* they are to be seen on the left side of the picture. The judge-puppet is tied down on both sides by three cords. The red robe with the white stole collar and sleeve cuffs on top of a lilac undergarment is, with its broad gown, an allusion to the style and dress of the German Renaissance, like that of Erasmus of Rotterdam in Dürer's engraving of 1526 (illus. 208). With the much more general hints of a robe of honour, the colouring and the folds distinguish it from that of the judge figure in version II which bring to mind clearer suggestions of the clothing of Nazi judges and of later ones. Harking back to the noble robe of the Humanists in the third version draws attention to the dress of judges across the ages, seemingly in the end nothing but showy appearance, the bourgeois adornment of a mechanical judge-puppet. For the seated figure of the 'evil Judge of the World', Beaucamp already identified the similarities often seen in the case of Tübke to Brueghel, pointing to the punishing teacher in Pieter Brueghel the Elder's parable *The Ass in the School*[199] (illus. 209). Schulze, the judge-puppet, is shown in front of a

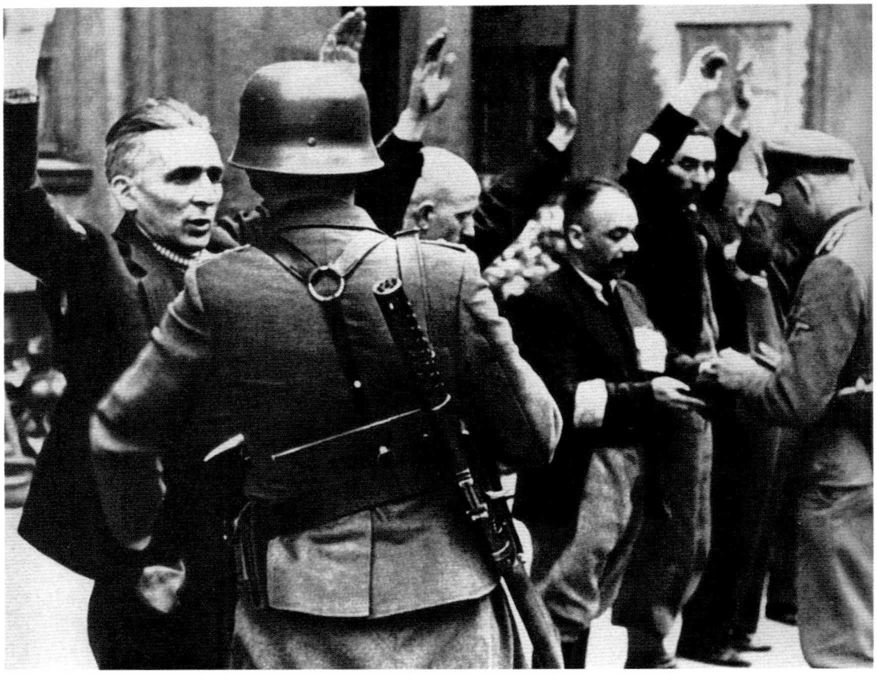

210 *Arrest of the Management of the Brauer Firm, Warsaw,* 1943 (Stroop Report: *The Brauer Firm*), photograph publ. in Schoenberner 1960.

tower-like structure full of holes reminiscent of photos of the ruins of the tall building in Warsaw.[200] Tübke is thus able to portray, more powerfully than in version II, his idea of the Nazi past conditioned by knowledge of the history in line with the representation of landscape in the style of the early Renaissance and a sky like that in Altdorfer's *The Battle of Alexander*.[201] He was concerned above all with the early bourgeois culture of Northern and Southern Europe and their social struggles, with violence and beauty. Only gradually is the public forced away from the historical background and only gradually do they become aware that in the *Memoirs* Tübke is portraying the murder of the Jews by the Germans during the Nazi period. Following a 'therapy of deterrence',[202] a concept that Tübke shared with Schoenberner and the Western occupying powers,[203] on the left side, in greater detail than in *Schulze II*, he displayed 'Victims Terror Criminals of the Nazi period'.[204]

On the ground in the left-hand corner a tortured man is hanging on a stake; his agonized posture reminds one of a photographed scene of a shooting by Nazi henchmen, the origin of which it was impossible to trace.[205] Above another man lying with a red jacket, one notices the figure covered by a cloth up to its chin and grieved over, as in *Schulze II*, by a kneeling woman on his right. The folds of the bright blue material revealing, as in the previous image of the court, a violent leg movement still in the onset of rigor mortis, have once again been copied, like the water can, from the Buchenwald photo (see illus. 195). The execution scene from Schoenberner 1960, p. 100 (see illus. 206), seen in *Schulze II* (see illus. 203), is visible again between a green bubble and skulls below an SS figure. Only, in this version, the executioner has acquired a

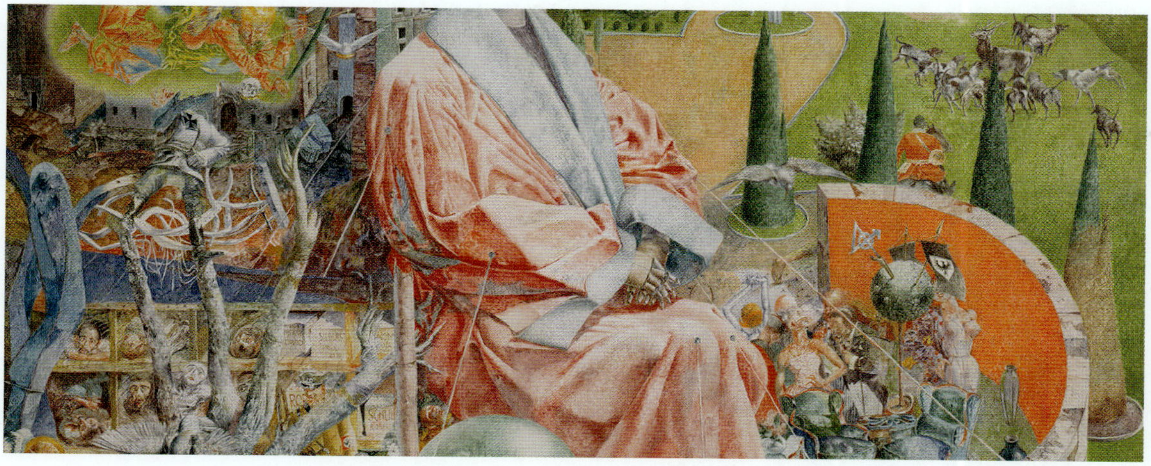

211 Detail of Werner Tübke, *Memoirs of Dr. jur. Schulze III*, 1965.

cloven hoof,[206] and he shows a similarity to Heinrich Himmler by being given spectacles.[207] Again references to photographs with fragments remembered from other historical and mythical narratives are added to the painting and realized by the use of collage made up of details copied from different photographs in a riot of colour and at the same time portrayed in isolation from their original context: for example, the bodies of the couple lying holding one another (see illus. 204), the SS officer's back (illus. 210) to which Tübke gave the skull of a dead man, and the fan-like iron grille in a ray shape (see illus. 201) behind a camp prisoner. The painting makes it possible to place, on the right next to the woman in the yellow coat, a group of figures in uniform, located in time and identifiable with National Socialism, and on the left a scene for which the model could have been the Descent from the Cross in Christian iconography.[208]

Further up in the picture (illus. 211) there is the floating figure of an angel with scales onto which the glove of a uniform, worn by a dead body, is placing a skull. The scales and the gesture remind one of the figure in *Schulze II* (see illus. 203), except that the uniform has now been made SS black, and the horse, on which the figure was seated in the picture previously discussed, has disintegrated into a pile of unidentifiable white parts. Like a mounted tin soldier without his cavalry unit, it is hanging in the air, proclaiming with the oversize Iron Cross on its chest its scorn for chivalric virtues by these very acts.[209]

In the wooden structure behind the grey branches there are inscriptions written on cardboard urns (illus. 212) and turned towards the viewer. Tübke makes it plain to see and read whose skulls weigh heavier than the Dove of Peace and who is represented by the tortured and murdered on the left side of the court. Unlike Beuys (see illus. 176) and Vostell (see illus. 171), Tübke did not build the type of structure where visitors could physically imagine the experience of being in the camp. Instead, he painted a wooden construction consisting, as it were, of compartments – a variation of the bunks photographed by Harry Miller (illus. 213) at Buchenwald and

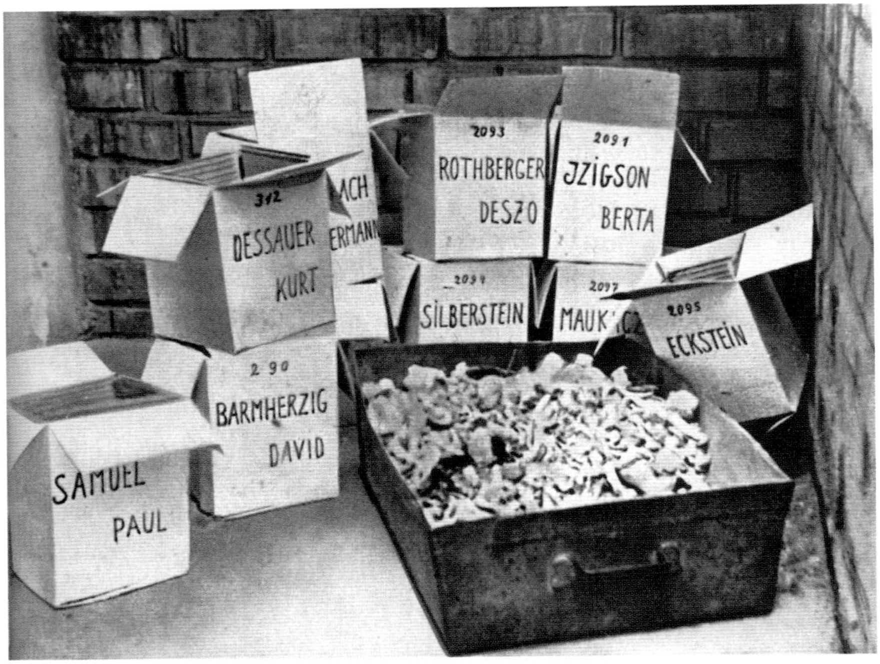

212 *Cardboard Urns for the Ashes of the Dead from Theresienstadt*, photograph publ. in Schoenberner 1960.

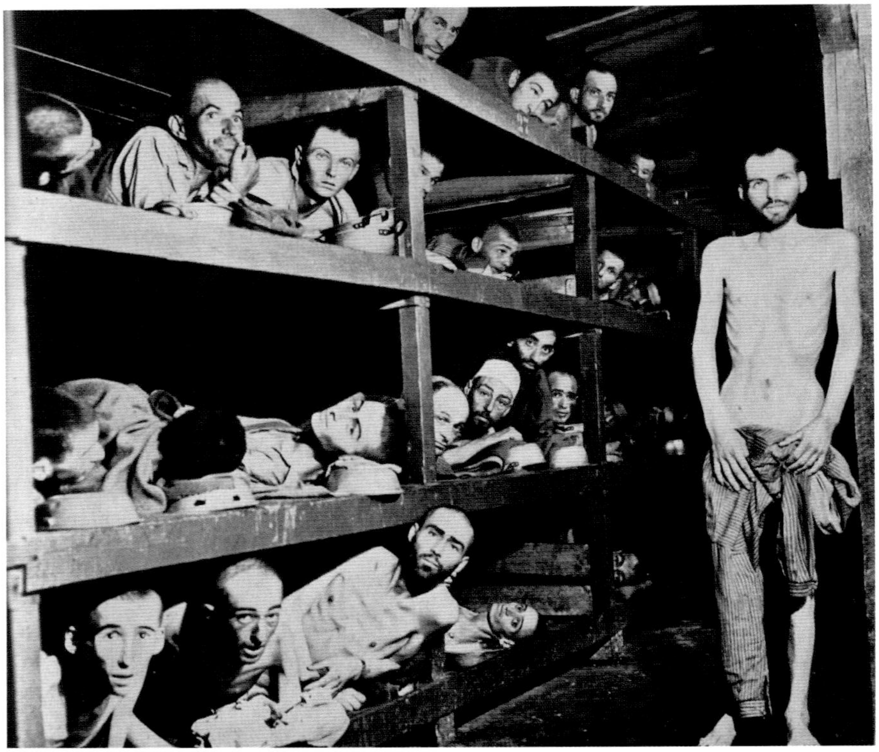

213 Harry Miller, *Living Hut at Buchenwald*, 1945, photograph publ. in Schoenberner 1960.

reproduced in *Der Gelbe Stern*. Tübke showed both the emaciated bodies of the inmates and also the cardboard urns with numbers and parts of Jewish surnames such as 'Silberst' or 'Herzig David' in the right-hand half. One can only presume that these memoirs by *Dr. jur. Schulze* awakened memories on the part of many visitors to the museum.

As well as the names of those who had been murdered, Tübke referred to the places in which the crimes occurred, on the left side of the picture: Warsaw by the ruins of the tall building and the Warsaw Ghetto by the grille behind the couple lying on the ground, now in front of the trunk, and in several places he indicated the camps. Thus the branches in front of the wooden structure remind one, not just metaphorically of the Tree of Life, but of the bare tree that is seen in the documentation about the camp at Auschwitz published by the International Auschwitz Committee in 1963.[210] On the left side of the picture, its growth seems to be echoed in metal which, however, by comparing the images, proves to be in the bizarre shape of the pipe work of the crematory installations from the camp destroyed by the Germans before they abandoned Auschwitz,[211] and at the level of the judge figure's head one can see a lamp typical of the camp lighting. The fact that Tübke used pictures of the camp and the gas chambers at Auschwitz for his work is illustrated once more by the fragments of a roof visible in the middle at the bottom of the picture. On close inspection, one can make out, not just a walled chimney, but at the front the rectangular opening for inserting the gas.[212]

The whole left side of the picture of the court, devoted to Auschwitz and the Warsaw Ghetto, turns into a Hell on earth, an image imbued with the language of nearly all the accounts by survivors of the camps.[213] As ones condemned by their actions, most of the tormentors bear skulls while those being tormented show their faces, albeit contorted with pain. Like Willi Sitte, who in *Massacre II* (see illus. 134) painted the Nazi soldiers as faceless beings, Tübke reversed tradition. The perpetrators, whose faces and often whose names too are known from the photographs and the accompanying text, become in his painting nameless, unidentifiable figures; Tübke attempted, on the other hand, to bring to an end the anonymity of those incinerated in the crematoria and shovelled into mass graves. Even in the scenes that he created from photographs of piles of anonymous corpses, he tried to give to the nameless differentiated positions and the space not granted by the mass grave.

A special position was likewise allotted to the female figure coming forward in the left-hand half of the picture in a coat of 'shocking yellow'. The colour was intentional for Tübke; he chose it, 'so as not to let the viewer take it easy, so as not to lull him aesthetically, so as to stay tough in its colourfulness'.[214] The figure is emphasized by this use of colour, only shared by the stream of material wafted by the angel with the scales in the top part of the picture and the clothing of the female figure positioned in the centre of the picture. As a lively individual figure firmly occupying space, the pregnant woman steps forward in her open, greenish-yellow coat out of the

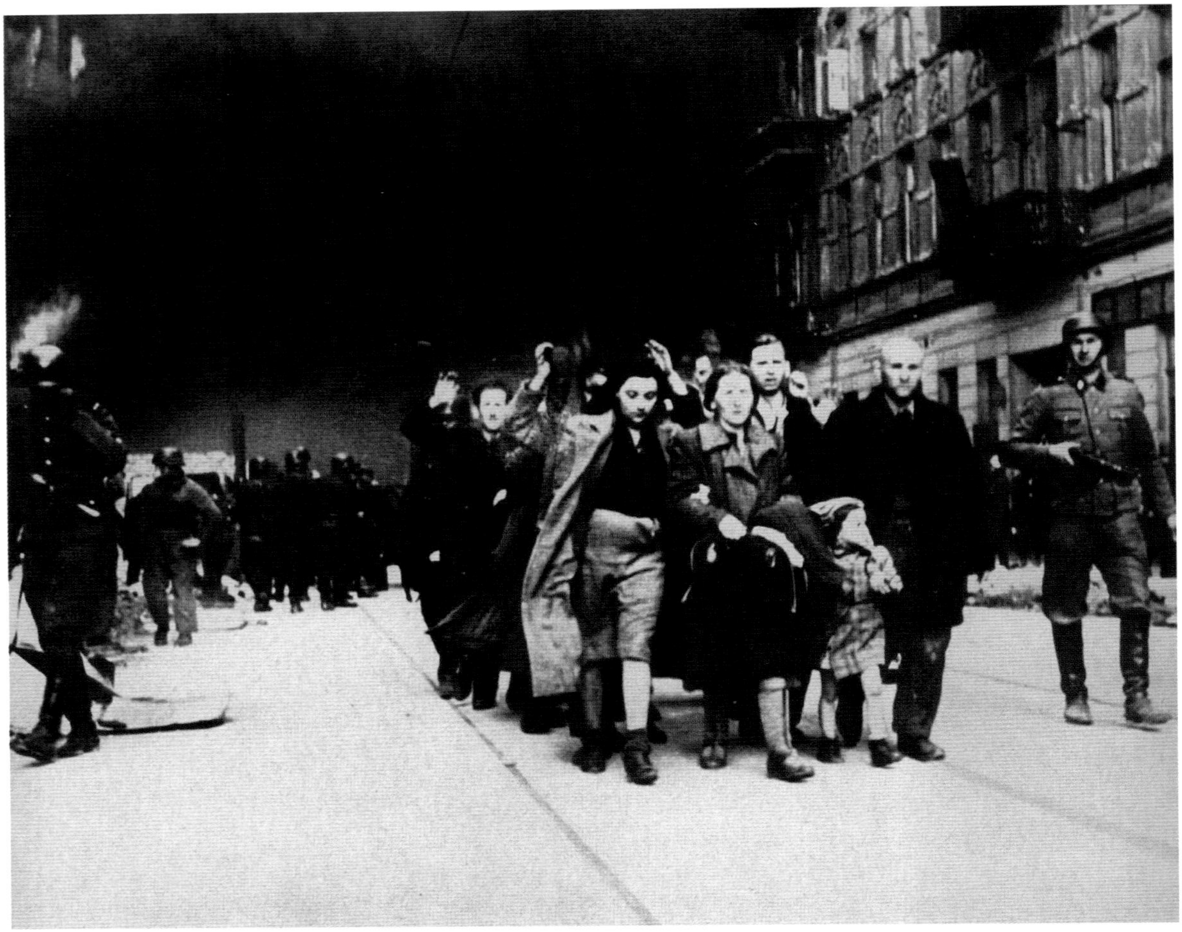

214 *The March to the Trans-shipment Point*, Warsaw, 1943 (Stroop Report: *Pulled from the Bunkers by Force*), photograph publ. in Schoenberner 1960.

Hell-like events. Again, as for that of the young man in *Schulze II*, Tübke took as a model a photo from the Stroop Report[215] about the suppression of the Warsaw Ghetto Uprising by the Germans. The female figure is repeated as an enlarged detail from the seventh photograph of the 'pictorial report' in the documentary, showing a group of persecuted Jews walking closely together being transported, under SS guard, to an extermination camp (illus. 214).[216] The photo that is now so moving to us was given the caption 'Pulled from the Bunkers by Force'[217] and intended to be attached to the pictorial report, with the photographic trophies of the prisoners to be handed over to Heinrich Himmler after the murder of all the Jews and the destruction of the ghetto under the overall title *The Jewish Quarter of Warsaw No Longer Exists*. After photographs of the eviction of the 'Brauer armaments firm' and a 'March to the Umschlagplatz (Trans-shipment Point)', the one selected by Tübke is the first to make direct mention of the 'eviction' of the Ghetto in the caption. The same caption is given to the fourteenth photo with the little boy that Schoenberner used as a poster for his 1960 exhibition (see illus. 153) and which came to be better-known than the one being discussed

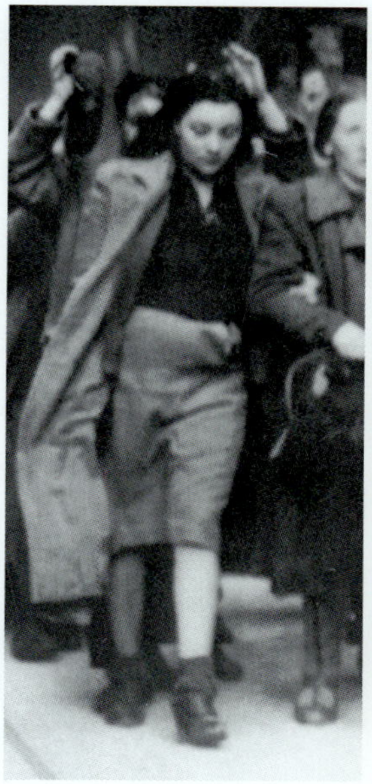

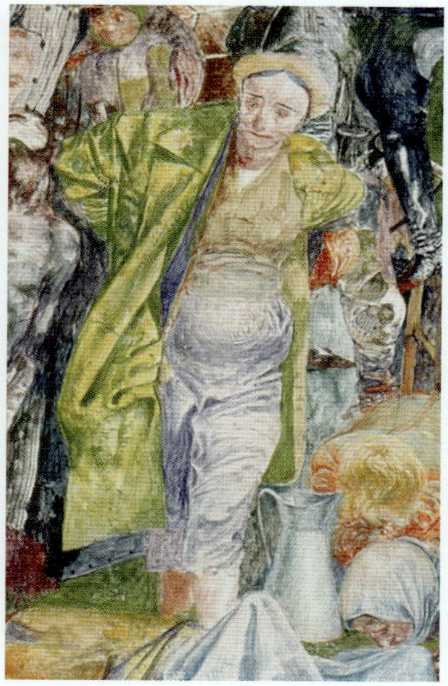

215 Detail of *The March to the Trans-shipment Point*, Warsaw, 1943, from Schoenberner 1960.

216 Detail of Werner Tübke, *Memoirs of Dr. jur. Schulze III*, 1965.

here. Reading the meagre daily bulletins, couched in official German, expressing extreme brutality and, without further commentary, a readiness to exterminate the Jews, is hard to endure, but it then becomes relatively easy to interpret the moment shown in the photograph. Despite daily engagement of the military, the SS and their auxiliary troops were by no means able to capture all of the inhabitants of the Ghetto, transport them or shoot them on the spot, since the 'Jews and Bandits', as they say over and over again, hid in underground bunkers and sewers. Stroop therefore continually gave orders to blow up buildings and start fires. How many people came to light as a result, were captured or shot was precisely noted in the daily reports and comments added with photos. Reading the text reveals the background to the photo, clouded by smoke as a result of the explosions and fires mentioned. In front of the burning buildings, the group of captured people is seen from slightly below, guarded on each side – albeit at a distance – by an SS officer with a gun in his hand, while in the background a lot of soldiers are looking in the direction of the destroyed buildings. The image, used so often before the Nazi period, of left-wing United Front demonstrations (see illus. 90) marching towards the viewer singing, is transformed into a group of people who have surrendered, guarded by the SS and huddling closely together, facing their murder.[218] All those being photographed knew this as much as the observers. The photo in the Stroop Report shows the inversion of revolutionary iconography in which the front row is now occupied by a Jewish family consisting of several generations doomed to die.[219] Tübke for his part turned the fascist perversion of the United Front into a representation of the future. The young woman in the family, the one he singled out from the front row in the SS photo, the same position at the front in which formerly the female

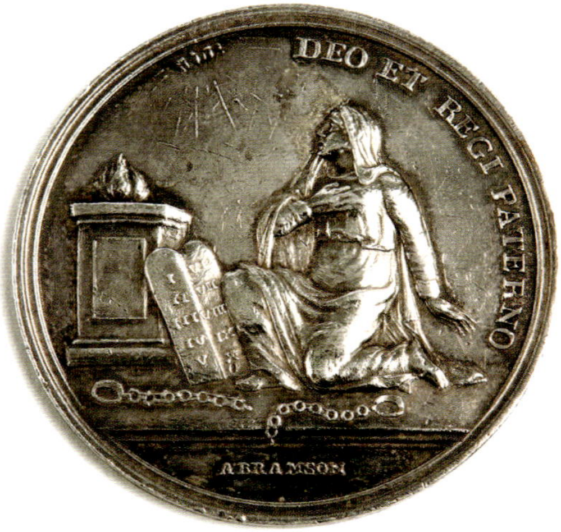

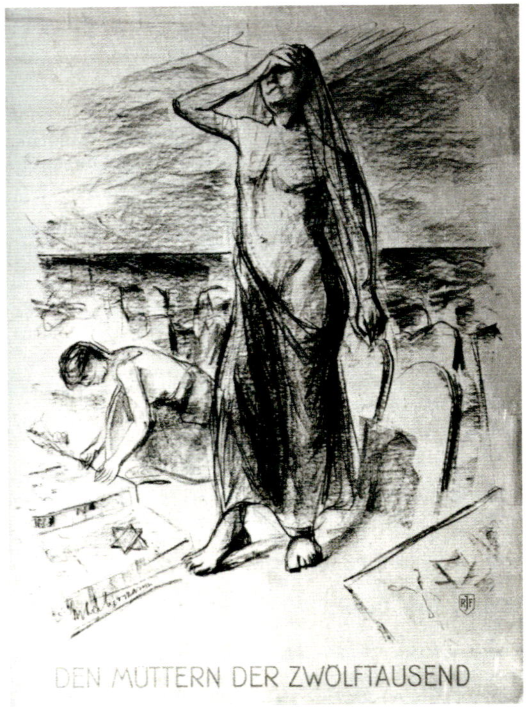

217 Abraham Abramson, *Enfranchisement of the Jews of Westphalia*, 1808, obverse, medal, silver and bronze.

218 Max Liebermann, *To the Mothers of the Twelve Thousand*, 1924, lithograph.

allegorical figure of Liberty or the Republic had been on display, is to be seen in the photo in a tight skirt with her coat flying in front of two people with their arms raised next to her mother-in-law with her daughter. She is looking straight ahead whereas the other captives appear to be looking at the camera. She is a helpless captive to be transported to the extermination camp, like the people on the 'March to the Trans-shipment Point' in the previous photo. However, the photograph chosen for the report, unlike the previous one, does not document the usual marching columns of Jews to the trans-shipment or collection point, and the goods wagons, but shows those defeated by the ss as being caught 'in the bag'. The photo does not just represent, like every other one, what Roland Barthes calls an analogon – here a capture – but is at the same time accompanied by a connotation,[220] underlining here, by the monumentalizing shot below, the defeat of the opponent.

In adapting it, the painter significantly altered the connotation of the original by means of small corrections to the perpetrators' perspective of the photograph (illus. 215 and 216): he slightly raised the face of the terrified, persecuted woman looking down at the ground, drew her pregnant body more clearly and, to judge from the folds newly added to the left side of the coat, had her supporting her right arm forcefully at the waist emphasizing her upright posture. In the painting she is no longer part of a group of persecuted people with arms raised. Tübke arranged the whole figure in the picture in such a way that she – turning away a little – is now no longer seen from slightly below but from above. She is the only one placed in the centre of the

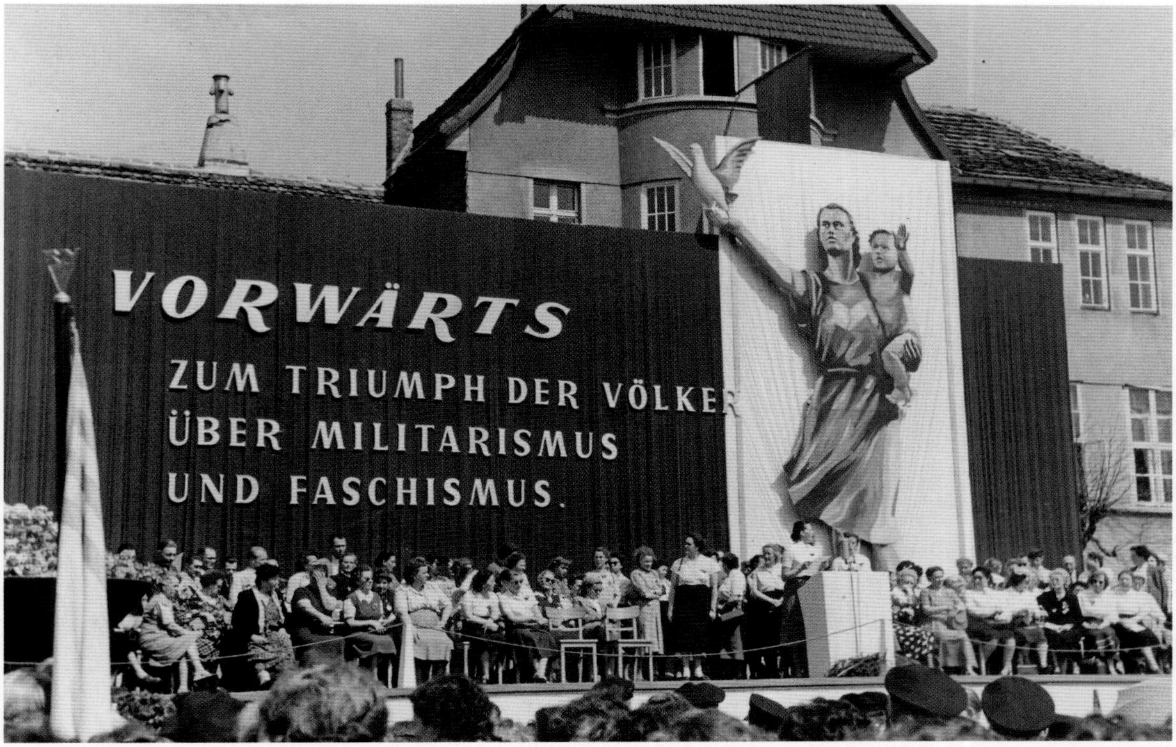

219 Ceremony to commemorate the liberation of Ravensbrück Concentration Camp on the marketplace of the City of Fürstenberg, 1955, photograph.

left side of the painting, seemingly walking forwards, and yet she is in suspended animation, as the space for the next step is not shown in the painting. Between those being tormented and the dead, she is the only one with her face turned straight towards the beholder and moving, unlike in the photograph, from right to left. On her left-hand coat lapel in the painting, but not in the photo in the Stroop Report, one can make out a slightly obscured yellow star. But it is not just this yellow star but her function in the picture that alters the figure.

Interpreting this borrowing from the photograph, one notices a significant difference as regards references to males as models in the case of *Schulze II* (see illus. 203). Whereas representations of the male hero indicate an agent, a specific person, here for example the underground fighter from the Ghetto captured by the SS, pictures of females in West European culture do not necessarily refer to individual women but rather to themes; they are used as allegories. 'Female allegorical figures represent what unites the agents [men – K.H.C.] in their imagination, what should unite them,' according to Silke Wenk in her analysis of 'petrified femininity'.[221] Representations of female figures signify, depending on the period and context, allegories of beauty, truth or the imagined community, the nation and the Jewish people, as shown on an 1808 medal for the enfranchisement of the Westphalian Jews (illus. 217) and Liebermann's 1924 graphic representation *To the Mothers of the Twelve Thousand* (illus. 218). In the visual culture of the GDR, the society that

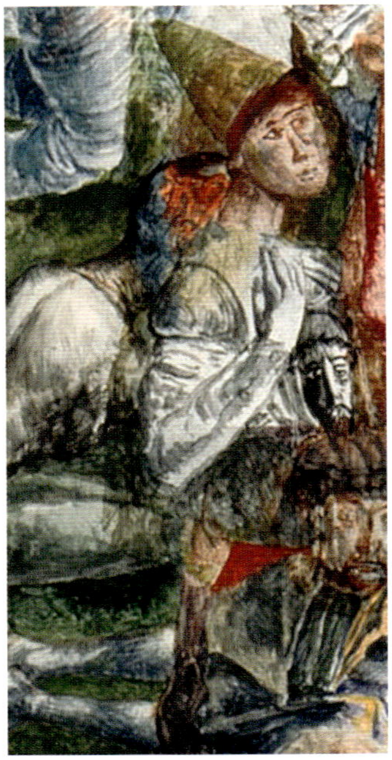

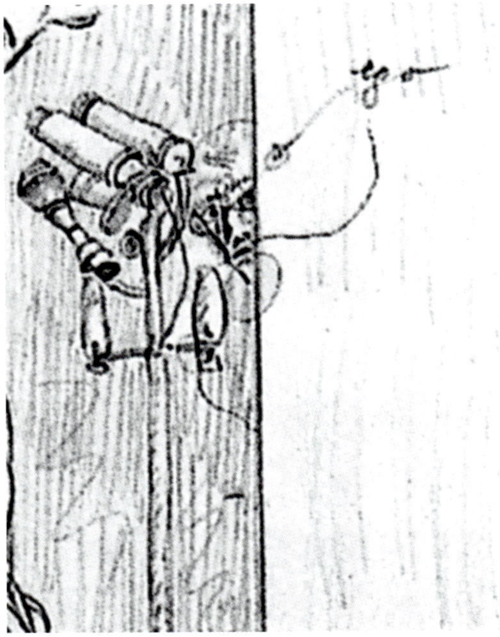

220 Detail of Werner Tübke, *Memoirs of Dr. jur. Schulze* III, 1965.

221 Detail of Werner Tübke, Sketch for the composition of *Memoirs of Dr. jur. Schulze* III, 1965, pencil.

affected Tübke, heroes marching forward as on the monument for the camp at Buchenwald by Fritz Cremer,[222] and much less often heroines, were an essential element of the future-directed state policy. If ever a woman appeared in a flowing gown, as at the celebration of the tenth anniversary of the liberation of the women's camp at Ravensbrück on the marketplace in Fürstenberg (illus. 219), then the stage was not dominated by the representation of a former female prisoner but by an allegory of Peace, in this case constructed probably out of painted cardboard, bearing a dove like a torch. Without any personal name, the image of the feminine, whether or not clothed, becomes a representation of something – without an individual history. In Tübke's initial plan, the female figure indicates the nation's power of reproduction. In *Schulze III*, precisely by the use of the direct reference to the photograph, the recoding of this moving and emotional female figure becomes apparent. Her flowing coat is now no longer explicable by the draught from the burning houses on the side of the street in Warsaw but is simultaneously the classical 'image of pathos' in a psychological dramatization of the figure by means of what Aby Warburg calls 'emotional accessories'.[223] Analogous with this ambivalence, her allegorization also remains in suspended animation between the portrayal of the Jewish woman, Yehudit Neyer, driven to the extermination camp, whose name Tübke definitely did not know, and the representation of the expectant mother advancing ever onwards, appearing to be stepping over those lying there, as the bearer of hope for the future survival of the Jewish people.

The fact that both the figure placed centrally in the image of torture and murder and the surrounding scenes frequently refer to photographs from the report on the completion of the liquidation of the Warsaw Ghetto is not a coincidence but can be taken to be Tübke's honouring of the members of the resistance. Shortly before he started work on the cycle he was reminded, by events staged in the GDR in 1963 and documentaries on the radio and television, about the Uprising by the captured Jews in the Ghetto twenty years previously. Presumably he had at least read in the newspapers about the commemorations organized in the GDR. An edition of the Stroop Report, put out by Verlag Rütten & Loening ahead of the commemoration, made the group known to the public, from where Tübke got the conspicuous woman in the coat.[224] As with Lea Grundig, Tübke also integrated the Jewish resistance into the history of the overthrow of fascism.

On the left side of the picture below the torso of an angel with golden red hair and a halo, the upper body of a kneeling Harlequin and his troubled face are visible (illus. 220). Bearing witness, he is holding the drawing of a head[225] done in black and white, a scene reminiscent of St Veronica's Veil. Here, however, it is not the image of Christ we see but the prisoner's head[226] preserved in Buchenwald. As Tübke frequently adopted the ambivalent role of the fool, he identified with it[227] and in a watercolour of the *Memoirs of Dr. jur. Schulze* he even put a Star of David on the hat of the Harlequin standing in the centre of the watercolour.[228] This character looking on aghast can be taken as Tübke's own position on the events in the picture and as an identification with those suffering. At the same time he was here identifying his authorship as being related to the events, while in the composition study WVZ Z7/65 (illus. 221) he added 'ego' on the right side of the picture behind a corner of the wall and possibly seeking to catch the eye of the viewer outside of the events. Another sign of his ego can also be revealed in the red and green harlequin figurine on the large white staircase to the right of the picture, on which the doll, all alone like a rejected toy, seems nevertheless to be clambering.

An angel in red and shocking yellow with a palm branch is a reference to the one weighing souls at the Last Judgement. Towards the right side of the picture, the 'paradise' side associated with desire and seduction, a connection is being made, on the one hand, by a soldier's multi-tailed whip and, on the other, by the female figure in the shocking yellow colour in the dress of a dominatrix, as also by the transparent green bubble between the two sides, suggesting pleasure in violence. Tübke turned the globe at the feet of the Judge of the World into 'a soap bubble of comfortable twosomeness'[229] next to Dr Schulze, providing a multifaceted commentary on the cluster of his disparate thoughts. In the right-hand half of the picture, the varied items from his Dr Schulze's memoirs are partly added to by the painter's autobiographical ones, such as the boy reading in the sailor suit and the hotel establishment that Tübke saw while staying with Kurella in the Caucasus.[230] Violence – so the whip suggests – appears to be involved even in sexual seduction. Tübke's intention to represent the desire to kill becomes clear from the pursuit of the stag by the hounds in the green countryside accompanied by a mounted huntsman dressed in red, whose broad back corresponds both to that of the SS officer with the death's head seen on the ladder in front of the execution scene next to the extinguished candle and also to the rider without a horse underneath the scales.

It was Irma Emmrich who noted in the first monograph on Tübke in 1976 that the painter, unlike in *Schulze II* (see illus. 203), 'integrated into the Berlin version . . . the Ecce homo motif . . . to a much greater extent, portraying the idea of the "Last Judgement" in a tragic inversion of value norms'.[231] By choosing to place those pleasing unto God on the right hand of the Lord at the Last Judgement, as in Matthew 25:33, Tübke was signalling his honouring of the abused, tortured and executed Jews who had actually been through the torments of Hell. In a period when the male hero of the communist resistance still defined the anti-fascist debate in the GDR, Tübke used the court setting to portray the suffering and the torments of the Jews along with their tormentors.

Study for the Memoirs of Dr. jur. Schulze IV

In his drawing now in Altenburg (illus. 222), regarded as a study for the never completed version IV of Schulze's *Memoirs*, he even drew the suffering prisoner on almost the same scale as the judge and placed a laurel wreath above his head. Michel Chaumont's 2001 revaluation of heroism, to honour the overwhelming majority of the camp prisoners simply for the torments they had to suffer,[232] Tübke brought to sight already in 1965, thus contradicting public positions in the Eastern as well as in the Western politics of memory. Eduard Beaucamp remarked that 'right from the first design, Tübke directed his attention towards the central fate of the Jews as victims and did not go along with the required party-political "anti-fascism"'.[233]

In his representations of the violence of the twentieth century, Tübke linked references to photographs directly to pictorial references to earlier periods, not limiting his involvement with the tradition of painting to a response to nineteenth-century painting devoted to realism. In doing this, he did not totally copy any photo from *Der Gelbe Stern*, like Tisa von der Schulenburg, later to become Sister Paula.[234] She worked, at the same time as Tübke, with Schoenberner's book but attempted in the course of several variations to emphasize even more the drama of the events through the intensive use of black ink in a late Expressionist style.[235] For his paintings Tübke also did not copy the almost filmic dramatic technique of pictures in sequence that Schoenberner used to illustrate the phases of murder. Instead, in his studies based on the photos, he avoided the disrespectful perpetrator's perspective of the Nazi photographers towards the victims; nor did he display piles of corpses, and children were shown only in studies for drawings.[236] At the same time, he used the many references to photos in the same revaluation of the Christian system of reference as Peter Weiss, whom he appreciated and who made use of statements from the Auschwitz trial in his

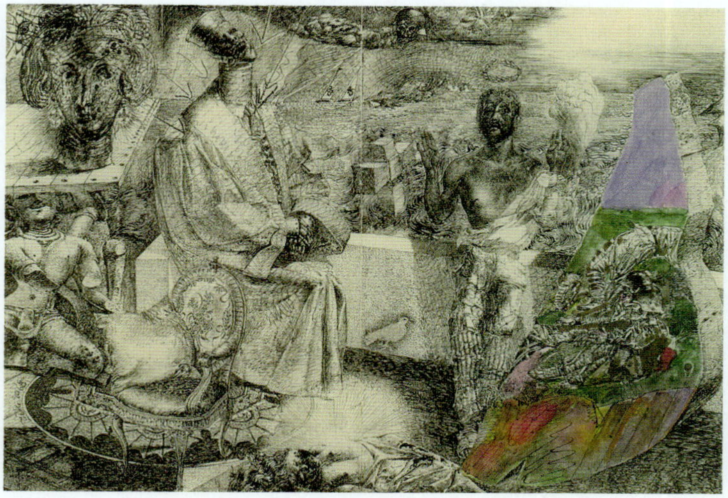

222 Werner Tübke, sketch for *Memoirs of Dr. jur. Schulze IV*, 1965, watercolour over pen and black ink.

play *Die Ermittlung* (The Investigation), the trial being the 'radically negative Paradiso of the Divina Commedia project'[237] following Dante. It premiered in October 1965 on the same day in East and West Germany.[238] Tübke's references to photos, however, are integrated in coded form into his painterly monologues.[239] As under the protective umbrella of reproducing from the book of photos, he developed in his paintings, which refer to the tradition of realism of early panel painting, his reinterpretations of the art-historical models and of photography.

The change of media between the arrested moment of the photograph and the painting suggests an overcoming of time and the detail identifiable within it. Even though the gestures and the folds simulate snapshots, he painted his pictures on a fluid time scale. 'The art of Tintoretto, El Greco, Veronese are so present to me as though they were my contemporaries. I paint in my way because I have to paint like that. I have no other possibility,'[240] he said in an interview with Emmrich. This concept of painting brought him room to manoeuvre as an artist in the GDR, offered the possibility of distancing himself from a Western avant-garde in the art scene that did not look back to former times, and allowed him to portray in many individual scenes the persecution of the Jews in the *Memoirs of Dr. jur. Schulze* as a historical continuum of cruelty and violence.

Arie Goral: *Warsaw Ghetto*

Tübke's *Memoirs of Dr. jur. Schulze III* (see illus. 207) and Arie Goral's later large composition entitled *Triptychon zum Warschauer Ghetto* (Triptych on the Warsaw Ghetto) (illus. 223)[241] were the only works of fine art hanging in the exhibition *Holocaust* at the Deutsches Historisches Museum in Berlin in 2002. A large-format panel is placed in the centre of Goral's collage, the whole

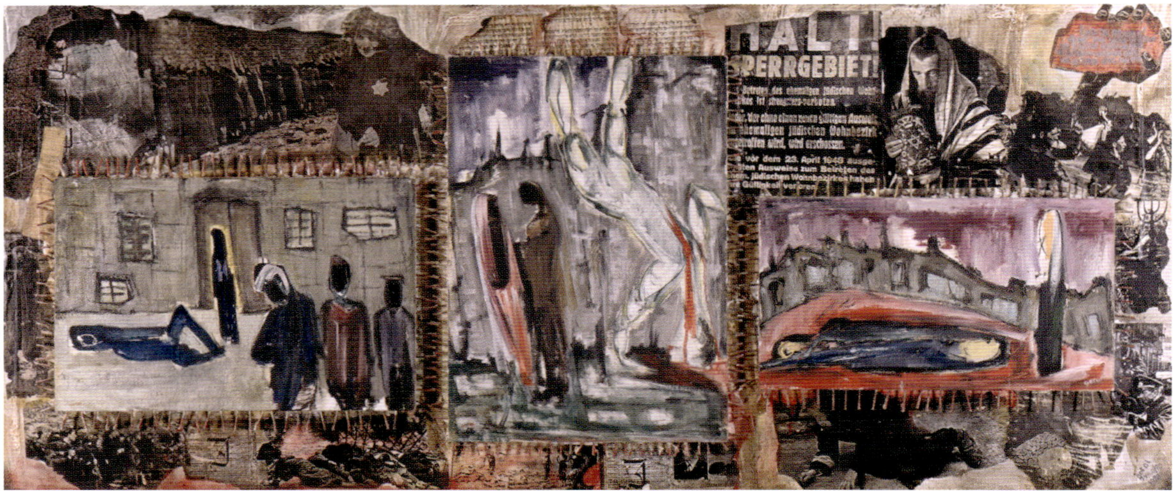

223 Arie Goral, *Triptych on the Warsaw Ghetto*, 1960–c. 1983, collage on hardboard, oil on wood.

right half of which is occupied by the distorted silhouette of the bleeding, naked body of a person hanged upside down. It is painted greenish white. To the left, two women are turning away as if unconcerned. In the background there is a suggestion of the outline of a city. The application comes across as a brutal reference to the picture *Sacrificial Animal and Boatman* (see illus. 148). The rectangular panel on the left shows a person lying on the ground in blue with his left leg bent, a woman passer-by and three figures outlined in the foreground. From the way they are drawn it is difficult to see whether they are grieving, observing or about to move on. On the right-hand panel, Goral painted in blue two dead bodies lying in front of a greyish-blue townscape against a lilac sky, framed by red paint, presumably a reference to Hans Grundig's 1947 commemorative picture (see illus. 114), and a figure on the right standing upright, apparently grieving over the dead people lying opposite. The paintings on all three panels do not on their own give any precise idea about the relevant event. It is only in combination with the background panel, to which the three oil paintings are attached in the form of a triptych and onto the free surface of which Goral collaged photos of the overthrow of the Uprising in the Warsaw Ghetto, that the small paintings can be seen as commentaries both on the Ghetto and on the other photographs of the Nazi atrocities against the Jews. The grid-like framing, caused by the nails placed close together along all the cut sides of the three panels, and showing red paint as well as white all over it, forms a link between Goral's paintings and the pictorial collage on the background panel.

He presumably conceived of this overall arrangement some time after the painted panels. Rommelfanger dates it to the 1980s, whereas the small paintings could have been produced in the 1960s and '70s.[242] At bottom and top left on the background panel, three photos from the Stroop Report are arranged, showing details from the destruction of the Warsaw Ghetto;[243] the large one at the top, 'Search and Interrogation',[244] had a photo stuck partly over it of the old Hungarian Jewish woman Perla Schwarz[245] marked by a Star of David in Auschwitz, from the ss album found by Lili Meier,[246] while the two photos underneath the left panel show inhabitants of the Ghetto herded together and people who had been shot in Warsaw. Between the photos at the bottom, there are two pages from the passport of a Jewish woman with the characteristic Nazi sign 'J' for Jewish. The left side is bordered by the photo of a half-starved camp prisoner after the liberation of Small Belsen (see illus. 202). In 1963 it was hung life-size in the Frankfurt exhibition on the Warsaw Ghetto[247] and was used by other painters such as Gerhart Frankl[248] and Werner Tübke (see illus. 199) as a model for painting and drawing.

The central part is framed at the top by three slightly charred pages with Hebrew text, and at the bottom, by one of the three photos which camp inmates took, under extremely dangerous circumstances, of the incineration of corpses at Birkenau in 1944 (see illus. 225, p. 29).[249] It is situated on the left next to two pages from the passport of a man similarly labelled with the characteristic Nazi sign 'J' for Jew and is to be found along with that of the Jewish woman on the left side on page 120 of the book *Der Gelbe Stern*. While on the extreme right side Stroop's prisoners, a photo probably of a ruined synagogue and the perpetrators are visible, the photo under the small panel of the painting of dead bodies shows an old Jew collapsing in a street in the Warsaw Ghetto and was taken by Ludwig Knobloch,[250] who also captured the Jew with a tallith and a Torah scroll on the top surface of the supporting panel.[251] On the left next to the one carrying the Torah, Goral placed the representation of a sign with the notice forbidding entry to the Warsaw Ghetto without a new valid identity card,[252] and on the right next to the Jew with the Torah, there is a detail from the photo in the Stroop Report of the defenders of the Ghetto forced to surrender.[253] The raised arms of the people about to be shot have towering over them a large, black hand holding a red sign that reads: 'Fight fascism! Remember by your own resistance the Jewish heroes and victims of the Uprising in the Warsaw Ghetto 45 years ago in April/May 1943.'

The collage, made up of oil paintings and photos[254] of the Warsaw Ghetto and other camps becoming well-known again at the time, reveals in the mixture of photographs of various places and times how little account Goral took, albeit in line with the Ghetto exhibition in Frankfurt and many other contemporary publications of photos, of the differences in the course of individual actions in the different camps and over the years. What seemed important instead was the indexicality of the photos from the Nazi period. As a framework, it lent a certain monumental character to Goral's schematic representations of grief, death and torture, which fitted in well with the first public presentation of Goral's picture in the *Freie Berliner Kunstausstellung* (Independent Berlin Exhibition of Art) commemorating the 45th anniversary of the Ghetto Uprising. The small panels are highlighted as representations of the inhabitants of the ghetto and also verified by the photos, and the collage of the action shots frames the painting that exposes the system of violence.

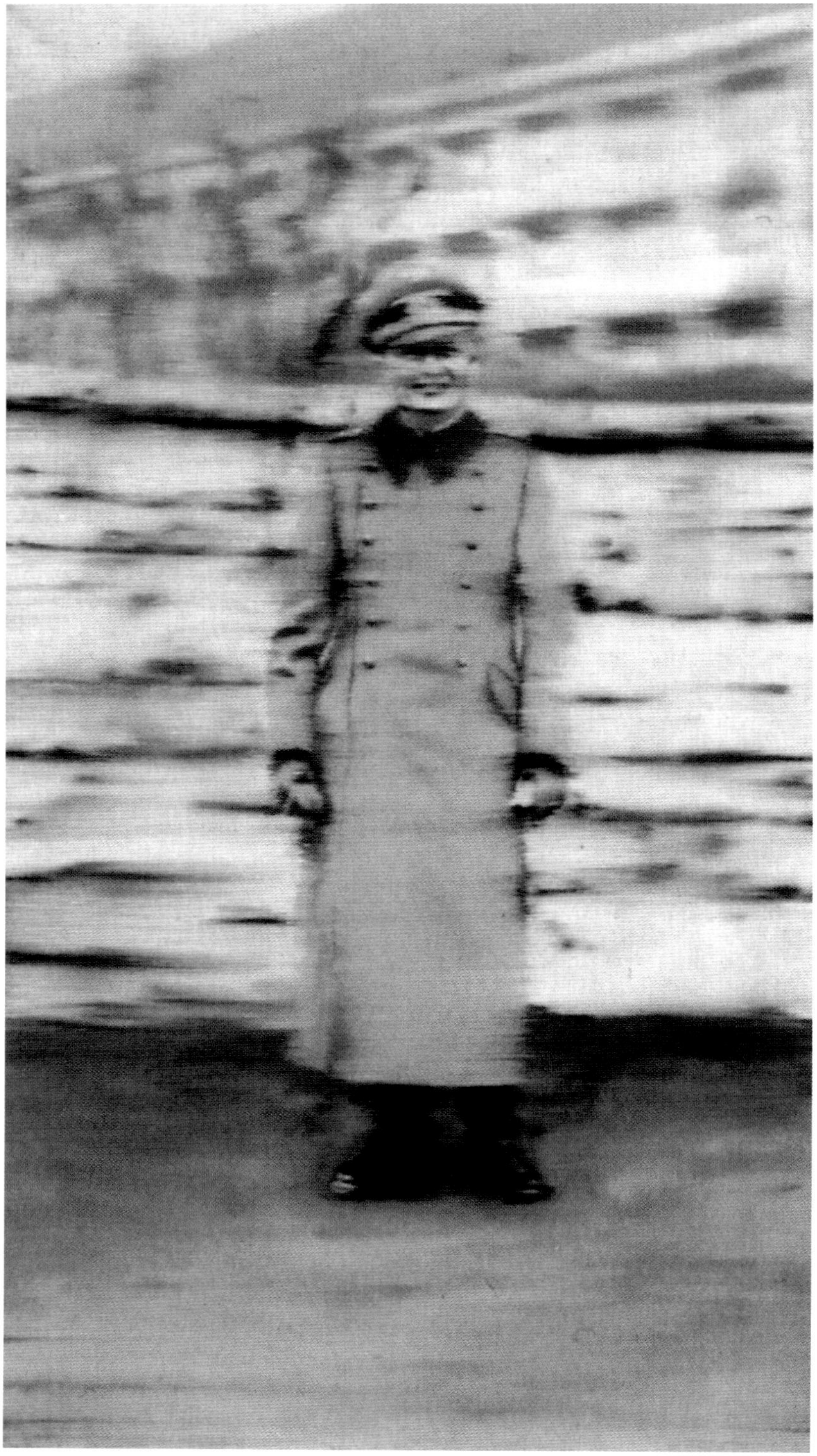

224 Gerhard Richter, *Uncle Rudi*, 1965, oil on canvas.

Out of the documentation of the history of Nazism, Goral developed an object demonstrating in favour of resistance against violence in the present.

Gerhard Richter

While Vostell and Goral obviously copied parts of photos as such into their provocative works and Tübke adapted individual references to Schoenberner's book of photos only in his paintings, in the 1960s Richter placed photography at centre stage of his artistic involvement. Shortly after 1961 when he had fled from the GDR to Düsseldorf, the West German art metropolis, he devoted himself to the unspectacular photographs of mass culture in two ways; he began to set out an *Atlas* of various pictorial worlds, and on canvas he copied large-format paintings photos that he had carefully picked out from the print media and private snapshots of family life.[255]

Richter studied the photographs of the persecution and murder of the Jews during the Nazi period since 1957, but not until 2014 did he represent the subject in oil painting. Nevertheless, for his work with the photographs and his involvement with the subject in the reunited Germany, it is illuminating to go beyond the time frame set here at 1965 and include the present because the exhibitions and reviews of Richter's latest works on the subject of Judenmord have revealed the contrast with the former decades of memorializing. There have been innumerable publications in art, literature and film, and in the meantime the danger becomes relevant that the system of the extermination camps and its function for the Nazi state disappear behind the mass phenomenon of the different narratives.

Uncle Rudi

The history of the Nazis appears in seven out of a total of 65 in Richter's 1965 series of blurred oil paintings based on photographs of everyday and holiday scenes.[256] Due to his unspecific use of titles based on his relatives and their first names, the models for the grisaille paintings were for a long time not questioned as regards their historical significance.[257] The photos used do not include a single picture of the genocide of the Jews but, within the many reproduced photos of post-war society, their amusements and everyday activities, they show individual, also dead, members of his family and the family of Ema Eufinger, his wife at the time. Richter produced an oil painting in 1964 based on a 1959 newspaper photo of *Dr. Heyde* who, as chief of the medical department of the Euthanasia Section under the Nazis, bore joint responsibility for thousands of murders during the Nazi period.[258] Closely associated with this we find the childhood picture of his *Aunt Marianne* murdered on account of schizophrenia,[259] as well as that of *Uncle Rudi*, the lieutenant in uniform killed in 1944 (illus. 224).[260] Paul Jaskot recognized in Richter's choice of such apparently harmless subject-matter for his paintings,

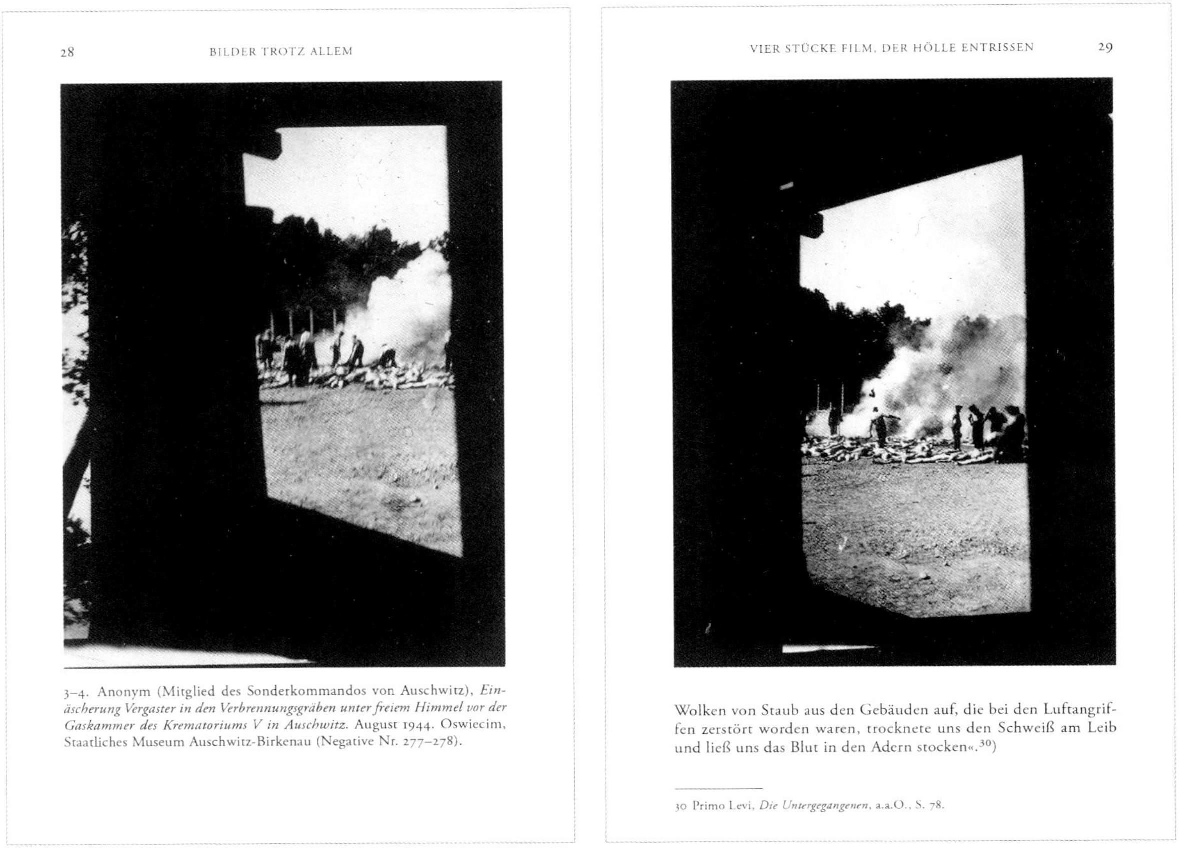
28 BILDER TROTZ ALLEM

3–4. Anonym (Mitglied des Sonderkommandos von Auschwitz), *Einäscherung Vergaster in den Verbrennungsgräben unter freiem Himmel vor der Gaskammer des Krematoriums V in Auschwitz.* August 1944. Oswiecim, Staatliches Museum Auschwitz-Birkenau (Negative Nr. 277–278).

VIER STÜCKE FILM, DER HÖLLE ENTRISSEN 29

Wolken von Staub aus den Gebäuden auf, die bei den Luftangriffen zerstört worden waren, trocknete uns den Schweiß am Leib und ließ uns das Blut in den Adern stocken«.[30])

30 Primo Levi, *Die Untergegangenen*, a.a.O., S. 78.

in addition, a response to the Eichmann trial in Jerusalem and Hannah Arendt's report on the 'banality of evil'.[261] Even more than the Auschwitz trial, which concentrated on the extreme acts of violence committed by the individuals accused, the trial in Jerusalem gave rise, according to Jaskot, to the uncomfortable question about the quite normal perpetrators.[262] The profound involvement of the members of Richter's family in the Nazi past, the fact that they were both perpetrators and victims, only became publicly known later, since Richter did not provide any further explanation of the pictures and concealed this knowledge behind the titles of the pictures and the usual, albeit much revised, interpretation of the theory of photography,[263] at the time describing it ambiguously:

> A photo, as long as it is not 'structured' by art photographers, is simply the best image that I can imagine. It is perfect, it is absolute, i.e. independent and unconditional, it has no style. The photo is the only image that can truly inform . . . I am fascinated by the human, the time-bound, the real, the logical, in an event, which is simultaneously so unreal, incomprehensible and timeless. And I should like to represent it in such a way that the simultaneity is kept.[264]

225 Anonymous, four photographs taken from and outside Crematorium V in Auschwitz-Birkenau, August 1944, publ. in Georges Didi-Huberman, *Bilder Trotz Allem*, Munich, 2007, pp. 28–31.

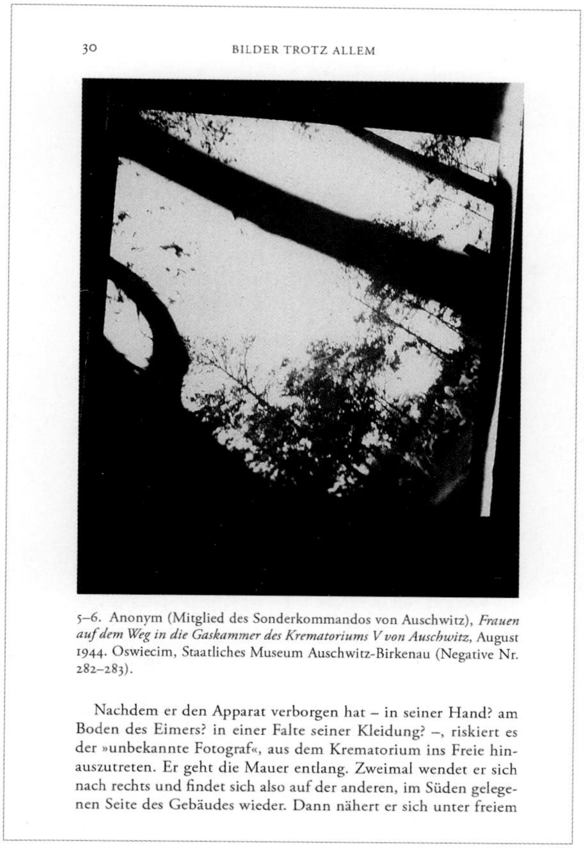

30 BILDER TROTZ ALLEM

5–6. Anonym (Mitglied des Sonderkommandos von Auschwitz), *Frauen auf dem Weg in die Gaskammer des Krematoriums V von Auschwitz*, August 1944. Oswiecim, Staatliches Museum Auschwitz-Birkenau (Negative Nr. 282–283).

Nachdem er den Apparat verborgen hat – in seiner Hand? am Boden des Eimers? in einer Falte seiner Kleidung? –, riskiert es der »unbekannte Fotograf«, aus dem Krematorium ins Freie hinauszutreten. Er geht die Mauer entlang. Zweimal wendet er sich nach rechts und findet sich also auf der anderen, im Süden gelegenen Seite des Gebäudes wieder. Dann nähert er sich unter freiem

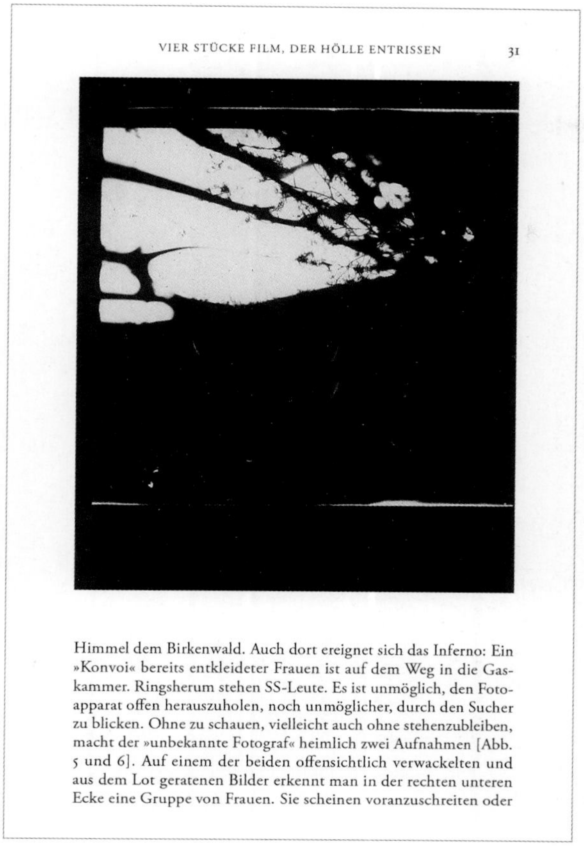

VIER STÜCKE FILM, DER HÖLLE ENTRISSEN 31

Himmel dem Birkenwald. Auch dort ereignet sich das Inferno: Ein »Konvoi« bereits entkleideter Frauen ist auf dem Weg in die Gaskammer. Ringsherum stehen SS-Leute. Es ist unmöglich, den Fotoapparat offen herauszuholen, noch unmöglicher, durch den Sucher zu blicken. Ohne zu schauen, vielleicht auch ohne stehenzubleiben, macht der »unbekannte Fotograf« heimlich zwei Aufnahmen [Abb. 5 und 6]. Auf einem der beiden offensichtlich verwackelten und aus dem Lot geratenen Bilder erkennt man in der rechten unteren Ecke eine Gruppe von Frauen. Sie scheinen voranzuschreiten oder

Simultaneity, thought of as periods of time merging 'timelessly' into one another, is particularly relevant in the case of the painting *Uncle Rudi*. According to Richter, with the 'unpleasant wall'[265] it points towards the continuity of the exclusion of people and the readiness to shoot them. The mounds of the wall visible in the photo, consisting of rough blocks,[266] were so blurred – Richter only leaves horizontal outlines – that this wall can also be associated with the wall made of smooth concrete in Berlin and the simultaneity 'is kept' in the form of a vision of the Second World War and the Cold War.[267] In the foreground Richter, as in the photo the painting was based on, showed the dead brother of his mother in dress uniform made to 'look like a hero' in the eyes of his family, as being 'young, charming, happy, vain in this uniform'. 'All round, straightforward. A regular chap,'[268] is his commentary on the choice of photograph on the occasion of the exhibition in Hamburg in 2011. The fact that Richter put this painting in the 1967 exhibition *Hommage à Lidice*[269] reveals his political judgement on the Nazi past and the crimes of the Wehrmacht; his commentary comes across as particularly provocative due to the copying of photographic documents of what is familiar.

Richter confronted the viewer with an allegedly authentic reality;[270] at the same time the media shift to prestigious art heightened the significance of the photographed everyday life. The painting became authenticated by the photograph still shining through, and in the painting, the banal acquired an aura. The private albums that Richter referred back to in exposing the 'banality of evil' did not attract public attention until the 1990s.[271] Thus indeed, in what was for the period an unusual manner, his oil paintings made public the presence of photographs of the perpetrators and the murdered in families, handed down from generation to generation, and he published them at a time when the perpetrators were standing trial, not just in the Eichmann and Auschwitz trials but in the second Treblinka trial in Düsseldorf as well. What was being publicly remembered in the trial was able to be linked to what was present in one's private thoughts about people but which did not become the subject at issue. Richter's paintings have a longer-lasting effect in exhibitions and postcards[272] than ephemeral press photos and television images, and they can draw people's attention, once more and continually, to the question of perpetrators within their own families.[273]

Atlas

In the 2011 documentary film *Gerhard Richter Painting*,[274] a copy of a photo of Auschwitz-Birkenau is visible on the studio wall in front of Richter's desk (illus. 226). Alex, a Greek man, took it, under extremely dangerous circumstances, from the gas chamber in Crematorium V at Birkenau to capture the disposal of gassed prisoners in the open-air incineration pits in front of the gas chamber of the crematorium (illus. 225, p. 28).[275] It hung in the studio in one shot in the film between the study of a head by Picasso and a picture of

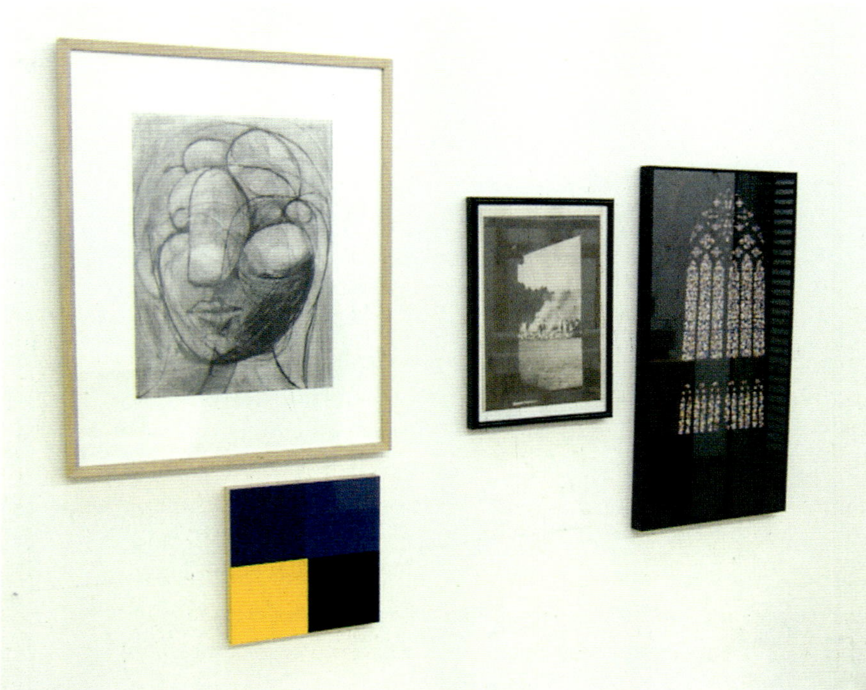

226 Still from *Gerhard Richter Painting* (dir. Corinna Belz, Germany, 2011).

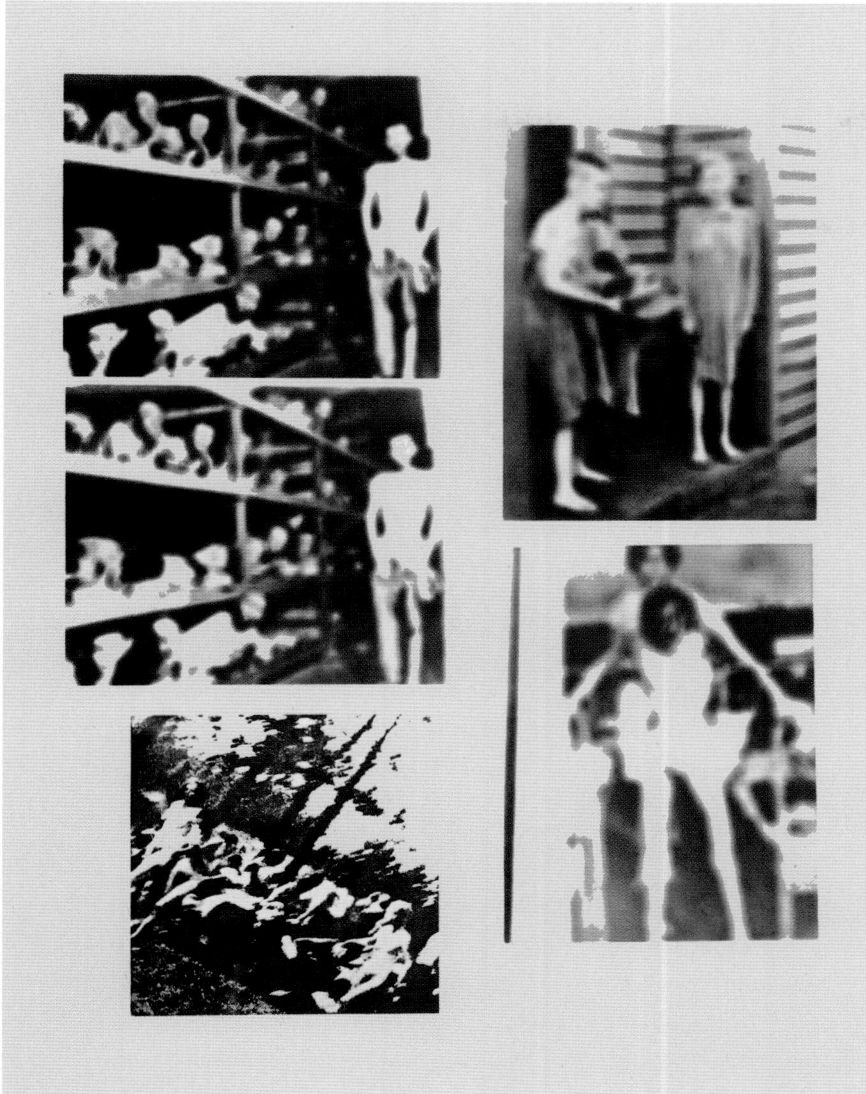

227 Gerhard Richter, *Photographs from Books*, 1977, 5 clippings in black and white, *Atlas*, sheet 19.

the stained-glass windows in Cologne Cathedral. In a later scene, the Picasso study of a head had been exchanged for another, unidentified picture. The enlarged reproduction of the photo from Auschwitz has a white passepartout and a black frame and, according to what Richter said, in such a version it became a 'new object'.[276] He had already known it for years and the review of the publication *Bilder trotz allem* (Images in Spite of All) by Georges Didi-Huberman in the *Frankfurter Allgemeine Zeitung* of 11 February 2008, which deals exclusively with this and three other photos taken under the same terrifying circumstances by the Greek Alex, made him once again aware of it. He had it cut out and framed and it[277] was on his mind for years to come. For the artist it has a particular significance as he described during the filming:

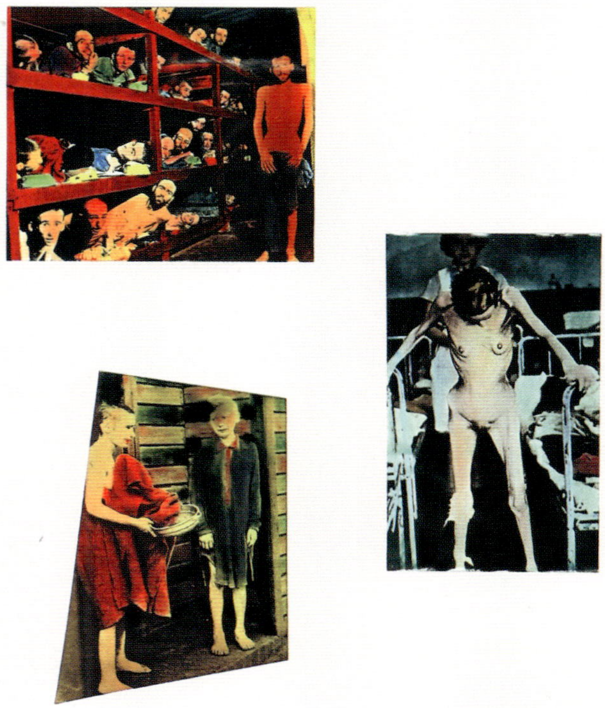

228 Gerhard Richter, *Photographs from Books*, 1967, 3 clippings in black and white, coloured, *Atlas*, sheet 20.

> RICHTER: And that is a crazy photo . . . I find it fascinating, because it looks so peaceful, so normal. If you look at it, they have – I don't know – nice people are chatting here. These are the Sonderkommando who have to incinerate the bodies. I can't tell you any more than that. It's crazy, how he keeps his balance here, acting as if walking on logs so normal.
>
> QUESTION FROM OFF-CAMERA: Can you remember when you first saw anything like that?
>
> RICHTER: At the Academy, right at the start, an American documentary, but not one smuggled, someone had it, and we looked at it and it has stayed with me ever since: images, reports on the atrocities.

While still in the GDR Richter had touched on Jewish history during the Nazi period in his works, producing in 1957 twelve drawings in ink on the subject of *Anne Frank* (see illus. 137 and 138). It was presumably also that time that he spoke about in a 1989 interview in the context of the Baader Meinhof

Gang. Asked by Jan Thorn Prikker whether he believed from the start that it was possible to paint the subject of terrorism, he answered:

> There was the desire for it to be possible to paint it, a need for it to be painted. But there were subjects that were not. When I was in my mid-twenties, I saw photos of the concentration camps which affected me very much. In my mid-thirties I collected them, photographed them and tried to paint them. I had to give it up. Then I put the photos together remarkably, seemingly cynically, in my *Atlas* of images.[278]

Exactly ten years after the ink drawings of *Anne Frank*, Richter arranged on sheets 16 to 20 of the *Atlas* a total of 23 photos of the murder of the Jews, of which the last eight photos on sheets 19 and 20 (illus. 227–8) are repeats of those on the previous sheets, with only one photo of the *Sonderkommando* at Birkenau newly added (illus. 225).[279] Richter's vague subtitle *Fotos aus Büchern* (Photographs from Books) can be used to identify them as being all from Schoenberner's book,[280] and remarkably, with the exception of the view of the barracks at Buchenwald after the liberation (see illus. 213) shown on pages 19 and 20, Richter chose a totally different selection than did Tübke two years previously. He did not select any photos of the resistance of the Jews during the Uprising in the Warsaw Ghetto to which Tübke had referred, but instead used the photos unaltered, which starkly show the mocking and the suffering of the Jews, the executions, the survivors and the dead.

Richter hardly took account of the historical process of persecution and murder of the Jews during the Nazi period, something which was dealt with by Schoenberner in eight stages over 212 pages as a development fraught with consequences.[281] He combined photos from different places and years, immediately illustrating the attack on the bodies of the persecuted Jews: whether this is the completely emaciated survivors in the camps (sheets 16, 18, 19, 20), or the humiliating denigration of female desire (sheet 16)[282] or the pillorying mutilation of the men (sheet 17), or facing the firing squad made up of Nazi marksmen shooting at undressed male and female Jews (sheets 17, 18) or the many corpses (sheet 18). Richter chose to make the series disjointed using a medium that freezes the moment and has always been associated with death,[283] documenting the murder via photographs of living as well as dead Jews. It could be that, in selecting these, he was also thinking of the metaphor, frequently used after the liberation of the camps, of the 'living corpse' or the 'living dead'.

Richter's out-of-focus new shots from photographs in sheet 19 (illus. 227), already published in sheets 16 and 18, add to this impression. The survivors become anonymous skeletons, and the blurred and duplicated photo by Private Miller of the camp inmates still alive on their bunks in Buchenwald now comes across as a view into a charnel house full of skulls. The photo at bottom left is clearly set apart. It is the detail from another photo by the Greek Alex which, taken during the daily murdering of thousands of people in August 1944, shows undressed women running into the gas chambers of Crematorium v in Birkenau (see illus. 225, p. 30). His lack of focus resulted from a technical inability to photograph while terrified to death.[284] Richter juxtaposed the reproduced original, its being out of focus giving it the status of documentary, with photos of the surviving camp prisoners at their liberation, in which he transferred his blurred painting technique into the medium of photography, it being the only one he did not alter. By being juxtaposed, similarities and differences become clear. The blurring of the frequently reproduced images photographed by perpetrators and liberators resembles that of the photo taken from the crematorium of the camp, and their all being generally out of focus on this sheet refers to the inconceivability of all events photographed. The wobbly photo from Birkenau, which Richter did not make any change to, comes into its own focus, however, in comparison with the other three reproductions. It seems as though Richter did not wish to expose this photo to the process of remembering and forgetting suggested by his paintings based on photos and by the other photographic reproductions on sheet 19 of the *Atlas*. In the case of all the photos on this sheet, none of which came from illustrated magazines or family albums, it could hardly be a question of the representation of the banal, and the extent to which the indexical character of the photos as documents could bear witness threatened, not just to be blurred, but even to be effaced. Possibly Richter here was exposing the danger that, through his commentaries 'as a painter', the photographs of those who had been abused and murdered might be defused and precisely the very thing that should be remembered might be made banal. On the following sheet, no. 20 (illus. 228), showing again some of the photographs that had already served as models in a different combination, Richter was no longer working with reproducing them out of focus, but experimented with cutting them diagonally and giving them gaudy colours; here he did not include the photo from Birkenau. Sheets 16–20 of the album document Richter's attempt to represent the crimes committed in the camps by reworking publicly available photos. The next six hundred sheets do not contain any more reproductions of camp photographs.

The fact that Richter and his fellow painter Konrad Lueg around 1966 planned another work with the photos of tortured and murdered Jews is documented by sheets 21ff. with the title *Photographs from Magazines*, following on directly from the photos of the murder of the Jews and exhibited alongside one another.[285] Dietmar Elger reports that Richter and Lueg prepared an exhibition for the Galerie Niepel in Düsseldorf which was to show documentary photos from the concentration camps of the Third Reich and pornographic images from cheap magazines under the title *Sex and Mass Murder*.[286] The photos of the camps shown on sheet 20 'in penetrating Pop colours',[287] reproduced there for the third or in part the fourth time, are supposed to have originated in connection with this plan that was abandoned again 'after some time'. The two artists, who happened to be studying Pop art from America at the time, were here in line with a concept that the American countercultural movement of Pop art, NO!art and in particular Boris Lurie, a camp survivor of Buchenwald, had already been carrying out in his collages by 1963.[288] It was not just the scandal, however, that this combination of images would have caused in Germany,[289] that made them distance themselves from it. As Richter in 2002 explained: 'I didn't see any moral or formal solution to how the camp and the porno pictures could have been exhibited . . . we would have caused a fuss, but it would have been particularly unprofitable, inappropriate – at least inappropriate.'[290]

Richter did not keep quiet about the project, however, but documented the intention in the *Atlas*. His selection of the photos of the murder of the Jews and the accompanying porno photographs draw a parallel with extremely obscene attacks on the female body, a composition attacking above all the scopophilia of the observer. The concept, admittedly not realized in the Gallery but shown in the *Atlas*, becomes a document of a period about which Ruth Klüger commented: 'And there was something resembling the pleasure at pornography about the interest at the time in the Holocaust which had not yet been given that name.'[291]

Black Red Gold

Thirty years later Richter added about two hundred other reproductions based on photos of the murder of the Jews in sheet 635 to sheet 646 of his *Atlas*, in connection with the commission to create a work of art for the former Reichstag that would become the building for the Parliament of the reunited Germany in Berlin. This time, unlike in 1967, he did not work with photos of ravaged bodies, but with pictures of marching columns of imprisoned men and women. Richter had sifted through other sources of images for this purpose. He was experimenting with this design at a time when the debate across the whole of Germany about erecting a *Memorial to the Murdered Jews of Europe* had reached a decisive phase and it seemed to be for certain that the abstract form of it would conceal the documentary element.[292] In the 'Kunst-am-Bau' ('Art for the Building') project, funded with 70 million Deutschemarks distributed among 26 artists by Götz Adriani and Karin Stempel, he and Sigmar Polke had been allocated the most prominent of sites, the side walls near the main Western entrance. In sheets 647 to 649 of the *Atlas*, Richter's original plan is published, setting up four 'large-format grey images' based on concentration camp photos on a narrow white wall made of large, brick-shaped stone plates in front of the elevator and right next to the entrance.[293] The model for the upper and the lower image is a photo published in 1995 from Lili Meier's album of the SS in Auschwitz; it shows a group of women in camp work clothes with a pregnant one at the front in the centre.[294] The second picture from the top also comes from this album

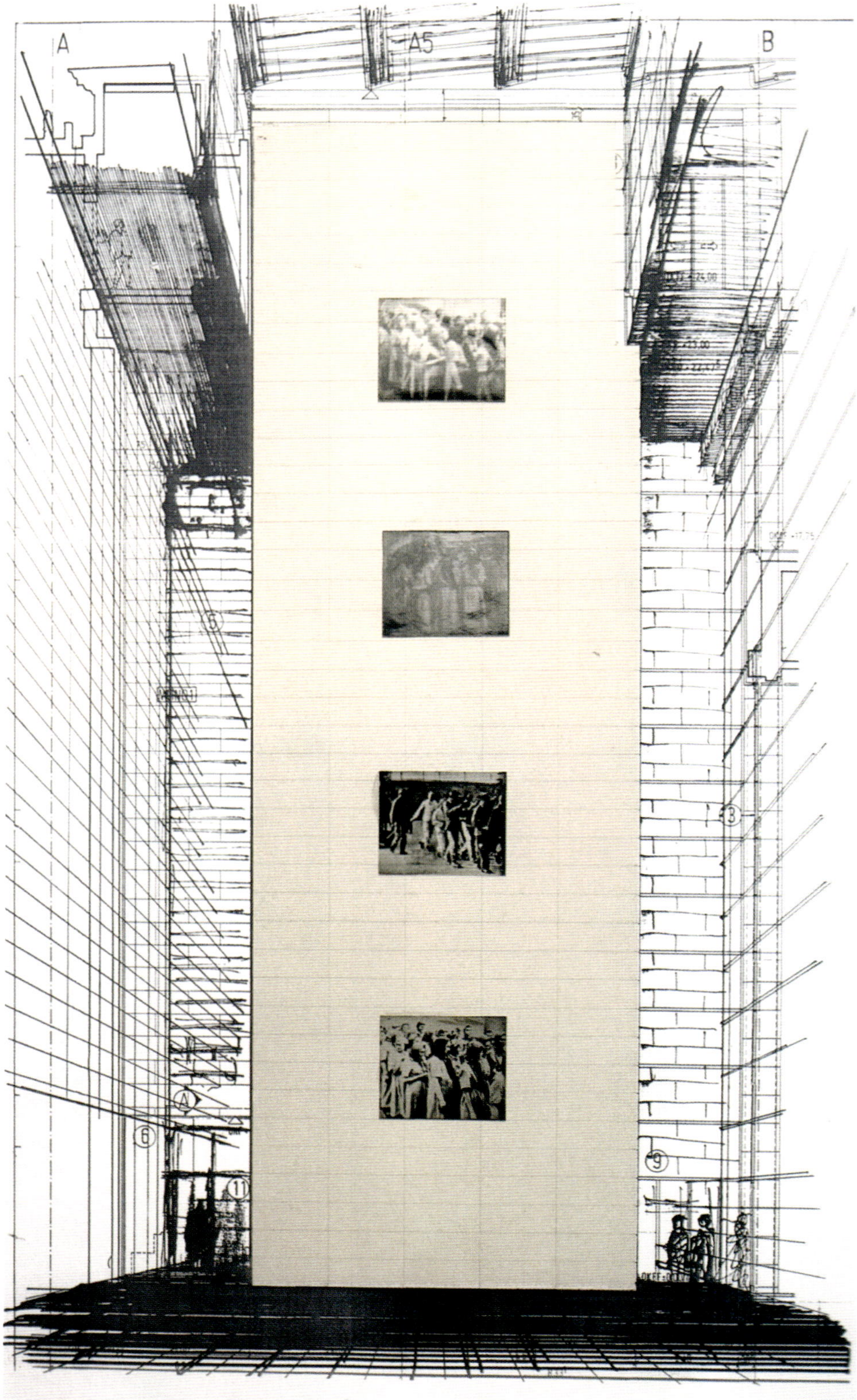
A
A5
B

230 Gerhard Richter, *Black Red Gold*, 1998, enamel on glass, 6 plates.

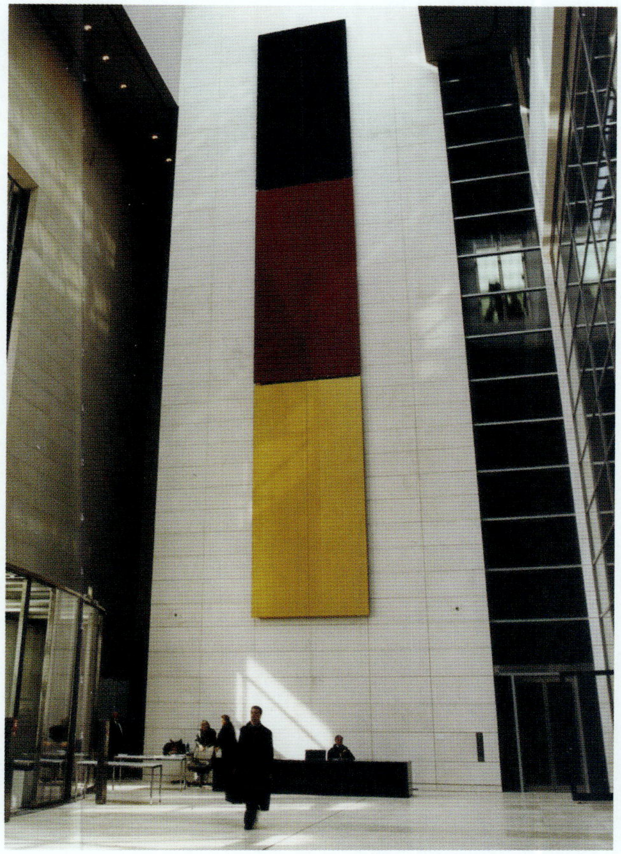

and shows women with headscarves 'After De-lousing', seen from the front. In the third position Richter placed the photo, shown several times in the *Atlas*, of the procession accompanied by music to the execution of the captured prisoner Bonarewitz at Mauthausen (see illus. 169) already used by Vostell.

The planned composition on sheet 648 can clearly be made out (illus. 229). But Richter abandoned the concept: 'Perhaps it was shame or pity or piety that held me back. I never figured it out,' he said in an interview in 2002.[295] Instead, he tried out various colour-field paintings using square and tall rectangular forms (see sheets 650–55). In the end he decided to place enamelled glass plates in the three colours, like the title of the work, recalling the flag of the Federal Republic.

Given the background to Richter's process of decision making, which can be looked up on the Internet and in the publication on the art of the Reichstag,[296] the *Black Red Gold* surfaces composed of six plates (illus. 230) on a white wall in the Bundestag building function as a blind in front of German history.

229 Gerhard Richter, *Reichstag*, 1997, sketch with four pictures, *Atlas*, sheet 648.

Birkenau

Richter carried out the commission of the Federal Government at a time when the debate around the *Memorial to the Murdered Jews of Europe* was occupying

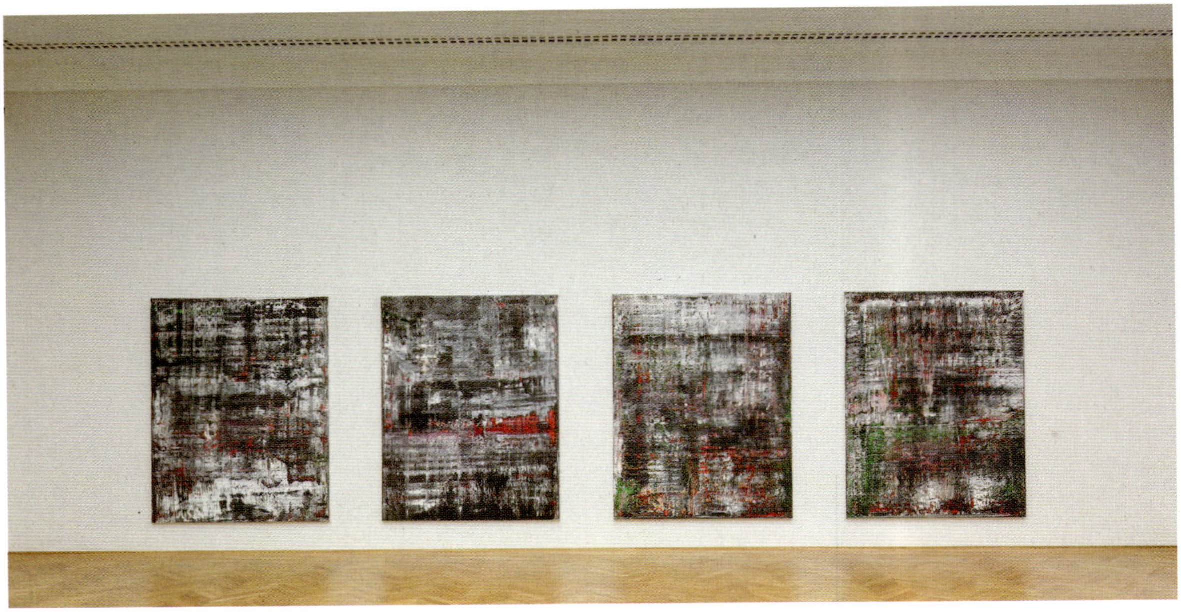

231 Gerhard Richter, *Abstract Pictures (937/1–4)*, 2014, oil on canvas.

considerable public attention and Martin Walser was warning of a 'moral cudgel' in his controversial speech at the award ceremony of the Friedenspreis des Deutschen Buchhandels in October 1998 at the Paulskirche in Frankfurt. Not until almost fifteen years later, when the memory of the Holocaust had become generally uncontroversial, did Richter once again confront the subject and the problem of representing it. In this work too, he totally concealed the photos that he had previously partly depicted on the canvases. Richter was in doubt but nevertheless copied the four photographs from Birkenau camp, taken under extremely dangerous circumstances (see illus. 225), onto the canvasses, finally realizing that 'it was not possible'[297] and that, once again, on none of the paintings would a photograph from Birkenau be recognized. Even more assertively than in the case of *Black Red Gold*, he made public the process by which he had discovered the images and permitted the subject photographs to be published along with photographs of the four canvases, still white and with only their priming coat.[298]

Finally in February 2015 he exhibited four *Abstract Pictures (937/1–4)*, their published titles at the time, at the Galerie Neue Meister in Dresden (illus. 231 and 232). A press release for the opening had made clear right from the start that the works were devoted to Birkenau; in later exhibitions and publications, first in the reproductions in matt printouts (*Birkenau 937/1–4, B*) exhibited at the Festival in Manchester,[299] they had this very title. In the volume of images in 2015, Richter wrote about all four canvases in the singular: '93 details from my picture *Birkenau*'.[300]

Richter had already in 1967 included a photo which belongs to the series from Crematorium v in an enlarged detail in his *Atlas* (see illus. 227); and since 2008 a framed cut-out has hung in his studio. For the year 2013 he documented

232 Gerhard Richter, *Birkenau (Abstract Pictures 937/3)*, 2014, oil on canvas.

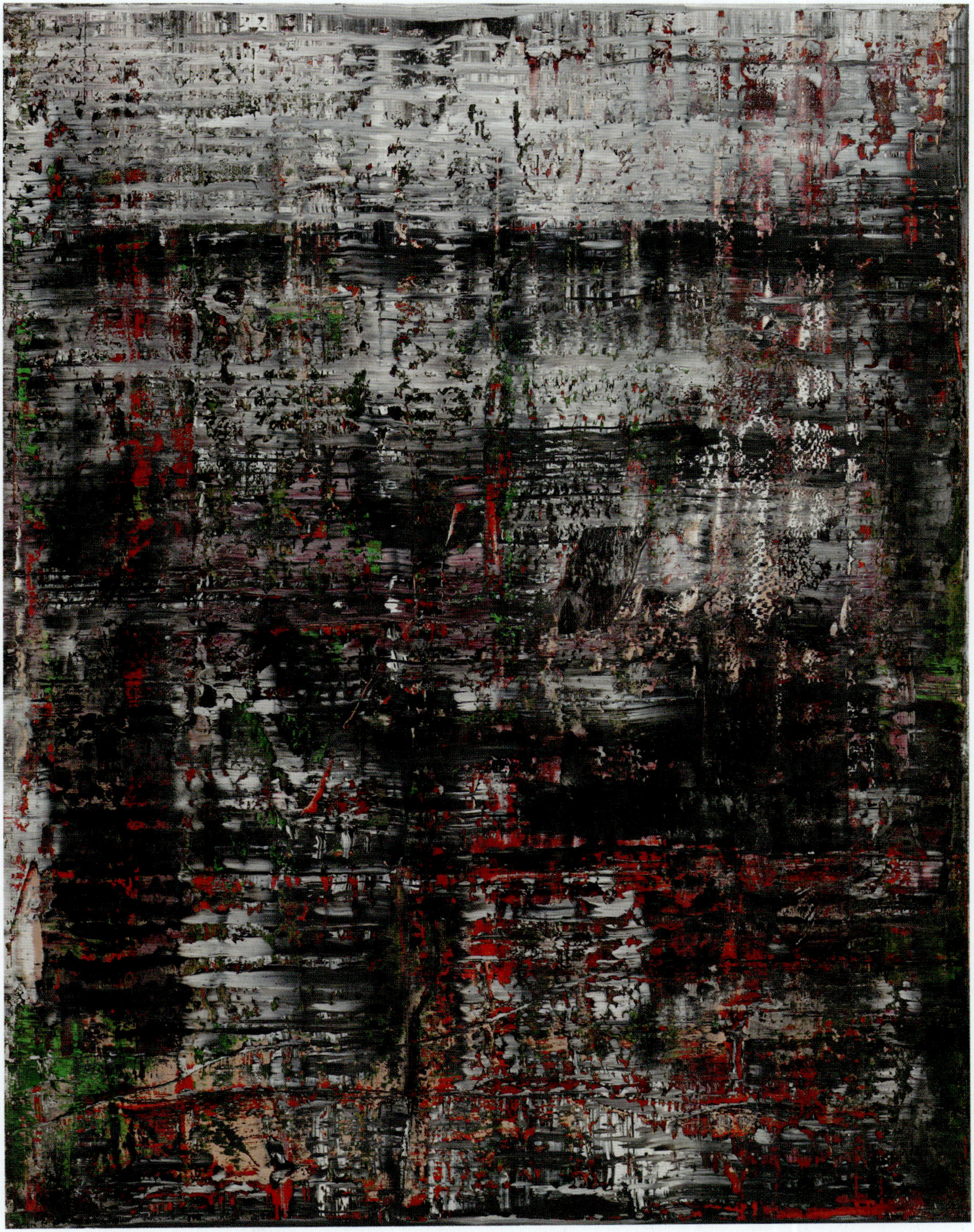

that he had started to work again on the representation of the murders by adding two sheets with studies of all four photographs to his *Atlas.*[301] When Georges Didi-Huberman visited Richter on 19 December 2013, he saw the empty canvases in his studio,[302] and Richter had also read the book *Borken*[303] about Didi-Huberman's visit to the Memorial Site at Auschwitz-Birkenau. At the exhibition *Gerhard Richter Birkenau* in Baden-Baden in 2016, the photographs were on display along with the oil paintings.[304]

The display of *Birkenau* along with other works by Richter at the Dresden gallery was supervised, if not to say curated, by Gerhard Richter himself and did not celebrate the process of producing the four paintings now called *Birkenau*, as in the Museum Frieder Burda.[305] Quite subtly but nevertheless obviously, it questioned the representation of historical events and, as if rethinking Walter Benjamin's famous thoughts of 1935, the reproducibility of art in the age of digital reprography. The four oil paintings were displayed in a room together with *Photographs based on Abstract Picture (937 1–4)* (2014–15). Didi-Huberman, along with Gelshorn, called them 'Nachbilder' ('copies', literally 'after-pictures').[306] The oil painting and its photographic copy were hung chiastically, that is, confronting one another in opposite order, and thus referring equally to one another.[307] The reproductions of photographs based on paintings, in their turn referring to photos, that are only copies of a snapshot of the crimes, were emphasized by the reproductions hanging on another wall based on 31 monotypes from 1957[308] and a work in grey reflecting the room and the viewer.[309]

Richter's changing of the title in different exhibitions and press releases is fairly remarkable. It was only after the first responses to the 2015 Dresden exhibition that he stopped having additional information published and designated the four abstract paintings a representation of the well-known extermination camp for the Jews. With the 93 details of photos[310] assembled in one volume and their further use on the covers of the book *Memoirs of Holocaust Survivors*,[311] Richter demonstrated another variation on the unavoidable process of reproduction. It can, on the one hand, enhance the significance of the original but, on the other, it is also part of the inescapable technology of reproduction, smoothing out the differences between the painted canvas and the photographic reproduction, between the original and the copy.[312] The four canvases forming one picture (see above) are not shown in their entirety in the two versions made public; the collection of the fragments highlights the fact that the work on the subject of Birkenau will always remain partial.

The viewer cannot recognize in the paintings that the artist had initially depicted photographs of Birkenau from the viewpoint of the terrified prisoner taking the photograph.[313] If it had been impossible for Richter to repeat the viewpoint of the Nazi photographer for the Reichstag, surely now he was not in a position to occupy that of the terrified prisoner. The copies of the photos are still present but no longer visible, as Richter concealed the original copy in the course of the summer using brown-grey-black, then green and finally black-grey-white paint layers and then peeled these away again using a squeegee. His 'aesthetics of absence',[314] given common knowledge about the Holocaust, can in the meantime take for granted associations with Auschwitz-Birkenau in the mind of the beholder. In order to decipher the absent presence of the Nazi images in the Reichstag in Berlin, on the other hand, one needs to have done some additional reading such as the *Atlas*, since neither the title *Black Red Gold* nor the shiny surface of the glass plates reveals the paintings initially planned based on the camp photos. In September 2017 Gerhard Richter finally succeeded in confronting German parliamentarians and visitors to the former Reichstag building with the German past in almost the same way as he had planned in his first design for *Black Red Gold* from 1998 and had then rejected. Four reproductions of *Birkenau*, a version D, similar to the one placed by Richter in the first exhibition in Dresden in 2015 across from the preliminary versions of them, are now hanging as a gift from the artist in the Reichstag and specially printed for the occasion. They occupy the north wall of the entrance hall opposite the panels of *Black Red Gold* on the south side and, just like them, are displayed in front of a white wall. Unlike the way they were hung in the previous exhibitions they are arranged vertically in the same way as the pictures from photographs of concentration camps in the never completed design of 1998 (see sheet 648, illus. 229).[315] This makes a clear statement against the revival of nationalism in Germany and in many other countries of the world, and against anti-Semitism as being still not confined to history. 'Anyone wishing to enter this site of German democracy, must pass this way – between Birkenau and the national flag', is how Norbert Lammert, President of the German Parliament, put it at the presentation on 4 September 2017.[316]

The knowledge that the photographs from Crematorium v are present is, in the paintings as well as in the mounted diasec prints entitled *Birkenau*, an integral element of the pictures, lending specific importance to the way they are painted, since the four paintings reveal over and over again the process of their production in the chalky dull colouring. Either this happens by tearing the paint into shreds and causing black holes, or earlier layers are breaking through again, forming vertical and horizontal bands and streaks of paint reminding one of the bunks in the camp sleeping quarters. They also make one think of the flaky bark of birch trees, after which Birkenau is named, as Didi-Huberman illustrated on the cover of the book *Borken* (Barks).[317]

Richter worked on the canvas, alone in his studio and without a commission, as though he was on an archaeological investigation with and within the paint. It is left up to the viewer to relate the specific colours white-grey-black-green and red to Birkenau and the mass murder of the Jews, to interpret the canvases as scraping away at the layers of history[318] and to reflect on his or her shreds of memory.

References

Introduction

1 Müller-Hill 2012, p. 121.
2 Fischer/Lorenz 2007, pp. 38f., and the debate about the photographs, sparked off once again around Didi-Huberman 2001: Wajcman, p. 47: 'Il n'y a pas d'images de la shoah . . . La shoah est irreprésentable' (There are no images of the Shoah . . . The Shoah cannot be represented), and Pagnoux 2001.
3 McCloskey 2009.
4 von der Bey 2000.
5 On its being banned in West Berlin in 1947 see Müller 1980.
6 On the attempts to impose this subject-matter through state commissions, exhibitions and university appointments, see Schütrumpf 1995 and Mathews 2006, particularly pp. 123–33, 'Socialist Realism and the Formalism Debate'.
7 This is typical of the tradition followed by art historians in the post-war period; see Friedrich, J. et al. 2013, as criticized by Fuhrmeister in the same volume.
8 Buchloh 2001, pp. 84f., talks about 'disavowal' and 'repression'; Fuhrmeister 2013, p. 237, about 'modernism as refuge'.
9 Amishai-Maisels 1993.
10 See McCloskey 2009; Amishai-Maisels 1993, p. 32.
11 Kuhirt 1982 and 1983.
12 Cat. Zwischen Krieg und Frieden 1980.
13 Ibid., pp. 14f.; both Hans Grundig's *To the Victims of Fascism 2* (see illus. 114) from 1947 and Horst Strempel's *Night over Germany* from 1946 were referred to in the catalogue, but could not be displayed in the exhibition. According to the exhibition handout, the only works displayed that are also commented on in this volume were Barz, *Inferno*; Geiger, *12 Years*; and Pankok, *Gelsenkirchen Memorial* and *Back from Auschwitz*.
14 In this context, especially the collection by Gerhard Schneider, see Cat. Entdeckte Moderne (Discovered Modernity) 2008 and Cat. Expressive Gegenständlichkeit (Expressive Figurativity), 2001.
15 Gillen, E. 1995, 1997, 2002 and 2009. Cat. Kunst und Kalter Krieg 2009; Cat. Art of Two Germanys 2009; on the cycles see Präger 2010.
16 This neglect meant that Andreas Huyssen was able to claim in 1993 'that in the visual arts (unlike literature) concern with the fascist past, even in the late 1960s, was almost totally absent'. Huyssen 1993, p. 138. In the same volume (Köppen 1993) Mittig deals with the problem of memorials since the 1950s.
17 Cat. Representations of Auschwitz, p. 7.
18 Köppen/Scherpe 1997.
19 Eitz/Stötzel 2007; Fischer/Lorenz 2007 mention photography, film, recent memorials and Art Spiegelman's graphic novel *Maus* (1986).
20 Kramer, S. 2003a.

21 'Aktuelle Symbolisierungsstrategien im Umgang mit dem System Auschwitz', pp. 171–98.
22 Wladyslaw Strzeminski, *To my Friends, the Jews*, 1945–7; Jean Fautrier, *Sarah* from the series *Otages*, 1944; Barnett Newman, *Stations of the Cross*, 1958–64; and Joseph Beuys, *Auschwitz Demonstration*, 1958–64 (see illus. 180); Buchloh 2016, p. 10.
23 Vogel-Klein 2010.
24 Braese 2001.
25 See Klüger 1994, pp. 9–38; Hahn 2005, pp. 46–72, which includes consideration of visual media. For the GDR see bibliography in Kirchner 2010.
26 Cat. Stunde Null 1998, p. 5.
27 Engler 2012, pp. 173 and 176.
28 Cat. Die Sammlung 2014.
29 Wahnsinnige Harlekine vor den Trümmern des Krieges (*II*) (Harlequins Raving at the Devastation of the War (II), 1945/51, illustrated at bpk-images.de/shop-site.
30 *Composition jaune*, 1947, illustrated at bpk-images.de/shop-site.
31 Klee 1988, III, p. 366, No. 952.
32 *Der Hai*, 1955, illustrated at bpk-images.de/shop-site.
33 *Invasion der braunen Tiere*, 1947, illustrated at bpk-images.de/shop-site.
34 *Eisheiligentag*, 1952, and *Pfingstlag*, 1952,
35 *Selbstbildnis*, 1946, illustrated at bpk-images.de/shop-site.
36 Illustrated in Knigge 1998, p. 131.
37 Sculpture *Strike*, 1950–52, Cat. Lörcher 1988, illus. 25, No. 17.
38 Particularly useful in this respect was Held 1981; it does not deal with the murder of the Jews, however.
39 The majority of the sculptural works are memorials, see Hoffmann-Curtius 2002a and 2010; no Jews are represented except on the 1948 Warsaw memorial to the Ghetto Uprising, and the concentration camps are mentioned on the inscription only in the case of the 1949 memorial in Hamburg.
40 Herding 1988, p. 292.
41 Held 1981, p. 364; the titles of the pictures purchased by museums in Germany, pp. 367–82.
42 Maximilian Feuerring, 'Kunstausstellung der Displaced Persons', *Prisma*, 1 June (April 1947), pp. 33f.
43 See works by Johannes Steyer at chgs.umn.edu/museum/responses/steyer (12 March 2014); on the persecution see Hacke 2011.
44 See e.g. American Office of War Information 1945. Hahn 2007, pp. 54–6, develops the generalization of the role of victim as early as 1946 in Wolfgang Staudte's Film *Die Mörder sind unter uns* (The Murderers Are Among Us), which only indirectly characterizes Herr Mondschein as a Jewish survivor.
45 Levy/Sznaider 2001, p. 68, with the explanation that this was not the case because of lack of information, but was due to a lack of cognitive framework such as that provided by the term 'Holocaust remembrance'.
46 Alain Resnais, *Nuit et Brouillard* (Night and Fog), France 1955–6.
47 On the vagueness of references or lack of mention of the murder of the Jews despite its being common knowledge among the population of West Germany, see the summary of the literature in Halbinger 2010, pp. 81–90.
48 Eitz/Stötzel 2007, pp. 166 and 101–14.
49 On the history of the term Eitz/Stötzel 2007, pp. 318–41; Wenk/Eschebach 2002, pp. 20f.
50 Agamben 2003, pp. 25–8.
51 Atze 2004, p. 645.
52 Welzer et al. 2002.
53 Arendt 1951/86, p. 446. Further examples in Agamben 2003, p. 36. Levi 1993, pp. 85f., talks of 'Muselmänner' who were the actual witnesses: 'Those condemned to death would never have written down any witness statements, even if they had had pencil and paper, as their death had already begun before the extermination of their bodies.' See for example Miller's photograph and the references to this and other photos in Werner Tübke in *Memoirs of Dr. jur. Schulze II* and *III* (see illus. 203 and 207) and the studies on this as well as Gerhard Richter's *Atlas Sheets* (see illus. 227 and 228).
54 Hartewig 2000, pp. 436–42, outlines the use of the word *Todesfabrik* (death factory) in communist vocabulary after the liberation of Lublin in 1944; it is likely that it influenced the choice of title for the film *Todesmühlen* (Death Mills) as in American usage 'mill' can mean both factory and mill. See Wiesenthal 1946: 'the death factory is working incessantly, day and night'.
55 On the role of photography in German remembrance, see Brink 1998 and 2000; Knoch 2001, pp. 237–47, reports on the collection and publication of the many photos of the persecution of the Jews by the survivors in diaries, camp newspapers, albums and exhibitions immediately after 1945; see also Cat. Mémoire 2001; on films see Weckel 2012; Egyptien 2012.
56 Leo Haas was invited with his drawings as a witness in the Theresienstadt (Terezin) trials; see Wagner, W. 1987, p. 155.

57 Vismann 2011, pp. 241–6.
58 Barthes 1984, pp. 87 and 96, emphasis in the original.
59 Longerich 2007 sees the root of this refusal as an unwillingness to admit knowledge of the 'open secret' in the Nazi period.
60 Stroop 1943/2009.
61 This is also the case for Richter's 2014 *Birkenau*, included in this English edition.
62 Godfrey 2007 in *Abstraction and the Holocaust* mentions in relation to the 1950s only the two American artists Morris Louis and Barnett Newman.
63 Gillen, E. 1995, pp. 27–47, indeed, points to the 'refusal to comment on the part of the black pictures' (p. 31) by abstract painters, but still comes to argue that 'only around 1960 did artistic engagement with the mental rejection of the recent past begin' (p. 30).
64 Monika Wagner outlines the 'path of suffering' of colour, see Wagner 2001, pp. 42–6.
65 Cat. Vernichtungskrieg 1995.
66 Brink 2007.
67 For details see Brink 1998, pp. 146–77, and Brink 2007.
68 Fritta was commenting on shots taken in the making of the Nazi propaganda film *Theresienstadt – Ein Dokumentarfilm aus dem jüdischen Siedlungsgebiet* (Theresienstadt/Terezin – A Documentary Film from the Jewish Area of Settlement); see also on the background to the production of the film Cat. Theresienstadt-Konvolut 2002.
69 Wagner, W. 1987, pp. 101–19. Fritta's drawings prompted allegations of portraying a false image of the camp and the suspicion that they had been distributed outside. They led to a trial by the SS under Adolf Eichmann over the drawings and Fritta was transferred, along with Leo Haas, to the notorious 'small camp' at Theresienstadt and then on to Auschwitz, where he died on 5 November 1944 in the hospital block. The first exhibition devoted to Bedřich Fritta was at the Jewish Museum Berlin in 2013; see the review by Markus Huth, 'Zeichnen, was zu sehen ist' (Drawing What is There to See), in *Die Tageszeitung*, 1 and 2 June 2013.

1 Prequel Images

1 Thanks to Hildegard Frübis for extensive advice about this chapter and Yael Rosenmann for the translations of the Hebrew and Yiddish texts.
2 Schedel 1493/1975, pp. ccxx (verso), ccxxx (verso), cclvii (verso).
3 Approximately 1,500 pogroms were carried out in 1,300 locations. Issachar Ber Ryback in his Pogrom Series portrayed the events in his home town of Yelizavetgrad (Kirovograd); the watercolours were shown in 1924 in Berlin. See Meidler-Waks 2012, as well as the illustrations in Cat. Transit 2012, 3.1–9.
4 On the significance of these pogroms for Zionism and their effects on art and literature see Cohen 1998, pp. 223–55; Penkower 2004, pp. 187–225; Jockusch 2012, e.g. pp. 19f.; Weik 2015, pp. 162f.
5 Neugebauer 2003, pp. 47ff. points out the increase in the use of the motif of flight in the nineteenth and twentieth centuries, in the context of those cycles of pictures 'taking as their subject-matter the terrors of violent power struggles'.
6 see Amishai-Maisels 1993, illus. pp. 19f., illus. 45, Cohen 1998, pp. 230–34, and Weik 2015, pp. 75–82.
7 See Weik 2015, pp. 229–31; Cat. Steinhardt 1959, Nos. 13 and 14.
8 See https://de.wikipedia.org/wiki/Hep-Hep-Unruhen#/media/File:Hep-hep_riots.jpg.
9 See Cat. Steinhardt 1995.
10 Cat. Liebermann 1979, No. 482. In the Russian provincial town of what was then Bessarabia in April 1903, 46 per cent of the population were murdered, that is, 50,000 Jews; see Penkower 2004, p. 187.
11 See Kathrin Hoffmann-Curtius 2015.
12 See Grundig 1958/1978, p. 175.
13 On this topic also: Cat. Art from the Holocaust 2016, pp. 234f.; it remains unclear whether the drawing dates from before or after the start of the war on 1 September 1939.
14 Yud Zayn 10 Chesvan Tarzat 5699.
15 After 1945 there is only one sketch by Horst Strempel with this title; see bildindex.de (7 March 2016).
16 On the debates in the camps for displaced persons see Holian 2011, pp. 153–84.
17 Jockusch 2012, p. 144.
18 Jockusch 2012, in particular pp. 141–7.
19 Yerushalmi 1988, p. 22.
20 On the authors see Jockusch 2012, p. 265, n. 162.
21 Ibid., p. 142.
22 Vesalius 1543/2014, vol. 1, p. 323.
23 Weik 2015, pp. 114–18; Cat. Le Juif errant 2001, pp. 158f.
24 Illustrated in Cohen 1998, p. 232, illus. 117 and wikipedia.org/wiki/file:Kishinev_Martyrs.jpg (4 February 2016).

25 Jockusch 2012, p. 144.

26 This is the Yiddish term derived from the Hebrew *churban* for the genocide of the Jews prior to the term Holocaust; see Jockusch 2012, p. 3. n. 2; on Khurbn-Forshung see Jockusch 2012, pp. 18–45.

27 Rajner 2011 and Rajner/Cohen 2015, further representations of pogroms in Amishai-Maisels 1993.

2 The Human Figure, 1945–9

1 Klemperer 1947, p. 140.

2 See Walser Smith 2008, pp. 24ff. for discussion of the Holocaust in historiography.

3 Semprun 1997, pp. 198ff.

4 Details of the re-education and re-orientation measures Brink 1998, pp. 40–93, Goldstein 2009. A view of 1945 with photographs of the time is also available in Schirmer/Frei 2015.

5 Analysis of *Die Neue Zeitung*, 27 November 1994–1 September 1945, *Berliner Zeitung* and *Neue Zeit*, 21 May 1945–31 September 1945, *Frankfurter Rundschau* 1 August 1945–31 September 1945.

6 On the biography see www.hall-of-fame-sport.de (12 January 2016). The stadium, again available for use, was opened with the ceremonial placing of its urn at the entrance to the stadium and a memorial ceremony. Remembrance of the communist resistance fighters was overturned by the Federal Republic, and with the start of the Cold War the stadium was renamed the Neuköllner Stadion in September 1949. Not until 2004, after the reunification of the two German states, was it once more named after Seelenbinder.

7 Illustrated in http://berlin.vvn-bda.de/wp-content/uploads/sites/3/2013/06/Septemberheft-OdF-2011-08-24kl.pdf, p. 17 (7 March 2016).

8 See the table of concentration camp insignia in the period 1936–44 in Bundesarchiv, Bilddatenbank: Bild 146-1993-051-07.

9 See *Berliner Zeitung*, 11 September 1945.

10 Strempel was a Communist and emigrated to France in 1933 where he was interned several times after 1939. He returned voluntarily to Germany, was imprisoned by the Gestapo and finally released to take part in the war. Details of his biography in Saure 1990.

11 Pointed out by Saure 1992, p. 85. Saure refers to a picture that has disappeared (WVZ 176, p. 272) and emphasizes that 'Strempel aimed to portray a Jewish family'.

12 Illustrated in Cat. Deutsche Kunstausstellung 1946; see also Wilhelm Lachnit, *The Death of Dresden*, 1945, illustrated in Kuhirt 1982, illus. 1.

13 The booklet 'Lest We Forget' published in London in the *Daily Mail* in 1945 describes how visits to the concentration camps had been part of leisure activities: 'And sometimes the local population, in their off-hours and on Sundays, would come to peer and jeer through the wires and throw in bits of offal to see the skeletons scramble' (p. 6, statement by Lord Vansittart on 1 May 1945). 'Germans living near these camps told Farr that they "had no idea such things were being done" – but Nordhausen civilians, out for a walk with their girls, used to go near the "extermination centre", point out the prisoners and crack jokes about them' (p. 16).

14 See this subject in the case of Zielezinski (illus. 83) and Brock (illus. 154).

15 *Die Todesmühlen* (Death Mills), Germany/U.S. 1945, directed by Hanuš Burger, adapted by Billy Wilder, produced by Information Control Division (ICD), newsreel department; on the background of the Office of Military Government for Germany United States (OMGUS) see Weckel 2012, pp. 151–72; on the production of the German text by Oskar Seidlin, pp. 611–15.

16 Edel 1983, No. 14, with the remark: 'Based on sketches from Auschwitz, drawn at the end of 1944 in Sachsenhausen concentration camp. Berlin, in the papers left by the regional rabbi Dr Martin Riesenberger.'

17 Manuscript for the Bergen-Belsen report of 15 October 1945, p. 2, quoted in Bayer/Wagner 2012, unpag.

18 See Hoffmann-Curtius 2010, in particular pp. 126ff.

19 In German an anachronistic term for people of Islamic faith, used in the concentration camps. Wittler 2013, see also Amishai-Maisels 1993, p. 19.

20 *Neues Deutschland*, 17 April 1947, review of the exhibition *Horst Strempel* at Galerie Franz, Berlin.

21 *Neue Zeit*, 21 October 1947, review of the exhibition *Meistenverke deutscher Bildhauer und Maler* (Masterpieces by German Sculptors and Painters), Berlin.

22 N. Orlow: 'Wege und Irrwege der Kunst', *Tägliche Rundschau*, 20 January 1951, with illustration of the left-hand panel, reprinted in Cat. Zone 5, p. 123.

23 See www.horch-und-guck.info/hug/archiv/2000-2003/heft-39/03904-Strempel (21 March 2012).

24 May/Obenau 2016, p. 255.
25 Cat. Nationalgalerie 1986, p. 8; included in this canon were Hermann Bruse (see illus. 110), Hans Grundig (see illus. 114) and Heinrich Ehmsen (see illus. 123); see also Cat. Die Schwarzen Jahre 2015, pp. 250–55.
26 Scholz, D. 1991.
27 Hans Grundig, *The Thousand Year Reich*, triptych with the panels *Carnival* (1935), *Vision of a Burning Town* (1936), *Chaos* (1938) and *The Sleepers* (1938), illustrated in Olbrich 1990, pp. 270f., 352.
28 Saure 1992, p. 272, No. 173–87.
29 Saure mentions '9 Paraphrases'.
30 Most probably it was already exhibited in the 'anti-fascist exhibition "niemals wieder" (never again)' in Vienna in 1947, which Edel took part in with his concentration camp drawings. See Schieber 2007, p. 51.
31 See Edel 1979.
32 Cat. Kunst in Auschwitz (Art in Auschwitz) 2005, p. 362.
33 Edel 1947.
34 Actually her real name was Lieselotte Reichmann, whom he married in 1941. Schieber 2007, p. 51.
35 Edel 1983, No. 12, 'Esther the wife murdered in Auschwitz of the author, drawn in the winter of 1943' Edel's Autobiography from 1979, p. 623, on the other hand and with reference Cat. Kunst in Auschwitz 2005, p. 127, gives: 'Peter Edel, Esther Edel, (sic!) 1944, 34 × 52 cm, Private collection.'
36 Jean Fautrier, *La Juive,* 1943, Cat. L'art en guerre 2012, illustrated p. 190; in detail see Haas 1997, pp. 166–74, in particular p. 173; see Hoffmann-Curtius 2008.
37 In the way Edel drew her from Esther's photo in the hospital hut in Auschwitz, he even referred to her very wide nose, the alleged characteristic of a Jew (Edel 1947, pp. 182, 184).
38 Frübis 1997; Feldmann 2012.
39 Illustrated also in Cat. Kunst in Auschwitz 2005, p. 623; Amishai-Maisels 1993, p. 5, illus. 1.
40 Zimmermann 1972, p. 64.
41 Held 1981, p. 177.
42 Presumably the same as *The Nameless Ones*, illustrated in Hofmann, L. et al. 1982, p. 97, illus. 83.
43 *Aachener Nachrichten*, 25 September 1945. Reproduction: Michael Jaspers; thanks particularly to Ulrich Schirbach, Zentralarchiv *Aachener Zeitung/ Aachener Nachrichten* for the helpful research.
44 Cat. Rheinische Secession 1946, Nos. 187–96: *The House for the Jews* (see illus. 24), *They Are Coming* (see illus. 25), *The Synagogue* (see illus. 19), *Sitting Jew*, *Jews in the Street*, *Village Street*, *Violinist in the Ghetto* (see illus. 27) (illus. 1 in the catalogue), *Jewish Cemetery*, *Violinist in the Cemetery*. The exhibition could presumably take place with the help of Werner Doede, head of the Kunstsammlungen der Stadt Düsseldorf, who had an unblemished record and was kindly disposed towards modern art; see Heymer 2013, pp. 56–62.
45 Cat. Pankok 1947 (not in Held 1981), pp. 29–32, copy in the Stadtarchiv Hamburg. In the introduction Ludwig Benninghoff writes in reference to Pankok's representations of the 'suffering of the people who were murdered and maltreated': 'Today it is the suffering of us all, now we are the people who are murdered and tortured' (p. 12).
46 Cat. Pankok 1948.
47 See the crudely defamatory publication *Der Untermensch*, put out by the ss in 1942.
48 Pankok Werksverzeichnis 3, pp. 17–22.
49 Hofmann, L. et al. 1982, p. 19. Pankok left behind a large number of works that still ought to be more thoroughly researched, including around 6,000 charcoal drawings which he himself regarded as charcoal paintings and for which there is no catalogue of the oeuvre.
50 Cat. Berlin Transit 2012, p. 51, No. 2.19; on the photographs of the Berlin Scheunenviertel see Pilarczyk 2012.
51 Pankok, having used Friedrich as early as 1937 as a source for his 'pacifist' drawings *Liquidated* and *Extinguished* (see Hofmann, L. et al. 1982, pp. 70, 76), is mentioned by Overbeck/Müller 1995, p. 210.
52 Four men standing on a pavement in front of a shop window with Hebrew letters, in place of the advertisement for 'Sunlight Soap' in Gircke's photograph 'The Jewess', 1943, illustrated in Cat. Pankok 1961, p. 63.
53 Renamed Almstadtstrasse in 1951, http://berlin.kauperts.de/Strassen/Almstadtstrasse-10119-Berlin#Geschichte (12 September 2013).
54 *Illustrierter Beobachter*, Edition 31, 1939, p. 1206, quoted from Franco Fratini 1999, illustrated on p. 114.
55 Cat. Rheinische Secession 1946.
56 Cat. Pankok 1946/47.
57 Pankok, Hulda 1955.
58 On the concentration of Düsseldorf Jews in 'Judenhäuser' (House for the Jews) from 1941 see Schmidt 2005, pp. 85 and 92.

59 There were estimated to be 1,000 of them: see Ulrich Herbert, 'Leben oder Tod ist keine akademische Frage', *Frankfurter Allgemeine Zeitung*, 6 March 2013, No. 55, p. 27. On the desperate conditions in the 45 'Judenhäuser' in Hamburg and the life of the Jews in the overcrowded rooms there, see Grenville 2012, pp. 247–50.
60 Overbeck/Müller 1995, p. 275 from 20 June 1948.
61 Pankok WVZ 2, WR 656; Pankok WVZ 3, WM 216; Cat. Pankok 1968 WP 118.
62 In existence there are another large charcoal drawing of 1941, showing a violinist standing with bended knees in the street in the ghetto, a woodcut of the same year and a 1954 monotype of this subject. All three are illustrated in Pankok WVZ 3, 1995, pp. 8f., illus 1, 2 and 3.
63 Illustrated in Cat. Pankok 1993, p. 164.
64 Cat. Chagall 1959, No. 43, *Violinist*, 1911–14.
65 Else Lasker-Schüler in a letter to Hulda Pankok, 10 August 1933, Lasker-Schüler 1969, p. 150, describes him as having more beard than face.
66 See the juxtaposition of *Self-portrait* and *Violinist in the Ghetto* in Hofmann, L. et al. 1982, pp. 92–3.
67 Here I am keeping to the term 'Sinti' used by Hulda Pankok and the Catalogue 'Sinti-Porträts' 2008 (Cat. Pankok 2008).
68 Cat. Pankok 2008, see in particular pp. 204–13.
69 Pankok 1958, p. 8.
70 Zimmermann 1972, pp. 43f.
71 See for example illus. 28.
72 Pankok 1958, p. 9.
73 Ibid., p. 8.
74 Ibid., p. 9.
75 Pankok 1947, Introduction pp. 7f, while in the new foreword to the second edition (Pankok 1958) he predicted their disappearance once more due to 'cold, hard-hearted mercantilism' and technology: 'The cities will devour them in the end lock, stock and barrel.' And Pankok criticized the 'incredible rules set up by the police' (p. 5). In West Germany, as Reuter describes in 2012, the criminalization of victims succeeded right up until the 1970s, as did letting the guilty off the hook.
76 Hofmann, L. et al. 1982, p. 22.
77 There is a surprising similarity between the portrait reproduced in Cat. Lingner 1988, No. 47, p. 75, *Old Jewish Woman in the Concentration Camp*, tempera on canvas, of 1947 by the press artist Max Lingner, at the time living in France 'as a recognized immigrant anti-fascist German', and the portraits of Sinti by Otto Pankok. The portrayal of a woman looking distraught is unusual for Lingner, but not for the period.
78 Cat. Pankok 2008, p. 232. Only in this recent publication has 'Gaisa in front of the wall' been added to the title, altering the subject of the picture, presumably in order to distinguish it from the other pictures of her by Pankok. Comment by Pankok on Gaisa after her return from the concentration camp, ibid., p. 222.
79 'In the concentration camp she had children several times by the guards,' Zimmermann 1972, p. 68.
80 Pankok brought an end to the business and threw him out of the window. Cat. Pankok 1993, pp. 174f.
81 On this whole question see Schwelling 2011.
82 Cat. Am Anfang 1986, p. 32.
83 Ottomeyer/Czech 2009, pp. 321f.; Hoffmann, D. 1998, pp. 58–61; Marcuse 2001, pp. 192–4; Hoffmann-Curtius 1996a, pp. 293–6.
84 See Hoffmann-Curtius 1996a, pp. 284–7.
85 See in this context Hoffmann, D. 1998, p. 58, illus. 40 and 41.
86 In the case of the photographs in Ebensee, an external camp of the concentration camp at Mauthausen, the camera ends the sequence with a recreation of the Mercy Seat. Moving from the two prisoners standing in the centre, who in the previous scene were carried and supported by a third, the shot only pans towards the father-like one doing the carrying and one of those being carried.
87 Besides criticism of Koelle's activities as a sculptor during the Nazi period, the accusation arose, according to Hoffmann, D. 1998, p. 59, of 'plain Naturalism', and the survivor Hans Schwarz, according to Marcuse 2001, p. 478, n. 39, did not want to see the horror prolonged forever.
88 This pose was also given by Taslitzki to the central figure in his oil painting *The Little Camp at Buchenwald*, 1945, Amishai-Maisels 1993, colour plate 14; according to Antelme 1947/1992, pp. 9ff., it was strictly forbidden for camp prisoners.
89 See Hoffmann-Curtius 1999a, 2002 and 2010.
90 Verspohl 1990, pp. 36–44; Verspohl 1987.
91 Later Pinchas Shaar, brief biography in Shapiro 1999, p. 293; Jockusch 2012, pp. 128–59, here also for the first time an illustration of the poster as a frontispiece.
92 Jockusch 2012, p. 143, see also p. 320, note 26.
93 Shvarts had already worked with collage in Lodz before the war; see Shaar 1999.
94 Shaar 1999, p. 134, illus. 8. Shaar had got this from a photographer friend in the Lodz Ghetto, Mendel

Volkman, who was shot in the last days of the war. Grossman, in his effort to record everything, had resorted to secretly capturing in photographs as many as possible of the ghetto dead.

95 Quoted in Jockusch 2012, p. 142.

3 Early Series

1 Feuerring had survived as a Polish soldier in a POW camp near Murnau; 52 members of his family including his wife and parents had been murdered in a concentration camp; for a bibliography see http://judaica.library.usyd.edu.au/histories/artists.html (28 May 2013). A painter belonging to the 'Neo-Humanists', he did not choose subjects from the period of the extermination of the Jews for his pictures and exhibited his own works at the DP exhibition. The illustration in tempera of a female 'Half figure' is brought together on the same page in the review with Zielezinski's charcoal drawing *When Will It Be My Turn?*, *Prisma* 1, 6 (April 1947), pp. 33f., illus. p. viii.

2 *Prisma* 1, 6 (April 1947), p. 34.

3 Even in retrospective exhibitions of graphic art devoted to the war they were ignored; see the gap in the Cat. Schrecknisse des Krieges 1983.

4 *Majdanek Death Camp – The Cemetery of Europe*, directed by Aleksander Ford, USSR 1944, announcement in the *Berliner Zeitung*, 10 August 1945. Weckel 2012, pp. 93–9. On this and the following Soviet films see the remarkable study by Hicks 2012.

5 *Berliner Zeitung*, 10 August 1945.

6 *Auschwitz: Film Documents of the Monstrous Crimes of the German Government in Auschwitz*, dir. Elizaveta Svilova, USSR 1945; Weckel 2012, pp. 99–105.

7 *Berliner Zeitung*, 14 September 1945.

8 Directed by Roman Karmen and Elizaveta Svilova; USSR 1946. Review in the *Berliner Zeitung* from 21 March 1947. Version from the 1960s, supplemented by pictures from the Bonn Republic and Nazi officials still in office there (see the campaign in the GDR pp. 224–6) in Russian available on YouTube (21 August 2017): www.youtube.com.

9 Directed by Marc Donskoi and Boris Gorbatov, USSR 1945; shown in New York in 1946 with the title *The Taras Family* and as *Taras* in 1947 during the Film Festival at the Berlin Haus der Kultur of the USSR; see *Neues Deutschland*, 12 December 1947.

10 Quoted in Löser 2012, p. 309.

11 Held 1981, p. 14.

12 Introduction to the exhibition, quoted in Cat. Zone 5, p. 236.

13 See Hoffmann-Curtius 2002a.

14 On the development and function of graphic art in the GDR see Kuhirt 1982, pp. 169–84.

15 On the graphic works by émigré Jewish artists produced after the war the basic source is Neugebauer 1997.

16 Präger 2010; as Präger is preparing a publication on all the graphic cycles about the crimes of the Nazis produced in the years immediately after the war, only a few key examples are dealt with here.

17 Hahn 2005, pp. 37f.

18 See Gorny 2012.

19 Maas 1990, vol. IV, pp. 206–14, Senior Editor Johannes R. Becher. After the invasion of the Soviet Union and particularly towards the end of the war, the journal published less literary material and more political news and commentary.

20 Lustiger 1995.

21 See summary in Hartewig 2000.

22 Amishai-Maisels 1993, pp. 131–54.

23 On her imprisonment in Nazi Germany and her flight see Heiner 2016, pp. 41–52.

24 *In the Valley of Slaughter*, drawings by Lea Grundig, Kibbuz-Hame'uchad (United Kibbuz), Tel Aviv 1944. The German edition edited by Liebmann is in parts rather free in its use of Grundig's English titles.

25 See Schätzke 1996a and b.

26 Grundig, L. 1947, p. 7; on the 'brief reviews' of *Im Tal des Todes* in East and West Germany see Schätzke 1996a, p. 58, n. 13.

27 The Expressionist writer, who during the Nazi period had been excluded from the Reichsschrifttumskammer and became secretary of the Kulturbund after 1945, also wrote the Introduction. On Liebmann see Streubel 1982.

28 Liebmann in Grundig, L. 1947, pp. 8f., and Neugebauer 2004, p. 75; on Arnold Zweig see Schätzke 1996a, p. 58, n. 12.

29 Liebmann in Grundig, L. 1947, p. 8.

30 Ibid., pp. 9f.

31 The extension of the iconography of the pogrom to the representations of the murder of the Jews by the Germans was discussed in Amishai-Maisels 1993, pp. 19, 21ff. and 73ff.; see also Neugebauer 2004.

32 Amishai-Maisels 1993, pp. 45f. and 74f. In addition Grundig was able to look at photos of those

murdered, e.g. in the newspaper *Al Hamishmar* from 23 July 1944, p. 2.
33 Neugebauer 2004, p. 76.
34 Chaim Nachman Bialik, *In the City of Slaughter*, see Amishai-Maisels, p. 75.
35 Ibid., p. 75; see Cat. Steinhardt 1995.
36 New Soviet documents 1943, illus. 10, following p. 33, bodies of Soviet prisoners of war who died in a fascist camp.
37 On the liberation of Majdanek as seen by Communists in exile see Hartewig 2000, pp. 436–42.
38 See also Lea Grundig, *In the Gas*, 1949, watercolour, Jewish Historical Institute in Warsaw, illustrated in Feist 1975, pl. 5.
39 Amishai-Maisels 1993, p. 44, and Kantor 1987, introduction, unpag.
40 According to Chéroux 2001a and 2001b it was not a straightforward matter for the Nazis to see and photograph simply what was happening in the gas chambers. Chéroux describes the debate that took place in France in the 1990s about how one was to deal with any photos that possibly existed.
41 Liebmann in Grundig, L. 1947, p. 36.
42 In cinemas from 16 November 1948, script by Gustav Kampendonk from an idea by the Jewish producer Artur Brauner, who survived the war underground, directed by Eugen York, camera: Werner Krien, cccFilm Berlin/West, ref. in www.cineholocaust.de (6 May 2013).
43 In the publication mentioned by Amishai-Maisels, New Soviet documents 1943, p. 10.
44 On the use of photographs as trophies and signs to ward off evil see Hoffmann-Curtius 2002b.
45 Gillen, E. 2005a, p. 66; on the differing positions of Hans and Lea Grundig see Gillen, E. 2002, pp. 342ff.; see also Schätzke 1996a, pp. 60–64.
46 Amishai-Maisels 1993, p. 75.
47 Ibid., p. 98.
48 Grundig, L. 1958/1978, p. 285.
49 Ibid., p. 287.
50 Amishai-Maisels 1993, p. 98, wrote in her summary that Jewish artists who had not been in concentration camps 'tended to require more distance between themselves and the subject both visually and thematically and rarely made direct comments'.
51 Grundig, L. 1958/1978, p. 287.
52 Brüne 1996a, p. 48, nn. 153 and 154.
53 Ibid., p. 51, n. 162.
54 Amishai-Maisels 1993, p. 25, was the first to analyse Lea Grundig's part in the development of the iconography of the horrors of this murderous event and called her 'one of the major non-inmate documentary artists of the Holocaust'; on the reception history of Grundig's drawings about this subject see also Brüne 1996a, pp. 40f.
55 Along with other pictures about the persecution of the Jews and landscapes in Palestine, see Cat. Grundig 1949.
56 Hoffmann-Curtius 2010, pp. 141–3.
57 Amishai-Maisels 1993, p. 103.
58 Something emphasized by Amishai-Maisels 1993, p. 103, and in addition in the other faces she thought she recognized Hans Grundig and friends. For the type of heroic fighter pure and simple, see Cat. Kunst im Dritten Reich 1974, pp. 195f.
59 See the view of Jerusalem in Schedelsche Weltchronik 1493, fol. xvii.
60 Illustrated in Hütt 1969, p. 22.
61 See Amishai-Maisels 1993, p. 103.
62 Ben Shem 1947; many thanks to Ayatala Laufer for the translation from Hebrew. Nündel 1986 quoted the German title used by Grundig, *Hinter den Mauern der Ghettos* (Behind the Walls of the Ghetto), p. 19. Access to the edition was kindly provided by the University Library at Tübingen, the only publicly accessible one in Germany.
63 Whether this book was seen as a children's book at the time is not clear. On the twenty children's books that Grundig illustrated while in exile, see Heiner 2016, pp. 64–83.
64 Weinbaum 2010.
65 See here Wenk 2003.
66 Petrowskaja 2014, p. 166.
67 Entry stuck into the Akademie der Künste archive of Grundig 320/1, typescript: 'Potsdam, 1956, Bezirksmuseum: 4 Kompositionen aus dem "Ghetto-Zyklus", Hunger, Kommandeuse' ('Potsdam, 1956, Local Museum: 4 Compositions from the "Ghetto Cycle", Hunger, Female Kommandant').
68 *Al Hamishmar*, 11 May 1945, p. 12; and as enlarged single photo in *The Palestine Post*, 13 May 1945, p. 4; in Schoenberner 1960, p. 206, they are referred to as 'Die Auschwitzer Aufseherinnen' (the female Auschwitz guards). This photo has also received much attention in Germany, having shattered the usual association of violence with maleness and showed these women in a particularly negative light in comparison with the hundreds of male concentration camp guards; see Hoffman-Curtius 1996b, pp. 64f.

69 The illustration of acts of human sympathy in 'terrifying' images was emphasized by Grundig in *Gesichte und Geschichte* (Grundig, L. 1958/1978), p. 287: 'Innumerable images, and again and again marvellous displays of love, bowing before the gate of salvation through which those seeking protection are fleeing, children along with parents, the weak along with the strong; the most terrible thing and the most beautiful thing that human beings are capable of.'

70 Wagner 1994, pp. 238–42; Cat. Abgestempelt 1999, p. 91. See also *Ahasver* (illus. 93).

71 Illustrated in Hütt 1969, p. 60.

72 Illustrated in Cat. Lea Grundig 1975, p. 71.

73 Ibid., p. 73.

74 Illustrated in Hütt 1969, p. 62.

75 AdK, Kunstsammlung, Lea Grundig 2435.

76 Not mentioned in the essays by Lanwerd 1999 and Hoffmann-Curtius 1999a on this memorial.

77 Illustrated in Hütt 1969, p. 61.

78 Brüne 1996a, pp. 53f.

79 *Terror* (see illus. 57–9), *In the Streets of Poland* (see illus. 51), *The Shooting* (Akademie der Künste, Kunstsammlung, Lea Grundig, 2425), *The Way into the Gas* (see illus. 58), *Children Being Transported to Auschwitz* (illustrated in Ben Shem 1947, p. 109) (Akademie der Künste, Kunstsammlung, Grundig 2427), *Children in Auschwitz* (Akademie der Künste, Kunstsammlung, Lea Grundig 2428), *The White Flag – Germany before the World Court* (see illus. 56).

80 Frommhold 1958.

81 As the order and dates vary in the publications which appeared while Grundig was alive, no indication of the order or the exact dates is given.

82 Hans Grundig, *Über die Technik des Fotografierens* (Im Verhältnis zum Werk des Künstlers), typescript, 2 pages, undated, in Akademie der Künste, Nachlass Grundig V.2.22.042.

83 Cat. Mémoire 2001, p. 106, illus. 138, first printed in *The Illustrated London News*, 28 April 1945.

84 Cat. Mémoire 2001, p. 107, illus. 139, p. 113, illus. 147 of April 1945, which appeared in *Time-Life*.

85 *Nada. El lo dira*; illustrated in Hofmann, W. 2003, illus. 164, p. 174.

86 Lustiger 1995.

87 Annuss 2011, p. 141, shows that as early as 1933 at an event in the Berlin Sportpalast, 100 policemen formed a swastika.

88 Similar to Meidner's charcoal drawing *The Woes of the Messianic Age* of 1938, illustrated in Cat. Meidner 1991, illus. 11, p. 264.

89 *Arbeiter Illustrierte Zeitung*, Prague, No. 22, 31 May 1934, p. 352, illustrated in Cat. Heartfield 1991/92, p. 429, No. 271.

90 Brüne 1996b, pp. 87f., documents the letter of 24 July 1957, in which Lea and Hans Grundig complain to Alfred Kurella about the 'boycott of our work, which is being carried out systematically and – as we see – successfully and is of a political nature'. Lea Grundig's ink drawing *Terror* from the cycle *Never Again!* was published as an illustration to the section about 'The crisis of ugliness', see the article by N. Orlow, 'Wege und Irrwege der modernen Kunst' (Part 2), in *Tägliche Rundschau*, 21 February 1951, reprinted in Brüne 1996b, pp. 85f.; see also Brüne 1996a, p. 55, and Schätzke 1996a, pp. 63ff.

91 The extent to which Meidner was forgotten in post-war Germany may be clear from the following episode: 'Recklinghausen 1960, opening of the exhibition "Synagoga": the speaker mentions Ludwig Meidner and remarks that, if he has survived the Nazi period, he would be able to supply a lot of facts or correct them. At this a little old man in the back row gets up and shouts "Here I am – Meidner!"', quoted in Cat. Herausgefordert 1998, p. 30.

92 Cat. Meidner 1970; Erik Riedel, Jewish Museum Frankfurt am Main, adds further drawings to the cycle under the archive numbers and titles such as *Behind Barbed Wire* or *Herded Together* (email 20 June 2012).

93 Nor does Grochowiak 1966 mention the cycle in the chapter 'Unter der Last des Leids – England 1939', pp. 198–209.

94 This is the translation of the working title used by Meidner in letters of 23 October 1943 (Cat. Meidner 1991, vol. II, p. 474) and 23 October 1949 (p. 281).

95 Riedel 2003, on the massacres p. 242 and illustrated p. 244. The Jewish press in Great Britain continually reported the murders from the beginning of the war in 1939; see Gorny 2012, pp. 176–84. From June 1942 at the latest, the BBC broadcast news about the crimes committed by the Germans against the Jews in Chelmno, Wilna and Belzec that had begun in 1941; quoted in Lustiger 1995, pp. 110ff. etc., as noted by the Ringelblum archive; see Wulf 1960, p. 339. The *Daily Telegraph* published detailed reports on 25 June 1942 about 'the physical extermination of the Jewish population in Poland'.

96 Information kindly supplied by Erik Riedel, Jewish Museum Frankfurt am Main.

97 Some of the drawings are available on the Internet: http://juedischesmuseum.de/lm_werke.html (21 March 2014)

98 Cat. Meidner 1991, vol. II, p. 474.

99 Henkel/Schöne 1967, pp. 174f.; see also, among others, Dürer's images of Hercules and Orpheus in Panofsky 1930, figs 30, 50, 104, 107, 12.

100 Amishai-Maisels 1993, pp. 297–300.

101 *Life*, 7 May 1945, p. 32. Rodger's photographs commissioned for *Life* were published at the same time in the British *Picture Post*, see Rodger 2009, p. 9.

102 Meidner may have seen the photo in *Lest We Forget*, p. 74, or else at the popular exhibition by the *Daily Express, The Horror Camps: Seeing is Believing*, at the end of April 1945 in London; see Schulze, R. 2011, pp. 57ff.; thanks to Klaus Tätzler, Bergen-Belsen, for the information. A booklet of the American Office of War Information, 1945, unpag. published it with the subtitle 'Spread out through the silent wood there were endless rows of bodies belonging to those who had died of hunger, beating and disease.' On the dates and the large number of copies published see Brink 1998, pp. 58ff. Shulamith Behr in Cat. Meidner 2016, p. 158, quotes in this context Jeremiah 9:22: 'Even the carcases of men shall fall as dung upon the open field, and as the handful after the harvestman, and none shall gather them.' Clearly Meidner derived the metaphors from the Old Testament in selecting contemporary press photographs. Was he too thinking here about God's punishment of the Jews?

103 The bent birch tree suggests that Meidner was possibly influenced by another photo of the liberation of Germany from the Nazis by the Allies: *Illustrated London News*, 28 April 1945, p. 455. The photo shows the Germans marching into Czechoslovakia near Asch, overlooked by two intertwining birches standing in front of a field with two dark strips running across it.

104 Cat. Meidner 1991, vol. II, p. 278.

105 Amishai-Maisels 1993, p. 290.

106 Präger 2010, p. 240.

107 See for example the illustration of corpses and cremation ovens in *Die Neue Zeitung*, 19 May 1945.

108 See Cat. Nachkriegskunst 1994.

109 For political reasons, in 1933 Geiger was dismissed from his professorship at the Staatliche Akademie für Graphik und Buchkunst in Leipzig and moved back to Chiemsee and Munich where he once more occupied a professorship after 1946; see the biography on www.archiv-geiger.de/willi-eigerbiografie.html (10 January 2014).

110 Präger 2010, p. 222, which also quotes the *Neue Zeitung* of 8 February 1946, in which this drawing is printed with the subtitle *They Died in Poland, 1947*; it was also displayed with this title in the exhibition of cycles of graphic art at the Deutsche Akademie der Künste East Berlin, 1956, see Cat. Der Graphische Zyklus 1956, p. 74.

111 'And later another 17,000 Jews, and even later they were not counted any more,' Petrowskaja 2014, p. 186, about Babi Yar.

112 Franz Roh, Introduction to Willi Geiger, *12 Jahre – 20 Zeichnungen*, Wiesbaden: Limes Verlag 1946, pp. 3f.

113 Quoted thus in Präger 2010, pp. 224f., emphasis in original; the copy in the Deutsches Historisches Museum in Berlin does not contain this note.

114 Eduard Winkler, 'Zum Geleit' (accompanying remarks), album *Der Braune Tod*, Munich: Graf 1946, unpag.; emphasis in original.

115 Ibid., Afterword, no author given. This assessment is shared by an exhibition review in the magazine *Der Spiegel* of 23 August 1947, in which the series of images based on the Dance of Death with its distorting dances and masks of death and monsters is referred to and presented by Maxon as 'problematic art' lurking in the shadows (see Cat. Maxon 1999).

116 Jerzy Zielezinski, *K.Z.Album*, Monachium Wydawn. 'Slowo Polskie', Buchdruckerei W. Schütz, München 22, Kanalstr. 1, 1946 with preface, list of illustrations in Polish, German, French and English; volume kindly made available by the Benedictine Abbey of Plankstetten.

117 The related titles of the illustrated reports alone point to Zielezinski's knowledge of the photographs via albums and films and to a conscious differentiation between his series of drawings and them; see e.g. American Office of War Information 1945; on the publications about Dachau see Hoffmann-Curtius 1996a, pp. 284f. on 'Dachau! Ein Tatsachenbericht in Bildern, München: Heinrich Wiegand 1945' and pp. 285–7 on 'Album: Conc. Camp Dachau'.

118 On his biography see: collections.ushmm.org/search/catalog/irn8787 and http://lynn-munroe-books.com/list_62/GEORGE_ZIEL2.htm,

with a collection of his illustrations for mystery books and novels (8 January 2017).

119 Cornelia Brink discovered the album *24 Drawings* in a flea market in 1990 and published plates from it in 1993. Research carried out by her at memorial sites, research institutes and in the local press in Munich did not come up with anything; see Brink 1993, p. 4.

120 Not discussed here from *K.Z.Album* are: fol. 1: *Transport*, fol. 3: *Before the Bath*, fol. 6: *Roll-call inside the Barbed Wire*, fol. 8: *The Knife at the Throat*, fol. 11: *I am cold*, fol. 12: *Spleen*, fol. 13: *Shadows on the Square*, fol. 14: *The Light Criminals*, fol. 15: *The Lice*, fol. 16: *Typhoid Fever*, fol. 17: *These are free*, fol. 18: *Evacuation*.

121 Eljott says in the accompanying French text to the 1946 edition of *24 Drawings* about a second printing: Car c'est une seconde édition, bien améliorée au point de vue technique (Being a second edition, it is greatly improved with regard to technique).

122 The text sounds like a reaction to the fifteen photos out of a total of 23 pictures from *Dachau! Tatsachenbericht in Bildern* from 1945, showing corpses and photos of the torture of prisoners as acted out on dolls.

123 Emphasis in the original.

124 Wiechert 1946/2007; the afterword to the edition gives 'First published by Rascher Verlag Zürich, December 1945 (date of publication 1946)' (p. 183).

125 Princeton University, Marquand Library, Call Number: NE735.P7 Z6f.

126 United Nations Relief and Rehabilitation Administration. Unfortunately the search facilities available online from UNESCO, the official successor to UNRRA, do not give any further information about exhibitions of the period.

127 *Prisma* 1, 6 (April 1947), p. 33.

128 'the present period of transition is not advantageous to artistic creations. This applies to the German population in general, above all, however to the homeless Displaced Persons . . . What shall he present? And how is it to present? . . . the exhibitors have not made special efforts to create supermodern works. In their opinion that would only destroy national characteristics. We hope this exhibition may help to remove the existing differences and discords between the public and the Displaced Persons and may establish a better understanding of their sorrows and needs.' Cat. UNRRA 1947, pp. 5f.

129 See the 1899 ink drawings *Grave Diggers* and *The Prisoner's Dream* in Cat. Kubin 1999, Nos 23 and 24, as well as *Anatomy*, 1901/2 in Cat. Kubin 1977, No. 23.

130 The miniature on the cover of *24 Drawings* is a pointillist copy of drawing No. 10.

131 In particular resembling the 1847/50 oil *Wandering Saltimbanques*, see Wechsler 2013, p. 33.

132 On *Kapo* see Weinmann et al 1990, p. 49.

133 Brink 1998, p. 48.

134 Chaumont 2001, pp. 236f.

135 Unlike for example classical modernism, as represented for us by Picasso's *The Charnel House*, also inspired besides by concentration camp photos of the liberation of the camps, see Amishai-Maisels 1993, pp. 57ff.

136 According to information kindly supplied by the Marquand Library, the drawings from the editions of *24 Drawings* of 1946 and 1948 are identical.

137 See in Amishai-Maisels 1993 front and side views, figs 16–21.

138 Different covers of the 1946 edition suggest that the small rotogravures glued onto the covers might have been different as well.

139 Wagner, W. 1987, p. 150.

140 Twelve lithographs in *12 [dvanáct] původních litografií z německých koncentračních táborů*, Prague 1947: Svaz osvobozených politických vězňů a pozůstalých po politických vězních; cycle of aquatint etchings *Terezin/Theresienstadt*, completed in 1964, and another unpublished one about *Auschwitz*; see Wagner, W. 1987, p. 155. On the painters in Theresienstadt see also Amishai-Maisels 1987.

141 Wagner, W. 1987, p. 155.

142 Schulenburg 2008 was the start of the academic study of him.

143 Illustrated with the caption *Leo Haas (Czechoslovakia) Ejected and Driven Out. (Lithograph)*. On the discussion about the VVN exhibition *The Other Germany* in *Bildende Kunst*, 1 (1949), p. 27; on later exhibitions see *Neues Deutschland* 15 June 1961; *Berliner Zeitung*, 14 June and 1 July 1961.

144 In the collection of the Akademie der Künste, Berlin.

145 Antelme 1947/1992, p. 137.

146 Edel 1983, illus. 8.

147 Amishai-Maisels 1993, illus. 31, 32.

148 Art Spiegelman, *Maus II. A Survivor's Tale. And Here My Troubles Began.* New York: Pantheon Books 1991, p. 91.

149 Cohen 1998, pp. 234f. and figs 119 and 120.

150 Tolnay 1973, illustrated pp. 310f.; Nelly Sachs dedicated the poem *Crowned with Thorns* to Hieronymus Bosch, printed in Sachs 1961, p. 235.

151 Haas employed this stylistic means very consciously; the ink drawing of a related subject *Transport* does not display any of these distortions; see Wagner, W. 1987, p. 59.

152 On his imprisonment see Wagner, W. 1987.

153 Sommer 2009, pp. 128–39; the SS, but also the Soviet POWs and the Jews, were not allowed to visit what was referred to as the Special Building.

154 On works by them and others see Täuber 1997.

155 Poster with the Czech heading *A Louse – Your Death*. The German version is illustrated in http://auschwitz-ag.org/unternehmen_auschwitz/3.3.1.6b.htm (19 February 2013).

156 See the discussion of the association between the vagina and the bell of a musical instrument in Hoffmann-Curtius 2004, pp. 296ff.

157 Wickert 2002; Eschebach 2008 and 2010.

158 Gert Wollheim emigrated to America in 1947. There in 1962 he painted a picture, *Millions,* about the murder of the Jews, that did not come to Germany until 1985 as a gift from his widow to the Düsseldorf City Museum (Index No. B2204). It shows an endless procession of old-fashioned harvesting wagons filled with corpses, passing across a burial ground against a gloomy sky. See Cat. Wollheim 1993, illus. p. 185, No. 64, and the pencil sketches *Human Transport I* and *II*, p. 184, Nos 209 and 210.

159 Johanna Ey, a gallery owner in Düsseldorf since the First World War, was called mother (in German: Mutter) by the artists she cared for; see Cat. Das Junge Rheinland 1996; Cat. Am Anfang 1986. All the artists mentioned here were opponents of the Nazi tyranny; Julo Levin was murdered in Auschwitz and Ludwigs in custody in Düsseldorf, Barz lived in hiding with his Jewish wife, Wollheim and Schwesig were imprisoned in camps in France.

160 Despite the fact that he sent innocuous studies to exhibitions permitted by the regime. On this subject Wieland König in Cat. Lauterbach 1981, pp. 26f.; Cat. Das Junge Rheinland 1996, p. 333 and 'Lauterbach – Maler im Zwielicht' at http://nachrichten.rp-online.de/regional/lauterbach-maler-im-zwielicht-1.2732908 (28 May 2013).

161 Cat. Lauterbach 1981, p. 28.

162 The ninety drawings, spread over three albums by Lauterbach, that are now in the Düsseldorf City Museum, are not catalogued and still not definitely identified. Also drawings, that are mentioned in the literature as belonging to the album, are difficult to identify, as many of the titles are missing or the information available doesn't make it possible to put them in any precise order.

163 Cat. Lauterbach, 1947, unpag., Nos 51–104; the *Ghetto Album* is mentioned under No. 55.

164 According to the latest state of research, it is not clear whether he continued to work on this subject-matter, which was certainly not very popular, and added new images to the album.

165 Lauterbach 1948; the photo-lithographs appeared in an edition of 1,000 copies.

166 The 1947 Düsseldorf exhibition (Cat. Lauterbach 1947) listed seven exhibited works which were signed with *Old Jew*, *Old Man* or *Man with Fur Cap*.

167 Possibly the same as Cat. Lauterbach 1947, No. 103 *A Mother.*

168 Cat. Ludwigs 1983, single volume and illus. 55 *Mother B.* of 1937. Painting of his mother in Frommhold 1968, illus. No. 331.

169 Known under various titles: Cat. Lauterbach 1947, No. 84, *Transport*; Frommhold 1968, illus. No. 391, *Transport 1943*; in the Cat. Lauterbach 1981, illus. 111, and in Alberg 1994, p. 153, it is captioned *Abtransport* (Deportation) *1943*, and Alberg adds it to *Aus der Ghetto-Mappe* (From the Ghetto Album).

170 See illus. 90 as well as Otto Griebel, *The Internationale* of 1928–30 on www.dhm.de/lemo/kapitel/weimarer-republik/kunst-und-kultur.html (24 August 2017); Max Lingner, *Nous sommes la Jeune France, Nous sommes les gars de l'avenir!* In *L'Avant-garde, Le Journal des Jeunes*, 14 July 1936, XVI/663, illus. in Cat. Lingner 1988, p. 141.

171 See illus. 90 and his lithography *Departure* of 1916 and his album *Croquis de temps de guerre* (Sketches of War Times) in Cat. Steinlen 1978, pp. 227 and 295–305.

172 The 941 Jews from the Düsseldorf area, who were transported to Trawniki near Lublin on 22 April 1942, had to go on foot through several streets as far as the loading ramp of the Düsseldorf abattoir, Schmidt 2005, p. 125. Schmidt comments: 'Nobody in Düsseldorf in the summer of 1942 admits to having seen anything at all of the procession of several hundred people from the "abattoir" to the "loading ramp" at the Derendorf station! Were then the inhabitants of the Rather- und Tussmannstrasse all blind?' (p. 126).

173 This is what Jakob Witsch says at the beginning of his introductory remarks to the 1947 album by

Fritz Ketz; see also Hartmann 1993; on the album in particular Gillen, O. 1993 and Präger 2010, pp. 230f.

174 Reutlingen: Buchhandlung Witsch 1947; see Präger 2010, pp. 230f.

175 After he was reported to the Gestapo in 1944, Ketz himself destroyed part of his work; other works were almost completely destroyed by air-raids in Stuttgart in 1944; see Zimmermann 1980, pp. 365f.

176 Schoenberner 1960, p. 35, first published in *The Black Book of Polish Jewry* (1943), pp. 65f.

177 Hartmann 1993, p. 39.

178 Amishai-Maisels 1993, pp. 178–97; Amishai-Maisels 2003, pp. 234f.; and Stahl 2012.

179 See Walter Carl Rauh, *Raving Demon* from 1947 in Präger 2010, p. 215, illus. 1.

180 See Weik 2015, pp. 44–7. Details in Weik 2015, pp. 59f.

181 Details ibid.

182 Neugebauer 2003, pp. 256–68.

183 The drawings were exhibited in 1947 in the Graphics Gallery of the Kulturbund in Berlin, for which a 'catalogue' was published, by which is probably meant *Nie Wieder. Tagebuch in Bildern*, Berlin Volk und Welt, undated; see review in *Bildende Kunst*, 1 June (1947), p. 28.

184 Präger 2010, p. 233.

185 Otto 1949, pp. 1f.

186 Brecht 1955/1983. English translation: Willett 1998.

187 Berlau 1983.

188 See Amishai-Maisels 1993, p. 22, within the chapter 'Chagall's Wandering Jews'.

189 Translation by Michael Roloff in Nelly Sachs, *Selected Poems*, Hamburger et al. 1968, p. 3.

190 Information kindly supplied by Katja Jedermann, Berlin. According to a 1981 letter from Stern (1911–1986) to Ralf Seilheimer, Solingen, who kindly supplied it, Stern was banned from working during the Nazi period because one of his grandparents was of Jewish origin and he was enlisted in a punishment unit; up to 1964 he was a self-employed artist, then a university lecturer, and from 1970 professor at the Hochschule der Künste Berlin.

191 How Stern knew about the Nazi photos is unfortunately not clear. The earliest photo known to me is available in Oświęcim-Brzezinka 1956, illus. 35; it is possible, however, that it was displayed at one of the exhibitions that took place immediately after the war that the occupying powers, the association of those persecuted by the Nazi regime (VVN) and others organized (see Schmid 2012); see also '12 Jahre Schmach, Original-Bilddokumente aus der Zeit der Nazi-Herrschaft', Berlin 1946 (Bundesarchiv/Bildarchiv Plak 100-011-023).

192 A drawing with the title *The Incomprehensible* in which the black smoke combines with the black of the crematorium, from which a prisoner is turning away, was also drawn by Peter Edel; see Edel 1983, Drawing No. 13, dated 1943.

193 Details in the edition referred to.

194 Alfred Kantor made the drawings in July 1945 in the DP camp at Deggendorf in Bavaria (Kantor 1987).

195 See the study by Frahm 2006, pp. 209–29.

196 Celan 1948, published by A. Sexl; see Celan 2003, pp. 40f; and the commentaries by Wiedemann ibid., pp. 581ff., 606ff. English translation: 'Death Fugue', Michael Hamburger 2007, p. 70.

197 Celan/Jené 1948, in an edition of 700 copies, unpag.

198 Poster reproduced in Ivanovic 2002, p. 65.

199 Ibid., p. 62; see *Herzzeit* 2015, p. 251.

200 Jené, *Begegnungen*, 1980, in Költzsch 1984, p. 70.

201 Celan 2003, p. 16.

202 See Wiedemann 1985, p. 87, n. 199.

203 Many thanks to Roland Augustin, Saarlandmuseum Saarbrücken, for his help in the research.

204 Inv. No. NI 396 (1).

205 Reproduced in colour in Cat. Phantastischer Realismus 2008, p. 49. Even though the date 'Jené 44' is visible there, Bugs writes: 'Jené uses motifs from the poem', thus establishing a line of interpretation that has become the norm in the research on Celan/Jené; Költzsch 1984 compares the signed and dated drawing with Celan's text and dates the title of the image to 1947; see also Könneker 1995 as well as Gossens in Celan-Handbuch 2012.

206 Edgar Jené, Zeichnungen, *Dessins des années de guerre 1939–1945*, Vienna: Erwin Müller, 1945, edition of 100 copies with a foreword by Otto Basil. The volume contains 25 drawings that clearly show acts of brutality committed by the Nazis. Basil summed it up as 'Traum und Trauma' (dream and trauma). The drawing *The Rampart* shows a pile of corpses reminiscent of those photographed at Buchenwald. See illustration in Knigge 1998, p. 96.

207 According to Könneker 1995, p. 109, added between the frontispiece and the title drawing on p. 1. The drawing was also published in Celan/Jené 1948, pl. 4.

208 Celan/Jené 1948, pp. 7–12.

209 Letter to Max Rychner, quoted by Ivanovic 2002, p. 69.

210 According to an email from Miriam Häfele, Deutsches Literaturarchiv Marbach, of 17 June 2014 the illustrations on the two pasted-in sides are also removed from the correction copy stored there (Celan, D. 90.1.20a).

211 Ernst 1929, p. 37.

212 Kleist 1952, vol. II, pp. 231–44.

213 On music and text see Olschner 1989.

214 Wiedemann 1985, p. 87

215 Wiedemann 2011, p. 448.

216 Illustrated in Költzsch 1984, p. 8. Likewise in the drawings done with pen, ink and pencil without titles, but dated 1937 and 1938, probably depicting a *Raft of Medusa*, the shipwreck that Theodore Géricault painted in 1819. Jené 1988, illus. 4 and 5.

217 Celan 2003, p. 607.

218 See the use of female figures as allegories of the nation or of the Jewish people in the images Liebermann (see illus. 5) Jaeckel (see illus. 6), by Lea Grundig (illus. 46), Sitte (illus. 134), Richter (illus. 137 and 138), Claus (illus. 150), Meyer-Vax (illus. 115 and 164), Beuys (illus. 181), Szymanski (illus. 191) and Tübke (illus. 207).

219 As Jené often included this; see Költzsch 1984, illus. p. 21, 31, 71, 79, 81, 94, 96.

220 See Költzsch 1984, pp. 35f.; likewise in the disintegrated figure or statue in *O Blume der Zeit*, Celan/Jené 1948, No. 4.

221 Wiedemann in Celan 2003, pp. 607f.

222 Jené 1988, No. 32, signed EJ 45.

223 Wiedemann 1985, p. 18.

224 Celan/Jené 1948, illustration section unpag.

225 Ibid., p. 11.

4 Captured in One Picture

1 Goldstein 2005, p. 748.

2 Gillen, E. 2009a, p. 18.

3 Goldstein 2005, p. 753; ibid., pp. 20f.

4 Congressmen and the Hearst Press, among others, regarded socially critical and Expressionist-Cubist works as anti-American and communistic. An exhibition put together by the head of the Walker Art Centers in Minneapolis, J. Leroy Davidson, *Advancing American Art* with works by Stuart Davis, George Grosz, John Martin, Georgia O'Keeffe, Ben Shahn and Ben Zion, which was intended to tour Europe and South America, had to be cancelled. Here too the issue was not the opposition between figurative and non-figurative, but the rejection of critical images. See Goldstein 2005, pp. 753–5.

5 For details of the different interpretations of the Holocaust in the abstract painting of the Western hemisphere see Amishai-Maisels, pp. 243–87.

6 Office of the U.S. Military Government in Germany.

7 Goldstein 2005, pp. 764–6.

8 Ibid., pp. 771f.

9 Bugs 2001 and 2008.

10 Goldstein 2005, pp. 773ff.

11 *Time*, 28 April 1947.

12 Werner Doede, on his return from being a British POW, was from 1945 until 1953 the commissioning head of Düsseldorf City Art collection; he was considered to be politically untainted. In 1953 Fred Kocks, who had been a 'Mitläufer' (fellow traveller), was reappointed in his place; see Heymer 2013 and www.wz-newsline.de/lokales/duesseldorf/kultur/museumkunstpalast-ein-neues-bild-zum-jubilaeum-1.1362465 (29 April 2014).

13 Cat. Ernst 1991, pp. 232f.

14 Since the time of the portraits associated with mummies in ancient Egypt, portrait painting has been closely connected with this subject-matter and since the nineteenth century has been replaced by photographs of the dead; see Sykora 2009, pp. 95–130.

15 Cohen 1998, pp. 234f. and illus. 119 and 120.

16 Cat. Pankok 1946–7, unpag. (p. 1).

17 Cat. Rheinische Secession 1946, No. 7; Goebbels 1987, p. 123.

18 The longest spell in hiding for himself and his wife sought by the Gestapo was with Otto Pankok in the Eifel hills, see Overbeck/Müller 1995, pp. 253–6; see also Arntz 2012, p. 77; Goebbels 1987, p. 125.

19 Goebbels 1987, p. 123.

20 See the inventory of the Stadtmuseum Düsseldorf Inv. No. SMD.B. 2147. The Museum also owns the first design that already closely resembles the final version. It is possible that it was purchased in connection with his exhibition at the Schirn Kunsthalle in Frankfurt am Main, see the addendum to the Cat. Zwischen Krieg und Frieden 1980.

21 The caption to the picture added by Arntz in 2012 – 'Under the influence of the Catholic priest Josef Thyl, the Jewish star is intended to remind one of Auschwitz' – probably refers to the internment of the later abbot of the monastery of Tepl, Herman

Josef Tyl, in the concentration camps at Auschwitz and Buchenwald. See also 1979, pp. 179 and 215. No other connection between Tyl and Barz could be identified.

22 Illustrated in Cat. Ensor 1973, p. 256, Cat. No. 280 and commons.wikimedia.org/wiki/File:Christ%27s_Entry_Into_Brussels_in_1889.jpg (17 April 2013)

23 Illustrated in Cat. Ensor 1973, p. 254, Cat. No. 104 and www.moma.org/collection/object.php?object_id=65244 (17 April 2013).

24 Which was much more pronounced compared with his 1932 painting *Jews in Antwerp* and *4th Class Carriage* of 1928. Illustrated in Cat. Am Anfang 1986, p. 277; on the cover of Goebbels 1986.

25 Goebbels 1987, p. 33; p. 36 also the illustration of a sketch, produced by Barz from memory in the 1970s, of his 1934 painting of a crucifixion with Christ holding his arm in similar way, in which by showing a Roman soldier he wanted to counter the legend that the Jews had crucified Christ.

26 Zimmermann 1972, p. 64, n. 14. 'Mathias Barz friends with Pankok already from the time in the "Ey"'; see also Arntz 2012.

27 See Cat. Barz 1980 and Cat. Am Anfang 1986, p. 313: 'In 1919 he became a member of the KPD (German Communist Party).'

28 Cat. Barz 1980, unpag.; Goebbels 1987, pp. 33–6.

29 On his biography and oeuvre see Cat. Bruse 1979.

30 On Anton Saefkow, a communist and resistance fighter executed after 20 July 1944, see www.gdw-berlin.de/nc/de/vertiefung/biographien/biografie/view-bio/saefkow (14 August 2013).

31 Notes by Hermann Bruse on the Formalism debate, Cat. Bruse 1959, unpag.

32 Cat. Bruse 1959 and 1979.

33 See on the origin of the pictorial subject Ilya Repin's representations of the forced labour of the Volga boatmen in Amishai-Maisels 1993, p. 10, illus. 16–20.

34 Blatmann 2011.

35 *Berliner Zeitung*, 28 October 1947.

36 See Sgt Hewitt's photo of Margit Schwartz on her sickbed at Bergen-Belsen on 16–17 May 1945 in Cat. Mémoire 2001, p. 164, illus. 209.

37 Office of U.S. Military Government in Germany.

38 Goldstein 2005, p. 773; Goldstein 2009.

39 Cat. Koerner 1947.

40 In 1973 Koerner completed a linocut based on the oil painting, see www.nationalacademy.org, object number 2000.5 (10 March 2014).

41 Goldstein 2005, p. 773; the exhibition was welcomed as a great event by the big American magazines *Time* and *Life* and the *New York Times*; see Goldstein 2009, p. 93.

42 Goldstein 2009 (see pp. 107–8).

43 Gillen 1981, pp. 243–87; and on the subject of Koerner's use of photography in Cozzolino 2011, pp. 103–10.

44 In 1944 when Koerner in the U.S. was still ignorant about the fate of his parents, he painted them in their living room in Vienna looking towards the viewer. His mother is sewing, his father asleep in the rocking chair with a book in his hands. Illustrated in Cat. Koerner 1997, p. 76, on the dating also p. 146.

45 Of 1 April 1947 with the heading 'Heightened Reality: On the Exhibition of the American Painter Henry Koerner': 'Henry Koerner, originally from Vienna, then New York, who has established his style as a virtuoso draughtsman . . .' Redslob compared Koerner to Dix and Grosz: 'Basically, however, Koerner's heightening of reality reminds one of altar paintings of the 15th century, on which the Passion of Christ is portrayed with terrifying force.'

46 Goldstein 2009, pp. 93f. thinks, however, that the 'exhibition brochure' reported on the murder. In the catalogue quoted here this is not the case. No other brochure was available.

47 *Der Spiegel*, 6 March 1948, p. 23.

48 Presumably this was the publicist and art historian Carl Linfert, who worked for various newspapers and journals in Berlin after 1945, see Heukenkamp 1996, p. 546; the title of his contribution to the catalogue on Koerner is: 'About the object in the image.'

49 Titles of the pictures in it include: *The Zealot*, *The Empty Square*, *The Beaten Ones*, *Numb*, *We Pretend*. Even in the explanatory afterword by an unidentified author, E.O.H., *My Parents* is not mentioned. It remains to be established whether the painting *Vanity Fair* (illustrated in the catalogue in black and white and in *Life* magazine, pp. 77f., full-size and in colour), with the artist looking fearfully at the people wrapped up in their own concerns, all of whom are marked by the murder by Cain of Abel, does not also refer to the Nazi tyranny in Germany.

50 Letter from Hans Grundig to Lea Grundig of 16 February 1947, in Grundig, H. 1966, pp. 122f.; see also Cat. Kunst in der DDR 2003, p. 120, Cat. No. 14.

51 Amishai-Maisels 1993, illus. 155.
52 'This version was first exhibited in Dresden in the exhibition that opened on 8 April 1948 "150 Jahre soziale Strömungen in der Kunst" (150 Years of Social Trends in Art) in a room devoted to the victims of fascism among drawings by Käthe Kollwitz,' wrote Gillen, E. 2002, p. 342; on the various versions and conditions see Sander 1988.
53 Illustration of concentration camp badges *c.* 1936/1944 in Bundesarchiv, Bilddatenbank: Bild 146-1993-051-07.
54 On this and on the classification by the *Opfer des Faschismus* (*OdF*) into fighters, that is, mainly Communists, and 'the defenceless', see Gillen, E. 2002, pp. 342f.
55 Grundig, H. 1966, p. 122.
56 Hoffmann-Curtius 2002a.
57 On the Grundigs' friends Christel Beham and Fritz Schulze, murdered in the concentration camps, see Gillen, E. 2002, p. 344, n. 1417f.
58 Helen Ernst, member of the KPD (German Communist Party) and of the 'Asso' (Association of Revolutionary Artists), friend of Hans Grundig and Carl Meffert, was arrested as early as 1933, imprisoned from 1941 until 1945 in the women's concentration camp at Ravensbrück; accused in 1947 of alleged activity as an informer; and died after being acquitted in 1948. Her artworks were only displayed in a retrospective in 1994 in the Verborgenes Museum (Hidden Museum) in Berlin (Cat. Ernst 1994).
59 Agamben 2003, p. 141.
60 See Cat. Meyer-Vax 1965, painting No. 3, *Impressions*, 1945; No. 4, *War Widow*, 1948; and No. 5, *The Waiting Ones*, 1948.
61 See Cat. Meyer-Vax 1965, print No. 7, *Nazi Judge*, 1959, lithograph; No. 98, *Fascism*, 1947, linocut; No. 105, *Child of Buchenwald*, 1961, linocut.
62 See Cat. Meyer-Vax 1965.
63 Cat. Expressive Gegenständlichkeit 2001, pp. 570f.; Lang 1960, pp. 453ff.
64 Cat. Schwesig 1983.
65 Illustrated in Cat. Schwesig 1984, p. 91.
66 Jung 1984, p. 92; illustrated ibid.
67 Illustrated in Cat. Abb. Schwesig 1984, p. 96.
68 Schwesig in the foreword to *Les Inutiles*, ibid., p. 101.
69 Illustrated ibid., pp. 102–6.
70 Illustrated ibid., pp. 98f.
71 Cat. Schwesig 1984, pp. 99 and 111. It is worth noting that this picture hung in the office of the director of a ministry; see ibid., p. 111, n. 7.
72 Max Lingner was the only other one at the time to address this subject (see p. 232, n. 77).
73 They have not been published in their entirety; on the 'Odyssey of the Legacy' see Barth 1984, p. 117.
74 Cat. Schwesig 1984, p. 108.
75 Vasari describes it as a 'wonderful and marvellous head of Christ, to whom a vulgar Hebrew [un villano ebreo] is showing Caesar's coin'. Vasari 1832–8, p. 1054.
76 Biography and illustrations in Cat. Ehmsen 1986a; Cat. Ehmsen 1986b; Schweitzer 2013, pp. 228–40. The studio photo and *Street of Horror* illustrated in Cat. Ehmsen 1986a, No. 37.
77 See p. 70; 'death factories'.
78 Hansen 2016; on the history of the term Auschwitz in West Germany in the 1950s see Eitz/Stötzel 2007, p. 321.
79 Buchheister wvz 2, Inv. No. 33/1949, p. 147; according to information from the present owner, along with the official title, the subtitle *Concentration Camp Picture* (vol. 1, p. 165) also referred to in the monograph as the 'usual' one, was already the one in use at the time of the first purchase in 1952; the handwritten note on the reverse of the picture does not include the subtitle.
80 Cat. Max Lachnit 1991, pp. 7 and 84f., illustrated 63f.
81 Röger 2007.
82 And thus contradicting the claim in Eitz/Stötzel 2007, pp. 29–33, that around this time the name was not yet in use in this sense.
83 Cat. Max Lachnit 1991, p. 7, n. 5.
84 Hoffmann-Curtius 1999b.
85 Gillen 2009a, p. 65.
86 Cat. Wilhelm Lachnit 2000, pp. 31, 65–7.
87 On the redirection of the process of coming to terms with grief in the GDR see in detail Hoffmann-Curtius 1999a, in particular pp. 58f. and illus. 44 and 45.
88 Hoffmann D. 1998b, p. 60.

5 A Confession

1 See Cat. Georgi 2001, p. 11.
2 On fear of revenge by the dead from a psychological perspective see Jureit/Schneider 2010, pp. 187ff.
3 Only the émigré Teo Otto, who was himself not in the Wehrmacht, as early as 1944 in Switzerland had shown the bloodstained hands of the murderers in an ink drawing, see Otto 1949, unpag.

6 Remembering in the 1950s

1 Schmid 2012, pp. 333f.
2 In 1958 alone, two full-length films and a documentary on 9 November 1938 were shown; see Classen 1999, p. 87. Halbinger 2010 notes a change of direction in the course of the 1950s due to the generational change of journalists.
3 Puvogel et al. 1995, pp. 505ff.
4 In the case of the earlier memorials outside of the camps, only in Hamburg and Cologne do the inaugurations mention the Jews; see Hoffmann-Curtius 2002a and Hoffmann-Curtius 2010.
5 For details on this see Halbinger 2000.
6 DEFA 1959; as already in the case of *Night and Fog*, the West Germans also tried to prevent the showing of *Sterne* (Stars) at international festivals; see Löser 2012, p. 316.
7 Löser 2012.
8 Discussion of the debate over the amnesty law of 1949 in Frei 1999, pp. 29–53.
9 France 1955–6; on the content see www.cine-holocaust.de/cgibin/gdq?efwoofbw001721.gd (27 January 2014).
10 On the reception history in Germany see the varied and careful studies by Knaap 2008, in particular pp. 61–124; on the omission of the Jews pp. 32–4 and Lindeperg 2010, pp. 198–232.
11 Lindeperg 2010, pp. 233–59.
12 Knaap 2008, pp. 32 and 129.
13 Celan Werke 1983, vol. IV, pp. 96f.
14 Godfrey 2007, pp. 16f.
15 Ibid.
16 Pankok WVZ 3, pp. 56f.; WL 73 A, 73 B *Ringela Grieving*. On one of the copies it is stated: 'This girl was murdered at Oranienburg.'
17 Cat. Pankok 1968, No. 32, plate XI.
18 Cat. Pankok 1955, No. 186.
19 Cat. Pankok 1968, No. 160, *Jewish Memorial* or *Jewish Monument*, 1950, with all the references to the earlier works and plaster models. What is certain, according to an entry in the inventory of the Gelsenkirchen Museum, is 'that the work was purchased in 1955 directly from Otto Pankok himself for the art museum', information kindly communicated in a letter of 5 February 2013 from the head of the museum, Leane Schäfer.
20 Cat. Pankok 1968, No. 118.
21 Cat. Pankok 1955, unpag.
22 Overbeck/Müller 1995, pp. 263f.
23 'Abstract painting is wandering off into play, avoiding the truth by straying into uncontrolled areas . . . It is freedom in a vacuum, in a land devoid of people' (Pankok 1951, p. 26). 'The only thing that is important for me is whatever is still whole and human' (Pankok 1958 quoted in Zimmermann 1972, p. 67).
24 Gillen, E. 2009a, pp. 129–35.
25 This was the way the dead were honoured at the time following the conservative and nationalist tendency of the powerful Kriegsgräberfürsorge association supported by the state; see Lurz 1986, pp. 432–46.
26 Thanks to the Institut für Stadtgeschichte in Gelsenkirchen, and in particular Birgit Klein, for their kind help in sending photocopies of the press, catalogues and other material.
27 *Recklinghäuser Zeitung*, 7 March 1955.
28 See Susanne Timm in Pankok WVZ 3, pp. 17–22: the complete text is available at https://archive.org/details/ssHauptamt-Der-Untermensch (29 March 2014).
29 Pankok WVZ 1, *Jew Walking* (WH 128), illustrated p. 67.
30 Pankok WVZ 1, WH 134, illustrated p. 69.
31 Pankok WVZ 2, p. 157, WR 627, illustrated p. 157.
32 See p. 23.
33 Haibl 1999, pp. 91f.; Cat. Die Macht der Bilder 1995, p. 225; Franco Fratini 1999, pp. 62–4.
34 Cat. Abgestempelt 1999, p. 189, illus. 3 and p. 306, illus. 7; Cat. Die Macht der Bilder 1995, pp. 226f.
35 Weidemann 1993, p. 200.
36 Illichmann 1997, in particular pp. 87f.
37 Hütt 1995, pp. 110f.
38 Documented in Willi Sitte, Handzeichnungen 1940–92, pp. 8f., pp. 124–33.
39 Details of the whole *Lidice* cycle Schirmer 2011, on the fate of the picture that was still unexplained in 2014, pp. 114–29.
40 A large number of them were exhibited in 1986 at the Altes Museum in Berlin, when Sitte had long ceased being a controversial artist and had become a politically influential one, see Cat. Sitte 1986, pp. 44–55.
41 Horst Strempel, *Lidice*, 1949, oil painting, illustrated in Saure 1992, Cat. No. 285, illus. 19.
42 See www.lidice-memorial.cz/world_de.aspx (20 January 2014); on the Memorial Site and the documentation centre at Lidice in the year that Sitte visited them, see Wheeler 1957; on this

massacre and the ones committed in neighbouring Kladno and Lezàky, as well as post-war treatment of those who were responsible, see Steinkamp 2003 and Klemp 2012.

43 The secondary literature op. cit. gives no figures for this.

44 On this picture Schirmer 2011, p. 110; see also Rehberg 2012, pp. 264f.; Gillen, E. 2009a, pp. 167–74.

45 It is unclear whether Sitte was aware of the murder of the 33 men and women in neighbouring Lezàky, see Steinkamp 2003, p. 130.

46 There is a short list of contents of the films shown there in Wheeler 1957, pp. 13f.

47 Schirmer/Sitte 2003, pp. 75–8.

48 'In the film I saw their faces, saw them laughing and boasting about it . . . It was inexplicable to me that people who commit such acts can be involved in any process of thought or feeling. So I painted them as faceless heads in steel helmets.' Schirmer/Sitte 2003, p. 77.

49 Hütt 1972, p. 39, quoted in Gillen, E. 2009, p. 170.

50 Sitte in discussion with Schirmer 2010; see Schirmer 2011, p. 112, n. 2001.

51 Illustrated in Hütt 1995, p. 33.

52 Fröhlich 2011.

53 Illustrated in Schoenberner 1960, p. 36.

54 Becker 2002, p. 134.

55 Ibid., pp. 38–47.

56 See Seiler 1942.

57 See Hoffmann-Curtius 2002b.

58 Musée National d'Arts Moderne, Centre Pompidou, Paris, illustrated in Cat. L'art en guerre 2012, p. 193.

59 Becker 2002, p. 40.

60 Ibid.

61 See ibid., in particular pp. 48–85.

62 Elger 2002, p. 30. On the popular view of Anne Frank as an unharmed child in the second half of the 1950s, see Frübis 2014.

63 Richter in the film by Corinna Belz *Gerhard Richter Painting*, Germany 2011.

64 On the success of the book, see Scholz 2011, in particular pp. 78f. and p. 82: 'The diary has become a symbol of the Holocaust, without the Holocaust ever being mentioned in it.'

65 *Jacqueline with the Black Scarf*, 1958, lithograph, repr. in Cat. Picasso 2002, p. 331; *Kentaur und Menade*, 1947, Cat. Picasso 1974, illus. 91.

66 Which Eduard Beaucamp referred to in the review of the German edition of this book in the *Frankfurter Allgemeine Zeitung* of 19 February 2015, and presumably meaning here the way the lines of his drawings in profile were done.

67 Frank 1954, p. 54: 'Countless friends and acquaintances have gone to a terrible fate. Evening after evening the green and grey army lorries trundle past. [The green ones are the German ss and the 'black' ones are the Dutch Nazi police.] The Germans ring at every front door to inquire if there are any Jews living in the house. If there are, then the whole family has to go at once.'

68 Gerhard Richter Archiv, Staatl. Kunstsammlung Dresden, Inv. No. 499/13.

69 Frank 1954, p. 55: 'I feel wicked sleeping in a warm bed, while my dearest friends have been knocked down or have fallen into a gutter somewhere out in the cold night. I get frightened when I think of close friends who have now been delivered into the hands of the cruellest brutes that walk the earth. And all because they are Jews!'

70 Ibid.: 'But Dussel was immediately plied with questions from all sides, and the stories he told us were so gruesome and dreadful that one can't get them out of one's mind. Yet we still have our jokes and tease each other, when these horrors have faded a bit in our minds. It won't do us any good, or help those outside, to go on being as gloomy as we are at this moment. And what would the object be of making our "Secret Annexe" into a "Secret Annexe of Gloom"?'

71 Gerhard Richter Archiv, Staatl. Kunstsammlung Dresden, Inv. No. 500/13.

72 Frank 1954, p. 109: 'Believe me, if you have been shut up for a year and a half, it can get too much for you some days. In spite of all justice and thankfulness, you can't crush your feelings. Cycling, dancing, whistling, looking out into the world, feeling young, to know that I'm free – that's what I long for; still, I mustn't show it, because I sometimes think if all eight of us began to pity ourselves, or went about with discontented faces, where would it lead us?'

73 Details of both editions: Kirschnick 2009, pp. 8–18; 59–82.

74 Kirschnick 2009, p. 11.

75 Ibid., pp. 35–58; on Dresden pp. 37–42.

76 These were analysed via the data bank *zefys* of the articles from *Neues Deutschland*, the *Berliner Zeitung* and *Neue Zeit* for 1955–7, available at the Staatsbibliothek Berlin.

77 Kirschnick 2009, p. 40; it is no longer possible to see any similarity to the portraits of the actresses in the publication. Harald Hakenbeck too in his oil painting dated 1961, *Anne Frank*, Galerie Neue Meister Dresden, did not aim at similarity but followed the cliché of the 'Jewess' as regards her dark hair, emphasized nose, sensuous mouth and big eyes; see illus. 6 in Horn 1973.

78 Hellwick/Deicke 1959, unpag., three studio photographs; see also Kirschnick 2009, pp. 83–98.

79 See his pen drawing, dated 16 July 1956, and the pencil drawing, simply signed 'Richter 1957', in the Gerhard-Richter-Archiv in Dresden.

80 Scholz, S. 2011, p. 86 points out that already in the first German edition of the Diary, published by Lambert Schneider in 1950, in the appendix at the end it is stated that Anne Frank's account 'can be said to stand symbolically for us all'.

81 A survey of the six volumes on loan from the Lea Grundig archive in the Akademie der Künste shows that *Roll-call in the Concentration Camp* is the most frequently exhibited drawing by the artist. The sculptor Georg Türke took the drawing as a model for the relief of a memorial in Meissen as early as 1956; see Heiner 2016, p. 113.

82 Edel 1983, No. 11, ink drawing; see similar scenes in the film *Death Mills*, Germany/U.S. 1945.

83 On the Jews who allegedly had not put up any resistance and were not mentioned also along with the Communists at the national memorial sites, see Gillen, E. 2002, pp. 342f.

84 This is how it is put in a protocol of the Organisation of the Victims of Fascism (OdF) in Mecklenburg-Vorpommern of November 1946, quoted in Knigge 1998, pp. 103f.; the allocation of ID cards corresponded to just this pattern, distinguishing between resistance fighters, the persecuted and the partly persecuted, but was increasingly made dependent on loyalty to the system.

85 The concentration camp number in mirror writing is presumably not intended to indicate any particular person; according to information kindly provided by Astrid Ley, from the Memorial Site at Sachsenhausen on 8 February 2013, a Polish prisoner under preventive arrest 'SP' Kasimir Sroka is listed under this number from 6 April 1940 up to 30 September 1940, but not registered as a Jewish prisoner. Hans Grundig, who was in Sachsenhausen from 30 March 1940, could have known him. It is unlikely that Lea Grundig knew of him.

86 Knigge 1998, p. 102.

87 Ibid., p. 132, illustration of the design, p. 131.

88 Stengel 2012, p. 282.

89 Spielmann's study focuses primarily on the competition. The numbers given in the contemporary press and in Spielmann 1990 differ; the total number of 618 is taken from the official record of the competition according to what was left by Langbein to the Austrian State Archive: 'Information for the participants in the competition for the setting up of an international memorial at Auschwitz' undated (1957), signed by the Secretariat of the International Auschwitz Committee (Allgemeines Verwaltungsarchiv, Nachlass Langbein E 1797:292/8). In the following quoted as: Auschwitz Competition 1957. Many thanks to Pia Wallnig from the Austrian State Archive in Vienna for her kind assistance in the research. The number of submitted models is given by Spielmann 1990, p. 293, but his figures seem to differ slightly from the way they are listed in the section of the catalogue, pp. 294–369. For the GDR he lists eleven entries there.

90 Stengel 2012, p. 289; see also Broszat 1958.

91 Huener 2003, pp. 150f., Aloszko 2011, pp. 160–79.

92 For details on the history of the IAC Stengel 2012, in particular on the competition, pp. 313–25.

93 Auschwitz Competition 1957.

94 Ibid., pp. 2 and 6; see Sehn 1956 and 1957.

95 Quoted in Spielmann 1990, p. 171.

96 Stengel 2012 and the review of it by Philipp Neumann on http://hsozkult.geschichte.hu-berlin.de/rezensionen/2013-2-076 (27 January 2014); the following remarks are based on Stengel's research.

97 Ibid., p. 97.

98 His critical stance towards the Communist Party after the Hungarian Uprising finally led to his exclusion in September 1958. He was no longer invited to the inauguration of the Memorial Site at Buchenwald in the same month. He was declared an 'enemy of the Party'. In 1960, at the time of the move of the Secretariat of the IAC to Warsaw, he was being defamed as discredited and voted out of office; see Stengel 2012, p. 300.

99 Ibid., pp. 59 and 235.

100 Even in a critical statement on the plan for the competition on the part of the museum at Auschwitz it says: 'A considerable percentage of the victims at Auschwitz were Jews from numerous countries. Even if we can in no way endorse the view that in Auschwitz it was exclusively Jews who

were exterminated, account must nevertheless be taken of the fact that the number of victims was very large.' Quoted in Stengel 2012, p. 316.

101 Ibid., pp. 248f.; Langbein sought 'independence from political blocks' (p. 300).

102 The third submission, which used a Jewish symbol, came from the Netherlands by B. H. Ringer. It was to show a cross, prisoner's stripes and a Star of David. Spielmann 1990, pp. 172 and 348.

103 On the circulation of the draft by the sculptor Waldemar Grzimek, then successful in the GDR, showing the relief of a man with a dove of peace in the centre of the arrangement and which is recorded without comment in Spielmann 1990, p. 313, nothing is known; see Grzimek WVZ 1979, No. 203, p. 71 and 211.

104 See www.josephlonas.com/bio.htm (27 January 2014).

105 All the information as per the description in Spielmann 1990, p. 330.

106 Ibid; on p. 180 there is a description of the design also with a picture of the motif of the three men in the Fiery Furnace and it is presented under the heading 'Christliche Interpretationen' (Christian Interpretations).

107 As early as 1947 Hermann Claasen published a popular volume of photos with the title *Gesang im Feuerofen. Köln. Überreste einer zerstörten Stadt* (Canto in the Fiery Furnace, Cologne: Remnants of a Destroyed City). In 1964–5 a sculpture was erected, at the entrance to the discussion area in the Protestant Church of Reconciliation in Dachau, of the three men in the Fiery Furnace by Carel Kneulmann as an offering from Dutch Protestants. Kappel 2010, p. 62.

108 In 1952 she was awarded the Berlin art prize for sculpture, Cat. Lüttwitz 1992, pp. 4, 12 and 82.

109 In which, like Lea Grundig (see illus. 59), she took up John Heartfield's image of a human being tortured on a swastika wheel, *Arbeiter Illustrierte Zeitung*, Prague, 31 May 1934, p. 352. The inscription on the memorial reads: 'Every philosophy based on violence breaks the human being on its symbols turned into wheels of torture'; see Endlich/Lutz 1998, p. 146. The teak sculpture of 1956 *The Voice from the Burning Bush* (Cat. Lüttwitz 1992, p. 34) documents her reading of the Old Testament not just for her model at Auschwitz-Birkenau.

110 Spielmann 1990, pp. 330f. The other model submitted by Lüttwitz with the number K86 (191512), recorded in Spielmann without explanation, based on a photo preserved at Auschwitz, shows a human figure lying horizontally on the points of flaming shapes or branches. Her commentary: 'As a warning the human being soars above the fire that consumed so many in this inhuman place. The work is conceived in painted bronze. It is intended to be placed together with the urn.' Thanks to Anna Odimłodszy dokumentalista, Państwowe Muzeum Auschwitz-Birkenau Oświęcim for kindly supplying the text.

111 Spielmann 1990, pp. 124–7 and 366.

112 Bauwelt, 1958, No. 22, pp. 588f.

113 Illustrated in Cat. Wien Berlin 2013, p. 63, illus. 42.

114 The art historian Eduard Trier 1962, p. 497, talked of a 'Cyclopean wall, through which they had to pass in order to relive in a realistic symbol the fate of human beings subject to a pitiless machinery of extermination'.

115 Quoted in Spielmann 1990, p. 124.

116 Trier 1962, p. 497.

117 The building of the Berlin Wall in 1961.

118 Ladendorf 1963, p. 662, claims he can see in its 'tank-like armoured form' both 'the dismissive rigidity of violence' and also 'the vital forces destroying the cohesion of the block from inside through an almost imperceptible movement'.

119 Rieth 1968, p. 24.

120 In the commentary on the first design by Eisenman Architects and Richard Serra, it says: 'The spaces thus created, condensed, narrowed and deepened, open up at any random point the possibility of a multi-layered experience'; Heimrod 1999, pp. 882 and 1,112 in a slightly altered version of Eisenman Architects on the reworked design.

121 Joseph Beuys 1980 in *Penthouse*, quoted in Kramer, M. 1997, p. 293.

122 On this crash and Beuys's mythologizing of his recovery by means of felt and fat with the Tartars see the biography by Riegel 2013, pp. 65–71: 'Tatarenlegenden'.

123 About which he said in 1979: 'This period was not positive for me as that was when my best friends were killed in the war,' quoted in Quermann 2006, p. 229, n. 46.

124 Illustrated in Beuys WVZ Aktionen 1994, p. 49.

125 Rosenthal 2005, p. 10.

126 On the association between trauma and the memory of German history in Beuys's work see also Antoine 2011.

127 Körffer et al. 1999.

128 Kölner Stadtanzeiger of 22 May 1959, p. 15, quoted in Fischer, H. 1999, pp. 154ff. There is no mistaking a connection between the event, under the aegis of Federal President Theodor Heuss, and the setting up of the enlarged copy of the Kollwitz figure *Mother with Dead Son* in the central Memorial Site of the Federal Republic at the Neue Wache in Berlin in 1993, which was essentially arranged by Federal Chancellor Helmut Kohl.

129 Cat. Beuys 1985a, pp. 8, 60, 68, Cat. Nos. 115–23, illus. 1, 69, 70, 79–83; on the significance of the crucifix for Beuys see ibid., illus. 17; see also Riegel 2013, pp. 139f.

130 The watercolour can be included under the series of early letter drawings, see Naef 2011, pp. 50ff., the drawing is not given; Naef excludes 'strategies of *Vergangenheitsbewältigung* (dealing with the past)' (p. 24) in her analysis.

131 Cat. Beuys 1996, No. 48, and Ray 2001b, p. 60.

132 Beuys proved the multifaceted nature of this form of image when he used it in another drawing that showed something not stamped at Auschwitz, but a label advertising 'Beck's guter Kaffee' (Beck's good coffee), illus. 116, in Cat. Beuys 2010, p. 141.

133 Knöll 2008.

134 By contrast, Winkler in his series *Brown Death* portrayed the specific political situation.

135 According to the whole tenor of Ray 2001b.

136 A study with three gates is also mentioned by Kramer, M. 1997, p. 294, and 2010, p. 147. A summary of all available documents and materials on the competition design is repeated, albeit without references, Rössler 2011. On the other designs of gates in the competition see Spielmann 1990, pp. 176f.

137 Cat. Beuys 2008, p. 95, Cat. No. 04 15c.

138 Kramer, M. 1997, p. 294; Cat. Beuys 2008, p. 97, No. 04 18, ibid., pp. 90–101. A summary of documents and materials on the competition is printed there along with evidence of various activities under the heading 'zeige Deine Wunde' (show your wound) and traced by Eugen Blume (pp. 76–7) to Christian iconography.

139 Cat. Beuys 2008, p. 94, illus. 04 14, and Kramer, M. 2010, illus. 131, p. 158.

140 The participants in the competition were free to reuse it; see the booklet of the Auschwitz Competition 1957, p. 10.

141 On his engagement with Steiner see Koepplin 1994; Beuys considered Steiner 'the greatest man of our time' (p. 91).

142 Riegel 2013, p. 144; Pohl 1995.

143 Pohl 1995, p. 25; see also Blume 2008, p. 156: 'The path through the gate led up to the resurrection symbolized by the light of the rock crystal or "solar mirror" erected in line with the gates.'

144 Kramer 1997, p. 305, No. 281, and p. 294 are given the title *Berglampen* (miner's lamps); they resemble for example the paraffin lamps also still used at the time in agriculture, where Beuys had worked during his crisis.

145 Cat. Beuys 1997; many thanks to Klaus-D. Pohl, the co-author, for his suggestions, particularly on the *Ulysseshefte*; Lerm Hayes 2001, pp. 29ff., dates the beginning of his reading of Joyce as some time in the 1950s at the latest.

146 On these see Lerm Hayes 2001, pp. 265 and 266f., illus. 18; Lerm Hayes/Walters 2011, illus. 1. Lerm Hayes 2001 sees a connection with the passage grave at Newgrange and mentions that the ashes of a corpse were discovered in a stone bowl at the end of the passage there 'and the sun shining along the passage at the winter solstice illuminates the bowl' (p. 269). However, the astronomical nature of the site was discovered no earlier than during the winter solstice on 21 December 1969 in the course of systematic excavation there by Michael J. O'Kelly; see O'Kelly 1982, pp. 123f.

147 Seen several times in the film *Night and Fog*.

148 See in particular the integration of the concertina fold from Sehn 1956 into the display case *Auschwitz Demonstration* (illus. 180).

149 Koepplin 1996, pp. 28ff.; van der Grinten 1996, pp. 201ff.

150 Van der Grinten 1996.

151 Jaskot 2012, p. 52, without knowing this drawing, associates the form of the gates with the polyhedron in Dürer's *Melencolia*.

152 A painting that Beuys could have been thoroughly familiar with, as it is reproduced in Haftmann 1950, p. 160. Werckmeister 1987, p. 50, interprets it as 'both anthromorphic and also political. "Aus der Reihe treten" (Not in line with the norm)'. If there were not another drawing done in the style of the young Klee with the title *Dwarves' Memorial in the Forest*, 1956, illustrated in Koepplin 1996, p. 28, illus. 13, it would be appropriate to see the title as an ironic distancing from the cult of Huns and Heroes.

153 Van der Grinten 1996, pp. 201ff.

154 Ibid.

155 Koepplin 1996, p. 28.

156 Kramer, M. 1997, p. 295, mentions 'the scaffold-like arches of the gates'; van der Grinten 1985, p. 10, talks of the 'guillotine-like arches of the gates'; Gillen, E. 2009a, p. 214, writes: 'the gates are marked in red and look like bloody guillotines.'
157 Kramer, M. 1997, pp. 294f.
158 Spielmann 1990, p. 150.
159 Sehn 1957.
160 Cat. Goral 2007; Rommelfanger 2008.
161 Rommelfanger 2007, pp. 36–9; Rommelfanger 2008, pp. 40–46.
162 Goral 1962; on Goral's decision to leave Hamburg, which he already expressed in 1960, see the details in Rommelfanger 2008, pp. 74–83.
163 *Animal Sacrifice Hanging Above the Alster Lake in Hamburg*, Rommelfanger 2008, pp. 70f., and the *Hanging Animal Sacrifices* which he painted in oil on wooden breakfast boards; see the archive of the Jewish Museum in Frankfurt Inv. No. 1997-0026-1-150 and 1997-0026-1-151, dated between 1960 and 1962; see also Rommelfanger 2008, pp. 59–64.
164 Rommelfanger 2008, p. 62, claims to be able to identify this view of the city in the view from the window of his newly occupied studio.
165 Cat. Chagall 1959, No. 100.
166 In the colour lithograph *Nativity*, 1950, as an addition to *Behind the Mirror* published by Maeght, Chagall's symbols for sacrifice or martyrdom appear together with the old Jew in the sky, the old town and the flickering candles of a candelabra between a white disc and a wall-clock with a pendulum.
167 Not considered by Rommelfanger 2007 and 2008.
168 Cat. Chagall 1959, No. 126, exhibited in 2006 in Baden-Baden with reference to the art-historical background (Rembrandt, Soutine) but without referring to the murder of the Jews; see Cat. Chagall 2006, pp. 160f. On Goral's own engagement with Soutine see Rommelfanger 2008, pp. 56–60; she indeed cites in Cat. Goral 2007, p. 40, Soutine's representation of *Plucked Turkey with Tomatoes* from about 1924, but not the *Flayed Ox* dating from around 1925.
169 Cat. Chagall 1959, Nos 120, 130, 100, 105, 109. See on all the pictures Amishai-Maisels 2004. Among the colour reproductions in this article there is as Cat. 84, illus. 104, p. 140 both a gouache from 1947 of the *Flayed Ox* and the oil painting from 1947 (No. 83, p. 141, illus. 106); neither of the pictures, however, is mentioned in her text. Schulze, T. 2005 attempts to make up for this lack in relating the picture and the biography.
170 Alpers 1989, p. 191, plate 10.
171 Here as a symbol of betrayal, see Cat. Chagall 1959, No. 115, *Listening to the Cock*, of 1944 and No. 127, *The Cock*, of 1947.
172 On Chagall's pictures of the Crucifixion and the Mother and Child that he used as a symbol of Jewish martyrdom, see the foundational chapter 'The Crucified Jew' in Amishai-Maisels 1993, pp. 178–97, and Amishai-Maisels 2003, pp. 128–31, arguing that Chagall's pictures are imbued with the intention of drawing the attention of the Christian world through the use of typical Christian imagery, at the same time not presenting the Crucifixion or the Mother and Child as symbols of the Holocaust but as indicating the actual events by means of added details.
173 See Grenville 2012.
174 Rommelfanger 2008, p. 63, n. 208.
175 The titles are *Lamentation for the Pogrom Sacrifice* and *Grieving over the Sacrifice* and it shows a victim hanging by the legs with a grieving woman in blue nearby on the left; the date is given by the Jewish Museum in Frankfurt 1961-72-85 (Inv. No. JMF 1997-0026-1-619).
176 Rommelfanger 2008, p. 133, illus. 278.
177 On the biography see Cat. Claus 2011, pp. 42–4.
178 Cat. Claus 1990, No. Z 142, p. 173; Gillen, E. 2009a, p. 209.
179 Celan 2003, pp. 113–18; pp. 643ff.; pp. 667–70. English translation: Hamburger 2007, pp. 158ff.
180 Ibid., p. 114. English translation: Hamburger 2007, p. 163.
181 On this see also Coche de la Ferté 1982, illus. 441–50.
182 Cat. Claus 1990, No. Z 243.
183 Cohen 1998, pp. 114–53.
184 'Kabbalah means literally "reception" from the Latin "receptio".' Kilcher 1998, p. 7.

7 Remembering Again: The Early 1960s

1 Fröhlich 2011.
2 Theodor Oberländer, from 1953 until his retirement in 1960 West German Minister for 'Vertriebene' (Germans forced out of Eastern Europe in 1945), Refugees and War Invalids, was accused of having taken part, as the leader of battalions made up of collaborators, in pogroms in Lemberg (Lviv) and in the Caucasus. In the GDR he was sentenced to life imprisonment in his absence. Both German states

were operating in this case with incorrect and denied statements. See the biography putting a gloss on things by Wachs 2000 and Schröder, D. 2007.

3 Hans Globke, Ministerial Director in the Federal Chancellor's Office, was referred to in the GDR as the 'Eichmann of Bonn' (*Neues Deutschland*, 29 July 1960) because of his activities in the Reich Interior Ministry, in particular his participation in a commentary on the Nuremberg Race Laws, and was sentenced to life imprisonment, like Oberländer, in his absence, but unlike him Adenauer kept him in office as having been 'exonerated'.

4 Erwin Leiser, *Mein Kampf* (originally released under the title *Den blodiga tiden*), Sweden 1960; Leiser 1961. On the background and reception see the details in Thiele 2001, pp. 207–34.

5 After the images, intended to be propaganda for the Nazis, did not produce the required responses at a trial showing, the material became part of the archive.

6 Germany 1934.

7 Originally released under the title *Das Urteil von Nürnberg*, Germany 1940; directed by Veit Harlan.

8 Germany 1940; directed by Fritz Hippler.

9 For Roland Buck, Tübingen, whom I have to thank for the information, the images, which he saw as a pupil in Friedrichshafen in 1961, are still fresh in his memory and recall the Nazi past.

10 U.S. 1961, directed by Stanley Kramer.

11 See Weckel 2009.

12 On Edel's testimony as a witness in the trial against Globke see Cat. Auschwitz-Prozess 2004, pp. 673ff.

13 American Office of War Information 1945, presumably already published at the end of May 1945 in an edition of approx. 250,000 copies; see Brink 1998, pp. 58–70.

14 Schulze, R. 2011.

15 Ibid., p. 56, saw in this a classic example of British culture which regarded the Jews as citizens of states, a definitive move away from the racial ideology of the Nazis, but also a latent anti-Semitism in the British upper classes and the related problem of Palestine. Right from the start of the first British reports, 'Belsen' became for Britain a place of remembrance of the atrocities that were not examined more closely as to how they came about.

16 Mazur et al. 1962, p. 5.

17 Ibid., p. 2.

18 On Schoenberner 1960 see Schmid 2012; summary analyses of the volume of photos and its place in critical history in Brink 1998, pp. 146–77, and Knoch 2001, pp. 699–721.

19 Schmid 2012, p. 339.

20 Stroop 1943/2009, the photograph there on p. 203 with the caption 'Pulled from the Bunkers by Force' looking like a response to Grundig's drawing *Pogrom* (see illus. 7); *Night and Fog* of 1956, it is the first picture of people being deported, see also Hirsch 2002, Raskin 2004, and Frübis 2014.

21 Schmid 2012, p. 340.

22 Arendt 2006 [1963], p. 134.

23 For example Poliakov/Wulf 1955.

24 Engl. edn 1969.

25 See Brink 2007.

26 See Schirmer 2015, p. 115.

27 Mentioned in particular by Schoenberner 1960, p. 222. The report was published in three copies with, in part, slightly different photos; as Andrzej Wirth writes in the foreword to the 1960 Luchterhand edition, his edition is based on the copy Stroop kept for himself, now in the Historical Institute in Warsaw; the others went to Himmler and Stroop's superior Krüger.

28 Raskin 2004, pp. 25–8.

29 Moczarski 1982, p. 202.

30 Stroop 1943/1960.

31 Raskin 2004, pp. 32ff.

32 Wulf 1960 and 1961.

33 Moczarski 1982, p. 156.

34 Stroop 1943/1960, p. 3; see also Grabitz/Scheffler 1993, pp. 285–327; Klemp 2013, pp. 135–74.

35 'The result is invaluable historical material for the Führer, for Heinrich Himmler and for future researchers into the history of the Third Reich, for our National Socialist poets and writers and for the instruction of the SS. Above all, however, this material will record what effort it took and what hard, bloody sacrifices the Nordic race and the Germanic peoples had to make to rid Europe and the whole world of the Jews', SS-Obergruppenführer Krüger explained in a concluding discussion of the situation. Moczarski 1982, p. 156.

36 Arani 1997, Part 2, p. 34.

37 Quoted in Jahn 2009, p. 74; Raskin 2004, pp. 31f., mentions more, possible authors apart from Konrad.

38 Errell 1961, in which eight of the 132 illustrated pages were devoted to the persecution of the Jews.

39 The material was kindly made available to me in 2012 by Matthias Griebel in Dresden.

40 Quoted in Brock 1977, p. 986.

41 Brock 2012, p. 159. Now also on this Cat. Beuys Brock Vostell 2016, pp. 48–51.
42 Becker 2012, p. 168.
43 Quoted in Brock 1977, p. 980.
44 Cat. Hundertwasser 2012, p. 61.
45 Quoted in Brock 1977, p. 979.
46 Brock 2012, p. 157.
47 Ibid.
48 Published in different languages and several editions since 1959, see Mazur et al. 1962, 2nd edn.
49 According to information kindly provided by Stephan Matyus, Fotoarchiv der KZ-Gedenkstätte Mauthausen on 18 November 2015, such photographs were staged and served as 'unnatural cases of death' for the internal SS administration to disguise the killing of concentration camp prisoners as alleged escape attempts or suicides (Inv. No. M-14-3-2).
50 See portraits of the different authors in Cat. dadaglobe 2016.
51 Brock 1960 no page given.
52 Martin Heidegger, Brief über den 'Humanismus' (Letter on 'Humanism') (published 1947): Gesamtausgabe, 9, p. 334.
53 'The "Reich" that we are fighting for receives its legitimation and its nobility from German poetry.' Burger 1942, p. 7.
54 König/Wägenbaur 2003, pp. 300–302.
55 See Broszat 1958, pp. 129f. Brock left out the relations described in it between the family and the prisoners.
56 See Cat. Beuys Brock Vostell 2016, p. 54.
57 On the reception of this photo and the story of the Jewish boy Sieg Mandaag from Holland, who had survived, see Sollors 2014, pp. 57–82.
58 Mandaag was born in 1937, Brock in 1936.
59 Cat. Beuys Brock Vostell 2016, pp. 63–6.
60 Knaurs Spielbuch 1953, p. 214.
61 'An Execution in Cracow', Mazur et al. 1962, p. 62; Cat. Beuys Brock Vostell 2016, p. 51.
62 Following Brock's instruction in 1977, p. 780, compared with Knaurs Spielbuch 1953, p. 214.
63 Cat. 'Wollt Ihr das totale Leben?', p. 22.
64 Note to the illustration of the postcard, Brock 1977, p. 780.
65 At the Berlin Sportpalast in 1943: 'Do you want total war?' This sentence was played in a continuous loop at the Aachen Festival of New Art on 20 July 1964; see the contribution by Vostell pp. 192f.
66 See Cat. 'Wollt Ihr das totale Leben?' 1995.
67 From 1913, see Cat. Steinhardt 1995, the picture hung in the entrance hall of the Jewish Museum in the Oranienburger Strasse in Berlin opened on 24 January 1933 (p. 75).
68 Cat. Vernichtungskrieg 1995.
69 Antelme 1947/1992, pp. 9ff.
70 Amishai-Maisels 1993, colour plate 14.
71 See the later version in the Deutsches Historisches Museum in Ottomeyer/Czech 2009, pp. 290f.
72 Stechow 1977, No. 12.
73 Kramer, S. 1993b, pp. 225–48, in general on this Chaumont 2001, pp. 207–58, chap. 6: 'Schäbigkeit, Scham und Grösse' (Shabbiness, Shame and Greatness) about the fundamental change in normal human values for the concentration camp inmates.
74 Schubert possibly knew about the 'intimate affair' that Rudolf Höss had had with a Jewess as Kommandant at Auschwitz and which had almost caused him to be put on trial by an SS court; see Broszat 1958, p. 19.
75 Eschebach 2010, p. 73.
76 Wenk 2008; Stiglegger 1999; Bartov 1997, pp. 44, 50f. and 55–7.
77 Cat. Dresdner Sezession 1919–1923. Milan/Munich 1977, unpag.
78 Meissner 1989, p. 75; in 1960 Tübke argues for artists to deal with 'the historically necessary, lawful realization of a communist Weltanschauung' and for the 'physically graphic quality' of the cultural tradition of early bourgeois art.
79 Beckmann 2011; Zöllner 2012, pp. 277–80; Cat. Klopfzeichen 2002, pp. 32–6; Zöllner 2009, pp. 73ff.; Meissner 1989, pp. 75–83.
80 Meissner 1989, p. 76.
81 Beckmann 2011, pp. 43f.
82 Ibid., pp. 37–42; on Saefkow see p. 114, n. 29.
83 Cat. Tübke-Stiftung 2009, p. 90, illus. 47; Beckmann 2011, p. 65.
84 Gillen, E. 2009a, p. 344: 'with these frivolous historical ramblings in the style of a diorama'.
85 Two triptychs were displayed in 1961 at the 6th Leipzig Regional Exhibition, see Meissner 1989, p. 80.
86 Buchenwald 1959.
87 Meissner 1989, p. 79.
88 Ibid., p. 75; Tübke 1960, pp. 198f.
89 'For the day rooms (bar etc.) I recommend a subject from a more pleasant aspect of our new socialist life. And if there are to be pictures from earlier decades of the German workers' movement, then

they should not be history painting . . . Tübke with his tendency to melancholy . . . should be actively encouraged to take on a cheery subject,' is what Georg Kaufmann, the chief editor of the house magazine of the Verband Bildender Künstler Deutschlands *Das Blatt*, wrote to Alfred Kurella on 12 September 1959, quoted in Cat. Klopfzeichen 2002, pp. 34f.; see also Kurella's related criticism in a letter to Tübke from 24 June 1960 in Beckmann 2011, p. 147.

90 Quoted in Gillen, E. 2009b, pp. 57f. On the important support nevertheless given to Tübke by Kurella up until the 1970s see Gassner 1996, pp. 70–674 and Gillen 2012, pp. 175–83. The letter from Kurella to Tübke from 24 June 1960 is given in Beckmann 2011, p. 147.

91 By Lothar Lang in the Weltbühne of 28 February 1962, quoted in Meissner 1989, p. 83.

92 Given in Thur 2009, pp. 125f.

93 Beckmann 2011, p. 148, giving the certificate of reception of 24 November 1966 at the Museum der bildenden Künste in Leipzig.

94 Soviet Union 1947, directed by Roman Karmen and Elizaveta Svilova.

95 Wenzel 2012, p. 338.

96 Akademie der Künste, Heartfield Archive 579, letter of 20 January 1960.

97 Speech published in March 1981, pp. 462f.

98 Cat. Sandberg 1965; in this autobiographical report on his political career and his time in the camp at Buchenwald there are no Jews mentioned.

99 Immediately after the end of the war Waldemar Grzimek for Halle (1946–7) and Fritz Cremer for Vienna (1948) worked on memorials to the victims of fascism; see Hoffmann-Curtius 2002a.

100 Review of the exhibition in *Bildende Kunst* 5/1960, pp. 342–5.

101 Source: Lea Grundig, Einträge zum Leihverkehr in 6 Bänden, here vol. 1, entry under 'Überschrift: Club der Kulturschaffenden', in Akademie der Künste, Grundig Archive, 320/1, unpag. loose sheet, added at the back, dated 2 February 1960.

102 Grundig, Lea WVZ 1973, illus. 43–8.

103 Akademie der Künste, Grundig Archive, No. 250, letter of 19 May 1960 and 8 November 1960.

104 *Neues Deutschland*, 6 July 1963, p. 2.

105 Research into the archive and art collection left by Hans and Lea Grundig; clues were found in the books, in which Lea Grundig listed loans, occasionally also sales and gifts as well as plans of work (Akademie der Künste, Grundig Archive, 320/1, 2, period from 1957 to 1968).

106 See *Dass ein gutes Deutschland blühe*, Grundig, Lea WVZ 2016 (unpag.); here the two drawings identified in 2014 as being from the Globke cycle are discussed.

107 Grundig, Lea WVZ 1973, No. 81, drawing 12 from the series *War Threatens*, 1936.

108 Brüne 1996a, p. 38, persuasively interpreted the footprints as an omen frequently used by Grundig and 'with hindsight a symbol for genocide by the Nazis in general'.

109 Didi-Huberman 1999, p. 10.

110 Cat. Lea Grundig 1977, illus. 26, No. 55; the catalogue entry notes: 'This street was built by prisoners on the orders of the SS from the ashes of their fellow prisoners incinerated at Theresienstadt.'

111 Hütt 1969, illus. 44; Feist 1975, Bl. 1.

112 Hütt 1969, illus. 120.

113 Grundig, Lea WVZ 2016 identifies her as a self-portrait of the artist.

114 Cat. Meyer-Vax 1965, unpag.

115 Ibid.

116 Antelme 1947/1992, p. 55.

117 Dürer WVZ 1973, p. 151, No. 72.

118 Schwerte 1962, pp. 258ff.

119 Cat. Wilhelm Lachnit 2000, p. 31.

120 Classification of the Berlinische Galerie Berlin, which exhibited the whole installation in 2010, on *Treblinka* and Vostell WVZ 1988, pp. 54 and 186ff. The date is questioned in Decker 1988, pp. 40–60. All the dates of Vostell's works are based on what the artist gave. To what extent there were lapses in his memory over this will have to be left for research into the whole of his oeuvre in this period that will only be possible in the archive being set up at the Museo Vostell in Malpartida in Spain. One thing for sure is that the *Auschwitzscheinwerfer* was exhibited in 1963 in connection with *Bus Trip 9 Decollages* at the Galerie Parnass in Wuppertal, as it is shown on a photo of the event: Cat. Treffpunkt Parnass 1980, illustrated p. 226.

121 According to information kindly provided by Rafael Vostell, the searchlight should be permanently shining as the only source of light in *Black Room*.

122 *Der Spiegel*, 12, No. 37, 10 September 1958, title page. Fumasoni-Biondi was Prefect of the Congregatio de Propaganda Fide.

123 *Der Spiegel*, 1 January 1958, p. 14.

124 Hackenschmidt 2014, pp. 444–57.

125 Cat. Vostell 1992, pp. 75ff.

126 See Hoffmann, D. 1998b.
127 The '"No-Book" is so fragile that it cannot be leafed through in its present position. Taking it out of its case of objects, securing the pages and photographing would be too much work for our restorers and photographers to carry out in the foreseeable future.' Email of 9 March 2012 from Dr Werner Esser, Conservator at the Kunstarchive-Archiv Sohm Staatsgalerie Stuttgart.
128 The catalogue of the Stuttgart exhibition of 2012, without giving any further details, mentions a new title and another date: *Nein-Buch Oradour*, 1959–1966, see Cat. FLUXUS 2012, No. 16.2.
129 Cat. documenta 6,3 1977, pp. 348–9.
130 Cat. NO!art 1995.
131 The connection is further supported by the insects (*Flea Siphomaptera*) preserved in resin, which are not shown in the photo in Cat. documenta 6,3 1977, but are now in the Nein-Buch and are comparable with the chickens' heads preserved in resin called *Death's Sculptures* by Boris Lurie, see Cat. NO!art 1995, illustrated p. 55.
132 Schoenberner 1960, pp. 40, 91, 96 and 152. The photo of Mauthausen was not reproduced there, according to the kind information by telephone from G. Schoenberner on 24 February 2012; it appeared only in the edition of 1998.
133 Photo of the camp band at Mauthausen illustrated in Mazur et al. 1960, p. 122; Fackler 2005 deals in detail with the history and the reception of the photo and three others that were taken of the event, and gives precise facts about its use in the Nuremberg trials (n. 4); information kindly supplied by Stephan Matyus, Fotoarchiv der KZ-Gedenkstätte Mauthausen.
134 Mazur et al., 1962, p. 123.
135 Cat. Vostell 2005, pp. 30f., No.1967: 3.
136 Schoenberner 1960, p. 163.
137 Repr. in Goldhagen 1996, p. 190. Knoch 2001, p. 953, see also Mazur et al. 1962, pp. 106f.

8 The Past in the Present: Commenting on the Auschwitz Trial

1 On the public response, see Atze 2004.
2 The much discussed book *Eichmann in Jerusalem: A Report on the Banality of Evil* (1963) was published in German in 1964.
3 See Jaskot 2012, pp. 65f.; Cat. Auschwitz-Prozess 2004, on the public response in particular see Atze, pp. 637–47.
4 See Brink 2000, pp. 36f., illus 5, 6.
5 Kosmala 2014; Knoch 2001, p. 803; Brink 2000, pp. 13 and 17.
6 *Berliner Zeitung*, 18 April 1963, p. 8, 'The Ghetto is a Warning', with the advance publicity.
7 Poland 1948.
8 *Berliner Zeitung*, 18 April 1963.
9 Cat. Monumenta Judaica 1963, B 730–93.
10 Brink 2000, pp. 12–16; Kosmala 2014; Knoch 2001, pp. 797ff.
11 Presumably *Tagebuch eines Verzweifelten* (Diary of a Man in Despair) by Friedrich Percyval Reck-Malleczewen, published posthumously in 1947 by Bürger-Verlag.
12 According to research by Hartewig 2000, p. 437, n. 9, Becher published the poem as a response to the news of the liberation of the Lublin concentration camp at Majdanek in the Moscow exile journal *Internationale LiteraturPresse* in October 1944; see Becher 1967, pp. 335–40.
13 *Frankfurter Allgemeine Zeitung* of 22 November 1963, p. 1, and in the local news section, pp. 33f. 'The Way of the Maltreated and Martyred: The Exhibition "Warsaw Ghetto" at the Paulskirche'.
14 Brink 2000.
15 Oellers 1997.
16 Cat. Vostell 1992, p. 315 and Vostell 1970, p. 342, documents and dates the concept to 1954. Cat. Vostell 1992, p. 88, identifies the first happening in 1958 in Paris, in which the public were requested to read texts from posters, constantly changing these by tearing them off.
17 Illustrated in Beuys WVZ Aktionen 1994, p. 66.
18 Cat. 'Wollt ihr das totale Leben?' 1995, p. 10.
19 Hackenschmidt 2014, p. 40.
20 See the commentaries in Cat. 'Wollt ihr das totale Leben?' 1995, p. 12.
21 Cat. 'Wollt ihr das totale Leben?' 1995, in particular pp. 38f. and 71.
22 Cat. Vostell 1992, p. 91.
23 Score and illustrations of the happening in Cat. Vostell 1975, pp. 120–35.
24 Morschel 1965, p. 39.
25 See the 'Partitur' ('score') in Cat. Vostell 1975, pp. 120–35, on this see p. 123.
26 Langston 2008, on p. 151, sees the whole happening in the context of the Nazis; see ibid., pp. 138–52.
27 Morschel 1965, p. 26.
28 On the directions for this happening on 5 June 1965 in Wuppertal see Vostell 1970, p. 204.

29 Berlinische Galerie Berlin; under the heading quoted in the title of the picture, the newspaper reported on 30 October 1964 about the witness statement to the Frankfurt trial by Piotr Mishin a Russian POW imprisoned at Auschwitz; see on this work Hoffmann-Curtius 2005, pp. 72–5.
30 Kuhn 1964 gives an insight into the parallel being drawn at the time.
31 Schoenberner 1960, p. 191.
32 John Profumo had to resign as British Secretary of State for War in 1963 for having deceived Parliament over his affair with Christine Keeler. The scandal occupied the press for months.
33 Wenzel 2009, pp. 200ff.
34 Quoted in Beuys WVZ Aktionen, pp. 43f.
35 Cat. Beuys 2008, p. 97 and 379, No. 04 18. Ibid., pp. 90–101.
36 Kramer, M. 1997, p. 295.
37 Information kindly supplied by the artist Galli.
38 Quoted from the 1980 edition, p. 35. For Beuys it is supposed to 'indicate something spiritual as a substance for dissolving sense impressions'. Joseph Beuys, *Die Materialien und ihre Botschaft*, Schloss Moyland 2007, Press release 2006, quoted at: www.kulturpunkt.ch/ereignisse/er-moylandbeuys06-11.htm (3 December 2013). On the Brown Cross as a 'sign of extreme diversity' see Cat. Beuys 1985a, pp. 12f; also Cat. Beuys 1985b.
39 See www.walkerart.org/archive/C/9C43F9ACA34F1B386167.htm (14 November 2013).
40 Following Rudolf Steiner, Beuys sees the Christ Impulse as the message from the crucified Christ to mankind, which does not mean salvation, but in Steiner's words calls upon them: 'You have come down into the material world, and now you must redeem yourself, free yourself again from it . . . and you can do that by taking on the power of Christ, revealed to you by the outside world in its reality!', Rudolf Steiner, *Der Christus-Impuls* (1910), quoted in Riegel 2013, p. 199; on the Christ Impulse in Beuys see also Malaka 2007, pp. 100f., and Maur 1988.
41 On this display case in particular Theewen 1993, pp. 29–32, and Cat. Beuys 1993, Cat. No. 11, pp. 29 and 67ff. In 1976 the box was acquired as display case 3 from the former private collection Herbig in 1992 by the Hessische Kulturstiftung with support from the Kulturstiftung der Länder and exhibited in a room for Joseph Beuys in the Neue Galerie in Kassel. We won't go any further here into the change of significance by being reassembled in the box.
42 Cat. Beuys 1986.
43 It is a question whether one should mention here the maltreatment inflicted on the Jews by the Nazis, e.g. in Vienna, when they were forced to clean the streets with brushes designed for personal hygiene, as recorded by Alfred Hrdlicka in his Memorial in Vienna.
44 Biro 2003, pp. 118f.
45 Buchloh 2001, pp. 85–9.
46 Tomberger 2002, p. 8, observes: 'Instead of the usually dominant way of handling material in Art Informel associated with aggression, Beuys was more for placing the emphasis on therapeutic, healing work and going along with the material. The artistic process was explicitly related to a society which was, in his way of understanding, in need of healing.'
47 Beuys in discussion with Caroline Tisdall 1979, pp. 21f.; similarly in discussion with H. Rywelski 1970, quoted in Koepplin 1977, p. 6.
48 Albrecht Goes writes in 1955 in the foreword to the paperback edition of the Diary of Anne Frank: 'It is necessary to listen to this voice in the world of 1955, which has not ceased to be a concentration camp' (Goes 1955, p. 7).
49 Riegel, 2013, p. 305, in his discussion of the *Auschwitz Demonstration* comes to the conclusion that Beuys 'interpreted the Holocaust as proof of the unhealthy effect of materialism', 'Auschwitz' being for him simply a 'metaphor' for this.
50 Cat. Beuys 1988, p. 179, No. 48.
51 See the explanation for the 1965 installation, in which this object was shown for the first time in Cat. No. K 37: 'K 37 1965 me and my loved one's abandoned sleep. Did not come about for nothing. The subject is breaking through this abandonment of oneself and others that he loves. It is a long time and there are many that it is our task to reach, created and referred to as a (stack).' Beuys 2010, p. 32. In addition the sheet 'CLAN' is reproduced (p. 40), in which the artist's parental and maternal ancestors are listed in a handwritten note as an 'example of a possible stack' (p. 42).
52 Ray 2001b, pp. 63ff., and Malaka 2007, p. 39.
53 Summary of this in Julia Voss, 'Stoff aus Schweigen', in *Frankfurter Allgemeine Zeitung*, 24 December 2009.
54 Wagner 2001, p. 216; Ray 2001b, pp. 63–5; see also on this the illustrations in Sehn 1957, p. 176.
55 As the *Block Beuys* is not accessible owing to the closure of the Hessisches Landesmuseum

Darmstadt since 2007, this is based above all on Beuys, E. et al. 1990.

56 For details of the exhibition and the background to the *Block Beuys*: see Beuys E. et al. 1990, pp. 395–403, and Malaka 2007, pp. 32–4.

57 Spielmann 1990, p. 298.

58 Illustrated in Cat. Beuys 1969, illus. 21; both Gate Models are on display there with the numerals of Beuys's date of birth.

59 Beuys wvz Aktionen 1994, p. 88.

60 Beuys, E. et al. 1990, pp. 40–54; Malaka 2007, pp. 124–7.

61 Beuys 1973, quoted in Beuys, E. et al. 1990, p. 307.

62 Ibid., p. 307. Huber 1995 describes the installation as 'selective' and 'subjective': 'Similarity and difference, order and disorder is the first thing one notices, Beuys forces the viewer, to put up with his works like a good liberal, to remain politely silent faced with the pleasures and rejections that he doesn't share with him' (p. 73).

63 Malaka 2007, pp. 126f., largely follows Huber 1995, pp. 73–84, who reads the word 'stag hunt' as its being endangered by the scientific method and simplistic materialism according to Beuys. The death of the stag whose sacrifice, he writes in line with Beuys, 'signifies, however, the resurrection of faith, thought and feeling. In the freedom achieved through death there arises a new, spiritual life' (p. 84). On animals such as the hare, elk, bee, horse and swan, 'loved by the average citizen', according to Beuys 1971; see Meink 2010 (quoted on this on p. 99).

64 Bächtold-Stäubli 1927–1942.

65 Fritz 2007, p. 60; on the stag in Beuys's work see also Bastian 1996, pp. 20f.

66 St Hubertus, whose image is the stag, or hart, with a crucifix between its antlers, is particularly revered in Cologne (BBKL vol. II), and one of the oldest representations of the saint is in the *Book of Hours* of Katherina von Kleve, the duchess who had once been a resident of Beuys's home town; illustrated on www.sankt-hubertus.de/bild28.htm (17 December 2013). *Crucifix on the Plate* of the *Auschwitz Demonstration*, used in the 1966 installation *Manresa*, could have been as much inspired by this as were the antlers with the halo in the drawing *Giant Stag with Slices of Sun and Moon*, 1957, illus. 92 in Cat. Beuys 2010, p. 114.

67 Beuys, E. et al. 1990, p. 158.

68 All the designations ibid., p. 158.

69 On the following see Malaka 2007.

70 Beuys in the interview with Dr Müller 1968, quoted in Cat. Beuys 1969, p. 35.

71 Beuys, E. et al. 1990, p. 182.

72 Ibid., p. 184.

73 Kramer, M. 1997, p. 301.

74 According to Kramer, M. 1997, p. 296, it is occasionally called *Celtic Sun Disc* and is supposed to bear a close relationship to Beuys's oil drawing *Druidic Measuring Device*. Perhaps Beuys, placing the end bits of the sausage on the disc, was recalling the photo of the camp prisoners' daily ration (see illus. 175), on which a thin slice of bread is visible.

75 Despite suggestions to the contrary, according to Ray 2001b, p. 62, there are no concrete indications that Beuys, in this happening that subsequently became famous, was referring to Auschwitz and the murder of the Jews; see the documentation of *Kukei, akopee-Nein! Braunkreuz, Fettecken, Modellfettecken im Rahmen der Fluxus-Veranstaltung Actions/Agit Pop/De-Collage/Happening/Events/ Antiart/L'Autrisme/Art total/Refluxus-festival der neuen Kunst* in Beuys wvz Aktionen 1994, pp. 42–66, in particular pp. 47ff. Only Tomas Schmit had written about 'genocide' before the event in the Aachen student magazine *Prisma* in the course of a polemic, ibid., pp. 43f.

76 Kramer, M. 1997, p. 298.

77 It is hardly surprising that Beuys referred to Ignatius Loyola, the initiator of Christian 'spiritual exercises'; after all they shared the experience of being wounded in war and reading theological texts during their convalescence. Manresa is the place in Spain where the later founder of the Jesuit order, through mystical experiences, turned away from the court and the military towards a life of service. Details of the installation in the Galerie Schmela in Düsseldorf Beuys wvz Aktionen 1994, pp. 146–65.

78 Sehn 1957, from p. 16.

79 Official designation of Auschwitz during the Nazi period, see Kramer, M. 1997, p. 300.

80 Date and designation according to Kramer, M. 1997, p. 302.

81 Malaka 2007, p. 347, describes it also as if it were obvious: 'The human being manifests itself as one sick unto death in the drawing "Sick Girl"'.

82 In 1976 he was to display two real undertaker's stretchers in his notorious environmental installation *Show Us Your Wound* in a pedestrian subway in Munich. Beuys talked on the occasion about 'indications that rigor mortis can be overcome'. Tomberger 2002, p. 1.

83 Malaka 2007, p. 348.
84 Exhibited in 1968 in Eindhoven with the title *Worst*, given in the meantime to another object from the same display case, see the exhibition list in http://alexandria.tue.nl/vanabbe/public/publiciteit/zaalteksten/1968/Zaaltekst-NEDBeuys1968.pdf (14 November 2013).
85 On the first exhibition of the objects in 'a totally different context in a four-level glass display case' see Kramer, M. 1997, p. 296, n. 23.
86 Malaka 2007, pp. 61–6, 346–53.
87 Ibid., p. 207.
88 On Beuys's 'totalitarian concept of art' Malaka 2007, pp. 17, 61 and 66: 'The "Auschwitz Demonstration" seems to be infused with the spirit of occultism, within which artistic creativity, the longing for religious salvation and the pursuit of scientific knowledge come together.'
89 Malaka 2007, pp. 349–51.
90 Ibid., pp. 221, 294, 342, 352; Bunge 1998, p. 155, writes about the four sausages, 'which remind one of half-burnt bodies such as were found in the hastily abandoned concentration camps'.
91 Gillen, E. 2009a, p. 216, likewise referring to Beuys's objects and installations to do with Auschwitz, talks about his attempt 'to liberate himself from his traumatic past' and 'as a representative of the Germans to redeem them symbolically'.
92 Fritz 2007, p. 22.
93 Here it needs to be noted that it was not just Beuys's works in Kassel but also the *Block Beuys* in Darmstadt that were acquired by the Kulturstiftung der Länder and the Deutsche Bank in 1989; see Malaka 2007, p. 34; also Beuys, E. et al. 1990, p. 403.
94 Emphasis in the original.
95 Kramer, M. 1997, p. 303.
96 Buchloh in the reprint of his article of 1979 in Ray, 2001d, pp. 199–211.
97 See for example the design for *Genoveva* of 1942, illustrated in Cat. Oppenheim 2013, illus. p. 92.
98 The common features go beyond the arrangement of objects in cases and boxes: both Beuys and Cornell based their art on the reading of theology (on Cornell and Christian Science see Doss 2007) outside of the main denominations and had the aim of healing mankind with their art. A comparative analysis of both artists would appear to be worth doing.
99 Tomberger 2002, p. 9; Quermann 2006, pp. 47–53; and the work by Kuni 2006 with the reception history as the background to the phenomenon of Beuys the 'magician'.
100 Kreidler, 1988a, pp. 129–33; Kreidler 1988b, p. 43; Cat. Berke 1992, pp. 106ff.; Cat. Berke 2008, p. 49.
101 Bartels/Berke 2008.
102 Kreidler 2004, pp. 11ff., illus. 7–13.
103 Berke 1992, p. 84.
104 Cat. Widerstand 1978, pp. 100f.
105 Haftmann 1954, S. 453 and 485; Berke was represented at *documenta 2* in 1959 by *Pain* from 1958 (illustrated in Cat. documenta 2,1 1959, p. 92). The only picture exhibited in 1959 in Kassel dealing with the murder of the Jews was *Otages: La Juive* from 1943 by Jean Fautrier, who was persecuted under the Nazis; see Hoffmann-Curtius 2008.
106 From Act 1 of the biblical drama by Friedrich Gerke from 1946, illus. 7 in Cat. Berke 1962, pp. 30f.
107 Amishai-Maisels, p. 164.
108 See Hoffmann-Curtius 2010, pp. 128f.
109 As far as one can see, thanks to the help of Michael Berke, the group of works consists of nine oil paintings on canvas and approximately seventy watercolours and ink drawings.
110 Kreidler 1988a, p. 133.
111 Newman was represented by *Tundra* (1950) and *Cathedra* (1951); Berke by *Schmerz* (1958); see Cat. documenta 2,1 1959, pp. 300f. and p. 92.
112 At moma.org/collection/works/79601, 15 October 2016.
113 Godfrey 2007, pp. 51–78.
114 An outcome of his discovering Newman's paintings appears to be the oil painting *Ritual* from 1958, illustrated in Cat. Berke 2008, p. 60.
115 Kreidler 1988a, p. 130.
116 Ibid., n. 407, mentions press photos with the titles 'Inhabitants of the Ghetto are driven out of their hiding-places' and 'Nameless victims of the organized mass murder at Bergen-Belsen'. The text of the press photo from the cuttings no longer traceable in the archive indicates the photo from the Stroop Report (see illus. 214), and Kreidler's description of the second photo 'The photo from Bergen-Belsen shows bodies stretched out and laid out like crosses, which one finds again in the series of "Hängende"' probably refers to Schoenberner 1960, p. 193.
117 Bronfen 2012.
118 Theweleit, 'Die zwei Seiten der Folter' (The Two Sides of Torture), ibid. 1995, pp. 47–55.
119 Kreidler 1988b, illus. 48.
120 Ibid., illus. 49.
121 Cat. Auschwitz-Prozess 2004, pp. 388–437.
122 See two of the drawings in Cat. Berke 1992, pp. 124f.

123 Kaschnitz 1945.
124 Hahn 2005, pp. 54–66.
125 Haftmann 1964, p. xiv; in the same introduction he said that both the owners of works by Chaim Soutine and also Mark Rothko with his own works refused to exhibit in Germany. He added the statement 'The wound which our country inflicted on humanity has not healed,' p. xvi.
126 Cat. documenta 3,1 1964, p. 390.
127 Roters 1964.
128 Szymanski wvz 1975, 62/3.
129 Szymanski wvz 1975, 59/6.
130 Roters 1964.
131 Wenk 1997.
132 In the Tate collection, London, illustrated at: www.tate.org.uk/art/artworks/moore-upright-motive-no-1-glenkiln-cross-t02274 (13 January 2014).
133 Roters 1964.
134 Szymanski requested the information but did not submit a proposal; see Spielmann 1990, p. 358.
135 Szymanski wvz 1975, 61/3.
136 See Roters 1964: 'The sculptor says that the impression made on him by the Strasbourg figures also influenced the creation of the sculptures.'
137 Szymanski wvz 1975, 63/2. Since 2008 the sculpture at the height planned by Szymanski has stood in front of the building of the Hannover Rückversicherung AG (Insurance Company) and in the garden of the Westend Clinic in Berlin, see www.brusbergfineart.com/html/bb/kataloge/r_szymanski_zum_80.pdf (13 January 2014).
138 Dirks 2006, pp. 59–72; on the 'Blutrichter' campaign and the trial against Theodor Oberländer and Hans Globke; see also Herbert 2013.
139 Copy in Thur 2009, p. 117.
140 Herbert 2013, p. 57, comments in the study of their Nazi past: 'The extraordinarily successful self-defence of their political past on the part of the former Nazi lawyers, who have been almost totally restored to West German positions since the 1950s, is certainly remarkable for its aggression.'
141 Thur 2009, p. 122.
142 Ibid., p. 123.
143 According to Beaucamp's classification 2008, p. 4; Thur 2009, p. 3, n. 1, carefully lists the different numbers of related works produced up until 2008. Gillen 2009b, p. 344, talks of '1964/5 up to 1967 12 paintings, approx. 70 drawings and 16 watercolours'.
144 Beaucamp 2009b, p. 62, with the only mention in the literature: 'Many of the representations are based on photographs and documentary film from the camps.' Quoted again in Thur 2009, p. 19.
145 Schoenberner 1960. For the pictures examined in this current volume, Tübke mainly used this publication. In the GDR an equivalent by the Jewish historian Eschwege was not published until 1966. Research into the background sources met with no success, on the other hand, via searches through: Jindrich/Lukas 1959, Buchenwald 1959, Buchenwald 1960, Wulf 1960, Errell 1961, Leiser 1961, Gumkowski et al. 1963, Cat. Warschauer Ghetto 1963, Huber/Müller 1964. In volumes such as: Stroop 1943/2009, Poliakov/Wulf 1955, Mark 1960, Rutkowski/Stempelberg 1960, Scheffler 1960, Jewish Historical Institute Warsaw 1960, Neumann 1961 and Zentner 1965, there are illustrations of individual photographs, particularly those from Stroop 1943/2009, which Tübke also referred to, but the pile of photos used by Tübke which are all collected in Schoenberner 1960, is likewise evidence of Tübke's principal study of that volume, as is the fact that Tübke only worked with those photos from the Stroop Report about the extermination of the ghetto that are also illustrated in Schoenberner's book.
146 Discussed and illustrated for the first time in Meissner 2009, pp. 10–17, illustrated p. 11.
147 The form of a triptych without a curved top section with three framed areas on each of the side wings, four planned in each in the sketch, is also what Tübke already chose for the 1960 preparatory drawing wvz z68/61 *Zur Geschichte der deutschen Arbeiterbewegung*, see Beckmann 2011, pp. 47–61, illus. 11 and p. 160.
148 Brink 2007, p. 65, quotes the *Deutsche Volkszeitung*, linked to the SED, the East German Socialist Party, of 11 November 1960, which mentions, apropos of Schoenberner's book, photos about the 'Passion of the Jews'.
149 Möbius 1989; Hoffmann-Curtius 2002a, pp. 372f.; see also the powerful female nude in Max Lachnit's group of sculptures *Death and Life* from 1945/1948 in Cat. Max Lachnit 1991, p. 74, illus. 53.
150 Beaucamp 2009a, p. 42.
151 In Cat. Tübke 1972 Roland März wrote: 'From the ruins of the old world there arises, after all, in the beautiful, unscathed physicality of the female nudes the pictorial antithesis: the new, free human being,' unpag.
152 Kantor 1987.
153 Cat. Galerie Neue Meister 2010, pp. 557f.;

1966 acquired by the City Council of Leipzig (Department of Culture) Gal.-No. 3636.

154 See Gillen 2009a, p. 345. Roland März writes in the Cat. Tübke 1972: 'The cycle of the Memoirs of Dr. jur. Schulze begins with the memorial painting "Requiem", a searing mass for the dead, dark and tragic in tone.'

155 The drawing referred to by Schwesig (illus. 120) of Daumier's (illus. 119) and in other representations known in all probability by Tübke: Rössing 1947, No. 7, *The Next Morning*; David Alfaro Siqueiros, *Victims*, 1945, addition to the left side of the mural painting *New Democracy*, Palacio de Bellas Artes, Mexico City, illustrated in Frommhold 1968, illus. 449.

156 Emmrich 1976, p. 21: 'the intellectual connection to the Dresden Memorial to the anti-Fascist fighters in the former state court is evident'.

157 Tübke 1960, p. 198.

158 Schoenberner 1960, p. 211; in the reference to this, p. 222, only the 'Imperial War Museum' is given. According to information kindly supplied by G. Schoenberner of 24 February 2012 it is a photograph of Bergen-Belsen camp.

159 Schoenberner 1960, p. 207.

160 The photo of the corpses of prisoners in Block 11 at Auschwitz was taken between mid-February and mid-March by Stanislaw Mucha (Cat. Mémoire 2001, p. 103, illus. 134).

161 Schoenberner 1960, p. 203.

162 Weiss 1960/1964, p. 48.

163 Tübke Skizzenbuch, p. 34 (the 'Green' Sketchbook of Werner Tübke is kept by the university library at Leipzig, which kindly supplied me with a CD; the quotations from it follow Tübke's pagination. Meissner 1989, p. 126, and Thur 2009, p. 76, refer to *Die Ermittlung* (The Investigation) by Peter Weiss, written and performed in the same period, emphasizing its 'scenic documentation'.

164 See the full-page illustration in Frommhold 1958, pp. 94 and 78.

165 On the *Requiem* the catalogue of the museum owning it only states, 'that the dead bodies in the "Requiem" are only distantly reminiscent of the victims of the Holocaust and in minor details such as the striped trouser leg of the dead body on the extreme left'. Fleischer 2010, p. 557.

166 See here also Emmrich 1976, p. 34, who felt reminded, in the case of one of the figures from the Halle version of *Dr. jur. Schulze*, of the Leipzig painter and graphic artist Alfred Frank murdered in 1945. The interesting thing about her remark 'although the artist by his own statement did not intend such a portrait either consciously or deliberately', is that Tübke did not reveal in this discussion that he based it on the Stroop Report (see Stroop 1943/2009) according to Schoenberner 1960, p. 180.

167 Schoenberner 1960, p. 89, top.

168 Information kindly supplied by Christiane Hess, Lüneburg.

169 Illustrated in Cat. Zeitenwende 2016, Cat: No. 90, p. 129.

170 WVZ Z 9/65 from 1965, illustrated in Cat. Tübke 2009, p. 43; illustration of the torso WVZ Z16/65 in Thur 2009, illus. 25.

171 The title of this watercolour and pen drawing is verified by Cat. Tübke 1976, p. 71, No. 58.

172 Wenzel 2009, p. 13.

173 See Gillen, E. 2009b.

174 Cat. Tübke 1972, unpag.

175 Thur 2009, p. 124. From this statement of Tübke's, the later selection of his works and the technique, Thur convincingly proves that the picture now called *Memoirs of Dr. jur. Schulze I* in Frankenhausen, which does not show a judge as a figure, should be considered a preliminary study. Thur 2009, pp. 56f. and 96.

176 Tübke Skizzenbuch, p. 62: 'The main thing! It must express generality (not everyday political illustration).'

177 Emmrich 1976, p. 34.

178 Illustrated in Zöllner 2012, illus. 263.

179 See Thur 2009, p. 123.

180 Not, as could be heard in the audio presentation at the Neue Nationalgalerie Berlin (May 2012) on *Schulze III*, just a reference to wealth.

181 Emmrich 1976, p. 35, similarly interpreted by Meissner 1989, p. 119, 'Memorial stele with the relief portrait of the person on trial'.

182 One thinks here of Benozzo Gozzoli's frescoes of the Journey of the Magi in the Palazzo Medici Ricardi, Florence from 1459 or Filippino Lippi's Altar of the *Adoration of the Magi* in the Uffizi in Florence from 1496. Illustration: http://bpkgate.picturemaxx.com, picture nos 00016807 and 00065412 (2 June 2013).

183 Schoenberner 1960, p. 22.

184 Presumably prompted by this scene, Emmrich 1976, p. 33 thought: 'The Halle picture is devoted to the subject of the Apocalypse.' The reference to the Apocalypse is taken up again by Zöllner 2012, p. 282.

185 Emmrich 1976, p. 34.

186 Tübke Skizzenbuch, p. 68.
187 Thur 2009, pp. 82–90, with a press review.
188 Lang 1978, illus. S. 91 and 94; Heisig destroyed the picture in 1966 after criticism; see Thur 2009, p. 83.
189 Thur 2009, p. 84.
190 Alfred Kurella, 'Alle Karten auf den Tisch – die besten ins Spiel. Die VI. Deutsche Kunstausstellung im Lichte des VII. Parteitages', *Neues Deutschland*, 26 February 1967.
191 Quoted from the inventory card of the Neue Nationalgalerie Berlin.
192 Thur 2009, pp. 91–4. Eduard Beaucamp, 'Ankunft über einen Umweg. Die Ausstellung der Bilder Werner Tübkes in Mailand', in *Frankfurter Allgemeine Zeitung*, 17 September 1971, quoted in Cat. Tübke 2004, pp. 159f.
193 To my knowledge the complete cycle has only been shown up to now at the exhibition in 1972; see Cat. Tübke 1972 for painting No. 4.
194 Cat. documenta 6,1 1977, p. 132, illus. 133.
195 Last Judgement triptych, around 1500, Vienna, Akademie der bildenden Künste.
196 See p. 105 for the same metaphor in Wiechert 1946.
197 Cat. Tübke 1972, unpag.
198 Ibid.
199 Beaucamp 1997, p. 204.
200 See the five last photos in the Stroop Report of the ruins of the Warsaw Ghetto, available at pamiec.pl/ftp/illustracje/Raport_stroopa.pdf (12 August 2017). The model for the skyscraper behind the judge-puppet was possibly the ruins of the building in Warsaw of the Prudential Insurance, built by Marcin Weinfeld in the 1930s as the second tallest building in Europe; see the illustration of the destroyed building in Mazur et al. 1962, p. 212, and at http://commons.wikimedia.org, wiki/File:Prudential_Building_Warsaw,_1945.jpg (7 October 2013).
201 Albrecht Altdorfer, *The Battle of Alexander at Issus*, 1528–9, Alte Pinakothek Munich.
202 Tübke Skizzenbuch, p. 68; Meissner 1989, p. 119, as well as Tübke's formulation in Cat. Tübke 1972 and the interview of June 1966 reprinted there, with the Berliner Rundfunk.
203 See Brink 1998, chap. 1 and p. 176.
204 Cat. Tübke 1972, unpag.
205 Photo in Amishai-Maisels 1993, illus. 172, with the caption: 'Photograph of prisoners shot by Nazis'.
206 See the metaphors of the Devil in human form in Schoenberner 1960, p. 5; Ernst Wiechert 1948 in the foreword to Zielezinski's *24 Drawings*; and Hannah Arendt's *Images of Hell* of 1946, reprinted in Arendt 1989, pp. 49–62.
207 Beaucamp 1997, p. 202.
208 Related to this in Tübke's own oeuvre are the pencil drawing *Prisoners* Z 3/65 in the Beaucamp collection and the oil study *White Terror in Hungary*, 1956–7; *Being Taken Down from the Lamppost* Gem. No. 29, illustrated in Cat. Tübke 1976, illus. 4.
209 For details on how the SS cavalry units were included in representing the Nazi state and in the actions carried out against Jews and partisans in Poland, see Dorondo 2012, pp. 166ff.
210 KL Auschwitz 1963, p. 75.
211 Ibid., pp. 77 and 81; see also the photo from 1945 of Hendryk Makarewicz in Swiebocka 1993, p. 192, illus. 218.
212 See KL Auschwitz 1963, p. 61; see at www.whale.to/b/auschwitz_gas_chamber.html (2 October 2013).
213 According to Didi-Huberman 2007, pp. 72f., even those of the executioners.
214 Cat. Tübke 1972, unpag.
215 Stroop 1943/2009, p. 196, Dok. N. 6/202 z. Inv. 4500.
216 A possible enlarged model could also be the one published in Gumkowski et al. 1963, unpag.
217 Schoenberner 1960, who was working with the copy from Warsaw, took the caption of another photograph in this copy: 'Der Marsch zum Umschlagplatz' (The March to the Trans-shipment Point). Raskin 2004, p. 49, pointed out that in a second copy of the Stroop Report, now in the National Archive in Washington, the attached photo shows the group shortly before the photo in the Warsaw copy was taken and has the subtitle 'Nach dem Umschlagplatz'. What is meant here is the collection point for transporting to Treblinka.
218 See the pictorial composition also with title page drawn by Max Lingner in the magazine *L'Avant-garde, Le grand journal de la jeunesse* of 7 April 1939 for the 10th Congress of the Young Communists, showing a marching column flanked by a barefoot *sans-culotte* armed with an axe and with a Phrygian cap and a soldier of the Garde Nationale from the period of the French Revolution. Cat. Lingner 1988, p. 142.
219 Laqueur 2001, p. 693 (also Raskin 2004, p. 67, n. 32), names them, but without giving any source. According to this, the young woman is Yehudit Neyer, née Tolub, next to her are her mother-in-law and Yehudit's daughter and Avraham Neyer, who is

walking behind his daughter and was the only one to survive.

220 Barthes 1984, pp. 87–109.

221 Wenk 1996, p. 102.

222 See Buchenwald 1959 and Knigge 1998.

223 Warburg 1906, p. 59; compare Hurttig 2011.

224 The documentary work *Faschismus – Getto – Massenmord* (Jewish Historical Institute Warsaw 1960) was published by this publishing house with close links to the GDR.

225 Thur 2009, p. 71, n. 340 describes it as 'the face of Christ'.

226 Illustrated in Buchenwald 1959, p. 71, with the caption 'head of a murdered prisoner preserved by shrink process. It stood on the desk of the camp Kommandant.'

227 Michalski 2009.

228 Watercolour with the Inv. No. A 84 of 1967 in the Panoramamuseum Bad Frankenhausen.

229 Meissner 1989, p. 119; the model for Tübke was probably the bubble with the couple of lovers inside on the left of the central panel in the *Garden of Earthly Delights* by Hieronymus Bosch in the Prado in Madrid. The Judge of the World can be found on the sphere in Bosch's *Last Judgement* in the Groeninge Museum in Bruges as well as on graphic works by Schongauer, Dürer and others.

230 Experience of the Soviet Union in Meissner 1989, pp. 84–96, and possibly reference to the Second World War Russian Campaign.

231 Emmrich 1976, p. 37.

232 Chaumont 2001, in particular pp. 252–7.

233 Beaucamp 2004, p. 46.

234 See Schoenberner 1960, p. 146, the illustration of the burning synagogue, and von Schulenburg *Fire 1938*, illustrated in Cat. Schulenburg 1989, p. 27.

235 Compare for example the drawings shown in Schröder, A. 1983, illus. 35 and 36, with Schoenberner 1960, pp. 142 and 22, and illus. 39 and 40 in Schoenberner 1960, pp. 36 and 193.

236 See *Study of Jews in Concentration Camp*, 1965, illus. 25, in Cat. Tübke 2010, in which mothers and many children appear. He based this on only five photos from Schoenberner 1960, p. 63, child on right side; p. 143 for the left half of the drawing; p. 149 the children standing bottom right with yellow star; p. 190 the camp wall at Dachau in the sketch top left and in front, from p. 192 the one lying and the prisoner with the water can from Buchenwald (see illus. 195).

237 Wenzel 2009, p. 293.

238 Ibid., pp. 285–324.

239 Tübke Skizzenbuch, p. 68: 'Technique of addition = painting a list also monological reflection (painting) is legal.'

240 Emmrich 1976, p. 9; other quotations about this in Beaucamp 2004, p. 12.

241 Title taken from Rommelfanger 2008, pp. 131ff., also resembling the one used at the first public exhibition of the picture in 1988 at the Freie Berliner Kunstausstellung: *Triptychon Judenghetto 1943*. The entry describing the object in the inventory of the Jüdisches Museum Frankfurt am Main reads: *Triptych on the Theme of the Uprising in the Warsaw Ghetto*.

242 Rommelfanger 2008, p. 131, presumes the production of the panels to have been 'in the 1960s and '70s' with them having been put together with the 'pictorial documents' in the 1970s or '80s.

243 See from left to right: Schoenberner 1960, pp. 169, 182 (see illus. 201).

244 Schoenberner 1960, p. 174.

245 Cat. Auschwitz-Prozess 2004, p. 516, Schoenberner 1960, p. 147.

246 The deported woman found the album, showing photos from Auschwitz taken by SS photographers, in the concentration camp at Dora in quarters recently vacated by the SS (whole album: www.yadvashem.org/yv/en/exhibitions/album_auschwitz/index.asp, 21 September 2017). On its sporadic reception in Germany up to 1960 Knoch 2001, pp. 830f. See Gesichter 1995. For Perla Schwarz see https://collections.ushmm.org/search/catalog/pa8575 (31 January 2017).

247 See Brink 2000, Sp. 36.

248 Gerhart Frankl, *Survivor II* from 1964–5, illustrated in Amishai-Maisels 1993, illus. 281.

249 In the same straightened detail illustrated in Schoenberner 1960, p. 162; details about it Didi-Huberman 2007; see also Gerhard Richter's involvement with the image.

250 Bundesarchiv/Bildarchiv: Bild 101I-134-0782-12 from the inventory of the propaganda companies of the Wehrmacht – Army and Airforce from May 1941. The photo next to it on the right, lightly crossed through, of a girl lying with a headscarf in front of her face, of a man with a moustache and a worker's cap on his head could not be identified.

251 Detail of the cantor from one of eight photos of the Warsaw Ghetto by Ludwig Knobloch from 24 May 1941: 'Jews with their rabbi praying. The one carrying the Torah reads from the rolled-up Torah,

the first written book of prayer and the law of Judaism,' with the note: 'freigegeben Bildpresse: 6 June 1941' (photo released to the press 6 June 1941). Bundesarchiv/Bildarchiv: Bild 1011-134-0791-20A.

252 Notice 'HALT! SPERRGEBIET! Das Betreten des ehemaligen jüdischen Wohnbezirkes ist strengstens verboten' (STOP! EXCLUSION ZONE! Entry to the former Jewish living area is strictly forbidden) from April 1943 'sgd SS and the Police Chief for the District of Warsaw, Jürgen Stroop' April 1943 (Bundesarchiv/Bildarchiv: Plak 003-037-080). Where Goral got the pictures from that he did not find in Schoenberner 1960 and Stroop 1943/2009 could not be identified. Goral, who was intensively involved in dealing with the crimes of the Nazis, had a wealth of material at his disposal from the end of the 1960s (for his visits to the trials see Rommelfanger 2008, pp. 110–16).

253 Schoenberner 1960, illustrated p. 181. Text for this: 'The defenders of the Ghetto are led away for execution.'

254 Knoch 2001, p. 769, identifies the 'return of the images' as being at the end of the 1950s.

255 Cat. Richter 2012; Cat. Richter 2011; Elger 2007; Kai 2010.

256 Jaskot 2005, p. 472; see also the interpretation of Wolfi in Richter's picture *Christa und Wolfi*, 1964, which Jaskot puts into the context of the artistic and political controversies around 1960: 'the issues concerning understanding the role of past perpetrators in contemporary politics' (p. 460).

257 Gelshorn 2007, in her analysis of the reception history as an integral part of the history of the artist's work, shows the renewed interest in the 1990s on the part of art historians about the subjects of Richter's pictures, see in particular pp. 83–90; see also Jaskot 2012, p. 48, who convincingly links and identifies the way in which he dealt artistically with the Nazi and with the relevant political fact of conservative government in West Germany: 'I argue that the Nazi past was much more omnipresent after 1945 than art historians have supposed and this was true of Richter's work as well.'

258 Senior Person Responsible for Euthanasie-Aktion-T4, and as a member of the SS-Totenkopfverbände (Death's-Head Units) also responsible for euthanasia in the concentration camps. Rübel 2007, pp. 50ff.; an in-depth analysis of this picture in particular is also in Cat. Richter 2011, p. 140, No. 27.

259 Gillen 2009a, pp. 277f.

260 All three pictures are also dealt with in Jaskot 2005, pp. 465–6.

261 Jaskot 2012, pp. 67ff. and Jaskot 2005, pp. 475f.; Richter himself uses this famous definition of Hannah Arendt's; see Cat. Richter 2011, p. 23.

262 Jaskot 2012, p. 66.

263 In 2002 looking back, Richter talked in an interview with Robert Storr, printed in Richter 2008, pp. 408f., apropos of the pictures of *Onkel Rudi* and *Tante Marianne*, of 'a strategy of disguising and rendering harmless', which he and the public 'had to resort to. That's how it worked. People thought it was audacious or absurd and not really meant seriously, so it was much easier to deal with.'

264 Gerhard Richter 1966, quoted in Schmied 1974, p. 254.

265 Elger 2002, chap. 5, in particular pp. 175, 182f.; see also Richter's notes on the picture in Cat. Richter 2011, p. 110 and 200.

266 Illustrated in Rübel 2007, p. 49.

267 Curley 2010 describes the political context and points out the 'ideological ambiguity' (p. 28).

268 Cat. Richter 2011, p. 110.

269 Cat. Pro Lidice 1997, unpag.; Elger 2002, pp. 182f.

270 In his 'n.s 1964–1965' Richter wrote: 'The photo changes one's way of seeing and thinking: photos are thought to be true and pictures to be artificial. The painted picture could not be believed any more, its representation did not move [sic] any more, because it was not authentic, but invented.' Quoted in Richter 2008, p. 30; see also on this Elger 2011, p. 65 (where by leaving out the German word 'sich' the sense is altered from 'not move anymore' to 'not move anybody').

271 Cat. Knipser. München Stadtmuseum 1995; Kat. Fremde 2009; and W. G. Sebald, who described a moment of recall on looking at photographs in the private album: 'Again and again, from front to back and from back to front, I leafed through the album that afternoon, and since then I have returned to it time and again, because, looking at the pictures in it, it truly seemed to me, and still does, as if the dead were coming back, or as if we were on the point of joining them.' Sebald 1996, pp. 45–6.

272 The exhibition at the Bucerius Kunstforum in Hamburg in 2011 and the book shop Walther König had a postcard of *Onkel Rudi* on sale.

273 See Rübel 2007, p. 54: 'The fascinating thing about Richter's pictures is that one can already sense what became clear much later: that no-one can or wants

to say any more what is being portrayed by whom. In them the hope is made manifest that the images of the Nazi past have to be understood as being part of everyday life.'

274 Information supplied by Kerstin Küster, Gerhard-Richter-Archiv Dresden.

275 Alex, surname unknown, member of a resistance group within the *Sonderkommando* at Birkenau, See on this Didi-Huberman 2007, pp. 27–31.

276 Richter in the interview with Storr 2002, admittedly in connection with a multiple exposure: 'It turned into quite a different object due to the frame, due to the plexi-glass plate over the photo . . . Here the frame and the distance belong to the glass and to the border. It became a new object, not a copy of the image.' (Richter 2008, p. 420).

277 Didi-Huberman 2015, p. 38.

278 Richter 1989, p. 175.

279 On the *Atlas* see Richter 2011 and Buchloh 2001; sheets 1–809 of the *Atlas* are available via the Gerhard-Richter-Archiv: www.gerhard-richter.com/art/Atlas (11 December 2016); on the first edition of these *Atlas* sheets in 1998 in a book by the Lenbachhaus in Munich and their subsequent circulation throughout the world, including China and Japan, see Richter 2011, pp. 7 and 14ff.

280 According to the order in the *Atlas*: sheet 16: pp. 159, 210, 21; sheet 17: pp. 35, 38, 37, 60, 71, 91; sheet 18: pp. 96, 94, 199, 160, 203, 193; sheet 19: repeated pp. 199 and 210, p. 162 newly added, repeated p. 159; sheet 20: repeated pp. 199, 210 and 159.

281 It is only interpretable on sheet 17 from the two top rows of photos of the humiliating denigration of Jewish men; below them, in the third and last row, are two photos of corpses (from the Warsaw Ghetto) and of undressed men about to be shot, now standing facing the viewer.

282 For 'defiling the race' a woman in Hamburg in 1935 was publicly branded by having the following sign hung round her neck: 'Ich bin am Ort das grösste Schwein und lass mich nur mit Juden ein!' (I am the biggest swine in the place and only consort with Jews!). Richter only illustrates the left side of the drawing, the right side showing a man with the sign 'Ich nehm als Judenjunge immer nur deutsche Mädchen mit aufs Zimmer!' (I as a Jewish boy only ever take German girls up to my room!); the photo is still popular with Neo-Nazis, see www.politische-bildung-brandenburg.de/node/6929 (15 October 2013).

283 Sykora 2015.

284 Didi-Huberman 2007, pp. 30ff. The photographer too did not survive the extermination camp.

285 See the exhibition *Gerhard Richter Atlas MikroMega* at the Lenbachhaus in Munich in 2013–14.

286 Elger 2002, pp. 137f.

287 Ibid., p 137.

288 Hoffmann-Curtius 1996b, pp. 62ff.; on NO!art see Lurie/Krim 1988.

289 Thorn Prikker in 1989, in his interview with Richter, still speaks of it seeming 'impermissible' to juxtapose 'concentration camp photos and pornography' and asks Richter: 'Did you never have the feeling that there could be a ban on pictures?' Richter replied: 'No, I never did. For the reason that I have always seen the photos as *pictures*.' Richter 1989, p. 175.

290 Richter in the interview with Storr in 2002, repr. in Richter 2008, p. 416.

291 Klüger 1996, p. 35.

292 Heimrod 1999; Kirsch 2003.

293 Adriani et al. 2002, pp. 18–29.

294 See Gesichter 1995. The photo referred to was known to the public in Prague by 1955, see Kraus/Kulka 1955, unpag., published in Germany with the title: *The Death Factory. Reports from Birkenau Concentration Camp* by Kongress-Verlag, East Berlin, in 1955.

295 Quoted in Elger 2002, p. 418.

296 Adriani et al. 2002, pp. 18–29.

297 Telephone conversation with Gerhard Richter, 7 May 2015.

298 Didi-Huberman 2014, p. 156.

299 Whitworth Art Gallery, Manchester, July 2015, see *The Guardian*: www.theguardian.com (21 March 2016); see also Cat. Richter 2016.

300 Richter 2015, subtitle.

301 Studies for Birkenau, pls. 807 and 808; Cat. Richter 2016, pp. 14f.

302 About this visit on 19 December 2013 see Didi-Huberman 2014.

303 Published in 2012, personal communication by Didi-Huberman on 17 July 2015.

304 Cat. Richter 2016.

305 The essays of Krankenhagen (2016) as well as Brauneis/Hafner (2016) concentrate on the Baden-Baden exhibition as a spectacular staging of the chef d'oeuvre and its master.

306 Didi-Huberman 2016, p. 47.

307 The mounted diasec prints (937/1–4, A) of the oil paintings are printed in high gloss and divided into four with each quarter framed. Richter described

them as 'Kreuze' (crosses). Telephone conversation with Gerhard Richter, 7 May 2015. In September 2017 there were four different reproductions of *Birkenau* (937/1–4, A–D) which were exhibited together with the paintings or alone in: *Richter/Pärt*, The Witworth, Manchester International Festival, Manchester, UK, 2015, *Birkenau* (937, 1–4, B); *Black Sun*, Riehen, Switzerland, 2015 (paintings); *Birkenau*, Museum Frieder Burda, Baden-Baden, FRG, 2016 (paintings and *Birkenau* (937/1–4, B)), Gerhard Richter: Abstraction and Appearance, Jewish Museum and Tolerance Center, Moscow, 2016 (paintings); *Birkenau*, BBK Galerie, Munich, 2016 (*Birkenau* (937/1–4, A)); *Gerhard Richter*, Nàrodni Galerie, Prague (paintings); *Gerhard Richter: The Life of Images*, Queensland Art Gallery, Brisbane, Australia, 2017 (paintings); and again in Albertinum Dresden (937/1–4, A). *Birkenau* (937/1–4, C) was not yet exhibited; see www.gerhard-richter.com (accessed 6 September 2017) and information kindly provided by Dietmar Elger, Gerhard Richter archives, Dresden (email to author, 7 September 2017).

308 Gerhard Richter, *Elbe*, 31 digital ink jet prints, 2012.
309 Gerhard Richter, *Mirror, Grey* (735-3), 1991.
310 Richter 2015.
311 Lefkovits 2016.
312 For details of the relation of the oil painting (still not for sale at the end of 2016) to the reproduction Buchloh 2016, pp. 26ff.
313 See Buchloh 2016, state of the painting on 15 July and 29 July 2014, illustrated p. 30; Cat. Richter 2016, pp. 12ff.
314 See Lehmann/Weibel 1994, and Jochen Gerz, *Platz des unsichtbaren Mahnmals* (Place of the Invisible Memorial) in Saarbrücken; on this Schmidt-Wulffen/Gerz/Gerz 1994 and www.gerz.fr/html/main.html (21 March 2016).
315 They replace Sigmar Polke's illuminated display cases 'Vor Ort Sein' (Being on the Spot) from 1998/99 that are having to be restored.
316 Quoted from www.bundestag.de/dokumente/textarchiv/2017/kw36-richter-birkenau/525720, accessed 14 September 2017.
317 Didi-Huberman 2012.
318 Iden 2016 talks of 'layered clusters', p. 15.

Bibliography

Adriani, Götz (ed.) (2002), *Kunst im Bundestag*. Cologne: DuMont.

Agamben, Giorgio (2003), *Was von Auschwitz bleibt. Das Archiv und der Zeuge*. Frankfurt a.M.: Suhrkamp.

Alberg, Werner (1994), *Carl Lauterbach. Maler und Sammler*. Düsseldorf, private publisher: Lauterbach.

Album (1945/1946), *Conc. Camp Dachau*. Ed. the International Information Office for the Former Concentration Camp Dachau. Dachau, no date given.

Aloszko, Stefan Ludwik (2011), *Auschwitz: Art, Commemoration and Memorialisation. 1940 to the Present Day*. Diss., University of Plymouth; pearl.plymouth.ac.uk/handle/10026.1/1194 (20 September 2016).

Alpers, Svetlana (1989), *Rembrandt als Unternehmer. Sein Atelier und seine Macht*. Cologne: DuMont.

American Office of War Information (ed.) (1945), *KZ. Bildbericht aus 5 Konzentrationslagern*. No place or date given.

Amishai-Maisels, Ziva (1987), *The Complexities of Witnessing*. In: *Holocaust Genocide Studies*, 2, pp. 123–47.

—— (1993), *Depiction and Interpretation. The Influence of the Holocaust on the Visual Arts*. Oxford, New York: Pergamon Press.

—— (2003), *Der jüdische Jesus*. In: Cat. *Das Recht des Bildes*, pp. 223–37.

—— (2004), *Chagall und der Holocaust*. In: Cat. *Verehrt und Verfemt. Chagall und Deutschland*. Berlin, Frankfurt a.M., Munich: Prestel, pp. 124–46.

Annuss, Evelyn (2011), *Das Theater der Hunderttausend historisieren*. In: *Forum Modernes Theater*, 26/1, pp. 135–50.

Antelme, Robert (1947/1992), *The Human Race*. Trans. Jeffrey Haight and Annie Mahler. Marlboro, VT: The Marlboro Press.

Antoine, Jean-Philippe (2011), *La Traversée du XXe siècle. Joseph Beuys. L'image et le souvenir*. Geneva: Les presses du réel.

Arani, Miriam Yegane (1997), *Aus den Augen, aus dem Sinn? Publizierte Fotografien aus dem besetzten Warschau 1939 bis 1945 Teil 2, Fotogeschichte*, 66, pp. 33–50.

Arendt, Hannah (1951/1986), *The Origins of Totalitarianism*. London: Deutsch.

—— (1963/2006), *Eichmann in Jerusalem. A Report on the Banality of Evil*. Harmondsworth: Penguin.

—— (1989), *Nach Auschwitz. Essays and Kommentare*. Ed. Eike Geisel and Klaus Bittermann. Berlin: Tiamat.

Arnold, Karsten (2007), *Wolf Vostell. Auf Strassen und Plätzen . . . durch Galerien*. In: *Sediment*, 14.

Arntz, Hans-Dieter (2012), *Der Maler Otto Pankok als Lebensretter im Dritten Reich. Ein Beitrag zur Judenverfolgung in der Eifel.* In: *Eifel-Jahrbuch*, pp. 71–81, hans-dieter-arntz.de (28 May 2013).

Atze, Marcel (2004), '*An die Front des Auschwitz-Prozesses*' *zur zeitgenössischen Rezeption der Strafsache gegen Mulka und andere.* In: Cat. *Auschwitz-Prozess 2004*, pp. 637–47.

Bächtold-Stäubli, Hanns, with Hoffmann-Krayer, Eduard (eds) (1927–42), *Handwörterbuch des Deutschen Aberglaubens*, 10 vols, Berlin & Leipzig, reprint Berlin: de Gruyter 1987.

Bartels, Ulrich, with Berke, Hubert (2008), *Verzeichnis der illustrierten Bücher und Schriften, der Schriften und Mappen mit Originalholzschnitten und einem Anhang über seine Glaskunstarbeiten und Mosaiken.* Münster: private print Ulrich Bartels.

Barth, Peter (1984), *Schwamm Drüber? Niemals!* In: Cat. *Schwesig*, pp. 107–20.

Barthes, Roland (1980/1984) *Camera lucida: Reflections on Photography.* Trans. Richard Howard. London: Flamingo.

—— (1990), *Der entgegenkommende und der stumpfe Sinn.* Frankfurt a.M.: Suhrkamp.

Bartov, Omer (1997), *Kitsch and Sadism in Ka-Tzetnik's Other Planet. Israeli Youth Imagine the Holocaust.* In: *Jewish Social Studies*, vol. 3, no. 2, pp. 42–76.

Bastian, Heiner (1996), *Formen der Initiation*. In: Cat. *Joseph Beuys, The Secret Block for a Secret Person in Ireland. Sammlung Marx*. Ed. and introduced by Heiner Bastian. Munich: Schirmer/Mosel, pp. 11–28.

Bayer, Florian, and Wagner, Hans-Ulrich (2012), *How Media Portrayed the Holocaust for the First Time. The Radio Coverage on the 1. Bergen-Belsen Trial.* Abstract of the Simon Wiesenthal Conference, Vienna, 29 November 2012.

BBKL = *Biographisch-bibliographisches Kirchenlexikon* (1990), founded and ed. Friedrich Wilhelm Bautz, continued by Traugott Bautz; vol. II. Hamm: Bautz.

Beaucamp, Eduard (1997), *Werner Tübke. Lebenserinnerungen des Dr. jur. Schulze III.* In: Cat. *Deutschlandbilder*, pp. 202–4.

—— (2004), *Tübke. Meisterblätter.* Munich: Prestel.

—— (2009a), *Mysterien des Schmerzes. Apokalypsen, Passionen und Auferstehungen im Werk Tübkes.* In: Cat. *Tübke-Stiftung 2009*, pp. 40–47.

—— (2009b), *Zeitgeschichtliche Interventionen*. In: Cat. *Tübke-Stiftung 2009*, pp. 61–4.

Becher, Johannes R. (1967), *Gesammelte Werke*, vol. V. Berlin: Aufbau.

Becker, Astrid (2012), *Die Linie von Hamburg 1959.* In: Cat. *Hundertwasser 2012*, pp. 164–9.

Becker, Wolfgang (2002), *Gerd Baukhage. 30 Jahre Malerei.* Cologne: Wienand.

Beckmann, Karin (2011), "*Die Geschichte der deutschen Arbeiterbewegung*" *von Werner Tübke.* MA Diss. Universität Leipzig.

Behr, Shulamith (2016), *Ludwig Meidner: Exile. Creativity and Holocaust Awareness.* In: Cat. *Eavesdropper on an Age, Ludwig Meidner in Exile.* Museum Giersch der Goethe-Universität. Frankfurt a.M.: Hirmer, pp. 148–61.

Beier, Martin (1996), *Bibliographie und Ausstellungsverzeichnis.* In: *Grundig, Lea WVZ 1973*, pp. 258–93.

Ben Shem (Reuben Feldschuh) (1947), *Between the Walls of the Ghetto. Stories from the Warsaw Ghetto* (in Hebrew), illustrated by Lea Grundig. Tel Aviv: N. Twerski 5707.

Berlau, Ruth (1983), Foreword to Bertolt Brecht, *Kriegsfibel*. Berlin: Eulenspiegel, 4th edn 1983, 1st edn 1955.

Beuys, Eva, et al. (1990), *Joseph Beuys. Block Beuys.* Munich: Schirmer Mosel.

Biro, Matthew (2003), *Representation and Event. Anselm Kiefer, Joseph Beuys, and the Memory of Holocaust.* In: *The Yale Journal of Criticism*, 16, no. 1, pp. 113–46.

Blatmann, Daniel (2011), *Die Todesmärsche 1944/45. Das letzte Kapitel des nationalsozialistischen Massenmordes.* Reinbek bei Hamburg: Rowohlt.

Blume, Eugen (2008), *Der Erfinder der Dampfmaschine.* In: Cat. *Beuys*, pp. 154–73.

Bracher, Karl Dietrich (1969) *Die Deutsche Diktatur. Entstehung, Struktur, Folgen des Nationalsozialismus.* Cologne, Berlin: Kiepenheuer & Witsch.

Braese, Stephan (2001), *Die andere Erinnerung. Jüdische Erinnerung in der westdeutschen Nachkriegsliteratur.* Berlin, Vienna: Philo.

Brauneis, Wolfgang and Hans Jürgen Hafner (2016), *Das Richtersche Rakel-Treatment.* In: perlentaucher.de (8 July 2016).

Brecht, Bertolt (1955/1983), *Kriegsfibel.* Berlin: Eulenspiegel, 1st edn 1955; *War Primer.* Trans. John Willett. London: Libris, 1998.

Brink, Cornelia (1993), *Georg Zielezinski. Zeichnungen aus deutschen Konzentrationslagern.* In: *Kritik and Krise,* No. 6, pp. 4–6.

—— (1998), *Ikonen der Vernichtung. Öffentlicher Gebrauch von Fotografien aus nationalsozialistischen Konzentrationslagern nach 1945.* Berlin: Akademie.

—— (2000), *Auschwitz in der Paulskirche. Erinnerungspolitik in Fotoausstellungen der sechziger Jahre.* Marburg: Jonas-Verl.

—— (2007), *'Ein Buch der Toten.' Gerhard Schoenberners Fotodokumentation der Judenverfolgung.* In: Danyel, Jürgen (ed.), *50 Klassiker der Zeitgeschichte.* Göttingen: Vandenhoeck & Ruprecht, pp. 62–5.

Brock, Bazon (1960), *DASERSCRECKENAMS. Anwendung jenes Prinzips des Unvermögens. Strukturen Childs.* Basel: Panderma-Verl. Laszlo (unpag.).

—— (1977), *Ästhetik als Vermittlung. Arbeitsbiographie eines Generalisten.* Ed. Karla Fohrbeck. Cologne: DuMont.

—— (2012), *Wellenlinien in gestautem Wasser.* In: Cat. *Hundertwasser 2012*, pp. 157–63.

Bronfen, Elisabeth (2012), *Picassos Kriegsfrauen.* In: *Frauen, Picasso – Beckmann – de Kooning.* Ed. Carla Schulz-Hoffmann. Munich: Cantz, pp. 254–65.

Broszat, Martin (ed.) (1958), *Autobiographische Aufzeichnungen von Rudolf Höss. Quellen und Darstellungen zur Zeitgeschichte*, Münchner Institut für Zeitgeschichte, vol. v. Stuttgart: Deutsche Verlagsanstalt.

Brüne, Gerd (1996a), *Von Dresden nach Tel Aviv. Zu Themen und Motiven in den Werken der 1930er und 1940er Jahre.* In: *Grundig, Lea* WVZ *1973*, pp. 16–55.

—— (1996b), *Von Kunst und Politik. Lea Grundig in publizierten und unpublizierten Dokumenten.* In: *Grundig, Lea* WVZ *1973*, pp. 82–105.

Buchenwald (1959), Ed. Komitee der antifaschistischen Widerstandskämpfer in der DDR. Berlin: Kongress-Verlag.

—— (1960), *Mahnung und Verpflichtung.* Fédération internationale des resistants, des victimes et des prisonniers du facisme et al., ed. Walter Bartel. Berlin: Kongress-Verlag.

Buchloh, Benjamin (2001), *Reconsidering Joseph Beuys. Once Again.* In: Ray 2001b, pp. 75–90.

—— (2002), *Gerhard Richters Atlas. Das anomische Archiv.* In: *Paradigma Fotografie. Fotokritik am Ende des fotografischen Zeitalters.* vol. 1., ed. Herta Wolf. Frankfurt am Main: Suhrkamp, pp. 399–427.

—— (2016), *Gerhard Richters Birkenau-Bilder.* Cologne: König.

Bugs, Monika (2008), *Pionier des Surrealen: Edgar Jené in Wien.* In: Cat. *Phantastischer Realismus 2008*, Agnes Husslein-Arco (ed.). Vienna: Belvedere, pp. 45–53.

Bunge, Matthias (1998), *Kunst der Nachkriegszeit. Kunst nach Auschwitz.* In: Raab, Josef (ed.), *Das 20. Jahrhundert. Nachkriegszeit.* Regensburg: Pustet, pp. 105–62.

Burgbacher-Krupka, Ingrid (1977), *Prophete rechts, Prophete links. Joseph Beuys.* Nuremberg: Edition für Moderne Kunst.

Burger, Heinz Otto (ed.) (1942), *Gedicht und Gedanke, Auslegungen Deutscher Gedichte.* Halle/S.: Max Niemeyer.

Celan, Paul (1948a), *Edgar Jené. Der Traum vom Traume.* Vienna: Agathon.

—— (1948b), *Der Sand aus den Urnen.* Vienna: Sexl.

—— (1983), *Gesammelte Werke in fünf Bänden*, vol. IV. Frankfurt a.M.: Suhrkampp.

—— (2003), *Die Gedichte.* Ed. and commented by Barbara Wiedemann. Frankfurt a.M.: Suhrkamp; *The Poems of Paul Celan.* Trans. Michael Hamburger. London: Anvil, 2007.

Celan-Handbuch (2012) ed. Markus May, Peters Gosens and Jürgen Lehmann. Stuttgart: Metzler.

Chaumont, Jean-Michel (2001), *Die Konkurrenz der Opfer. Genozid, Identität und Anerkennung.* Lüneburg: zu Klampen.

Chéroux, Clément (2001a), *L'épiphanie negative. Production, diffusion et réception des photographies de la libération des camps. Les chambres noires ou l'image absente?* In: Cat. *Mémoire*, pp. 103–27.

—— (2001b), *Les chambres noires ou l'image absente?* In: Cat. *Mémoire*, pp. 213–17.

Classen, Christoph (1999), *Bilder der Vergangenheit. Die Zeit des Nationalsozialismus im Fernsehen der Bundesrepublik Deutschland 1955–1965.* Cologne: Böhlau.

Coche de la Ferté, Etienne (1982), *Byzantinische Kunst.* Freiburg: Herder.

Cohen, Richard I. (1998), *Jewish Icons. Art and Society in Modern Europe.* Berkeley: University of California Press.

Cozzolino, Robert (2011), *Henry Koerner, Honoré Sharrer, and the Subversion of Reality. 'Magic Realism' and the Photograph.* In: Barbara Buhler Lynes et al., *Shared Intelligence. American Painting and the Photograph.* Berkeley, Los Angeles, London: University of California Press, pp. 103–21.

Curley, John J. (1972), *Gerhard Richter's Cold War Vision.* In: *Gerhard Richter. Early Work, 1951–1972.* Los Angeles: J. Paul Getty Museum 2010, pp. 11–35.

Dachau! Ein Tatsachenbericht in Bildern (1945), Munich: Heinrich Wiegand.

Daily Mail (ed.) (1945), 'Lest We Forget'. London.

Decker, Edith (1988), *Paik. Video.* Cologne: DuMont.

Dengler, Steffen (2010), *Die Kunst der Freiheit? Die westdeutsche Malerei im Kalten Krieg und im wiedervereinigten Deutschland.* Munich: Fink.

Der Untermensch. Ed. Reichsführer der SS, SS-Hauptamt. Berlin: Nordland-Verlag 1942, archive.org (21 April 2014)

Didi-Huberman, Georges (1999), *Ähnlichkeit und Berührung, Archäologie, Anachronismus und Modernität des Abdrucks.* Cologne: DuMont.

—— (2007), *Bilder trotz allem* (*Image malgré tout*, Paris: Paradoxe 2003). Trans. Peter Geimer. Munich: Fink.

—— (2012), *Borken.* Trans. Horst Brühman. Paderborn, Konstanz: Univ. Press.

—— (2014), *Aus dem Planen heraus.* In: Cat. *Gerhard Richter. Bilder/Serien.* Riehen/Basel: Fondation Beyeler, pp. 155–73.

—— (2016), *Die Malerei in ihrem aporetischen Moment.* In: Cat. *Richter 2016*, pp. 31–55.

Dillon, Sandra L. (2010), *Audacious Rhetorical Devices in Paul Celan's 'Todesfuge' and Nelly Sachs', 'O die Schornsteine'.* In: *Rocky Mountain Review*, 64, no. 1, pp. 32–46.

Dirks, Christian (2006), "*Die Verbrechen der anderen*". *Auschwitz und der Auschwitz-Prozess der DDR. Das Verfahren gegen den KZ-Arzt Dr. Horst Fischer.* Paderborn: Schöningh.

Dorondo, David R. (2012), *Riders of the Apocalypse. German Cavalry and Modern Warfare, 1780–1945.* Annapolis, MD: Naval Institute Press.

Doss, Erika (2007), *Joseph Cornell and Christian Science.* In: Edwards, Jason, and Taylor, Stephanie L. (eds), *Joseph Cornell. Opening the Box.* Oxford: Lang, pp. 113–35.

Edel, Peter (1947), *Schwester der Nacht.* Vienna: Erwin Müller.

—— (1979), *Wenn es ans Leben geht. Meine Geschichte.* Berlin: Verlag der Nation.

—— (1983), *Wenn es ans Leben geht. 20 Zeichnungen zu seiner Autobiographie.* Berlin: Staatliche Museen Berlin DDR, Kupferstichkabinett und Sammlung der Zeichnungen.

Eitz, Thorsten, and Stötzel, Georg (eds.,) (2007), *Wörterbuch der 'Vergangenheitsbewältigung'. Die NS-Vergangenheit im öffentlichen Sprachgebrauch.* Hildesheim, Zürich, New York: Olms.

Elger, Dietmar (2002), *Gerhard Richter. Maler.* Cologne: DuMont.

—— (2007), *Wer war Helga Matura wirklich? Die Bilder und ihre Vorbilder.* In: *Vorträge über Gerhard Richter.* Ed. Dietmar Elger and Jürgen Müller. Gerhard-Richter-Archiv, Staatliche Kunstsammlungen Dresden. Cologne: König, pp. 31–45.

—— (2011), *Das gemalte Foto. Gerhard Richter im Atelier.* In: Cat. *Richter*, pp. 60–69.

Emmrich, Irma (1976), *Werner Tübke. Schöpfertum und Erbe.* Vienna: Edition Tusch.

Endlich, Stefanie, and Lutz, Thomas (1998), *Gedenken und Lernen an historischen Orten. Ein Wegweiser zu Gedenkstätten für die Opfer des Nationalsozialismus in Berlin.* Berlin: Landezentrale für politische Bildungsarbeit, 2nd edn.

Engler, Martin (2012), *Von Quadraten und Gittern. Die Welt als Geometrie und Vorstellung.* In: *Gegenwartskunst 1945-heute im Staedel Museum.* Ostfildern: Hatje & Cantz, pp. 164–203.

Ernst, Max (1929), *La Femme 100 têtes.* Trans. Dorothea Tanning. New York: George Braziller, 1981.

Errell, Richard (1961), *Bilderbuch für Vergessliche.* Frankfurt a.M.: Europäische Verl.-Anst.

Eschebach, Insa, et al. (eds) (1999), *Die Sprache des Gedenkens, Zur Geschichte der Gedenkstätte Ravensbrück.* Berlin: Hentrich & Hentrich.

—— et al. (eds) (2002), *Gedächtnis und Geschlecht. Deutungsmuster in Darstellungen des nationalsozialistischen Genozids,* Frankfurt a.M., New York: Campus.

—— and Mühlhäuser, Regina (eds.) (2008), *Krieg und Geschlecht. Sexuelle Gewalt im Krieg und Sex-Zwangsarbeit in NS-Konzentrationslagern.* Berlin: Metropol.

—— (2010), *Sex-Zwangsarbeit in NS-Konzentrationslagern. Geschichte, Deutungen und Repräsentationen.* In: *L'Homme,* no. 1, pp. 65–73.

Eschwege, Helmut (1966), *Kennzeichen J. Bilder, Dokumente, Berichte zur Geschichte der Verbrechen des Hitlerfaschismus an den deutschen Juden 1933–45.* Berlin: Verlag der Wissenschaften.

Fackler, Guido (2005), *Panoramen von Macht und Ohnmacht. KZ-Bilder als ikonisierte Erinnerung und historisches Dokument.* In: Helge Gernt et al. (eds), *Der Bilderalltag. Perspektiven einer volkskundlichen Bildwissenschaft. Münchner Beiträge zur Volkskunde,* vol. XXXIII, Münster: Waxmann.

Feist, Günter (1975), *Lea Grundig. Blätter wider den Imperialismus.* Leipzig: Seemann.

—— et al. (eds) (1996), *Kunstdokumentation 1945–1990 SBZ/DDR. Museumspädagogischer Dienst.* Berlin: DuMont.

Feldmann, Petra (2012), *Die 'Schöne Jüdin'. Jüdische (Geistes) Schönheit zwischen erotisierter Begierde und judenfeindlicher Abwehr als exemplarisches Phänomen einer Legitimierung hegemonialer Wahrnehmungsordnungen.* In: *Nebulosa. Zeitschrift für Sichtbarkeit und Sozialität* 1, pp. 105–20.

Fings, Karola, and Opfermann, Ulrich Friedrich (ed.) (2012), *Zigeunerverfolgung im Rheinland und in Westfalen. 1933–1945. Geschichte, Aufarbeitung und Erinnerung.* Paderborn: Schöningh.

Fischer, Alfred M. (1994), *Hubert Berke. Abstraktion des Wirklichen.* In: *Kölner Museums-Bulletin* 3, pp. 4–19.

Fischer, Hannelore (1999), *Käthe Kollwitz, die trauernden Eltern – ein Mahnmal für den Frieden.* Cologne: Käthe-Kollwitz-Museum.

Fischer, Torben, and Lorenz, Matthias N. (eds) (2007), *Lexikon der, "Vergangenheitsbewältigung" in Deutschland. Debatten und Diskursgeschichte des Nationalsozialismus nach 1945.* Bielefeld, transcript.

Fleischer, Simone (2010), *Werner Tübke. Requiem.* In: Cat. *Galerie Neue Meister.*

Frahm, Ole (2006), *Genealogie des Holocaust. Art Spiegelmans Maus. A Survivor's Tale.* Munich: Fink.

Franco Fratini, Iris (1999), *Das Bild der Juden in der Bildberichterstattung der Nationalsozialisten. Ein Vergleich der Ghettoreportagen in der "Berliner Illustrirte Zeitung" und dem "Illustierter Beobachter".* MA Diss. Universität Kiel.

Frank, Anne (1954), *The Diary of Anne Frank.* Trans. B. M. Mooyart-Doubleday. London: Pan, 1954.

Frei, Norbert (1999), *Vergangenheitspolitik. Die Anfänge der Bundesrepublik und die NS-Vergangenheit.* Munich: Beck.

Friedrich, Ernst (1924), *Krieg dem Kriege!* (Berlin, Verl. Freie Jugend, 1924) Reprint: Zweitausendeins, 1980.

Friedrich, Julia, et al. (eds) (2013), *'So fing man einfach an, ohne viele Worte'. Ausstellungswesen und Sammlungspolitik in den ersten Jahren nach dem Zweiten Weltkrieg.* Museum Ludwig. Berlin: Akademie.

Fritz, Nicole (2007), *Bewohnte Mythen. Joseph Beuys und der Aberglaube.* Nuremberg: Moderne Kunst.

Fröhlich, Claudia (2011), *Der Ulmer Einsatzgruppen-Prozess 1958. Wahrnehmung und Wirkung des ersten großen Holocaust-Prozesses.* In: Jörg Osterloh et al. (eds), *NS-Prozesse und deutsche Öffentlichkeit. Besatzungszeit, frühe Bundesrepublik und DDR.* Göttingen: Vandenhoeck & Ruprecht, pp. 233–62.

Frommhold, Erhard (1958), *Hans und Lea Grundig.* Dresden: Kunst.

—— (1968), *Kunst im Widerstand. Malerei, Graphik, Plastik 1922–1945.* Dresden: Kunst.

Frübis, Hildegard (1997), *Die 'Schöne Jüdin'. Bilder vom Eigenen und vom Fremden.* In: Friedrich, Annegret et al. (eds), *Rassismus und Sexismus in der Visuellen Kultur.* Marburg: Jonas, pp. 112–24.

—— (2014), *(Kinder)-Ikonen des Holocaust.* In: Peter Seibert et al., *Anne Frank: Mediengeschichten.* Berlin: Metropol, pp. 12–36.

Fuhrmeister, Christian (2013), *Statt eines Nachworts. Zwei Thesen.* In: Friedrich, J., et al., pp. 234–9.

Gassner, Hubertus (1996), *Alfred Kurella. Wandervogel auf bitterem Feldweg. Eine Porträtskizze.* In: Feist et al., pp. 654–73.

Gelshorn, Julia (2007), *Rezeptionsgeschichte und Geschichtsrezeption. Zur Zeugenschaft Gerhard Richters.* In: *Sechs Vorträge über Gerhard Richter.* Ed. Dietmar Elger and Jürgen Müller. Gerhard-Richter-Archiv, Staatliche Kunstsammlungen Dresden. Cologne: König, pp. 71–95.

Gesichter der Juden in Auschwitz. Lili Meiers Album (1995). Ed. Hans-Jürgen Hahn. Yad Vashem & Berlin: Arsenal.

Gillen, Eckhardt (1995), *Kunst nach Auschwitz? Stichworte zum Umgang mit der Vergangenheit in der deutschen Kunst nach 1949.* In: Cat. *Kunst in Deutschland 1945–1995. Beitrag deutscher Künstler aus Ost- und Mitteleuropa.* Museum Ostdeutsche Galerie. Regensburg, pp. 27–47.

—— (1997), *Phänomenologie des Verdrängten. Wolf Vostell: 'Deutscher Ausblick'.* In: Cat. *Deutschlandbilder*, pp. 240–45.

—— (2002), *'Schwierigkeiten beim Suchen der Wahrheit'. Bernhard Heisig im Konflikt zwischen verordnetem Antifaschismus und der Auseinandersetzung mit seinem Kriegstrauma. Eine Studie zur Problematik der antifaschistischen und sozialistischen Kunst der SBZ/DDR 1945–1989*, Diss. Heidelberg, ub.uni-heidelberg.de/archiv/4475 (2 October 2013).

—— (2009a), *Feindliche Brüder? Der Kalte Krieg und die deutsche Kunst. 1945–1990.* Berlin: Nicolai.

—— (2009b), *Werner Tübke. Ein postmoderner Maler 'avant le lettre'?* In: Cat. *Tübke*, pp. 54–62.

—— (2012), *Alfred Kurella Der Bitterfelder Weg 1959 und die sowjetische Kulturrevolution 1929.* In: Cat. *Abschied*, pp. 175–83.

Gillen, Otto (1993), *Fritz Ketz. Gestalten und Bilder.* In: Hartmann, pp. 103–7.

Godfrey, Mark (2007), *Abstraction and the Holocaust.* New Haven, London: Yale University.

Goebbels, Günter (ed.), *Mathias Barz. 30.8.1895 Düsseldorf –19.10.1982 Margraten.* No place given (Düsseldorf), no date given (1987), reproduced in manuscript, copy in the Stadtmuseum Düsseldorf.

Goes, Albrecht (1955), *Vorwort.* In: *Das Tagebuch der Anne Frank*, Frankfurt a.M.: Fischer, pp. 5–7.

Goldhagen, Daniel J. (1996), *Hitler's Willing Executioners: Ordinary Germans and the Holocaust.* New York: Knopf.

Goldstein, Cora (2005), *Before the CIA. American Actions in the German Fine Arts (1946–1949).* In: *Diplomatic History*, 5, pp. 747–78.

—— (2009), *Capturing the German Eye. American Visual Propaganda in Occupied Germany.* Chicago and London: University of Chicago Press.

Goral, Arie (1962), *Kein Weg in Deutschland.* Reprinted in: *Goral. An der Grenzscheide. Kein Weg als Jude und Deutscher?* Münster, Hamburg: LIT 1994, pp. 6–11, first publication of this essay 1962.

Gorny, Yosef (2012), *The Jewish Press and the Holocaust, 1939–1945.* Cambridge: University Press.

Grabitz, Helge, and Scheffler, Wolfgang (1993), *Letzte Spuren. Ghetto Warschau, SS-Arbeitslager Trawniki, Aktion Erntefest. Fotos und Dokumente über Opfer des Endlösungswahns im Spiegel der historischen Ereignisse.* Berlin: Hentrich, 2nd revd edn 1993, 1st edn 1988.

Grenville, John A. S. (2012), *The Jews and the Germans of Hamburg. The Destruction of a Civilisation 1790–1945.* Abingdon, New York: Routledge.

Grochowiak, Thomas (1966), *Ludwig Meidner.* Recklinghausen, Aurel Bongers.

Grundig, Hans (1966), *Künstlerbriefe aus den Jahren 1926 bis 1957.* Rudolstadt: Greifenverlag.

Grundig, Lea (1944), *In the Valley of Slaughter. Drawings.* Tel Aviv: Kibbuz-Hame'uchad.

—— (1947), *Im Tal des Todes.* Introduction and text by Kurt Liebmann. Dresden: Sachsenverlag.

—— (1958/1978), *Gesichte und Geschichte.* Berlin: Dietz, 9th edn 1978, 1st edn 1958.

Gumkowski, Janusz, et al. (1963), *Treblinka*, Warszawa. Rat f. Schutz d. Denkmäler d. Kampfes u. d. Heldentums, no date given (*c.* 1963).

Haas, Mechthild (1997), *Jean Dubuffet. Materialien für eine 'andere' Kunst nach 1945.* Berlin: Reimer.

Hacke, Gerald (2011), *Die Zeugen Jehovas im Dritten Reich und in der DDR. Feindbild und Verfolgungspraxis.* Göttingen: Vandenhoeck & Ruprecht.

Hackenschmidt, Sebastian (2014), *Knochen. Ein Material der zeitgenössischen Kunst.* Munich: Silke Schreiber.

Haftmann, Werner (1950), *Paul Klee. Wege bildnerischen Denkens.* Munich: Prestel.

—— (1954), *Malerei im 20. Jahrhundert.* Munich: Prestel.

—— (1964), 'Einführung'. In: Cat. documenta 3,1 1964, pp. xvi–xvii.

Hahn, Hans-Joachim (2005), *Repräsentationen des Holocaust. Zur westdeutschen Erinnerungskultur seit 1979.* Heidelberg: Winter.

—— (2007), *'Die von denen man erzählt hat, dass sie die kleinen Kinder schlachten'. Deutsche Leiderfahrung und Bilder von Juden in der deutschen Kultur nach 1945. Zu einigen Texten Wolfgang Weyrauchs.* In: Helmut Schmitz (ed.), *A Nation of Victims? Representations of German Wartime Suffering from 1945 to the Present.* Amsterdam, New York: Rodopi, pp. 51–70.

Haibl, Michaela (1999), *Juden in der Bildpolemik.* In: Cat. *Abgestempelt*, pp. 79–96.

Halbinger, Monika (2010), *Das Jüdische in den Wochenzeitungen Zeit, Spiegel und Stern (1946–1989).* Munich: Meidenbauer.

Hansen, Imke (2016), *Als Auschwitz noch nicht Holocaust bedeutete.* In: Fritz, Regina, et al., *Before the Holocaust had its name; Beiträge zur Holocaustforschung des Wiener Wiesenthal Instituts für Holocaust-Studien (VWI)*; vol. II, Vienna: New Academic Press, pp. 201–22.

Hartewig, Karin (2000), *Zurückgekehrt. Die Geschichte der jüdischen Kommunisten in der DDR.* Cologne, Weimar, Vienna: Böhlau.

Hartmann, Rainer (1993), *Fritz Ketz.* Grafenau: Edition Schlichtenmaier.

Heidegger, Martin (1976), *Gesamtausgabe, Abt. 1, Veröffentlichte Schriften*, vol. 9, Frankfurt a.M., Klostermann.

Heimrod, Ute, et al. (eds) (1999), *Der Denkmalstreit. Das Denkmal? Die Debatte um das 'Denkmal für die ermordeten Juden Europas'. Eine Dokumentation.* Berlin: Philo.

Heiner, Maria (2016), *Lea Grundig. Kunst für die Menschen.* Berlin: Hentrich & Hentrich.

Held, Jutta (1981), *Kunst und Kunstpolitik. Kulturaufbau in Deutschland nach dem 2. Weltkrieg.* Berlin (West): VAS.

Hellwig, Joachim, and Deicke, Günther (1959), *Ein Tagebuch für Anne Frank.* Berlin: Verlag der Nation.

Henkel, Arthur, and Schöne, Albrecht (eds) (1967), *Emblemata. Handbuch zur Sinnbildkunst des 16. und 17. Jahrhunderts.* Stuttgart: Metzler.

Herbert, Ulrich (2013), *Justiz und NS-Vergangenheit in der Bundesrepublik 1945–1970.* In: Görtemaker, Manfred and Safferling, Christoph (eds), *Die Rosenburg. Das Bundesministerium der Justiz und die NS-Vergangenheit. Eine Bestandsaufnahme.* Göttingen: Vandenhoeck & Ruprecht, pp. 43–59.

Herding, Klaus (1988), *Humanismus und Primitivismus. Probleme früher Nachkriegskunst in Deutschland.* In: *Jahrbuch des Zentralinstituts für Kunstgeschichte*, vol. IV, pp. 281–311.

Herter, Renate, and Katja Jedermann (eds) (2014), *Spuren, Hohlräume, Leerstellen – Jüdisches Leben am Kurfürstendamm 1933–1945. Dokumentation eines künstlerischen Projektes am Kurfürstendamm April bis November 2013.* Berlin: Universität der Künste.

Herzzeit (2015), *Ingeborg Bachmann – Paul Celan, der Briefwechsel; mit den Briefwechseln zwischen Paul Celan und Max Frisch sowie zwischen Ingeborg Bachmann und Gisèle Celan-Lestrange.* Ed. and commented by Bertrand Badiou et al. Frankfurt a.M.: Suhrkamp, 4th edn.

Heukenkamp, Ursula (ed.) (1996), *Unterm Notdach. Nachkriegsliteratur in Berlin 1945–1949.* Berlin: Schmidt.

Heymer, Kay (2013), *Die Kunstsammlungen der Stadt Düsseldorf 1945–1953.* In: Friedrich et al., pp. 56–62.

Hicks, Jeremy (2012), *First Films of the Holocaust. Soviet Cinema and the Genocide of the Jews. 1938–1946.* Pittsburgh: University Press.

Hirsch, Marianne (2002), *Täterfotografien in der Kunst nach dem Holocaust. Geschlecht als ein Idiom der Erinnerung.* In: Eschebach et al., pp. 203–26.

Hoffmann, Detlef (ed.) (1998), *Das Gedächtnis der Dinge. KZ-Relikte und KZ-Denkmäler 1945–1995.* Fritz-Bauer-Institut Frankfurt a.M., Wissenschaftliche Reihe des Fritz-Bauer-Instituts, vol. IV.

Hoffmann-Curtius, Kathrin (1996a), *Denkmäler für das KZ Dachau.* In: *Die Nacht hat zwölf Stunden, und dann kommt schon der Tag. Antifaschismus. Geschichte und Neubewertung.* Berlin: Aufbau, pp. 280–309.

—— (1996b), *Feminisierung des Faschismus.* In: *Die Nacht hat zwölf Stunden, dann kommt schon der Tag. Antifaschismus. Geschichte und Neubewertung.* Berlin: Aufbau, pp. 45–69.

—— (1999a), *Caritas und Kampf. Die Mahnmale in Ravensbrück.* In: Eschebach et al., pp. 55–68.

—— (1999b), *Sieg ohne Trauer – Trauer ohne Sieg. Totenklage auf Kriegerdenkmälern des Ersten Weltkrieges.* In: Gisela Ecker (ed.), *Trauer tragen – Trauer zeigen. Inszenierungen der Geschlechter.* Munich: Fink, pp. 259–86.

—— (2002a), *Feminisierte Trauer und aufgerichtete Helden. Figürliche Denkmäler der frühen Nachkriegszeit in Deutschland.* In: Eschebach et al., pp. 363–94.

—— (2002b), *Trophäen in Brieftaschen. Fotografien von Wehrmachts-, SS- und Polizeiverbrechen.* In: Gisela Ecker et al. (eds), *Dinge. Medien der Aneignung – Grenzen der Verfügung.* Königstein: Helmer, pp. 114–35.

—— (2005), *Zeitgenossenschaft als Herausforderung.* In: *kritische berichte*, no. 4, pp. 70–82.

—— (2008), *Zwischen Heroisierung und Viktimisierung. Anmerkungen zur visuellen Erinnerungskultur nach 1945.* Unpublished manuscript of lecture, Sommeruniversität der Mahn- und Gedenkstätte Ravensbrück.

—— (2010), *Deutsche Denkmalpolitiken nach 1945.* In: Maja Figge et al. (eds), *Scham und Schuld.* Bielefeld: transcript, pp. 121–46.

—— (2009), *Terror in Germany 1918/19: Visual Commentaries on Rosa Luxemburg's Assassination.* In: *Colvin, Sarah and Watanabe-O'Kelly, Helen (eds.), Women and Death, vol. II, Warlike Women.* London: Camden House, pp. 127–166.

Hofmann, Ludwig et al. (eds) (1982), *Otto Pankok. Zeichnungen, Grafik, Plastik.* Berlin: Elefanten-Press.

Hofmann, Werner (2003), *Goya.* Munich: Beck.

Holian, Anna Marta (2011), *Between National Socialism and Soviet Communism: Displaced Persons in Postwar Germany.* Ann Arbor: The Univ. of Michigan Press.

Horn, Ursula (1973), *Harald Hakenbeck.* Dresden: Kunst.

Huber, Hans Dieter (1995), *Joseph Beuys' 'Szene aus der Hirschjagd' Ein selektives und subjektives Inventar.* In: *Vorträge zum Werk von Joseph Beuys.* Arbeitskreis Block Beuys. Darmstadt (ed.) Darmstadt: Häusser, pp. 73–98.

Huber, Heinz, and Müller, Artur (1964), *Das Dritte Reich. Seine Geschichte in Texten, Bildern und Dokumenten*, 2 vols. Wiesbaden: R. Löwit.

Huener, Jonathan (2003), *Auschwitz, Poland, and the Commemoration, 1945–1979.* Athens: Ohio University Press.

Hurttig, Marcus Andrew (2011), *Die entfesselte Antike. Aby Warburg und die Geburt der Pathosformel in Hamburg.* Hamburg: Hamburger Kunsthalle.

Hütt, Wolfgang (ed.) (1969), *Lea Grundig.* Berlin: Kunst.

—— (1972), *Willi Sitte.* Dresden: Kunst.

—— *Willi Sitte. Gemälde 1950–1994.* Bönen: Kettler, no date given (*c.* 1995).

Huyssen, Andreas (1993), *Anselm Kiefer. Mythos, Faschismus und Geschichte.* In: Köppen, pp. 137–50.

Iden, Peter (2016), *Anblicke einer verheerenden Welt. Zu Gerhard Richters 'Birkenau'-Bildern.* In: Lefkovits, pp. 12–19.

Illichmann, Jutta (1997), *Die DDR und die Juden. Die deutschlandpolitische Instrumentalisierung von Juden und Judentum durch die Partei- und Staatsführung der SBZ/DDR von 1945 bis 1990.* Frankfurt a.M., New York: Lang.

Ivanovic, Christine (2001), '*Des menschen farbe ist freiheit*'. *Paul Celans Umweg uber den Wiener Surrealismus.* In: Gosens, Peter, and Marcus G. Patka (eds), Cat. *'Displaced'. Paul Celan in Wien 1947–1948.* Vienna, Jüdisches Museum, Frankfurt am Main: Suhrkamp, pp. 62–70.

Jahns, Joachim (2009), *Der Warschauer Ghettokönig.* Leipzig: Dingsda.

Jaskot, Paul B. (2005), *Gerhard Richter and Adolf Eichmann.* In: *Oxford Art Journal*, 28, no. 3, pp. 457–78.

—— (2012), *The Nazi Perpetrator. Postwar German Art and the Politics of the Right.* London, Minneapolis: University of Minnesota Press.

Jené, Edgar (1945), *Zeichnungen. Dessins des annees de guerre 1939–1945.* Foreword by Otto Basil. Vienna: Müller.

—— (1988), *Zeichnungen, mit einem einfuhrenden Text von Friedhelm Haring.* Worms: Wernersche Vertragsgesellschaft.

Jindrich, Lion, and Lukas, Jan (1959), *Das Prager Ghetto.* Prague: Artia.

Jockusch, Laura (2012), *Collect and Record! Jewish Holocaust Documentation in Early Postwar Europe.* Oxford: University Press.

Joseph Beuys Symposium Kranenburg 1995, ed. Förderverein Schloss Moyland e. v. Basel: Wiese, 1996.

Jüdisches Historisches Institut Warschau (ed.) (1960), *Faschismus – Getto – Massenmord. Dokumentation über Ausrottung und Widerstand der Juden in Polen während des Zweiten Weltkrieges.* Selected, presented and introduced by Tatiana Berenstein et al. Berlin: Rütten & Loening.

Jung, Peter (1984), *'Du musst es aushalten . . .' Karl Schwesig im Exil 1933–1935.* In: Cat. *Schwesig*, pp. 81–106.

Junghanns, Kurt (1956), *Lea Grundig und der Faschismus.* In: *Bildende Kunst*, no. 4, pp. 193–6.

Jureit, Ulrike, and Schneider, Christian (2010), *Gefühlte Opfer. Illusionen der Vergangenheitsbewältigung.* Stuttgart: Klett-Cotta.

Kai, Michael Robert Alois (2010), *Die Rezeption deutscher Geschichte im Werk Gerhard Richters.* Diss. University of Vienna, othes.univie.ac.at/8651.

Kantor, Alfred (1987), *Das Buch des Alfred Kantor.* Frankfurt a.M.: Jüdischer Verlag bei Athenäum, German 1st edn 1971.

Kappel, Kai (2010), *Religiöse Erinnerungsorte in der KZ-Gedenkstätte Dachau.* Munich: Deutscher Kunstverlag.

Kaschnitz, Marie Luise (1945), *Von der Schuld.* In: *Die Wandlung 1945/46*, no. 2, pp. 143–7.

Ketz, Fritz (1947), *Gestalten und Bilder.* Reutlingen: Buchhandlung Witsch.

Kilcher, Andreas (1998), *Die Sprachtheorie der Kabbala als ästhetisches Paradigma.* Stuttgart: Metzler.

Kirchner, Renate (2010), *The Jewish Press and the Holocaust, 1939–1945.* Cambridge: University Press.

Kirsch, Jan Holger (2003), *Nationaler Mythos oder historische Trauer? Der Streit um ein zentrales Holocaust-Mahnmal für die Berliner Republik.* Cologne: Böhlau.

Kirschnick, Sylke (2009), *Anne Frank und die DDR. Politische Deutungen und persönliche Lesarten des berühmten Tagebuchs.* Berlin: Christoph Links.

KL Auschwitz; ed. the Comité International d'Auschwitz; Krakow, no date given (*c.* 1963).

Klee, Paul (1988), *Tagebücher 1898–1918.* Ed. Paul-Klee-Stiftung, Kunstmuseum Bern, presented by Wolfgang Kersten. Stuttgart: Hatje.

Kleist, Heinrich von (1952), *Gesammelte Werke in 2 Bänden*, ed. Helmut Sembner. Munich: Hanser.

Klemp, Stefan (2012), *Rücksichtslos ausgemerzt. Die Ordnungspolizei und das Massaker von Lidice.* Münster: Geschichtsort Villa ten Hompel der Stadt Münster.

—— (2013), *Vernichtung. Die deutsche Ordnungspolizei und der Judenmord im Warschauer Ghetto 1940–43.* Münster, Berlin: Prospero.

Klemperer, Victor (1947), *LTI: Notizbuch eines Philologen*, Berlin: Aufbau. Published in English as *LTI: The Language of the Third Reich, A Philologist's Notebook* (2006).Trans. Martin Brady. London: Continuum.

Klüger, Ruth (1994), *Katastrophen. Über deutsche Literatur.* Göttingen: Wallstein.

—— (1996), *Von hoher und niedriger Literatur.* Göttingen: Wallstein.

Knaap, Ewout van der (2008), *"Nacht und Nebel". Gedächtnis des Holocaust und internationale Wirkungsgeschichte.* Göttingen: Wallstein.

Knaurs Spielbuch (1953), ed. and illustrated by Johanna Preetoris. Munich: Droemer.

Knigge, Volkard (1998), *Buchenwald.* In: Hoffmann, D., pp. 94–173.

Knoch, Habbo (2001), *Die Tat als Bild. Fotografien des Holocaust in der deutschen Erinnerungskultur.* Hamburg: Hamburger Ed.

—— (2003), *Die Grenzen des Zeigbaren. Fotografien der NS-Verbrechen und die westdeutsche Gesellschaft 1955–1965.* In: Kramer 2003a, pp. 87–116.

Knöll, Stefanie (2008), *Death and the Maiden. A German Topic?* In: Helen Fronius (ed.), *Women and Death: Representations of Female Victims and Perpetrators in German Culture 1500–2000.* Rochester N.Y. Camden House, pp. 9–27.

Koepplin, Dieter (1977), *Inkarnation. Ausscheidung, Potential.* In: Cat. *Joseph Beuys: The Secret Block for a Secret Person in Ireland.* Basel: Kunstmuseum, pp. 3–8.

—— (1994), *Beuys aktualisiert Steiner.* In: Cat. *Rudolf Steiner. Tafelzeichnungen – Entwürfe – Architektur.* Württembergischer Kunstverein Stuttgart. Ostfildern: edition tertium, pp. 85–106.

—— (1995), *Hirschdenkmäler und Zwergendenkmäler im Werk von Joseph Beuys.* In: *Joseph Beuys Symposium 1995*, pp. 24–41.

Kogon, Eugen (1979), *Der SS-Staat – Das System der deutschen Konzentrationslager.* München: Heyne, 5th edn.

Kohn-Waechter, Gudrun (ed.) (1991), *Schrift in Flammen, Opfermythen und Weiblichkeitsentwürfe im 20.Jahrhundert.* Berlin: Orlanda.

Költzsch, Georg-W. (1984), *Schön ist nur das Wunderbare. Leben, Werke, Begegnungen des Malers Edgar Jené,* with texts by Jené and his friends André Breton, Paul Celan, Jerry Glenn. Saarbrücken: Die Mitte.

König, Christoph, and Wägenbaur, Birgit (eds) (2013), *Internationales Germanistenlexikon.* Berlin: de Gruyter.

König, Wieland (1981), *Einführung.* In: Cat. *Carl Lauterbach. Gemälde Grafik Dokumente.* Stadtmuseum Düsseldorf, pp. 6–38.

Könneker, Sabine (1995), *'Sichtbares, Hörbares'. Die Beziehung zwischen Sprachkunst und bildender Kunst am Beispiel Paul Celans.* Bielefeld: Aisthesis.

Köppen, Manuel (ed.) (1993), *Kunst und Literatur nach Auschwitz.* Berlin: Schmidt.

—— and Scherpe, Klaus R. (eds) (1997), *Bilder des Holocaust. Literatur – Film – Bildende Kunst.* Cologne, Weimar, Vienna: Böhlau.

Körffer, Sonja, et al. (1999), *Dokumentation zur Aufstellung der Trauernden Eltern in St. Alban, Köln.* In: Fischer, Hannelore (ed.), *Käthe Kollwitz. Die trauernden Eltern, ein Mahnmal für den Frieden.* Cologne: DuMont, pp. 125–9.

Kosmala, Beate (2014), *Ghettoaufstand. Helden wider Willen.* In: Hans Henning Hahn and Robert Traba (eds), with Maciej Gorny and Kornelia Konczal, *Deutsch-Polnische Erinnerungsorte*, vol. 1: *Geteilt/Gemeinsam*, pp. 375–400.

Kramer, Mario (1997), *Joseph Beuys. Auschwitz Demonstration 1956–1964.* In: Cat. *Deutschlandbilder*, pp. 293–307.

—— (2010), *Reflektor und Lichtschein. Zu den Entwürfen von Joseph Beuys für ein Mahnmal für Auschwitz.* In: Cat. *Beuys*, pp. 145–55.

Kramer, Sven (ed.) (2003a), *Die Shoa im Bild.* Munich: Ed. Text + Kritik.

—— (2003b), *Nacktheit in Holocaust-Fotos und -Filmen.* In: Kramer 2003a, pp. 225–48.

Krankenhagen, Stefan (2016), *Von der Kunst, Auschwitz darzustellen.* In: *Merkur*, no. 12, merkur-zeitschrift.de (12 November 2016).

Kraus, Ota, and Kulka, Erick (1955), *Továrna na smrt.* Prague: Naše Vojsko.

Kreidler, Richard (1988a), *Formensprache und Thematik im Gesamtwerk des Kölner Malers Hubert Berke (1908–1979).* Diss., University of Bonn.

—— (1988b), *Hubert Berke.* Recklinghausen: Aurel Bongers.

—— (2004), *Der Maler Hubert Berke in Köln 1934–1945.* In: *Kölner Museums-Bulletin*, no. 2, pp. 4–18.

Kuhirt, Ullrich (1982), *Kunst der DDR. 1945–1959.* Leipzig: Seemann.

—— (1983), *Kunst der DDR. 1960–1980.* Leipzig: Seemann.

Kuhn, Manfred (1964), *Auschwitz und Nagold.* In: *Gewerkschaftliche Monatshefte*, no. 3, pp. 143–5.

Kuni, Verena (2006), *Der Künstler als 'Magier' und 'Alchemist' im Spannungsfeld von Produktion und Rezeption. Aspekte der Auseinandersetzung mit okkulten Traditionen in der europäischen Kunstgeschichte nach 1945. Eine vergleichende Fokusstudie – ausgehend von Joseph Beuys.* http://archiv.ub.uni-heidelberg.de/artdok/volltexte/2006/192

Lacroix, Paul (2010), *La légende du juif errant, illustrée par Gustave Doré.* Paris: Éditions Interférences.

Ladendorf, Heinz (1963), *Denkmäler und Mahnmale seit 1945.* In: Cat. *Monumenta Judaica, Handbuch*, pp. 656–67.

Lang, Lothar (1960), *Die Nürnberger Malerin Dore MeyerVax.* In: *Bildende Kunst*, no. 7, pp. 453–5.

—— (1978), *Malerei und Grafik in der DDR.* Leipzig: Edition Leipzig.

Langston, Richard (2008), *Visions of Violence. German Avant-gardes after Fascism.* Evanston, IL: Northwestern University Press.

Lanwerd, Susanne (1999), *Skulpturales Gedenken. Die 'Tragende' des Bildhauer Will Lammert.* In: Eschebach et al., pp. 39–54.

Laqueur, Walter (2001), *The Holocaust Encyclopedia.* New Haven: Yale University Press.

Lasker-Schüler, Else (1969), *Briefe, Teil 2: Wo ist unser buntes Theben.* Munich: Kösel.

Lauterbach, Carl (1948), *Zeichnungen. Auswahl und Vorwort von Anna Klapheck.* Solingen-Ohligs: Kaloso.

Lefkovits, Ivan (ed.) (2016), *'Mit meiner Vergangenheit lebe ich'. Memoiren von Holocaust-Überlebenden.* Berlin: Jüdischer Verlag im Suhrkamp Verlag.

Lehmann, Ulrike, and Peter Weibel (eds) (1994), *Aesthetik der Absenz. Bilder zwischen Anwesenheit und Abwesenheit.* Munich: Klinckhardt & Biermann.

Leiser, Erwin (1961), *'Mein Kampf'. Eine Bilddokumentation.* Frankfurt a.M., Hamburg: Fischer.

Lerm Hayes, Christa Maria (2001), *James Joyce als Inspirationsquelle für Joseph Beuys.* Hildesheim: Georg Olms.

—— and Walters, Victoria (2011), *Beuysian Legacies in Ireland and Beyond. Art, Culture and Politics.* Berlin: Lit.

Levi, Primo (1986), *The Drowned and the Saved.* Trans. Raymond Rosenthal. Washington: Summit.

Levy, Daniel, and Sznaider, Natan (2001), *Erinnerung im globalen Zeitalter: der Holocaust.* Frankfurt a.M.: Suhrkamp.

Lindeperg, Sylvie (2010), *'Nuit et Brouillard'. Ein Film in der Geschichte.* Trans. Stefan Barmann. Berlin: Vorwerk 8.

Longerich, Peter (2007), *'Davon haben wir nichts gewusst!'. Die Deutschen und die Judenverfolgung 1933–1945.* Munich: Pantheon.

Löser, Claus (2012*), Liebe und Schuld im Zeichen des Holocaust. Konrad Wolfs Spielfilm 'Sterne' 1959.* In: Bruns, Claudia, et al. (eds), *'Welchen der Steine du hebst.' Filmische Erinnerung an den Holocaust.* Berlin: Bertz & Fischer, pp. 309–20.

Lurie, Boris, and Krim, Seymour (1988), *NO!art.* Berlin and Cologne: Ed. Hundertmark.

Lurz, Meinhold (1986), *Kriegerdenkmäler in Deutschland.* vol. VI, *Bundesrepublik.* Heidelberg: Esprint.

Lustiger, Arno (ed.) (1995), *The Black Book of Polish Jewry.* Reprint of the 1943 edition. Frankfurt a.M.: Syndikat.

Maas, Lieselotte (1978/1990), *Handbuch der deutschen Exilpresse 1933–1945.* Ed. Eberhard Lammert, vols II and IV. Munich: Hanser.

McCloskey, Barbara (2009), *Dialektik im Stillstand. Ostdeutscher sozialistischer Realismus in der Stalin-Ära.* In: Cat. *Kunst und Kalter Krieg*, pp. 105–17.

Malaka, Stephan (2007), *Die Aktualisierung der Alchemie im Werk von Joseph Beuys – Der Beuys-Block als Manifestation eines okkultistisch geprägten Weltbildes.* Diss. Universität Braunschweig, opus.hbk-bs.de/volltexte/2009/50.

Marcuse, Harold (2001), *Legacies of Dachau. The Uses and Abuses of a Concentration Camp, 1933–2001.* Cambridge: University Press.

Mark, Bernard (1960), *Der Aufstand im Warschauer Ghetto.* Berlin: Dietz.

März, Roland (ed.) (1981), *John Heartfield. Der Schnitt entlang der Zeit.* Dresden: Kunst, no date given.

Mathews, Heather Elizabeth (2006), *Making Histories: The Exhibition of Postwar Art and the Interpretation of the Past in Divided Germany, 1950–1959*. Austin. Tex.: University of Texas Libraries, catalog.lib.utexas.edu (4 April 2016).

Maur, Karin von (1988), *Joseph Beuys und der 'Christusimpuls'*. In: Cat. *Beuys*, pp. 45–68.

May, Jan, and Maria Obenaus (2015), *Horst Strempel. Nacht über Deutschland 1945/46*. In: Cat. *Die Schwarzen Jahre 2015*, pp. 250–55.

Mazur, Tadeusz, et al. (eds) (1960), 1939–1945. *We have not forgotten/Wir haben es nicht vergessen/Nous n'avons pas oublié*. Warsaw: Polania, 1st edn 1959.

Meidler-Waks, Sigalit, *Die Pogromserie vom Issachar Bar Ryback*. In: Cat. *Berlin Transit*, pp. 37–41.

Meink, Anke (2010), *Joseph Beuys und die Tiere. Über Hirsch und Elch. Schwan und Biene und deren Einordnung in den Energieplan*. In: Cat. *Beuys*, pp. 97–121.

Meissner, Günter (1989), *Werner Tübke. Leben und Werk*. Leipzig: Seemann.

—— (2009), *Bildfolge Lebenserinnerungen des Dr. jur. Schulze im Schaffen Werner Tübkes*. In: Cat. *Tübke*, pp. 10–17.

Meyer-Vax, Dore (1965), Ein Bilderbuch des Lebens. In: *Bildende Kunst*, pp. 534–6.

Michalski, Annika (2009), *Selbst als närrische Figur. Zur Inszenierung der Künstlerexistenz im Werk Werner Tübkes*. In: Cat. *Tübke*, pp. 30–39.

Mittig, Hans-Ernst (1993), *Auf der Suche nach Alternativen zum Mahnmal*. In: Köppen, pp. 151–65.

Möbius, Helga (1989), *Zeichen für Vitalität und Schönheit. Frauenfiguren im städtischen Raum der DDR*. In: Ines Lindner et al. (eds), *Blick-Wechsel. Konstruktionen von Männlichkeit und Weiblichkeit in Kunst und Kunstgeschichte*. Berlin: Reimer, pp. 271–80.

Moczarski, Kazimierz (1982), *Gespräche mit dem Henker*. Frankfurt a.M.: Fischer.

Morschel, Jürgen (1965), *In Ulm und um Ulm und um Ulm herum*. In: *Das Kunstwerk*, no. 7, pp. 26, 27 and 39.

Müller, Henning (1980), *Das Exempel Kulturbund: Anatomie eines Verbots. Zur Geschichte des 'Kulturbundes zur demokratischen Erneuerung Deutschlands' in den Westsektoren Berlins 1945–1947*. In: Cat. *Zwischen Krieg und Frieden*, pp. 175–82.

Müller-Hill, Werner Otto (2012), *'Man hat es kommen sehen und ist dennoch erschüttert.' Das Kriegstagebuch eines deutschen Heeresrichters 1944/45*. Munich: Siedler.

Naef, Maja (2011), *Josef Beuys: Zeichnung und Stimme*. Munich: Fink.

Neugebauer, Rosamunde (See also Schulenburg, Rosa von der) (1997), *Der Holocaust in der Sicht deutsch-jüdischer Künstler und Künstlerinnen*. In: *Argonautenschiff. Jahrbuch der Anna Seghers Gesellschaft Berlin und Mainz*, 6, pp. 181–99.

—— (2003), *Zeichnen im Exil – Zeichen des Exils? Handzeichnungen und Druckgraphik deutschsprachiger Emigranten ab 1933*. Weimar: VDG.

—— (2004), *Kunst im Exil oder im 'Land der Väter'? Anmerkungen zum Werk von Jakob Steinhardt und Lea Grundig in Palästina und Israel*. In: *Jahrbuch der Deutschen Exlibris-Gesellschaft e.V.* Wiesbaden: Deutsche Exlibris-Ges., pp. 69–89.

Neumann, Robert (1961), *Hitler. Aufstieg und Untergang des Dritten Reiches. Eine Bildbiographie*. Munich, Vienna, Basel: Desch.

New Soviet Documents on Nazi Atrocities. London, New York, Melbourne: Hutchinson, 1943.

Nündel, Ursula (1986), *Lea Grundig – antifaschistische Folgen aus Palästina. Zum Gedenken des 80. Geburtstages am 23. März 1986*. In: *Mitteilungen. Akademie der Künste der Deutschen Demokratischen Republik*, 2, pp. 18–19.

O'Kelly, Michael J. (1982), *Newgrange: Archeology, Art and Legend*. London: Thames and Hudson.

Oellers, Adam C. (1997), *Fluxus an der Grenze. Aachen 20. Juli 1964*. In: Cat. *Deutschlandbilder*, pp. 232–9.

Olbrich, Harald (ed.) (1990), *Geschichte der Deutschen Kunst 1918–1945*. Leipzig: Seemann.

Olschner, Leonard (1989), *Fugal provocation in Paul Celan's 'Todesfuge' and 'Engführung'*. In: *German Life and Letters*, 43, 1, pp. 79–89.

Otto, Teo, *Niemals wieder. Tagebuch in Bildern*. Berlin: Volk und Welt, 1949.

Ottomeyer, Hans, and Czech, Hans Jörg (eds) (2009), *Deutsche Geschichte in Bildern und Zeugnissen*. Berlin: Deutsches Historisches Museum.

Overbeck, Cyrus, and Müller, Oliver (1995), *Otto Pankok. Maler, Grafiker, Bildhauer. Eine Biographie.* Düsseldorf: Droste.

Pagnoux, Elisabeth (2001), *Reporter photographe à Auschwitz.* In: *Les Temps Modernes*, ed. Claude Lanzmann. No. 613, pp. 84–108.

Pankok, Hulda (1955), *Otto Pankok.* In: Cat. *Pankok*, unpag.

Pankok, Otto (1947), *Zigeuner.* Düsseldorf: Drei Eulen, 1st edn.

—— (1951), *Der Glaube an das Leben.* In: *Jahrbuch der staatlichen Kunstakademie Düsseldorf 1948–50.* Düsseldorf: Giersen, pp. 25–8.

—— (1958), *Zigeuner.* Düsseldorf: Progress-Verl. Fladung, 2nd edn.

Panofsky, Erwin (1930), *Herkules am Scheidewege.* Leipzig, Berlin: Teubner.

Penkower, Monty Noam (2004), *The Kishinev Pogrom of 1903: A Turning Point in Jewish History.* In: *Modern Judaism*, 24, no. 3, pp. 187–225.

Perotti, Berto (1959), *Begegnung mit Otto Pankok.* Düsseldorf: Progress.

Petrowskaja, Katja (2014), *Vielleicht Esther. Geschichten.* Frankfurt a.M.: Suhrkamp, pp. 165–7.

Pilarczyk, Ulrike (2012), '*Ostjuden*' *im Scheunenviertel. Eine bildanalytische Recherche.* In: Cat. *Transit*, pp. 65–9.

Platt, Kristin (2012), *Bezweifelte Erinnerung, verweigerte Glaubhaftigkeit. Überlebende des Holocaust in den Ghettorenten-Verfahren.* Munich: Fink.

Pohl, Klaus-D. (1995), *Der Kristall im Werk von Joseph Beuys. Frühe Arbeiten – ein Überblick.* In: *Vorträge zum Werk von Joseph Beuys.* Arbeitskreis Block Beuys Darmstadt (ed.) Darmstadt: Häusser, pp. 19–34.

Poliakov, Leon, and Wulf, Josef (1955), *Das Dritte Reich und die Juden. Dokumente und Aufsätze.* Berlin: Arani.

Präger, Christmut (2010), '*Vergessen? – Niemals!*' *Zur Darstellung nationalsozialistischer Verbrechen in graphischen Zyklen der frühen Nachkriegszeit.* In: Carsten Dutt (ed.), *Die Schuldfrage. Untersuchungen zur geistigen Situation der Nachkriegszeit.* Heidelberg: Manutius, pp. 212–45.

Puvogel, Ulrike, Stankowski, Martin et al. (1995), *Gedenkstätten für die Opfer des Faschismus. Eine Dokumentation.* Bonn: Bundeszentrale für Politische Bildung, vol. II.

Quermann, Andreas (2006), '*Demokratie ist lustig.*' *Der politische Künstler Joseph Beuys.* Berlin: Reimer.

Rajner, Mirjam (2011), *The Continuity of Jewish Iconography.* In: *Legacy, Journal of the International School for Holocaust Studies*, no. 4, pp. 14–25.

—— and Cohen, Richard (2015), *Invoking Samuel Hirszenberg's Artistic Legacy—Encountering Exile. In: Images, Journal of Jewish Art & Visual Culture*, vol. VIII, i, pp. 46–65.

Raskin, Richard (2004), *A Child at Gunpoint. A Case Study in the Life of a Photo.* Aarhus: University Press.

Ray, Gene (ed.) (2001a), *Joseph Beuys. Mapping the Legacy. Ringling Museum's International Symposium.* New York: Distributed Art Publ.

—— (2001b), *Joseph Beuys and the After-Auschwitz Sublime.* In: Ray 2001a, pp. 55–74.

Rehberg, Karl-Siegbert (2012), *Apotheose des Schreckens. Leipziger Geschichtsbilder.* In: Cat. *Abschied*, pp. 259–71.

Reuter, Frank (2012), *Die Deutungsmacht der Täter: Zur Rezeption des NS-Völkermords an den Sinti und Roma in Norddeutschland.* In: Giercks, Herbert (ed.), *Die Verfolgung der Sinti und Roma im Nationalsozialismus.* Bremen: Ed. Temmen, pp. 127–43.

Richter, Gerhard (1989), *Gespräch mit Jan Thorn Prikker über den Zyklus '18. Oktober 1977'.* In: *Gerhard Richter. Text, Schriften und Interviews.* Ed. Hans-Ulrich Obrist. Frankfurt a.M., Leipzig: Insel, 1993, pp. 173–96.

—— (2008), *Text 1961 bis 2007: Schriften, Interviews, Briefe.* Ed. Dietmar Elger and Hans Ulrich Obrist. Cologne: König.

—— (2011), *Atlas.* Ed. Helmut Friedel. Städtische Galerie im Lenbachhaus Munich. Cologne: König, 2nd edn.

—— (2015), *Birkenau.* Cologne: König.

—— (2016), *Atlas in 4 Bänden. Tafeln 1 – 809.* Ed. Städtische Galerie im Lenbachhaus Munich. Cologne: König.

Riedel, Erik (2003), *Man lebt hier wie in der Wüste. Zu jüdischen Exilkünstlern und ihrer Rezeption*. In: Cat. *Das Recht des Bildes*, pp. 238–45.

Riegel, Hans Peter (2013), *Beuys. Die Biographie*. Berlin: Aufbau.

Rieth, Adolf (1968), *Den Opfern der Gewalt. KZ-Opfermale der europäischen Völker*. Tübingen: Wasmuth.

Rodger, George (2005), *unterwegs 1940–1949, Tagebuchaufzeichnungen eines Fotografen und Abenteurers*, ed. Andrea Holzherr and Siben, Isabel. Ostfildern: Hatje & Cantz.

Röger, Maren (2007), *Adorno-Diktum*. In: Fischer/Lorenz, pp. 38f.

Rommelfanger, Silke (2007), *Das künstlerische Werk Arie Gorals. 'Da mir von zweier Völker Erb/Geheimnis einzig Schicksal ward . . .'* In: Cat. *Goral*, pp. 32–61.

—— (2008), *'Mein Zuhause mein Exil. Das Leben und Werk des deutsch-jüdischen Malers Arie Goral.'* Diss., Johann-Wolfgang-Goethe-Universität Frankfurt a.M.

Rosenthal, Mark (2005), *Joseph Beuys Staging Sculpture*. In: Cat. *Joseph Beuys, Actions, Vitrines, Environments*. London: Tate Modern, pp. 10–135.

Rössing, Karl (1947), *Passion unserer Tage*. Diez/Lahn: Aldus.

Rössler, Stephan (2011), *Joseph Beuys' Modell für ein Mahnmal in Auschwitz-Birkenau*. In: *Rheinsprung 11 – Zeitschrift für Bildkritik*, Ausgabe 02, Basel, pp. 216–22.

Roters, Eberhard (1964), *Rolf Szymanski*. In: *Kunst in Berlin. Schriftenreihe: Das Kunstwerk*, 11–12; Baden-Baden: Agis, pp. 56–7.

Rübel, Dietmar (2007), *Die Fotografie (un)erträglich machen. Gerhard Richter gesehen mit W. G. Sebald*. In: *Sechs Vorträge über Gerhard Richter*. Ed. Dietmar Elger and Jürgen Müller. Gerhard-Richter-Archiv, Staatliche Kunstsammlungen Dresden. Cologne: König, pp. 47–69.

Rutkowski, Adam, and Stempelberg, Hermann (eds) (1960), *Męczeństwo, walka, zagłada żydów w Polsce 1939–1945*. Warsaw: Wydawnictwo Ministerstwa Obrony Narodowej.

Sachs, Nelly (1946), *In den Wohnungen des Todes*. Berlin: Aufbau.

—— (1961), *Fahrt ins Staublose*. Frankfurt a.M.: Suhrkamp; 'Journey into a Dustless Realm', trans. Michael Roloff. In: *Nelly Sachs, Selected Poems*, ed. Michael Hamburger et al. London: Jonathan Cape, 1968, p. 3.

Sander, Dietulf (Bearb.) (1988), *Hans Grundig. Opfer des Faschismus. Meisterwerke aus dem Museum der bildenden Künste Leipzig* 3. Leipzig.

Saure, Gabriele (1992), *'Nacht über Deutschland.' Horst Strempel. Leben und Werk*. Hamburg: Argument.

Schätzke, Andreas (1996a), *'Unendlich viel Neues . . .' Lea Grundigs Rückkehr aus dem Exil*. In: *Grundig, Lea WVZ 1973*, pp. 56–67.

—— (1996b), *Rückkehr aus dem Exil. Zur Remigration bildender Künstler in die SBZ/DDR*. In: Feist et al., pp. 96–109.

Schedelsche Weltchronik 1493. Reprint: Grünwald b. München: Kölbl, 1975.

Scheffler, Wolfgang (1960), *Judenverfolgung im Dritten Reich 1933–1945*. Berlin: Colloquium.

Schieber, Elke (ed.) (2007), *Recherche zu einem Fernsehfilm "Die Bilder des Zeugen Schattmann"*. Potsdam: Filmmuseum.

Schirmer, Gisela (2003), *Farben und Folgen. Eine Autobiographie mit Skizzen und Zeichnungen des Künstlers*. Leipzig: Faber & Faber.

—— and Sitte, Willi (2011), *Willi Sitte. Lidice. Historienbild und Kunstpolitik in der DDR*. Berlin: Reimer.

Schirmer, Lothar (ed.) (2015), *1945. Ikonen eines Jahres*. Mit einem Einführungstext von Norbert Frei. Munich: Schirmer/Mosel.

Schmid, Harald (2012), *'Die Vergangenheit mahnt.' Genese und Rezeption einer Wanderausstellung zur nationalsozialistischen Judenverfolgung (1960–1962)*. In: *Zeitschrift für Geschichtswissenschaft*, no. 4, pp. 331–49.

Schmidt, Herbert (2005), *Der Elendsweg der Düsseldorfer Juden. Chronologie des Schreckens 1933–1945*. Düsseldorf: Droste.

Schmidt-Wulffen, Stephan (1994), *The Monument Vanishes: A Conversation with Esther and Jochen Gerz*. In: Cat. *The Art of Memory: Holocaust Memorials in History*, Jewish Museum New York, ed. James E. Young. New York: Prestel.

Schmied, Wieland (1974), *Malerei nach 1945 in Deutschland, Österreich und der Schweiz.* Frankfurt a.M.: Propyläen.

Schoenberner, Gerhard (1969), *The Yellow Star: The Persecution of the Jews in Europe, 1933–1945*, revd edn, trans. Susan Sweet. London: Corgi.

—— (1960), *Der gelbe Stern. Die Judenverfolgung in Europa 1933 bis 1945.* Hamburg: Rütten & Loening.

Scholz, Dieter (1991), *'Das Triptychon Der Krieg.'* In: Cat. *Otto Dix zum 100. Geburtstag.* Galerie der Stadt Stuttgart, ed. Wulf Herzogenrath. Stuttgart: Hatje, pp. 260–67.

Scholz, Stephan (2011), *'Seltsamer Triumphzug.' Zu den Ursachen des bundesdeutschen Erfolgs des ‚Tagebuchs der Anne Frank' in den 50er Jahren.* In: *Geschichte in Wissenschaft und Unterricht*, 62, no. 1/2, pp. 77–91.

Schröder, Anneliese (1983), *Tisa Schulenburg.* Recklinghausen: Aurel Bongers.

Schröder, Dominique (2007), *Fälle Globke und Oberländer.* In: Fischer and Lorenz, pp. 101–3.

Schulenburg, Rosa von der (See also Neugebauer, Rosamunde) (2008), *Die Grafikfolgen zu Terezin/Theresienstadt von Fritz Lederer (1878–1949) und Leo Haas (1901–1983).* In: Cat. *Entdeckte Moderne*, pp. 30–46.

Schultheiss, Gabriele (1980), *Vom Mythos und seinen Bildern. Krisenbewältigung in der nachkriegsdeutschen Kunst.* In: Cat. *Zwischen Krieg und Frieden*, pp. 10–24.

Schulze, Rainer (2011), *Britain's Finest Hour. Bergen-Belsen in der britischen Erinnerungslandschaft – eine Annäherung.* In: Wilfried Wiedemann and Joachim Wolschke-Bulmahn (eds), *Landschaft und Gedächtnis Bergen-Belsen. Esterwegen, Falstad, Majdanek.* Munich: Martin Meidenbauer, pp. 51–74.

Schulze, Theodor (2005), *Abendmahl und Schlachtopfer. Übergänge zwischen Leben, Ritual und Ikone in Autobiographie und Bildern von Marc Chagall.* In: Christoph Wulf et al. (eds), *Ikonologie des Performativen.* Munich: Fink, pp. 104–29.

Schütrumpf, Jörg (1995), *Auftragspolitik in der DDR.* In: *Auftragskunst der DDR 1949–1990*, pp. 13–29.

Schweitzer, Cara (2013), *Heinrich Ehmsen.* In: Cat. 1938, *Kunst – Künstler – Politik.* Ed. Eva Atlan et al. Jüdisches Museum Frankfurt a.M., Göttingen: Wallstein, pp. 228–40.

Schwelling, Birgit (2011), Rezension zu Agazzi, Elena/Schütz, Erhard (eds), *Heimkehr. Eine zentrale Kategorie der Nachkriegszeit. Geschichte, Literatur und Medien. Berlin.* hsozkult.de, 12 August 2011.

Schwerte, Hans (1962), *Faust und das Faustische, ein Kapitel deutscher Ideologie.* Stuttgart: Klett.

Sebald, W. G. (1996), *The Emigrants.* Trans. Michael Hulse. London: Harvill.

—— (1998), *The Rings of Saturn.* Trans. Michael Hulse. London: Harvill.

Sehn, Jan (ed.) (1956), *Obóz koncentracyjn Oświęcim-Brzezinka (Auschwitz-Birkenau), Na podstawie dokumentów i źródeł opracował Jan Sehn. Główna Komisjabadania zbrodni hitlerowskich w Polsce.* Warsaw: Wydawn. Prawnicze, 1956.

—— (1957), *Konzentrationslager Oświęcim-Brzezinka (Auschwitz-Birkenau), Zentralkommission zur Untersuchung der Naziverbrechen in Polen. Aufgrund von Dokumenten und Beweisquellen* (trans. Rita Tertel). Warsaw: Wydawn. Prawnicze, 1957.

Seiler, Harald (1942), *Das Bild des Krieges. Die Ausstellung Kunst der Front.* Ed. Luftgaukommando VI, Münster i. W. Essen: Giradet, no date given [1942].

Semprun, Jorge (1997), *Literature or Life.* Trans. Linda Coverdale. New York: Viking Penguin.

Shaar, Pinchas (1999), *Mendel Grossman: Photography Bard of the Lodz Ghetto.* In: Shapiro 1999, pp. 125–32.

Shapiro, Robert Moses (ed.) (1999), *Holocaust Chronicles: Individualizing the Holocaust through Diaries and Other Contemporaneous Personal Accounts.* Hoboken: KTAV Publ. House.

Sitte, Willi, *Handzeichnungen 1940–1992.* Bönen: Kettler, no date given (*c.* 1993).

Sollors, Werner (2014), *The Temptation of Despair, Tales of the 1940s.* Cambridge Mass., London: Belknap of Harvard University Press.

Sommer, Robert (2009), *Das KZ-Bordell. Sexuelle Zwangsarbeit in nationalsozialistischen Konzentrationslagern.* Paderborn: Schöningh.

Spiegelman, Art (1991), *Maus. A Survivor's Tale, vol. II. And Here my Troubles Began.* New York: Pantheon.

Spielmann, Jochen (1990), *Entwürfe zur Sinngebung des Sinnlosen. Zu einer Theorie des Denkmals als Manifestation des "kulturellen Gedächtnisses". Der Wettbewerb für ein Denkmal in Auschwitz.* Diss., Freie Universität Berlin.

Stahl, Neta (ed.) (2012), *Jesus among the Jews. Representation and Thought.* New York: Routledge.

Stechow, Wolfgang (1977), *Pieter Brueghel der Ältere.* Cologne: DuMont.

Steinkamp, Peter (2003), *Lidice 1942.* In: Ueberschär, Gerd R. (ed.), *Orte des Grauens. Verbrechen im Zweiten Weltkrieg.* Darmstadt: Wiss. Buchgesellschaft, pp. 126–35.

Stengel, Katharina (2012), *Hermann Langbein. Ein Auschwitz-Überlebender in den erinnerungspolitischen Konflikten der Nachkriegszeit.* Frankfurt a.M., New York: Campus.

Stiglegger, Marcus (1999), *Sadiconnazista. Faschismus und Sexualität im Film.* St Augustin: Gardez!

Streubel, Manfred (1982), *Zum Tode Kurt Liebmanns.* In: *Neue Deutsche Literatur*, 1, pp. 164–9.

Stroop, Jürgen (1943/1960), *Es gibt keinen jüdischen Wohnbezirk in Warschau mehr! (Stroop-Bericht über die Vernichtung des Warschauer Ghettos)*, with a foreword by Andrzej Wirth. Warsaw, Neuwied: Luchterhand.

—— (1943/2009), *Es gibt keinen jüdischen Wohnbezirk in Warschau mehr!* Warsaw 2009; pamiec.pl/ftp/ilustracje/Raport_STROOPA.pdf

Swiebocka, Teresa (ed.) (1993), *Auschwitz. A History in Photographs.* Oświęcim: Panstwowe Muzeum.

Sykora, Katharina (2009), *Die Tode der Fotografie,* vol. I: *Totenfotografie und ihr sozialer Gebrauch.* Paderborn: Fink.

—— (2015), *Die Tode der Fotografie*, vol. II: *Tod, Theorie und Fotokunst.* Paderborn: Fink.

Täuber, Rita E. (1997), *Der hässliche Eros. Darstellungen zur Prostitution in der Malerei und Grafik 1855–1930.* Berlin: Gebr. Mann.

Theewen, Gerhard (1993), *Joseph Beuys. Die Vitrinen, ein Verzeichnis.* Cologne: König.

Theweleit, Klaus (1995), *Das Land, das Ausland heisst.* Munich: dtv.

Thiele, Martina (2001), *Publizistische Kontroversen über den Holocaust im Film.* Münster: Lit.

Thur, Nicole (2009), *Die 'Lebenserinnerungen des Dr. jur. Schulze' I–III.* MA Diss., Universität Leipzig.

Tisdall, Caroline (1979), *Joseph Beuys.* New York: Salomon Guggenheim Foundation.

Tolnay, Charles de (1973), *Hieronymus Bosch.* Baden-Baden: Holle.

Tomberger, Corinna (2002), *Zeige Deine verwundete Männlichkeit: Heilsversprechen im Werk von Joseph Beuys.* Lecture at the 2nd conference of the *Arbeitskreis für interdisziplinäre Männer- und Geschlechterforschung. Kultur-, Geschichts- und Sozialwissenschaften (AIM Gender)*: Mannsein und Männlichkeiten, 9 November 2002, Stuttgart, ruendal.de/aim/pdfs02/tomberger.pdf (6 January 2014).

Trier, Eduard (1962), *Notizen zum neuen Denkmal.* In: *Der Mensch und die Künste. Festschrift für Heinrich Lützeler*. Ed. Günter Bandmann et al. Düsseldorf: Schwann, pp. 494–9.

Tübke, Werner (1960), *Zu einigen theoretischen Problemen der Malerei.* In: *Bildende Kunst*, no. 3, pp. 196–200.

van der Grinten, Franz (1985), *Joseph Beuys und das Zeichen des Kreuzes.* In: Cat. Beuys 1985a, pp. 6–13.

—— (1996), *Beuys' Beitrag zum Wettbewerb für das Auschwitzdenkmal.* In: *Joseph Beuys Symposium 1995*, pp. 199–203.

Vasari, Giorgio (1832–8), *Il resto delle vite degli artefici, l'appendice alle note delle medesime, l'indice generale e le opere minori dello stesso autore, parte seconda.* Florence: Passigli.

Verspohl, Franz (1990), *Die Moderne auf dem Prüfstand. Pollock, Wols, Giacometti*. In: Monika Wagner et al. (eds), *Funkkolleg Moderne Kunst, Studienbegleitbrief 10*; Weinheim, Basel: Beltz, pp. 11–52.

—— (1987), *Die konkreten Dinge stehen im zweiten Rang. Wols und Sartre*. In: *Idea*, no. 6, pp. 109–39.

Vesalius, A. (1543/2014), *The Fabric of the Human Body: An Annotated Translation of the 1543 and 1555 Editions of De Humani Corporis Fabrica Libri Septem by D. H. Garrison and M. H. Hast*. Basel: Karger.

Vismann, Cornelia (2011), *Medien der Rechtsprechung.* Ed. Alexandra Kemmerer und Markus Krajewski. Frankfurt a.M.: Fischer.

Vogel-Klein, Ruth (Ed.) (2010), *Die ersten Stimmen. Deutschsprachige Texte zur Shoah 1945–1963.* Würzburg: Königshausen & Neumann.

von der Bey, Katja (2000), *Nationale Codierungen abstrakter Malerei. Kunstdiskurs und -ausstellungen im westlichen Nachkriegsdeutschland 1945–1952.* Diss., Carl von Ossietzky University of Oldenburg.

Vostell, Wolf (1970), *Happening und Leben.* Neuwied, Berlin: Luchterhand.

Wachs, Philipp-Christian (2000), *Der Fall Theodor Oberländer (1905–1998). Ein Lehrstück deutscher Geschichte.* Frankfurt a.M., New York: Campus.

Wagner, Monika (1994), *John, der Frauenmörder.* In: Hamburger Kunsthalle (ed.), *Konstruktionen der Moderne.* Hamburg: Christians, pp. 237–46.

—— (2001), *Das Material der Kunst. Eine andere Geschichte der Moderne.* Munich: Beck.

Wagner, Wolf H. (1987), *Der Hölle entronnen. Eine Biographie des Malers und Grafikers Leo Haas.* Berlin: Hentschel.

Wajcman, Gérard (2001), *De la croyance photographique.* In: *Les Temps Modernes*, ed. Claude Lanzmann. No. 613, pp. 47–83.

Walser Smith, Helmut (2008), *The Continuities of German History. Nation, Religion, and Race across the Long Nineteenth Century.* Cambridge: University Press.

Warburg, Aby (1906), *Dürer und die italienische Antike.* In: *Verhandlungen der 48. Versammlung deutscher Philologen und Schulmänner in Hamburg vom 3. bis 6. Oktober 1905.* Leipzig: Teubner, pp. 55–60.

Wechsler, Judith (2013), *Daumiers 'Saltimbanques'.* In: Cat. *Daumier*, pp. 29–37.

Weckel, Ulrike (2009), *Amerikanischer Traum von einem deutschen Schuldbekenntnis: Der Spielfilm Judgment at Nuremberg (1961) und seine Rezeption in der deutschen Presse.* In: Georg Wamhof (ed.), *Das Gericht als Tribunal, oder: Wie der NS-Vergangenheit der Prozess gemacht wurde* (Veröffentlichungen des Zeitgeschichtlichen Arbeitskreises Niedersachsen, vol. XXV). Göttingen: Wallstein, pp. 163–85.

—— (2012), *Beschämende Bilder. Deutsche Reaktionen auf Alliierte Dokumentarfilme über befreite Konzentrationslager.* Stuttgart: Steiner.

Weidemann, Friedgund (1993), *Otto Nagel und Otto Pankok. Künstlerfreunde im geteilten Deutschland.* In: Cat. *Pankok*, pp. 194–203.

Weik, Lea (2015), *Jüdische Künstler und das Bild des Ewigen Juden. Vom Antijüdischen Stereotyp zu jüdischen Indentifikationsfigur.* Heidelberg: Universitätsverlag Winter.

Weinbaum, Laurence (2010), *'Shaking the Dust Off.' The Story of the Warschaw Ghetto's Forgotten Chronicler, Ruben Feldschu (Ben Shem).* In: *Jewish Political Studies Review*, 22, nos 3–4, jcpa.org.

Weinmann, Martin (1990), with contributions by Anne Kaiser and Ursula Krause-Schmitt, *Das nationalsozialistische Lagersystem*, Frankfurt a.M.: Zweitausendeins, p. 49.

Weiss, Peter (1964), *Der Schatten des Körpers des Kutschers.* Frankfurt a.M.: Suhrkamp (1st edn 1960).

—— (1966), *Die Ermittlung. Oratorium in 11 Gesängen.* Berlin, Rütten & Loening, 2nd edn (licence for the GDR); *Marat/Sade; The Investigation. Oratorio in 11 Cantos; The Shadow of the Body of the Coachman*; ed. Robert Cohen. New York: Continuum, 1998.

Welzer, Harald, et al. (2002), *'Opa war kein Nazi.' Nationalsozialismus und Holocaust im Familiengedächtnis.* Frankfurt a.M.: Fischer.

Wenk, Silke (1991), *Nike in Flammen. Gründungsopfer in der Skulptur der Nachkriegszeit?* In: Kohn-Waechter, pp. 193–218.

—— (1996), *Versteinerte Weiblichkeit. Allegorien in der Skulptur der Moderne.* Cologne, Weimar, Vienna: Böhlau.

—— (1997), *Henry Moore. Two Large Forms. Eine Allegorie des modernen Sozialstaates.* Frankfurt a.M.: Fischer.

—— and Eschebach, Insa (2002), *Soziales Gedächtnis und Geschlechterdifferenz. Eine Einführung.* In: Eschebach et al., pp. 13–38.

—— (2003), *Happy End nach der Katastrophe. La 'Vite è bella' zwischen Medienreferenz und 'Postmemory'.* In: Frölich, Margrit, et al. (eds), *Lachen über Hitler – Auschwitz-Gelächter? Filmkomödie, Satire und Holocaust.* Munich: Ed. Text + Kritik, pp. 199–224.

—— (2008), *Expositionen des Obszönen. Zum Umgang mit dem Nationalsozialismus in der visuellen Kultur.* In: Eschebach/Mühlhäuser, pp. 279–95.

Wenzel, Mirjam (2009), *Gericht und Gedächtnis. Der deutschsprachige Holocaust-Diskurs der sechziger Jahre.* Göttingen: Wallstein.

—— (2012), *Vom Zeugnis zum Tribunal.* In: Bruns, Claudia, et al. (eds), *'Welchen der Steine du hebst.' Filmische Erinnerung an den Holocaust.* Berlin: Bertz & Fischer, pp. 332–43.

Werckmeister, O. K. (1987), *Von der Revolution zum Exil.* In: *Paul Klee, Leben und Werk.* Ed. Paul-Klee-Stiftung Bern: Kunstmuseum, pp. 51–7.

Wheeler, Eleanor (1957), *Lidice.* Prague: Orbis.

Wickert, Christel (2002), *Tabu Lagerbordell. Vom Umgang mit der Zwangsprostitution nach 1945.* In: Eschebach et al., pp. 41–58.

Wiechert, Ernst (2007), *Der Totenwald. Ein Bericht mit einem Essay von Klaus Briegleb.* Frankfurt a.M.: Suhrkamp (first publication: Rascher Verlag Zürich, 1946); *The Forest of the Dead.* Trans. Ursula Stechow. London: Gollancz, 1947.

Wiedemann, Barbara (1985), *Antschel Paul – Paul Celan. Studien zum Frühwerk.* Tubingen: Max Niemeyer.

—— (2011), *Welcher Daten eingedenk? Celans Todesfuge und der Izvestija-Bericht über das Lemberg Ghetto.* In: *Wirkendes Wort*, 61, no. 3, pp. 437–52.

Wiesenthal, Simon (1946), *KZ Mauthausen. Bild und Wort.* Linz: Ibis.

Wittler, Kathrin (2013); *'Muselmann'. Anmerkungen zur Geschichte einer Bezeichnung.* In: *Zeitschrift für Geschichtswissenschaft,* 61, no. 12, pp. 1045–56.

Wrocklage, Ute (1998), *Auschwitz-Birkenau – Die Rampe.* In: Hoffmann, D. 1998, pp. 278–309.

Wulf, Josef (1960), *Vom Leben, Kampf und Tod im Ghetto in Warschau.* Bonn: Bundeszentrale für Heimatdienst.

—— (1961), *Das Dritte Reich und seine Vollstrecker. Die Liquidation von 500 000 Juden im Ghetto Warschau.* Berlin: Arani.

Yerushalmi, Yosef Hayim (1988), *Zachor: Erinnere Dich!* Berlin: Wagenbach.

Zentner, Kurt (1965), *Illustrierte Geschichte des Dritten Reiches.* Munich: Südwest.

Zimmermann, Rainer (1972), *Otto Pankok. Das Werk des Malers, Holzschneiders und Bildhauers.* Berlin: Rembrandt.

—— (1980), *Die Kunst der verschollenen Generation. Deutsche Malerei des expressiven Realismus.* Düsseldorf, Vienna: Econ.

Zöllner, Frank (2009), *Auftragswerke.* In: Cat. *Tübke-Stiftung*, pp. 71–100.

—— (2012), *Apokalypse und Erlösung. Zum Geschichtsbild im Werk Werner Tübkes.* In: Cat. *Abschied*, pp. 273–83.

Catalogues of Exhibitions and Collections

Altenbourg WVZ 2004

Janda, Annegret, *Gerhard Altenbourg. Monographie und Werkverzeichnis.* Ed. the Lindenau-Museum Altenburg. Cologne: Wienand, vol. 1.

Beuys WVZ Aktionen 1994

Beuys, Joseph (1994), *Die Aktionen. Kommentiertes Werkverzeichnis mit fotografischen Dokumentationen.* Ed. Uwe M. Schneede. Ostfildern-Ruit: Hatje.

Buchheister WVZ 1998

Kemp, Willi, and Buchheister, Elisabeth (eds), *Carl Buchheister, vol. 1: Monographie. Band 2: Werkverzeichnis der abstrakten Arbeiten.* Cologne: König.

Dürer WVZ 1964

Dürer. Das graphische Werk. Text von Karl-Adolf Knappe. Vienna, Munich: 1964.

Dürer WVZ 1973

The Complete Engravings, Etchings and Drypoints of Albrecht Dürer. Ed. Walter L. Strauss. New York: Dover Publ. 2nd edn.

Grundig, Lea WVZ 1973

Lea Grundig. Werkverzeichnis der Radierungen. Ladengalerie Berlin 1973, Berlin (West): Ladengalerie.

Grundig, Lea WVZ 2016

Werkverzeichnis Lea Grundig. Unpublished Manuscript, ed. Maria Heiner.

Grzimek wvz 1979

Pankok wvz 1

Pankok, Otto. Werkverzeichnis. Otto-Pankok-Gesellschaft, ed. Hulda and Eva Pankok, vol. 1: *Die Holzschnitte.* Rev. and intro. by Rainer Zimmermann. Düsseldorf: Droste 1985.

Pankok wvz *2*

Otto Pankok. Werkverzeichnis. Otto-Pankok-Gesellschaft, ed. Eva Pankok, vol. II: *Die Radierungen.* Rev. by Rolf Jäger. Intro. by Rainer Zimmermann. Düsseldorf: Droste 1990.

Pankok wvz *3*

Pankok, Otto. Werkverzeichnis. Otto-Pankok-Museum Hünxe-Drewenack, ed. Eva Pankok, vol. 3: *Die Lithographien, Steinätzungen und Monotypien.* Rev. by Susanne Timm. Düsseldorf: Droste 1995.

Roters, Eberhard: *Der Bildhauer Waldemar Grzimek.* Frankfurt: Propylaen.

Szymanski wvz *1975*

Rolf Szymanski. Werkverzeichnis der Plastiken 1958–1975. With texts by Rolf Szymanski et al., ed. Dieter Brusberg. Hannover: Galerie Brusberg.

Vostell wvz 1988

Vostell, Wolf, *Vostell. Das plastische Werk 1953–87.* Intro. by Jürgen Schilling. Milan: Mult(h)ipla.

Catalogues of Works

Cat. Abgestempelt 1999

Abgestempelt. Judenfeindliche Postkarten. Exh. Jüdisches Museum Frankfurt a.M. and Museum für Post und Kommunikation Frankfurt a.M. 1999. Ed. Helmut Gold. Heidelberg: Umschau/Braus.

Cat. Abschied 2012

Abschied von Ikarus. Bildwelten in der DDR – neu gesehen. Weimar 2013. Ed. Karl-Siegbert Rehberg et al. Cologne: König.

Cat. Am Anfang 1986

Am Anfang: Das Junge Rheinland. Zur Kunst- und Zeitgeschichte einer Region 1918–1945. Ed. Ulrich Krempel. Düsseldorf: Claassen.

Cat. Art from the Holocaust 2016

Art from the Holocaust. 100 Works from the Yad Vashem Collection. Exh. Berlin, Deutsches Historisches Museum. Cologne: Wienand.

Cat. Art of Two Germanys 2009

Art of Two Germanys – Cold War Cultures. Stephanie Barron and Sabine Eckmann (eds). Exh. Los Angeles, Calif., Nuremberg, Berlin 2009. New York 2009: Abrams.

Cat. Auschwitz-Prozess 2004

Auschwitz-Prozeß 4 Ks 2/63 Frankfurt a.M. Exh. Haus Gallus Frankfurt a.M., ed. Fritz Bauer Institut, Cologne: Snoeck.

Cat. Barz 1980

Mathias Barz. Gemälde, Grafiken, zum 85. Geburtstag des Künstlers. Exh. Düsseldorf: Stadtmuseum.

Cat. Berke 1962

Hubert Berke. Dokumentation seines 30jährigen künstlerischen Schaffens. Mainz 1962. Ed. Friedrich Gerke (= Kleine Schriften der Gesellschaft für bildende Kunst in Mainz, 5, 1962).

Cat. Berke 1992

Hubert Berke. Masken im Sumpf. Ed. Sabine Fehlemann and Werner Schäfke. Exh. Wuppertal and Cologne: Kölnisches Stadtmuseum.

Cat. Berke 2008

Hubert Berke. Exh. Aachen, Bonn, Münster, Linnich, Gelsenkirchen. Cologne: DuMont.

Cat. Berlin Transit 2012

Berlin Transit. Jüdische Migranten aus Osteuropa in den 1920er Jahren. Exh. Jüdisches Museum in Berlin. Göttingen: Wallstein.

Cat. Beuys 1969

Joseph Beuys. Werke aus der Sammlung Ströher. Basel: Kunstmuseum Basel.

Cat. Beuys 1985a

Kreuz + Zeichen. Religiöse Grundlagen im Werk von Joseph Beuys. Aachen: Suermondt-Ludwig-Museum & Museumsverein.

Cat. Beuys 1985b

Joseph Beuys. Braunkreuz. Westfälisches Landesmuseum für Kunst und Kulturgeschichte Münster und Landschaftsverband Westfalen-Lippe.

Cat. Beuys 1986

Ute Klophaus: Sein und Bleiben. Photographie zu Joseph Beuys. Bonner Kunstverein, Bonn.

Cat. Beuys 1988

Joseph Beuys. Teil 1: Skulpturen und Objekte. Exh. Berlin and Tübingen 1988. Munich: Schirmer-Mosel.

Cat. Beuys 1993

Joseph Beuys. Raum in der Neuen Galerie. Ed. Kulturstiftung der Länder in association with the Staatliche Museen Kassel. Berlin und Kassel.

Cat. Beuys 1996

Joseph Beuys. Eine Werkübersicht. Zeichnungen und Aquarelle, Drucksachen und Multiples, Skulpturen und Objekte, Räume und Aktionen. 1945–1985. Intro. by Alain Borer, ed. Lothar Schirmer. Munich: Schirmer/Mosel.

Cat. Beuys 1997

Joseph Beuys. 'Joseph Beuys verlängert im Auftrag von James Joyce den Ulysses um sechs weitere Kapitel.' Undated, 6 vols, ed. Klaus-D. Pohl and Peter Märker. Darmstadt: Hessisches Landesmuseum, Graphische Sammlung.

Cat. Beuys 2008

Joseph Beuys. Die Revolution sind wir. Ed. Eugen Blume and Catherine Nichols. Nationalgalerie im Hamburger Bahnhof, Museum für Gegenwart, Berlin. Göttingen: Steidl.

Cat. Beuys 2010

Joseph Beuys. Energieplan. Zeichnungen aus dem Museum Schloss Moyland. Exh. Bedburg-Hau.

Cat. Beuys Brock Vostell 2016

Beuys Brock Vostell Aktion Demonstration Partizipation. Peter Weibel (ed.) zkm Karlsruhe. Ostfildern: Hatje & Cantz.

Cat. Bruse 1979

Hermann Bruse 1904–1953. Gedenkausstellung anlässlich seines 75. Geburtstags. Exh. April to June 1979, Museen, Gedenkstätten und Sammlungen Magdeburg, Kulturhistorisches Museum.

Cat. Chagall 1959

Marc Chagall. Exh. Hamburg, Munich, Paris 1959. Hamburg: Christians.

Cat. Chagall 1991

Marc Chagall. Die russischen Jahre 1906–1922. Frankfurt a.M.: Kunsthalle Schirn.

Cat. Chagall 2006

Chagall in neuem Licht. Ed. the Stiftung Frieder Burda, exh. Museum Frieder Burda. Baden Baden. Ostfildern: Hatje & Cantz.

Cat. Claus 1990

Carlfriedrich Claus. Erwachen am Augenblick Sprachblätter, with the theoretical texts by Carlfriedrich Claus and a commented list of works. Exh. Karl-Marx-Stadt, Hamburg 1991. Karl-Marx-Stadt: Städtische Museen.

Cat. Claus 2011

Carlfriedrich Claus. Geschrieben im Nachtmeer. Berlin: Akademie der Künste.

Cat. dadaglobe 2016

Dadaglobe reconstructed. Ed. Adrian Sudhalter et al., exh. Kunsthaus Zürich and Museum of Modern Art New York. Zürich: Scheidegger & Spiess.

Cat. Das junge Rheinland 1996

Das Junge Rheinland. Künstler – Werke – Dokumente. Düsseldorf: Galerie Remmert und Barth.

Cat. Das Recht des Bildes 2003

Das Recht des Bildes. Jüdische Perspektiven in der modernen Kunst. Museum Bochum 2003–2004. Ed. Hans Günter Golinski et al. Heidelberg: Braus.

Cat. Daumier 2013

'Daumier ist ungeheuer!' (Max Liebermann) Gemälde, Zeichnungen, Graphik, Bronzen von Honoré Daumier. Exh. Max Liebermann Haus, Berlin. Berlin: Nicolai.

Cat. Der Geteilte Himmel 2014

Die Sammlung der Nationalgalerie 1945–1968. Der geteilte Himmel. Berlin: Distanz-Verlag.

Cat. Der Graphische Zyklus 1956

Der Graphische Zyklus von Max Klinger bis zur Gegenwart. Ed. Gerhard Pommeranz-Liedtke. Berlin: Deutsche Akademie der Künste.

Cat. Deutsche Kunstausstellung 1946

Deutsche Kunstausstellung der Deutschen Zentralverwaltung für Volksbildung in der Sowjetischen Besatzungszone. Berlin: Zeughaus Unter den Linden.

Cat. Deutschlandbilder 1997

Deutschlandbilder. Kunst aus einem geteilten Land. Berlin. Ed. Eckhart Gillen. Cologne: DuMont.

Cat. Die Macht der Bilder 1995

Die Macht der Bilder. Antisemitische Vorurteile und Mythen. Ed. the Jüdisches Museum der Stadt Wien. Vienna: Picus.

Cat. Die Schwarzen Jahre 2015

Die Schwarzen Jahre. Geschicht einer Sammlung 1933–1945. Für die Nationalgalerie, Staatliche Museen zu Berlin ed. Dietzer Scholz and Maria Obenaus. Berlin: Verbrecher Verlag.

Cat. documenta 2,1 1959

documenta 2,1: Malerei. Cologne: DuMont Schauberg.

Cat. documenta 3,1 1964

documenta 3,1: Malerei und Skulptur. Cologne: DuMont Schauberg.

Cat. documenta 6,1 1977

documenta 6,1: Einführung, Malerei Plastik/Environment, Performance. Kassel: Dierichs.

Cat. documenta 6,3 1977

documenta 6,3: Handzeichnungen, utopisches Design, Bücher. Kassel: Dierichs.

Cat. Dresdner Sezession 1977

Dresdner Sezession. 1919–1923. Exh. Milan and Munich: Galleria del Levante.

Cat. Ehmsen 1986a

Heinrich Ehmsen 1886–1964. Gemälde, Aquarelle, Zeichnungen. Ausstellung zum 100. Geburtstag. Exh. Berlin (Ost) Nationalgalerie. Berlin: Staatliche Museen 1986.

Cat. Ehmsen 1986b

Heinrich Ehmsen. Gemälde aus dem Bestand der Heinrich-Ehmsen-Stiftung. Exh. Berlin (West) and Kiel/Kiel 1986. Kiel: Heinrich-Ehmsen-Stiftung.

Cat. Ensor 1973

James Ensor. Catalogue illustré des ses gravures, leur description critique et l'inventaire des plaques. Ed. Auguste Tavernier. Ghent: Ledeberg.

Cat. Ensor 1992

James Ensor. Catalogue raisonné of the paintings, vol. 1, 1875–1902. Ed. Xavier Tricot. Antwerp: Wienand.

Cat. Entdeckte Moderne 2008

Entdeckte Moderne. Werke aus der Sammlung Gerhard Schneider. Rolf Jessewitsch and Gerhard Schneider (eds), exh. Salzburg, Altenburg, Bayreuth, Berlin, Solingen 2008–2010. Bönen: Kettler.

Cat. Ernst 1991

Max Ernst. Retrospektive zum 100. Geburtstag. Werner Spies (ed.): exh. London, Stuttgart, Düsseldorf, Paris. München: Prestel.

Cat. Ernst 1994

Helen Ernst, 1904–1948, Berlin Amsterdam Ravensbrück, Stationen einer antifaschistischen Künstlerin. Berlin: Das Verborgene Museum.

Cat. Europa 1989

Europa 1789. Aufklärung, Verklärung, Verfall. Ed. Werner Hoffmann. Hamburg: Hamburger Kunsthalle.

Cat. Expressive Gegenständlichkeit 2001

Expressive Gegenständlichkeit. Schicksale figurativer Malerei und Graphik im 20. Jahrhundert. Werke aus der Sammlung Gerhard Schneider. Exh. Osnabrück, Halle, Hamm, Bönen: Kettler.

Cat. Fluxus 2012

Fluxus! >Antikunst< ist auch Kunst. 50 Jahre Fluxus – das Archiv Sohm gratuliert. Texts and Eds: Werner Esser et al. Cologne: Snoeck.

Cat. Fremde 2009

Fremde im Visier. Fotoalben aus dem Zweiten Weltkrieg. Exh. Oldenburg, Frankfurt a.M., Jena. Ed. Petra Bopp and Sandra Starke. Bielefeld: Kerber.

Cat. Galerie Neue Meister 2010

Galerie Neue Meister Dresden. Illustrierter Katalog in zwei Bänden. Staatliche Kunstsammlungen Dresden. Ed. Ulrich Bischoff. Cologne: König.

Cat. Georgi 2001

Hanns Georgi (1901–1989), Maler, Grafiker, Buchillustrator. Sebnitz.

Cat. Goral 2007

Kein Weg als Jude und Deutscher? Der Maler, Publizist und Dichter Ariel Goral. Frankfurt a.M.: Museum Judengasse.

Cat. Heartfield 1991/92

John Heartfield. Eine Ausstellung der Akademie der Künste Berlin. Exh. Berlin, Bonn, Tübingen 1991/92. Cologne: DuMont.

Cat. Herausgefordert 1998

Herausgefordert – Bilder des Widerstandes. Zum Gedenken an Hubert Berke und Karl Schwesig. Ed. Leane Schäfer. Gelsenkirchen: Städtisches Museum.

Cat. Hundertwasser 2012

Friedensreich Hundertwasser. Gegen den Strich. Werke 1949–1970. Exh. Kunsthalle Bremen 2012. Ostfildern: Hatje Cantz.

Cat. Klopfzeichen 2002

Klopfzeichen. Kunst und Kultur der 80er Jahre in Deutschland. Begleitbuch zur Doppelausstellung Mauersprünge und Wahnzimmer. Exh. Leipzig and Essen 2002; Leipzig: Faber & Faber.

Cat. Knipser 1995

Knipser. Die Bildgeschichte der privaten Fotografie in Deutschland und Österreich von 1880 bis 1980. Ed. Timm Starl. München: Stadtmuseum.

Cat. Koerner 1947

Henry Koerner. USA Gemälde, Graphik, 1945–1947. Berlin: Haus am Waldsee, Amt für Kunst Zehlendorf.

Cat. Koerner 1997

Unheimliche Heimat. Henry Koerner, 1915–1991. Intro. by Joseph Leo Koerner. Vienna: Österreichische Galerie Belvedere.

Cat. Koerner 2003

The Early Work of Henry Koerner. Ed. Edith Balas. Pittsburgh (USA): Frick Art and Historical Center; Estate of Henry Koerner.

Cat. Kubin 1977

Alfred Kubin. Das zeichnerische Frühwerk bis 1904. Hans Albert Peters (ed.), exh. Baden-Baden, Munich, Vienna, Baden-Baden: Staatliche Kunsthalle.

Cat. Kubin 1999

Alfred Kubin 1877–1959. Ed. Annegret Hoberg with Ines Engelmann, with contributions by Peter Assmann. Exh. Munich and Linz. Munich: Hirmer.

Cat. Kunst im Dritten Reich 1974

Kunst im Dritten Reich. Dokumente der Unterwerfung. Exh. Frankfurt a.M., Hamburg, Stuttgart, Ludwigshafen, Wuppertal 1974/75, Frankfurt a.M.: Kunstverein.

Cat. Kunst in Auschwitz 2005

Kunst in Auschwitz 1940–1945. Begleitbuch zu der Ausstellung der Stiftung Neue Synagoge Berlin – Centrum Judaicum, im Kulturgeschichtlichen Museum Osnabrück/Felix-Nussbaum-Haus und dem Muzeum Tradycji Niepodległościowych w Łodzi 2005. Bramsche: Rasch.

Cat. Kunst und Kalter Krieg 2009

Kunst und Kalter Krieg. Deutsche Positionen 1945–89. Exh. Los Angeles, Nürnberg and Berlin 2009/10, Cologne 2009. Ed. Stephanie Barron and Sabine Eckmann. Cologne: DuMont.

Cat. Kunstfreunde 1912

Katalog der Vereinigung der Kunstfreunde. Farbige Nachbildungen von Gemälden der königlichen National-Galerie und anderer Kunstsammlungen. Berlin, no date given (1912)

Cat. L'art en guerre 2012

L'art en guerre, France 1938–1947. Musée d'Art Moderne de la Ville de Paris 2012/13, Paris: Editions Paris Musées.

Cat. Lauterbach 1947

Carl Lauterbach. Dokumente der Zeit. Exh. by Kulturbund zur demokratischen Erneuerung Deutschlands, Düsseldorf: Städt. Kunsthalle.

Cat. Lauterbach 1981

Carl Lauterbach. Gemälde Grafik Dokumente. Texts by Wieland König. Düsseldorf: Stadtmuseum.

Cat. Lea Grundig 1949

Jüdische Gesellschaft zur Verbreitung der Schönen Künste unter Mitarbeit des Verbandes Polnischer Bildender Künstler (eds), *Lea Grundig, Ausstellung Grafik und Zeichnungen*, with a text by Jozef Sandel. Warsaw.

Cat. Lea Grundig 1975

Lea Grundig. Zeichnungen, Grafik. Ed. Horst-Jörg Ludwig. Exh. Berlin, Leipzig and Dresden, Berlin: Akademie der Künste.

Cat. Lea Grundig 1977

Lea Grundig. Grafik und Zeichnungen im Kulturhistorischen Museum Magdeburg, no date given.

Cat. Lea Grundig 1996

Lea Grundig. Jüdin, Kommunistin, Graphikerin. Exh. Galerie St Etienne and New York 1996/97, Berlin: Ladengalerie.

Cat. Le Juif errant 2001

Le Juif errant, un témoin du temps. Musée d'art et d'histoire du Judaisme, Paris.

Cat. Liebermann 1979

Max Liebermann in seiner Zeit. Ed. Sigrid Achenbach and Matthias Eberle. Berlin: Nationalgalerie Staatliche Museen Preußischer Kulturbesitz.

Cat. Lingner 1988

Max Lingner 1888–1959, Gemälde, Zeichnungen, Pressegraphik. Ed. Gisela Josten, exh. Berlin 1988/89. Berlin: Staatliche Museen.

Cat. Lörcher 1988

Alfred Lörcher: Plastiken und Zeichnungen. Stuttgart: Staatsgalerie.

Cat. Ludwigs 1983

Peter Ludwigs. Malerei, Grafik, Dokumente. Düsseldorf: Stadtmuseum.

Cat. Lüttwitz 1992

Lidy von Lüttwitz. Skulpturen. Exh. München and Oberhausen 1992. Munich: Barbara-Gross-Galerie.

Cat. Max Lachnit 1991

Max Lachnit 1900–1972. Plastik Malerei Grafik. Magdeburg: Magdeburger Museen.

Cat. Meidner 1970

Ludwig Meidner. Zeichnungen aus dem Nachlass. Darmstadt: Kunstverein.

Cat. Meidner 1991

Ludwig Meidner: Zeichner, Maler, Literat. Ed. Gerda Breuer and Ines Wagemann, Institut Mathildenhöhe Darmstadt. Stuttgart: Hatje, 2 vols.

Cat. Mémoire 2001

Mémoire des camps, Photographies des camps de concentration et d'extermination nazis, 1933–1999. Ed. Clément Chéroux. Paris: Marval.

Cat. Menschenbilder 1998

Menschenbilder. Figur in Zeiten der Abstraktion (1945–1955). Exh. Kunsthalle Mannheim 1998/1999. Ed. Manfred Fath. Ostfildern-Ruit: Hatje.

Cat. Meyer-Vax 1965

Dore Meyer-Vax. Exh. Nürnberg and Berlin, ed. Verband Bildender Künstler Deutschlands and Neue Berliner Galerie.

Cat. Moderne Zeiten 2014

Moderne Zeiten, die Nationalgalerie der Staatlichen Museen zu Berlin zu Gast in der Kunsthalle Würth in Schwäbisch Hall. First shown in Berlin 2010/11. Ed. Udo Kittelmann. Künzelsau: Swiridoff.

Cat. Monumenta Judaica 1963

Monumenta Judaica. 2000 Jahre Geschichte und Kultur der Juden am Rhein. Ed. Konrad Schilling. Cologne: Stadtmuseum.

Cat. Nachkriegskunst 1994

Nachkriegskunst in Karlsruhe 1945–1955. Karlsruhe: Bezirksverband Bildender Künstler Karlsruhe in Zusammenarbeit mit dem Badischen Kunstverein.

Cat Nationalgalerie 1986

Nationalgalerie. Sammlung Kunst der DDR. Gemälde. Bildhauerwerke. Vollständiges Verzeichnis des Sammlungsbestandes und der Dauerleihgaben. ed. Hans Jürgen Papies and Fritz Jacobi. Berlin: Henschelverlag.

Cat. No!Art 1995

No!Art. Redaktion: Ulrike Abel, Matthias Reichelt, Klaus Theuerkauff. Berlin: Neue Gesellschaft für Bildende Kunst.

Cat. Oppenheim 2013

Meret Oppenheim. Retrospektive. Wien, Berlin 2013. Ed. Heike Eipeldauer et al. Ostfildern: Hatje und Cantz.

Cat. Pankok 1946/1947

Kollektivausstellung. Otto Pankok. Ein Maler der Gegenwart. Ed. Kulturbund zur demokratischen Erneuerung Deutschlands in Düsseldorf, Kunsthalle Düsseldorf.

Cat. Pankok 1947

Otto Pankok. Blätter der Kunstfreunde, 1, Hamburg.

Cat. Pankok 1948

Otto Pankok. exh. Pfälzische Gewerbeanstalt, Kaiserslautern 16 September–1 October 1948.

Cat. Pankok 1955

Otto Pankok. Gelsenkirchen: Städtische Kunstausstellung.

Cat. Pankok 1961

Otto Pankok. Handzeichnungen, Druckgraphik, Plastik. Berlin Deutsche Akademie der Künste.

Cat. Pankok 1968

Otto Pankoks Plastische Gestalten. Werkkatalog der Skulpturen. Ludwigshafen 1968. Ed. Bertold Roland. Drevenack: Otto-Pankok-Ges.

Cat. Pankok 1993

Otto-Pankok-Gesellschaft (ed.), *Otto Pankok: 1893–1966, Retrospektive zum 100. Geburtstag.* Oberhausen: Plitt.

Cat. Pankok 2008

Pankok, Eva, and Romane Rose (eds.), *Otto Pankok, Sinti-Porträts 1931–1949.* Exh. Heidelberg, Hünxe: Damm und Lindlar.

Cat. Picasso 1974

Picasso und die Antike. Karlsruhe: Badisches Landesmuseum.

Cat. Picasso 2002

Picasso et les femmes. Ed. Irene Mössinger et al. Kunstsammlungen Chemnitz. Cologne: DuMont.

Cat. Pro Lidice 1997

Pro Lidice, 52 umělc u z Německa. 52 Künstler aus Deutschland. Exh. Prag 1997, Concept by René Block. Prague: České Muzeum Vytśvarných Umění.

Cat. Representations of Auschwitz 1995

Representations of Auschwitz. 50 Years of Photographs, Paintings, and Graphics. Exh. Krakow 1995, Oświeçim: Auschwitz-Birkenau State Museum.

Cat. Rheinische Secession 1946

Rheinische Secession. Düsseldorf: Kunsthalle.

Cat. Richter 2011

Gerhard Richter. Bilder einer Epoche. Kunsthalle Hamburg, exh. and catalogue by Uwe M. Schneede, Munich: Hirmer.

Cat. Richter 2012

Gerhard Richter. Panorama (Retrospektive). Ed. Mark Godfrey et al., exh. Berlin, London, Paris, Munich: Prestel.

Cat. Richter 2016

Gerhard Richter. Birkenau. Ed. Helmut Friedel. Museum Frieder Burda Baden-Baden. Cologne: König.

Cat. Sandberg 1965

Herbert Sandberg. Der Weg, 70 Aquatintaradierungen. Exh. Berliner Kupferstichkabinett im Bodemuseum. Berlin: Staatliche Museen.

Cat. Schrecknisse des Krieges 1983

Schrecknisse des Krieges. Druckgraphische Bilderfolgen des Krieges aus fünf Jahrhunderten. Ludwigshafen: Wilhelm-Hack-Museum.

Cat. Schulenburg 1989

Tisa von Schulenburg. Begegnungen, Zeichnungen, Plastiken, Reliefs. Kolvenburg Billerbeck: Kulturzentrum des Kreises Coesfeld.

Cat. Schwesig 1983

Karl Schwesig. Schlegelkeller. Galerie Remmert und Barth (eds). Düsseldorf: Frölich & Kaufmann.

Cat. Schwesig 1984

Karl Schwesig. Leben und Werk. Ed. Herbert Remmert. Berlin: Frölich & Kaufmann.

Cat. Sitte 1986

Willi Sitte. Epochenbilder. Gemälde, Zeichnungen, Druckgraphik. Exh. Altes Museum Berlin, by Ministerium für Kultur, Verband Bildender Künstler der DDR, Staatliche Museen zu Berlin, Hauptstadt der DDR, Nationalgalerie.

Cat. Steinhardt 1959

Leon Kolb (ed.), *The Woodcuts of Jakob Steinhardt.* San Francisco: Genuart.

Cat. Steinhardt 1995

Jakob Steinhardt. Der Prophet. Exh. and collection catalogue, Jüdisches Museum im Berlin Museum.

Cat. Steinlen 1978

Theophile-Alexandre Steinlen. Berlin: Staatliche Kunsthalle.

Cat. Stunde Null 1998

Stunde Null. Deutsche Kunst der späten vierziger Jahre. Stuttgart: Staatsgalerie.

Cat. Theresienstadt-Konvolut 2002

Das Theresienstadt-Konvolut. Exh. Heine Haus Hamburg, Hamburg. Munich: Dölling & Galitz.

Cat. Treffpunkt Parnass 1980

Treffpunkt Parnass. Wuppertal: 1949–1965. Exh. von der Heydt Museum Wuppertal 1980, Ed. Will Baltzer et al. Cologne: Schriften des Rheinischen Museumsamtes, no. 11.

Cat. Tübke 1972

Werner Tübke. Variationen zum Thema ‚Lebenserinnerungen des Dr. jur. Schulze'. Exh. Studio Altes Museum Berlin. Berlin: Staatliche Museen, Nationalgalerie.

Cat. Tübke 1976

Werner Tübke. Gemälde, Aquarelle, Druckgrafik, Zeichnungen. Exh. Dresden, Leipzig, Berlin, concept and cat. by Günter Meissner and Horst Schulze. Dresden, Leipzig, Berlin: Ministerium für Kultur der DDR.

Cat. Tübke 2004

Werner Tübke. Faszination Mittelmeer. Bad Frankenhauen 2004. Ed. Gerd Lindner. Bad Frankenhausen: Panorama-Museum.

Cat. Tübke 2009

Werner Tübke. Die Retrospektive zum 80. Geburtstag. Exh. Museum der Bildenden Künste Leipzig and Berliner Volksbank Berlin 2009/10, ed. Hans Werner Schmidt. Leipzig: Seemann Henschel.

Cat. Tübke 2010

Werner Tübke. Zeichnungen 1962–1969. Leipzig: Ed. Galerie Schwind.

Cat. Tübke-Stiftung 2009

Tübke-Stiftung Leipzig: Bestandskatalog der Zeichnungen und Aquarelle. Leipzig: Ploettner.

Cat. UNRRA 1947

Catalogue of the International Art Exhibition of the UNRRA Team 1041: Printing, Graphic, Plastic, Art Handicraft, Ansbach Castle.

Cat. Vernichtungskrieg 1995

Vernichtungskrieg. Verbrechen der Wehrmacht 1941–1944. Touring exh., ed. Hannes Heer for Stiftung Hamburger Institut für Sozialforschung. Hamburg: Hamburger edition.

Cat. Vostell 1975

Vostell Retrospektive 1958–1974. Exh. Nationalgalerie Berlin, Staatliche Museen Preussischer Kulturbesitz, organized by Neuer Berliner Kunstverein and Neue Nationalgalerie.

Cat. Vostell 1992

Vostell. Exh. Rheinische Landesmuseum Bonn, Josef-Haubrich-Kunstalle Köln, Stadtmuseum Leverkusen, ed. Rolf Wedewer. Heidelberg: Ed. Braus.

Cat. Vostell 2005

Wolf Vostell. Die Druckgrafik. Exh. Städtische Villa Sanders Bergisch Gladbach, Kunsthalle Bremen, Museo Vostell Malpartida, Cáceres 2005–7. Bergisch Gladbach: Städtische Villa Zanders.

Cat. Warschauer Ghetto 1963

Warschauer Ghetto. Ausstellung in der Paulskirche in Frankfurt a.M. Foreword: Eugen Kogon. Frankfurt a.M.: Union Dt. Widerstandskämpfer u. Verfolgtenverbände; no year given (1963).

Cat. Widerstand 1978

Zwischen Widerstand und Anpassung. Kunst in Deutschland 1933–1945. Exh. concept by Janos Frecot, cat. ed. Barbara Volkmann. Berlin: Akademie der Künste.

Cat. Wien – Berlin 2013

Wien – Berlin. Kunst zweier Metropolen. Exh. Berlinische Galerie, Österrichische Galerie Belvedere, cat. ed. Agnes Husslein-Arco. Munich: Prestel.

Cat. Wilhelm Lachnit 2000

Wilhelm Lachnit 1899–1962. Gemälde. Ed. Gabriele Werner. Dresden: Staatliche Kunstsammlungen, Gemäldegalerie Neue Meister.

Cat. Wollheim 1993

Gert H. Wollheim: 1894–1974. Eine Retrospektive. Exh. Kunstmuseum Düsseldorf im Ehrenhof 1993. Cologne: Wienand.

Cat. 'Wollt ihr das totale Leben?' 1995

'Wollt ihr das totale Leben?' Fluxus und Agit-Pop der 60er Jahre in Aachen, exh. cat., ed. Adam C. Oellers and Sibille Spiegel. Aachen: Neuer Aachener Kunstverein.

Cat. Zeitenwende 2016

Zeitenwende. Von der Berliner Secession zur Novembergruppe. Exh. Bröhan-Museum Berlin. Munich: Hirmer.

Cat. Zielezinski 2013

George Ziel [Jerzy Zielezinski], lynn-munroe-books.com/list62/GEORGE_ZIEL2.htm (15 April 2013).

Cat. Zwischen Krieg und Frieden 1980

Zwischen Krieg und Frieden. Gegenständliche und realistische Tendenzen in der Kunst nach 1945. Exh. Frankfurter Kunstverein. Berlin: Elefanten-Press 1980.

Cat. Zone 5 1989

Zone 5. Kunst in der Viersektorenstadt 1945–1951. Ed. Eckhart Gillen and Diether Schmidt. Berlin: Berlinische Galerie.

Archives

Auschwitz Wettbewerb 1957

Unterlagen fur die Teilnehmer am Wettbewerb zur Errichtung eines internationalen Denkmals in Auschwitz (1957): Ed. Secretariat of the International Auschwitz Committee, Auschwitz. Copy in: Osterreichisches Staatsarchiv, Allgemeines Verwaltungsarchiv, Nachlass Langbein E 1797:292/8.

Nachlass Grundig

Akademie der Künste, Berlin, Archiv: Nachlass Grundig; V.2.22.042; Nr. 250; Lea Grundig: 6 vols. 1957–68 (320/1).

Nachlass Heartfield

Akademie der Künste, Berlin, Archiv: Nachlass Heartfield 579.

Collection Lea Grundig

Akademie der Künste, Berlin, Kunstsammlung

Acknowledgements

Selecting and commenting on the images was a long process that was supported by many people. I should like to express my gratitude to them. The invitation by Mirjam Wenzel and Cilly Kugelmann to the lecture on 27 January 2010 at the Jewish Museum in Berlin led to my work involving a systematic attempt to find an answer to a question that had concerned me for a long period of time. The planned essay turned into a book for which Sigrid Philipps became irreplaceable in the process of research, writing, rewriting and, last but not least, translating this book.

Much of this would have been impossible without help: had it not been for Atalya Laufer's translation of the story *Zwischen den Ghettomauern* (Between the Walls of the Ghetto) by Ben Shem, the context in which the illustrations by Lea Grundig were produced would have gone unrecognized. Eduard Beaucamp generously allowed me to share his knowledge about Tübke, and Dorothea Dornhof helped me to research the history of the Jews in the GDR.

New knowledge was discussed in the *Villigster Forschungsforum zu Nationalsozialismus, Rassismus and Antisemitismus*, leading to some creative reflection extending beyond the boundaries of the subject area. Hajo Hahn invited me to present my work to a group of students at the Villigster Spring Academy in Wittenberg (in March 2013) on the subject of *Genocide as a Challenge to 'Cultures of Memory'*, at which lively discussion on the part of the students was encouraging. With Linda Hentschel and Katharina Sykora I was able to think through some still unformed ideas in considerable depth.

Silke Wenk's notes and questioning of the way to proceed stimulated me into thinking more precisely and pointed the way ahead. Barbara Hahn still took the project seriously even when the end of the work was no longer in sight, commenting on the trial structure and the first samples of the text.

My neighbour and respected artist, Barbara Jedermann, provided me with insight into Jewish life in the course of her youth in 1930s and '40s Berlin. Katja Jedermann pointed me in the direction of difficult-to-find materials from the post-war period and read a first draft while she herself in 2013, along with Renate Herter, was curating display-case installations on the Kurfürstendamm that commented in current artistic works on the exclusion of the

Jews from that famous street. The good wishes of my family and many of my friends have given me much encouragement.

Museums and archives preserve the works of art that have been paid little attention over the years, and almost without exception, they have enabled me to work with them. I have to thank the many owners of artworks who once again allowed me their copyright, at a time when many public museums demand such high fees that scholarly work and the publication of it in and outside the institutions are becoming more and more difficult. Mention must be made particularly to:

Aachen, Zentralarchiv Aachener Zeitung and Aachener Nachrichten: Ulrich Schirbach; Ludwig Forum: Sonja Benzner and Anette Lagler; *Altenburg*, Lindenau-Museum: Thomas Matuszak; *Bedburg-Hau*, Stiftung Museum Schloss Moyland, Sammlung van der Grinten: Maurice Dorren; *Bergen-Belsen*, Gedenkstätte: Klaus Tätzler; *Berlin*, Akademie der Künste, Kunstsammlung und Archiv: Antje Keller-Harnack, Anita Metelka and Rosa von der Schulenburg; Bazon Brock; Kupferstichkabinett, Staatliche Museen: Andreas Heese; Nationalgalerie Staatliche Museen: Dieter Scholz and Ute Smeteck; Zero one film GmbH; *Boston*, Leo Koerner; *Chemnitz*, Carlfriedrich Claus-Archiv: Brigitta Milde; *Cologne*, Michael Berke, Gerhard Richter; Stadtmuseum: Sibylle Schmitt; Hünxe-Drevenack, Otto-Pankok-Museum: A. Burger, Eva Pankok and Katrin Reuscher; *Darmstadt*, Hessisches Landesmuseum: Klaus-D. Pohl; *Dresden*, Matthias Griebel and Maria Heiner; Gerhard Richter Archiv: Dietmar Elger, Kerstin Küster Staatliche Kunstsammlungen: Alexandra Schellenberg and Angela Rietschel; *Düsseldorf*, Stadtmuseum: Christoph Danelzik-Brüggemann and Bernd Kreuter; Galerie Remmert und Barth; *Eichstätt*, Bibliothek der Katholischen Universität: Anna Maria Siebers; *Frankfurt a.M.*, Jüdisches Museum, Meidner-Archiv: Erik Riedel; *Gelsenkirchen*, Institut für Stadtgeschichte: Birgit Klein; *Hannover*: Ernst August Rödiger; *Karlsruhe*, zkm: Ulrike Havemann; *Leipzig*, Kunsthistorisches Institut: Karin Schumann; Museum der bildenden Künste: Frédéric Bussmann; *Malpartida de Cáceres*, Museo Vostell: Rafael Vostell; *Marbach*, Deutsches Literaturarchiv: Miriam Häfele; *Minneapolis*, Curtis Gallery; *Nuremberg*, Neues Museum Staatliches Museum für Kunst und Design: Jutta Birle and Thomas Heyden; *Olpe/Solingen*, Gerhard Schneider and Susanne Vieten; *Oranienburg*, Gedenkstätte und Museum Sachsenhausen: Astrid Ley; *Oświęcim*, Państwowe Muzeum Auschwitz-Birkenau: Wojciech Płosa and Anna Odi; *Princeton*, Marquand Library of Art & Archaeology: Rebecca Friedman; *Saarbrücken*, Saarlandmuseum: Roland Augustin; *Vienna*, Fotoarchiv der KZ-Gedenkstätte Mauthausen: Stephan Matyus; Österreichisches Staatsarchiv: Pia Wallnig; *Washington*, Steven Spielberg Film and Video Archive, United States Holocaust Memorial Museum.

These acknowledgements that I am sincerely pleased to give would never have seen the light of day even in the German version, had not Regina Nössler read the proofs and had not Kathrin Brömse, Dieter Mayer-Gürr and Simone Tavnrath from Jonas Verlag been so considerate and patient over its production and printing and so sensitive to the close relationship between text and illustration.

The English translation was financed by the Börsenverein des Deutschen Buchhandels, by the Federal German Foreign Ministry, by the vG Wort and the Fritz Thyssen Foundation. The translation was undertaken by Anthony Mathews showing careful consideration and sensitivity to the subject.

Thanks must also go to Marcia Pointon for her thoughtful commitment and to Michael Leaman's decision to include this book in his list of publications. And, last but not least, to the team at Reaktion Books, especially Jess Chandler, for an excellent job in preparing the book for publication.

List of Illustrations

1 Bedřich Fritta, *Film und Realität* (Film and Reality), Theresienstadt, 1944, pen and black ink, 31.1 × 56.1 cm. Thomas Fritta-Haas, long-term loan to the Jewish Museum Berlin. © Jewish Museum Berlin; photo: Jens Ziehe/Fritta-Haas via Jewish Museum Berlin.

2 Hartmann Schedel, 'Burning Alive of Jews', from *Schedelsche Weltchronik* (Nuremberg, 1493), woodcut.

3 Samuel Hirszenberg, *Golus* (Exile), 1904, postcard. © Musée d'art et d'histoire du Judaïsme, Paris.

4 Jakob Steinhardt, *Pogrom*, 1913, dry-point etching, 22.3 × 27.1 cm. © Jüdisches Museum, Berlin; photo: Jens Ziehe, Ankauf aus Mitteln der Stiftung Deutsche Klassenlotterie, Berlin.

5 Max Liebermann, *Kischinew, An meine geliebten Juden (Der Zar)* (Kischinew: To my Beloved Jews (The Czar)), from *Kriegszeit Künstlerflugblätter*, III/16 (September 1916), lithograph. © Universitätsbibliothek Heidelberg.

6 Willy Jaeckel, *Juden-Massaker* (Massacre of the Jews), from *Kriegszeit Künstlerflugblätter*, XXXII/24 (March 1915), lithograph. © Universitätsbibliothek Heidelberg.

7 Lea Grundig, *Pogrom*, drawing 5 from the series *Der Jude ist schuld!* (The Jew is Guilty), 1935, etching. © photo: Ludwig Meidner-Archiv, Jüdisches Museum, Frankfurt am Main/Akademie der Künste, Berlin, Kunstsammlung.

8 Ludwig Meidner, *In Memory of our Destroyed Synagogues in Germany*, 1939, chalk and charcoal on paper. Collection of the Yad Vashem Art Museum, Jerusalem. © Yad Vashem Art Museum, Jerusalem/jmf/Ludi-Meidner-Archiv.

9 P. Shuldenreyn, *Remember What Amalek Did to You*, for the competition 'Collect and Record!', Munich, 1947, poster. © Yad Vashem Archive, Jerusalem.

10 Horst Strempel, *Nacht über Deutschland* (Night over Germany), 1946, oil on sack-cloth. Central panel: 150 × 168 cm; side panels: 150 × 78 cm; predella: 79 × 166 cm. Staatliche Museen zu Berlin, Nationalgalerie. © photo: bpk/Jens Ziehe/SMB, Nationalgalerie/VG Bildkunst, Bonn 17.

11 *Liberation of Auschwitz*, Poland, 1945, part of the film *Death Mills*. © Steven Spielberg Film and Video Archive, United States Holocaust Memorial Museum.

12 Teo Otto, *Kinder im Lager* (Children in the camp), from *Nie Wieder. Tagebuch in Bildern* (Berlin, 1949), photolithograph.

13 Peter Edel, *Kinder in Auschwitz-Birkenau* (Children in Auschwitz-Birkenau), 1944, fol. 14 from the series *Wenn es ans Leben geht, 20 Zeichnungen zu seiner Autobiographie* (When Life is Threatened: 20 Drawings from his Autobiography), (Berlin, 1983). © bpk/Kupferstichkabinett, SMB/VG Bildkunst, Bonn 17.

14 Peter Edel, *Self-portrait*, pencil on cardboard, 29.5 × 20 cm. © Państwowe Muzeum, Auschwitz-Birkenau, Oświęcim/VG Bildkunst, Bonn 17.

15 Peter Edel, *Esther*, 1944, from *Märkische Volksstimme* (16 April 1961). © VG Bildkunst, Bonn 17.

16 Otto Pankok, *Pogrom in Düsseldorf*, 1940, charcoal on paper, 96 × 129 cm. Otto Pankok Museum, Hünxe-Drevenack. © Otto Pankok Stiftung Hünxe-Drevenack.

17 'Those coming from the dark, stinking ghettos of Eastern cities', in *Der Untermensch*, ed. Reichsführer ss Office (Berlin, 1942).

18 Otto Pankok, *Rabbiner 2* (Rabbi 2), 1942, charcoal on paper, 119 × 99 cm. Otto Pankok Museum, Hünxe-Drevenack. © Otto Pankok Stiftung Hünxe-Drevenack.

19 Otto Pankok, *Die Synagoge* (The Synagogue), 1940, charcoal on paper, 97 × 129 cm. Otto Pankok Museum, Hünxe-Drevenack. © Otto Pankok Stiftung Hünxe-Drevenack.

20 'Behold the Constructive Work of Capitalism', in Ernst Friedrich, *Krieg dem Kriege!* (Berlin, 1924), p. 193.

21 Walter Gircke, *Berlin Scheunenviertel*, 1928, photograph. © bpk/Walter Gircke.

22 Otto Pankok, *Wartende Männer (Ghetto)* (Waiting Men (Ghetto)), 1939, charcoal on paper, 117 × 99 cm. Otto Pankok Museum, Hünxe-Drevenack. © Otto Pankok Stiftung Hünxe-Drevenack.

23 Otto Pankok, *Pogrom mit ss-Mann* (Pogrom with ss Officer), 1940, charcoal on paper, 100 × 130 cm. Otto Pankok Museum, Hünxe-Drevenack. © Otto Pankok Stiftung Hünxe-Drevenack.

24 Otto Pankok, *Judenhaus* (House for the Jews), 1945, charcoal on paper, 149 × 99 cm. Otto Pankok Museum, Hünxe-Drevenack. © Otto Pankok Stiftung Hünxe-Drevenack.

25 Otto Pankok, *Sie Kommen* (They Are Coming), 1943, charcoal on paper, 120 × 100 cm. Unknown Grammar School in Göttingen. © Otto Pankok Stiftung Hünxe-Drevenack.

26 Marc Chagall, *Le Violoniste* (The Fiddler), 1912–13, oil on canvas, 188 × 158.5 cm. Stedelijk Museum Amsterdam © Stedelijk Museum Amsterdam/vg Bildkunst, Bonn 17.

27 Otto Pankok, *Alter Geiger (Geiger im Ghetto)* (Old Violinist (Violinist in the Ghetto)), 1941, charcoal on paper, 150 × 97 cm. Otto Pankok Museum, Hünxe-Drevenack. © Otto Pankok Stiftung Hünxe-Drevenack.

28 Otto Pankok, *Blume*, 1947, etching, 36.4 × 29.5 cm. Otto Pankok Museum, Hünxe-Drevenack. © Otto Pankok Stiftung Hünxe-Drevenack.

29 Otto Pankok, *Von Auschwitz zurück oder Gaisa an der Wand* (Back from Auschwitz, or Gaisa against the Wall), 1948, charcoal, 99 × 117 cm. Otto Pankok Museum, Hünxe-Drevenack. © Otto Pankok Stiftung Hünxe-Drevenack.

30 Fritz Koelle, *Inferno*, 1946, bronze, 180 × 52 × 52 cm. Deutsches Historisches Museum, Berlin. © dhm, Berlin/Fritz Koelle.

31 Postcard from album *Conc. Camp Dachau*, 1946, kz-Gedenkstätte Dachau.

32 Scene from *Death Mills*, Germany/u.s., 1945, dir. Hanuš Burger, abridged version by Billy Wilder. © Steven Spielberg Film and Video Archive, United States Holocaust Memorial Museum.

33 Peter Edel, *Mauthausen*, January 1945, fol. 15 from the series *Wenn es ans Leben geht, 20 Zeichnungen zu seiner Autobiographie* (When Life is Threatened: 20 Drawings from his Autobiography), Berlin: Staatliche Museen, 1983. © bpk/Kupferstichkabinett, smb/vg Bildkunst, Bonn 17.

34 Wols, *Composition*, 1947, oil and grattage on canvas, 91 × 65 cm. Haniel Collection. © photo: Sammlung Haniel/vg Bildkunst, Bonn 17.

35 Gerhard Altenbourg, *Mein Bruder das frasslüsterne Schwein* (My Brother, the Greedy Pig), 1949, pastel on paper, 30 × 26 cm. Kupferstichkabinett, Staatliche Museen zu Berlin. © bpk/Kupferstichkabinett, smb/Jörg P. Anders/Stiftung Gerhard Altenbourg, Altenburg.

36 Gerhard Altenbourg, *Mein Bruder das frasslüsterne Schwein frisst immer noch* (My Brother, the Greedy Pig, is Still Feeding his Face), 1949, pastel and stabilo pen on paper, 274 × 27 cm. Kupferstichkabinett, Staatliche Museen zu Berlin. © photo: bpk/Kupferstichkabinett, smb/Volker-H. Schneider/Stiftung Gerhard Altenbourg, Altenburg.

37 Eugen Schönebeck, *Toter Mann* (Dead Man), 1962, oil on canvas, 140 × 120 cm. Private collection. © Michael Habes, Fotografie/vg Bildkunst, Bonn 17.

38 Pinkhes Shvarts, *Helft schraiben! Die Geschichte fun letsten khurbn* (Help with the Writing! The History of the Latest Destruction), poster for the competition 'Collect and Record!', Munich, 1947, poster. © Yad Vashem Archive, Jerusalem.

39 Lea Grundig, *CURSED BE THE ONE WHO CLOSES HIS EYES AS NOT TO SEE! / CURSED BE THE ONE WHO SHUTS HIS EARS AS NOT TO HEAR! / CURSED BE THE ONE WHO REFUSES TO HELP*, fol. 1 from the series *In the Valley of Slaughter*, Tel Aviv, 1944. © adk, Berlin, Kunstsammlung.

40 Lea Grundig, *IN THE DEATH WAGONS*, fol. 4 from the series *In the Valley of Slaughter*, Tel Aviv, 1944. © adk, Berlin, Kunstsammlung.

41 Lea Grundig, *TREBLIANCA*, fol. 11 from the series *In the Valley of Slaughter*, Tel Aviv, 1944. © adk, Berlin, Kunstsammlung.

42 Ludwig Meidner, *Gaskammer* (Gas Chamber), from the series *Massacres in Poland*, 1942–53, charcoal on paper, 56.7 × 76.1 cm. Jüdisches Museum der Stadt Frankfurt am Main. © jmf/Ludwig Meidner-Archiv.

43 Lea Grundig, *UNDERGROUND*, fol. 14 from the series *In the Valley of Slaughter*, Tel Aviv, 1944. © adk, Berlin, Kunstsammlung.

69 *Photographs of Polish Jews*, publ. in Schoenberner 1960, p. 89.

70 Eduard Winkler, *Der Tod im KZ* (Death in the Concentration Camp), from the series *Der braune Tod*, 1946, heliogravure, 29.6 × 21.7 cm. Deutsches Historisches Museum Berlin. © photo: DHM Berlin.

71 Jerzy (George) Zielezinski, *Those Strangled in the W.C. – Everybody can't die on a battle-field*,, fol. 10 from the series *K.Z.Album*, Munich, 1946, rotogravure, 29 × 21.6 cm.

72 Jerzy (George) Zielezinski, *The New Inmate – I don't know what I should fear more, death or life in the camp*, fol. 10 from the series *K.Z.Album* and fol. 2 in *24 Drawings from the Concentration Camps in Germany*, Munich, 1946, rotogravure, 29 × 21.6 cm.

73 Jerzy (George) Zielezinski, *Special Mission – The one lying at the bottom of the cart is very fat, that's why it is so heavy to pull today*, fol. 7 from the series *K.Z.Album*, Munich, 1946, rotogravure, 21.6 × 29 cm.

74 Jerzy (George) Zielezinski, *Meditation – He is breathing deeply and quietly, his glance roves over the heads of the 'Muselman'. There are several slices of bread and margarine in his stomach*, fol. 9 from the series *K.Z.Album*, Munich, 1946, rotogravure, 21.6 × 29 cm.

75 Jerzy (George) Zielezinski, *The Prominents*, fol. 20 from the series *24 Drawings from the Concentration Camps in Germany*, Munich, 1946, rotogravure, 39.9 × 29.8 cm.

76 James Gillray, '*Un petit Soupér, a La Parisienne – or – A Family of Sans Culotte refreshing, after the fatigues of the Day*', 1792, etching, 25 × 35 cm.

77 Jerzy (George) Zielezinski, *When will it be my turn?*, fol. 6 from the series *24 Drawings from the Concentration Camps in Germany*, Munich, 1946, rotogravure, 39.9 × 29.8 cm.

78 *Starving KZ-Inmate*, from *Mitteilungen*, published by 12. Amerikanischen Heeresgruppe, 5 May 1945. Brink, Cornelia (1998): *Ikonen der Vernichtung. Offentlicher Gebrauch von Fotografien aus nationalsozialistischen Konzentrationslagern nach 1945*. Berlin: Akademie.

79 Jerzy (George) Zielezinski, *Roll-call in the Women's Camp. – There are women inside the barbed wire, they are all there, – some of them holding their suckling babies, and those who lost their children last night*, fol. 5 from the series *K.Z.Album* and *The Women's Roll-call*, fol. 17 from the series *24 Drawings from the Concentration Camps in Germany*, Munich, 1946, rotogravure, 29 × 21.6 cm.

80 Jerzy (George) Zielezinski, *I am hungry*, fol. 4 from the series *24 Drawings from the Concentration Camps in Germany*, Munich, 1946, rotogravure, 39.9 × 29.8 cm.

81 Jerzy (George) Zielezinski, *Work is freedom – One more loading and I'll have done twenty-eight until noon. And in the afternoon?*, fol. 4 from the series *K.Z.Album*, Munich, 1946, rotogravure, 21.6 × 29 cm.

82 Jerzy (George) Zielezinski, *Work is Liberty*, fol. 11 from the series *24 Drawings from the Concentration Camps in Germany*, Munich 1946, rotogravure, 29.8 × 39.9 cm.

83 Jerzy (George) Zielezinski, cover of the series *24 Drawings from the Concentration Camps in Germany*, after fol. 22, *To the Wire!*, Munich, 1946, screen printing on cardboard and rotogravure on paper, 40.5 × 30.5 cm.

84 Leo Haas, *Hunger (Auschwitz)*, fol. 4 from the series *Deutsche KZ*, 1947, colour lithograph, 28.3 × 45 cm. Akademie der Künste, Berlin, Kunstsammlung © adk, Berlin, Kunstsammlung/Fritta-Haas via Jewish Museum Berlin.

85 Leo Haas, *Todesmarsch* (Death March), 1947, fol. 11 from the series *Aus deutschen konzentrationslagern*, colour lithograph, 28.7 × 44.7 cm. Akademie der Künste, Berlin, Kunstsammlung © adk, Berlin, Kunstsammlung/Fritta-Haas via Jewish Museum Berlin.

86 Leo Haas, *Von Theresienstadt ins Gas* (From Theresienstadt into the Gas), 1947, fol. 2 from the series *Aus deutschen konzentrationslagern*, colour lithograph, 29 × 44.5 cm. Akademie der Künste, Berlin, Kunstsammlung © adk, Berlin, Kunstsammlung/Fritta-Haas via Jewish Museum Berlin.

87 Leo Haas, *Auschwitz*, 1947, fol. 5 from the series *Aus deutschen konzentrationslagern*, colour lithograph, 29.5 × 45.5 cm. Akademie der Künste, Berlin, Kunstsammlung © adk, Berlin, Kunstsammlung/Fritta-Haas via Jewish Museum Berlin.

88 Carl Lauterbach, *Aus der Ghetto-Mappe* (From the Ghetto Album), 1940, charcoal, from *Carl Lauterbach Zeichnungen* (Solingen-Ohligs, 1948). © Stadtmuseum Düsseldorf.

89 Carl Lauterbach, *Abtransport, Aus der Mappe: Ghetto* (Deportation, From the Ghetto Album), 1943, charcoal, 70 × 50 cm. Stadtmuseum Düsseldorf © Stadtmuseum Düsseldorf.

90 Théophile Alexandre Steinlen, cover illustration, *Le Chambard socialiste*, 14 (17 April 1894). © Bundesarchiv Berlin.

91 Carl Lauterbach, *Jüdische Mutter* (Jewish Mother), 1940, charcoal, from *Carl Lauterbach Zeichnungen*, Solingen-Ohligs, 1948. © Stadtmuseum Düsseldorf.

92 Fritz Ketz, *Flehende* (The Ones Pleading), 1941, from the album *Gestalten und Bilder* (Figures and Images), Reutlingen, 1947, 39.7 × 30 cm. © Joern-Uwe Droemann.

93 Fritz Ketz, *Die Ausgemerzten* (The Ones Eridicated), 1946, pen, brush and ink, wash, 44 × 33 cm. Collection Fritz Ketz. © Joern-Uwe Droemann.

94 Fritz Ketz, *Ahasver*, 1941, pen, brush and ink, wash, 39.7 × 31.2 cm. Collection Fritz Ketz. © Joern-Uwe Droemann.

95 Gustave Doré, *Ahasverus*, woodcut for *La légende du juif errant, 12 compositions*, Paris, 1856. © bpk/BnF, Dist. RMN-GP/image BnF.

96 Fritz Ketz, *Selbstbildnis* (Self-portrait), 1948, brush and ink, 49.9 × 34.9 cm. Collection Fritz Ketz. © Joern-Uwe Droemann.

97 Teo Otto, *Hitler: Der Krieg wird als Ergebnis die Ausrottung der Juden in Europa bringen* (Hitler: The war will have the result of bringing about the eradication of the Jews of Europe), from *Nie wieder. Tagebuch in Bildern* (Berlin, 1949), photolithograph.

98 Teo Otto, *Wenn Steine reden könnten* (If only stones could speak), from *Nie wieder. Tagebuch in Bildern* (Berlin, 1949), photolithograph.

99 Teo Otto, *Deportiert ins Vernichtungslager* (Deported to the extermination camp), from *Nie wieder. Tagebuch in Bildern* (Berlin, Verlag Volk und Welt, 1949), photolithograph.

100 Rudi Stern, illustration for Nelly Sachs, *Dein Leib im Rauch durch die Luft* (Your Body Dissolves as Smoke Through the Air), from *In den Wohnungen des Todes* (Berlin, 1947), p. 11.

101 Auschwitz-Birkenau, Crematorium III during the Construction in 1943, photograph publ. in Sehn 1957, p. 166. © Państwowe Muzeum, Auschwitz-Birkenau Oświęcim.

102 Edgar Jené, *Todesfuge* (Death Fugue), 1944, pen and ink, 34 × 24.5 cm, signed 'Jené 44'. Saarland Museum Saarbrücken. ©Stiftung Saarländischer Kulturbesitz, Saarbrücken.

103 Max Ernst, *L'Immaculée conception* (The Immaculate Conception), 1929, collage, from *La Femme 100 têtes* (Paris, 1929). © VG Bildkunst, Bonn 17.

104 Edgar Jené, *Das rote Meer geht über Land* (The Red Sea Passes Over the Land), 1949, painting (missing), from Paul Celan, *Edgar Jené* (Vienna, 1948). © bpk/Staatsbibliothek zu Berlin PK.

105 Edgar Jené, *Die Gefangenen* (The Prisoners), 1941–2, oil on wood, 60 × 73 cm. Saarland Museum, Saarbrücken. © Stiftung Saarländischer Kulturbesitz, Saarbrücken.

106 Edgar Jené, *Das Lager* (The Camp), 1945, oil on wood, 60 × 73 cm. Saarland Museum, Saarbrücken. © Stiftung Saarländischer Kulturbesitz, Saarbrücken.

107 Otto Pankok, *Max und Alice Stern* (Max and Alice Stern), 1945, charcoal on paper, 96 × 128 cm. Otto Pankok Museum, Hünxe-Drevenack. © Otto Pankok Stiftung Hünxe-Drevenack.

108 *Max and Alice Stern*, *c.* 1930, photograph. © commons.wikimedia.org.

109 Mathias Barz, *Inferno*, 1946, oil on wood, 151 × 151 cm. Stadtmuseum Düsseldorf. © Stadtmuseum Düsseldorf.

110 Hermann Bruse, *Hungermarsch* (Hunger March), 1945–6, oil on hardboard, 127 × 93.5 cm. Stiftung Stadtmuseum Berlin. © photo: bpk/smb.

111 Hermann Bruse, *Ecce Homo*, 1948, oil on canvas, 70 × 53.5 cm. Nationalgalerie, Staatliche Museen zu Berlin. © Nationalgalerie, smb.

112 Henry Koerner, *Meine Eltern II* (My Parents II), 1946, oil on hardboard, 63.5 × 72.2 cm. Curtis Gallery Minneapolis. © Curtis Galleries, Inc. and Myron Kunin Collection, Minneapolis/Leo Koerner.

113 Henry Koerner, *Ruins on Schillerplatz*, Vienna, 1946, photograph. © Leo Koerner.

114 Hans Grundig, *Den Opfern des Faschismus 2* (To the Victims of Fascism 2), 1947, oil on hardboard, 110 × 200 cm. Staatliche Kunstsammlungen Dresden, Galerie Neue Meister. © photo: Gal. No. 3182/Elke Estel/Hans-Peter Klut, skd/adk, Berlin, Kunstsammlung.

115 Dore Meyer-Vax, *Todesmosaik* (Death Mosaic), 1948–51, oil on hardboard, 82.5 × 122 cm. Collection Gerhard Schneider. © photo: Gerhard Schneider.

116 Karl Schwesig, *Judenlazarett in Noé* (Jewish Infirmary at Noé), 1947–8, oil on canvas, 116 × 136 cm. Stadtmuseum Düsseldorf. © Stadtmuseum Düsseldorf.

117 Karl Schwesig, *Badenser Jüdinnen im Camp de Noé* (Jewish Women from Baden in Noé Camp), about 1948, brush and ink, 58 × 50.5 cm. © Galerie Remmert und Barth, Düsseldorf.

118 Karl Schwesig, *Jüdinnen mit Kind im Lager* (Jewish Women with a Child in the Camp), about 1948, brush and ink, 21.9 × 15.7 cm. © Galerie Remmert und Barth Düsseldorf.

119 Honoré Daumier, *Rue Transnonain, 15 April 1834*, 1834, lithograph, 28 × 44 cm.

120 Karl Schwesig, *Der Ermordete ist schuldig* (The One Murdered is Guilty), 1948–9, etching, 20.6 × 28.2 cm. Stadtmuseum Düsseldorf. © Stadtmuseum Düsseldorf.

121 Karl Schwesig, *Der Harlansgroschen* (The Harlan's Groschen), 1949, etching, 28.1 × 20.6 cm. Stadtmuseum Düsseldorf. © Stadtmuseum Düsseldorf.

122 Engraving after Titian, *The Tribute Money*, *c.* 1516, Gemäldegalerie Alte Meister, Dresden, from *Katalog der Vereinigung der Kunstfreunde* (Berlin, 1912), p. 113.

123 Heinrich Ehmsen, *Auschwitz*, 1948, oil on plywood, 215.5 × 101 cm. Nationalgalerie, Staatliche Museen zu Berlin. © photo: bpk/smb/Staatliche Museen

zu Berlin, Nationalgalerie, smb/Heinrich Ehmsen Stiftung Kiel.

124 Carl Buchheister, *Komposition mit brutalen Gegensätzen (KZ-Bild)* (Composition with Brutal Opposites (Concentration Camp Picture)), 1949, material picture, 76.5 × 55.7 cm. Private collection. © VG Bildkunst, Bonn 17.

125 Max Lachnit, *Auschwitzgruppe I* (Auschwitz Group I), 1949–52, bronze, h: 28.5 cm. Private collection. © Erbengemeinschaft Lachnit.

126 Max Lachnit, *Auschwitzgruppe II (Fliehender Engel)* (Auschwitz group II (Fleeing Angel)), 1949–52, bronze, h: 51.5 cm. Private collection. © Erbengemeinschaft Lachnit.

127 Hanns Georgi, *Vision (Verfolgung der blutigen Hände 1945* (Vision (Persecution of Bloodstained Hands)), *c.* 1946–8, oil on hardboard, 50 × 69.8 cm. Collection Gerhard Schneider. © photo: Gerhard Schneider.

128 Otto Pankok, *Jüdisches Ehrenmal* (Memorial to the Jewish People), 1932–50, 10 sculptures in bronze on stone, up to 40 cm high. Museum Gelsenkirchen. © Otto Pankok Stiftung Hünxe-Drevenack.

129 Otto Pankok, *Gehender Jude* (Jew Walking), 1942, woodcut, 45.5 × 17.4 cm. Otto Pankok Museum, Hünxe-Drevenack. © Otto Pankok Stiftung Hünxe-Drevenack.

130 Otto Pankok, *Stehender Jude* (Jew Standing), 1942, woodcut, 52 × 53 cm. Otto Pankok Museum, Hünxe-Drevenack. © Otto Pankok Stiftung Hünxe-Drevenack.

131 Wlodzimierz Kuhn, *Mąż Biegły w Piśmie* (A Perfect Man in the Newspaper), 1922, lithograph, 34.9 × 19.9 cm. © Jüdisches Museum der Stadt, Wien, Inv. No. 11297, Sammlung Schlaff.

132 Caricature, 'A Student of the Imperial University in Approved Clothing, publ. in Pluvium 1906', from Eduard Fuchs, *Die Juden in der Karikatur, ein Beitrag zur Kulturgeschichte* (Munich, 1921), p. 276.

133 Otto Pankok, *Gehender Jude* (Jew Walking), 1957, bronze, h: 44 cm. Akademie der Künste, Berlin, Kunstsammlung. © adk, Berlin, Kunstsammlung/Otto Pankok Stiftung Hünxe-Drevenack.

134 Willi Sitte, *Massaker II* (Massacre II), 1959, oil on hardboard, 150 × 207 cm. Willi Sitte Galerie Merseburg. © Willi Sitte Galerie Merseburg/VG Bildkunst, Bonn 17.

135 Gerd Baukhage, *Die Gehenkten* (The Ones Hanged), 1957, charcoal on watercolour on paper, *c.* 50 × 60 cm. Stadtmuseum Köln. © photo: Rheinisches Bildarchiv Köln, rba_d033248/Estate Baukhage.

136 Gerd Baukhage, *Gehenkter Jude mit Hut* (Hanged Jew With a Hat On), 1957, charcoal on watercolour on paper, *c.* 50 × 60 cm. Stadtmuseum Köln. © photo: Rheinisches Bildarchiv Köln, rba_d033249/Estate Baukhage.

137 Gerhard Richter, *Anne Frank*, 1957, brush and black ink on paper, 29.6 × 21 cm. Gerhard Richter Archiv, Staatliche Kunstsammlungen Dresden, Inv. No. 498/13. © Gerhard Richter 2016 (A1002).

138 Gerhard Richter, *Anne Frank*, 1957, brush and black ink on paper, 29.7 × 21 cm. Gerhard Richter Archiv, Staatliche Kunstsammlungen Dresden, Inv. No. 497/13. © Gerhard Richter 2016 (A1002).

139 Lea Grundig, *Appell im KZ* (Roll-call in the Concentration Camp), 1956, etching, 36 × 27 cm. © adk, Berlin, Kunstsammlung.

140 Lidy von Lüttwitz, *Model for an International Memorial in Auschwitz-Birkenau*, 1958. © Państwowe Muzeum, Auschwitz-Birkenau Oświęcim.

141 Helmut Wolff, *Model for an International Memorial in Auschwitz-Birkenau,* 1958. © Państwowe Muzeum, Auschwitz-Birkenau Oświęcim.

142 Joseph Beuys, *Der Tod und das Mädchen* (Death and the Maiden), 1957, brush and ink on an envelope, 17.6 × 25.2 cm. Collection Ludwig Rinn. © Ludwig Rinn/VG Bildkunst, Bonn 17.

143 Joseph Beuys, *Sketches for the Auschwitz Memorial,* 1957, collage on book paper, with two photographs and a picture, 33.1 × 49.5 cm. Museum Schloss Moyland, Collection van der Grinten. © Stiftung Museum Schloss Moyland; photo: Maurice Dorren/VG Bildkunst, Bonn 17.

144 Joseph Beuys, *Model for an International Memorial in Auschwitz-Birkenau,* 1958. © Państwowe Muzeum Auschwitz-Birkenau Oświęcim./VG Bildkunst, Bonn 17.

145 Joseph Beuys, Sketch from the notebook *Joseph Beuys verlängert im Auftrag von James Joyce den Ulysses um 2 weitere Kapitel* (Joseph Beuys Extends Ulysses by 2 Chapters on the Order of James Joyce), 1957, Book 2, p. 3. Hessisches Landesmuseum Darmstadt. © Hessisches Landesmuseum Darmstadt; photo: Wolfgang Furmanek/VG Bildkunst, Bonn 17.

146 Joseph Beuys, *Zwergengräber* (Dwarves' Graves), 1953–4, pencil and opaque white on paper, 12.7 × 9 cm. Museum Schloss Moyland, Collection van der Grinten. © Stiftung Museum Schloss Moyland; photo: Maurice Dorren/VG Bildkunst, Bonn 17.

147 Paul Klee, *Revolution des Viaducts* (Revolution of the Viaduct), 1937, oil on cotton, 60 × 50 cm. Hamburger Kunsthalle. © photo: Elke Walford/ bpk.

148 Arie Goral, *Opfertier und Ewerführer (Hängendes Opfertier über Hamburger Alsterbucht)* (Sacrificial Animal and Boatman (Sacrificial Animal Hanging Above the Lake Alster in Hamburg)), 1959, oil on hardboard, 105 × 52 cm. Jüdisches Museum

accompanied their comrades to the execution site, from *We Have Not Forgotten/ Wir haben es nicht vergessen/ Nous n'avons pas oublié* (Warsaw: Polonia, 1st edn 1959), p. 122.

170 Wolf Vostell, *In Ulm und um Ulm und um Ulm herum*, Station 21: *Die Infragestellung der inneren Behaglichkeit – oder wo waren Sie heute vor 20 Jahren?* (In Ulm and around Ulm and all around Ulm; Station 21 (Calling Peace of Mind into Question – Or Where Were You 20 Years Ago?)), from *Das Kunstwerk*, XVIII/7 (January 1965), p. 27. © Rafael Vostell/The Vostell Estate.

171 Wolf Vostell, *Die Folgen der Notstandsgesetze* (Consequences of the Emergency Laws), happening with audience participation, *24 Stunden* (24 Hours), 1965. Galerie Parnass, Wuppertal. © Rafael Vostell/The Vostell Estate.

172 Wolf Vostell, *Eine Autofahrt Köln-Frankfurt auf überfüllter Autobahn kostet mehr Nerven als eine Woche lang angestrengt arbeiten* (A Car Journey on the Crowded Autobahn Cologne–Frankfurt Takes More Out of You Than a Week of Hard Work), 1964, screen printing and spray can colour on canvas, 123 × 450 cm. Forum Ludwig, Aachen. © Rafael Vostell/The Vostell Estate.

173 Josef Beuys, *Auschwitz*, 1963, pen and ink, brush and oil (brown cross), brush and opaque white on map of Birkenau Concentration Camp on book paper, 50 × 75.5 cm. Museum Schloss Moyland, Collection van der Grinten. © Stiftung Museum Schloss Moyland; photo: Maurice Dorren/VG Bildkunst, Bonn 17.

174 Joseph Beuys, *KZ=Essen 1* and *2* (Concentration Camp Essen 1 and 2), 1963, part of the installation *Block Beuys*, box 3, china dish, painted white and with sinter, diam. *c.* 21 cm, nail brush at the rim; open tin painted, h.: *c.* 20 cm, gypsum mortar, 3.5 × 10 × 8 cm. Neue Galerie Kassel. © bpk/Stiftung Museum Schloss Moyland/Ute Klophaus/ VG Bildkunst, Bonn 17.

175 *Häftlingsration* (Prisoner's Meal Ration), publ. in Comité International d'Auschwitz, ed., *KL Auschwitz Krakau* (*c.* 1963), p. 13. © Państwowe Muzeum, Auschwitz-Birkenau Oświęcim.

176 Joseph Beuys, *Mein und meiner Lieben verlassener Schlaf* (My and My Loved Ones' Abandoned Sleep), 1965, part of *Block Beuys*, wooden shelf with felt, 150 × 152 × 62 cm. Hessisches Landesmuseum Darmstadt. © Hessisches Landesmuseum Darmstadt; photo: Wolfgang Furmanek/VG Bildkunst, Bonn 17.

177 Stanislaw Mucha, *Inneres einer Wohnbaracke im Männerlager in Brzezinska (Pferdestallbaracke Typ 260/9)* (Inside of a Living Hut in the Brzezinska Men's Camp (Temporary Horse Stable Barrack Type 260/9)), photograph, publ. in Sehn 1957, p. 51. © Państwowe Muzeum, Auschwitz-Birkenau Oświęcim.

178 *Nach der Befreiung vorgefundene Ballen Schneiderrosshaar, das von den Nazis fabrikmässig aus den Haaren vergaster Frauen hergestellt wurde* (Found After the Liberation: Bundles of Hair for Tailors, Manufactured on an Industrial Scale by the Nazis from the Hair of Women Gassed), photograph publ. in Sehn 1957, p. 176. © Państwowe Muzeum, Auschwitz-Birkenau Oświęcim.

179 Joseph Beuys with the arches from his model for the Auschwitz Memorial, performance *und in uns . . . und unter uns . . . landunter* (And Inside Of Us . . . And Beneath Us . . . Everything Flooded), happening with audience participation, *24 Stunden* (24 Hours), 1965. Galerie Parnass, Wuppertal. © bpk/Stiftung Museum Schloss Moyland/Ute Klophaus.

180 Joseph Beuys, display case *Auschwitz Demonstration*, part of *Block Beuys*, 1956–64, assemblage. Hessisches Landesmuseum Darmstadt. © Hessisches Landesmuseum Darmstadt; photo: Wolfgang Furmanek/VG Bildkunst, Bonn 17.

181 Joseph Beuys, *Sick Girl, Ambulance Behind*, 1957, from the display case *Auschwitz Demonstration*, part of the *Block Beuys*. Hessisches Landesmuseum Darmstadt. © Hessisches Landesmuseum Darmstadt; photo: Wolfgang Furmanek/VG Bildkunst, Bonn 17.

182 *Kinder im Lager Brzezinska. Die Aufnahme stammt aus der Sammlung des SS-Arztes Dr Mengele* (Children in the Brzezinska camp, photograph from the collection of Dr Mengele, SS physician), publ. in Sehn 1957, p. 61. © Państwowe Muzeum, Auschwitz-Birkenau Oświęcim.

183 Hubert Berke, *Hängende (KZ-Serie)* (The Ones Hanged (Concentration Camp Series)), 1964, oil on canvas, 136 × 150 cm. Private collection. © photo: Thomas Beier, Köln/Erbengemeinschaft Hubert Berke.

184 Hubert Berke, *Hängender* (Hanged Male Figure), 1964, oil on canvas, 150 × 89.5 cm. Private collection. © photo: Thomas Beier, Köln/Erbengemeinschaft Hubert Berke.

185 Hubert Berke, *Hängende* (Hanged Female Figure), 1964, oil on canvas, 150 × 100 cm. Private collection. © photo: Thomas Beier, Köln/Erbengemeinschaft Hubert Berke.

186 Hubert Berke, *Ohne Titel (KZ-Serie)* (Untitled (Concentration Camp Series)), *c.* 1964, tempera on Ingres paper, 62 × 48 cm. Private collection. © photo: Thomas Beier, Köln/Erbengemeinschaft Hubert Berke.

187 Hubert Berke, *Ohne Titel (KZ-Serie)* (Untitled (Concentration Camp Series)), *c.* 1964, oil on canvas, 100 × 80 cm. Private collection. © photo: Thomas Beier, Köln/Erbengemeinschaft Hubert Berke.

188 Hubert Berke, *Boger*, from the series *Figurinen der Vorhölle* (Figurines of the Anteroom to Hell), 1964,

brush and black ink, wash, yellow and red watercolour, 62 × 48 cm. Private collection. © photo: Thomas Beier, Köln/Erbengemeinschaft Hubert Berke.

189 Hubert Berke, *KZ Häftling* (Concentration Camp Prisoner), from the series *Totenbüsten (Busts of the Dead)*, 1964, ink wash and tempera, 62 × 48 cm. Private collection. © photo: Thomas Beier, Köln/ Erbengemeinschaft Hubert Berke.

190 Hubert Berke, *KZ Häftling* (Concentration Camp Prisoner), from the series *Totenbüsten (Busts of the Dead)*, *c.* 1963, ink wash and tempera, 62 × 48.5 cm. Museum Ludwig, Köln. © photo: Thomas Beier, Köln/Erbengemeinschaft Hubert Berke.

191 Rolf Szymanski, *Synagoge* (Synagogue), 1963, bronze, h: 207 cm, model for a sculpture of 6 m height. Private collection. © Galerie Brusberg, Berlin/VG Bildkunst, Bonn 17.

192 Poster for the Christian Democratic Union (CDU), elections for the State Parliament of Baden-Württemberg 1946: 'Save Western culture, Vote Christian Democrat'. Print: Esslingen 1946. © Konrad-Adenauer-Stiftung e.v., Archiv für Christlich-Demokratische Politik, Plakatsammlung.

193 Werner Tübke, sketch for a triptych dedicated to the persecution of the Jews, Skizzenbuch, 1964. Universitätsbibliothek Leipzig. © Universitätsbibliothek Leipzig, NL 300/2/VG Bildkunst, Bonn 17.

194 Werner Tübke, sketch for the series *Dr. jur. Schulze*, 1965, graphite, 18.5 × 18 cm, Tübke-Stiftung Leipzig. © photo: Tübke-Stiftung Leipzig/VG Bildkunst, Bonn 17.

195 *Buchenwald 1945*, photograph publ. in Schoenberner 1960, p. 192.

196 Werner Tübke, *Requiem*, 1965, oil on canvas on plywood, 28 × 44 cm. Staatliche Kunstsammlungen Dresden, Galerie Neue Meister. © Gal. No. 3636; photo: Elke Estel/Hans-Peter Klut, skd/VG Bildkunst, Bonn 17.

197 *Bergen-Belsen, May 1945*, photograph publ. in Schoenberner 1960, p. 211.

198 Stanislaw Mucha, *Kadaver der Häftlinge im Block II in Auschwitz* (Corpses of the Prisoners in Block II in Auschwitz), photograph publ. in Schoenberner 1960, p. 155.

199 Werner Tübke, *Erschiessung an der Mauer* (Shot Against the Wall), sketch for *Lebenserinnerungen des Dr. jur. Schulze III*, 1965, watercolour over pen and black ink, 25.4 × 44.2 cm. Neues Museum Nuremberg, long-term loan from the City of Nuremberg. © Neues Museum, Nuremberg/VG Bildkunst, Bonn 17.

200 *Small Belsen*, 1945, photograph publ. in Schoenberner 1960, p. 161.

201 *Erschossene Aufständische im Warschauer Ghetto* (Rebels Who Had Been Shot in the Warsaw Ghetto) (Stroop Report: 'Im Kampf vernichtete Banditen'), photograph publ. in Schoenberner 1960, p. 182.

202 Photograph, probably Bergen-Belsen, May 1945, publ. in Schoenberner 1960, p. 196.

203 Werner Tübke, *Lebenserinnerungen des Dr jur. Schulze II* (Memoirs of Dr. jur. Schulze II), 1965, technique of superimposing different colours on canvas on wood, 40 × 53 cm. Kunstmuseum Moritzburg Halle (Saale). © photo: Klaus E. Göltz, Halle (Saale)/VG Bildkunst, Bonn 17.

204 *Aus den Bunkern geholt.* (Pulled from the bunker), Warsaw, 1943 (Stroop Report: 'Soeben aus einem Bunker hervorgeholt' (Just Pulled from a Bunker)), photograph publ. in Schoenberner 1960, p. 179.

205 *Die Verteidiger des Ghettos werden zur Hinrichtung geführt* (The Defenders of the Ghetto are Led Away to be Executed), Warsaw, 1943 (Stroop Report: 'Banditen' (‚Bandits')) photograph publ. in Schoenberner 1960, p. 180.

206 *Erhängung eines russischen Bauern* (Hanging of a Russian Peasant), photograph publ. in Schoenberner 1960, p. 100.

207 Werner Tübke, *Lebenserinnerungen des Dr. jur. Schulze III* (Memoirs of Dr. jur. Schulze III), 1965, tempera on canvas on wood, 188 × 121 cm. Nationalgalerie, Staatliche Museen zu Berlin Berlin. © photo: bpk/Jörg Anders/, Nationalgalerie smb/VG Bildkunst, Bonn 17.

208 Albrecht Dürer, *Erasmus of Rotterdam*, 1526, copperplate engraving, 24.9 × 9.3 cm. Kupferstichkabinett, Staatliche Museen zu Berlin. © photo: bpk/ smb/Jörg P. Anders.

209 Pieter van der Heyden after Pieter Brueghel the Elder, *The Ass in the School*, 1556, etching and copperplate engraving, 23.3 × 29.7 cm, Kupferstichkabinett, Staatliche Museen zu Berlin. © photo: bpk/smb/ Volker H.-Schneider.

210 *Verhaftung der Betriebsleitung der Firma Brauer* (Arrest of the Management of the Brauer Firm), Warsaw, 1943 (Stroop Report: 'Firma Brauer'), photograph publ. in Schoenberner 1960, p. 170.

211 Detail of illus. 207.

212 *Pappurnen für die Asche der Toten in Theresienstadt* (Cardboard Urns for the Ashes of the Dead from Theresienstadt), photograph publ. in Schoenberner 1960, p. 73.

213 Harry Miller, *Baracke in Buchenwald* (Living Hut at Buchenwald), 1945, photograph publ. in Schoenberner 1960, p. 199.

214 *Der Marsch zum 'Umschlagplatz'* (The March to the Trans-shipment Point), Warsaw, 1943 (Stroop Report: 'Mit Gewalt aus Bunkern hervorgeholt' (Pulled from

the bunkers by force)), photograph publ. in Schoenberner 1960, p. 175.

215 Detail from Schoenberner 1960, p. 175.

216 Detail of illus. 207.

217 Abraham Abramson, *Enfranchisement of the Jews of Westphalia*, 1808, obverse, medal, silver and bronze, diam. 0.43 cm. The Israel Museum, Jerusalem. © The Israel Museum, Jerusalem; photo: Yair Hovav.

218 Max Liebermann, *Den Müttern der Zwölftausend* (To the Mothers of the Twelve Thousand), 1924, lithograph, 69 × c. 48 cm.

219 Ceremony to commemorate the liberation of Ravensbrück Concentration Camp on the marketplace of the City of Fürstenberg, photograph, 1955. Mahn- und Gedenkstätte Ravensbrück. © Mahn- und Gedenkstätte Ravensbrück; photo: Erich Riedel.

220 Detail of illus. 207.

221 Detail of Werner Tübke, Sketch for the composition of *Lebenserinnerungen des Dr. jur. Schulze* III (Memoirs of Dr. jur. Schulze III), 1965, pencil, 69.6 × 49.4 cm. Tübke-Stiftung Leipzig WVZ Z7/65. © Tübke Stiftung Leipzig, photo: Martin Weicker/VG Bildkunst, Bonn 17.

222 Werner Tübke, sketch for *Lebenserinnerungen des Dr. jur. Schulze* IV (Memoirs of Dr. jur. Schulze IV), 1965, watercolour over pen and black ink, 29.6 × 42.2 cm. Lindenau-Museum, Altenburg. © Lindenau-Museum, Altenburg/VG Bildkunst, Bonn 17.

223 Arie Goral, *Triptych on the Warsaw Ghetto*, 1960–c. 1983, collage on hardboard, oil on wood, nails, 65 × 149.5 cm. Jüdisches Museum der Stadt Frankfurt am Main. © jmf/Ludwig Meidner-Archiv.

224 Gerhard Richter, *Onkel Rudi* (Uncle Rudi), 1965, oil on canvas, 87 × 50 cm. Národni Galerie, Prague. © Gerhard Richter 2016.

225 Anonymous, four photographs taken from and outside Crematorium V in Auschwitz-Birkenau, August 1944, publ. in Georges Didi-Huberman, *Bilder Trotz Allem*, Munich, 2007, pp. 28–31. © Państwowe Muzeum Auschwitz-Birkenau Oświęcim. Courtesy of Wilhelm Fink Verlag, Paderborn.

226 Still from *Gerhard Richter Painting* (dir. Corinna Belz, Germany, 2011). © zero one film GmbH, Berlin.

227 Gerhard Richter, *Fotos aus Büchern* (Photographs from Books), 1977, 5 clippings in black and white, 66.7 × 51.7 cm, *Atlas*, sheet 19. © Gerhard Richter 2016.

228 Gerhard Richter, *Fotos aus Büchern* (Photographs from Books), 1967, 3 clippings in black and white, coloured, *Atlas*, sheet 20. © Gerhard Richter 2016.

229 Gerhard Richter, *Reichstag*, 1997, sketch with 4 pictures, *Atlas*, sheet 648. © Gerhard Richter 2016.

230 Gerhard Richter, *Schwarz Rot Gold* (Black Red Gold), 1998, enamel on glass, 6 plates, 2072 × 317 cm. Deutscher Bundestag im Reichstag, Berlin. © Gerhard Richter 2016.

231 Gerhard Richter, *Abstrakte Bilder (937/1–4)* (Abstract Pictures (937/1–4)), 2014, oil on canvas, each 260 × 200 cm. Installation Albertinum Dresden 2015. © Gerhard Richter 2017 (25082017); photo: David Brandt.

232 Gerhard Richter, *Birkenau, Abstrakte Bilder 937/3* (Birkenau (Abstract Pictures 937/3)), 2014, oil on canvas, 260 × 200 cm. Possession of the artist. © Gerhard Richter 2017.

Index

Illustration numbers are indicated by *italics*